Human Rights and Reformist Islam

Based at the Aga Khan Centre in London, the Aga Khan University Institute for the Study of Muslim Civilisations is a higher education institution with a focus on research, publications, graduate studies and outreach. It promotes scholarship that opens up new perspectives on Muslim heritage, modernity, religion, culture and society. The Institute aims to create opportunities for interaction among academics and other professionals in an effort to deepen the understanding of pressing issues affecting Muslim societies today.

In Translation: Modern Muslim Thinkers

Series Editor: Abdou Filali-Ansary

This series aims to broaden current debates about Muslim realities which often overlook seminal works produced in languages other than English. By identifying and translating critical and innovative thinking that has engendered important debates within its own settings, the series seeks to introduce new perspectives to the discussions about Muslim civilisations taking place on the world stage.

Available titles:

Islam: Between Message and History
Abdelmadjid Charfi
Translated by David Bond

Islam and the Foundations of Political Power
Ali Abdel Razek
Translated by Maryam Loutfi

The Sorrowful Muslim's Guide
Hussein Ahmad Amin
Translated by Yasmin Amin and Nesrin Amin

Secularism in the Arab World: Contexts, Ideas and Consequences
Aziz al-Azmeh
Translated by David Bond

Human Rights and Reformist Islam
Mohsen Kadivar
Translated by Niki Akhavan

Blasphemy and Apostasy in Islam: Debates in Shi'a Jurisprudence
Mohsen Kadivar
Translated by Hamid Mavani

edinburghuniversitypress.com/series/tmmt

Human Rights and Reformist Islam

MOHSEN KADIVAR

Translated by
Niki Akhavan

EDINBURGH
University Press

IN ASSOCIATION WITH

THE AGA KHAN UNIVERSITY
INSTITUTE FOR THE STUDY OF MUSLIM CIVILISATIONS

Edinburgh University Press is one of the leading university presses in the UK. We publish academic books and journals in our selected subject areas across the humanities and social sciences, combining cutting-edge scholarship with high editorial and production values to produce academic works of lasting importance. For more information visit our website: edinburghuniversitypress.com

© Mohsen Kadivar, *Haqq al-Nas: Islam va Hoquq-e Bashar*, Tehran: Kavir Publications, 2008 and Preface to the English Translation, 2021, 2023

English Translation © Niki Akhavan, 2021, 2023

Edinburgh University Press Ltd
The Tun – Holyrood Road
12 (2f) Jackson's Entry
Edinburgh EH8 8PJ

First published in hardback by Edinburgh University Press 2021

Typeset in 10.5/13 Adobe Garamond by
IDSUK (DataConnection) Ltd

A CIP record for this book is available from the British Library

ISBN 978 1 4744 4930 4 (hardback)
ISBN 978 1 4744 4931 1 (paperback)
ISBN 978 1 4744 4933 5 (webready PDF)
ISBN 978 1 4744 4932 8 (epub)

Contents

Section Five: Other Debates in Human Rights

Acknowledgements

I dedicated the Persian original of this book to my mentor Ayatollah Hossein-Ali Montazeri Najaf-Abadi (1922–2009). At the time, it was not possible to explicitly mention his name due to censorship and political restrictions in Iran. The book was released when I left Iran and since he passed away a few months later, I am not sure he ever saw the book. I learned from him that most *shariʿa* rulings related to human interactions are not dictated and are not beyond rational (*tawqifiyya*) rulings. This includes human rights, which is one of the major points of this book. Grand Ayatollah Hossein-Ali Montazeri Najaf-Abadi (1922–2009) read the first draft of Chapter 5 and gave me his advice. God bless him.

It is a pleasure to record my gratitude to a number of scholars and institutions who had a role in shaping the chapters of this book. These include Nasser Hadian (School of Law and Political Science, Tehran University) in Chapter 3; Saeed Hajjarian, Alireza Alavitabar and Reza Kaffash Tehrani (editors of the daily magazine *Sobh-e Emrouz*) in Chapter 4; Isa Saharkhiz and Alireza Alavitabar (editors of the bimonthly journal *Aftab*) in Chapter 5; Ali Ghodsi (Department of Statistics, University of Waterloo, Canada) in Chapter 6; Ardeshir Amirarjomand and Amir Nikpay (both from the School of Law, Department of Human Rights, Shahid Beheshti University, Tehran) in Chapter 6; Mohammad Jaʿfar Habibzadeh (Department of Law, Tarbiat Modares University, Tehran) in Chapter 11; Ali-Akbar Shobeyri-Nejad (1941–2009) (Director, Research Council of the Institute of Advanced Research on Social Security) and Bahram Panahi (Research Deputy, Research Council of the Institute of Advanced Research on Social Security) in Chapter 14; Mofid University in Qom in Chapters 8 and 12; the women's unit of the Mosharekat political party in Chapter 10; and the Islamic Association of Students of Iranian Universities in Chapters 1 and 9.

I extend my profound appreciation to Mohamad Javad Mozaffar (Kavir Publishers, Tehran) for publishing the original Persian book. Although the book was a best-selling title and was reprinted four times in less than a year, it was banned in June 2009 because of my criticism of the Islamic Republic. As a result, the publisher incurred losses for several years.

I benefited from consultation with Abdulaziz Sachedina (George Mason University) in my Preface to the English translation. He brought certain essential matters to my attention. Locating the sources for the Preface and the first draft of the translated manuscript would have been impossible without the help of the librarians at Duke University. The final drafts of the Preface and the translated manuscript were completed during my fellowship at the National Humanities Center (NHC) at Research Triangle Park (North Carolina). I would like to express my deep gratitude to both Duke University and NHC.

I would like to sincerely thank Niki Akhavan (Associate Professor and Chair, Department of Media and Communication Studies at the Catholic University of America) for her excellent work on the translation; Charlotte Whiting (Manager, Publications Department at the Aga Khan University, Institute for the Study of Muslim Civilisations) for her editorial work and a great deal of support and cooperation; as well as Edinburgh University Press for all their help and patience. In addition, I would like to thank Mirjam Künkler (Professor at the Swedish Collegium for Advanced Study) for her contribution to the volume, excellent Foreword and her help with the translation. Lastly, I thank the two reviewers for their insightful remarks and useful critique, which I have tried to incorporate to the best of my ability. However, it goes without saying, that ultimately, I am solely responsible for any flaws and errors.

Transliteration: the IJMES transliteration guide has been followed for the most part.

Qur'an Translation: M. A. S. Abdel Haleem's translation of the Qur'an has been used throughout.

Mohsen Kadivar

Foreword: Revising Shari'a in the Light of the Universal Declaration of Human Rights

Mirjam Künkler

Introduction

Mohsen Kadivar (b. 1959) is one of Iran's leading reformist scholars of Islam. He is the author of twenty-two books in Persian and the editor of three books in Arabic, and writer of numerous academic articles. This is his first book translated into English, with a second forthcoming shortly.[1] Since 2008, Dr Kadivar has been forced to live and work outside Iran, and since 2009 has been a research professor of Islamic Studies at Duke University, North Carolina. Despite the fact that he has been living in exile in recent years, his works are read widely in Iran and the wider Shi'ite world. This is due not least to the dissemination of his works via his website, where most of his writings can be downloaded and which Dr Kadivar updates regularly.

The current book *The Rights of People: Islam and Human Rights* (*Haqq al-Nas: Islam va Hoquq-e Bashar*) was first published in Persian in 2008, and brings together Dr Kadivar's writings from the early 2000s until 2007. For the purposes of this English edition, he has added new epilogues to many of the chapters, thus indicating the evolution of his thinking since the original Persian publication. He has also added a weighty Preface to the English translation, in which he juxtaposes his reformist thinking with that of five other scholars of Islam and human rights.

---

1 *Mujazat-e Ertedad wa Azadi-ye Mazhab: Naqd-e Mujazat-e Ertedad wa Sabb al-Nabi ba Mawazin-e Feqh-e Estedlali* (*Apostasy, Blasphemy and Religious Freedom in Islam: A Critique Based on Demonstrative Jurisprudence*), 2014 (published in English as *Blasphemy and Apostasy in Islam: Debates in Shi'a Jurisprudence*, trans. Hamid Mavani (Edinburgh: Edinburgh University Press in association with Aga Khan University Institute for the Study of Muslim Civilisations, 2021).

This contribution is divided into six sections. Section 1 provides a brief biography; section 2 presents Kadivar's intellectual trajectory; section 3 introduces the main themes of the book; section 4 outlines Kadivar's methodology; section 5 points to the consequences of his methodology for three selected topics; section 6 summarises his notions of democratic secularism, democracy and social security; before the Conclusion closes with a brief summary.

1 Biography

Mohsen Kadivar's biography has been chronicled in several encyclopaedia entries and Kadivar's own website features a detailed overview.[2] Therefore, a short summary shall suffice here. Kadivar was born in Fasa, southeast of Shiraz, in 1959, and in 1977 began to study electrical engineering at the University of Shiraz. These studies were interrupted by the 1979 revolution, in the course of which universities were closed until 1981 and a cultural revolution carried out with the aim of Islamising the educational sector. During that time, Kadivar enrolled in the Shiraz Seminary (in October 1980) and in June 1981 transferred to the Hawzeh-ye 'Elmiyyeh-ye Qom, continuing the first stage of seminary studies (*muqaddamat*). In 1984, he was turbaned by the conservative scholar and expert in Qur'anic exegesis Abdollah Javadi Amoli and began the intermediate courses (*sutuh*). After completing them at the top of his class, he began the third cycle (*dars-e kharej*) in 1987.

Kadivar studied *usul al-fiqh* (principles of jurisprudence) under the mentorship of grand ayatollahs Mirza Jawad Tabrizi (1926–2006), Seyyed Kazem Husseini Ha'eri (1938–), as well as Seyyed Mahmoud Hashemi Shahroudi (1948–2018), who would later serve as Iran's Head of Judiciary from 1999 to 2009 (he was generally considered a mentor to Supreme Leader Ali Khamenei and believed to have largely written the latter's *resale-ye amali-ye*, which is one important criterion towards becoming a source of emulation (*marja'*) for Shi'ite believers).

Kadivar completed his advanced studies in jurisprudence (*kharej-e fiqh*) under the supervision of grand ayatollahs Mirza Jawad Tabrizi (1926–2006)

2 See, for example, Ahmad Sadri, "Kadivar, Mohsen", in *The Oxford Encyclopaedia of the Islamic World*, Oxford Islamic Studies Online, available at: http://www.oxfordislamicstudies.com/article/opr/t236/e0961, last accessed 29 April 2019.

and Sayyid Mohammad Husseini Rohani (1920–1997). His most important mentor in jurisprudence, with whom he studied for more than a decade, was Grand Ayatollah Shaykh Hossein-Ali Montazeri (1922–2009), who was a key drafter of the Iranian 1979 constitution, and initially designated Ayatollah Khomeini's successor as Supreme Leader of Iran until Montazeri became a vocal critic of the Islamic Republic – in particular of its persecution of internal opponents. Following Montazeri's lead, Kadivar developed his in-depth comparison of notions of government in the thought of leading Shi'ite scholars, which culminated eventually in a three-volume work on *Government in Islamic Thought*. He was also inspired by Montazeri in his interests in political economy, particularly regulations on almsgiving (*zakat*) and forbidden businesses (*al-makasib al-muharramah*).

In 1998, Kadivar received his *ijazah al-ijtihad* (certification of being trained in interpreting Islamic law and issuing *fatawa*, the highest degree in the seminary) at the age of thirty-nine. In 2000, he obtained a doctorate from Tarbiyat Modarres University (Teacher Training University) in Tehran, where he henceforth taught at the faculty of philosophy. Due to political pressure, he had to give up his teaching appointment there in 2007, and in the following year worked at the Research Center of the Iranian Institute of Philosophy, before leaving the country in 2008.

Kadivar shot to domestic fame when he published his treatise *Theses on the State in Shi'ite Jurisprudence* (*Nazariya-ha-ye Dawlat dar Fiqh-e Shi'a*) in 1997, which presented Khomeini's theory of government as one among many recognised Shi'ite views on notions of government. Implicitly, Kadivar's treatise documented that Khomeini's theory of government was a minority view and a rather novel one that lacked broader support among Shi'ite juristic opinions. In a follow-up book a year later, *Governance by Guardianship* (*Hokumat-e Wela'i*, 1998), Kadivar explicitly refuted Khomeini's theory of government step by step on the basis of Shi'ite jurisprudential principles.[3]

In the same year, he published *The Book of Intellect*, a collection of philosophical and theological articles (*Daftar-e Aql: Madjmou'eh Maqalat-e Falsafi va Kalami*). Partly as a result of that book, he was arrested by the Special

---

3 For an excellent overview of the debate, see Said Amir Arjomand, "The Reform Movement and the Debate on Modernity and Tradition in Contemporary Iran", *International Journal of Middle East Studies* 34 (2002): 719–731.

Court for the Clergy and imprisoned for eighteen months. During the trial, he served as his own defence counsel and his defence speech was broadcast in reformist news media, further disseminating his arguments which proved to be a thorn in the side of the Islamic Republic.

Kadivar published a third collection of articles on government in 2000, collectively titled *The Appointive/Non-Elective Government* (*Hokumat-e Entesabi*), which, once published as a book, has come to form a trilogy together with *Nazariya-ha-ye Dawlat dar Fiqh-e Shi'a* and *Hokumat-e Wela'i*.[4] *Hokumat-e Entesabi* is an evaluation of the lessons to be learned from the experience of thirty years of the Islamic Republic, and amounts to a devastating indictment, laying bare the disappointments and disenchantments that the *Hokumat-e Wela'i* has brought about.

Kadivar has also made an important contribution to the history of constitutionalism in Iran by publishing in 2006 the political writings of the constitutionalist Grand Ayatollah Akhund Mulla Muhammad Kazim Khorasani (1839–1911).[5]

2 Intellectual Trajectory

Kadivar describes his own intellectual trajectory as having undergone three paradigm shifts: while being trained in traditional *ijtihad* with a focus on secondary *fiqhi* rulings, he evolved to engage instead in *ijtihad* in principles and foundations (*al-usul wa al-mabani*), focusing on *ijtihad* of the Qur'anic verses and the hadith rather than comparing and discussing secondary commentaries.[6] His second shift consisted of regarding *shari'a* as a system of law to considering it as a system of moral virtues and ethical values. A third shift took place when he discarded his view that an Islamic democratic state was

4 The collection was published as an ebook in 2010 once Kadivar had left Iran.
5 Mohsen Kadivar (comp. and ed.), *Siyasat-nameh-ye Khorasani* (*Political Works of Akhond Molla Mohammad Kazem Khorasani*) (Tehran: Kavir, 2006).
6 Kadivar calls *ijtihad* in principles and foundations also "structural *ijtihad*". See Mohsen Kadivar, "Ijtihad in Usul al-Fiqh: Reforming Islamic Thought through Structural Ijtihad", *Iran Nameh* 30(3) (2015): 20–27, and Chapter 5 in this volume.

Foreword

possible and instead moved to regard the secular state (in the sense of a state not identifying with any particular religion) as the only option for a democratic state, albeit buttressed by a civil society in which religion ideally flourishes. Kadivar's notion of justice encompasses both political and economic justice. He fully endorses the centrality of human rights: "In Islamic teachings humans have inherent dignity (Q. 17:70). Regardless of colour, race, gender, nationality, religion or sect, all come from one mother and father (Q. 4:1) and enjoy the same minimum of human rights."[7] His notion of justice is political, while also placing great emphasis on the importance of redistributive mechanisms in society so that every citizen is in a position to live a life in dignity.

While Kadivar is thought of (and self-identifies) as a member of the *roshanfekran-e dini* (reformist intellectuals) in Iran, together with Abdulkarim Soroush, Mohammad Mojtahed Shabestari, Mohammad Khatami, Hasan Yusefi Eshkevari and others, out of this group Kadivar enjoys the deepest grounding in Shi'ite *fiqh*. While Mojtahed Shabestari grounds his reformist approach predominantly theologically and hermeneutically, and Abdolkarim Soroush mystically, Kadivar's foremost methodology is theological and jurisprudential. He follows traditional *ijtihad* and reinterprets it with new ijtihadic principles both in *usul al-fiqh* (Islamic legal theory) and in expanded foundations. Specifically, he reconstructs *usul al-fiqh* in the light of linguistic philosophy, hermeneutics, historicity and critical thinking, and in his *ijtihad* draws not on secondary *fiqhi* rulings, but instead on the foundations of Islam, including its epistemological, cosmological, ontological, anthropological, sociological, psychological, theological and ethical foundations. With its strong jurisprudential methodology, Kadivar's approach is arguably also the most effective in the context of the Islamic Republic, as it has the potential to shake the polity at its core. Iran's hardliners are not necessarily moved by Islamic theological or mystical arguments. Jurisprudential arguments, however, which are firmly grounded in the Twelver Shi'ite tradition and moreover in the particular Iranian canon that has been created around the idea of *velayat-e faqih*, hit the polity where it is most vulnerable.[8]

---

7 Chapter 14, p. 388.
8 One of Kadivar's most daring publications in this regard has been a series published on the website of Iran's Green Movement in 2013, titled *Ebtezal-e Marja'iyyat-e Shi'a: Estidhah-e Marja'iyyat-e Maqam-e Rahbari S. Ali Khamenei (The Trivialization of Shi'ite Marja'iyyat: Impeaching Iran's Supreme Leader on his Marja'iyyat)*.

3 *This Book*

Over the years, Kadivar developed a clear profile as a democratic thinker, embracing human rights, the equality of men and women, the equality of Muslims and non-Muslims, and underlining also the importance of social rights which ensure that every citizen can live a life in dignity and is provided for by the state with the fundamental standards of living (water, electricity, health care) and education.

Kadivar's life work presents in essence an attempt at reviewing Islamic legal teachings in the light of contradictions with democracy and human rights. He works primarily within Shi'ite jurisprudence, but understands most of his key arguments and his methodology to be relevant also to Sunni jurisprudence and other schools of Islamic law.

Translated as *The Rights of People: Islam and Human Rights* (*Haqq al-Nas: Islam va Hoquq-e Bashar*), *Haqq al-Nas* literally means "The Right of the People". *Haqq* stands for "rights" in Arabic (and Persian) but also means truth and reality. Kadivar comments: "It has been said that *haqq* means 'duty as well as right, obligation as well as claim, law as well as justice' . . . For this book I have chosen the title *Haqq al-Nas*, a traditional term used with a modern meaning, to claim that the Islamic legal tradition has the potential for a modern reading. *Haqq al-Nas*, the rights of the people, literally also means human rights." [9]

The book was written and revised between 2001 and 2008, and has been reprinted several times since. [10] But since Kadivar's writings remain banned in Iran, they are disseminated there nearly exclusively on the internet. The book has fourteen chapters, many endowed with new epilogues. These epilogues are often revealing, sometimes because Kadivar's thinking has evolved significantly since the original publication (in some cases more than fifteen years ago), often deepening and expanding the reformist interpretation of the topic under discussion, and sometimes because the circumstances of the publication did not allow him to be as explicit in the implications of his intellectual position as his life in exile now does. Therefore, some of the more

---

9 Preface, p. xiv.

10 It was reprinted three times in less than a year, but the fifth print was not allowed to be released. The pdf of the 4th edition was posted online as an ebook in May 2015.

radical implications of the arguments come to the fore only in the newly added epilogues.[11]

To the original short Introduction of the 2008 Persian book, Kadivar has now also added a much longer Preface to the English translation, in which he places his own thought in relation to that of five other leading scholars of Islam and human rights. With this he has done an enormous service to his readership and a readership generally interested in Islam and democracy, demarcating his own approach from that of several other scholars engaged in reforming Islam from within. Notably, he has also included here as one of his interlocutors a woman, and engaged with a non-Muslim's perspective on the topic.

The chapters of the book, all written between 2001 and 2008 (and sometimes revised since, as they were published as individual articles elsewhere), cover the topics of freedom of belief and models of secularism, the rights of non-Muslims, the rights of political opposition, women's rights (with a separate chapter on women's rights in the Hereafter), slavery, international human rights covenants, and Islamic rules on welfare and charity.

In many of the chapters, Kadivar presents traditional viewpoints from Islamic jurisprudence on a given matter, then revisits the relevant Qur'anic verse or hadith to critique the given interpretations and discuss what counts as legitimate sources and methodology, in order to then present his alternative interpretation. In doing so, he engages with classical as well as contemporary literatures, and does so not only from within Shi'ite Islam, but also providing Sunni perspectives and occasionally engaging arguments also from minority schools of jurisprudence and writings outside the tradition. As diverse an array of scholars are being cited and discussed as al-Tabari, Zayn al-Din al-Juba'i al-'Amili, Mulla Sadra, Theodor Nöldeke, Christoph Luxenberg, Amina Wadud, to name only a fraction, as well as the five contemporary scholars prominently featured in the Preface: Mahmoud Mohamed Taha, Abdullahi An-Na'im, Mohammad Mojtahed Shabestari, Ann Elizabeth Mayer and Abdulaziz Sachedina. Along the way, Kadivar engages with literatures in Arabic, Persian, English, French and German.

Kadivar's main aim is to outline an interpretation of Islamic law that is compatible with human rights. *Shari'a* regulations (*al-ahkam al-shari'a*) are

---

11 Note, for example, his conclusion in the epilogue to Chapter 14 that the duty to pay *khums* was based on a temporal ruling and as such *khums* should no longer be considered an obligatory tax.

to be reviewed to probe whether they still apply today and, if so, in what form. To do so, as will be elaborated below, he asks whether they fulfil the four criteria of justice, reason, morality and superior functionality compared with alternative rulings.

His approach is developed in contradistinction to what he refers to as historical Islam and traditional Islam. Historical Islam stands for the conviction that notions of what we today call human rights can be found in the Qur'an and hadith, and hence the earliest practices among Muslim communities. Traditional Islam, by contrast, here denotes an understanding of Islam according to which human rights have always been embedded in broader rights understandings that also recognise God's rights and those of animals and plants, which all delimit human rights.

Diverging from these two perspectives, Kadivar holds that human rights have to be recognised as deriving from sources other than the Qur'an, hadith or the rulings of the *madhahib*. Human rights have modern intellectual sources and cannot be read back into the religious texts. Moreover, in contrast to adherents of traditional Islam, he does "not expect law from Islam".[12] *Shari'a* shall be a source to guide believers in their behaviour, as an ethics, but not as a basis for state law.

Further, in the reformist perspective, which is also Kadivar's, the mere presence of an issue in the Qur'an does not render it an eternal ruling. The Qur'an (and even Islam) should not be viewed as an exclusive source guiding Muslims' behaviour and beliefs. There are norms Muslims may follow today which are not contained in the Islamic sources.

Kadivar believes that all Qur'anic verses have to be interpreted within their context and as such subjected to contextual analysis. "The mentality of the seventh-century Hijaz is not Islam, but simply the custom (*'urf*) of that specific time and place. Arab customs were not, and especially *are* not, part of *shari'a* and Islam." He goes as far as to hypothesise that "most of the problematic issues concerning human rights are these ancient customs".[13]

Since all Qur'anic verses are a reflection of their context, they all need to be reviewed with regard to their validity today: either they are time-bound and ephemeral, or they are permanent and eternal. In order to decide into which category verses fall, Kadivar applies the four mentioned criteria: they need to be just, reasonable, moral and superior in their functionality to

---

12 Preface, p. lxxxv.
13 Preface, p. lxxxvii.

alternative rulings. His review of Qur'anic verses leads him to the conclusion that "most (not all) of the abrogated rulings belong to the Medinan period, including Qur'anic verses and prophetic hadiths (and the hadiths of other Shi'ite Imams)". Kadivar is careful, however, to distinguish his approach from that of Mahmoud Mohamed Taha, Abdullahi An-Na'im and others who argue that the permanent verses in general originate in the Meccan period, while those from the Medinan period reflect the norms of the time and as such have lost their imperative character today. While their methodology is based on a chronological distinction, his is rational, Kadivar argues. There is, in other words, coincidence in some of the outcomes of his methodology with that of Taha and An-Na'im, but the methodologies are radically different.

4 Review of Shari'a *Rulings in the Light of Four Criteria*

Kadivar argues that at the time of their formulation, all *shari'a* rulings were reasonable, just, moral and more efficient (or functional) than possible alternatives, and he connects this to a sociological insight when he argues that "The first addressees of Islamic teachings might not have accepted these teachings if they were unreasonable, unjust, immoral, or less functional than others. These people were the same as other human beings: reasonable people, and these four criteria are general criteria for accepting vital teachings. [. . .] The Qur'an is full of emphasis on reasonableness, justice and morality."[14]

Kadivar has identified the four criteria by way of induction (*istqra*), and their identification is finite. He suggests that the same criteria that were applied then have to be applied today. Those *shari'a* verdicts that are immoral, unjust, unreasonable or inferior to (less functional than) alternative rules according to the conventions of our time should be abrogated as "divine law cannot be unjust, immoral, unreasonable and inferior in function."[15]

All four criteria need to be met for a ruling to be considered valid today, but internally the criteria are also related to one another. He explains "the

---

14 See p. lxxxvii.
15 P. xxvi. Notably, Kadivar had first outlined the three criteria of justice, reasonability and superior functionality to other rules, and only added the fourth criterion of morality in 2006 after extensive writings on the issue of slavery (Chapter 12).

three criteria of reasonability, justice and morality are inseparable. This means that we cannot find any reasonable injustice or immorality, nor a just, unreasonable or immoral case, nor a moral but unjust or unreasonable case. In other words, reasonableness, justice and morality are three dimensions of a single overarching criterion, and removing any one of them correlates to removing the other two. This point strengthens our evaluation."[16]

The four criteria are in turn complemented by narrative "confirming" criteria (*mu'yyid*). Such narrative confirmers can be found mostly (but not exclusively) in the generalities (*'umumat*) and in absolute expressions (*itlaqat*) in the Meccan period, including in the Qur'anic verses and in the prophetic hadith (and for Shi'ites in the hadith heritage of Imam 'Ali).

Approaches that ask for the objectives of *shari'a* (*maqasid al-shari'a*) and probe the validity of *shari'a* rulings with regard to the question of whether they serve the broader objectives of *shari'a* are not as persuasive in his view. Such legal frameworks "do not offer a complete rational approach that could solve any problem, until their position regarding reasonableness, justice, morality and functionality by comparison to other frameworks is clarified".[17]

How precisely should this probing of *shari'a* rulings be carried out?

The method of evaluating a *shari'a* ruling in the light of Kadivar's four criteria consists of scholarly discussion and debate. He does not intend to subject *shari'a* rulings to this test alone, but he wishes to subject them to scholarly probing. In the meantime, all rulings will be considered permanent unless reason is given for why they should be considered conditional and temporary.[18]

It should be borne in mind that abrogation applies only to the ruling, not its reading and recitation. No verse or hadith shall be removed from the corpus of Scripture or hadith collection. Also, considering a ruling to be permanent or changing does not diminish its authenticity as a Qur'anic ruling.[19]

---

16 Preface, p. lxxxviii.
17 Preface, p. lxxxvii.
18 Kadivar expands this discussion in Chapter 5, "Human Rights and Reformist Islam".
19 "If this point is accepted, we can say that these types of rulings [now abrogated] were made in accordance with the time of the Revelation and as long as those conditions remained, so did these rulings retain validity. The eternal nature of the Qur'an is due to its containing eternal rulings. This does not cancel belief in rulings which are abrogated, temporary, and historical." See Chapter 10, p. 297.

But who can claim that a ruling may be abrogated? Kadivar's method begs the question as to who will be accepted as a worthy interlocutor in this scholarly debate. Will non-Muslims be accepted as participants? Will women? Will those from different *madhahib*? Based on the selection of five scholars Kadivar himself chose for the Preface to the English translation, it would appear as if he would answer all of these in the affirmative. Participants in this debate need not be Muslim, male, trained *'ulama* or from a particular Islamic school of law.

Drawing such a conclusion would be misleading, however. Kadivar clarifies that those probing Islamic rulings for their congruence with the four criteria ought to be *mujtahid*s, and, moreover, not *mujtahid*s trained predominantly in secondary ruling of *fiqh*, but those who, like he, embrace the methodology of structural *ijtihad* and advance to the sources and fundamental principles.[20] This is so because the topos of abrogation has a long history in Islamic legal debates and requires great familiarity with casuistry as well as the sources and consequences of disagreements over abrogation.[21]

Kadivar justifies that rulings need to be revisited in the light of the conventions of the time with reference to the experience of the Prophet himself. "It was not the case that the rulings were accepted because the Prophet was

---

20 "It requires the most expert Islamic studies based on modern methodology and scholarship. Islamic jurisprudence or *fiqh* is a prerequisite, but it is not sufficient. To be qualified for such a sensitive responsibility the scholar should have holistic, comprehensive and multidisciplinary knowledge of Islamic studies. This must include Qur'anic studies, hadith studies, Islamic theology, Islamic ethics, Islamic jurisprudence and its prerequisites (such as its methodology or *'usul al-fiqh*), the history of Islam, Islamic philosophy, Islamic mysticism and Arabic literature. In other words, only a *mujtahid* (agent of *ijtihad* or scholar of independent reasoning) is qualified, but not within the framework of traditional or conventional *ijtihad* that is restricted to the subsidiary rulings of *fiqh* (*furu' fiqhiya*), but structural *ijtihad* or *ijtihad* in the principles and foundations, or revision in the principles and foundations of Islamic thought." See Preface, p. xc.

21 "Abrogation (*naskh*) is a familiar term in Qur'anic studies and the discipline of jurisprudence (*'usul al-fiqh*). Abrogating (*nasikh*) is exclusive to the Qur'anic verses, if the abrogated (*mansukh*) is an earlier Qur'anic verse. Abrogating (*nasikh*) can be achieved only by Qur'anic verses or Prophetic Traditions, if the abrogated (*mansukh*) is an earlier Prophetic Tradition. In other words, the abrogating (*nasikh*) is restricted to transmitted indications (*al-adillah al-naqliyya*) or textual indications. Although abrogation has been an accepted part of Islamic scholarship since early Islam, there are nonetheless a lot of disagreements in three areas: the type of abrogation; the particulars of the abrogating verses; and the particulars of the abrogated verses. The thinking on these three areas differs very widely, which has a profound effect on the perspective of Islam, especially in modern times." See Preface, p. xci.

a good person. Rather, the rulings were accepted in accordance with the conventions of the time."²² ... "Let us suppose that the Prophet wanted to carry out *ijtihad* in his own time, did he have to take into consideration the conditions of his time or not? Was it possible to issue a ruling of *shari'a* without taking into consideration the conditions of that time and place? Is it possible to speak with Arab-speakers in a language and culture that is other than the language and culture of Arabs? It was not possible. The Prophet has spoken in the language and culture of the reasonability of his time. Today it is we who must separate the stable and permanent rulings of the Prophet from the margins that were the conventions of that time."²³

In other words, Kadivar suggests that as the issuing of rulings by the Prophet was embedded in a particular socio-political, economic, geographic context, so must the review of rulings today. This, of course, begs the question of whether scholars operating in different contexts today might not come to different conclusions in subjecting a particular ruling to his four criteria. Kadivar does not discuss the possibility.

5 Excavating Normative Plurality

Before closing with a discussion of Kadivar's notion of democratic secularism, his innovative approach of "excavating normative plurality" shall briefly be highlighted. That is, by meticulous comparison of extant rulings on a given subject matter, Kadivar demonstrates far greater plurality of normative positions than is often assumed. Three examples shall illustrate this: his discussion of the right to resist despotic power, women's rights and the rights of non-Muslims.

Kadivar asks whether there is a right in Islam to resist an unjust ruler and notes that such a right has hardly been recognised in Islamic law. This is partly because the relevant discussions have almost exclusively been limited to two concepts: those of *baghi* (rebel) and *muharib* (secessionist, someone who has risen up in war). The latter also has the connotation of gangster. A *muharib* has committed one of the gravest crimes and the punishments fall into the area of *hudud*.

---

22 Chapter 10, p. 293.
23 Chapter 10, p. 295.

In contrast to the *muharib*, the *baghi* fights for change in rulership and his actions are deeply political. Whether he is fighting for justice must be determined on the basis of the political order he is fighting against and the alternative political order he is fighting for. The *hudud* punishments do not apply to him. Kadivar lays out that Hanbali *fiqh*, as well as the majority opinions in the other three Sunni *madhahib*, do not recognise justified political opposition. And while Shi'i *fiqh* does in limited circumstances recognise it, de facto Shi'ite rulers, like their Sunni counterparts, have not tolerated any concept in Islamic law that would legitimise challenges to their rule. He notes that even Iran's former Head of the Judiciary, Ayatollah Shahroudi, recognised that there is a category of political opposition that does not qualify as *muharib* and that is legitimate. Kadivar reminds the reader that in Islamic history, Husain is neither *muharib* nor *baghi*. Rather, as Shi'ites see it, he is a political opponent who with the aim of preventing wrongdoing, did not pledge allegiance to the corrupt government of his time. Thus, Islamic juristic thought has recognised the possibility of legitimate opposition to illegitimate government, and Islamic history has seen examples of this. Nevertheless, Islamic jurisprudence has not acknowledged this intellectual possibility with its own legal concept, and Kadivar sees predominantly political reasons for this failure.

With regard to the topic of women's rights, Kadivar points out that in the area of public life the discussion boils down to five positions which women are "allegedly excluded from holding" according to traditional Islam. These are: source of emulation (*marja'-i taqlid*); Friday prayer leader; prayer leader in general; political leader or ruler; and judge. Kadivar indicates that he rejects the prohibition against women in the position of *marja'*. If a woman has the capacity to carry out *ijtihad*, why can she not be a source of reference for *shari'a* affairs, he asks?[24] He does appear to make a qualified advance in this regard, asking why female believers cannot at least emulate a female *mujtahid*. His pondering begs the question as to why he theoretically restricts women's authority to female followers. If a woman can be a source of emulation and a reference for *shari'a* affairs, then why should she be emulated by women only and not also by male believers?[25] On the topic of whether women can be

---

24 On this discussion, see also Karen Bauer, "Debates on Women's Status as Judges and Witnesses in Post-Formative Islamic Law", *Journal of the American Oriental Society* 130(1) (2010): 1–21; Sedigheh Vasmaghi, *Zan, Fiqh, Islam* (Tehran: Nashr-e Samadiyah, 2008).

25 Chapter 11, p. 292.

prayer leaders, Kadivar points to the fact that "in the case where the general prayer leader is a male and women are praying, we segregate the two by a curtain and no problems arise. Why can the same not be done if the prayer leader is a woman, or why can the prayer leader not stand in a deep prayer niche (*mihrab*) [if there are males in the congregation]?" In other words, Kadivar does not see a general prohibition against women leading the prayer even for male believers as long as they can be concealed from the male gaze. With regard to the question of whether women may function as rulers, he points to the works of Mohammad Mehdi Shamseddin (1936–2001), who in Kadivar's view has disproved as invalid all traditional Islamic arguments against women exercising political and sociological authority. On the question of whether women may serve as judges, he notes that in the view of reformist Islam, women's right to judge is the same as that of men.[26] In his particular case, given that he argues Islamic law should be limited to the realm of the ethical orientation for individuals, but not serve as the basis for state law, the reservations against female judges would presumably disappear. Reservations in traditional Islam against women judges are based on the idea that women lack the mental faculties to interpret Islamic law and the sociological faculties to enact it. But if Islamic law is not applied in courts, then the reservation against women judges becomes obsolete. In a very innovative separate chapter, Kadivar explores women's rights in the Hereafter: are there indications in Islamic teachings that women will be held to a different standard on Judgement Day? Are women believed to have fewer or different rights than men in the Hereafter? Based on an analysis of Qur'anic verses, and after disqualifying alternative sources as unsound, Kadivar concludes that the sources "explicitly and transparently prove the equality of men and women in the Hereafter and the absence of a role for gender in [final] Judgement".[27]

On the question of the rights of non-Muslims, Islamic law has developed different categories of non-Muslims, each of which is accompanied by different sets of rights and duties. One of the chief contributions of Kadivar in this area consists in his insistence on a category that is often

26 He explained his reasoning on the topic in Mohsen Kadivar, "Revisiting Women's Rights in Islam: 'Egalitarian Justice' in Lieu of 'Deserts-based Justice'", in Ziba Mir-Hosseini, Lena Larsen, Christian Moe and Kari Vogt (eds), *Gender and Equality in Muslim Family Law: Justice and Ethics in the Islamic Legal Tradition* (London: I. B. Tauris, 2013), 213–234.
27 Chapter 11, p. 308.

neglected, that of non-Muslims who are not protected by *dhimmi* status or by treaty, but who deserve peace and security because they are also not in the category of those warring with Muslims. Kadivar lays out that non-Muslims are usually discussed in Islamic law as falling into three categories: first, there are the "People of the Book", that is, adherents of the Abrahamic religions Judaism and Christianity. Second, there are non-Muslims other than Jews and Christians who have entered bilateral treaties with Muslims, the so-called "People of Treaty" (*mu'ahad*). These may include believers of other religions as well as all types of non-believers such as pagans, agnostics, idolaters, polytheists and atheists. Third, there are non-Muslims at war with Muslims (*kafir harbi*), who are not accorded human rights in Islamic law. But, importantly, there is a fourth category that must be recognised: non-Muslims who do not fall into the first two categories but who also are not part of the third, because they have not taken up arms against Muslims. According to the explicit textual meaning of Qur'anic verses 60:8–9, Muslims are not allowed to wage war against unbelievers who have not initiated war against Muslims and did not try to expel them from their homes or violate their religious affairs. Apart from those of *dhimmi* status, the vast majority of non-Muslims in the world fall into this latter category and therefore should be accorded full human rights, according to Kadivar.

At the same time, Kadivar also demonstrates the multiple ways in which the rights even of those non-Muslims who enjoy *dhimmi* or treaty status suffer severe limitations compared with Muslims, if one subscribes to the viewpoint of what Kadivar calls traditional Islam. These range from inferior rights in marriage, to considerations of their inferior dignity, limitations on their own rights of religious practice, to inferior status in criminal law and with regard to property rights.[28] Kadivar is clear on the implications of *dhimma*, which accords protection but nevertheless does not accord non-Muslims equality in their dignity. "The way in which the *jizya* is paid must be humbling and the people of *dhimma* must always feel lowly . . . From the point of view [of traditional Islam], these people [non-Muslims] are not 'the holders of sacred life' (*al-nafs al-mohtarama*). Their blood has neither sanctity nor value. It is the religion of truth that creates the value of life. Adhering to false religions and beliefs takes the value from life."[29]

---

28 Chapter 5.
29 Chapter 5, p. 96.

Overall, Kadivar's interventions on these three topics illustrate the strength of his methods. He follows traditional *ijtihad*, discussing the conclusions in the prevalent majority opinions of what he refers to as traditional Islam in order to then apply his own method of *ijtihad* in principles and foundations (*al-usul wa al-mabani*), which leads him to eliminate unsound sources and contradictory arguments, and to revive indications that other interpretations have overlooked in order to then reinterpret given conclusions. In doing so, he expands the discursive space of methodologically sound interaction with a given legal problem and frequently documents greater normative plurality in jurisprudential perspectives in the history of Islamic law than most contemporary discussions allow for.

6 Democratic Secularism and Democracy

Kadivar's notion of religious freedom encompasses several dimensions, notably the freedom to choose a religion, the freedom to leave a religion, the freedom to either practice a religion or not, and the freedom to religious education. The secular state is one that does not identify with a particular religion. Accordingly, its law is secular (as mentioned earlier, *shari'a* ruling should be the basis for individual people's ethics, but not state law, according to Kadivar). Further, religious officials have no special political right of representation and their qualification as religious officials does not empower them to political privileges.

Like other scholars of democratic religion–state relations, Kadivar distinguishes a distancing model of state neutrality, often associated with the French model, that prioritises freedom *from* religion, with models of secularism where religion is not relegated to the private sphere but instead may be a force in civil society. This latter model of open (as opposed to distancing) neutrality, which takes the freedom *to* religion as seriously as the freedom *from* religion, is often associated with the United States, Germany, the northern European countries and India.

Kadivar favours the model of open neutrality which allows for a strong presence of religion in civil society. He also appears to favour a model of public education that accommodates (non-devotional) education in religion, although he does not specify whether he favours denomination-based instruction or, by contrast, integrated instruction where pupils are taught about several religions together. It appears to be clear that he does not advocate a model where religious content would inform the teaching of other subjects, such as history, philosophy or biology. Kadivar further suggests that public media ought to be sensitive to content that might be deemed offensive to adherents of a religion, and as such appears to be in favour of laws against blasphemy and defamation. In all of these cases, the safeguarding of human rights would appear to be the highest standard, with the notable specification that the freedom to religion (positive religious freedom) be considered as important as (and not less important than) the freedom from religion (negative religious freedom).

Accordingly, Kadivar writes that the impermissibility of personal religious symbols such as women's headscarves in the public sphere (in countries such as France, in Turkey in government buildings and public educational institutions) is against human rights.[30] Other scholars would agree that such prohibitions are actual violations of the right to religious freedom, specifically the right to exercise one's religion not only in private but also in public spaces.[31]

With these views, Kadivar is in the mainstream of thinkers who endorse secularism combined with the possibility of a strong role for religion in public life, such as Rajeev Bhargava, Ernst-Wolfgang Böckenförde, Alfred Stepan and Charles Taylor.[32]

What further unites the last three thinkers (Bhargava is more ambiguous on the matter) is the principle of reciprocity: no religious group can claim rights and benefits for itself that it would not also grant to other religious groups in the same polity, as well as to non-believers. Kadivar appears to take the same position, which is all the more striking as he writes with Muslim

---

30 At the same time, he also suggests that veiling is not mandatory in Islam: "Covering woman's hair, head and neck is unnecessary and, in the first place, never was obligatory, and depends on the conditions and customs of time and place." Interview: Muslim Attitudes Towards Democracy, interview with Islamic Studies Section, Research Center Crisis and Conflict in Iraqi Kurdistan, 7 August 2017, available at: https://kadivar.com/16102, last accessed 30 July 2019.

31 Heiner Bielefeldt, Nazila Ghanea and Michael Wiener, *Freedom of Religion or Belief* (Oxford: Oxford University Press, 2016); Ernst-Wolfgang Böckenförde, "The Fundamental Right of Freedom of Conscience", *Religion, Law, and Democracy. Selected Writings* (Oxford: Oxford University Press, 2020).

32 Rajeev Bhargava, "Reimagining Secularism: Respect, Domination and Principled Distance", *Economic and Political Weekly* 48(50) (2013): 79–92; Böckenförde, *Religion, Law, and Democracy. Selected Writings*; Alfred C. Stepan, "The World's Religious Systems and Democracy: Crafting the Twin Tolerations", *Arguing Comparative Politics* (Oxford: Oxford University Press, 2001), 213–253; Charles Taylor, "The Meaning of Secularism", *The Hedgehog Review* 12(3) (2010).

majorities in mind. Repeatedly, he insists that religions are not permitted to assert themselves anywhere other than in personal lives and in civil society. And he has approvingly pointed elsewhere to the few Muslim countries experimenting with secular democracy. "Models of secular democratic rule are now exemplary at least in Turkey and Tunisia. Senegalese and Indonesian models can also be studied."[33]

Kadivar identifies six points of conflict between *shari'a* and the UN Universal Declaration of Human Rights (UDHR, 1948): religious discrimination, gender discrimination, the acceptance of slavery, inequality between religious officials and lay people, lack of religious freedom and violent punishments. All *shari'a* regulations that violate human rights as defined in the UDHR must be abrogated, he writes, because they do not pass the review based on his four criteria. "Divine law cannot be unjust, immoral, unreasonable and inferior in function."[34]

But the international definitions of Human Rights have expanded since the 1948 UDHR, and many democratic governments have since passed legislation further breaking down discrimination based on criteria such as sex, religion or race.

It is in this light that Kadivar also addresses the topics of sexual relations outside marriage, euthanasia and homosexuality. Here he clearly rejects the positions of traditional Islam which criminalise all three phenomena, but leaves his own position unspecified. He reminds the reader that he discusses them purely from the perspective of lawfulness, not sin, and adds that there is no question these acts are sinful.[35] With regard to homosexuality, Mehrdad Alipour has concluded that although Kadivar has not explicitly accepted the human rights of homosexuals as homosexuals, "his theological repertoire is extensive enough to have the capacity to permit practicing homosexuality in Islam".[36]

---

33 Interview: Muslim Attitudes Towards Democracy, interview with Islamic Studies Section, Research Center Crisis and Conflict in Iraqi Kurdistan, 7 August 2017, available at: https://kadivar.com/16102, last accessed 30 July 2019. He adds: "I think that secular democratic rule is growing among Muslim thinkers."

34 Preface, p. xxvi.

35 A sin is something that has consequences in the hereafter. A crime is something that may be punished in this world." Chapter 9, p. 250.

36 Mehrdad Alipour, "Shi'a Neo-traditionalist Scholars and Theology of Homosexuality: Review and Reflections on Mohsen Kadivar's Shifting Approach", *Theology & Sexuality* 24(3) (2018): 200–218, at p. 200.

Foreword

Finally, it has already been mentioned that Kadivar envisions a democratic state where religious authority has no bearing on political authority
and where state law is exclusively secular. But it also bears mentioning that
democracy is strongly connected with social rights in Kadivar's thought. The
last chapter of the book is in fact the one that was written earliest and it
discusses the institutions of social welfare in Islamic law in depth, inspired
by his mentor Montazeri, who accorded great merit to the social dimension
of justice in Islam. Kadivar emphasises that social security is not among the
elements considered recommended (*mustahabb*) in Islamic law, but instead
is among the necessities (*ilzami*) and as such is obligatory. He clarifies that
the instruments in this regard are multiple, that they serve different ends, are
undertaken by different subjects, and also differ in their shares. Overall, he
outlines fourteen different kinds of taxes, fees and social institutions which
help to alleviate poverty and need in society. The most important of these are
the taxes of *zakat* and *khums*, but there also penances, charity, endowments,
shares of wills, interest-free loans and other mechanisms to ensure that social
security is being provided for.

Kadivar makes three major points in this regard. First, providing social
security is obligatory according to notions of just government and thus a government cannot absolve itself of this responsibility. Notably, in contemporary
times this also includes the provision of insurances, such as health insurance,
unemployment insurance, retirement funds and disability insurances. Their
fulfilment is obligatory and, according to Kadivar, such measures should be
established "with the participation of citizens, the government, and employers". Discussions along these lines were particularly acute in Iran during the
long process of revising the labour law in the 1990s and 2000s, during which
the parliament pushed for higher social standards (with arguments supplied
by Montazeri and Kadivar among others), and the Guardian Council vetoed
draft legislation as it views labour contracts as part of the private sphere
which the government does not have the mandate to regulate.[37]

Second, Kadivar criticises that according to what he refers to as traditional Islam, faith (as defined in each *madhab*) is a condition for receiving
khums (20 per cent) and *zakat* (2.5 per cent). The poor and orphaned of the

---

37 Asghar Shirazi, *Constitution of Iran: Politics and the State in the Islamic Republic* (London: I. B.
Tauris, 1997), ch. 10, "Circumventing the Sharia through Secondary Contractual Conditions",
pp. 206ff.

mukhalif (people of other *madhahib*) are not eligible to receive *shariʿa* funds. *Khums* and *zakat* are exclusive to the *muʾmin* (true *madhab*) Muslims.[38] Thus, according to traditional Islam, minorities (even Muslims of another sect) in a Muslim-majority society are not eligible for these kinds of social security support.

In contrast to such a position, Kadivar insists that social security is a human right and as such is a right for all citizens irrespective of their "religion, sect, gender, colour, race, etc.".[39] According to his re-interpretation, "social security counts as a right and providing it is the responsibility of the government".[40]

Third, somewhat surprisingly, in the epilogue, Kadivar clarifies that his methodology of applying *ijtihad al-usul wa al-mabani* led him to conclude that *khums* was a temporal ruling at the time of the seventh Shiʿite Imam. As it is not a permanent ruling, the annual obligatory Islamic tax for each Muslim is *zakat* only, amounting to around 2.5 per cent of all profits. Businesses are then absolved from paying 20 per cent of their profits on social causes (half of *khums* is traditionally spent on the Prophet and his descendants, while the other half is spent on orphans, the needy and travellers in need). Kadivar does not address how social causes would be financed once *khums* funds fall away, and he does not address the larger question of the relationship between regular state taxes and religious taxes. For example, one could ask whether Muslim citizens in high tax countries, such as Sweden, where taxes are used to pay for countrywide free education (including university education), health care, various insurances, social institutions (such as orphanages, retirement homes), as well as generous pension schemes, must still pay the additional 2.5 per cent *zakat* or whether

---

38 Chapter 5, p. 94: "In *sharʿi* discussions and the *fiqhi* rulings, the term *muʾmen* (believer) is different from that of Muslim. A believer is a Muslim who is a believer in the True sect (*al-madhab al-haqq*). Muslims who believe in other sects (*madhahib*) of Islam are called the opposite (*mukhalif*). For example, from the perspective of Shiʿite religious leaders, a believer is a Shiʿite Muslim and a Sunni is a *mukhalif*. To hold religious positions such as ruler (*wilayat al-amr*), source of emulation (*al-marjiʾayyat al-diniyah*), judge, witness, Friday and congregational prayer leader (*imam*), having faith (as defined in each *madhab*) is an additional condition to being Muslim. That is to say, Muslims of other sects do not meet the necessary requirements to serve in the six positions named above. Their testimony is not heard, their judgement is not credible."

39 Chapter 14, p. 401.

40 Chapter 14, p. 401.

this should be considered paid in their regular taxes which are invested also on social causes. Since Kadivar advocates the secular state that does not identify with any particular religion, where all law is secular, and where moreover it is the responsibility of the state to provide for basic standards of social welfare, it is worth clarifying what role the fourteen different kinds of Islamic taxes and charity payments ought to play.

7 Conclusions

With his approach of reviewing *shari'a* regulations with regard to their compatibility with human rights as defined in the UDHR, Kadivar has developed a ground-breaking methodology that concentrates on the source texts and prioritises the social effect of rulings. Rather than suggesting that notions of what we call human rights today can be found in the Qur'an and hadith, and instead of aiming to reinterpret rulings in order to bring them in line with contemporary rights notions, Kadivar calls for their abrogation in the case of contradictions with human rights. In order to do so, he has identified four criteria that rulings must fulfil in order to stand the test of time: they must meet the requirements of reasonability (*'uqala'i*), justice (*'adala*), morality and superior functionality over alternative solutions. He suggests that these four criteria are criteria that Islamic rulings were always meant to fulfil and that this explains why these rulings were issued by the Prophet and accepted by believers in the first place.

Kadivar's method of abrogation applies to *shari'a* rulings only and not to recitation or reading. His intention is certainly not to alter the Scriptures. But it means changing the source material from which *shari'a* rulings are derived and the methodology through which source material is being interpreted.

Kadivar holds that human rights have to be recognised as deriving from sources other than the Qur'an, hadith or the rulings of the *madhahib*. Human rights have modern intellectual sources and cannot be read back into the religious texts. Moreover, in contrast to adherents of traditional Islam, he does "not expect law from Islam".[41] *Shari'a* should be a source to guide believers in their behaviour, as an ethics, but not as a basis for state law.

---

41 See Preface, p. lxxxv.

Apart from providing answers to the question of whether a given ruling ought to be abrogated or not, the application of Kadivar's methodology bears great benefits. He follows traditional *ijtihad,* discussing the conclusions in the prevalent majority opinions of what he refers to as traditional Islam in order to then apply his own method of *ijtihad* in principles and foundations (*al-usul wa al-mabani*), which leads him to eliminate unsound sources and contradictory arguments, and to revive indications that other interpretations have overlooked, in order to then present his own conclusions. In doing so, he expands the discursive space of methodologically sound interaction with a given legal problem and frequently documents greater normative plurality in jurisprudential perspectives in the history of Islamic law than most contemporary discussions allow for.

Fully executing Kadivar's research programme will take decades to complete and may involve large communities of scholars. Furthermore, the review of *shari'a* rulings is an ongoing task as new normative questions arise (one need only think of the field of biotechnologies) and as attitudes change and rights notions may expand further. One can only hope that Kadivar's research programme will inspire debates and mobilise emulators in scholarly communities around the world. Whether his four-criteria test will prove to be durable or not, Kadivar has raised the level of the debate on Islam and human rights, and it will be difficult for future voices to make substantive contributions without being able to draw on a similar depth of familiarity with the multiple disciplines of Islamic studies and without applying the same rigour in *ijtihad al-usul wa al-mabani*.

Preface to the English Translation

Haqq al-Nas: Islam va Hoquq-e Bashar (*The Rights of People: Islam and Human Rights*) was originally written in Persian, and its first edition was published in Tehran in 2008. Less than a year later, all of my publications were banned by the present government in Iran and I was fired illegally from my tenured academic professorship. In Suhrawardi's terminology, I became an "Occidental Exile"![1] Now, twelve years later, the English translation of *Haqq al-Nas* is published here as *Human Rights and Reformist Islam*. The story of *Haqq al-Nas* is a real-life, ironic tragicomedy of "Islam and human rights", not in theory but in practice.

This Preface to the English Translation discusses the literature on Islam and human rights in order to situate *Haqq al-Nas* within it. By human rights I mean the Universal Declaration of Human Rights (UDHR) by the United Nations (1948). This is a much narrower definition than the notion of human rights in general, such as, for example, ideal human rights or metaphysical human rights. These general terms are ambiguous and unclear even to their advocates. In using "Reformist Islam", I distinguish between three readings of contemporary Islam: traditionalist, fundamentalist and reformist. I criticise the former two and follow the latter. By "reformist Islam" I mean the reading of Islamic scripture in the twenty-first century by a Muslim loyal to Islamic values and permanent criteria on the one hand, and awareness of rationality, the sciences and the conventions of the time, on the other. Neglecting this diversity in contemporary Islam, and generalising or identifying traditional or fundamentalist Islam as "Islam" is misleading and gives the wrong impression.

Although my perspective is clearly from a reformist Usuli Ja'fari Shi'ite Muslim point of view, this Preface also covers Sunni Islamic (traditionalist

---

1 "Qissat ul-Ghurbat il-Gharbiyya", in Shahabuddin Yahya Suhrawardi, *Majmu'a Mussanafat-i Shaikh Ishraq* (*Complete Works of the Master of Illuminative Philosophy*), vol. II, ed. Henry Corbin (Tehran: Institute of Humanities and Cultural Research, 1993), 273–297; "A Tale of Occidental Exile", in *The Mystical Visionary Treatises of Shahabuddin Yahya Suhrawardi*, trans. W. M. Thackston Jr. (London: Octagon Press, 1982), 100–108.

and reformist), as well as non-Muslim, perspectives. Islam is, therefore, one of two major subjects discussed in this Preface which covers a vast spectrum of interpretations. Furthermore, this Preface takes account of the English-language, Arabic and Persian literature relating to this subject.[2] I restricted myself to scholarly and academic literature. The authors included in my discussion are Mahmoud Mohamed Taha, Abdullahi Ahmed An-Na'im, Ann Elizabeth Mayer, Mohammad Mojtahed Shabestari and Abdulaziz Sachedina. Taha represents the Arabic literature on Islam and human rights in this review, Shabestari the Persian, and the other three the English-language literature. Mayer is the author of the most popular book on Islam and human rights from a non-Muslim and Western perspective. The other four could be considered to be the most outstanding Muslim reformist thinkers regarding Islam and human rights.[3]

This Preface contains six sections. I analyse the works of each thinker respectively in the first five sections. Each section has two parts: the first is a brief description of the thinker's opinion on human rights, and the second is a brief critical analysis, reviewing the advantages and disadvantages of that opinion. The last section is the longest and contains four parts. The first outlines my opinion on Islam and human rights, and the second compares my approach to the other five approaches. The third presents a comparative chronology of the six approaches, and the fourth and last part discusses the present book and the advantages of its English translation.

Section One: Taha's Second Message of Islam

Mahmoud Mohamed Taha (1909–1985) was one of the grandsons of a well-known Sudanese Sufi master,[4] and a civil engineer involved in political activities in Sudan during British colonialism. In 1945, together with others of like mind, he founded the "Republican Party" with the aim of achieving Sudan's independence and establishing a republican regime. He was imprisoned for his political activities. During his second term of imprisonment,

---

2 Although I also looked at French and German works, in this case indirectly.
3 This does not mean that there are no scholarly works on Islam and human rights except these five. I could only select a small number of authors, and this is my selection.
4 Hassan Wudd Balil.

having undertaken specific Sufi rituals,[5] he concluded that God had prepared him for a new invitation to Islam. He isolated himself from other people and, after his release from prison in 1948, spent three years in religious contemplation (*'i'tikaf*), completing what had been ignited in his mind in prison, focusing on the soul and spiritual illumination. He thought that his new ideas were a direct, divine inspiration straight to his heart. Finally, he laid his plan, titled *al-madhabiya al-islamiyya al-jadidah* (new Islamic school), which was based on absolute personal liberty and pervasive social justice, before a meeting of the Republican Party in 1951. Prior to this, the Republican Party had not had a religious framework. Taha started publishing his political manifesto, *al-Fikrat al-Jumhuriyya* (*Republican Thought*) which included explanations of his new approach to Islam: *Qul Hazihi Sabili* (*Say: This is my Way*, 1959) and *Usas Dastur al-Sudan* (*The Foundations of the Constitution of Sudan*, 1955). Taha's advocacy for a social democratic federal presidential republic was set out in his book, *Islam* (1960). It is one of Taha's major works, and could be said to be the manifesto of the Republican Party, setting out its call to a new Islam. Other works include *Risalat al-Salat* (*The Message of Prayer*, 1966) and *Tariq Muhammad* (*The Way of Muhammad*, 1966).

Mahmoud Mohamed Taha published *al-Risalat al-Thaniya min al-Islam* (*The Second Message of Islam*) in 1967. This is the most important of Taha's books and, together with *Islam*, contains the theoretical principles of the Republican Party. Publication of Taha's books was banned in Sudan around 1960, and in 1965 he was accused of apostasy *in absentia*. Taha wrote more than thirty books in the last two decades of his life, clarifying and explaining the major themes of his 1967 book. As a result of the publication and distribution of *al-Hawas al-Dini Yuthiru al-Fitnah Liyasila ila al-Sultah* (*Religious Obsession Incites Civil Strife to Gain Power*) by the Republican Party in 1983, Taha and more than fifty of the main party members were detained and imprisoned for eighteen months.

In the same year, Islamic *shari'a* law was ratified and started to be implemented in Sudan. Taha and other Republicans began criticising the new law from both inside and outside prison. Taha and four other high-ranking members of the Republic Party were detained in late 1984, accused of releasing a new book published by the Party: *Haza wa Toufan* (*This and Storm*),

---

5 Such as *Samadi* fasting (seven consecutive days and nights of abstinence from eating and drinking).

again criticising *shari'a* law and defending their interpretation of Islam. Taha and his four followers were sentenced to death, accused of apostasy and of acting against national security. But only Taha was executed, after the sentence was approved by Ja'far Numayri, the President of Sudan, on 7 November 1985.[6] Taha's religious thought is inseparable from his political thought, and combines a type of Sufi thought (*tariqa*) common in Sudan with his own specific Islamic intellectualism. He was unrealistically accused of apostasy on two grounds: the first was his inclination to Sufi doctrines such as the Unity of Existence (*wahdat al-wujud*), which provided the reason for the baseless accusation that he had claimed to be divine and had thereby dishonoured the Lord. The second was his innovative ideas about *shari'a* or Islamic law, which gave rise to two charges. The first was an erroneous accusation of "prophesy of the second Islam"; and the second was "denying the essentials of Islam" (*dharouriyyat al-din*), such as denying *zakat*, *jihad*, *talaq* (divorce), eternal punishment in hell, and disqualification of implementation of *shari'a* in modern times. The *fatwas* of apostasy that were issued against him in Khartoum, Mecca and Cairo, and the books that were published in criticism of his thoughts, all indicate the intense fear that conservative Muslims have of broader perspectives and the influence of his innovative ideas.[7]

Mahmoud Mohamed Taha did not have a background in classical Islamic studies. His works are completely unrelated to any scientific tradition in the Islamic world. He tried to resolve the socio-political problems of Sudan in the second half of the twentieth century through a "free interpretation" of the Qur'an. Taha distinguished between *shari'a* – what he saw as the product of

---

6 The main source on Taha's life and thoughts is this comprehensive and detailed book: 'Abdullah al-Fakki al-Bashir, *Sahib al Fahm al-Jadid lil-Islam, Mahmud Muhammad Taha wa al-Muthaqqafun: Qarat-un fi al-Mawaqif wa Tazwir al-Tarikh (The Holder of a New Understanding of Islam: Mahmud Muhammad Taha and Intellectuals, A Reading of Situations, and the Deception of History)* (Cairo: Roueya, 2013). The second source is the introduction by Taha's daughter Asma and his student an-Nur Muhammad Hamad to the first publication of Taha's selected works in the Arab world: *Nahwa Mashru' Mustaqbali lil-Islam (Towards a Future Project of Islam)* (Morocco and Lebanon: Al-Markaz al-Thaqafi al-'Arabi, 2002), 5–66. It contains three of Taha's major works: *al-Risalat al-Thaniya min al-Islam, Risalat al-Salat* and *Tatwir Shari'a al-Ahwal al-Shakhsiyya (Developing the Shari'a of Civil Status)*. The third source is the translator's introduction by Abdullahi Ahmed An-Na'im in Mahmoud Mohamed Taha, *The Second Message of Islam* (Syracuse, NY: Syracuse University Press, 1987), 1–30.
7 The full text of the *fatwas* of apostasy against Taha can be found in al-Bashir, *Sahib al Fahm al-Jadid lil-Islam*, 1158–1162.

the *fuqahas'* (jurists') understanding of the Qur'an and Prophetic Tradition –
and the Qur'an and the Tradition that are the origins of Islam. He believed
that the only solution to human problems was to return to Islam, following Muhammad's example, and the implementation of unabrogated verses
of the Qur'an. But his most innovative idea was his fresh understanding of
the Qur'an and the Tradition. His principal work, *al-Risalat al-Thaniya min
al-Islam* (*The Second Message of Islam*), contains the major themes of his ideas
on this subject.

Taha believed that Islam has two main missions. The first is that of the
mu'minun (believers) whose Islam was framed in the time of the Prophet in
Medina during one decade from 622 to 632. Most of their non-ritual rulings
were not originally (*bil-asalah*) Islamic but were adapted to the conditions of the
time, and human ability. This first mission is based on the subsidiary matters
(*furu'*) of the Qur'an. The second mission is that of the *muslimun* (Muslims;
from Taha's perspective all monotheists are Muslims) of the last days (*akhir al-
zaman*) – by which he means modern times – and is based on the *usul* (principles) of the Qur'an. These principles were revealed in Mecca over the course
of thirteen years (610–622). This Islam (the second mission) was not born in
fossilised form and its actualisation is inevitable. It will be actualised by distancing from the verses of subsidiary matters (*ayat far'iyyah*) and by approaching the
'principal verses' instead. It looks forward to preparing an appropriate atmosphere, an appropriate *ummah* (community) and appropriate figures.[8]

According to Taha, an egregious error is to imagine that the Islamic *shari'a*
of the seventh century (first century AH), with all its details, is appropriate for
implementation in the twentieth century (the time of writing his book), given
the undeniable difference between the horizons of the seventh and twentieth
centuries. He clarified this important point in his book *al-Islam fi Risalatahi
al-Ula la Yaslahu li Insaniyyat al-Qarn al-'Ishrin* (*Islam's First Message is not
Qualified for the Humanitarianism of the Twentieth Century*, 1969). He explicitly and frankly declared that *jihad* and *qital* (war), slavery, capitalism, gender inequality, polygamy, *talaq* (divorce), *hijab* and segregation of the sexes
(in public places) were not among the principal verses of the Qur'an.[9] These

8 Mahmoud Mohamed Taha, *al-Risalat al-Thaniya min al-Islam in Nahwa Mashru' Mustaqbali
lil-Islam* (*Towards a Future Project of Islam*) (Morocco and Lebanon: Al-Markaz al-Thaqafi
al-'Arabi, 2002), 149–156 and 167–173 (chs 5 and 6).
9 Ibid., 156–166.

verses were revealed in Medina, and it was imagined that they abrogated the principal verses that had been revealed in Mecca. From his point of view, human freedom, the absence of compulsion in religion, socialism in property ownership, gender equality in all its aspects, monogamy, the continuity of marriage, spiritual modesty and chastity of both man and woman, and de-segregation or mixing between women and men, were some of the principal verses of the Qur'an.

The structure of religion is pyramidal, with God at its peak, and at its base humanity. *Shari'a* is descending (*tanzil*) from that transcendent peak and taking human capacity into account. The pyramid's base was proportional to the conditions at the time of revelation. The nearer one gets to the pyramid's peak, the closer one is to the principal goals. Humanity has matured and grown out of its childhood, the consequence being its ascent from a dense *shari'a* to a light *shari'a*, that is, from subsidiary statements (*al-nusus al-far'iyya*) to the principal statements (*al-nusus al-asliyya*).[10]

A good society is based on three equalities: economic equality (socialism), political equality (democracy), and social equality (lack of discrimination and social inequality).[11] According to Taha, the objective of the second Islam is to approach the principal verses and put aside the subsidiary verses, in accordance with the specific conditions of the times. Islamic *shari'a* is perfect, but its perfection is its flexibility and its capacity for transformation and evolution, making it compatible with different individual and collective conditions. What is called Islamic *shari'a* today is based on the texts of the second period of Islam (Medina).[12]

Although Taha critically analysed abrogation of the principal verses by the subsidiary verses of Medina,[13] I have not found a single "abrogation of Medina verses by Meccan verses" in his major books, including his master work *al-Risalat al-Thaniya min al-Islam* (*The Second Message of Islam*).[14] The clearest piece on abrogation in his books could be this:

---

10 Ibid., 185–189 (conclusion).

11 Ibid., 172–184.

12 Ibid., 76–78.

13 Ibid., 75, 120, 151, 157. Taha did not use "abrogated" on p. 181, but in An-Na'im's translation "which were temporarily abrogated" was added to the text (*The Second Message of Islam*, 161).

14 I could not find anyone (be they Taha's proponents or opponents) who refers to Taha's books for attribution of the "abrogation of Medina verses by Meccan verses". In which of his books does he mention this explicitly?

It is as if the abrogated verses were abrogated in accordance with the needs of the time, and postponed until their appropriate time comes. When it does, they become the suitable and operative verses and are implemented, while those that were implemented in the seventh century become abrogated. The dictates of the time in the seventh century were the subsidiary verses. For the twentieth century, they are the primary verses. This is the rationale of abrogation, [in other words, it was not intended to be] final and conclusive abrogation, but merely postponement until the appropriate time. In this evolution, we consider the rationale beyond the text. If a subsidiary verse, which used to overrule the primary verse in the seventh century, has served its purpose completely and become irrelevant for the new era, the twentieth century, then the time has come for it to be abrogated and for the primary verse to be enacted. In this way, the primary verse has its turn as the operative text in the twentieth century and becomes the basis of the new legislation. This is what the evolution of *shari'a* means. It is shifting from one text that served its purpose and was exhausted to another text that was postponed until its time came. Evolution is therefore neither unrealistic or premature, nor expressing a naïve or immature opinion. It is merely shifting from one text to the other.[15]

Undoubtedly, abrogation of Medina verses by Meccan verses is consistent with the teachings of Taha. His teachings are based on the implementation of principal verses (Meccan verses from his perspective) and ignoring subsidiary verses (Medina verses from his perspective). He classified the rulings of the Qur'an and Tradition in two categories: the principal, and permanent rulings, and the subsidiary and temporal rulings. Implementation of the former is the original mission of Islam. The subsidiary and non-ritual rulings of *shari'a* – that were specific to the first mission of Islam, and are known as subsidiary verses of the Qur'an – are temporal rulings. Therefore, it is not incorrect to conclude that, from his perspective, the Meccan verses abrogated the Medina verses. The abrogating (*nasikh*) – as he explicitly noted – is the Qur'anic statement, nothing else.

---

15 Taha, *al-Risalat al-Thaniya min al-Islam*, 78; An-Na'im's translation in Taha, *The Second Message of Islam*, 40–41. This is part of Taha's introduction to the 4th edition of *The Second Message of Islam*.

We can find the first usage of "reverse abrogation" in the writings of Taha's students, but still without explicit abrogation of Medina verses by Meccan ones: "The evolutionary principle of interpretation is nothing more than reversing the process of *naskh* or abrogation so that those texts which were abrogated in the past can be enacted into law now, with the consequent abrogation of texts that used to be enacted as *Shari'a*."[16]

From the Sunni perspective, there are three types of abrogation in the Qur'an: abrogation of the ruling and elimination of the verse from the Scripture; elimination of the verse from the Scripture without abrogation of the ruling; and abrogation of the ruling, but retention of the verse in the Scripture.[17] Taha did not discuss the first two types of abrogation, but focused on the third, that is, *naskh al-hukm bi la talawa* (abrogation of the ruling, without elimination of its verse from Scripture). This type of abrogation is also divided into two categories. In the first category, the abrogating verse observes the ruling of the abrogated verse and describes its cancellation, that is, the conflict between the two verses is essential. The second category does not have this characteristic, and although the later verse abrogates the earlier one it is because of a non-essential conflict.[18] It appears that Taha did not have any problem with the first category. His challenge focused on the second category of abrogation of the Qur'an by the Qur'an, that is, non-essential conflict. This category of abrogation is extremely common among Sunni exegetes. The best example is the "sword verse" (Q. 9:5) and the abrogation of more than 140 verses of the Qur'an,[19] including the most liberal one,[20] *la ikraha fi al-din* (no compulsion in religion, Q. 2:256).

Taha's idea is innovative and helpful, because many verses – all of the liberal verses of the Qur'an – which contain the principal rulings on human rights are protected from being destroyed by abrogation (*mansukhiyyat*).

---

16 Abdullahi Ahmed An-Na'im, *Toward an Islamic Reformation: Civil Liberties, Human Rights and International Law* (Syracuse, NY: Syracuse University Press, 1990), 56.

17 Muhammad Ibn 'Abdullah al-Zarkashi, *Al-Burhan fi 'Ulum al-Qur'an (The Perfect Guide to the Sciences of the Qur'an)* (Cairo: Maktaba Dar al-Turath, 1984), 2:36–40.

18 Sayyid Abu al-Qasim al-Khu'i, *Al-Bayan fi Tafsir al-Qur'an (Explanation of Qur'anic Exegesis)* (Qom: Anwar al-Huda, 1981), 286; English translation: *The Prolegomena to the Qur'an*, introduction and trans. Abdulaziz A. Sachedina (Oxford: Oxford University Press, 1998).

19 Mustafa Zayd, *Al-Naskh fi al-Qur'an al-Karim, Dirasah Tashri'iyah, Tarikhiyah, Naqdiya (Abrogation in the Qur'an, a Legal, Historical and Critical Study)* (Cairo: Dar al-Wafa, 1987), 508.

20 Taha used the term *at-Tasamuhi* (tolerated) verses.

Shi'ite scholars restricted abrogation to the first category of the third type and denied the first two types explicitly, and the second category of the third type implicitly.[21] Contemporary Shi'ite scholars expressed the opinion that the second category of abrogation never occurred in the Qur'an.[22] Although the abrogation of the principal verses on human rights are not accepted in Shi'ite Islam, most scholars did not accept the priority of these verses in the conflict with the subsidiary verses (in Taha's terminology), so Taha's idea is innovative for these too.

Advantages and Shortcomings of Taha's Approach

Taha's approach injected fresh blood into the veins of the *shari'a* corpus. He reconstructed Islam in two ways: first, he designated the principal verses of the Qur'an on human rights, that is to say, the liberal verses that were revealed in Mecca, as permanent essentials of Islam; second, he abrogated all the verses that are known as obstacles to human rights, democracy and modernity, which were revealed in Medina as temporal and which were appropriate for conditions in the past. Like a proficient physician, Taha diagnosed the illness of Islamic thought: the subsidiary rules of the Qur'an or Tradition are not essentials of Islam. They were rulings for different conditions and situations, and their time is over. They were abrogated by the Meccan verses, that is, the principal verses. This is his important surgical contribution. He eliminated the rulings that belonged to the past and that became the ugliness of Islam in the contemporary age, and released those rulings that had been imagined as abrogated, and manifested them as the beauty of Islam. He restructured the abrogation technique, and reversed it. The earlier text abrogates the later, and both the abrogating and the abrogated are verses of the Qur'an. The Meccan verses abrogated the Medina verses and hadiths. Taha's revision of Islam fits modernity, democracy and human rights. This is reform from the inside, revisiting the Qur'anic technique of abrogation. I believe that Taha's theory was the most progressive in the Islamic world, not only for his time but for several decades after his death.

---

21 Muhammad Hadi Ma'rifat, *al-Tamhid fi 'Ulum al-Qur'an* (*Introduction to the Sciences of the Qur'an*) (Qom: Dar al-Ta'aruf, 2011), 2:263–390.
22 Al-Khu'i, *Al-Bayan fi Tafsir al-Qur'an*, 287.

However, Taha's theory suffers from at least twelve major shortcomings.

First, Taha's theory is in essence a religious theory. After criticising Western philosophical theory, he concluded that although the West had made much progress in technology and science, in civilisation (which for him was ethics and its essence, absolute human freedom) it had failed both at an individual and on a community level. According to Taha, all Western philosophies are shallow in their attempts to attain happiness for human beings.[23] By contrast Islam has this ability based on its first principle of *tawhid* (unity of God). Islam bestows absolute freedom on human beings.[24] But which Islam? It is obvious that he meant the prevalent understanding of Islam. His new understanding of Islam, based on the principal Meccan verses of the Qur'an, is the key to opening all locks and for solving all problems, that is, the problems that Western philosophies, including capitalism and communism, could not solve. Therefore, from his perspective, Islam is a comprehensive set of teachings that solves all the individual and collective problems of humanity. Taha's new understanding of Islam as it was in Mecca is the primary source of all that is necessary for humans, including economic equality (socialism), political equality (democracy), justice and, most importantly, absolute human freedom. Taha's project for the happiness of all human beings is the "second message of Islam". It covers all aspects of human life, politics, economics, culture, and social affairs, and is not based on the *shari'a* of the seventh century, but on that of the modern age. It does not suffer from the fanatical rulings of fourteen centuries ago, but is a modern Islamic prescription for all aspects of life. In other words, Taha's expectation of Islam was as high as it could possibly be. The difference between him and conservative Muslims is not the belief in the necessity of an Islamic formula for all aspects of life; both of them agree on this fundamental point. The big difference is in the understanding of Islam: Islam as it was understood in Medina in the context of the seventh century that fixed *shari'a* as a permanent law forever (conservative Islam), and Islam as it is understood in modern times based on the permanent principal Meccan verses of the Qur'an and on the teachings of the Prophet (Taha's approach). The point of conflict is the understanding of Islam, not Islam itself, nor its universal sphere of reference. Islam, for Taha, is the source of *all* good outcomes. There

---

23 Taha, *al-Risalat al-Thaniya min al-Islam,* 88–91.
24 Ibid., 101.

is no good whose roots cannot be found in the principal Meccan verses of the Qur'an or in the Tradition of the Prophet. In the matter that concerns us, that is, human rights, Meccan Islam is the source of human rights for everyone, Muslim and non-Muslim, male and female alike. Meccan Islam is neither historical, nor is it restricted to the specific context of seventh-century Mecca. These are the eternal/timeless teachings and rulings on all aspects of life for all human beings. It means that the Universal Declaration of Human Rights was in the mind of the Lawmaker (*shari'*) and was possible not only in the context of the premodern period, but also that the Qur'an and the Prophetic Tradition in the Meccan period expressed it explicitly and implicitly. Taha references these textual sources of evidence repeatedly. His claim is much broader than "Islam is not inconsistent with modern notions of human rights". His claim is "Meccan Islam is the unique and only correct source of human rights". This is a very big, fundamental epistemic claim. I will return to it in the last section of this Preface.

Second, Taha's approach is a textual approach. Textual means scriptural, and scriptural means Qur'anic and Prophetic Tradition-oriented argumentation. There is no difference in this case between Taha and the original conservative mainstream Muslims. The difference lies in the domain of the Scripture, not in the scriptural approach itself. While the Scripture for conservative Muslims means the Qur'an and the Prophetic Tradition in both the Meccan and the Medina period, the major reference in *shari'a* rulings is the verses and hadiths of the Medina period, based on the abrogation of many verses of the Meccan period, or the priority of the specific (*khass*) over the general (*'amm*), or restricted (*muqayyad*) rather than absolute expression (*mutlaq*). In contrast, Taha restricted the Scripture in practice (not in recitation) in his time in two ways. First, it contains only Meccan verses and hadiths, just as the second mission of Islam. Second, the verses and hadiths of the Meccan period, as principal rulings of Islam, abrogate the Scripture of Medina as subsidiary rulings now out of their temporal context. In other words, while the principal rulings of the Meccan period are timeless and eternal, the Medina Scripture contains only subsidiary and temporal rulings that belonged in a specific context. So, it is obvious that from Taha's perspective the *shari'a* or Islamic law of the seventh century does not fit the different context and different situations of recent centuries. We should keep in mind that, based on the maximal expectation of Islam, the Scripture is the unique source of human rights (and other modern affairs). Again, Taha's specific scriptural approach correlates not only with the possibility, but also with the occurrence, of modern notions such as human rights in the context of the seventh century. This means that these notions are beyond history. In other words, in contrast to Medina Scripture, Taha's view on Meccan Scripture is ahistorical and non-critical. He did not provide any evidence or argumentation to uphold this claim.

Third, the indication (*dilala*) of the Scripture is not arbitrary. The methodology of indication has been discussed in detail in *usul al-fiqh* in the long chapter on the indication of utterances (*dilalat al-alfaz*). This discipline forbids imposing personal meaning on the text, describing that as interpretation by opinion (*al-tafsir bi al-ra'y*). The meaning of the Scripture has two levels: the apparent or *prima facie* meaning (*zahir*), and the internal or hidden meaning (*batin*). Interpretation of the Scripture (*tafsir*), especially in theology, ethics and jurisprudence (*fiqh*), is based on the former meaning. Interpretation of the Scripture in mysticism and Sufism is based on the latter meaning and is called *ta'wil*, which is close to symbolic language. Taha neither had any regard for the regulation of scriptural interpretation as it was explained in *usul al-fiqh*, nor gave an explanation of his methodology of textual interpretation in his writings. His scriptural interpretation is a combination of Sufi *ta'wil* and of interpretation by opinion (*al-tafsir bi al-ra'y*). The former methodology is acceptable in the domain of mysticism, such as his Recital of Prayer (*risala al-salat*), but most of his scriptural interpretations are classified under the latter type. This style of undisciplined interpretation is problematic and includes his interpretation of both the Qur'an and hadith.

Fourth, reference to weak hadith in jurisprudence and theology is problematic. All reporters in the chain of transmitters of hadith should be qualified in *rijal* (biographical evaluation or evaluation of the narrators of hadith). It is not acceptable to rely on a weak hadith. Taha used some weak hadiths that were attributed to the Prophet in his argumentations. He thought that there was no problem in using such hadiths if their indications supported his opinion. His non-critical approach to the transmission (*isnad*) of hadith is problematic, especially since we know that the majority of hadiths are not authentic.[25]

---

25 The second, third and fourth critiques were briefly discussed altogether first by Basim al-Makki in the first chapter titled "Mahmoud Mohamed Taha" in *'Alam tajdid al-fikr al-dini (Outstanding Men of the Renewal of Religious Thought)*, vol. I: *Tajdid al-fikr al-Islami: muqaraba naqdiyya (Renewing Islamic Thought: A Critical Approach)*, ed. Bassam al-Jamal (Rabat, Morocco: Mominoun without Borders, 2016), 31–32.

Fifth, Taha's concern was to convince his followers and challenge his political opponents. He was a social reformer in a low-tolerance religious community. He was a forceful preacher (*da'i*) and the charismatic leader of a political and modern Islamic party in opposition to a dictator. Such responsibility excites emotions, affections and passions, and is of epic proportions. The rational and critical approach of a scholar has different requirements and Taha's argumentations are made in a far from scholarly manner. Taha was a civil engineer, a political activist, a modernist Muslim thinker and a leading social reformer; but he had no background in either Islamic studies or philosophy. His critique of the latter, especially his generalisation about the lack of absolute freedom in *all* Western philosophical schools, is superficial. Although his critical approach to traditional Islamic studies was courageous and correct, his solution – which is the subject of this discussion – is problematic.[26]

Sixth, Taha divided the mission of the Prophet Muhammad and the teachings of Islam, at least for the modern era, into two periods, Mecca and Medina, respectively, as the second mission of Islam and its first mission. He clarified his innovative opinion that although the Prophet and the Qur'an codified the permanent outline of Islam in Mecca, there was not enough time to expand it theoretically, nor to implement it practically. It was in Medina that the first mission of Islam was described in detail and completely put into practice. However, it was adapted to fit the specific situation of that time, that is, it was temporal and time-bound. Today is the time to expand the second mission of Islam (the Islam of Mecca), implementing and practising it as the eternal teaching of Islam. But the message of the Prophet encompassed all of the revelations and teachings in Mecca and Medina, not just a part of them. The Prophetic mission is indivisible; it is a whole. In all of his works Taha's explanation of his innovative theory of the second mission of Islam was not able to break the integrity of the Prophetic mission. That would require a much stronger argumentation, and that is beyond Taha's knowledge and ability.[27]

Seventh, The key point in Taha's theory is the distinction between the Meccan verses – the principal and permanent teachings of Islam – and the

---

26 Ibid., 32–33.
27 Ibid., 33. See also 'Abd al-Majid Sharafi (or Abdelmadjid Charfi), *al-Islam wa al-Hidathah* (*Islam and Modernity*) (Tunisia: Al-Dar al-Tunisiyya, 1991), 156–160.

verses of the Medina period – the temporal and abrogated verses of the Qur'an. But how can we distinguish the Meccan verses? His criterion is the audience to whom the verses are addressed, and the use of specific phrases, such as *ya ayuha allazina amanu* (O, believers / *muminun*), which is a phrase specific to the Medina verses (except in *Sura* 22: Hajj), as well the use of the words *munafiq* (hypocrite) and *jihad*. But Meccan verses have several identifying characteristics. These are, first, that every sura mentions prostration (*sajdah*); second, that every sura opens with an alphabetic letter (*al-huruf al-muqatta'a*), except suras 2 and 3; and, third, that every sura uses the phrases *ya ayuha al-nas* (O, people) and *ya bani adam* (O, the children of Adam), except suras 2 and 4.[28] But Taha's criteria are not accurate in these matters. First, the term hypocrite (*munafiq*) is used in a Meccan sura, 29:11. Second, the term *jihad* is used in another Meccan sura, 25:52.[29] Third, prostration is used twice in this Medina sura, 22:18 and 77. These three criteria at least are neither comprehensive (*jami'*) nor inclusive (*mani'*), that is, they neither cover all Meccan and Medina verses nor exclude all non-Meccan or non-Medina verses. There are many places where these rules are violated. Distinguishing Meccan verses from Medina verses therefore cannot be determined by these qualitative criteria. It needs accurate critical and historical research such as was undertaken by Theodor Nöldeke (1836–1930) and his students.[30] There is no evidence that Taha was aware of this academic research. Nevertheless, if we revisit Taha's theory through Nöldeke's chronology, is it defensible? I will respond to this question in the next point.

Eighth, based on the chronology of Nöldeke and his students, there are many principal verses from the Medina period that ought to be permanent and eternal (in Taha's framework), as well as verses on subsidiary matters from the Meccan period that ought to be temporal and restricted to the time of early Islam (again in Taha's framework). These principal verses were

---

28 Taha, *al-Risalat al-Thaniya min al-Islam*, 150.

29 *Jihad* as a verb is used in these Meccan suras: 16:110, 29: 6, 8, 69 and 31:15. Suras 16 *al-Nahl* (Bee), 25 *al-Furqan* (Differentiator), 29 *al-'Ankabut* (Spider) and 31 *Luqman*. The meaning of *jihad* as a verb in these verses is not *qital*, so they do not violate Taha's claim.

30 Theodor Nöldeke, *Geschichte des Qorâns* (Leipzig: Dieterich, 1860, 2nd edn 1909–38). Its Arabic translation: *Tarikh al-Qur'an*, George Tamer (Beirut: Konrad-Adenauer-Stiftung, 2004); its English translation: *The History of the Qur'an*, by Theodor Nöldeke, Friedrich Schwally, Gotthelf Bergsträßer and Otto Pretzl, ed. and trans. Wolfgang H. Behn (Leiden: Brill, 2013).

revealed in Medina: "There is no compulsion in religion" (Q. 2:256); "By an act of mercy from God, you [Prophet] were gentle in your dealings with them – had you been harsh, or hard-hearted, they would have dispersed and left you – so pardon them and ask forgiveness for them. Consult with them about matters, then, when you have decided on a course of action, put your trust in God: God loves those who put their trust in Him" (Q. 3:159); "The Messenger's duty is only to deliver the message" (Q. 3:20, 5:92 and 99, 24:54, 64:12); the lack of a cardinal penal code or any worldly punishment for apostasy (Q. 2:217, 3:85–90, 4:137, 5:5 and 54, 47:25–28), the lack of any punishment, especially of any arbitrary cardinal code of punishment, for blasphemy, that is, for one who insults the Prophet *sabb al-nabi* (Q. 3:186, 4:40, 6:68 and 108, 9:49 and 61, 33:45–48 and 57); and religious diversity (Q. 2:113). I have explained in detail the indication (*dilalat*) of all of these verses elsewhere.[31] There are many more principal verses that were revealed in Medina concerning the rights of women and non-Muslims. These are discussed in the next section. Taha recognised only the first verse (Q. 2:256) as an exception to his criteria. On the other hand, verse 43:18, which is one of the discriminative verses in the case of women's rights, is Meccan! These instances (*mawadd al-naqdh*) seriously challenge the validity of Taha's theory of the second mission of Islam. These Medina verses are principal, permanent and cannot be abrogated, but because they were revealed in Medina they should be abrogated according to Taha's theory. This is a clear contradiction. Taha's ultimate goal was to preserve the principal verses of the Qur'an, which is a defensible aim. But restricting the principal and permanent verses to the Meccan period is neither correct, nor defensible. The complete inductive argument (*al-istiqra' al-tamm*) does not open any ground for inconclusive deductive syllogism (*al-qiyas al-'aqim*). This premise, that all principal verses were Meccan, was the backbone of Taha's theory and is wrong and unacceptable. The common ground of principal permanent verses of the Qur'an requires another theory. I will return to this key point in the last section of this Preface.

Ninth, highlighting the principal verses of the Qur'an is a brilliant point in Taha's theory, and he should be admired for it. In a previous remark,

---

31 In my monograph, *Blasphemy and Apostasy in Islam: Debates in Shi'a Jurisprudence.*

I argued that the point of principality could not be Meccan, and there is another problem here. The principles of dignity, justice, liberty, peace and so on are clear. But the principles of socialism, democracy, and lack of divorce are ambiguous and questionable. Divorce is not like polygamy, to be classed as temporal. Although marriage is highly recommended in Islam, and divorce is undesirable, nevertheless it is permissible, permanently. The problem concerning notions such as democracy and socialism is their derivation from the Scripture and the claim that Scripture was in a position to give such teachings. This means that managing economics and politics (not political ethics, nor the ethics of economics) is the role of religion, and especially of Islam, and that we should find the outline of correct politics and economics in the Qur'an and the Prophetic Tradition. Taha's claim went even further than this: socialism and democracy are two of the principal teachings of the second mission of Islam. This is another reading of political Islam, and is a very big claim. The key concept of "principal verses" is not defined clearly in Taha's works: he did not give us a comprehensive criterion for this important subject.

Tenth, abrogation is a legal term, regardless of whether the context is religious or secular, and it has two major elements, abrogating (*nasikh*) and abrogated (*mansukh*). These two elements have several essential characteristics. Abrogation is the cancellation of *previous* legislation – that its apparent meaning (*zahir*) requires its continuity – by *later* legislation, and concatenating the validity of these two laws is impossible. The abrogated is the previous law, and the abrogating is the new law. The *contradiction* between abrogated and abrogating legislation is essential and definite. Observing the general conditions of abrogation is required in the abrogation of Qur'anic verses. It is necessary for the abrogated to be the older verse and for the abrogating to be the later verse in time.[32] What Taha called abrogation – that is, abrogation of the Medina verses by Meccan verses, which is called *reverse abrogation* – does not observe the essentials of abrogation. Cancellation of the later verses by the earlier verses is *not* abrogation, neither in legal terminology, nor in scriptural terminology. It is a meaningless term that is not supported by any legal or scriptural scholarship. So-called "reverse abrogation" is unacceptable by definition. In addition, not only is there no evidence in support of its

---

32 Ma'rifat, *al-Tamhid fi 'Ulum al-Qur'an*, 2:267–274.

validity (*hujjiyaa*), but there are also strong arguments for it not being valid. Abrogation of a Qur'anic verse needs strong evidence. Such strong evidence is only available for less than seven verses of the Qur'an.[33] If the conflict between two verses is not in their essence, and compromise between them, even partial, is possible, then abrogation does not occur. More than two hundred cases of so-called abrogation in exegeses of the Qur'an are unacceptable because of the lack of this necessary condition of abrogation.[34] The most famous example is the abrogation of "there is no compulsion in religion" (Q. 2:256) by the Sword verse (Q. 9:5).[35]

This type of abrogation was the point of contention between mainstream Sunni Islam and Taha. Taha correctly concluded that abrogation in this category was baseless. If abrogation was decided by humankind, then that practically gave Taha permission to apply abrogation in his particular framework. To be fair, both of them are baseless: both the abrogation of liberal verses by the Sword verse and its sisters, and the abrogation of all non-ritual rulings of the Medina verses, including the Sword verse, by Meccan verses. In the medieval period, Sunni exegetes promoted the abrogation of all the liberal verses of the Qur'an by the Sword verse (and its sisters) in justification of their political agenda. In the twentieth century, Mahmoud Mohamed Taha formulated the theory of "reverse abrogation" to justify his political agenda in support of his democratic humanistic activities. The motive of both abrogation techniques was political: two different policies of course, autocratic theocracy and social democracy. We cannot blame Taha for abusing (or using) religion as an instrument for politics, unless we also blame the mainstream of Sunni exegetes for exactly the same abuse. I have discussed this important point elsewhere.[36]

In any case, transmitted abrogation (*al-naskh al-naqli*) or abrogation of the Qur'an by the Qur'an is restricted to abrogation of the earlier verse by the later verse if, and only if, their conflict is in their essence. These four types of so-called abrogation are completely invalid and without foundation:

---

33 Abrogation of Q. 58:12 by 58:13, 8:65 by 8:66, 2:240 by 2:234, 4:15–16, 8:72 by 33:6, and 2:142–150. See al-Khu'i, *al-Bayan fi Tafsir al-Qur'an*, 287–326.

34 Ma'rifat, *al-Tamhid fi 'Ulum al-Qur'an*, 2:318–413.

35 Zayd, *Al-Naskh fi al-Qur'an al-Karim*, 508.

36 See my chapter "Genealogies of Pluralism in Islamic Thought: A Shi'a Perspective", in Mohammed Hashas (ed.), *Pluralism in Islamic Contexts: Ethics, Politics and Modern Challenges*, Philosophy and Politics – Critical Explorations Series (Basel: Springer, forthcoming).

abrogation of the ruling and the recitation (*naskh al-hukm wa al-talawa*); abrogation of the recitation but not the ruling (*naskh al-talawa bi la hukm*); abrogation of the ruling but not the recitation (*naskh al-hukm bi la talawa*) in non-essential conflicts; and, finally, 'reverse abrogation', that is, abrogation of Medina verses by Meccan verses. The first three are abrogation specific to Sunni mainstream exegetes of the Qur'an, and the latter is Taha's innovative idea. The only valid type of transmitted abrogation (*al-naskh al-naqli*) is abrogation of the ruling but not the recitation (*naskh al-hukm bi la talawa*) in the case of essential conflicts. This is the consensus of both Sunni and Shi'ite schools of thought and is accepted by Taha too.

Eleventh, Taha is a well-known and leading Muslim reformer, first, because of his strong criticism of the implementation of seventh-century *shari'a* in the twentieth century, and, second, because of his classification of *shari'a* as principal and permanent teachings of Islam, on the one hand, and subsidiary and temporal teachings, on the other hand; focusing on principal verses of the Qur'an and the Prophetic Tradition, and neglecting the permanence of (or marginalising, abrogating) the other teachings (the Medina verses and hadith) and introducing them as subsidiary and temporal teachings.

However, his innovative theory of reverse abrogation has not been accepted by scholars of Qur'anic studies. More than half a century after the publication of *al-Risalat al-Thaniya min al-Islam* (*The Second Message of Islam*), "reverse abrogation" has been discussed neither in major books of *'ulum al-Qur'an* (Qur'anic studies),[37] nor in monographs on abrogation in the Qur'an,[38] nor in the articles on *naskh* (abrogation) in the major encyclopaedias of Islam[39] or the Qur'an.[40] This means that "reverse abrogation" in Qur'anic or Islamic studies is accepted neither in Muslim nor in Western scholarship. If it is said that the former is under the domination of conservative Muslims, nonetheless

---

37 Ma'rifat, al-*Tamhid fi 'Ulum al-Qur'an*.

38 Zayd, *al-Naskh fi al-Qur'an*; John Burton, *The Sources of Islamic Law: Islamic Theories of Abrogation* (Edinburgh: Edinburgh University Press, 1990); Louay Fatoohi, *Abrogation in the Qur'an and Islamic Law: A Critical Study of the Concept of "Naskh" and its Impact* (London: Routledge, 2014).

39 John Burton, "*Naskh*", in *The Encyclopedia of Islam*, 2nd edn (Leiden: Brill, 1993), 7:1009–1012. There is a short article by Annette Oevermann, "Taha, Mahmud Muhammad", in *The Encyclopaedia of Islam*, 2nd edn (Leiden: Brill, 2000), 10:96–97, that briefly mentions his religious theory and specific abrogation.

40 John Burton, "Abrogation", in Jane Dammen McAuliffe (ed.), *An Encylopaedia of the Qur'an* (Leiden: Brill, 2001), 1:11–19.

the latter, for all its eagerness to embrace modern approaches to Islam and the Qur'an, has not acknowledged Taha's theory as a scholarly discipline of Qur'anic studies. I have not found any scholars who support Taha's theory (except his students, of course).

Twelfth, and final remark, distinguishing between principal verses and subsidiary ones is not a textual and transmitted (*naqli*) discipline. It requires a strong methodology and a rational framework. Taha started a radical reform that could be called a revolution in Islamic thought, but without preparing a methodology and rational framework for it. Because of this shortcoming, although he constructed a wonderful building, the foundations on which it stands are weak and problematic. Traditional Islamic studies and *ijtihad* do not have the capacity, nor are they prepared, for such a radical reform or revolution. Sunni theology, jurisprudence and ethics do not recognise independent human reason (*al-'aql al-mustaqil*) as one of the epistemic sources of Islam and *shari'a*. There is, therefore, a deep resistance to acceptance of such structural reform. *Maqasid al-shari'a*, or the objectives of Islamic law, are restricted to the subjects on which there is no ruling in *shari'a* (*ma la nass fih*).[41] The main problem of Islamic law is the subjects about which there are rulings in the Qur'an and Prophetic Tradition. Although Shi'a (Usuli school) theology, jurisprudence and ethics theoretically recognised reason as one of the epistemic sources of Islam, in practice it was not used, and Shi'ite scholars have not been brave in applying it, especially in challenging cases of *ma nass fih* (the challenge between the Scripture and reason). We have come very close to the key point of this discussion, to which I will return in the final section of this Preface.

Section Two: An-Na'im's Toward an Islamic Reformation

In 1987, Abdullahi Ahmed An-Na'im[42] (b. 1946 in Sudan) published an English translation of the work of his teacher, Mahmoud Mohamed Taha,

---

41 See Abu Ishaq al-Shatibi, *Al-Muwafaqat fi Usul al-Shari'a* (*The Reconciliation of the Fundamentals of Islamic Law*) (Saudi Arabia: Dar Ibn 'Affan, 1997), 1:125–138 (the tenth and eleventh introduction on human reason). English translation: *The Reconciliation of the Fundamentals of Islamic Law*, trans. Imran Ahsan Khan Nyazee, reviewed by Raji M. Rammuny (Reading: Centre for Muslim Contribution to Civilization in association with Garnet Publishing, 2011), vol. 1.

42 Charles Howard Candler Professor of Law at Emory Law, Associated Professor in the Emory College of Arts and Sciences, and Senior Fellow of the Center for the Study of Law and Religion at Emory University.

titled *The Second Message of Islam.*[43] In his first book, *Toward an Islamic Reformation: Civil Liberties, Human Rights and International Law,*[44] An-Na'im described his "adequate reform methodology" (ch. 3) and *"Shari'a* and basic human rights concerns" (ch. 7). This was the first book to discuss Islam and human rights from the critical viewpoint of a Muslim reformer. An-Na'im is a prolific author and has published several books, each of which touches on Islam and human rights, for example, *Islam and the Secular State: Negotiating the Future of Shari'a*[45] and *Muslims and Global Justice.*[46]

Taking all his works on Islam and human rights into consideration, we can say that An-Na'im has stuck to the same path for more than three decades and has advocated the same ideas from the beginning. All of his numerous works carry the same message, defending the UDHR and other UN human rights documents on the one hand, and attempting to reconcile Islam and human rights on the other. An-Na'im is without doubt a pioneer of the reconciliation of Islam and human rights. We cannot discuss this subject without comparing our standpoint with his, either to confirm or to criticise. An-Na'im's approach to the reconciliation of Islam and human rights is in two parts. The first is the innovative idea of his *ustadh* (teacher) Mahmoud Mohamed Taha, and the second is his attempt to apply that idea to human rights issues. I analysed the former above, but I would like to briefly mention An-Na'im's perspective on his teacher, and then to discuss the second part in detail.

An-Na'im correctly pointed out that Taha's work was a turning point in Islamic law. "From the tenth century, up to the present time, Muslim jurists have confined themselves to the study and elaboration of the work of those early masters."[47]

---

43 An-Na'im trans. of Taha, *The Second Message of Islam.*
44 An-Na'im, *Toward An Islamic Reformation.*
45 Abdullahi Ahmed An-Na'im, *Islam and the Secular State: Negotiating the Future of Shari'a* (Cambridge, MA: Harvard University Press, 2008).
46 Abdullahi Ahmed An-Na'im, *Muslims and Global Justice* (Philadelphia, PA: University of Pennsylvania Press, 2011). His other works include: Abdullahi Ahmed An-Na'im (ed.), *Human Rights in Cross-Cultural Perspectives: A Quest for Consensus* (Philadelphia, PA: University of Pennsylvania Press, 1992); Abdullahi Ahmed An-Na'im, *Islam and Human Rights: Selected Essays of Abdullahi An-Na'im,* ed. Mashood A. Baderin (Farnham: Ashgate, 2010).
47 An-Na'im's introduction to the translation of Taha's book, *The Second Message of Islam,* 21.

1

As Ustadh Taha explained, the earlier universal message of Islam, of peaceful propagation and non-discrimination, was contained in parts of the Qur'an that were revealed in Mecca (610–622). But when the Prophet migrated with his few persecuted followers to Medina in 622, the Qur'an had to provide for the concrete needs of the emerging community, which had to struggle for survival in an extremely harsh and violent environment. In this light, it is clear that traditional *Shari'a* principles of *qawama*, *dhimma*, and violently aggressive jihad were in fact concessions to the social and economic realities of the time and not the message of Islam intended for humanity at large into the indefinite future. Since those principles were developed by early Muslim jurists applying their own methodology of interpretation, which was not sanctioned as such in the Qur'an or Sunna of the Prophet, different conclusions can be drawn by applying a new methodology.[48]

An-Na'im correctly first said that "The techniques of creative juristic reasoning (*ijtihad*) could not remove all discrimination against women and non-Muslims because *ijtihad* itself has its limitations. In particular, *ijtihad* is not permitted in any matter governed by an explicit and definite text of the Qur'an or Sunnah",[49] and later, "Since *ijtihad* was defined and regulated through human reason in the past, rather than being the direct revelation as such, it can be redefined and regulated through human reason today and in the future."[50] His final destination is nothing other than that "*Ijtihad* should be reformulated to apply even to matters governed by clear and categorical texts of the Qur'an, as suggested by the late Sudanese Muslim reformer Ustadh Mahmoud Mohamed Taha."[51]

In his reformist journey, An-Na'im's position on the secular state evolved from a starting point of denial of the secular state: "Neither implementation of historical *Shari'a*, nor establishing a secular state, but the way of Ustadh Mahmoud, i.e., evolving Islamic law to a fresh plane",[52] to one where,

---

48 An-Na'im, *Islam and the Secular State*, 284.
49 An-Na'im trans. of Taha, *The Second Message of Islam*, 23.
50 An-Na'im, *Muslims and Global Justice*, 146.
51 Ibid., 193.
52 An-Na'im trans. of Taha, *The Second Message of Islam*, 23.

twenty-one years later, he saw the secular state as the future of *shari'a*. He correctly focused on civic reasoning, constitutionalism and citizenship in the modern state and politics. "*Shari'a* principles, by their nature and function, defy any possibility of enforcement by the state; claiming to enforce *Shari'a* principles as state law is a logical contradiction that cannot be rectified through repeated efforts under any conditions."[53]

The most recent clarification by An-Na'im may be this one:

I am therefore calling for framing the issue in terms of the contextual nature of human understandings and practice of Islam, on the one hand, and the universality of human rights, on the other. This approach is more realistic and constructive than simplistic assertions of compatibility or incompatibility of Islam and human rights that take both sides of this relationship in static, absolute terms. This view does not uphold human rights as the standard by which Islam itself should be judged, but only proposes that these rights constitute an appropriate framework for human understanding of Islam and interpretation of *Shari'a* . . . Since traditional interpretations of *Shari'a* are human and not divine, they can change through the process of reinterpretation and consensus-building.[54]

The areas of conflict between *shari'a* and universal standards of human rights in An-Na'im's early writings were twofold: gender and religious discrimination under historical *shari'a*.[55] Later, it increased to three: there are no fundamental problems with *Shari'a* except for slavery and discrimination on grounds of gender and religion.[56] In a third stage he noticed cruel, inhuman or degrading treatment or punishment in *shari'a* criminal law,[57] and finally he added the freedom of religion and belief.[58]

After mentioning two types of abrogation – abrogation of both the ruling and the wording of the text, and abrogation of the ruling but not the

53 An-Na'im, *Islam and the Secular State*, 2.
54 Ibid., 112.
55 An-Na'im trans. of Taha, *The Second Message of Islam*, 22.
56 An-Na'im, *Toward an Islamic Reformation*, 172.
57 An-Na'im, *Human Rights in Cross-Cultural Perspectives*, 29, 32.
58 An-Na'im, *Islam and the Secular State*, 111.

wording of the text – he focused on the latter. "Without this device for reconciling apparently contradictory verses of the Qur'an, it would have been impossible to develop *Shari'a* as a coherent and internally consistent legal system."[59] He correctly continued by saying that the theory of *naskh* as developed and applied by the jurists cannot be traced back to the Prophet. The principle of *naskh* was the cornerstone of their conception of *shari'a*. Why should modern Muslims be denied the opportunity to rethink the rationale and application of *naskh*?[60]

This is an explicit criterion of An-Na'im's approach: "The only effective approach to achieve *sufficient* reform of *Shari'a* in relation to universal human rights is to cite sources in the Qur'an and Sunna which are inconsistent with universal human rights and explain them in a historical context, while citing those sources which are supportive of human rights as the basis of the legally applicable principles and rules of Islamic law today."[61] And "An *Islamic* alternative to *Shari'a* is provided as the appropriate framework for Muslims to exercise their right to self-determination while fully respecting the rights of others, whether within their own countries or in other lands."[62]

An-Na'im's most recent approach can be interpreted as stating that "there is no such thing as the only possible or valid understanding of the Qur'an, or conception of Islam . . . A change in the viewpoint of Muslims will contribute to a transformation of their understanding of the Qur'an, and hence of their conception of Islam itself."[63] Or it can be seen as an anthropological approach to Islam: an organic relationship between the Qur'an and Islam, on the one hand, and the nature of human beings (that is, their understanding, imagination, judgement, behaviour, experience and so forth), on the other hand.[64] Reconciliation of universal human rights with *shari'a* is neither possible nor required.[65] It is possible to achieve Islamic authenticity and legitimacy for a set of human rights by distinguishing between Islam and *shari'a*, the divinity of Islam and the temporality of *shari'a*.[66]

---

59 An-Na'im, *Toward an Islamic Reformation*, 57.
60 Ibid., 58–59.
61 Ibid., 171.
62 Ibid., 185.
63 An-Na'im, *Muslims and Global Justice*, 187.
64 Ibid., 189.
65 Ibid., 191.
66 Ibid., 192.

For this precept (that Islam is suitable/valid for all times and places) to be true, there must be flexibility in the understanding and capacity for change in the implementation of Islam over time and place. *Shari'a* principles must be reformulated before they can be applied today, whether in themselves or as criteria for accepting and implementing a normative system of universal human rights.[67]

Advantages and Disadvantages of An-Na'im's Approach

The brilliant points and major advantages of An-Na'im's viewpoint that I admire and with which I agree are these: the inadequacy of traditional Islam; the insufficiency of non-structural reform and *ijtihad*, especially with regard to the incompatibility of traditional Islam and human rights; the need for secular states for Muslims; the necessity of abrogation techniques for non-structural reform in Islamic thought; and the need to revisit abrogation in the modern age. However, I have three main concerns or critical comments in response to An-Na'im's ideas.

First, Taha's innovative abrogation theory is the backbone of the approach of his loyal student An-Na'im. Although I have already criticised Taha's theory above, I want to add some further comments concerning the rights of women and non-Muslims to demonstrate that demarcation of Medina verses from Meccan verses is not the point in abrogation. All the verses cited in this section were revealed in Medina in support of equal rights for women and men, on the one hand, and for Muslims and non-Muslims, on the other hand.

> People, We created you all from a single man and a single woman, and made you into races and tribes so that you should recognise one another. In God's eyes, the most honoured of you are the ones most mindful of Him: God is all knowing, all aware. (Q. 49:13)

This verse is addressed to *nas* (people) not *mu'minun* (believers), and all people, regardless of their gender and faith, are created in the same way, and ethnic diversity is attributed to God, so cannot be a reason for discrimination. The

---

67 Ibid.

important thing is the virtue of piety and not gender, race, colour, faith, social status and so on.

> People, be mindful of your Lord, who created you from a single soul, and from it created its mate, and from the pair of them spread countless men and women far and wide . . . (Q. 4:1)

This verse is also addressed to *nas* (people) and it is one of the verses of the Qur'an that is clearest in its support of gender equality. There are other verses in support of gender equality: Q. 33:35, 9:71–72, 48:5, 6 and 25, 57:12–13, 5:38, 24:2, 3 and 26, and 2:187.[68] Can we say that these verses should be abrogated because they were revealed in Medina?

These verses are the foundation of foreign policy in the *shari'a* and define the relationship with non-Muslims:

> He does not forbid you to deal kindly and justly with anyone who has not fought you for your faith or driven you out of your homes: God loves the just. But God forbids you to take as allies those who have fought against you for your faith, driven you out of your homes, and helped others to drive you out: any of you who take them as allies will truly be wrongdoers. (Q. 60:8–9)

The foundation of modern public life is social contracts. These verses on the necessity of protecting a contract or treaty, especially with non-Muslims, were revealed in Medina: Q. 5:1, and 9:4 and 7. How can Taha's abrogation theory be supported when these liberal verses of the Qur'an were revealed in Medina? If An-Na'im had himself examined the Meccan and Medina verses of the Qur'an he would have recognised that the categorisation of Mecca–Medina as principal–subsidiary and abrogating–abrogated is neither comprehensive nor inclusive and, given of the large number of instances that do not conform to the theory, it is an indefensible and inadequate criterion for abrogation.

Second, the problem of discriminatory and anti-human rights verses of the Qur'an cannot be solved by the Mecca–Medina differentiation. In

---

68 I classified and analysed these verses in "Revisiting Women's Rights in Islam", pp. 213–234.

contrast to An-Naʿimʾs justification, the important difference between these two periods was not to whom the verses were addressed nor the different socio-political situations. The point was the difference between the principal verses as abrogating, and the subsidiary (*furʾu*) verses as abrogated. An-Naʿim ignored this fundamental point and highlighted the Mecca–Medina differentiation and tried his best to justify it. Although almost all of the discriminatory verses were revealed in Medina, we cannot say that all or even most of the principal verses were revealed in Mecca: they were revealed both in Mecca and Medina.

We know that, on the one hand, the principal verses are to be considered permanent and timeless and, on the other hand, that the verses dealing with subsidiary matters, if they are discriminatory and against human rights (which not all of the subsidiary matter verses are), are considered to be time-bound, temporal and abrogated. But there is a big problem. Although the abrogated should be the verses and not the words and recitation, the problem is on the abrogating side. In other words, it is not necessary for the abrogating to be textual, it could also be based on non-textual evidence, that is, certain reason (*ʿaql*).

The validity and authenticity of human rights is not that it has scriptural support. The UDHR was not submitted or accepted because of any religious or scriptural teachings. Nevertheless, the root of many of its articles can be found in the Scriptures, so why were they not discovered before the modern age? The modern understanding that gave rise to the UDHR and the notion of modern human rights came from something else. This "something else" was not the principal verses of the Qurʾan nor other scriptures, but these principal verses can guide us to that "something else". In other words, the abrogating is that "something else", and not its indicator (principal verses). This "something else" is the key point in our discussion and successful abrogation theory. I will introduce this "something else" in the last section of this Preface.

Third, the idea of a secular state is a turning point in An-Naʿimʾs thought. Before that, he was an interpreter of, and commentator on, Taha, preaching and expanding the teachings of his *ustadh*. *Islam and the Secular State: Negotiating the Future of Shariʿa*[69] was a celebration of An-Naʿimʾs maturity

---

69 An-Naʿim, *Islam and the Secular State*.

and independence. Before that, the correlations and consequences of belief in a secular state were not present in An-Naʿimʾs thought. He had not yet clarified the role of Meccan verses as the textual and scriptural source of human rights. The Mecca-oriented *shariʿa* in Tahaʾs framework was Islamic law appropriate for modern times, and it is clear that the abrogated Medina verses were not a cause for concern in modern times, unlike the Meccan verses. These verses are essential in Tahaʾs theory. However, there is substantial inconsistency in An-Naʿimʾs approach to a secular state. If the role of shariʿa in his secular state is the same as the role of *shariʿa* in Tahaʾs non-secular state, this means that An-Naʿim does not acknowledge the consequences of a secular state. Deriving human rights from the socio-political, cultural and economic situations of premodern times, on the one hand, and the necessity of justifying human rights by scripture, on the other, are essentially problematic and contradictory to the idea of a secular state. An-Naʿim should clarify the requirements of his theory of a secular state with regard to the Mecca-oriented *shariʿa*. He needs to demonstrate the possibility of the notion of human rights occurring in premodern times and the impossibility of human rights in modern times without relying on Meccan verses.

Section Three: Mayer's Islam and Human Rights: Tradition and Politics

Ann Elizabeth Mayer (b. 1945 in the US)[70] published her first monograph on Islam and Human Rights in 1991: *Islam and Human Rights: Tradition and Politics*.[71] She focused precisely on the subject without deviating to discuss any additional issues. It is a well-organised book that is clear for the lay reader who has no background in the subject. The book has been re-issued five times in less than three decades.[72] The *Islam* in this book is the one represented in official documents of Muslim-majority countries.

These documents are divided into two types: first, universal Islamic declarations of human rights or their published drafts; and, second, the constitutions

---

70 Associate Professor Emeritus of Legal Studies in the Department of Legal Studies and Business Ethics at the Wharton School of the University of Pennsylvania.
71 Ann Elizabeth Mayer, *Islam and Human Rights: Tradition and Politics*, 5th edn (London: Routledge, 2019).
72 Mayer, *Islam and Human Rights*, 2nd edn (1995), 3rd edn (1998), 4th edn (2007), 5th edn (2013).

of Muslim-majority countries. The best examples of the former type are the "Draft of the Islamic Constitution" (published in 1979 in the journal *al-Azhar*), the 1981 Universal Islamic Declaration of Human Rights (UIDHR), and the 1993 Cairo Declaration on Human Rights in Islam (CDHRI). The best examples of the latter type are the constitution of the Islamic Republic of Iran, as well as the new constitutions of Afghanistan and Iraq. The main sources that Mayer draws on for her book are two pamphlets: *Muslim Commentary on the Universal Declaration of Human Rights* by Sultan Hussein Tabandeh (1915–1992)[73] and *Human Rights in Islam* by Abu'l A'la Mawdudi (1903–1979).[74]

Based on this understanding of Islam or "Islamic human rights schemes", Mayer started by "assimilating human rights in the Middle East" and correctly explored: (1) discrimination against women and restrictions of their rights; (2) discrimination against non-Muslims and restrictions placed on religious minorities; (3) the resistance to acknowledging human rights for sexual minorities; and (4) restrictions on freedom of religion. Finally, she concluded, "Once embodied in law, Islamic criteria limiting rights protections present obstacles to advancing human rights", and "The Islam and human rights nexus has been in a state of acute tension for decades."[75]

After introducing so-called "Islamic human rights schemes", Mayer confessed fairly, "None of these have been ratified by a universal Islamic consensus or by anything like democratic referenda; instead, they have been promoted by undemocratic governments and various ideologues with views hostile to rights and freedoms."[76] She was aware that, "As the burgeoning human rights movement in the Muslim world has demonstrated, many Muslims believe that Islam and human rights can be successfully integrated, even taking the position that Islam reinforces human rights."[77] Mayer justified her approach in the preface to the most recent edition of her book thus:

---

73 A Persian pamphlet published in Iran by Sultan Hussein Tabandeh, *Nazar-e Madhabi be E'lamiye-i Hoquq-e Bashar* (n.p., 1345/1966; reprinted in 1354/1975), 98 pp.; in English translation *Muslim Commentary on the Universal Declaration of Human Rights* by Sultan Hussein Tabandeh of Gunabad, Iran, trans. F. J. Goulding (London: F. T. Goulding, 1970), with a foreword by Abulfazl Hazeqhi and a letter of permission from the author to the translator, 96 pp.

74 A speech given in 1975 in Lahore, Pakistan; English translation published by Zahid Bashir Printers in Lahore in 1976.

75 Mayer, *Islam and Human Rights*, 5th edn, 2013, 207.

76 Ibid., 3.

77 Ibid., 13.

There is no intention, however, to imply that Islam is exclusively a legal tradition or that comparative legal history is the only legitimate way to approach this topic. In a more comprehensive study on the relationship of Islam and human rights, one would ideally want to include analyses of how principles of Islamic theology, philosophy, and ethics tie in with the treatment of human rights. This would carry one into areas beyond the comparative legal analyses of civil and political rights in international human rights law and in Islamic human rights schemes, which are the sole concern of this work.[78]

Advantages and Disadvantages of Mayer's Approach

Although I absolutely agree with Mayer on the incompatibility of so-called "Islamic human rights schemes" with the UDHR, and that conservative Muslims disagree with it, it is not correct to conclude that there is an "incompatibility of Islam and human rights". Mayer herself apologised for the overly general title of her book and offered a more accurate title,[79] but this does not justify the many misunderstandings implied by the overly broad title of her book. A more accurate title for the work might be *Islam and Human Rights: Approaches from Conservative Realpolitik Perspectives*.

In Chapter 5 of this book I strongly criticise so-called "Islamic human rights schemes". I think there is a kind of agreement, or even a consensus, among Muslim reformers and reformists that the approach of these schemes is not representative of Islam. It is a fact that conservative Muslims are in the majority and that they seek to justify discrimination on grounds of gender or religion and do not tolerate freedom of religion, but we cannot overlook the rapid growth among Muslims of a tendency towards the reconciliation of Islam and the UDHR in almost all of its details.

For the new generation of Muslims in Pakistan and the Indian subcontinent, Fazlur Rahman (1919–1988)[80] is much more acceptable than Abu'l A'la

---

78 Ibid., xiii.
79 Ibid., ix.
80 Fazlur Rahman is the author of *Islamic Methodology in History* (Karachi: Central Institute of Islamic Research, 1965); *Islam* (Chicago: University of Chicago Press, 1979); *Islam and Modernity: Transformation of an Intellectual Tradition* (Chicago: University of Chicago Press, 1982); *Revival and Reform in Islam* (Oxford: Oneworld, 2010); *Major Themes of the Qur'an* (Chicago: University of Chicago Press, 2013).

Mawdudi as the representative of Islam. It is interesting to note that Dr Nour-Ali Tabandeh Majzub-Ali-Shah (1927–2019), the younger brother of Sultan Hussein Tabandeh Reda-Ali-Shah, was the leader (*qutb*) of the Ne'matullahi Gonabadi Sufi order (*tariqa*) until recently (1997–2019). He was a lawyer, and was one of the most distinguished advocates of human rights in Iran since the 1970s.[81] Because of this democratic position, he was imprisoned in 1990 and placed under house arrest in Tehran in early 2018 for more than twenty months.

Mayer and conservative Muslims (as well as Muslim fundamentalists and the undemocratic regimes of Muslim-majority countries) have similar positions in comparing Islam with the UDHR. Both of them introduce so-called Islamic law or *shari'a* as the fossilisation of Islam and thus arrive at the incompatibility of Islamic law with the UDHR where the rights of women and non-Muslims are concerned, and in the matter of freedom of religion. Of course, Mayer concluded that this is a shortcoming of Islam, while conservative Muslims view it as the deviation of the Western legal regime from truth and metaphysical human rights.[82]

Section Four: *Mojtahed Shabestari's* A Critique of the Official Reading of Religion

Mohammad Mojtahed Shabestari (b. 1936 in Iran) is one of two leading Iranian Muslim reformists of the late 1980s.[83] He wrote on the UDHR

---

81 His articles and book chapters on human rights can be found in the following books: Nour-Ali Tabandeh, *Hoquq-e Tatbiqi* (*Comparative Law*) (Qom, Tehran University, College of Judicial and Administrative Sciences, 1978); Nour-Ali Tabandeh, *Majmou'e Maqalat-e Feqhi wa Ejtema'i* (*Collection of Fiqhi and Social Articles*) (Tehran: Haqiqat, 1999); Nour-Ali Tabandeh, *Majmou'e Maqalat-e Hoquqi wa Ejtema'i* (*Collection of Legal and Social Articles*) (Tehran: Haqiqat, 2002).

82 The best examples of conservative Muslims who wrote and published on the UDHR are Mohammad al-Ghazali (1917–1996), the distinguished Egyptian jurist, in his book *Huquq al-Insan bain Ta'alim al-Islam wa I'lan al-Umam al-Muttahidah* (*Human Rights between the Teachings of Islam and the Declarations of the United Nations*) (Cairo: Nahdet-I Misr, 1965), in Sunni Islam; and 'Abdollah Javadi Amoli (b. 1933) in his book *Falasafe-ye Huquq-e Bashar* (*The Philosophy of Human Rights*) (Qom: Esra', 1996), in Shi'a Islam. The best representative of Shi'ite fundamentalism is Mohammad Taqi Mesbah Yazdi (b. 1934) in his book *Negahi Gozara be Hoquq Bashar az Didgah Eslam* (*Human Rights from an Islamic Perspective: A Brief Review*), ed. 'Abdul-Hakim Salimi (Qom: Imam Khomeini's Educational and Research Institute, 2013). He even openly justified slavery in the modern era! The head of Iran's judiciary (1989–1999) was Mohammad Yazdi (b. 1931) another Shi'ite fundamentalist, not Mesbah Yazdi. Mayer (*Islam and Human Rights*, 5th edn, 2013, 35) mixed these two Yazdis up with each other.

83 The other is Abdolkarim Soroush.

from a reformist perspective. Although Shabestari did not publish any books specifically focusing on human rights, he paid particular attention to this subject in his work in general.[84]

His most extensive discussions of human rights are to be found in his book *Naqdi bar Qaraát-e Rasmi az Din: Bohranha, Chaleshha va vah-e Halha (A Critique of the Official Reading of Religion: Crisis, Challenges and Solutions)*,[85] and additional points are made in two other books: *Táammolati dar Qaraát-e Ensani az Din (Reflections on a Humane Reading of Religion)*[86] and *Naqd-e Bonyadha-ye Feqh va Kalam: Sokhanraniha, Maqalat va Gofteguha (Critique of the Foundations of* Fiqh *and Theology, Speeches, Articles and Dialogues)*.[87]

He divided his career into two periods. His aim in the first period was the codification of *sharia* goals (*maqasid al-sharia*) from a Shi'ite perspective.[88] In *Jamée-ye Ensani-e Eslam, Ketab-e Avval: Osoul-e Fekri (Humanistic Society of Islam, Book One: The Theoretical Principles)*,[89] Shabestari wrote that "The issue of human rights – that is, based on the principle of equity and brother-hood of human beings – is an Islamic thought, more than a European gift."[90]

---

84 Mojtahed Shabestari has not published any monographs so far. His books consist of collections of all of his speeches, interviews, round tables (using edited tape recordings) and articles, not selections thereof. Thus, his books are full of overlaps and repetition.

85 Mohammad Mojtahed Shabestari, *Naqdi bar Qaraát-e Rasmi az Din: Bohranha, Chaleshha va vah-e Halha (A Critique of the Official Reading of Religion: Crisis, Challenges and Solutions)* (Tehran: Tarh-e No, 1379/2000).

86 Mohammad Mojtahed Shabestari, *Táammolati dar Qaraát-e Ensani az Din (Reflections on a Humane Reading of Religion)* (Tehran: Tarh-e No, 1383/2004).

87 Mohammad Mojtahed Shabestari, *Naqd-e Bonyadha-ye Feqh va Kalam: Sokhanraniha, Maqalat va Gofteguha (Critique of the Foundations of Fiqh and Theology: Speeches, Articles and Dialogues)*, published online, 1395/2017.

88 He started as a writer of the first monthly *Darsha-yi az Maktab-e Eslam (Lessons from Islamic School)* in the Qom seminary in the 1960s. He was the co-author of a book with four other clerics, *Zan va Entekhabat (Woman and Election)* (Qom: n.p., early 1340s/1960s) (publication date not mentioned), 146 pp, which justified election as a masculine right. This was one of two slogans of the Shi'ite authorities in their struggle against the Shah at that time.

89 Mohammad Mojtahed Shabestari, *Jamée-ye Ensani-e Eslam, Ketab-e Avval: Osoul-e Fekri (Humanistic Society of Islam, Book One: The Theoretical Principles)* (Tehran: Sherkat-e Sahami-ye Enteshar, 1347/1968).

90 Shabestari, *Jamée-ye Ensani-e Eslam, Ketab-e Avval*, 66. Shabestari was appointed Imam of the Islamic Centre in Hamburg (1348–1357/1969–1978) by the Shi'ite authorities. He learned German and taught himself modern Christian theology. He was elected as one of the representatives of Tehran in the first Iranian parliament after the revolution (1359–1363/1980–1984). Shabestari touched on the real meaning of the "Islamic State" in practice and understood the shortcomings of an administration based on *fiqh* and *sharia*. Shabestari taught as a faculty member of the School of Theology at Tehran University (1363–1385/1984–2006), focusing on theology and mysticism.

His second period began with a series of articles titled *Din va 'Aql (Religion and Reason)*[91]: religiosity is only possible in the light of human sciences and knowledge. He was the first Iranian Shi'ite thinker to apply hermeneutics to Islamic textual understanding.[92] He correctly criticised the traditional semantic discussions (*mabahith al-alfaz*) in *'usul al-fiqh* (principles of jurisprudence) and explicitly expressed that all *tafsir* (interpretation) – without *any* exceptions – is based on the knowledge, interests and expectations of the interpreter.[93]

According to Shabestari: "Understanding is a historical issue, the same as language. Understanding should be discussed precisely as a type of epistemic subject. This is first-level knowledge that will be discovered by second-level knowledge, i.e., philosophical hermeneutics." He correctly emphasised: "By which criterion can a *faqih* (jurist) distinguish that a specific ruling – which is expressed in the Scripture or Tradition – is either permanent and eternal or time-bound and temporal, restricted to a specific time, place and situation. The criterion for distinguishing the correctness of a *fatwa* (*shari'a* verdict) is that the *fatwa* is intended to supply justice."[94]

Shabestari clarified this approach: ahistorical interpretation of the Scripture and Tradition is impossible and would be a misunderstanding. Many of the rulings in the time of the Prophet – be they in the Qur'an or in the Tradition – were accidental and related to the subsidiary goals of *shari'a*. This duality was not clear to the companions of the Prophet.[95] It is not possible to distinguish between the essential and the accidental goals simply by turning to the verses (of the Qur'an) or sayings (of the Prophet). Historical phenomenology is the only method that can be used for this important issue, and in this way we can distinguish the main focus of prophetic phenomena from their socio-material and spiritual-historical framework. The primary and essential goals are those that are inseparable from *tawhid*

---

91 Mohammad Mojtahed Shabestari, *Din va 'aql (Religion and Reason)* (Tehran), *Kayhan-e Farhangi* monthly, 1366/1987.

92 His books *Hermeneutic, Ketab va Sonnat (Hermeneutics, the Scripture and the Tradition: The Process of Interpretation of the Revelation)* (Tehran: Tarh-e No, 1375/1996), and *Iman wa Azadi (Faith and Freedom)* (Tehran: Tarh-e No, 1376/1997) were the turning point not only of Shabestari's career but also of Islamic thought in Iran.

93 Shabestari, *Hermeneutic, Ketab va Sonnat*, 9.

94 Ibid., 42–43, 64.

95 Shabestari, *Naqdi bar Qara'at-e Rasmi az Din*, 267–268.

(God's unity), so that when *tawhid* appears in any culture, those goals are necessarily attached to it. Identifying the five goals of *shari'a* – and all rulings of *shari'a* must seek to supply them – is one way of distinguishing the essential from the accidental.[96]

If the Prophet had been sent on a prophetic mission in another social situation, these subsidiary rulings and norms would have been different. This is what is meant by accidental and non-essential.[97] Perhaps, if Meccan pagans had not prevented the Prophet's mission, and he had not relocated to Medina, and had not accepted the political leadership there, other historical events might have occurred and other rulings might have been sent down from Heaven to the Prophet.[98]

The domination of *fiqh* over religion is equivalent to taking the soul of religion and drying out its root from which grows religious emotion, religious experience and the message of religion. The main functions of religion are to nurture religious emotion, improve ethical values and to give meaning to life.[99] Political *fiqh* has lost its rational context. We should turn to the general divine commands and prohibitions, such as the requirement for justice, the protection of the five goals of *shari'a* (*maqasid shari'a*) in political and criminal matters, and seek to establish a just socio-political, economic and cultural system based on those principles. This means the replacement of most *fatwa*s and jurisprudential (*fiqhi*) theories in political as well as criminal matters with laws and administrative systems based on the justice of human rights. This replacement never harms the perfection and comprehensiveness of Islam (in their acceptable meaning, according to Shabestari).[100]

The validity of a *shari'a* ruling in any given era is determined by whether or not it makes *tawhid*-oriented conduct (*suluk-e tawhidi*) possible.[101] The only way that Muslims can remain loyal to Islam, to faith, justice, morality and love in the present era is through the establishment of systems

---

96 Ibid., 271.
97 Ibid., 273.
98 Ibid., 278.
99 Ibid., 50.
100 Ibid., 182–183. Shabestari holds that some meanings of the perfection and comprehensiveness of Islam in books by conservative scholars are unacceptable. In his work, he provides an explanation for the meanings that he considers to be acceptable and reasonable.
101 Ibid., 271.

based on human rights.[102] There were four characteristics in the discourse of Muhammad the Prophet of Islam. The first is his reasonableness. Religious discourse in any era should not be inconsistent with the rationale of that era. The second characteristic is justice. His mission was to change the oppression of his time to justice as understood at that time. We should understand justice and its interpretation in our time. The message of religion cannot be unjust. We as Muslims can and should accept human rights as the foundation of our political, social and economic organisations. I am talking about the *message* of Mohammad's sayings and deeds, not their utterances (*mantuq*) and meanings (*madlul*). The third characteristic is realism, not imagination or idealism. The fourth and final characteristic is teaching mercy and opposing violence and revenge.[103]

In his last book, Shabestari mentioned the elements of Islamic reform in this way:

> What is discussed by Muslim scholars in the last century in the name of belief, religious virtues, or *Shari'a* rulings should be validated against three criteria: first, rationality, irrationality, anti-rationality; second, ethical goodness and evilness; the third being usefulness or harmfulness. It is necessary to check continuously all religious beliefs, religious moralities and *Shari'a* rulings with these three criteria.[104]

The essence of his fourth book *Reflections on a Humane Reading of Religion* can be summarised as follows. The movement of revisiting and reconstructing Scripture and Tradition is nothing more than making those experiences accessible, as well as creating new experiences, through participation in the experiences that were started by Prophet Muhammad. Reinterpretation of Scripture and Tradition is continuity of that path in the age of modernity. There is a new combination and reorganisation of the limits of *shari'a*. Although what is divinely permissible and prohibited (*halal wa haram*) and His command and prohibitions remain, the main changes are in their meanings, particulars and domains. In the light of this revisiting and reconstruction of Scripture and Tradition, human rights have become acceptable to

---

102 Ibid., 297.
103 Ibid., 344–348.
104 Shabestari, *Naqd-e Bonyadha-ye Feqh va Kalam*, 146 (speech of December 1385/2003).

Muslim societies because of the religious background of the discussion, as well as becoming the axis of Muslim political organisation. *Shari'a* orders have very clearly changed in the case of human interactions (*mu'amalat*) and political and criminal issues (*siyasat*).[105]

Shabestari summarises all the articles of the UDHR into three general and public principles: freedom of thought and belief, and freedom of expression of those thoughts and beliefs; the equality of all human beings in rights and obligations; and the participation of all human beings in society. He does not deny that a distant anthropological basis for human rights can be found in different cultures and religions, but the discussion, refinement and standardisation of the details has taken place in modern times, and particularly in the twentieth century in Western countries.[106] He emphasises that human rights discourse is one of the essential foundations of modern-day social life, and that this discourse is not exclusive to a specific culture.[107] The rights of human beings cannot be the same at different points in history. The genesis, validity and codification of the rights of human beings are subordinate to cultural and social evolution through the ages. The current organisation and codification of human rights could only exist in the twentieth/twenty-first century. The language used to express moral rights in religious texts is the language of "obligations". That is different from the term "rights" that is used in the philosophy of law.[108]

Shabestari is clear about the right of freedom of religion. If the UDHR recognises the freedom of religion even in denying God or in converting from one faith to another, it means that no individual or state can force a person to accept the existence of God or to remain in any given religion.[109] He distinguishes between "metaphysical human rights" and the UDHR. The former comes from God alone, and He expressed it in Scripture and Prophetic Tradition. Shabestari explicitly says that resistance to metaphysical human rights leads to meaningless and multifaceted sayings and denying the accepted philosophical and historical premises.[110]

---

105 Shabestari, *Ta'ammolati dar Qara'at-e Ensani az Din*, 25–26.
106 Shabestari, *Naqdi bar Qara'at-e Rasmi az Din*, 201.
107 Ibid., 223.
108 Ibid., 203–204.
109 Ibid., 226.
110 Ibid., 239–264.

In the latter part of his career, Shabestari prepared two books of his collected works, but could not publish them in Iran, so he posted them on his website.[111] The germ of this line of thought can be observed in his earlier works, but the clarification and detailed explanation of his new approach are given in these two books. In the first phase of the second stage, Shabestari was a reformist, offering a new interpretation and understanding of Islamic Scripture and Tradition, but in the second phase he appears as a radical reconstructionist and reformist of Islam itself, not its interpretation or understanding. His concern at this stage is not religious text (Scripture and Tradition) at all.

Comparing the experiences of Christian theologians, such as the neo-orthodox theology of Karl Barth (1886–1968), the secular theology of Rudolf Karl Bultmann (1884–1976), and the liberal theology of Friedrich Schleiermacher (1768–1834) and his followers Paul Tillich (1886–1965) and Wolfhart Pannenberg (1928–2014), Shabestari favoured the third approach, liberal theology. That is to say, discovering religious experience and learning about the founders of religion through historical and phenomenological methods, and demonstrating the validity of those experiences and their divinity to the contemporary human being.[112]

He highlights the deep contrast between the traditional approach to revelation and his modern approach. In the former, revelation as a non-human or meta-human phenomenon is unseen (*ghaib*) knowledge and rulings that come from God. In this approach, religion comes from an unseen world and humans are to live up to the expectations of this unseen agent. The content of revelation in this approach is different from human sciences and abilities and cannot be rationalised. But in Shabestari's modern approach, revelation and religion are created by human understanding as required by humanness.[113]

There is no room for God's agency nor any unseen world; everything, including religion and revelation, is made by man, his understanding and his reason. Shabestari clarifies the deep contrast between these two approaches later:

---

111 The first is *Qarâ'at-e Nabavi as Jahan* (*The Prophetic Reading of the World*). This is a collection of his presentations and notes posted on his website in thirty-one parts (January 2008–November 2015). The second is *Naqd-e Bonyadha-ye Feqh va Kalam*. I referred to the latter above.

112 Shabestari, *Ta'ammolati dar Qarâ'at-e Ensani az Din*, 48–50.

113 Ibid., 81–86.

We have two ways for learning this phenomenon (religion/revelation). The first is turning to the texts of verses (Scripture) and hadiths (Tradition), and the second is turning to the lived faith of Muslims. Faith is absorption in an address (*khitab*) and turning towards it and listening.[114]

He prefers to call his quest for meaning "*Verstehende* theology" (*elahiyyat-e tafahhomi*) or "theology of meaningful understanding", not "interpretive theology" (*elahiyyat-e tafsiri*). Interpretation (*tafsir*) has different types: *verstehende* (meaningful understanding) and non-*verstehende* (interpretive). His approach is the former. In this approach, God is "the meaning of the meanings", and the prophecy and the mission of the messengers of God also belong to the *verstehende* (meaningful understanding) type. In this theology, the Prophets and messengers of God were humans who wanted those to whom they spoke to understand what they understood.[115]

He called the theology of his rivals "dogmatic theology", especially the theology of jurists, and introduced the contrast between these two theologies in the following way: in his theology, what the Prophet of Islam offered to his audiences is a *verstehende* or meaningful understanding of matters, so they could understand them through their *verstehende* seeking. This is the only possible way. The crisis in the Islamic world is because of "dogmatic theology". The time has come to replace the juridical deduction (*istinbat*) of *shari'a* rulings from Scripture and Tradition with the continual moral *verstehende* of God's will. He declared that the methodology of modern *ijtihad*, that considers the requirements of time and place, is not the essential solution to the problems of the Islamic world. Our responsibility to religion and religiosity is nothing other than our continuous *verstehende* of the fact that "existence is God" in theory and practice. Continuous *verstehende* (*tafahhum*) is different from continuous obedience (*ta'abbud*).[116]

Although Shabestari did not divide his second period into two phases, I think we should distinguish between philosophical hermeneutics and reform in the understanding of religious text from radical reconstruction of and participation with the Prophet in monotheistic and just living. In other words,

---

114 Ibid., 100–102.
115 Shabestari, *Naqd-e Bonyadha-ye Feqh va Kalam*, 363.
116 Ibid., 345–346.

Shabestari reduces Islam, its Scripture and Prophetic Tradition to two concepts in theory and practice: *tawhid* (unity of God) and justice (*'idala*). A believer's way of life is to follow Muhammad in these two concepts.

In *The Prophetic Reading of the World*, Shabestari explained his final perspective on revelation and the Qur'an in detail. First, the Qur'an is a text of *verstehende* (understanding) letters, like a "narrative" using the original language of "metaphor". Second, the Qur'an is the product of revelation, not the revelation itself. The text of the Qur'an (*mushaf*) is a historical and gradually produced artefact, and its author is a human (the Prophet). It is not a metaphysical text. The text's significance becomes impossible if it is attributed directly to God without an intermediary. The Prophetic Reading that exists in the Qur'an has "humanness", and all of the shortcomings and restrictions of the human world are reflected in it. The possibility of our understanding and interpreting the text of the Qur'an comes from our knowledge of the human world, not from our knowledge of God.[117]

Shabestari agrees with Mahmoud Mohamed Taha and Abdullahi Ahmed An-Na'im that the Medina verses were restricted to the specific situation of that time and place, and on their temporality. But he disagrees with them that the Meccan verses are the source of human rights. His main reasons are: first, the meaning of terms such as freedom, justice, international peace, state and society as we understand them today did not exist in the time of revelation; second, those rights derived from these verses would be the public rights of Muslim countries and could not be called international human rights; and, third, the Meccan verses do not cover all thirty articles of the UDHR. He concluded that the theory of Taha and An-Na'im is not acceptable according to the principles of disciplined interpretation of the texts.[118]

Shabestari put forward his ideas about *fiqh* and its methodology. He postulated that the time of *usul al-fiqh* and *fiqhi ijtihad* was over and that they were no longer valid. Turning to Scripture and Tradition through the theory of rational intelligibility of praiseworthy and blameworthy (*al-husn wa al-qubh al-'aqli*) is not the solution. Scripture and Tradition cannot help to solve thousands of new (*mustahditha*) issues. *Fiqhi ijtihad* is completely

---

117 Shabestari, *Qara'at-e Nabavi as Jahan*, 2015. This work is not in book format with page numbers, so cannot be referenced as such.

118 Shabestari, *Naqd-e Bonyadha-ye Feqh va Kalam*, 667–669.

meaningless in the context of human interactions (*mu'amalat*), politics and criminal matters (*siyasat*). We must apprehend all of these issues through our reason, sciences and human experiences. To preserve spiritual health, we should remove the concept of obligation (*wujub*) in worship (*'ibadat*), and in its place we should put the concept of recommendation (*tawsiya*). The origin and foundation of closeness to God is noble morality, not the motions of ritual worship. Recommendations for the form of worship should not be obligatory.[119] The time of obligatory *fiqh* is over. My God is not an obligator. The authoritativeness of reason (*hujjiyyat al-'aql*) is the branch of obligation-oriented approach. The discussion of independent rational indications in *kalam* (theology) and *usul al-fiqh* (principles of jurisprudence) is incomplete and problematic.[120]

Advantages and Disadvantages of Shabestari's Approach

Concentrating on the second stage of Shabestari's career, the following are the advantages of his approach:

(a) Philosophical hermeneutics and historical phenomenology are two necessary disciplines in contemporary Islamic studies.
(b) Understanding is a historical issue; and it is not possible to distinguish between essential and accidental goals by turning to Scripture or Tradition.
(c) It is only in the twentieth century that it has been possible to organise and codify the modern notion of human rights, and it is different from the term "rights" as used in the language of religions, including Islam.
(d) The notion of metaphysical human rights is an absolutely meaningless term.
(e) Political issues and criminal law in *shari'a* should be classified as temporal matters. The decision in these cases will be made based on human reason and experience.
(f) It is necessary to continuously check all Islamic beliefs, moralities and rulings against these criteria: reasonableness, justice, ethical goodness and usefulness, based on the understanding of our time.

---

119 Ibid., 673–676.
120 Ibid., 679.

The following are some of the concerns, critiques or disadvantages of Shabestari's approach, especially in the second phase of his second stage.

First, if "liberal theology" is required, or at least acceptable, in Protestant Christian tradition, its justification in an Islamic framework requires a lot of argumentation: first, its correctness or validity in itself; and, second, whether it is necessary for the modernisation of Islam. The former is beyond the scope of this book. Briefly, the product of liberal theology in different traditions is somehow one thing: "deism" without any specific identity of this or that tradition. In Shabestari's case, his Islam has *only* two elements: *tawhid* – as the Sufis understand it, that is, an impersonal God or pantheism or unity of being (*wahdat al-wujud*) – and justice, nothing else. It is the most minimal Islam that we can imagine. No problem will remain at all, neither in human rights cases nor in any other modern phenomena, and all problems really will be solved by this ultra-progressive Islam. But this occurs by removing the subject of the issue (*surat-i mas'ala*). Of course, there will be no problem, because no issue remains! The issue was the Islam of the Qur'an and the Prophetic Tradition. Liberal Islam is a homonym of the Islam of mainstream Muslim scholars in its historical background. They are two different things under the same name. The contrast between *deism* in the name of Islam and Islam as a monotheistic faith with its Scripture and Tradition is very deep, essential and fundamental. We are talking about two different realities. I discuss the latter, that is, the necessity of liberal theology for Islam below.

Second, Shabestari's project is a type of "humanism" in Islamic theology. He is among the most radical advocates of the autonomy of human reason. He openly criticised the idea that revelation is a meta-human phenomenon or unseen (*ghaib*) knowledge and ruling that comes from God, and that humans should measure themselves against this unseen agent. On the contrary, he believes that revelation and religion are the product of human understanding, fashioned according to the needs of humans. On the other hand, that we can understand and interpret the text of the Qur'an is owing to our knowledge of the human world, not our knowledge of God. According to Shabestari, "speaking" is a human action, and God speaking is essentially *impossible.* This dumb God cannot send down verbal revelation. Shabestari's project is the "de-sacralisation" of revelation, the Qur'an, the unseen world (*ghaib*), and finally of Islam. "Human autonomous reason" takes the place of a metaphysical agent. It is a project of "secularising Islam". This type of Islam is absolutely inconsistent with an Islamic and Qur'anic perspective:

that Islam as a religion, the cosmos, and the seen and unseen worlds, are all full of God and secrets. It is not a project of "de-sacralisation of human interpretation or understanding of the divine" – that is correct – but it is a project of "de-sacralisation of divine elements of Islam" especially the Qur'an. When God does not and cannot speak, the scripture is not divine, because it is the narration of revelation by Muhammad as a human, so the ground is completely ready for human autonomous reason. This type of Islam carries the same name as conventional Islam that is based on the original texts of Islam, but has quite a different meaning. However, Shabestari does not care, and I discuss the reason for this below.

Third, if liberal theology was correct in itself, it would still need to prove its necessity for the modernisation of Islam. The argumentation of necessity has at least two premises: first, all other approaches to the modernisation of Islam are insufficient, incomplete and unacceptable; and, second, this approach comes at less of a cost than the other approaches. These two premises are not self-evident. The competing approaches are at least reverse abrogation and *ijtihad* in foundations and principles. Shabestari discussed his criticism of the former – I will examine this below – but although he briefly mentioned his lack of satisfaction with the insufficient methodology of modern *ijtihad* regarding the requirements of time and place, he did not provide any arguments in support of this claim. He neither discusses *ijtihad* in the foundations and principles (*ijtihad fi almabani wa l-al-usul*) nor presents any critical arguments in his books at all. As such, he did not prove the first premise. The second premise, that is, that it comes at less of a cost than others, was not discussed by Shabestari at all. And yet this economic premise is so important. Here are some examples of the price that has to be paid for this approach:

- first, replacing verbal revelation with existential revelation;
- second, replacing the Words of God with the Words of Muhammad as a human: "Its author is a human (the Prophet). It is not a metaphysical text";
- third, reclassifying the Qur'an not as the verbatim words of God, but as Muhammad's narration, reading and interpretation of revelation: "The Qur'an is the product of revelation, not the revelation itself. The Prophetic Reading that exists in the Qur'an has 'humanness', and all of the shortcomings and restrictions of the human world are reflected in it";

- fourth, abrogation of *usul al-fiqh* (principles of *fiqh*) and *ijtihad*: "The time of *usul al-fiqh* and *fiqhi ijtihad* is over and their age of validity has ended";
- fifth, complete abrogation of *Shari'a* in human interaction (*mu'amalat*), and in terms of rituals (*'ibadat*), abrogation of all obligations (*takalif/ wujub*) and changing these to recommended or advisory issues (*tawsiya*).

A critical analysis of each of these innovative points is beyond the scope of this book. I will briefly discuss the last two points below, because of their close relationship with the purpose of this book. Although Shabestari thoroughly clarified these points, his arguments were not strong, and they have not convinced either mainstream Muslim communities across the globe, nor to my knowledge, any Muslim scholars. Regardless of problematic argumentation, Shabestari's approach to modernising Islam is idealistic and unrealistic, imaginary and radical, and is far removed from the reality of Muslim communities and their scholars. Although his approach is admired by lay people, it is impractical and not a feasible solution to any problems of modernisation of Muslims including the problem of human rights in Muslim communities.

Fourth, the criteria for calling something Islamic, anti-Islamic or non-Islamic have been the original texts of Islam: the Qur'an and the authentic Tradition of the Prophet. The principles of consistency or inconsistency with the Scripture have been discussed by Muslim theologians and jurists in the books of *usul al-fiqh*, *fiqh* and *kalam*. We can say that conventional Islam, as well as almost all Islamic sciences, are "textual". The main discussions in the history of Islam are related to understanding the text of the Qur'an and Tradition and the validity of hadiths as vehicles of Tradition, and modern hermeneutics is essential for renewing the understanding of the original Islamic texts. Although Shabestari was a leading scholar in this subject, he destroyed his credibility in the last phase of his final period. He openly identified his approach as the opposite of textual Islam. In other words, he abrogated Islamic Scriptures and replaced them with the ambiguous term "*tawhid*-oriented conduct" (*suluk-e tawhidi*) or "lived faith of Muslims". It was not until later that he expanded his alternative to the original Islamic texts to "participation with the Prophet in monotheistic and just living". The manifestation of such teachings in conventional Islam is the texts of Scripture, that is, the Qur'an and Tradition. The detailed principles of deduction of these teachings were discussed in *usul al-fiqh*. However, in Shabestari's approach, all of the conventional bridges to Islam, that is, textual scriptures, their divinity, *ijtihad* and *usul al-fiqh*, are ruined. The alternative is the idealistic promotion of Muslims to the same stage of enlightenment as the Prophet in monotheistic and just living, and that is absolutely unrealistic and practically impossible for non-elite believers. This idealistic participation may work for a very small minority of elites such as the Sufis. It is a type of spiritual or mystical taste (*dhawq*) that is personal and undisciplined. Anyone can claim it as *their form* of spiritual participation in Prophetic monotheistic and just living. No one is able to reject this *personal* claim. Removing the original texts leads to anarchy in theory and practice. There will be far more disagreements and differences in non-textual Islam than textual Islam.

Fifth, tawhid-oriented conduct (*suluk-e tawhidi*) is an attractive proposition, but it requires principles. In the first phase of the second stage of his career, Shabestari emphasised the protection of five *shari'a* goals (*maqasid shari'a*), and that all rulings of *shari'a* must seek to supply them, as well as the need for justice. He found a correlation between *tawhid* (God's unity) and these five *shari'a* goals, on the one hand, and these five *shari'a* goals as a way of distinguishing essential Islam from accidental Islam, on the other. Although he did not pursue his discussion of these *shari'a* goals, he did not refute it either. What he wrote on the five *shari'a* goals is altogether problematic. He exaggerated their importance and was too optimistic about their functions.

- For example, their domain of validity is where there is no textual ruling: if there is a textual ruling and they are in conflict with it, then, they cannot be used, and they may not be used in worship. So, it is problematic to claim that *all* rulings of *shari'a* must seek to supply them. We may not refer to the five goals of *shari'a* when human rights are in conflict with *shari'a*, because of the existence of textual rulings.
- Second, the five *shari'a* goals require a rational framework in *usul al-fiqh*. Such rationality is not available in Sunni theology, except in Mu'tizilite theology, which was banned.
- Third, there is no evidence to restrict the *shari'a* goals to five, nor to accept some of these five as *shari'a* goals, for example, the protection of religion.
- Fourth, the correlation between *tawhid* and these five *shari'a* goals is not clear. Protection of life and ownership come before religion and

are accepted even by atheists. The point of these goals is therefore something else, not unity with God. They are essentially good. This is rational goodness and evil, yet Shabestari accused them of ambiguity and incompleteness!

Sixth, Shabestari's Islam is *shari'a*-less. In his project, the time of *usul al-fiqh*, *fiqh* and *fiqhi ijtihad* is over and their period of validity has ended. This termination applies not only to all aspects of human interaction (*mu'amalat*), but also covers all obligatory worship (*'ibadat*). Rituals are recommended, not required. After removing *usul al-fiqh*, *fiqh*, *fiqhi ijtihad* and *shari'a* what would be the alternative? His response: "We must apprehend all issues through our reason, sciences, and human experiences." Of course, the concept of human rights is one of his priorities. This is another example of his unrealistic and impractical approach. It is understandable that human interactions (*mu'amalat*), or the traditional *fiqh* or *shari'a* are suspended, but it is not clear that this is why the rulings of obligatory rituals,[121] and semi-rituals,[122] should be stopped. Shabestari neglected semi-rituals altogether, and justified the suspension of obligatory worship briefly for the protection of "spiritual health"! The Islamic Republic of Iran has indulged in the abuse of *fiqh* and *shari'a* in the form of state law and administrative policy. The reactionary approach of some Iranian thinkers is to completely remove *shari'a* and *fiqh*. Contrary to what Shabestari says, *shari'a* as the standard of Islamic virtues, ethical values[123] and the outline of Islamic beliefs, *fiqh* as the science of Islamic rituals and semi-rituals, *usul al-fiqh* as the methodology of *fiqh* and other textual Islamic sciences, and *ijtihad* in principle and foundations, are inseparable elements of Islam or Islamic sciences even today. Contrary to Shabestari's position, the discussion of independent rational indications (*mustaqillat al-'aqliyya*) is one of the advantages of Shi'ite *usul al-fiqh* (principles of jurisprudence) and Mu'tazilite and Shi'ite *kalam* (theology). It is obvious that this discussion should be held in the light of modern rationality, especially post-Kantian rationality. I will return to this point below.

---

121 I.e., prayer (*salat*), fasting in Ramadan (*sawm*), *zakat* and *hajj*.

122 I.e., rulings on drinking (such as prohibition of alcohol), eating (such as prohibition of pork) and sex (e.g., sex outside of marriage).

123 See Khaled Abou El Fadl, *Reasoning with God: Reclaiming Shari'a in the Modern Age* (Lanham, MD: Rowman & Littlefield, 2017).

Section Five: Sachedina's Islam and the Challenge of Human Rights

Abdulaziz Sachedina (b. 1942 in Tanzania)[124] is the most well-known international scholar advocating human rights from an Islamic perspective, close to the mainstream of the Muslim world. He is the co-author of *Human Rights and the Conflict of Cultures: Western and Islamic Perspectives on Religious Liberty*,[125] and his principal work on this subject is *Islam and the Challenge of Human Rights*.[126]

In his first publication on human rights Sachedina wrote: "The Qur'an maintains the universality and objectivity of basic spiritual and moral truths, and hence all human beings are not only equal but equally accountable for any violations. There is much concurrence regarding the underlying commitments of Islam and the West in respect to religious liberty. Both traditions share a common framework within which human beings may think about freedom of conscience and religious liberty."[127]

On the genealogy of "the clash of universalism: religious and secular in human rights", focusing on "the moral foundation of human rights", Sachedina believes that "The language of human rights is modern, firmly rooted in a secular liberalism that safeguards and promotes citizens' rights and that demands privatisation of religion from the public sphere to allow the development of a politics independent of religion."[128] In "Foundationless human rights?"[129] his concern is clear: "One of the major problems confronting the secular document from an Islamic point of view is the charge of relativity against the Eurocentric sources of the Declaration."[130]

Sachedina clarified his standpoint in his major work on human rights in the following way. First, "liberal views about human individuality, dignity,

---

124 Professor and International Institute of Islamic Thought Chair in Islamic Studies at George Mason University, Fairfax, Virginia. He is the author of *The Islamic Roots of Democratic Pluralism* (Oxford: Oxford University Press, 2000), and *Islamic Biomedical Ethics: Principles and Application* (Oxford: Oxford University Press, 2010).

125 David Little, John Kelsay and Abdulaziz Sachedina, *Human Rights and the Conflict of Cultures: Western and Islamic Perspectives on Religious Liberty* (Columbia, SC: University of South Carolina Press, 1988).

126 Abdulaziz Sachedina, *Islam and the Challenge of Human Rights* (Oxford: Oxford University Press, 2009).

127 Little, Kelsay and Sachedina, *Human Rights and the Conflict of Cultures*, 86.

128 Sachedina, *Islam and the Challenge of Human Rights*, 6.

129 Ibid., 7, section title.

130 Ibid., 13.

and agency are compatible with Islamic revelation as developed in Muslim philosophical theology and juridical methodology to human personhood." Second, "a critical analysis of Muslim theological resources [is needed] to propose a fresh understanding of Muslim theology to support universal human rights".[131]

Following a selective review of the literature on human rights in Eastern and Western languages, Sachedina classified the works in this way. There are, generally speaking, two identifiable trends in the Muslim scholarship that has investigated the Declaration (the UDHR) in terms of its conceptual formulations and effectiveness, in the Muslim understanding of modern rights language. The first trend is that of scholars speaking for the religious tradition, mainly centred in Muslim seminaries, who were not invited and therefore did not participate in the human rights formulations when the UDHR was being drafted. The methodology of traditionalist scholarship is problematic and full of self-congratulatory apologetics and non-critical scholarship in Islamic studies. This line of thinking continues to hold sway as the most authentic Islamic scholarship in the Muslim world. Traditionalist scholars regard human rights as belonging to the secular sphere of human thought and as an issue independent of the religious sphere.

The second trend is that of the secularly educated Muslim intellectuals. This group can be divided into two wings: those writing in the native languages of Muslims in support of the UDHR as it stands; and those writing in the West in European languages for Western academic audiences and government agencies. They are almost unknown in the Muslim world except among the educated. It is also possible to identify a third trend that takes the foundational sources of Islam seriously and at the same time argues for or against a liberal interpretation of the writings of the second group. They discuss the compatibility, or lack of it, by acknowledging substantial differences between some of the fundamental principles set forth in the UDHR and the Islamic tradition. Accordingly, this scholarship points out irreconcilable differences between the secular and religious foundations of human rights' norms and their origins in secular and Islamic political ideology and theology, respectively.[132]

131 Ibid., 16.
132 Ibid., 20–21.

According to Sachedina, three major tendencies can be identified in human rights discourse in contemporary Islamic thought. The first is the tendency to view the discourse in liberal secular terms. The second is the tendency to compare the UDHR with the CDHRI of 1990 without engaging with the philosophical–theological underpinnings of either document. And the third, which prevails mostly among the traditionalists, is to challenge the foundational sources of the UDHR in terms of Western politics against the Islamic world and to present an alternative revelation-based foundation for the inherency of human rights. Sachedina does not hesitate to say:

> My major interest is in the third tendency, because it asks the tough questions that Ignatieff would like us to downplay in the practical interest of protecting individuals' inalienable human rights. Moreover, since the majority of traditional leaders have a problem with the foundational origins of UDHR, they have worked and reworked metaphysical questions to argue against the authenticity of human rights norms and demonstrate their stark opposition to the secular-political affirmations of dominant Western culture.[133]

Sachedina follows in the footsteps of two scholars who wrote their studies at the time of the fifth anniversary of the UDHR, and had the advantage of hindsight that allowed them to examine the document and its impact on the development of human rights. These scholars are Johannes Morsink, *The Universal Declaration of Human Rights: Origins, Drafting, and Intent*,[134] and Michael Ignatieff, *Human Rights as Politics and Idolatry*.[135] Sachedina likes the question that they raised, which asks whether there is a single moral foundation for human rights that spans many cultures, or whether there are many culturally specific moral foundations, or none.[136]

The academic goals of Sachedina's project are, in his words, twofold. The first goal is an analytical aim, to identify the ethical–political formulation of

---

133 Ibid., 22–23.

134 Johannes Morsink, *The Universal Declaration of Human Rights: Origins, Drafting, and Intent* (Philadelphia, PA: University of Pennsylvania Press, 1999).

135 Michael Ignatieff, *Human Rights as Politics and Idolatry* (Princeton, NJ: Princeton University Press, 2001).

136 Sachedina, *Islam and the Challenge of Human Rights*, 8.

the sources of human dignity and human agency, as a major epistemic shift from a juridical to a theological–ontological view of the status of human personhood. This is a new theological–ethical vision of politics among traditionalist interpreters of political theology. The second goal is to investigate alternative ways to work out the foundational sources of Islam in order to think through different theological–ontological affirmations concerning universal moral values and the inherent nature of rights that occur to a human as human.[137]

Critically evaluating the universalist claims of the UDHR, in agreement with a number of Christian theologians, Sachedina concludes that:

> Without a universalist religious validation, any notion of universal morality is incomplete because secular culture is incapable of generating religion's sense of life's sacredness and human beings' possession of inherent dignity and rights. Religion, with its power of persuasion, not only provides cultural legitimacy to human rights; it can also become its staunchest advocate.[138]

He prefers "political theology" in an Islamic context rather than Max Stackhouse's "public theology" in a Christian context.[139]

In seeking the answer to the fundamental question "Can an Islamic foundation for human rights sit in dialogue with the Declaration?" Sachedina correctly identifies the lack of any theological–ontological articulation about human personality in the Cairo Declaration.[140] Keeping in mind the problem of the lack of foundations in human rights in building a secular–religious alliance, Sachedina looks at the foundational Islamic model with its own universal claim of offering a more comprehensive understanding as a defender of human rights.[141] His aim is to explore the ethical doctrine that underpins the legal tradition in Islam, because it is the ethical dimension of Islamic legal methodology that has the potential for an inclusive universal language that can engage the universal morality of the UDHR on several levels.[142]

---

137 Ibid., 23–24.
138 Ibid., 24.
139 Ibid., 24–25.
140 Ibid., 27.
141 Ibid., 36–39.
142 Ibid., 41.

According to Sachedina, Muslim reformers ignored the task of rethinking legal methodology to appreciate the universal content of its ethical underpinnings in favour of seeking textual proof for fresh rulings in the area of inter-human relationships. The same neglect of Islamic ethical resources occurred in drafting the CDHRI in August 1990.[143] Discussing religious reason in Muslim polities, Sachedina highlighted a very important point: the ethical–political obligation connected to public order in Islam has been identified by Western social scientists as "political Islam".[144]

Explaining the nature of Islamic juridical–ethical discourse, Sachedina concludes that the foundational question about the character of universal morality in Muslim political theology has provided us with an opportunity to delineate the relative adequacy of teleological and deontological models of human moral agency that underpin the legal tradition in Islam. These are the two sources of his claim. First, passage 5:48 of the Qur'an underscores the divine mystery that allows pluralism in matters of faith and law to exist in human society. This is the foundation for moral universality of human rights. Second, the idea of civic equality was introduced in the document written by Caliph 'Ali (d. 660) himself to underscore the fact that communitarian membership was not incompatible with civic equality based on human dignity.[145]

Sachedina's task is to provide an Islamic perspective on human dignity and justice in a universal idiom that appeals to all human beings and communities. This process had to rely on two hermeneutical moves applied to normative Islamic sources to bring the relevant materials in line with modern human rights discourse. The first hermeneutical move, of necessity, involved deconstructing the contextual aspects of the classical juridical heritage of Muslims by looking at the way religion and politics in Islam interacted to distort the original universal intent of the relevant texts for exclusivist political reasons. The second move involved providing a fresh interpretation that is consonant with the inclusive intent of the religious discourse and relevant to modern discourse on human dignity and justice.[146]

The backbone of Sachedina's project is a Mu'tazilite and Shi'ite ethical approach. Human rights discourse in the Muslim world could be based on

---

143 Ibid., 42.
144 Ibid., 45.
145 Ibid., 79–80.
146 Ibid., 111.

the foundational doctrine of natural law (*fitrah*), which treats human equality as its first and essential tenet. Natural law goes back to God, in the sense that its precepts derive their authority from the fact that they are confirmed and implemented by the revelation as the internal, immutable tradition of God (*sunnat allah*). Natural law, with its connection to inherent human capacity, has an inbuilt permanence, which renders it absolutely binding and which overrules all other laws. Muslim jurists should rethink some juridical decisions, both in historical Islam and in contemporary rulings, on the basis of ethical sensibilities that underpin juridical methodology in Islamic jurisprudence. Islamic ethics, rather than Islamic jurisprudence, must assume a central role in defining human rights that accrue to all humans as human. It derives from the justice of God, who never abandoned humanity without providing basic moral awareness.[147]

Defending the God-centred pluralism of the Qur'an, Sachedina concluded that the religious commitment to a community-oriented belief system necessarily led to the formulation of an exclusivist theology. The foundation of a civil society in Islam is based on equality in creation in which the privilege of citizenry attaches equally to Muslims and non-Muslims, entailing inclusive political, civil and social membership in the community. He finished his book in this way:

> Islam's founder, the Prophet Muhammad, underscored my unflinching support for the UDHR based on inherent human dignity and moral ability to negotiate its spiritual destiny without the interference of the state. The Prophet's non-interventionist policy in the matter of the enforcement of religious faith was based on the confidence generated by the Qur'an regarding the universal moral intuitive ability of all human beings who needed to work together to make this world an ideal for all human beings to live in harmony and peace.[148]

Advantages and Disadvantages of Sachedina's Approach

Like Ann Elizabeth Mayer, Abdullahi Ahmed An-Na'im and Mohammad Mojtahed Shabestari, Abdulaziz Sachedina is a sincere proponent of the

---

147 Ibid., 114.
148 Ibid., 205–208.

UDHR. Like them, he strongly criticised the stance of traditional Islam (especially *fiqh* and so-called Islamic law) on human rights. Like Mahmoud Mohamed Taha and An-Na'im, Sachedina believes that Islam in its foundations and principles, in the Qur'an and Tradition, is consistent with the modern understanding of human rights, including the UDHR.

But Sachedina is unique among the leading Muslim defenders of the modern idea of human rights and the UDHR in Western academic scholarship on at least two counts. First, he believes that the UDHR is rooted in a secular liberal philosophy that is not able to justify inherent human dignity and human rights, and, therefore, all the UN documents on human rights, including the UDHR, are "foundationless". Second, Abrahamic traditions, especially Islamic philosophical theology and juridical methodology, do have the capacity to support universal human rights. Sachedina is not alone in making either of these claims and cites his counterparts in contemporary Christianity.

It is a traditionalist standpoint. All traditionalist Muslims deny so-called "Western human rights" and support "metaphysical or real human rights" based on Islamic teachings. But Sachedina's standpoint differs from theirs in at least three ways. First, both his critiques and supporting arguments are acceptable in modern academic scholarship, and are far from the dogmatic, apologetic and ahistorical methodology of traditionalists. Second, he absolutely defends the UDHR. His challenge is to its roots, not its content. In contrast, Muslim traditionalists justify religious and gender discrimination, cardinal punishment for blasphemy and apostasy, other harsh punishments (*hudud shar'iyya*), and deny the right to freedom of religion and expression. Some even justify modern slavery. Third, he supports reform in *fiqh* based on the ethical Islamic foundations in the Qur'an and Tradition, but to be determined by qualified Muslim scholars. Sachedina's approach is a combination of Islamic traditionalism and reformism: traditionalist in its objectives, but reformist and modernist in its methodology.

The brilliance of Sachedina's work lies in his objective to convince Muslim traditionalist scholars that it is their duty to support the UDHR and human rights based on rich Islamic teachings. He started to integrate the culture of human rights into traditional Islam. This was a wake-up call, telling ordinary Muslims: this is your property! Maintain it carefully! Do not reject it! Sachedina addresses Muslim traditionalists, not secular or modernist elites. In his journey, Sachedina constructs a "political theology", focusing on Islamic theology and ethics. These are the foundations of a new jurisprudence or Islamic law, a discipline in need of renewal. His idea is made possible by revisiting the rational foundations of Islamic theology and ethics (the Mu'tazilite and Shi'ite approach). Be that as it may, Sachedina's proposal is the most acceptable in Muslim-majority countries where the majority of the population is traditionalist. It is the most practical and successful way to normalise human rights in developing Muslim countries.

Having said that, I have some comments on Sachedina's proposal:

First, the debate between the secular and monotheists is endless. Sachedina's argument, that all secular documents of human rights are "foundationless" and that monotheism is necessary for achieving human rights, is problematic. Rationality, justice and morality are not *a posteriori* to revelation. They are *a priori* concepts to revelation. This means that the need for rationality, reasonability, justice and morality is not based on any religious argumentation. The authority of these concepts outweighs all others, so that God, revelation and religious teachings ought to be reasonable, just and moral, not vice versa. It is one of the first debates in Islamic theology that "God ought to be just" or that "justice is meaningless outside the framework of revelation". The former was the slogan of the People of Justice (al-'Adliya), that is, Sunni Mu'tazilites and Shi'ites, and the latter was the slogan of other Sunni Muslims. Sachedina unconsciously took a position in opposition to his preferred[149] theological school (the People of Justice), which is self-contradictory.

Second, although no one can deny the general teachings of religions, especially the Abrahamic traditions and particularly Islam, on human dignity, individuality, agency and personhood, nevertheless the modern notion of human rights is not the product of any religious movement or organisation. I am not sure that scholars like Sachedina would remember to revisit their religious teachings to look for the roots of human rights if this secular event, the UDHR, had not occurred in the twentieth century. As Mary McCarthy wrote in her *Memories of a Catholic Girlhood*, "Religion makes good people better and bad people worse."[150] We cannot deny the abuse of religious traditions, including Islam, especially in the past two centuries, to justify religious

---

149 Sachedina is the author of *Islamic Messianism: The Idea of Mahdi in Twelver Shi'ism* (Albany, NY: State University of New York Press, 1981); and *The Just Ruler in Shi'ite Islam: The Comprehensive Authority of the Jurist in Imamite Jurisprudence* (Oxford: Oxford University Press, 1988).
150 Mary McCarthy, *Memories of a Catholic Girlhood* (New York: Open Road Media, 2013).

discrimination, gender discrimination, slavery, restriction of the freedom of religion and expression, the killing of dissidents accused of blasphemy or apostasy, and harsh punishments. These ugly aspects of religion in practice are highlighted more often than the beautiful theoretical aspects that he describes.

Third, the ugly anti-human rights understanding of monotheism among conservative believers, including Muslims, who are the majority in developing Muslim-majority countries, is an undeniable reality. It is not only fundamentalists, but also traditionalists who have many misunderstandings about human rights, arising from religious teachings that we think are wrong. The main problem is that there are some verses and statements in the original religious texts, including the Scriptures and teachings of the prophets, that are inconsistent with the concept of human rights. These verses or statements are the source of anti-human rights interpretations by conservative, fundamentalist or traditionalist believers. The Qur'an and the Tradition of the Prophet contain items that support human rights as well as items inconsistent with them. Traditional *shari'a* and *fiqh* were built on the principles of the latter teachings. An-Na'im followed Taha's belief that the Medina material should be retired and that the Meccan material should be used to build a new Islam. Mojtahed Shabestari's approach was to return to public reason and human experience, and reduce Islam to "*tawhid*-oriented conduct" (*suluk-e tawhidi*) or "lived faith of Muslims" and justice. In practice, this means the abrogation of Islamic Scripture. What is Sachedina's answer to this key question? Although he generally accepts the necessity of renewing *fiqh* based on the beautiful aspects of Islamic theology and ethics, I did not find any specific answers to this key question nor any solutions to this major problem in his works. Reconstruction of *fiqh* in the light of Islamic theology and ethics requires a detailed plan that Sachedina's work does not provide. In other words, there is no theory in his book for the reconciliation of Islam as it is with the UDHR. Sachedina did not engage with the most essential issue at the heart of the discussion around Islam and human rights.

Fourth, it is not sufficient to say that Islamic law or *fiqh* or *shari'a* should be reconstructed in the light of Islamic theology or Islamic ethics, because Islamic theology and ethics have the same problem in relation to human rights. They are not free of the ugliness of religious or gender discrimination, lack of freedom of religion or expression and so on. Islamic studies, including theology (*kalam*), Islamic ethics (*akhlaq*), Islamic law (*fiqh*), the exegesis of the Qur'an (*tafsir*), the science of hadith (*'ilm al-hadith*) and the principles of jurisprudence (*usul al-fiqh*), all need reconstruction. It is what I call structural *ijtihad* or "*ijtihad* in principles and foundations" (*ijtihad fi al-usul wa al-mabani*). In other words, any reconstruction of *fiqh* or other Islamic sciences requires certain criteria, and these criteria cannot be clearly found in Sachedina's works.

Section Six: Kadivar's Human Rights and Reformist Islam

This final section has four subsections: the outline of my approach; a comparison with other approaches; the comparative chronology of the approaches; and a note about this book.

The Outline of Kadivar's Approach

First, the idea of human rights is a modern phenomenon. It is impossible to find this concept in any premodern socio-political, economic or cultural context. By this I mean the rights of a human being as a human being, regardless of religion or gender, be they free or in slavery, without any discrimination. The prohibition of arbitrary punishments, harsh punishments and torture, and the absolute freedom of religion are also the product of modern times. The term "human rights" or its synonyms do not have the same meaning in premodern and modern contexts. The paradigm of premodern times was that of *responsibility* and *duty* to God, and was presented in *divine rulings*. Some of what are now called human rights can be found in these rulings. They are directly and explicitly duties, and indirectly and implicitly rights. For example, the *shari'a* ruling that prohibits the killing of an innocent person correlates with the right to live.

Second, so-called Islamic law, *shari'a* rulings or traditional Islam, as manifested in *fiqh*, is inconsistent with the concept of human rights and especially with the UDHR. These inconsistencies occur in six areas at least: religious discrimination; gender discrimination; discrimination between slaves and free people; discrimination between jurists and laymen; freedom of religion and punishment of apostasy; and arbitrary punishment, harsh punishment and torture. These inconsistencies are not found only in *fiqh*, that is, the understanding of jurists of Scripture and Tradition, but can also be seen in many authentic hadiths and a few verses of the Qur'an. The inconsistencies between traditional Islam and the UDHR are not accidental, but essential and structural, and conventional *ijtihad* or *ijtihad* in subsidiary *shariʿa* rulings cannot solve this problem.

Third, "traditional Islam" is not the same thing as Islam, rather, it is the reading and understanding of Islam by scholars of the past. It is possible to have a reading of the Qur'an and the Tradition of the Prophet that is consistent with the UDHR. In other words, a new understanding of *shariʿa* and *fiqh* is the product of modern-day scholars. It is obvious that although Scripture and Tradition are the same in the past and in the present, the understanding of scholars has differed deeply over time. Traditional Islam *was* the Islam of its time. But it is difficult to imagine that it *is* Islam today too. Confining Islam to traditional Islam and denying other readings, understandings and interpretations is a form of bullying and is unreasonable.

Fourth, whether or not Islam can be understood as being consistent with the UDHR is a completely different matter from deriving human rights from the Qur'an and Tradition. This juridical deduction is not possible because Scripture and Tradition were not in a position to declare (*maqam-i bayan*) human rights, since that was not a concept that existed at the time, as I explained in the first point above. On the other hand, human rights (as introduced in the UDHR) are completely different from Islamic human rights, such as those expressed in the 1993 CDHRI.

Fifth, a human rights scheme is not one of the attributes of religion. It is something entirely human, that only humans can attain, and which they have attained in the middle of the twentieth century. The expectations of religion are matters that are not achievable by most people within a reasonable timeframe and without mistakes. These are my expectations of Islam: that life be meaningful, including awareness of the transcendent (God), resurrection and the Hereafter, the spiritual unseen world (*ghaib wa malakut*), a guarantee of ethics and morality, training in rituals, worship and semi-rituals (the rules of eating, drinking and sexual affairs), and guidance in some social affairs (human interactions), for example, the prohibition of usury, or the necessity of consulting in public affairs with other human beings. Natural science, social sciences and humanities are not within the realm of religions, including Islam. In contrast to traditional Islam, we do not expect law from Islam. Law is constrained in time and cannot be one of the timeless expectations of Islam. A framework of human rights is a branch of law and not one of the expectations of Islam. This is a very important point.

Sixth, the revelation and the Prophet had two objectives; first, to solve the problems of their immediate audience, that is, the people of the Hijaz in the age of revelation; and, second, to provide guidelines for a happy existence for all human beings everywhere and for all time. It is obvious that the Prophetic Tradition addresses both, but it is important to note that some verses of the Qur'an were revealed explicitly to solve the problems of the time of the Prophet. Thus, the verses of the Qur'an are divided into two major categories: time-bound and temporal, and timeless and permanent. The former category includes the verses that are specific to a time, a place and an audience, and the latter includes the verses of the eternal mission of Islam and the Qur'an. Many problems have arisen through neglect of this vital classification, and the mistaken belief that all verses of the Qur'an are timeless and permanent. Although many time-bound and temporal verses were revealed in Medina, it is not correct to think that *all* verses revealed in Medina were temporal and time-bound, and that *all* Meccan verses were timeless and permanent. There is no doubt that many timeless and permanent verses were revealed in the Medina period. The classification of temporal or permanent is therefore *not* parallel or identical to the Meccan or Medina classification, but is a completely new classification. The Meccan–Medina period classification is a chronological division, while the temporal–permanent classification is a rational division based on precise criteria. All the verses that are problematic in the context of human rights are in the temporal and time-bound category. I will discuss the criteria for this classification and who is qualified to apply this classification below.

Seventh, the Islamic teachings in the original Islamic texts, that is, the Qur'an and Tradition, are considered to be the *culture* of the first addressees (*mukhatabun*) of Islam. By this I mean not only the Arabic language, but also the conventions, knowledge, science and reason of that time. The messages of Islam, especially the divine revelation, must be understandable to the people to whom it was first addressed. To be understandable it must be delivered in a specific language (Arabic) and have due regard for the conventions of that specific time (the seventh century) and place (the Hijaz). This is a general textual principle, and the divine texts or revelation are no exception to it. Although it is God speaking as revelation, it is humans who are to receive it, and humans are not able to understand God's message except in human language and according to the conventions of the time. However, these conventions are not divine and we do not have any Islamic responsibility to preserve them. The conventions of seventh-century Hijaz are not Islam, but simply the customs (*'urf*) of that specific time and place. Arab customs were not, and especially *are* not, part of *shari'a* and Islam. Most of the problematic issues concerning human rights are these ancient customs.

Eighth, all Islamic teachings, including *shari'a* rulings, *were* reasonable, just, moral and more functional as compared with other belief systems, in the context of the conventions of the age of early Islam. The first adressees of Islamic teachings might not have accepted these teachings if they were unreasonable, unjust, immoral or less functional than others. These people were the same as other human beings: reasonable people, and these four criteria are general criteria for accepting vital teachings. At least Islam never invited anyone to accept any unreasonable, unjust, immoral or less functional teachings. The Qur'an is full of emphasis on reasonableness, justice and morality. Rationality and justice were the key points of the first controversial discussions and theological division among Muslim scholars in the eighth century and onwards. One of these theological schools called itself the People of Justice (*'Adliyya*) and it established the first discipline of rational morality or philosophy of ethics among Muslims. Rationality and reasonability, justice and fairness, and morality and ethics have been the conventional criteria among Sunni Mu'tazilites and Shi'ites since the beginning of Islamic theology. The framework of objectives of *shari'a* (*maqasid al-shari'a*) and similar legal frameworks postulated by other Sunni legal schools do not offer a complete rational approach capable of solving any problem, until their position regarding reasonableness, justice, morality and functionality in comparison with other frameworks is clarified. It is clear to me that the problem of human rights in Islam cannot be solved except through the channel of these four criteria and any other attempts at solving the problem always come back to these. There are four criteria, no less, no more, because of induction (*istqra*). As such, there is no deductive argument that any new criterion is possible. Reasonableness is the key concept. Although justice is a vital part of any ethical framework, it is mentioned separately because of its high importance. Justice is a broader field than ethics, and covers politics, law and economics. There are many other ethical issues alongside justice that justify ethics as the third criterion. The fourth criterion is functionality. These four criteria are rational and are supported strongly by Scripture and Tradition. This is the most important point in this outline.

Ninth, it is necessary to evaluate each conventional Islamic teaching against these four criteria. The result of this evaluation is acceptable if, and only if, the conclusion is certain, decisive and definitive. Any speculative conclusion, presumption, conjecture, estimation or fantasy can never be an acceptable outcome of this process. Three cases may result. If none of the four criteria are met by a teaching, that teaching is determined to be invalid and cannot be called "Islamic", even though it *was* called Islamic in the past, which was a different context and situation. If three of the criteria (except functionality) are not met by a teaching, it means that we conclude that the teaching is unreasonable, unjust and immoral, and is therefore invalid and cannot be called "Islamic" anymore. But if only one or two of these three criteria (other than functionality) is not met, it is not easy to call a teaching "Islamic". We should be cautious in this third case. However, according to inductive inquiry, the three criteria of reasonability, justice and morality are inseparable. This means that we cannot find any reasonable injustice or immorality, nor a just, unreasonable or immoral case, nor a moral but unjust or unreasonable case. In other words, reasonableness, justice and morality are three dimensions of a single overarching criterion, and removing any one of them correlates to removing the other two. This point strengthens our evaluation.

Tenth, according to these four criteria, the Islamic teachings in the Scripture and Tradition were reasonable, just, moral and more functional than other teachings not only at the time of early Islam, but also in the whole premodern era. We should keep in mind that the human rights movements were started in the late eighteenth century. Many basic human rights were approved in 1789, first, in the United States Bill of Rights and then in the Declaration of the Rights of Man in France. Two more events occurred in the nineteenth century. The United States abolished slavery in 1865 in its 13th Amendment to the Constitution, and the state of Mississippi allowed women to own property in their own names. It was the first state to do so, in 1839, and in 1844 Maine became the first state in the United States to grant married women the right to "separate economy". Voting rights were extended to women in the second decade of the twentieth century (in Canada, Britain, Germany and the United States between 1917 and 1920). We can say that religious discrimination, lack of freedom of belief and of speech, unequal rights before the law (until the late eighteenth century), slavery (until the second half of the nineteenth century) and gender discrimination (until the second decade of the twentieth century) were not perceived as unreasonable, unjust or immoral across the globe. These were simply the conventions of the time. It is correct to say that until the nineteenth century there were not only no problems concerning Islam and human rights, given the conventions of that time, but also that the rights of women in traditional Islam were far greater than their rights in the Western legal system until the second decade of the twentieth century.

Eleventh, the "inconsistency of Islam and human rights" was perceived as a problem only in approximately the middle of the twentieth century. The reason was the gradual change in the thinking on human rights starting in the late eighteenth century. In this new way of thinking and modern epistemology, freedom of religion was required, and slavery, gender discrimination, religious discrimination, punishment for blasphemy or apostasy, arbitrary or harsh punishments, and torture were no longer tolerated. It is clear that traditional Islam, or conservative *fiqh* and *shari'a*, are inconsistent with the human rights scheme and the UDHR. In the modern way of thinking there are many matters, such as the rights of women and of non-Muslims, slavery, freedom of religion, blasphemy and apostasy, and punishments in the framework of traditional Islam that since the middle of the twentieth century have been found to be unreasonable, unjust, immoral and less functional than other approaches. In premodern contexts, the conventions of the times viewed them as reasonable, just, moral and more functional. These four criteria are not only criteria that were valid at the start, or the establishment, of Islam, but are also the criteria for attributing anything to Islam and *shari'a* at any time. In other words, these are the criteria of *being* Islamic. Anything that we call Islamic must always be reasonable, just, moral and more functional than other teachings. Clearly, therefore, anything that is unreasonable, unjust, immoral and less functional than other approaches, according to the conventions of the time, is *not* Islamic, even though it *might previously have been*. This is why Islam is dynamic. What should always be protected is not the *form* of *shari'a* rulings, nor the *shell* of Islamic teachings, but the *criteria* for those rulings or the *kernel* of those teachings. There is no doubt that the kernel of Islamic teachings and the criteria for *shari'a* rulings are always reasonableness, justice, morality and greater functionality than other approaches, based on the conventions of the time. In other words, there is a clear *correlation* between Islamic teachings and *shari'a* rulings, on the one hand, and reasonableness, justice, morality and functionality, on the other.

This clear correlation means that the lack of any criterion at any time, as viewed by the conventions of that time, is identical with being non-Islamic. That which is unreasonable, unjust, immoral or less functional in comparison with other teachings and according to the conventions of today cannot be called "Islamic". It is absolutely unreasonable to live today and refer to the conventions of a previous era. This is the major problem of conservative or traditional Islam.

Twelfth, distinguishing timeless or permanent from time-bound or temporal teachings and rulings is not only not an easy task, but is also a complex and advanced professional undertaking. This is not something that can be decided by each believer based on their daily desires and limited knowledge. It requires the most expert Islamic studies based on modern methodology and scholarship. Islamic jurisprudence or *fiqh* is a prerequisite, but it is not sufficient. To be qualified for such a sensitive responsibility the scholar should have holistic, comprehensive and multidisciplinary knowledge of Islamic studies. This must include Qur'anic studies, hadith studies, Islamic theology, Islamic ethics, Islamic jurisprudence and its prerequisites (such as its methodology or *usul al-fiqh*), the history of Islam, Islamic philosophy, Islamic mysticism and Arabic literature. In other words, only a *mujtahid* (agent of *ijtihad* or scholar of independent reasoning) is qualified, but not within the framework of traditional or conventional *ijtihad* that is restricted to the subsidiary rulings of *fiqh* (*furu' fiqhiya*), but structural *ijtihad* or *ijtihad* in the principles and foundations,[151] or revision in the principles and foundations of Islamic thought. This has two parts. "*Ijtihad* in principles" means restructuring *usul al-fiqh* (the methodology of Islamic law). It requires enrichment and continuity of *ijtihad* throughout itself, as well as being inspired by linguistic philosophy, hermeneutics, historicity and critical thinking. The second part is "*ijtihad* in foundations", that is, the epistemological, cosmological, ontological, anthropological, sociological, psychological, theological and ethical foundations of Islamic teachings. According to traditional or conventional *ijtihad*, *shari'a* is the system of Islamic law, but from the perspective of structural *ijtihad* it is the set of Islamic standards, virtues and values. Islamic rules at the time of the revelation were reasonable, just, ethical and more functional than other teachings, according to the conventions of that time. The

---

151 See my article "Ijtihad in Usul al-Fiqh: Reforming Islamic Thought through Structural Ijtihad".

school of structural *ijtihad* sees these criteria as the necessary characteristics for all particulars of Islamic teachings forever. Distinguishing timeless from time-bound teachings, and structural *ijtihad* are not tasks for one scholar alone; it is a collective responsibility of *mujtahids* (with the aforementioned characteristics) working in an academic atmosphere with critical scrutiny.

Thirteenth, after the careful evaluation of Islamic teachings against the four criteria, any teachings definitely classed as time-bound and temporal means that such teachings belong to a past context, and their time of validity is over. The technical name of this process is "abrogation" (*naskh*). Abrogation is a familiar term in Qur'anic studies and the discipline of jurisprudence (*usul al-fiqh*). Abrogating (*nasikh*) is exclusive to the Qur'anic verses, if the abrogated (*mansukh*) is an earlier Qur'anic verse. Abrogating (*nasikh*) can be achieved by Qur'anic verses or Prophetic Traditions only if the abrogated (*mansukh*) is an earlier Prophetic Tradition. In other words, the abrogating (*nasikh*) is restricted to transmitted indications (*al-adillah al-naqliyya*) or textual indications. Although abrogation has been an accepted part of Islamic scholarship since early Islam, there are nonetheless a lot of disagreements in three areas: the type of abrogation; the particulars of the abrogating verses; and the particulars of the abrogated verses. The thinking on these three areas differs very widely, which has a profound effect on the perspective of Islam, especially in modern times. Studying these three areas of challenging abrogation shows that abrogation in its particulars and types is indisputably a human action (*al-fi'l al-bashari*), without any divine intervention. Two of the three types of abrogation, that is, abrogation of the recitation or the removal of a verse from the Qur'an (*naskh al-talawa*), with abrogation of the ruling (*naskh al-hukm*) or without (*bi la hukm*) are absolutely problematic, or in other words, are misunderstandings and mistakes made by past exegetes of the Qur'an. Indeed, these two types of abrogation in addition to the first kind of the third type have resulted in abrogation of almost all of the principal verses of the Qur'an. In other words, more than two hundred verses – almost all of them considered as principal verses of the Qur'an – were abrogated by a few subsidiary verses. Their understandings were based on speculation, presumption and conjecture (*zanni*). According to structural *ijtihad*, abrogation of Qur'anic verses on speculative evidence (*al-dalil al-zanni*) is absolutely prohibited. Abrogation is unacceptable except by definitive evidence (*al-dalil al-qat'i*), either textual or non-textual. Non-textual evidence means rational demonstration (*al-dalil al-'aqli*) which must be restricted to definitive evidence. There is a fundamental principle in *usul al-fiqh* called the principle of correlation (*qa'ida al-mulazama*). There is a correlation between a rational ruling and a *shari'a* ruling. The acceptance of rational demonstration in *usul al-fiqh* is the consequence of this fundamental principle. There is also a correlation between rational ruling and rational abrogation. It is impossible to approve the former and disapprove the latter. Sunni theology (except for the banned Mu'tazilites) and Akhbari Shi'ites do not accept rational demonstrations and restrict themselves to textual or transmitted indications. It is obvious, therefore, that rational abrogation is not accepted in these schools. The Usuli Shi'ite traditionalists also accept the validity of independent rational demonstration (*al-dalil al-'aqliyya al-mustaqil*) in *usul al-fiqh*, but they do not practise it in *fiqh* and restrict themselves to textual or transmitted indications and dependent rational demonstrations (*al-dalil al-'aqliyya ghair al-mustaqil*). Therefore, they do not acknowledge the validity of rational abrogation either. However, rational abrogation based on the four criteria (reasonableness, justice, morality and functionality) is accepted, and all verses or hadiths that have been definitively determined to be unreasonable, unjust, immoral and non-functional are abrogated. This abrogation is only in ruling, not in recitation. This means that neither a verse nor a hadith is removed from Scripture or hadith collections, but the rulings of such verses and hadiths are abrogated. In other words, the indications of these verses are not used in any contemporary Islamic arguments. They are elements in the museum of the history of Islamic thought, but they do not play any role in contemporary Islamic teachings. For those who cannot accept permanent rational abrogation, they may consider it as temporal, which means that the time of this abrogation would be over, if the conventions of human beings return to those of a premodern period. I do not think this return is possible, and that rational abrogation is permanent and irreversible.

Fourteenth, in this approach all the verses and hadith that are problematic in relation to human rights issues (such as slavery, gender discrimination, religious discrimination, freedom of religion and punishment of blasphemy and apostasy, arbitrary punishments, harsh punishments, torture, and discrimination between jurists and laypeople) are abrogated according to the permanent criteria of reasonability, justice, morality and functionality. Nevertheless, this approach does not only concern human rights, but a much broader field, including democracy and all other aspects of modern life.

Comparison with the Five Other Approaches

I will now compare my approach to the reconciliation of Islam and human rights with the approaches of the five scholars discussed above: Mahmoud Mohamed Taha, Abdullahi Ahmed An-Na'im, Ann Elizabeth Mayer, Mohammad Mojtahed Shabestari and Abdulaziz Sachedina. Their approaches have been described above, together with my critical comments and a discussion of their similarities and common ground. Here I focus on their differences in a brief comparative study of each one. I will set out my position in the last part.

(a) My approach differs from that of Mahmoud Mohamed Taha in at least three major points:

First, the crux of Taha's approach is the distinction between the Meccan period as the major source of the principal and permanent Islamic teachings, and the Medina period as the source of time-bound, temporal, subsidiary Islamic teachings that were abrogated by the former. In contrast, the Meccan–Medina categorisation does not play a role in my approach.

Second, according to Taha, Meccan Islam is the only correct source of human rights. This is a major fundamental epistemic claim with which I do not agree.

Third, his approach is absolutely textual, while my approach is semitextual and more rational.

(b) The differences between Abdullahi Ahmed An-Na'im's approach and mine:

First, contrary to An-Na'im's point of view, demarcation of Medina verses from Meccan verses is not the point in abrogation. The categorisation of Mecca material and Medina material as principal and subsidiary, abrogating and abrogated, is neither comprehensive nor inclusive, and, given the high number of articles that do not conform to this division, it is an indefensible and inadequate criterion for abrogation.

Second, although the principal permanent verses (the Meccan verses according to Taha and An-Na'im) support human rights, they can be neither the source of a modern framework of human rights (including the UDHR), nor the standard for the reform of Islamic thought. Both of these are the result of a greater force, namely, modern rationality, that articulates the necessity for reasonableness, justice and morality. An-Na'im neglected the cause and engaged in the effects, whereas I focus the whole discussion on the major cause. The point is beyond the scriptural or textual attempts of An-Na'im.

(c) Differences between Ann Elizabeth Mayer's approach and mine:

First, neither conservative Islam nor so-called 'Islamic Human Rights schemes" are representative or unique interpretations of Islam. The undeniable and rapidly growing tendency among educated Muslims is to seek consistency between Islam and human rights.

Second, her focus is a conservative approach and a *realpolitik* standpoint, of course in the name of Islam, whereas my concern is providing a clear reformist Islam that is in harmony with human rights.

(d) Differences between Mohammad Mojtahed Shabestari's approach and mine:

First, in contrast to Shabestari's ultra-progressive liberal theology approach, that is, the de-sacralisation of revelation and the radical humanism that abrogates Scripture and Tradition, my approach is based on Scripture, as the verbatim words of God and the authentic Prophetic Tradition. His approach is not reminiscent of anything related to Islam in modern times, except in terms of *tawhid* – an impersonal God in a pantheistic way – and justice.

Second, Shabestari's Islam is *shari'a*-less. He declared that the time of *usul al-fiqh*, *fiqh* and *fiqhi ijtihad* is over and that this applies not only in all aspects of human interactions (*mu'amalat*), but also covers all obligatory worship (*'ibadat*). His alternative to *shari'a* is human reason, science and experience. In my approach *shari'a* embodiment of Islamic virtues, values and standards of life is permanent. *Fiqh* as the science of Islamic rituals (worship) and semi-rituals (the boundaries of drinking, eating and sex); *usul al-fiqh* as the methodology of *fiqh* and other textual Islamic sciences; and "*ijtihad* in principle and foundations" are inseparable elements of Islam or Islamic sciences even today.

Third, it is self-evident that after removing divine verbal revelation, *shari'a*, *fiqh* and *ijtihad*, there will be no problems of inconsistency between Islam and human rights at all. By contrast, my approach resolves the problem of conflict between Islam and human rights without removing the subject of the conflict.

(e) Differences between Abdulaziz Sachedina's approach and mine:

First, in contrast to Sachedina's approach, mine is not based on the "lack of foundation" of all secular documents concerning human rights. Reasonableness, justice, morality and efficiency are *a priori* issues of religions and revelation.

Second, Sachedina has not provided any criteria for distinguishing the beautiful aspects of Islamic theology and ethics (political theology in his words) from the ugly anti-human rights stance that is evident in traditional Islam. His approach is selective and without criteria.

Third, although he generally accepts the necessity of renewing *fiqh* based on the beautiful aspects of Islamic theology and ethics, he offers no specific solution for the conflict between Islamic Scriptures and teachings and human rights, and he does not engage with the fundamental issue of Islam and human rights.

(f) We can compare these five scholars of Islam and human rights and range them on a spectrum:

Ann Elizabeth Mayer, Abdulaziz Sachedina, Mahmoud Mohamed Taha, Abdullahi Ahmed An-Na'im and Mohammad Mojtahed Shabestari. The former restricted herself to proving the essential inconsistency of Islam and human rights. Sachedina is the more conservative in his view of the consistency of Islam and human rights, and Shabestari is the most radical. Sachedina, Taha and An-Na'im all believe that human rights can be derived from Islamic texts, Taha and his students believe that they can come only from Meccan texts, and Shabestari from the whole Scripture.

My position is between that of An-Na'im and Mojtahed Shabestari, more rational and less textual than the former, and more textual than the text-less position of the latter. Unlike Shabestari's position on liberal theology, existential revelation and humanism, he and I are on the same track in our understanding of human rights and the interpretation of Islamic texts. Although Taha, An-Na'im and I agree on the abrogation of the Islamic teachings which are anti-human rights as time-bound, we differ on this key point: their approach is based on the distinction between Mecca and Medina, whereas mine is rational and based on the pre-eminence of reasonableness, justice, morality and functionality as the certain causes of permanence and timelessness. My objective is not to derive human rights from Scripture, Tradition or *shari'a*, but to prepare a reformist reading of Islam consistent with human rights and other modern phenomena.

The Comparative Chronology of the Approaches

Haqq al-Nas (*The Rights of People: Islam and Human Rights*) was published in Persian in Tehran in September 2008, but most of its chapters had been previously published as journal articles or as chapters in other books several years earlier.[152]

Taha's books, An-Na'im's first two books, Mayer's book, and both Sachedina's and Shabestari's first books on this subject were published before my work, which was published in articles or chapters before being published as a book.[153] Shabestari's and Sachedina's second book and An-Na'im's third book were published after publication of my articles,[154] while Shabestari's third book and An-Na'im's fourth were published after my book.[155]

---

152 Here is a chronology of some of its major chapters: *Emam-e Sajjad wa Hoquq-e Mardom* (*Imam Sajjad and the Rights of Mankind*), Tehran, *Sobh-e Emrouz* (*This Morning*), daily magazine, 17 April 2000; "*Az Eslam Tarikhi fe Eslam-e Ma'navi*" ("From Traditional Islam to End-Oriented Islam"), presentation on 27 August 2001 at the annual meeting of the Islamic Association of Students of all Universities in Iran, Tehran; later in *Sonnat wa Secularism* (*Tradition and Secularism*), the presentations of Abdolkarim Soroush, Mohammad Mojtahed Shabestari, Mostafa Malekian and Mohsen Kadivar (Tehran: Serat, 2002), 405–431. "*Azadi-ye 'Aqidideh wa Mazhab dar Eslam wa Asnad-e Hoquq-e Bashar*" ("The Freedom of Belief and Religion in Islam and Human Rights Documents"), presentation at the first International Conference of Human Rights and the Dialogue of Civilizations, Mofid University, Tehran, 2 May 2001, *Conference Proceedings* (Qom: Mofid University, 2001), 263–265; later *Aftab* (*Sunshine*), bi-monthly, Tehran, March 2003, 23:54–63; "*Mas'ale-ye Bardedari dar Eslam-e Mo'aser*" ("The Issue of Slavery in Contemporary Islam"), presented at the second International Human Rights Conference (The Theoretical Bases of Human Rights), Mofid University, Qom, 18 May 2003, *Conference Proceedings*, 2005, 477–502; later *Aftab* (*Sunshine*) bimonthly, May 2003, 25:80–89; "*Hoquq-e Bashar wa Roshanfekri-ye Dini*" ("Human Rights and Reformist Islam"), *Aftab* bimonthly, June 2003, 27:54–59 and August 2003, 28:106–115; "*Roshanfekri-ye Dini wa Hoquq-e Zanan*" ("Reformist Islam and Women's Rights"), *A'yeen Monthly Journal of Culture, Society, and Politics* pre-issue 1 (December 2003): 9–17.

153 Taha, *al-Risalat al-Thaniya min al-Islam*; Taha, *The Second Message of Islam*, trans. and introduced Abdullahi Ahmed An-Na'im. Little, Kelsay and Sachedina, *Human Rights and the Conflict of Cultures*; Abdullahi Ahmed An-Na'im, *Toward an Islamic Reformation*; Mayer, *Islam and Human Rights*, 5th edn; Shabestari, *Naqdi bar Qara'at-e Rasmi az Din*.

154 Shabestari, *Ta'ammolati dar Qara'at-e Ensani az Din*; An-Na'im, *Islam and the Secular State*; Sachedina, *Islam and the Challenge of Human Rights*. Sachedina reliably cited my articles and ideas at 199, 213 and 219.

155 An-Na'im: *Muslims and Global Justice*; and, finally, Shabestari, *Naqd-e Bonyadha-ye Feqh va Kalam*.

Notes on the Present Book

This subsection has two parts: an overview of the first edition, and the advantages of the English translation.

The First Edition at a Glance

Haqq al-Nas: Islam va Hoquq-e Bashar (*The Rights of People: Islam and Human Rights*, 2008)[156] was a best-selling book in Iran and was reprinted three times in less than a year.[157] However, the publication of all of my books, articles, interviews and speeches, including the present work, were banned during Mahmoud Ahmadinejad's second term as president in spring 2009.[158] After Hassan Rauhani took office as president it was announced that "No author is banned and reprinting previously published books does not require new permission from officials." My publisher reprinted two of my books,[159] including the fifth reprint of *Haqq al-Nas* in Farvardin 1393/March 2013, but the Ministry of Guidance and Islamic Culture would not grant permission for the books to be released from the printer's premises.[160] This book, as well as all my other works, have been banned since spring 2009. My Persian writings were posted and circulated largely on social networks.

---

156 Mohsen Kadivar, *Haqq al-Nas: Islam va Hoquq-e Bashar* (*The Rights of People: Islam and Human Rights*) (1st print, Tehran: Kavir, Mehr 1387/September 2008).

157 Aban 1387/November 2008, Bahman 1387/February 2009 and Sharivar 1388/August 2009.

158 I was active in the Green Movement and posted many critical articles, speeches and interviews on social media and the internet.

159 The other book was the sixth reprint of *Hokumat-e Wela'i* (*Governance by Guardianship*) (Tehran: Nashr-e Ney, 1st edn 1998, 2nd edn 2001, 5th print 2007, 6th print 2009) (its release was not permitted however).

160 When the publisher asked what the reason was, the official who is now the Minister of Guidance and Islamic Culture replied that: "The author questioned the religious authority of the Supreme Leader and he expects to be free to reprint his books! It does not happen!" When the publisher asked when this ban would be terminated, the official responded, "At the release of the hidden Imam" (the end of the time)! The problem was posting a series of my articles online titled "*Ebtezal-e Marja'iyyat-e Shi'a: Estidhah-e Marja'iyyat-e Maqam-e Rahbari S. Ali Khamenei*" ("The Trivialization of Shi'ite *Marja'iyyat*: Impeaching Iran's Supreme Leader on his *Marja'iyyat*"), *JARS* (website of the Iranian Green Movement) (March/April 2013). I complained to the Minister of Guidance and Islamic Culture in an open letter of 23 July 2014, but received no response. The 4th edition of it was posted as a web book in May 2015.

The various chapters of *Haqq al-Nas* were reviewed at least twenty-five times between August 2001 and 2018.[161] Chapters 5, 10 and 1 were reviewed, respectively, ten, five and three times. The book as a whole was reviewed five times in Persian between November 2008 and January 2013.[162] My approach to human rights has been reviewed in English too.[163] It is ironic that although all of my publications are banned in Iran, my ideas, especially those on human rights, are discussed in Iranian academia. A Master's thesis on human rights titled "Human Rights from the Perspectives of Ayatollah 'Abdollah Javadi Amoli[164] and Dr Mohsen Kadivar" was defended at Mofid University, Qom, in 2013.[165]

Chapter 1 has been translated into German, English and Arabic.[166] Chapter 2 has been translated into Arabic.[167] Chapter 3 first appeared in English,[168] and chapter 5 has been translated into English.[169] Chapters 5 and

---

161 For example, by 'Abdollah Naseri, Behzad Hamidiyya, Mostafa Hoseini Tabataba'i, Nasser Imani, Sayyid Mohammad Ali Mahdavi al-Hoseini, Mohammad Reza Baqerzadeh, Ehsan Shoja'i and Ahmad Shoja'i. The full text and bibliography of all of these reviews is available at: https://kadivar.com/13826.

162 Rouzbeh Karimi, Reza 'Alijani, Sayyid 'Ali Mir-Mousawi, Reza Rasouli and Daniyal Eftekhari.

163 For example, Yasuyuki Matsunaga, "Human Rights and New Jurisprudence in Mohsen Kadivar's Advocacy of 'New-Thinker' Islam", *Die Welt des Islams* 51(3/4) (2011): 358–381.

164 Ustadh Javadi Amoli (b. 1933) was my teacher in *tafsir* (Qur'anic exegesis), Islamic philosophy and mysticism for more than a decade. He is one of the *maraji'-i taqlid* (Shi'ite authorities) in Qom. He is the most distinguished living scholar of conservative Shi'ite Islam, especially in Islamic philosophy and Qur'anic Studies. His book on human rights is *Falasafe-ye Huquq-e Bashar* (*The Philosophy of Human Rights*) (Qom: Esra', 1996).

165 Student: Farhad Ghaffari, supervisor: Dr Abdorrahim Soleimani, Mofid University, Faculty of Law, Department of Public Law and Human Rights, Qom, date of defence 2 February 2013. Mofid is a private university.

166 "Vom historischen Islam zum spirituellen Islam", in *Unterwegs zu einem anderen Islam, Texte Iranischer Denker*, ed., trans. and annotated by Katajun Amirpur (Freiburg: Herder, 2009), 80–105; "From Traditional Islam to Islam as an End in Itself", *Die Welt des Islams* 51(3/4) (2011): 459–484; Tawfiq Alsaif (trans.), "Fahm al-Islam bain al-Qara'at al-Taqlidiyya wa al-Qara'at al-Maqasidiyya", *Al-Kalema* (*The Word*) (quarterly), (Beirut), 25 (2018): 99:141–165.

167 "Usul Insijam il-Islam wa al-Hidatha", Mushtaq 'Abdi Manaf (trans.), *Qadaya Islamiyya Mu'asira* (quarterly) (Baghdad: Centre for Studies of Philosophy of Religion), 51/52 (2012): 302–314.

168 "An Introduction to the Public and Private Debate in Islam", *Social Research* (quarterly) (New School University, New York) 70 (2003): 3:659–680.

169 "Human Rights and Intellectual Islam", trans. Nilou Mobasser, in Kari Vogt, Lena Larsen and Christian Moe (eds), *New Directions in Islamic Thought: Exploring Reform and Muslim Tradition* (London: I. B. Tauris, 2009), 47–74. The second half of Ch. 5.

6 were translated and published in Germany as a book.[170] Chapter 8 was translated into English, and twice into Arabic.[171] Chapter 12 has recently been translated into English.[172]

Advantages of the English Translation

It has been impossible to revise or reprint *Haqq al-Nas* in Iran since 2009. Although it would have been possible to publish it online, I wanted a print copy of my book. Publishing it in Persian outside Iran, or publication in Arabic or English, were other options, each of which has its advantages and disadvantages. This is my first experience of publishing in English and the other options could be pursued in parallel.

The English translation of *Haqq al-Nas* was commissioned in 2015 for inclusion in the In Translation: Modern Muslim Thinkers series published by the Aga Khan University, Institute for the Study of Muslim Civilisations (AKU-ISMC) in association with Edinburgh University Press. The book was translated by Niki Akhavan, who translated the whole work, including those chapters that had been translated and published previously.[173]

---

170 *Gottes Recht und Menschenrechte. Eine Kritik am historischen Islam*, trans. and introduced Armin Eschraghi, Buchreihe der Georges-Anawati-Stiftung, Modernes Denken in der Islamischen Welt, Band 7, (Freiburg: Herder, 2017). It has two notes from the author as an appendix: LGBT rights and the rights of Baha'is.

171 "Freedom of Religion and Belief in Islam", in Mehran Kamrava (ed.), *The New Voices of Islam: Reforming Politics and Modernity – A Reader* (London, I. B. Tauris, 2006), 119–142; *Huriyyat ud-Din wa al-'Aqida fi il-Islam, Mutala'a Fiqhiyya*, trans. 'Ali al-Wardi, *Al-Ijtihad wa al-Tajdid* (quarterly), 3 (2008): 9–10:11–57; *Huriyyat ul-'Aqida wa ad-Din fi il-Islam*, trans. Haidar Najaf, *Qadaya Islamiyya Mmu'asira* (quarterly) (Baghdad: Centre for Studies of Philosophy of Religion), 13 (2009): 39–40:146–187.

172 "The Issue of Slavery in Contemporary Islam", trans. Sadiq Meghjee, Syed Ali Imran and Syed Hadi Rizvi, advisor Jonathan Brown (Georgetown University), *Iqra Online: Shi'ite Islamic Sciences Repository*, September 2018.

173 Five chapters, including 1,3, 5, 8 and 12: Ch. 1: "From Traditional Islam to Islam as an End in Itself", *Die Welt des Islams* 51 (2011): 459–484; Ch. 3: "An Introduction to the Public and Private Debate in Islam", *Social Research*, 2003, 659–680; Ch. 5 (second half): "Human Rights and Intellectual Islam", in *New Directions in Islamic Thought: Exploring Reform and Muslim Tradition*, 47–74; Ch. 8: "Freedom of Religion and Belief in Islam", in *The New Voices of Islam: Reforming Politics and Modernity – A Reader*, 119–142; Ch. 12: "The Issue of Slavery in Contemporary Islam", trans. Sadiq Meghjee, and Syed Ali Imran and Syed Hadi Rizvi *Iqra Online: Shi'ite Islamic Sciences Repository*, September 2018.

However, the appendix to Chapter 9 of the Persian original, "*Shari'a-based Rights of the Political Opposition and the Religious Jurisprudence Sentences for Rebellion, Enmity against God, and Corruption*", was omitted from this translation. It comprised the detailed responses of my mentor Hossein-Ali Montazeri Najaf-Abadi (1922–2009) to the fourteen questions I posed in this chapter. I included this appendix as a way to publish his ideas, since he was under house arrest at the time of writing his responses, and his publications were completely banned when my book was published in 2008. However, a few months later all my publications were banned too! I hope there will be future opportunities to publish his selected works in English.

The author carefully edited the translation. During this process, the project moved from being a pure translation of the original to a revised, updated and expanded version of *Haqq al-Nas* in English. While the original was published in 2008, I have not been idle in the twelve years since then. I have continued thinking, elaborating and deepening the ideas that were discussed in the book, and I have revised a few of them as well. This revision is reflected in the following ways.

First, there were a lot of typos in the original Persian book (text and footnotes). The last draft should have been corrected by the publisher's copy-editor, but it was not. The book was published after I left Iran and I received the first copy of the book several months later. All of these mistakes are corrected in the English translation.

Second, all of the references are revised in the English translation, and the bibliographies are updated.

Third, very minor changes in the text itself (less than 1 per cent) have been made.

Fourth, many footnotes have been revised and added for clarification of the text.

Fifth, epilogues have been added to nine of the translated chapters.[174] These epilogues outline the author's most recent ideas. This is one of the important updates included in the English translation.

Sixth, a critical analytical Preface has been added.

Seventh, a Glossary has been added at the end of the book.

---

174 These epilogues were added in Chapters 3–10 and 14.

Preface to the English Translation

The English translation of *Haqq al-Nas* has resulted in a more complete and comprehensive version of the Persian original.[175]

Although the English translation of *Haqq al-Nas* is consistent with my recent ideas on Islam and human rights, and the outline of my approach (Section Six of this Preface) can be considered the most recent manifestation of this, this does not mean that this book is completely comprehensive. Some aspects of human rights have not been discussed: the relationship between Islam and children's rights, the human rights of people with disabilities, LGBTQIA+ rights, environmental rights, various aspects of the right to life (such as capital punishment, war, abortion, euthanasia, justifiable homicide, suicide, animal welfare, public health care and so forth). The lack of discussion of these rights does not mean that I do not believe in them, and I hope that I can complete my research into these aspects in the future.

I believe my work requires completion through additional explanation of four of the criteria of my approach, that is, reasonableness, justice, morality and functionality or efficiency. Each of these requires detailed discussion to clarify their domain of validity, their conditions and characteristics, and their relationship with each other. What I have discussed in this book is akin to an introduction, which I would like to expand and deepen in the future.

Mohsen Kadivar
Duke University, Durham, North Carolina
3 April 2020

---

175 I may apply the same strategy to my other books, if the illegal ban on my publications in Iran continues.

Introduction to the 2008 Edition

In the name of God, the most gracious, the most merciful
Praise be to God, the lord of the worlds
May God bless his best creatures and the last of his
prophets Mohammad and His Households (*Ahl al-Bayt*)

1. Human rights are the subject of some of the most important debates in contemporary Iran, which officially accepted the United Nations Charter in 1945, the Universal Declaration of Human Rights in 1948, the International Covenant on Economic, Social, and Cultural Rights in 1975, and the International Covenant on Civil and Political Rights in 1975. Key parts of these international texts have also been included in the 1979 Iranian Constitution, such as Section Three of that document (amended 1989). Nonetheless, human rights in Iranian society are a problem in theory and practice. From the perspective of theory, many of its core principles (such as the equality of all humans regardless of gender, religion or political leanings) are seen to be incorrect or in conflict with divine teachings. In terms of practice, many aspects of the Universal Declaration, the two Covenants, as well as the related principles found in the Constitution are systematically violated.

In a society ruled in the name of religion, where all affairs are explained and understood from the perspective of religion (albeit a particular reading of religion), it is natural that discussions pertaining to the relationship of human rights and Islam are both necessary and challenging. This difficult debate is the subject of this book.

2. Numerous books have been published about Islam and human rights in Iran for almost a half century. The contents of most of these publications can be distilled into the following two points: first, human rights are not new. Human rights themes have been abundantly present for a long time in our religious texts. Then, various pieces of evidence from texts and tradition are presented to support these claims. Basically, although Muslims may have

neglected the relevant divine teachings, these teachings mean that we have no need for the likes of the Universal Declaration of Human Rights.

Second, human rights in Islam are much richer and more extensive than those in the Universal Declaration of Human Rights. The divine Lawmaker has determined the true rights of humans in religious decrees, while in the above-mentioned document only some rights are noted, and then only in an incomplete manner that is not based on divine sources. In addition, Islam not only heeds the rights of humans but also those of God, animals, plants and inanimate objects.

3. In addition to respecting the above viewpoint (which will be noted here as historic Islam or traditional Islam), this book explores "the relationship of Islam and human rights" from another perspective. This perspective can be summarised as follows:

First, human rights are among the most important new achievements of humankind in the recent century and, as such, were not a deep or wide-spread concern of people of the past.

Second, while the Abrahamic religions and Islam in particular have explicitly or implicitly considered that which is now known as human rights, in traditional readings of religions or in religions historically, especially in *shari'a* and religious jurisprudence, conflicts with human rights are funda-mental and undeniable.

Third, Islam is not synonymous with historical Islam or traditional read-ings of Islam. Spiritual or end-oriented Islam, which is a forward-thinking and intellectual version of Islam, is compatible with the system of human rights.

4. This book, *Haqq al-Nas* (literally translated: the rights of people), pro-vides a critical analysis of the traditional and the historical reading of human rights in Islam, on the one hand, and makes a humble attempt at providing a solution to the problem of human rights in Islam from the perspective of a spiritual or teleological reading, on the other hand. The ultimate message of the book is as follows:

Faith in God, belief in the Hereafter and following the teachings of the Messenger of Islam, in essence has no conflict with the human approach to human rights. One can be a Muslim from the bottom of one's heart and truly defend the idea of human rights.

5. The methodological framework of this book is based on the following:

A. While the idea of human rights is just, ethical and rational, like all other ideas of humankind, it is fallible and subject to critique and assessment.

B. While human rights have been codified by people in the West, it is not bound by geography and it is the achievement arising from human experience and collective human wisdom.

C. Interpretations of religion are human narratives about divine teachings, and, on account of the human element, are subject to critique and assessment. The same is true of the differences in opinion among various religious scholars and schools of religion, and their mutual criticisms of one another. Thus, while to be a Muslim means to submit absolutely to the Almighty, no human interpretative take on revealed truth is beyond criticism.

6. In a society that for multiple reasons has been accustomed to extremes, where, on the one hand, there are those with a tribal, narrow and harsh reading of the teachings of the Prophet of mercy, who have in their heads the idea that they have the full authority in adjudicating God's religion, and with this crude fantasy tame God's creatures away from his religion, and where, on the other hand, there are those whose reaction is to flee from whatever smells of religion and faith, and who believe that the only prescription to cure the pains of this society is to modernise and to reduce and ultimately eliminate the role of religion in the public sphere, to defend human rights in a manner that is pious, faithful and yet modern, is not acceptable to either the person who is bound by tradition or to the secular citizen. In addition to respecting both, this author believes that a third way of thinking that is critical of the above-mentioned officially sanctioned traditional and the secular currents has the right to exist; this author has a heart full to express and, of course, has an ear for listening as well. I sincerely welcome every scholarly critique, and believe that being subject to criticism is an advantage rather than a deficiency. I hope that this book will have the blessing of scholarly critique as my past work did, and that such critiques will lead to the greater growth of critical thought in Iran.

7. *Haqq al-Nas* is a familiar term in our society. Every Muslim, every Iranian, indeed, is familiar with sayings such as "*haqq al-nas* comes before *haqq Allah*", "Without observing *haqq al-nas* the satisfaction of God will not be gained", "The repentance of the person who is remiss in *haqq al-nas* will not be accepted" or "the first rule of generosity and religiosity is *haqq al-nas*".

Haqq al-nas is a compound word made up of the two Qur'anic terms "*haqq*" and "*nas*" and has no meaning other than the rights of the people. Scholars of religious jurisprudence have counted the following as included in *haqq al-nas*: the right to pre-emption (*shuf'a*); the right to choose in buying and selling (*khiyar*); the right of retaliation (*qisas*); the mother's right to custody; the father's right to guardianship; the right to property; the right to *qasm* (the right of wives in polygamy to have equal nights with the husband), etc. Without doubt, however, the rights of the people are not limited to past incidents of what counted as a "right". Nor is "right" limited to the *maj'ulat* (*shari'a*-made terms). The rights of humans are rational affairs that are *a priori*. Even if these rights were not officially recognised by religion, they would remain valid. What has been recognised in the language of religion as "*haqq al-nas*" is guided by the rule of reason and not something that has been established in opposition to reason. From the point of view of religious jurisprudence, the common division of *shari'a*-made terms into right (*haqq*) and rule (*hukm*) is not correct since both are religious rules (*ahkam*). To be more precise, what is referred to as rights in *shari'a* is no different than religious obligation.

In any case, this writer has not employed the term *haqq al-nas* in the sense in which it is used in religious jurisprudence. Rather, the term is used in its literal and conventional sense to mean the right of humans. It is a term that is the sum of the parts that make up human rights.

For this book, I have chosen the title "*Haqq al-Nas*" – a traditional term used with a modern meaning – to claim that this tradition has the potential for a modern reading. *Haqq al-nas* is the same as human rights, literally.

8. *Haqq al-Nas* is a collection of fourteen chapters on Islam and human rights, which have been organised topically into five sections. The first section is devoted to "The Bases for Discussions on Islam and Human Rights". The three chapters "From Traditional Islam to End-Oriented Islam", "The Principles of Compatibility between Islam and Modernity" and "An Introduction to the Public and Private Debate in Islamic Culture", lay the groundwork for the book's central discussion. The first chapter outlines the book's readings of Islam as compared with traditional readings. The second examines the relationship between Islam and modernity as a collection of issues which includes human rights. The third provides an overview of the public and private spheres as they relate to human rights.

The topic of the second section of the book is "Islam and Human Rights". The first chapter in this section, "Imam Sajjad and the Rights of Mankind" is an exploration of Imam Sajjad's treatise on rights and the meanings and aims of the notion of right in religious texts. The written interview, "Human Rights and Reformist Islam" is the second chapter in this section and the longest piece in the book. It consists of a reflection on the relationship between traditional Islam and the Universal Declaration of Human Rights and its related covenants, and provides a solution for making traditional Islam compatible with the idea of human rights. "Questions and Answers about Human Rights and Reformist Islam" is a written response to the questions posed by Iranian students in Canada about the aforementioned piece. The last chapter in this section "Human Rights, Secularism and Religion" provides a critical overview of the relationship between human rights and two competing contemporary currents of thought, namely, religious thought and secular thought.

The third section considers the "Freedoms of Belief, Religion and Politics". "The Freedom of Belief and Religion in Islam and Human Rights Documents" is the first chapter in this section, and includes a consideration of the punishments for apostasy. Using the Ashura movement and the way of Ali as case studies, "The Rights of the Political Opposition in an Islamic Society", proves that political freedoms are an integral part of the presence of Islam in the public sphere. This chapter has a religious jurisprudence addendum which provides an *ijtihad* inference on the technical nuances of the punishments for rebellion (*baghi*) and terrorism (*muharabe*) using the methods of past jurists and traditional religious jurisprudence.

The fourth section is devoted to "Women's Rights". The first chapter in this section, "Reformist Islam and Women's Rights", critically analyses traditional Islam's challenges in dealing with the notion of human rights as it relates to women's issues, and provides a solution using Qur'anic teachings. "Women's Rights in the Hereafter: a Qur'anic Theological Study" is another contemplation of various religious teachings from the perspective of human rights.

The last section of the book is devoted to "Other Debates in Human Rights". The first chapter in this section is titled "The Issue of Slavery in Contemporary Islam". The second chapter considers "The Rights of Non-Muslims in Contemporary Islam". Lastly, "Social Security in Islamic Teachings", makes up the final chapter of the book.

9. The chapters in this collection were written between the years 1998 and 2006, and have been published previously in Iran as separate pieces. The original publication details of each work are provided in a footnote in each chapter. Of these fourteen chapters, six have been presented at international gatherings (three of which were in Iran and three abroad). Three other chapters are the edited versions of three talks given to students or academics. Two of the pieces are transcribed interviews. Given that these chapters were written over nine years and in differing circumstances, they are not uniform or on the same level. Yet they all pursue one aim and one topic and express a shared pain. Each and every one of these pieces has arisen from pain. Perhaps pained writing may have more of an impact on eager hearts than writing in an ornamental or artificial manner. What happiness if these articles are of any help in solving the problem. Regardless, if there had been more opportunity for doing so, there is no doubt that this collection could be made richer and less flawed.

10. These fourteen chapters are not the only ones the author has written about human rights. Twelve articles published in *The Concerns of a Theocracy*[1] are all related to human rights debates. The article "Rights and Religious Obligation in Religion"[2] speaks to the chapters in Section One. The articles "The Political Rights of the People in Islam: The Right to Determine One's Destiny",[3] "The Foundations of Political Freedom in Islam",[4] "Ashura and Freedom",[5] "Freedom in the Religious State",[6] "The Epistemological Foundations of Freedom in the Religious State",[7] "Cultural Freedoms in Islam",[8] "The Boundaries of Freedom from the Perspective of Religion",[9] "An Introduction to the Relationship of Religion to the Idea of Tolerance",[10] "The Book, Supervision, and Religion"[11] and "A Religious Jurisprudential Investigation of Rights as

---

1 Mohsen Kadivar. *Daghdaghehaye Hokumat-e Dini* (*The Concerns of a Theocracy*) (Tehran: Ney, 2000).
2 Ibid., 305–319.
3 Ibid., 320–337.
4 Ibid., 352–383.
5 Ibid., 401–418.
6 Ibid., 419–434
7 Ibid., 435–441.
8 Ibid., 442–445.
9 Ibid., 495–543.
10 Ibid., 446–453.
11 Ibid., 468–483.

They Relate to Political and Press Crimes"[12] are also related to the chapters in Section Three about the freedoms of belief, religion and politics. In reality, the fourteen chapters of the present book constitute the second volume of the twelve articles mentioned above.

A notable number of my unpublished works are also devoted to the relationship between Islam and human rights. These include "Islam and Children's Rights", "Islam and Criminal Law", "The Rights of Women in the Qur'an" and, most importantly, "Islam and the Philosophy of Law".[13] I was determined to present all of my work on human rights in one volume. This is why the publication of this book was delayed. Unfortunately, I did not have the chance to edit four of my most recent works. God willing and with some luck, the above noted articles will make up the two volumes that follow this work.

This humble work is dedicated to my greatest teacher with whom I studied *fiqh* of the *ahl al-bayt* (the households of the Prophet). I owe to him the formation of my thinking in *fiqh*. It is for him, the scholar who is not only a master of *shari'a* and *fiqh*, but also a great teacher of generosity, sincerity, freedom, justice and seeking, as well as adhering to what is right: to the author of *Risalah Huquq* (*Apostle of Rights*) [Ayatollah Montazeri]. The gift of the Dervish is a green leaf.[14] May his glory be sustained and his life be long.

Mohsen Kadivar
Tehran
Anniversary of the Prophet's death
18 March 2007

---

12 Ibid., 484–494.

13 Many of my articles on women's rights and criminal law in Islam have been published on my website in Persian. They would comprise at least three volumes if I were to publish them as books. The most important one of the former is the series of articles titled *Ta'ammoli dar Mas'aleye Hejab* ("A Reflection on the Issues of *Hijab*" [women's head scarf]), July–September 2012, available at: https://kadivar.com/10843, last accessed 15 June 2020. Another article *Bazkhani-ye Hoquq-e Zanan dar Eslam: Edalat-e Mosavati bejaye Edalat-e Estehqaqi*, November 2011, available at: https://kadivar.com/8931, last accessed 15 June 2020, which was translated into English, Arabic and Turkish is another example: "Revisiting Women's Rights in Islam, 213–234. On the latter, i.e., criminal law and Islam, I published a series of articles titled *Layeheye Qesas wa Hokm-e Ertedad-e Jebhe-ye Melli* ("Retaliation Bill and Apostasy Sentence of the National Front"), October 2017–March 2018, available at: https//kadivar.com/16159, last accessed 18 June 2020.

14 *Translator's note*: The idea behind this saying is as follows: while the Dervish may only be able to gift a green leaf, a small and unworthy gift, this gift holds much meaning and should not be dismissed.

Section One

The Bases for Discussions on Islam and Human Rights

1

From Traditional Islam to End-oriented Islam[1]

The curve of change in religious thought in Iran, particularly in the last century, shows an accelerated growth. This change can be interpreted as a transition from a traditional approach to religion to an approach towards end-oriented Islam. Traditional Islam takes the culture and the exigencies of time and place and the special circumstances in the age of the Revelation to perfect and immutable forms and as ideals in Islamic thought (retrospective utopia). It is as though the mould and authentic form of Islam is the mould and form of the time of the Prophet, and the further we get from that sacred past and those historical circumstances, the further we have got from the real and authentic Islam: the best circumstances are the circumstances at the time of the Prophet and there is no other way to start a revival of religion than to rebuild those same circumstances and requirements.

In contrast, end-oriented Islam, while taking into account the circum-stances of the time and place of the religion's formative period, considers religiosity to be in the knowledge and realisation of the spirit of the religion and the goals and ends of Islam. Based on this reading, piety is the coor-dination in theory and practice with the aim of the mission and spirit of Islam rather than the observation of what appeared and what was a model

---

1 The first draft of this chapter was my presentation at the Annual Conference of the Islamic Asso-ciation of Students of Iranian Universities at Tehran University (summer 2000). Its second draft was published in *Sunnat wa Secularism* (*Tradition and Secularism: Collected Presentations*) (Tehran: Serat, 2002), 405–431. The title of the Persian version was *Az Eslam-e Tarikhi be Eslam-e Ma'navi* (*From Historical Islam to Spiritual Islam*).

at the specific place and time of the Revelation. Islam is as clear as the rain and as it took current in different historical contexts and lands, it took on the colour, taste and smell of various customs. Of course, among these the customs and ways of the time and the place of the Revelation have the biggest share. The shared task of far-sighted scholars of religion and Islam is to join the unadorned knowledge of religion and its refined rules from various circumstances of time and place, including the special circumstances of the time of the Revelation. This means to transcend time-dependent issues and arrive at the stable and timeless texts. Put another way, Islam must be freed from those rules which are no longer relevant, with nothing left but the shell of an appearance, no longer providing for the great aims and ends of religion. Instead, there should be a redoubled emphasis on the ends, contents and core of religious teachings. Overall, this characterises the common approach to the study of Islam and religion in our society. The approach that seeks perfection and growth benefits piety, and although it may seem to reduce the domain of religion, by approaching the true domain of religion, it will seriously deepen it; today's lost human seeks him- or herself in the depths of these pious meditations. The more religion is absorbed into the various issues and problems of knowledge and society, its reality, function, domain and what is expected of it becomes greater, better and more precise.

Here modernity is a turning point. Before Muslims came into contact with modernity, which was ushered into Iranian society with the Constitutional movement, the religious found fewer problems in their religiosity. In other words, they found their beliefs, ethics, *shari'a* and religious jurisprudence to be the norm. Thus, in dealing with various issues, they felt no difficulties. With the world's entry into the era of modernity and as Muslims gradually became familiar with the standards and debates of the new era, the relationship between religiosity and modernity became one of the most important issues for the contemporary Muslim. The problem started when some religious propositions seemed to be incompatible with the results of the new civilisation. Gradually the domain of this incompatibility expanded. Among various sectors of Islam, the realm of *shari'a* – meaning the sector of religious jurisprudence and the practice of Islamic rules – the abyss of this incompatibility grew more so than in the realms of Islamic faith, belief, ethics and ways of thinking. The problem became more serious when slowly the consequences of this new civilisation and the products of modernity became the customs (*'urf*), or in more technical terms, turned into the method of reasonable people (*sira-yi 'uqala'*) of this era and some religious propositions came into conflict with these customs and behaviours.

The first reaction by the religious was to vilify new standards and issues. They considered modernity to be an organised, satanic conspiracy to destroy the foundations of religion and thought that closing the doors of the country against the sewer of modernity was a religious duty. But their approach in facing modernity showed that floodwaters cannot be blocked with a slab of rock and another solution must be found. Alongside this, there was another group who completely lost themselves in the other extreme, and saw the road to happiness in absolute submission to modernity and relegation of religion to life's most private aspects. This group stayed on the level of the appearance of change and never reached the fruits of progress. Apart from these two extreme tendencies, far-sighted religious people found that one can neither flee from modernity and modernisation nor can one abandon tradition and religion. But how can one preserve the tradition of Islam in the modern world and the era of modernisation? Various answers have been given in response to this important question. These answers reflect the studious efforts of religious scholars to solve the problem of how Islam should respond to the circumstances of the new age. These answers are not perfect or timeless, but, in any case, show the preoccupations of religious scholars with this important issue. To be more precise, we will limit the discussion to the responses of Iranian Muslims, meaning we will examine the efforts of Shi'a Muslim thinkers in Iran. As will be seen, these thinkers saw the biggest incompatibility between religion and modernisation in the realm of *shari'a* and paid less attention to the two realms of belief and faith as well as ethics and the way of thinking. Thus, their answers are mostly focused on solving the conflicts that arise between the circumstances of the new world and the realm of *shari'a* or religious jurisprudence or the practical rules of Islam. An examination of how Muslim scholars in contemporary Iran dealt with the circumstances of the new age as they bear on the realm of *shari'a* shows that the most important solutions offered can be categorised in terms of three models or approaches. These three approaches consist of the following: the fixed and variable model; state religious jurisprudence or the jurisprudence of interest; and the model of end-oriented or teleological Islam.

First Approach: Fixed and Variable

The fixed and variable is the most famous and common approach of the last century. According to this approach, rules which are known as Islamic rules are of two types: fixed rules and variable rules. Fixed rules, unchanging and permanent, make up the text of *shari'a*, and variable rules are situated, temporary and are the function of local positions, and are subject to decline. Fixed rules are the same rules which were revealed by God to the Prophet. But variable rules are those that were established by humans in the shadow of those fixed rules, and while they are obligatory in religious society, they are not counted as part of the religious text. In order to determine who can set or legislate these variable rules, religious scholars have two conditions.

First View: Rulers as the Legislators of Variable Rules

For the first condition, the late religious scholar Seyyed Mohammad Hossein Tabataba'i[2] and his followers believe that the status of variable rules is the responsibility of the statesman of Islamic society. Based on the theory of the *wilayat-i faqih* (guardianship of the jurist), variable rules are the same as the rules of the leader or state rules which are issued for the benefit of Muslims. According to Seyyed Mohammad Hossein Tabataba'i, Islamic rules and laws are divided into two kinds. The first are those that protect the vital interests of humans as beings who live collectively, no matter what era or area or with what characteristics. These are those segments of beliefs and rules which capture humans' obedience and humility before the creator, who is not subject to any change or decline, and like all of the regulations that relate to the principles of human life, such as home and marriage and the defence of life and communal living, are those which humans always need to implement.

Second, there are rules and regulations that are temporary, local or specialised and are subject to change with changes in the way of life. Of course, these are subject to transformation with the gradual changes in civilisation, shifts in societies, and the appearance of new ways and the disappearance of

---

2 Seyyed Mohammad Hossein Tabataba'i (1904–1981) was one of the most prominent Muslim thinkers of the twentieth century. He was distinguished in two fields: Qur'anic exegesis and Islamic philosophy. His most famous book is *al-Mizan fi Tafsir al-Qur'an* (*Balance in the Exegesis of the Qur'an*) 20 vols (Qom: Jama'a al-Mudarissin, [1954–1972] 2009).

old ones. As such, Islam has divided its regulations into those that are fixed and those that are variable. The former are those that are built on the basis of creation and the specific characteristics of humans. These are called Islamic religion and *shari'a* and they provide the guiding light towards human prosperity. "Arise, turn to the Faith of the devotee. Be of the nature which God made human nature. There is no transformation of God's creation. That is the upright Faith" (Q. 30:30). In addition, one should note that those regulations that make up the second kind are subject to change and can be different depending on what is prudent in a particular place and time, as phenomena of the general guardianship (*wilayat-i 'amma*), are subject to the views of the Prophet and the successors designated by him who have recognised and implemented them under the arc of fixed religious regulations and based on what was prudent at the particular place and time. Of course, these types of regulations based on the reform of religion do not count as divine regulations and laws and they are not called religion. "O believers! Obey God and obey the Prophet and those in authority among you" (Q. 4:59). About these types of rules and regulations in Islam, we have a principle that in this discussion we will call "the authorities of the guardian". This principle in Islam provides the answer to those needs of people and society which are subject to change and transformation in any given time or place and in any region. It answers these needs in such a way that the fixed regulations of Islam are not undermined or nullified. The guardian of Muslims (*wali-yi amr*), who has been determined to be qualified from an Islamic point of view and rules over his province, and who is in fact the source of an Islamic society's ideas and has oversight over the society's actions, can make decisions about the general affairs of the public in the same way that he could if he were making decisions about his own affairs. In short, whatever new regulations that may be beneficial to the progress of the communal life of society and which are beneficial for Islam and Muslims, all fall under the authority of the guardian and there is no prohibition in their status or implementation. Of course, while these regulations in Islam are obligatory and the guardian is also obligated to follow them, these regulations do not count as *shari'a* or divine rules. The validity of this type of regulations is naturally based on the need that brought it about and as soon as that need is eliminated, it too is eliminated. In this case, the former or current guardian will announce the disappearance of the old rule and the appearance of a subsequent rule will cancel the former one. However, the divine rules which are the text of *shari'a* will always remain stable and standing and no one, not even the *wali-yi amr* (guardian), has the right to change them to fit the needs of the time or to revoke them if he thinks that part of them have been destroyed.[3]

Allameh Tabataba'i's reading of the fixed and variable type can be presented as follows:

One: Islamic rules, laws and provisions can be divided into two distinct types.

Two: the characteristics of the first type are as follows:

First, they provide for the vital needs of humans; second, unchanging and not subject to various versions; third, they are established by the legislator (*shari'*), meaning they were either revealed as inspiration from God to the Prophet or they were established by the Prophet or the Twelve Shi'ite Imams have informed us of their establishment by the Prophet; and, fourth, the meaning of religion and Islamic *shari'a* is limited to this category of rules.

Three: the characteristics of the second type are as follows:

First, they provide for the various time and place-specific needs and for the temporary and local benefits of people; second, they are changing and subject to decline and revision; third, they are established and revised by the *wali* (Islamic guardian/ruler) considering the fixed provisions of religion and based on what is prudent at the time; and, fourth, while these are obligatory in Islam, they do not constitute *shari'a* or divine rules.

This reading of the fixed and variable rules raises several questions:

First, do all the *shari'a* rules present in the Qur'an and in the tradition (or Sunna) count as fixed rules?

Second, if there were variable rulings among those issued by the prophets or the Imams, what are the criteria for distinguishing between the fixed and variable rules?

Third, if Islam and *shari'a* are limited to fixed rules, and if the variable rules, despite being obligatory, do not count as *shari'a* or divine rules, then how do the second type of rules count as Islamic rules and provisions?

---

3 Seyyed Mohammad Hossein Tabataba'i, "Eslam wa Ensan-e Moaser, Barresihay-e Eslami" (*Islam and the Needs of the Contemporary Human*), in *Barrasiha-ye Eslami* (*Islamic Investigations*), vol. II, ed. Seyyed Hadi Khosrowshahi (Qom: Resalat Publications, 1977), 36–43. See also "Guardianship and Leadership in Islam", in *Barrasiha-ye Eslami* I:180–1. Morteza Motahhari has likewise commented on this: *Eslam wa Muqtazayat-e Zaman* (*Islam and the Time Specific Requirements*) (Tehran, Sadra, 2001), 2:77–92.

Fourth, What are the procedures, criteria and limits of variable rules? And by what criteria does the Islamic guardian establish these rules?

The Second View: The Representatives of the People, Setter of Variable Rules

In the second approach, the conditional authority to set the variable rules is given to the representatives of the people. There are two expositions of this approach.

First Exposition: Non-*mansus* (Unauthorised) Rules

In the first exposition, Mirza Mohammad Hossein Gharavi Na'ini, author of *Tanbih al-Ummah wa Tanzih al-Milla* (*The Awakening of the Community and Refinement of the Religion*),[4] understands variable rules to be the same as unauthorised ones; the representatives of the people may be entrusted with setting them as long as they follow the principle of consultation and take into consideration the exigencies of the time and what is prudent in that period. According to Na'ini, the implementation of *shari'a* is exclusive to fixed and *mansus* (authorised) rules:

> The total duties pertaining to order and preserving the nation and the policies governing the affairs of the *umma* (Muslim world), whether they are the primary instructions on how human duties or whether they are the secondary ones which are the punishments for acting against the primary instructions, will not be external to the two types. If *mansus* (necessary or authorised), the duty to carry it out is particularly given and its rules are recorded in the pure *shari'a*. If non-*mansus* (unauthorised), due to it being unspecified and not included as part of a particular position, then the duty to carry it out is accorded to the *wali* (guardian/ruler) based on his views and preferences.

It is clear that just as the first type cannot be altered or varied in various times and places and is not exempt from being followed exactly (*ta'abbud*) as

---

4 Mirza Mohammad Hossein Gharavi Na'ini (1860–1936), Iranian *faqih* and *usuli*, was the most competent student of Akhond Mohammad Kazem Khorasani and the most famous theoretician of Iran's Constitutional Revolution (1905–1911).

stipulated in religious *mansus* and envisioned as obligatory until the time of judgement, the second type follows the interests and exigencies of times and places. With such variations, it may therefore vary and change, both with the presence and expansion of the power of the ruler (*wali*) appointed by God and even in other places, with the oversight and authority of those appointed on behalf of His Holiness (the Prophet) and in the Age of Occultation,[5] too, with the oversight and authority of the general deputies (of the Hidden Imam) (*nuwwab-i 'amm*) or someone who may take up the afore-mentioned duties and who has the mandate of being authorised by the authorised (*man lahu wilayat al-izn*). It follows plainly and with complete clarity that political derivations based on this principle shall be as follows:

First, those rules and commandments that shall be harmonised with the *shari'a* as they should, with care and precision, shall be limited to the first class (*mansus*). These rules and commandments are irrelevant in the second type and have no place there.

Second, the principle of consultation, on which is based the knowledge of the grounds for Islamic rule in accordance with the teachings of the Qur'an and the Sunna (Tradition) and the tradition (*sira*) of the Prophet, belongs to the second type. The first type, as has been pointed out previously, is outside this subject matter and consultation has absolutely nothing to do with it.

Third, just as the age of the presence of the Prophet and Imams and the free hand and even administrations (*tarjihat*) of the rulers and agents appointed by the universal ruler (*wali-yi kull*) (the Prophet) necessitated the second type, similarly in the time of Occultation, too, administrations of the general deputies (*nuwwab-i 'amm*) or those who are authorised by their permission (*ma'zunin*), in accordance with the exigencies of a firm and decisive deputyship, necessitates this second type.

Fourth, most of the general (*naw'iya*) politics is of the second type and is included under the heading of the guardianship of the Twelfth Imam (*wali-yi amr*) and his deputies, special deputies (during the Minor Occultation) or

---

5 In traditional Twelver Shi'a Islam, Occultation (*ghaybah*) refers to the belief that the *Mahdi* (or messianic figure), a male descendant of Prophet Muhammad and the Twelfth Imam, was born in 868 and went into Occultation in 872. This is still in effect and will last until the End of Time when the Mahdi is believed to come back and re-establish justice and peace on earth. The Hidden Imam is considered to be the "Imam of the Era", to hold authority over the community, and to guide and protect individuals as well as the Shi'a community.

general deputies (during the Major Occultation) and their administrations. The Shi'i principle of consultation is in the *shari'a* for this reason, and acting upon this necessary civil (*hisbiya*) duty (pertaining to the duty to "enjoin the proper and forbid the improper") under present circumstances and the suspension of its recognition and its promulgation are to issue from an official National Consultative Assembly (parliament). It has been previously made clear that it is through the responsibility of the deep wisdom and extensive capacity of the nation's deputies and by the signature and permission of all who bear the signature and permission that they shall gather all propriety and legitimacy and eliminate doubts and difficulties.

Fifth, since the understanding of the second class of general (*naw'iya*) politics is under definite criterion which is not included and accepts various interests and exigencies, it is not set down as authoritative (*mansus*) in the pure *shari'a*, but is consigned to consultation and the preference of those whose opinions are authoritative, surely the laws referring to this class will represent different perspectives of their interests and exigencies for various ages and will likely vary and are subject to annulment and amendment and cannot be like the first class, based as it is on permanency and confirmation. Thus far, it appears that such laws will necessarily be annulled or altered as is characteristic of the laws of this second class.[6]

Mirza Na'ini's exposition of the fixed and variable models can be summarised as follows:

One: a political rules and all social rules are of two types: first, those that are *mansus* (authorised) by *shari'a*; second, non-*mansus* (unauthorised) ones.

Two: rules authorised by *shari'a* are, first, fixed and unchangeable; second, they cannot be nullified; third, they are derived by the religious scholars; fourth, most political rules are not of this category.

Three: the second type of rules are those that are, first, unauthorised (non-*mansus*), meaning that they have not been specified in the *shari'a*; second, they are subject to what is prudent given the circumstances of time and place; third, they are changing, subject to deterioration, and may be

---

6 Mirza Mohammad Hossein Gharavi Na'ini, *Tanbih al-Ummah wa Tanzih al-Milla: Hokoumat az nazar-e Eslam (The Awakening of the Community and Refinement of the Religion: Governance in Islam)*, with an introduction and commentary by Sayyed Mahmoud Taleqani (Tehran: Ferdowsi, 1954), 98–102.

nullified, fourth, establishing these rules is the responsibility of the Islamic guardian; fifth, these rules are established following consultation with experts; sixth, the Islamic ruler may delegate the responsibility for establishing these rules to the people's representatives, for this category of rules, harmonising with the *shari'a* is irrelevant and pointless; seventh, most political rules fall into this category; eighth, these rules are obligatory to follow from the point of view of *shari'a*.

What sets Na'ini's exposition apart from the previously noted one is as follows:

First, the correlation of fixed and variable to authorised (*mansus*) and unauthorised (non-*mansus*); second, the necessity of consultation in the establishment of unauthorised rules; third, the unnecessity of harmonising the unauthorised (non-*mansus*) rules with the *shari'a*; fourth, the possibility of relegating the task of establishing the unauthorised (non-*mansus*) rules to the representatives of the people; fifth, the majority of political and social rules fall under the category of unauthorised (non-*mansus*) rules.

Na'ini's exposition of the fixed and variable models raises the following questions:

First, can all authorised (*mansus*) rules be considered fixed and unchangeable? Is it not possible that a variable rule established by the Prophet or the Imams have remained among the authorised (*mansus*) rules?

Second, if it is the case that the rules in the second category have not been specified in the *shari'a*, and that it is irrelevant and pointless to harmonise them with the *shari'a*, and they require consultation, and their establishment can even be relegated to non-jurists (the representatives of the people), then why does establishing these rules require that the Islamic guardian be a religious jurist (*faqih*)?

Third, does the necessity for the Islamic guardian to establish these rules or the obligation to follow them according to the *shari'a* derive from something other than the rational necessity of complying with the social order?

Fourth, if it is the case that all of the great policy perspectives and nearly all social rules belong to the unauthorised (non-*mansus*) category, then how can one speak of religious politics, religious rule, etc., and what would it mean to speak of such things?

Second Exposition: The Rules of the Discretionary Sphere

Using the neologism, "the discretionary sphere" (*mantiqat al-faragh*), Sayyid Muhammad Baqir al-Sadr[7] also considers variable rules to be limited to the sphere of what is permissible (*mubahat*) in *shari'a*. In his final decree, he considers the establishment of rules in the discretionary sphere to be the responsibility of the people's representatives in the legislative branch, who should set them in accordance with what is in the public interest. Sadr believes that in the case of contested rules, which include most religious (*fiqhi*) rules, the parliament consisting of those who solve problems and make connections will choose from among the views of the jurists (*faqih*) those views which are most compatible for the ruling system's overall well-being. According to Sadr:

Shari'a is the foundation for constitutional and ordinary laws, meaning that all laws are based upon it as follows:

First, the fixed rules of *shari'a* which are not subject to differences of opinion among the religious jurists. In accordance with their relationship to social life, this group of rules are among those that are considered to be a permanent part of the constitution. This is the case, whether or not they have been stipulated in the text of the law.

Second, the fixed rules of *shari'a* which are contested among numerous religious jurists. As a result, there is not one single position taken about them in accordance with *shari'a*. Therefore, it is conceivable that alternative positions can be presented about them in line with the *shari'a*. It is the responsibility of the legislative branch to choose among these various opinions based on what is in the general public interest.

Third, the area where the divine legislator has not issued a necessary order of obligation or prohibition, which includes all situations where the legislator has granted the legal agents (*mukallafan*) the ability to set rules. This area is called the discretionary sphere. The legislative branch has the

---

7 Sayyid Muhammad Baqir al-Sadr (1935–1980) is an Iraqi Shi'ite authority. He is famous for his innovative ideas in Islamic Studies, particularly in *usul al-fiqh* and logic. He was executed by Saddam Hussein along with his sister, Bintelhuda.

responsibility to set the obligatory rules in this sphere in accordance with the public interest and in keeping with the constitution.[8]

Sayyid Muhammad Baqir al-Sadr's exposition of the fixed and variable models can be summarised as follows:

First, Islamic laws are of three types: first, *shari'a* rules which are not subject to any disputes; second, *shari'a* rules which are not subject to any disputes among religious jurists (*faqih*); third, rules in the discretionary sphere (the sphere where there are no rules of obligation or prohibition under the *shari'a*).

Second, the rules of *shari'a* which are not contested among the jurists constitute the fixed and unchangeable rules (the sphere of necessary religious obligations (*zaruriyat-i fiqhi*)).

Third, in the case of contested rules of *shari'a*, choosing a *shari'a* rule that is compatible with the public interest is the responsibility of the people's representatives. In this sphere, it is not necessary for a special jurist (*faqih*), whether a Shi'ite authority (*marja'*) or the *wali*, to give a religious decree (*fatwa*). These rules are also considered to be fixed.

Fourth, in the discretionary or permissible sphere, the divine legislator has granted authority to the legal agents (*mukallafan*). The representatives of the people have the responsibility to set the obligatory rules in accordance with the constitution and public interest. It is clear that the rules in this sphere are variable.

What distinguishes Sadr's exposition from that of Na'ini is as follows:

First, Sadr divides the authorised (*mansus*) rules into contested and uncontested rules; second, he accepts the decision of the people's representatives in choosing among the contested authorised rules based on what is in the public interest; third, his interpretation gives the people's representatives the authority to set rules in the discretionary sphere; fourth, his interpretation limits the legal supervision of a righteous source of emulation to the setting of the rules in the discretionary sphere so that he may provide warning in cases there are violations of the *shari'a*.

The following questions may be raised about Sadr's exposition of the fixed and variable models:

---

8 Sayyid Muhammad Baqir al-Sadr, *Lamha Fiqhiya Tamhidiya 'an Mashru' Dustur al-Jumhuriya al-Islamiyat-i Iran, Majmu'at al-Islam yaqud al-Hayat* (*Introductory Juristic Glance at the Constitution of the Islamic Republic of Iran*), Majmu'a al-Islam yaqudu al-Hayat, Islam Guides Life Series, No. 1 (Qom: al-Khayyam, 1979), 18–19.

First, can all authorised (*mansus*) rules, including both contested and uncontested ones, be considered among the fixed and unchanging rules of *shari'a*? Is it not possible that some of these authorised rules of *shari'a* are those that have carried over from the variable rules that were issued by the Prophet and the Imams?

Second, if there are no rules of obligation or prohibition in the discretionary sphere, what does it mean for a jurist (*faqih*) to have supervision over the rules that have been set by the representatives of the people? Following Na'ini, could one not claim that harmonising with the *shari'a* in this sphere is out of place and irrelevant?

Third, is there a criterion based in religion or *shari'a* for assessing the public interest in the discretionary sphere and the contested authorised (*mansus*) rules?

A Critique of the Fixed and Variable Models

Given all of this, it is without doubt that the fixed and variable models have become more complete through these expositions. Nonetheless, the model faces problems in all three expositions.

First, the first exposition provides no criteria for distinguishing among the variable rules. In the second and third, it is not clear why all orders which are authorised (*mansus*) according to the *shari'a* are fixed. What has become of all the temporary and variable orders issued by the Prophet and the Imams?

Second, the problem of the incompatibility of the religious orders with modernity pertains to those orders which are considered to be fixed and authorised (*mansus*). This problem remains unsolved in the above.

Third, if religion and *shari'a* are limited to the fixed and authorised (*mansus*) orders, the variable or non-authorised orders, or those in the discretionary sphere, cannot be considered to be religious or in accordance with *shari'a*. This is especially the case given that no *shari'a*-based criteria have been provided for determining the public interest.

Fourth, considering that variable or unauthorised rules do not have set criteria in *shari'a*, harmonising them with the *shari'a* is irrelevant and out of place, and setting them requires consultation. There is no reason that an Islamic guardian or the Islamic Jurist as Guardian (*wali-yi faqih*) should have the task of determining the orders. In addition, there is no reason for the jurists to supervise them to ensure that there are no violations of *shari'a*.[9]

These problems lead to the ineffectiveness of the fixed and variable model and necessitate the creation of a new model.

Second Approach: Governmental or Expedient Jurisprudence

The second approach, that of governmental or expedient jurisprudence (*fiqh*), is the innovation of the late Ayatollah Khomeini (1902–1989), the leader of the Islamic Revolution and the founder of the Islamic Republic of Iran. This approach is the result of the practical encounter between religion and the administration of society, or to put it more precisely, it is the encounter of religion with social problems in the modern age. Recognising the shortcomings of the first approach, the innovator of this approach came up with another. Initially, following other jurists who leaned towards the first approach, Khomeini focuses on the variable rules and the authorities of the governor and the government, and by expanding and deepening this sphere, comes up with the "element of expediency". He concludes that independent reasoning (*ijtihad*) that is found in the seminaries, that is to say, that which is prevalent among the jurists, is not able to solve the problems of today, and to act in accordance with it can only lead to a dead end and shutdown of civilisation. From this perspective, he becomes aware of the determining role of time and place in independent reasoning (*ijtihad*). For him, the determining role of time and place is not limited to setting variable rules in accordance with *shari'a* but extends to all other orders, including the fixed rules (as based on the first approach). With this point, meaning with this kind of revision in the orders that were considered to be fixed in the previous approach, a new approach is founded. According to this account, taking

---

9 Na'ini did not consider it necessary to have a council of jurists (*mujtahid*s) supervise the people's representatives' bills in the sphere of non-*mansus* rules of *shari'a*. Rather, he thought that either the preliminary permission of the religious authorities or the presence of some jurists (*faqih*s) among the representatives would suffice, and even this was out of caution and not obligation: "To the best of one's ability, simply out of the caution which must be observed, the principle of election and the participation of the electees may occur with the permission of a jurist-ruler (*mujtahid-i nafiz al-ḥukumat*) or the inclusion of a council of deputies so that the rejection or approval should be the responsibility of a number of the system's *mujtahid*s, to approve and ratify the votes taken." *Tanbih al-Umma wa Tanzih al-Milla*, 79.

into consideration the exigencies of time and place leads to compatibility of the *shariʿa*, indeed of religion, with modernity, or, at least, it reduces many of the incompatibilities. Some of Ayatollah Khomeini's key statements in this regard are as follows:

> Islam is government in all its aspects, and it is the rules of the laws of Islam that make up the aspects of the government. Indeed, the orders are means to an end and mechanisms for governing and expanding justice.[10]

That is to say, *shariʿa* rules are not an end to themselves. They are the path to attaining a goal, not the goal itself. The end in itself is the expansion of justice by an Islamic government. The means to an end may be changed and overturned to achieve that end.

> If the powers of the government are in the framework of the second-ary divine rules, then the divine government and the absolute guard-ianship entrusted to the Prophet of Islam would be an empty and meaningless phenomenon. A government which is a branch of the absolute guardianship of the Prophet is one of the primary orders of Islam and takes precedence over all others even praying, fasting, tak-ing the pilgrimage to Mecca (*hajj*). The ruler may demolish a mosque or a home that is blocking a road and compensate the owner of the house. If necessary, the ruler may close a mosque or demolish a harm-ful mosque (*masjid-i zirar*) if what is harmful about it cannot be fixed without demolition. The government may unilaterally nullify the reli-gious contracts it has made with the people, should those contracts be against the interests of the nation and of Islam. The government may prohibit anything, whether related to worship or not, for as long as it is against the interests of Islam. The government may temporar-ily prevent the pilgrimage to Mecca (*hajj*), which is among the most important religious obligations, in instances when it is against the interests of the Islamic country. So far, what has been said or con-tinues to be said, has arisen from the lack of an understanding of the

10 Ruhollah Mousawi Khomeini, *Kitab al-Bayʿ* (*The Book of Selling*) (Tehran: Institute for Compilation and Publication of Imam Khomeini's Work, 2013), 2:672.

divine absolute guardianship. Regarding the rumour that sharecropping (*muzara'a*), silent partnerships (*muzaraba*), and the like will be destroyed, I will say explicitly, that even if we suppose this were true, it would be within the government's power; and even beyond this there are issues as well, with which I will not trouble you.[11]

Time and place are two determining factors in independent reasoning (*ijtihad*). An issue that in the past had had an order may require a different order in another context and in relation to the demands of another social and political system. This means that with a precise understanding of the economic, social and political relationships, that same issue which appears to be the same as the past has in fact become a new one which requires a new order. The jurist (*mujtahid*) must have a grasp of the issues of his own time.[12]

One of the very important issues in today's turbulent world is the role of place and time in independent reasoning (*ijtihad*) and in how we make decisions. The government determines a practical philosophy for dealing with idolatry and unbelief, as well as domestic and international challenges; these issues not only cannot be solved by the theoretical debates of seminarians, but also they may drag us to dead ends which will lead to the apparent violations of the constitution.[13]

I must express my regret at your understanding [here Khomeini was addressing Mohammad Hassan Qadiri, a member of his office] of the traditions (*akhbar*) and the rules . . . Based on how you have understood the traditions and narratives (*rawayat*), the new civilisation would be destroyed and people would have to go and live in caves or deserts forever.[14]

---

11 Ruhollah Mousawi Khomeini, "Open letter dated January 6, 1988, to Seyyed Ali Khamenei" [the leader of Friday prayers in Tehran and the President of the Islamic Republic of Iran at that time], in *Sahife-ye Imam* (*The Speeches and Declarations of Imam Khomeini*) (Tehran: Institute for the Compilation and Publication of Imam Khomeini's Work, 2010), 20:451–452.

12 Ibid., 21:289, declaration of 22 February 1989, Charter of the Clergies.

13 Ibid., 21:217–218, letter of 28 December 1988, to the Members of the Expediency Discernment Council of the System.

14 Ibid., 21:150–152, letter of 24 September 1988, to Mohammad Hassan Qadiri (a member of his office).

From the perspective of the true jurist (*mujtahid*), government is the practical philosophy of all aspects of the life of humankind. Government displays the practical aspect of *fiqh* in dealing with all social, political, military and cultural issues. *Fiqh* is the true and complete theory of managing individuals and society from the cradle to the grave.[15]

The above approach can be summarised as follows:

First, the prevailing religious jurisprudence (*fiqh*) and conventional independent reasoning (*ijtihad*) are ineffective for dealing with the problems of our time. It is clear that this lack of effectiveness is due to how the fixed rules have been understood (in the first approach).

Second, for orders to be effective, paying attention to the exigencies of time and place is a necessity in independent reasoning (*ijtihad*) in the case of all orders.

Third, religious jurisprudence (*fiqh*) is the true and complete theory of managing individuals and society from the cradle to the grave. The solution to all political, economic, social, cultural and military difficulties of Islamic societies and, indeed, of all human societies can be expected from *fiqh*.

Fourth, Islamic government is the practical philosophy of the entirety of jurisprudence (*fiqh*) applied to the entirety of human life. Protecting the government is an ultimate obligation. The government takes precedence over Islam's primary and secondary orders even praying, fasting and the pilgrimage to Mecca (*hajj*).

Fifth, the absolute guardianship (*wilayat*) over jurisprudence (*fiqh*) gives the jurist (*faqih*) expansive powers to secure the people's interests and spread justice. The guardian *faqih* (*wali-yi faqih*) may nullify all those orders of the *shari'a* for as long as they are not relevant to the time and place or do not secure the system's interests; and he may set the necessary orders to meet the system's interests or to address the exigencies of time and place.

Sixth, religious rules are a means to an end and not an end in themselves. The end in itself is the establishment of an Islamic government in order to spread justice.

---

15 Ibid., 21:298.

Assessment of the Governmental Jurisprudential Approach

The strengths of this approach to the fixed and variable orders can be noted as follows:

First, given that the incompatibility of the religious orders with modernity arose in the sphere of the fixed and unchangeable *mansus* orders, and that this issue remained unresolved in the first approach, the second approach resolves it with the absolute guardianship of the jurist (*wilayat-i mutlaqa-yi faqih*) on jurisprudence (*fiqh*) and by considering the exigencies of time and place in the case of all orders.

Second, the fact that the jurist (*faqih*), as the advocate of the interests of the people and the Islamic system and by observing exigencies of time and place, may set any order that he considers expedient and may nullify whatever religious orders that he finds contradictory to such interests, is a particular strength of this model towards updating the *shari'a*.

Nonetheless, this approach has several ambiguities and problems.

First, in this approach there are no general criteria (non-personal) provided for determining the exigencies of time and place. Given that assessing the exigencies of time and place is ultimately the responsibility of the person of the jurist-ruler (*wali-yi faqih*) himself and the survival of all religious orders rests on his understanding of the above-mentioned conditions, what is to guarantee that all or most of the orders will not change when he does? How can one consider religion and *shari'a* to be dependent on the personal understanding of a single individual?

Second, how does religiosity arise from such an approach? Considering the exigencies of time and place, the system's interests or the people's well-being are rational issues and may not necessarily be found in religious texts and may not shift with changes in religion. Simply placing the jurist (*faqih*) in the sole position and authority of recognising what is in the best public interest or determining exigencies of place and time is no guarantee that his understanding and perception will remain a religious one. If the jurist (*faqih*) roots his assessment of these two issues (recognising the interest and determining the exigencies of time and place) in something other than religion – which is how it is – then how can something outside religion be a criterion for understanding and elucidating religion? Also, more basically, in continuing with this approach, will anything remain of religion, or will the expediency and exigencies of time and place dissolve all religious orders.

Third, given the great importance of this approach to government, political power, strength and the absolute guardianship of the religious ruler over jurisprudence (*fiqh*), religious orders will in a sense become subordinate to the government's interests, will follow political power and become awash in the mundane. The ultimate result of this approach is "statist religion". A statist religion will, like a disease, destroy religious faith, spirituality and the religious conscience.

Fourth, this approach expects from religion in general and jurisprudence (*fiqh*) in particular those things which are to be expected from the humanities in general. To begin with, it is impossible to have a field of knowledge that could meet the vast expectations of solving all social, political, economic, cultural and military problems of all human societies. Second, such tasks, meaning organising the world and managing society, cannot be expected of religion and declaring otherwise requires proof, which has not been provided. Third, if determining public interest as well as the exigencies of time and place are rational, not religious, and are generally topical (*mawdu'i*) – as opposed to being like a religious rule (*hukmi*) – then why must these issues be entrusted to a jurist (*faqih*)?

Third Approach: End-oriented Islam

These serious problems led to a third approach which may be called end-oriented Islam. This approach aims to draw from the strengths of the previous approaches while resolving their problems. This approach takes several points into consideration. First, religion must remain religion and not be overshadowed; second, while the scope of religion in this approach is less than the previous, its depth is greater; third, the power of religion is strengthened in the sphere of what is expected of it in the new age and many of those things which are incompatible with it in the new age are placed outside its scope.

The religion of Islam was sent down to the Final Prophet, Muhammad bin 'Abdallah, by the wise God. Islam is a faith for all times and places and is based on virtues, norms and rules which are wise, just and reasonable. Matters of faith and belief, moral values, the orders of *fiqh* pertaining to worship (*fiqh-i 'ibadi*), as well as some of the principles in the jurisprudence of human interactions (*fiqh al-mu'amalat*) are the main parts of the religion which are all eternal and transcend time and place. However, in the jurisprudence of human interactions, that is to say, those orders which do not pertain to worship, there are very serious components of exigencies of time and place. All orders pertaining to criminal law and penal code, civil laws, international affairs and basic laws, some of which are rooted in the Qur'an and the Sunna (Tradition), are counted among those in the realm of the *fiqh* of human interactions. At the time they were issued, all of these orders were absolutely wise, just, moral and reasonable; otherwise, they would not have been issued by the Divine Legislator (*shari'*). At the time of the Revelation, none of these orders were considered to be oppressive, violent, immoral or unreasonable in the mind of the common, reasonable person.

The orders in the sphere of the *fiqh* of human interactions cannot be considered totally bound by *shari'a* (*tawqifi*) and to be accepted without question (*ta'abbudi*); it is not the case that human reason understands no expedience in them and that they should only be submitted to out of pure imitation (*ta'abbud*), particularly since the orders of secular interaction were a matter of orders of approval (*ahkam-i imda'i*) and not of innovation (*ta'sisi*). In other words, Islam either approved or reformed the customary pre-Islamic orders in such a way that one might consider these orders as being at the margins of what was common usage (*'urf*) at the time of the Revelation. It is clear that the common usage (*'urf*) of that time was not bound by *shari'a* (*tawqifi*), or by dictated and devotional (*ta'abbudi*) rulings in rituals, or the sacred (*qudsi*), or else they would not have been used by reasonable people (*'uqala'*). These orders were provided to achieve justice and advocate for the worldly interests of human societies.

On the other hand, one cannot deny that human issues, particularly in the spheres of the social and human societies' common usage (*'urf*), have changed greatly and that many things which were considered in past centuries to be just, moral, reasonable and normal are today seen to be oppressive, immoral, abnormal and contrary to the way of reasonable people (*sira-yi 'uqala'*). These changes have become serious and have deepened in issues of international law more so than in discussions regarding the general law, in discussions of general law more so than in criminal law and penal codes, and in matters pertaining to the penal code more so than in discussions of civil law. It is clear that among all the spheres of *fiqh*, the *fiqh* pertaining to matters of worship has been least impacted by these changes.

Given that justice is the standard for religion rather than religion being the standard for justice, and given that reasonableness (*'uqala'i*) is standard in the social sphere (the *fiqh* of human interactions (*muʿamalat*), one may conclude that juridical (*fiqh*) orders are legitimate and conclusive as long as they satisfy the exigencies of justice and do not contradict the way of reasonable people (*sira-yi ʿuqalaʾ*). In the case of the School of Justice[16] (*mazhab-i ʿadliya*) (Muʿtazilite and Shiʿite), can those rules which contravene the way of reasonable people (*sira-yi ʿuqalaʾ*) and the criteria of justice be considered religious and in accordance with *shariʿa*? The contradiction of an order with the way of reasonable people (*sira-yi ʿuqalaʾ*), its negation of the criteria of justice, or if it contributes to the spread of corruption (*mafsada*) over interest (*maslahat*), indicates that it is ephemeral and not permanent. This means that such orders were appropriate in relation to the exigencies of the time of the Revelation and are not among the permanent and constant legislation issued by the divine Legislator. According to the text of the Qurʾan and the Sunna, the philosophy behind the existence of such orders is that they were necessary for solving the problems of the time of the Revelation and similar premodern eras. If the divine Legislator had not legislated such orders (despite the urgent need of the people of those times), and the prophetic mission had not been relayed to the target audience, and if some people considered such orders that are tied to temporal and spatial exigencies of the time of Revelation to be eternal and fixed Islamic rules, they have not understood the meaning of religion, the aim of the Revelation and the spirit of Islam. End-oriented Islam means paying serious attention to the great goals of religion and to the meaning of Islam. Islam as an End means that we should not hold practical orders and models to be above the goal of religion, and that we should know with certainty that the rules which are a means to an end are not an end in and of themselves. The rules of the *shariʿa* are a way to achieve the great goals of religion; every path is legitimate as long as it gets us to our destination. If we are certain (and not merely guessing) that a path is no longer taking us to that goal, then it loses legitimacy and a new path for reaching that ultimate goal must be considered. Of course, this does not mean that all *fiqhi* rules which do not pertain to worship (non-*ʿibadi*) are as a matter of fact illegitimate. Rather, it indicates a serious probability. Paying

---

16 This school established the first discipline of rational morality or philosophy of ethics among Muslims. Rationality and reasonability, justice and fairness, and morality and ethics have been the conventional criteria among Sunni Muʿtazilites and Shiʿites since the beginning of Islamic theology.

attention to the exigencies of space and time in accordance with the criteria of the School of Justice (*mazhab-i 'adliya*), the teachings of the Qur'an, and the Sunna (Tradition) has no meaning other than this. Thus, the criteria for legitimacy, authority and persistence of the orders of *fiqh* rest on them satisfying two important tests[17]: first, they must not be in contravention of justice; and, second, they must not contradict the way of reasonable people. Albeit, both criteria ultimately return to a single criterion. Justice, too, is established by reasonable people, but the importance of justice has resulted in considering it separately from the other reasonable criteria.

In addition, unlike previous approaches, orders which do not satisfy the afore-mentioned important tests are considered to be variable rules and are situationally contingent; by losing their expediency or by contradicting reasonableness or justice, we realise that the legitimacy of this order has expired, and that it is a temporary and not a permanent rule. However, legislating a religious rule in that case is not relegated to a jurist (*faqih*) or theocratic ruler (*wali-yi faqih*) since that is restricted to God and the Prophet alone. In general, there is nothing in the preserved tablet (*lawh-i waqi'*) that can be used to indicate that there are any other *shari'a* rules to be given. In place of these variable rules whose time has come, rational laws are posited by the people's collective wisdom, and they are in no way attributed to religion. Thus, we gave no new variable religious orders, and legislation remains in the hands of the divine Legislator alone. It is wrong to determine orders using secular reason (*'aql-i 'urfi*) and then attribute them to religion and the *shari'a*. In addition, limiting religious orders to the just, rational and fixed orders in the Qur'an and the Sunna (Tradition) protects us from falling into the trap of relying on suppositional reason (*'aql-i zanni*) and its consequences.

While the domain of jurisprudence (*fiqh*) will steadily decrease if this approach is followed, and while it will gradually become clear that some of the rules of the *shari'a* were not permanent and are therefore to be considered variable rules that are no longer legitimate for the current time, by the grace of religion's true dimensions, the pious will find opportunities for deepening faith promoting greater wisdom. In accepting the approach of Islam as an end the true teachings of Islam will not be in confrontation with justice,

---

17 I added two more criteria to reasonability and justice: the third is functionality (see Chapter 5), and the fourth ethics (see my Preface to the English Translation, Section Six, subsection "*The Outline of Kadivar's Approach*", point eight).

the way of reasonable people and modernity. Therefore, the orders of the *shari'a* constitute a path towards the spread of justice, the achievement of the criteria of the reasonable (*'uqala'i*), and the advocacy of the public interest. It is not the case that the juridical (*fiqhi*) orders themselves will have become topical (*mawżu'iyat*) or that the form and appearance of *fiqh* would have sanctity. Thus, any *shari'a* order remains as long as it is a path to achieving religious ends, and as soon as it ceases to be such a path, it exits the circle of religious (*shar'i*) rules and is relegated to the museum of variable rules.

It is not only the responsibility of jurists (*faqih*s), but also mainstream scholars of religion and scholars of Islam to determine whether or not *shari'a* orders are in agreement with the criteria of justice and the way of reasonable people (*sira-yi 'uqala'*). Such great responsibility necessitates, in addition to a profound understanding of religion and religious texts, scholarly knowledge of the exigencies of the times, the way of reasonable people (*sira-yi 'uqala'*), and the criteria of justice as *a priori* religious criteria. The best approach for the way of reasonable people (*sira-yi 'uqala'*) and learning of the exigencies of time and place is to rely on mainstream scholars and specialists in various disciplines of the humanities.[18]

Dimensions of End-oriented Islam

The approach of end-oriented Islam may be summarised as follows:

First, at any time, the criterion for the legitimacy of a religious (*shar'i*) rule is justice and accordance with the way of reasonable people (*sira-yi 'uqala'*) of that time.

Second, at the time of Revelation, the *shar'i* rules were just, moral, reasonable (*'uqala'i*) and normal. These criteria are both the conditions for them to occur and to persist. Any rule that at the present time does not meet the above criterion should as a matter of fact be excised from the circle of permanent rules, and it will be determined that it is among the variable and impermanent rules of religion.

Third, only God and the Prophet are the Legislator and no one who is not infallible (*m'assoum*) can be a religious legislator. Those rules that leave the sphere of the religious on account of not being just or rational are not replaced

---

18 Here I mean mainstream scholars and specialists in general, not scholars of Islam.

by a religious order; rather, in these cases, action is taken in accordance with rational laws without affected (*mutakallifane*) reliance on religious texts.

Fourth, in this approach, the sphere of jurisprudence (*fiqh*) and the *shari'a* are gradually reduced, but the scope and depth of the sphere of religion is increased. Whatever is no longer a path to religious ends is voided. The religious path is that path that God and the Prophet presented. Other paths to reaching these ultimate goals are not closed. While reasonability and justice may seem incongruous with one another, the only limits to these two criteria are the limits of human thought and wisdom. We humans have nothing other than them for understanding Revelation. In any case, as compared with the previously noted approaches, the approach to end-oriented Islam is the least problematic, soundest and surest way for defending religiosity in the modern age.

Conclusion

There are three approaches to the discussion of the compatibility of Islam (or more precisely *shari'a* and *fiqh*) with modernity among Muslim Shi'ite thinkers in the past century and a half in Iran. Although the Constant and Variable Perspective in its different expositions by Na'ini, 'Allama Tabataba'i and Sayyid Muhammad Baqir Sadr, is the most famous perspective of the compatibility of Islam and modernity, it has four serious problems. Ayatollah Khomeini's Perspective of Governmental or Expedient *Fiqh*, which is the official policy of the Islamic Republic of Iran, aside from its flexibility, encounters four problems. The perspective of end-oriented Islam is the third approach that I argue has four advantages. It has the capacity to give a new interpretation of Islamic jurisprudence (*fiqh*) in the modern world based on the spirit of Islam and the goals of the Qur'an, the Sunna (Tradition) of the Prophet and his household (*ahl al-bayt*). I find that end-oriented Islam is a perfect perspective for the modern world.

2
The Principles of Compatibility between Islam and Modernity[1]

Modern culture is the dominant one in our time, such that it has somehow influenced all cultures and subcultures. Modernity in one sense covers humankind's biggest achievements and the changes it has brought about have shone a light on all aspects of human society, so much so that it has become a turning point in all individual and collective affairs as compared with what came before it. Yet this does not mean that modernity should be considered as an end in itself or a superior virtue to be used as a measuring stick for assessing human phenomena. Thus, while welcoming many of the achievements and consequences of modernity, one must not ignore its shortcomings and the criticisms that can be brought against it. One must consider it, after Habermas, "an incomplete project" that sets a way but is not itself a destination. Modernisation is a gradual process, and following that process requires the maturation of specific cultural, economic, political and social conditions; there is no reason why this process should be followed in the same way by different societies or for all societies to achieve the current situation of European and American ones. Every society has the right to take its own path towards modernity, and, most importantly, towards a modernity in which it believes.

---

1 This chapter is based on my presentation "*Osul-e Sazgari-ye Eslam wa Moderniteh*" ("The Principles of Compatibility of Islam and Modernity") at the International Symposium of Islam, Society and Modernity, held at the Interdisciplinary Centre for the Study of Religion and Laicity, The Free University of Brussels, Belgium, October 2004.

The Meaning of the Compatibility of Islam and Modernity

I should clarify at the outset that what I mean by the compatibility of Islam and modernity is not to say that Islam as a variable should harmonise itself with modernity as that what is fixed, resulting in "modern Islam" where all of the rules and laws of Islam should be coordinated with modernity and all of the rules and standards of modernity should be adopted as is and without condition in Islamic thought and action, and where modernity becomes the solid rock against which Islamic propositions are measured, accepted or rejected. Similarly, what I mean by compatibility is not to say that modernity as a variable should harmonise itself with Islam as that what is fixed, resulting in an "Islamic modernity" where every contrary act to Islam in modernity is cast away and Islam becomes the standard for accepting or rejecting modern propositions. In the first instance, Islam would be dissolved in modernity and in the second modernity would be dissolved in Islam.

If the aim of the compatibility of Islam and modernity is not to unquestioningly accept one and dissolve one into the other, what does compatibility mean? What I am setting out in this chapter is the possibility of the compatibility of one reading of Islam with a narrative of modernity; or, put another way, the possibility of the realisation of Islam and modernity in a society – a society whose members are believers in Islam, who think and act in an Islamic manner, and at the same time observe the standards of modernity. What I want to say is that it is possible to bring modernity and Islam together.

This is not to say that any reading of Islam is compatible with any reading of modernity and that there can be no incompatibilities between them. On the contrary, at present there are readings of Islam that are incompatible with modernity. Thus, I speak of the compatibility of Islam and modernity with the disclaimer that I have critiques of both, although the angle and extent of the critique of each varies. On the one hand, I consider the critique of thinkers such as Alisdair MacIntyre and postmodern intellectuals, and, on the other hand, which is more the focus of this chapter, I assess "traditional Islam" to be distant from the true message of Islam.

The Confrontation of Traditional Islam with Modernity

As the last of the three great Abrahamic religions and after fourteen centuries, Islam has become so embedded with the traditions and customs of its followers that it is difficult today to ascertain Islam's true message. In traditional Islam, the text of the holy book of the Qur'an, the sayings and actions of the Prophet Muhammad, and the ways and methods and consensus of Muslim scholars are taken as fixed rules that transcend time and space, and on these bases are considered sanctities that cannot be critiqued or debated.

In this approach, while this Islamic rationale is considered to be a *hikma* (wisdom), it is not a rationale that is understandable by human reason. Thus, given the limits of human rationality, the role of rationality is not much emphasised in deducing divine rules; religious understanding is "text-based" and understanding "appearances" is equated with religious understanding. In addition, in religious understanding formalism dominates; this formalism never allows those religious ends which cannot be relied on much via the limitations of the human mind to show themselves. For this reason, while independent reasoning (*ijtihad*) as a whole is accepted in some religions, it has not gone beyond independent reasoning (*ijtihad*) in minutiae.

In traditional Islam, carrying out the rules of *shari'a* is the criterion that determines whether a society is Islamic. Insofar as this approach considers the rules of *shari'a* to be human laws, there is no need for documents such as the International Declaration of Human Rights. This is because the *khalifa* or the jurist-ruler (*wali al-faqih*) enacts what is in the best interests of the people better than they can do themselves. In traditional Islam, the rules of *shari'a* void freedom of religion and belief. And in cases where the Islamic ruler or Muslim *faqih*s determine it to be so, violence can be used to enact *shari'a* or to expand the growth of the religion. Instituting the rules of *shari'a* or enacting religion does not require the consent of others, all are obligated to follow these rules and orders. Accepting Islam or accepting to live in an Islamic society means to agree at the outset to all its rules, and after this initial agreement there is no room for violations thereafter.

From this perspective, the time of the Prophet was the best of times and Muslims are obligated to build their societies in accordance with the model of the time of the Revelation. And when there are incompatibilities between modern phenomena and the model of the time of the Prophet, it is the modern phenomena which are the problem; those phenomena must either be eliminated or the sacred model must be incorporated within them. There is not much place for interpretation of texts when it comes to conflicts with the dictates of reason because the overwhelming majority are the rules of conjectural reason (*'aql zanni*) and have less influence than absolute and certain reason.

What has been noted thus far in brief is a summary of traditional Islam that includes a wide spectrum of Islamic sects such as the Salafi, Akhbari, Hanbali and Wahabi, as well as official interpretations of other sects. Despite the great number of people who hold this perspective, the doubtless fact of their being Muslim, and with respect for their interpretation, their view conflicts with modernity. In the current age, if their approach is carried out in the public arena, there will be no place in society for modernity. If someone considers Islam to be limited to this official reading, it leaves no room for compatibility with modernity. While the followers of traditional Islam may not face any problems in their private lives in meeting Islamic criteria, in the current age they will face serious difficulties in carrying out Islamic rules in society and will have no choice but to either turn a blind eye to the ways that rules of *shari'a* are carried out in society and by others and to consent to the shutdown of religion in society, or they must turn to force and violence for propagating Islamic criteria in society.

Traditional Muslims have mostly followed the first method, while fundamentalist Muslims have followed the second. To follow the first method means nothing other than to surrender traditional Islam to modernity and to withdraw to private life. Yet the issue does not end there, because traditional Muslims do not have a convincing reason for not acting in response to society's and others' failure to follow the rules of *shari'a* which according to their reading falls under the auspices of the fixed and permanent rules of Islam. The problems that arise for fundamentalist Muslims who turn to force for enacting rules of *shari'a* are worse and it results in presenting an abominable and violent face of Islam. Likewise, the face of Islam presented by traditional Muslims is a weak and powerless one.

The Principles of the Compatibility of Islam and Modernity

Now it is time to consider another reading of Islam as it relates to modernity. This growing reading is the result of the work of a number of Islamic thinkers who are known as Muslim reformists. In their work, they have brought together modernity and intellectualism on the one hand, with Islam on the other. In this intellectual and faith movement, human rights and divine obligation, individual freedom and social justice, collective wisdom and religious ethics, human rationality and the divine prophecy, peacefully coexist. The thinkers of reformist Islam have accepted the Islamic message together with the jewel of modernity.

The characteristics of reformist Islam or the principles of the compatibility of Islam and modernity are as follows:

First Principle: Re-reading the Texts of Religion on the Basis of its Higher Ends

Compared with official Islam, which was "formalist", reformist Islam is "teleological" (or end-oriented) and believes that all religious rules, rites and propositions are in the service of a higher end. In its most general sense, this higher end is "human dignity", which is also interpreted as closeness with God or nirvana (ultimate). Every single Islamic commandment, prohibition, rite, rule and proposition has a particular end. These ends are all in the service of that ultimate end and the lofty ideal; in the sum of its parts, religion is an orientation towards the Almighty to complete and free humans. The value of religious actions and rites are realised when this orientation is secured. Put another way, it is an appearance, face and a casing for reaching that which is the content, what is inside and what is at the core. Religious ends are fixed, permanent and transcend both time and place, but the tools and rules that result from them change in various circumstances of time and place.

Thus, it is natural that some rules that secured religion's higher ends at the time of the Revelation and for centuries after may not bring about these goals when the circumstances of time and place change. On this basis, these rules are time-based, temporary and impermanent. These types of variable and temporary rules can be found not only among the rules of *shari‘a* issued by Muslim *faqih*s, about the consensus of which information can be found, but can even be seen among the rules issued by the Prophet. In other words, it is not the case that all the narrations of the Prophet contain fixed and permanent rules. The Prophet has also issued Islamic rules that were limited to his time and place, and honest adherence to the way of the Prophet never means following rules of this type in varying circumstances of time and place. Rather, it means to preserve the spirit of his message and his main aim.

Based on this, even the Holy Book of Qur'an includes the two types of Islamic rules. There is no shortage of fixed and universal rules which transcend time and place, but it is not the case that all Qur'anic statements and propositions are of this type. Rather, in the Qur'an, one can also find propositions that are linked to the special circumstances of the time of the Revelation and are changing and temporary. The Qur'an and the Prophet could not remain indifferent to the problems of the time of Revelation and the early years of Islam, and there is no reason at hand for believing that the issues and problems of that time can be generalised to all times and places. Rather, an inductive and *a posteriori* study provides enough reason for the existence in God's Book of changing and temporary rules and statements linked to the specific circumstances of time and place of the time of the Revelation. Rules pertaining to slaves, the issue of punishments in accordance to *shari'a*, some forms of *jihad*, discrimination as it relates to the rights of women and non-Muslims are examples of these variable and temporary rules.

From another perspective, language is an historical affair. Even if the Divine message and the Word of God is presented in the mould of language, linguistic limitations which include historical ones apply. In any case, fixed propositions that transcend time also require proof and proving them is not an easy task. Followers of reformist Islam believe that Muslim *faqih*s have dealt with many of the variable and temporary rules in the Qur'an and hadith as though they are fixed and permanent, resulting in the prevailing problems of contemporary Muslims.

Second Principle: The High Place of Reason in the Understanding of Religion

While in some Islamic sects, "reason" is explicitly considered a source of deduction, it does not have much of a role in traditional Islam. Reason is ultimately that which discovers the rule of *shari'a* and nothing more, and due to the rarity of the rules of absolute reason and the lack of authority of speculative reason in the current face of religion, reason does not hold a high place. In critique of the earlier noted approach, thinkers of reformist Islam cite the speculative nature of the text-based reasons (the Book, Sunna and consensus), and do not accept the rejection of reason on the basis of it being speculative. They believe that it is not the case that human reason cannot understand the end of any of the rules; of course, they do not claim that they have understood the wisdom of all the rules of *shari'a*, but many of the rules of *shari'a*, in particular, the overwhelming majority of rules that do not pertain to worship can be discussed with reason.

Religious rules at the time of the Revelation were rational, and were understood and interpreted by the general rational custom of the time, they were not accepted just because they were propositions uttered by God or the Prophet, but were accepted because they were reasonable as such. Many of these propositions in the Qur'an or narrations of the Prophet drew in non-believers. They accepted these propositions because of their reasonable and correct content and accepted them in accordance to their reasonableness. The credibility of these utterances caused them to realise the credibility of the utterer, not the other way around. Those who heard the Islamic rules in the early years of Islam, found the rules in accordance to the customs of the time to be just and better than similar solutions. Today, too, if there is a rule that is to be linked to religion and considered to be an "Islamic rule", it must also be assessed in accordance to the rationality of our time to be rational, just and better than similar solutions. This means that religious propositions are debatable, and more important is the fact that these propositions are subject to debate, comparison and assessment. Muslims must be able to defend their rules and criteria in a rational manner and must have sufficient rational justification for their religious dictates as compared with other solutions.

Any proposition that today is understood to be unjust, or is in opposition to the dictates of absolute reason, lacks credibility, even if in the past it was considered to be a rule of *shari'a*. Thus, just as it is possible to void a rule of *shari'a* using evidence from the Book and Sunna, it is also possible to do so using reason. In reality, a rule becoming void shows its temporality and the expiration of its credibility.

If one does not accept that reason has such credibility and denies the role of reason in deducing rules of *shari'a* or in understanding religious propositions, it means that one considers the rules of *shari'a* and religious propositions to be devotional, imitative and not subject to rational justification, research or discussion. If this approach had a place in traditional Islam, it is not accepted in reformist Islam.

Thinkers of reformist Islam believe that the decline of Islamic culture and civilisation started when the Mu'tazila movement of justice and rationality was defeated by the conservative Ash'ari movement. Reformist Islam is a continuation of the Mu'tazila movement of justice and rationality. The Holy book of Qur'an has many times emphasised intellection and has asked its critics to offer "proof" for their words. Based on this, it is completely rational that others have this same expectation of Muslims that they should be able to provide arguments for their religious foundations. Providing proof is nothing other than entering the trade of reason, providing proof is to accept rationality. Traditional Islamic scholars also accept that in the arena of belief, imitation is not permissible and Muslims must have reasons for what they accept.

Put another way, there is no doubt about the rationality in debates of belief. It is also not debatable that devotional affairs and rites have no logic other than that of love and servitude; the differences in traditional and reformist Islam are over non-devotional rules of *shari'a*, which are called "*mu'amalat*" in the terminology of *fiqh*, and cover all legal issues including civil law, trade law, criminal law, constitutional law and international law. Reformist Islam does not consider this aspect of religion (meaning the rules of *mu'amalat* or the legal aspect) to be absolutely devotional or imitative and believes the understandings of reason in this arena are also credible.

Put another way, reformist Islam considers this important aspect of religion to be the function of rational criteria, and in engaging these and its concomitant criteria of justice considers many of the rules of this arena to be a part of the rules which are temporary, variable and obsolete. In contrast, for traditional Islam, being Muslim means to carry out the legal criteria of the time of the Prophet, all of which it considers to be a part of the fixed and permanent rules. In order to extend the rational method to the legal section of religion, it is clear that reformist Islam requires a new *fiqh* methodology; one that will be based on the rationality of *shari'a*. In fact, this rationality is the engine of the new *ijtihad*.

It goes without saying that defining this rationality, and the limits of its credibility, and their assessment is among those debates that, aside from big speeches, requires technical and expert research. To which approach of modern rationality is this closer and from which is it most distant? How is the justice that is at the centre of the rules of *shari'a* defined and where does it belong in the new categorisations of justice?

Reformist Islam has a long way ahead on this difficult path, we are in fact at the beginning of the road.

Third Principle: The Permanent Right to Choose How to Live

One of the biggest differences between traditional Islam and reformist Islam is the amount of intervention in the religiosity of others. If a member of society does not follow Islamic criteria, are other members of society permitted to force him or her to follow these criteria? Can one use force and violence towards this end and to carry out *shari'a* at any price? Relying on rules such as *al-amr bi al-ma'ruf wa al-nahy 'an al-munkar* (enjoining good and forbidding wrong) and on punishments of *shari'a* such as *hudud* and *ta'zirat*, traditional Islam argues that if people do not agree to follow their religious obligations after they have been asked to do so peacefully, then it is not problematic to turn up the heat using threats, force, intimidation and violence as necessary. After all, Divine criteria and limits must be respected.

Reformist Islam finds the society that is built and imagined by traditional Islam to be one that is closed and based on force and pressure, and believes that whatever is carried out by force will only have the form but not the content of religion. Religious faith cannot be realised through force. Faith is like love, can one fall in love through the force of decrees, directives and orders? Instead of religious faith, force and pressure will bring about shams, pretensions and hypocrisy; the place of religion will be taken by indifference and aversion towards religious practices. Each person may be as strict with him- or herself to whatever extent is deemed necessary, but as it relates to the "other", until such time that that person desires it, we are not permitted to impose anything, even the thing that we believe to be completely just.

The relationship "the other and I" is one that is intertwined with freedom and choice. Using force and violence in this relationship is strictly forbidden. Just as I am free to choose my religion and the way and manner of my life, the other also has the same freedom, choice and right to choose. If I find another's choice to be wrong, I am not permitted to force onto him or her that which I consider to be just but he or she does not. In such a case, I am able and, indeed, obligated to bring about circumstances that will convince the other so that he or she may freely choose to reform his or her ways; but if he or she is not convinced, I am not permitted to turn to force and violence. He or she has consciously chosen the path that I consider unjust and will pay for it in the Hereafter.

Al-amr bi al-ma'ruf wa al-nahy 'an al-munkar (enjoining good and forbidding wrong) has no other meaning other than bringing about the right cultural conditions for good deeds and creating the maximum cultural and legal obstacles for preventing evil deeds. Within an existing state, no citizen has the right to use force for the purposes of discipline and guidance. The prescriptive result of reformist Islam is "persuasive Islam", and the prescriptive result of traditional Islam is "compulsory Islam".

Thinkers of reformist Islam believe that human dignity cannot be spoken of without respect for the individual and the right of the individual to choose. Based on this freedom to choose, what people choose may not be correct from our point of view. The only thing that can limit this freedom of choice is a just law, a law with which each member of society is involved, meaning a democratic law. Thus, it is forbidden for members of society to put pressure or force others in the name of religion and *shari'a*; as such, the right of individual freedom remains immune against transgression by other members of society and no one has the right to use the delusion of religious obligation to intervene in the lives of others, much less if this intervention is accompanied by violence and battery.

We should remember that the right of individuals to choose does not expire after one use, lest it be said that they have chosen once and are forced to stay within the framework of their first choice. This is a permanent right, they can cancel their previous choices, or choose to carry out only some aspects of religion. That this is a right means that it is permitted and has no correlation with it being correct. Not recognising this right means a prescription for force, pressure or hate in religion that conflicts with the eternal rule "*la ikraha fiddin*" (there is no compulsion in religion).

Fourth Principle: The Possibility of Legislation and Public Policy on the Basis of Religious Values

Now the time has come for a more difficult question. The last three points covered the differences between reformist and traditional Islam. By rejecting dogmatic interpretations of texts, accepting rationality in the understanding of religion, and officially recognising people's rights to choose, believers of reformist Islam have stepped into the modern world. This fourth point covers the differences between reformist religious intellectuals and non-religious ones.

Intellectuals of reformist Islam have at least three differences with non-religious ones. First, those who are religious, including religious intellectuals (whether Muslim, Christian or Jewish), live piously in the arena of their personal and private lives, have faith in God and Judgement Day, and base their ethical conduct on religious models. They follow prayer, worship and religious rites.

Second, in the public sphere and in relationship with others, religious intellectuals are committed to religious ethics, and, more importantly, are grounded in religious criteria. If the thought and ways of reformist Islam are accepted by the general public and the majority of people in that society become convinced that this way will better bring about their happiness, then, on the one hand, this type of believer will democratically become brokers in the public sphere, and, on the other hand, society will freely accept that its laws will appreciate religious criteria and values, which are themselves accepted by the general public. For example, in such a society, the law would use democratic means to forbid homosexuality, free sexual relations outside marriage and before marriage in particular, and cases of abortion when it is not an emergency; and it would legally defend religious instruction in public schools.

Third, in such a society, public policy making would doubtlessly be influenced by religious values and criteria. Public policy making is different from and more vast than legislation. The religious and believers try to observe human dignity, justice and ethics in setting public policy. Solutions such as democracy and human rights have not been able to fill the empty place of ethics, justice and dignity. This is exactly where the French thinker Alexis de Tocqueville has affirmed democracy's need for religion.

If the national thinking is ever in conflict with human rights, justice, ethics or human dignity, what other than religious faith and ethical conscience would prefer these high human values to national interest? Or if the gross national production of one country is at the price of the extreme poverty of other countries, what other than religion and ethics would consider such a development to be bad?

Non-religious intellectuals have no issue with religious intellectuals on the first issue, meaning in the matter of being pious in one's private life. However, on the second and third, meaning the observance of religious values and criteria in legislation and public policy making, they are in great opposition and emphasise that modernity demands that we consider religion to be a private matter and do not allow it to intervene in the public sphere. Thus, the essential requirement of modernity is secularism, meaning the separation of legislation, policy-setting and public policy making from religion. The nature of modernity is secular and tolerates no religion in the public sphere, even if the majority of society requests that such values and criteria be observed because in that case the rights of the minority that does not believe in that religion will be trampled. Based on this, no one has the right to violate the nature and essence of modernity which is a secular rationality.

In response, religious intellectuals reason that this is the right of the members of a society to legislate as they wish or to set public policy. It is clear, first, that the minority must have the possibility of becoming a majority and at a time when they are generally accepted, they too will have the right to coordinate laws and public policy in accordance to their criteria and values. Second, fundamental rights, such as the right to life, the freedom of expression, the right to determine one's destiny, the right to a fair trial, are protected for all people without exception. Therefore, there is no dictatorship of the majority and a transgression against the rights of the minority.

About the disagreements between non-religious and religious intellectuals, numerous examples of which exist in past cases of legislation and public policy making, there is no single rationale that is accepted by both sides. In the language of philosophy, the reasons for and against each position are equally credible. Each side presents its own special rational reasons, which are not acceptable to the other side and do not convince the other for whatever reason. In such cases the practical solution – rather than the theoretical one – for determining which side will set the policy and ways of the society is the democratic solution, meaning referring to the majority.

That the religious have no right to consider religious rules and criteria in legislating or setting public policy, even though they may have come to power for a temporary time through democratic methods and will step aside in accordance to the general vote, and despite having general public support in ethical matters for which there are sufficient rational arguments, is a "modern taboo" and nothing other than unproven dogma. That this is secularism's red line and religious societies are obligated to accept laws and public policy that they believe are completely wrong, is nothing other than a recourse to force and the imposition of axioms as rationality.

Modernity does not have a nature or essence so there is need to worry that its nature or essence will be lost. If there is a nature or essence it is in affairs of truth rather than affairs of credibility. In addition, is modernity sacred that we should worry about stepping on its sacredness? Yes, one cannot forget that the modernity established in the West has this as a necessity, meaning it has been secular, but is it necessary that Islamic societies should follow exactly the path of Europe and the United States in their own experience?

Conclusion

The critical confrontation with modernity (rather than being dissolved in modernity) demands that reformist Muslims emphasise this important point that, given the above-mentioned, they consider themselves to be both deeply Muslim and completely modern, albeit modern in their own way. Islam does not exclusively belong to traditional Muslims, so there is no worry that disagreement with them would mean leaving Islam; nor does modernity exclusively belong to secular and non-religious intellectuals, so there is no worry that disagreement with them would mean leaving modernity. In all Islamic societies, reformist Islam is not to the liking of traditionalists, fundamentalists and secular and non-religious intellectuals and is growing and thriving. One cannot ignore it, and this is a reality.

3

An Introduction to the Public and Private Debate in Islamic Culture[1]

While in one sense the distinction of the private sphere from the public sphere has a meaning that is as old as human existence, the increasing attention being paid to the scope and importance of the private sphere and to protecting it against transgressors is a contemporary concern. If in the past, states were considered to be the biggest transgressors of the private sphere, due to the astonishing developments in technology, today electronic media threaten private life right along with states. Without doubt, the boundaries of the private and public spheres depend on a number of cultural, social, political and economic factors, and changes in these factors would mean changes in the scope and nature of private and public life. Culture, especially religion, is one of the most important factors determining the boundaries of these two domains.[2] Religions have given special attention to notions of private life. The Abrahamic religions have attempted to strengthen human identity through efforts pertaining to private life. This chapter investigates the "Public and Private Debate in Islamic Culture".

From what perspective does Islam, as one of the contemporary world's living religions, distinguish the private from the public? From an Islamic

---

1 This chapter is my presentation "*Daramadi bar bahth-e Omumi wa Khosusi dar Farhangh-e Eslami*" at the Social Studies Conference on Islam: Public and Private Sphere at New Scholl University, New York, 5 December 2002. It has previously appeared in English translation as "An Introduction to the Public and Private Debate in Islam", *Social Research*, 659–680. However, for inclusion in the present book, it was retranslated from the original Persian.

2 The importance of religion's role depends on the level of religiosity in each society.

standpoint, how far does the domain of private life extend? How does this domain compare and contrast with the Western understandings of private life? As a whole, what are the characteristics of the private lives of Muslims? Does this domain change, or perhaps shrink, in a society that is run in accordance to the criteria of *shari'a*? What are the limitations of the state's authority, including those of a religious state? How has Islam understood the meaning of notions such as the individual, family, society and state?

This chapter is an introductory discussion that sets the groundwork for providing responses to questions such as the above. This is why I have called it an introduction.

While the roots of the distinction between private and public exist in Islamic texts, especially those pertaining to ethics and *fiqh*, there is not much precedence for an independent discussion on the private and the public in Islam. Despite its importance, they have not received the necessary examination. This chapter will first present a brief explanation about the private and the public before establishing the fundamental principle of the matter. Using two of the criteria taken by private definition as the basis of discussion, the chapter will then consider the following two axes: the prohibition against prying and the right to freedom in action. Thereafter, the chapter will consider important issues pertaining to the private sphere, such as *al-amr bi al-ma'ruf wa al-nahy 'an al-munkar* (enjoining the proper and forbidding the improper), the office of accountability (*da'irat al-hisbah*) and the limits of the authority of an Islamic government. Finally, the chapter will conclude with a recommendation for raising religious conscience.

The Meaning of Private Affair

The two terms "private" and "public" do not exist in *shari'a*. They are not used in the Qur'an or in hadiths. Even in *fiqh*, these terms are not recognised. Thus, I will first articulate what I mean by these two terms and then will aim to find the closest Islamic terminology and rules for them. The meanings of public and private are the type of ideas which, although basic, are nonetheless not easy to explain. In addition, there is not much consensus among existing definitions. According to research on the private sphere,[3] the

---

3 Ruth Gavison, "Privacy: Legal Aspects", in Neil J. Smelser and Paul B. Baltes (eds), *International Encyclopaedia of Social and Behavioural Sciences* (Amsterdam: Elsevier, 2001), 12067.

following three meanings can be understood: first, that which is personal, individual and exclusive; second, that which a person wishes to keep hidden and inaccessible to others; third, that over which a person has the exclusive right of control and decision.

What I mean by "private" covers the second and third meaning, as the first meaning does not clarify much when it comes to the ambiguity of the term. In fact, an affair is private if these two criteria (or one of them) is realised: one is the desire to be clandestine or keep something out of the reach of others, the desire to hide and not be seen, to remain secret and to treat it like a closed book. Given this, it is the individual who decides who may have access to (part of) this private realm and who does not show most of that realm to anyone. Some parts of one's body, orientations, wishes and much of what is predicated on our past belongs to this sphere. There is also that over which only the individual has control and in relation to which only they are responsible for making decisions about. It is the sphere over which the individual has power and authority, no one else can determine what he or she should do in this sphere. The individual does not even need to consult anyone about this sphere.

While the first criterion denies information and supervision to others, the second criterion strips others from guardianship or authority over this sphere. Assets and properties, residence and profession, religion and belief, body and clothing, and socio-political policies are considered private according to this criterion. It is possible that something may be covered by both criteria or it may only coincide with one of them. The private is that about which only the individual knows or can make things known, or can exclusively arrange or make decisions about, and the individual has complete authority in both (or either). In some cases, seeing or knowing about them is of value and in other cases knowledge of them is not the criterion, what is important is who is at the helm in making decisions about them. Do others have the right to make decisions in directing them or not?

Are there any individuals who have no right to privacy? Inmates in prison, a hospitalised patient in affairs pertaining to his or her illness, the mentally ill in an institution, and a child before maturity – to these four one can add individuals living under totalitarian rule who may be deprived of private lives in accordance to the power of the state, and the state may make decisions about some or all of their affairs and tries to have knowledge about all aspects of their lives.

In contrast, the public sphere is one in which nothing is kept hidden or inaccessible, and it is the right of all citizens to arrange and make decisions about. The public sphere is the state's sphere of authority.[4] All citizens have joint ownership of this sphere,[5] and like a glass room its contents are in view of all of them (unless they all agree that some issues such as military and security affairs should be under the supervision of their representatives rather than everyone).

One cannot inquire about the affairs of the private sphere, it does not concern anyone else, and it is forbidden to investigate or inspect it; if somehow one finds out about its contents, it is not permissible to disclose them. The management of this sphere is the exclusive right of the individual, he or she has the right to determine his or her destiny and no one rules over him or her in this regard. Given the two criteria under consideration, we find that *fiqh* fully recognises the private sphere, since it has spoken at length, on the one hand, about the prohibition against investigating and exposing what a person has kept hidden about an individual's rights over their property and the management of their affairs, on the other. In general terms, there is no problem when it comes to the private sphere, what is at issue is where to delineate the line between the private and the public, and how to deal with those religious orders which at first sight may seem in conflict with the criteria of the private sphere.

The Requirement of the Fundamental Principle in the Private–Public Debate

Having discussed the meanings of the private and public spheres, it is necessary to determine the fundamental principle that is at issue. Establishing the fundamental principle (*ta'sis al-asl*) is useful because in dubious cases when it is not clear whether something belongs to the private or public sphere, referring to the fundamental principle will allow that determination to be made. That which is in accordance to the fundamental principle

---

4 "Public Sphere and Private Sphere", in Craig J. Calhoun (ed.), *Dictionary of the Social Sciences* (Oxford: Oxford University Press, 2003), 392.
5 Mehdi Haeri-Yazdi, *Hekmat wa Hokumat* (*Wisdom and Government*) (London: Shadi, 1994), 95, 99–108.

requires no further proof, but that which contradicts the fundamental principle necessitates proof.

According to *shari'a* criteria, the fundamental principle is against being public, that is to say, the status of something is private unless proven otherwise. One cannot inquire into the circumstances of another unless it is proven that what is at issue is of the public domain and subject to questioning. Preserving the sanctity of the private and the prohibition against investigation or inspection is in accordance with the fundamental principle.[6] The permission to investigate and inspect requires credible *shari'a* evidence. On the other hand, every person has the full authority to make decisions regarding his or her affairs and destiny, whereas the interventions of others require evidence. This criterion is called the "principle of excluded guardianship" (*asl 'adam al-wilaya*).[7] The requirements of the principle of excluded guardianship is that no one is allowed to intervene in human affairs without the specific permission of the Lawmaker (*shari'*). Interference in the political, economic, cultural and personal affairs of people requires evidence; non-interference in the person's personal affairs is in accordance to the fundamental principle and does not require evidence.

Based on this analysis, a person's affairs pertain to him or her; unless that person gives permission, it is not permitted to investigate, inspect, interfere, change or make decisions about said affairs. Inquiry and intervention into that sphere requires credible *shar'i* evidence. Similarly, in affairs that pertain to everyone (public affairs), no one person has the right to intervene without the consent of all unless it is with the express permission of the Lawmaker.

Now we must investigate which cases *fiqh* has been specifically exempted from, the prohibition against investigation and inspection or from intervening in and changing a person's individual affairs. Which affairs have been entrusted to a particular person irrespective of the consent of all? Reflecting

---

6 Hossein Ali Montazeri, *Dirasat fi Wilayat al-Faqih wa Fiqh al-Dawlat al-Islamiya* (*Studies on the Guardianship of the Jurist and Islamic State Law*) (Qom: Maktab al-I'lam al-Islami, 1988), 2:539: "In requirement of preserving the dignities (*al-a'rad*) and secrets of Muslims . . . Its meaning is in accordance to the fundamental principle."

7 Jaffar Kashif al-Ghita', *Kash al-Ghita'a an Mubhamat al-Shariat al- Gharra'* (*The Revealing of the Covering from the Ambiguities of the Brilliant* Shari'a) (Qom: Maktab al-I'lam al-Islami, 2001), 1:207–208; al-Shaykh Mortada al-Ansari, *Al-Makasib* (*Book of Buying*) (Qom: Majma' al-Fikr al-Islami, 1999), 3:546.

on this principle shows that the base of the discussion is reason-based (*al-ʿuqalaʾi*) and anything to the contrary requires credible *sharʿi* evidence.

The Requirement of Piety in the Private and Public Spheres

The pious person submits to God in all domains of life. He or she has accepted with free will that his or her happiness is tied to arranging human life in accordance to God's satisfaction. Islam is the name of all the Abrahamic religions[8] and has no meaning other than submission to God.

A faithful person is one who arranges all aspects of his or her life in accordance with divine criteria. On this basis, there is no difference between the private and public spheres. Only two entities are aware of the private life of the faithful individual (God and the individual). The individual manages that life, but he or she freely arranges his or her private life so as to satisfy God. The non-believer thinks that no one supervises his or her actions. The faithful person knows and accepts this ultimate supervision. The faithful person is not forced to give in to God's commandments. He or she may break some of God's commands and sin. Sinning is contrary to the criteria of faith and comes with punishment. This punishment follows in case the sinner does not regret and repent; whenever a sinner repents he or she is forgiven. In case he or she does not repent, there will be punishment on Judgement Day (*ʿiqab*). It is not necessarily the case that every sin is punished in the temporal world. The faithful person is not required to disclose to anyone sins that have been committed in private and have temporal punishments as long as these sins have not violated the rights of others. It is enough that he or she repents. Put another way, if in the private sphere the individual has violated God's right (*haqq Allah*) (committed a sin), it is not necessary for him or her to confess and be subject to *sharʿi* punishment (*al-hadd* or *al-tazir*); from the perspective of *shariʿa*, it is better that he or she does not make the sin known.[9] In Islam, the relationship between God and the individual is a direct one and to repent, no one, including clerics, are intermediaries. No one has the right to force a

---

8 Q. 3:19: "True Religion, in God's eyes, is Islam [devotion to Him alone]": Q. 22:78: "The faith of your forefather Abraham. God has called you Muslims, both in the past and in this [message]."

9 Montazeri, *Dirasat fi Wilayat al-Faqih wa Fiqh al-Dawlat al-Islamiya*, 2:544: "This type of hidden sexual and personal sin is not permitted to be investigated or pried into. *Shariʿa* recommends hiding them."

pious individual to carry out his or her religious obligations. If he or she, for whatever reason, does not practice religion, it is his or her life and decision.

Islam also has conventions (values and standards)[10] for the public sphere. Muslims consider themselves obliged to follow these. Thus, in managing the public sphere of an Islamic society, it is necessary to obtain the satisfaction of God along with the consent of Muslims. This satisfaction is obtained by adhering to religious criteria. The intended audience of the Qur'an's social addresses are Muslims.[11] As long as Muslims willingly arrange their society in accordance with Islamic criteria and standards, the management of that society will be "Islamic"; whenever those criteria are for whatever reason violated, the society is not Islamic, although one can still call it a "society of Muslims".

Has God appointed a specific person or group of people to manage the public sphere? Muslims in general concur that the Prophet Muhammad b. 'Abdullah was also a judge of disputes and a ruler of the public sphere. According to the clear verses (*al-nass*) of the Qur'an, following the Prophet is a religious duty for Muslims.[12] The verse "The Prophet is more protective towards the believers than they are themselves" (Q. 33:6) has absolute expression (*itlaq*) and covers all of the Prophet's commands, including those that may pertain to the private lives of Muslims.[13] In addition to the Prophet, the Shi'ite give similar authority to their Imams.[14] But after these, has God appointed another person as his deputy on earth? The collective response of Muslims to this question is negative, meaning no one person can say "I am God's deputy on Earth".[15] The question of the caliphate for Sunnis and the *wilayat al-faqih* (guardianship of the jurist) for Shi'ites will be considered later. But in general, neither of Islam's two great schools (*madhab*) unanimously accept either of these approaches.

---

10 These regularities are almost moral values and ethical standards, and less legal rules.

11 Montazeri, *Dirasat fi Wilayat al-Faqih wa Fiqh al-Dawlat al-Islamiya*, 1:499.

12 Q. 4:58–60; 24:62–63; 4:65 and 105.

13 See both Sunni and Shi'ite interpretations of Q. 33:6.

14 On the issue of the Imamate, see Nassir al-Din al-Tusi, *Tajrid al-E'tiqad* (*Abstraction of the Belief*), ed. Muhammad Jawad al-Hussaini al-Jalali (Qom: Maktab al-I'lam al-Islami, 1987) and Hassan b. Yusuf al-Helli, *Kashef al-Morad fi Sharh Tajrid al-E'tiqad* (*The Discovery of the Intention in Commentary of Tajrid al-I'tiqad*), ed. Hassan Hassanzadeh Amoli (Qom: Islamic Publication Institute, 2012).

15 I have extensively critiqued this "Theory of Appointment" in my book, *Hokumat-e Entesabi* (*Appointive/Non-Elective State*), Political Thought in Shi'ite Islam Series, vol. 3, Kadivar web-book, 2014.

The Strict Prohibition against Investigation and Inspection

The first criterion of private life is that a person may choose to keep it hidden or inaccessible to others. This criterion implies both a prohibition against investigation or inspection as well as a prohibition against the publication and distribution of material about a person's personal situation and the various aspects of his or her private life. Both of these orders have been explicitly addressed in the Qur'an:

> Believers, avoid making too many assumptions – some assumptions are sinful – and do not spy on one another or speak ill of people behind their backs: would any of you like to eat the flesh of your dead brother? No, you would hate it. (Q. 49:12)

In this verse, God has asked the faithful to refrain from being suspicious of others, and to also refrain from investigating and showing curiosity about their personal affairs. All three parts of this verse outline *shari'a* prohibitions. The issue at hand here is focused on investigation. Investigation means to seek whatever it is that an individual has chosen to keep hidden. The Qur'an has not only forbidden curiosity about people's private lives, but has also prohibited the dissemination of this information: "A painful punishment waits in this world and the next for those who like indecency to spread among the believers" (Q. 24:19).

Faith is the guarantor of private life. First of all, the faithful have no right to put thenself in a position to find out about others' private secrets; second, if for some reason, he or she becomes aware of these secrets, he or she has no right to disseminate this information. These two prohibitions clearly show that there is a guarantee in *shari'a* of the sanctity of the private sphere.

Does Islam only recognise the necessity to respect the sanctity of the private spheres of Muslims or is this sanctity respected for both Muslims and non-Muslims? While the prohibition against dissemination in verse Q. 24:19 is about believers, the prohibition against investigation in verse Q. 49:6 is absolute, and given the principle in question and the criteria for judgement, all residents of an Islamic society, including Muslims and non-Muslims, are included in the order to respect the sanctity of the private sphere. While the majority of religious narratives about the issue concern Muslims, there is first of all no *shar'i* evidence that would permit investigation into and curiosity about the private affairs of non-Muslims; second, the description (*wasf*) and title (*laqab*) do not have implicit meaning (*mafhum*), and the existence of a ruling (*hukm*) about Muslims does not constitute evidence of its opposite for non-Muslims.

The Prophet of Islam has said: "Oh those who have become Muslim in words but not in their heart, do not scrutinise the errors of Muslims, those who do so, God will scrutinise their errors, and the person whose errors God scrutinises will be exposed."[16]

Imam Ja'far b. Muhammad al-Sadiq said: "The *awrah* (intimate parts of the human body) of the believer is forbidden to another believer." When he was asked if he was referring to the genitalia of the believer, he replied, "No, I meant the dissemination of believer's secrets."[17] This prohibition against the dissemination of secrets is not only applicable to the secrets of others, the individual him- or herself need not reveal sins committed in secret. Imam 'Ali b. Abi Talib told a man who had confessed to adultery: "Couldn't you have kept this sin hidden in the same way that God has kept your sins hidden?"[18] *Shari'a* is inclined towards keeping the sins of private life undiscovered and hidden from the public. The Prophet warned: "A leader who scrutinises the errors of the people will corrupt them."[19]

The issue of inquisition is one of the particulars of the prohibition of investigation. If a person, for whatever reason, is not inclined to reveal his or her opinion about a matter, others are not permitted to seek his or her opinion. Indeed, even beyond that, it is not permitted to punish another for holding any specific ideas. Opinions may be considered correct or incorrect; but no opinion is subject to punishment. Punishments pertain to actions, not opinions. Opinions and ideas will not change with punishment. Not only does Islam not permit inquisition, but it also has not set worldly punishments

---

16 Muhammad b. Ya'qub al-Kulaini, *al-Kafi* (*The Sufficient*), ed. Ali-Akbar Ghaffari (Tehran: Dar al-Kutub al-Islmiyya, 1984–1988), 2:355.

17 Ibid., 2:385.

18 Muhammad ibn al-Hassan al-Hurr al-'Amili, *Tafsil Wasa'il al-Shi'a Tahsil Masa'il al-Shari'a* (*Details of the Means of the Shi'a regarding the Collection of Shari'a Issues*) (Qom: Mu'assasa Al al-Bayt li Ihya' al-Turath, 1994), 28:38.

19 Abu Bakr Ahmad ibn al-Hussain Al-Beyhaghi, *al-Sunan al-Kubra* (*Major Traditions*) (Haydarabad Dakan: Da'ira al-Ma'arif-'Uthmaniyya: 1936), 8:333; Abu 'Abdullah Muhammad ibn Ahmad al-Qurtubi, *Tafsir al-Qurtubi: Al-Jami' li Ahkam al-Qur'an* (*Comprehensive [Interpretation] in Rulings of the Qur'an*) (Beirut: Resalah, 2006), 16:333.

for having incorrect ideas. Elsewhere, I have proven the freedom of belief and religion in Islam and have shown that contrary to popular belief, no one can be punished or killed for their opinion or for converting to another religion.[20] There is no trace in the Qur'an about worldly punishment for the apostate. This, in spite of popular opinion about religious conversion.

Thawr b. Malik al- Kindi, one of the Prophet's companions, has reported the following: "One night the second caliph, Omar b. Khattab was walking about in Medina when he heard a man singing in his house. He climbed over the wall and began rebuking him: 'Oh enemy of God, do you think God will hide your sin when you are sinning against him?' The man said: 'Oh leader of the faithful, do not rush, for if I have sinned once against God, you have sinned against him three times. God has said: do not investigate and show curiosity about the affairs of others (Q. 49:12), and you have investigated.' God said: 'Enter homes through their front doors' (Q. 2:189), and you have climbed the wall. And you entered without permission even though God has said: 'Do not enter homes, unless it is your own home, without permission and without greeting the residents' (Q. 24:27). Omar said: 'Wouldn't it be better if you forgave me?' The man agreed, forgave him, and Omar left."[21]

This historic scene from early Islam, on the one hand, reflects the amount of freedom people at that time had, and, on the other hand, beautifully illustrates the sanctity of private life. Sinning in private life is not a concern of the state. If there is punishment for a sin (in case the person does not repent), it will be handed out in the other world by God and not in this world by the rulers. In general, one can say: Islam recognises the sanctity of private life. Private information and affairs are the concern of the individual only and no one, not even the state, has the right to be curious about or investigate it, and should that information somehow come to be known, has no right to disseminate the private secrets of another. Inquisition is forbidden. If a person sins in his or her private life, there is no necessity to confess to anyone, not even the state or a judge (in cases where no harm has been done to others). Rather, it is better to repent and hide the sin. In *shari'a*, transgressions against the private lives of others, interrogation and curiosity about it, and dissemination

---

20 "The Freedom of Belief and Religion in Islam and Human Rights Documents", Chapter 8, this book.
21 Ali al-Muttaqi ibn Hisam al-Din al-Hindi, *Kanz al-'Ummal fi Sunan al-Aqwal wa l-Af'al* (*Treasures of the Doers of Good Deeds*) (Beirut: Resalah, 1985), 3:808, No. 8827.

of information about it are considered a sin and are subject to punishment in this world and the next. Therefore, according to Islamic standards the guarantee of the sanctity of the private sphere is greater than in secular standards.

We know that one of the distinguishing characteristics of the private sphere is that one can keep it hidden from others, such that no witness may bear witness and no overseer can oversee. Now if someone transgresses against this sphere and watches a person's private life without his or her knowledge or consent – for example, watching women and girls in their private life – there will be heavy punishments in this world as well as on the Day of Judgement.[22] The respect for the private sphere in Islamic standards is very high.

The Freedom of Action in Private Life

One of the important criteria of private life is the freedom to make decisions in that sphere. That is to say, it is the freedom of the individual to arrange that sphere however he or she wishes, and no one else has the right to make decisions for the person contrary to his or her views. In a well-known hadith, the Prophet has said: "People have control over their property."[23] No one can seize another's property without consent. Using this hadith as the basis, jurists have created a legal principle known as the "sovereignty principle" (*qa'idat al-saltanat*), which implies that whoever owns property has control over it. As such, if individuals have control over their property, then they also have more control than others over their own destiny.[24] The other principle in Islamic culture that supports private life is the "principle of excluded guardianship" (*asl 'adam al-wilaya*).[25]

No one has the right of guardianship over the other or the right to encourage or forbid the other unless there is a legitimate reason based in

22 See, for example, Muhammad Hassan al-Najafi, *Jawahir al-Kalam fi sharh Sharay'i' al-Islam* (*Jewels of Speech in the Commentary of Sharay'i' al-Islam*), ed. 'Abbas Quchani (Tehran: Dar al- Kutub al-Islamiyya, 1988), 41:660.

23 Muhammad Baqir al-Majlisi, *Bihar al-Anwar al-Jami'a li Durar-i Akhbar al-A'ima al-Athar* (*Seas of Lights, the Collection of the Pearls of the Reports of the [Shi'i] Pure Imam*) (Qom: Ihya' al-Kutub al-Islamiyya, 2009), 2:272, hadith No. 7; Al-Hurr al-'Amili, *Tafsil Wasa'il al-Shi'a*, 19:297, hadith No. 2: "The owner of property can do anything [in his property] in his lifetime."

24 For example, see Montazeri, *Dirasat fi Wilayat al-Faqih wa Fiqh al-Dawlat al-Islamiya*, 1:495.

25 Ibid., 1:27.

shari'a that God has given that person permission to do so. What arises from these two principles is the freedom of people in their private lives within the framework of Islamic *shari'a*. Based on this, determining one's profession, place of residence, spouse, name, and lifestyle and dress are a part of private life and, while following religious criteria, individuals have complete freedom in them.

In his or her private sphere – which we call the home and which is often hidden from others – the individual is free to do anything, even if it is a sin. This freedom has only one stipulation, that it not be harmful to others. That is all. But once this same individual enters the public sphere, in every society there will be limitations accordance to the rule of the law. In the public sphere, individuals will have limitations on how they dress, their sexual behaviour, in social activities, and these will differ in various cultures and societies. In an Islamic society – a society wherein Islamic standards are part of its laws – there are special limitations for individuals in the public sphere. These are noteworthy for study in comparison with other societies, including Western ones. These limitations in areas such as dress, sexual relations, drinking and eating, economic relationships and even issues of worship, make it appear as though the private sphere in Islamic culture is smaller than that which prevails in the contemporary world, and, similarly, the public sphere is wider than that which is standard elsewhere. Failure to observe these limitations is a sin from a religious point of view, and in a society whose laws are based on *shari'a*, violating these limitations in the public sphere is considered a "crime" and can be prosecuted.

What is important to follow in the public sphere is the "appearance (*zahir*) of *shari'a*", whether this be in worship (*'ibadat*) or transactions (*mu'amalat*). It is clear that the essence of religiosity cannot be assessed except by God or a person's conscience. Therefore, even in the public sphere, a person's intentions or the essence of one's actions cannot be force, and only their external manifestations must be observed. Insofar as religious orders encompass all aspects of human life, and obligatory orders have divided a noteworthy segment of actions into those that are either required or forbidden, abstaining from that which is required and engaging in the forbidden in ways that negatively manifest in the public sphere are not permitted. *Al-amr bi al-ma'ruf wa al-nahy 'an al-munkar* (enjoining the proper and forbidding the improper) is among Islam's important requirements without consideration of which one cannot examine the public and private spheres in Islam. Put another way, the issue of the individual's freedom of action in the public sphere is framed by this necessity. Thus, it is important to first determine its domain and limits.

Al-amr bi al-ma'ruf wa al-nahy 'an al-munkar
(Enjoining the Proper and Forbidding the Improper)

Based on this incontrovertible Islamic principle, which has been confirmed in the Qur'an and in the Islamic tradition,[26] all Muslims are duty bound to be sensitive to adhering to the proper and avoiding the improper whether it comes from individuals or the government. They must also observe certain conditions such as assessing whether it will have an influence on the departure from the proper and committing the improper. If the person insists on continuing the act, one must sincerely object, then give a verbal warning, and in the third instance, if the previous two have not been effective, physical confrontation to stop him or her. The first phase includes showing distaste, turning one's back, or showing a sour disposition. The second phase of verbal objection is certainly interfering in people's private sphere and if it were not for the religious permission – and indeed the religious recommendation – it would not be allowed. These first two phases are required of everyone (*al-waifs al-kifa'i*), but if some people are enacting them, then others are excused from doing so. The third phase of physical confrontation, which includes hitting, wounding and even killing is among the state's duties in cases when there is a religious state in place[27] (which will be discussed further below). In the absence of a religious state, it is apparently the duty of civil society, although the final phase or the last two phases are not allowed without the permission of a *mujtahid* (a qualified jurist).

While the prohibition against investigation remains, all apparent prohibitions and requirements (*al-zawahir al-shar'iya*) are subject to *al-amr bi al-ma'ruf wa al-nahy 'an al-munkar*. The residents of an Islamic society are

---

26 For example, refer to Sayyid Ahmad Khwansari, *Jami'al-Madarik fi Sharh-i al-Mukhtasar al-Nafi'* (*The Comprehensive Evidence of the Commentary of al-Mukhtasar al-Nafi'* [fi Fiqh al-Imamiyya] *[Useful Manual on the Shi'i Fiqh of al-Muhaqiq al-Hilli]*), ed. 'Ali Akbar al-Ghaffari (Tehran: Maktabat al-Saduq, 1976–1981), 5:398–414.

27 Ruhollah Mousavi Khomeini, *Tahrir al-Wasilah* (*The Editing of* Wasilah al-Nijat *[The Means of Salvation by al-Sayyid Abul-Hassan al-Isfahani]*) (Tehran: Institute for Compilation and Publication of Imam Khomeini's Work, 2013), article 11, 1:511.

not permitted to openly sin or pretend to sin in the public sphere. Otherwise, they must expect the manifestation of dissatisfaction, verbal warnings or perhaps (following certain conditions) physical confrontation from Muslims. This shows the Lawmaker's emphasis on following the orders of *shari'a* in the public sphere. It also prevents careless and inattentive persons from holding the reins of the public sphere. In any case, in an Islamic society, private affairs within the public sphere are quite limited.

Al-amr bi al-ma'ruf wa al-nahy 'an al-munkar is a powerful level in the hands of Muslims for overseeing and confronting unjust governments, such that as long as Muslims adhere to this principle, it is possible to maintain the health of states, and in case it is forgotten, the fall of states from justice and fairness will be certain. A second aspect of this principle is that it is a good guarantee for maintaining the continuity of Islamic criteria and values among every member of an Islamic society. The sense of responsibility among the pious before other members of society and the uses of appropriate methods for deepening adherence to Islamic principles is among the blessings of this divine principle.

At the same time, one must not forget that in the absence of the exact adherence to the conditions of this religious requirement, it can be easily used as a weapon for inadmissible interference in the private lives of people. Put another way, superficial people can misuse *al-amr bi al-ma'ruf wa al-nahy 'an al-munkar* as a weapon to violate the rights and permitted freedoms of the people. Nonetheless, one cannot forget that the resident of an Islamic society must follow (or, at the very least, must not display their violations of) Islamic teachings. Put another way, Islamic *shari'a* does not tolerate individuals who do not comply with Islamic orders in the public sphere and who insist on explicit rejection of those orders. However, it does assure their freedom in the private sphere even for committing sin and acting against *shari'a* and does not permit investigation into their private affairs.

*The Office of Accountability (*Da'ira al-Hisbah)*

The *da'ira al-hisbah* was one of the institutions of the Islamic state whose duty it was to universalise and expand the proper and prevent the improper in society.[28]

---

28 Abd ar-Rahman ibn Muhammad Ibn Khaldun, *Muqaddimah (The Introduction)*, ed. Abdullah Muhammd al-Darwish (Damascus: Dar Ya'rib, 2004), s. 31 of ch. 3 of Bk 1:1407.

Put more precisely, a *muhtasib* (the director of *da'ira al-hisbah*) is assigned by the Islamic ruler to coordinate the public sphere in accordance with Islamic criteria, meaning that the *muhtasib* prevents the departure from the requirements and prohibitions of *shari'a*. And in cases where it is in the interests of society, the *muhtasib* can require the carrying out of acts that are recommended (*mustahabbat*) or even permitted (*mubahat*) and stop certain things that are deplorable (*makruhat*) and others that are permitted.[29] In fact, the *da'ira al-hisbah* was the institutional form of *al-amr bi al-ma'ruf wa al-nahy 'an al-munkar* which is carried out by the Islamic state in a targeted and orderly manner, rather than being carried out by volunteers in a disorderly way without a plan.

The *da'ira al-hisbah* encompasses the entire public sphere, and includes widespread authorities. It is as extensive as the orders of *shari'a*. It not only covers transactions but also includes matters of worship. The *muhtasib* is not only sensitive to the rights of the people (*haqq al-nas*) and the shared rights between God and people, but is also watchful lest *haqq Allah* (human duty before God) not be violated in the public sphere. The *muhtasib* can remind and even force Muslims to pray, if they have forgotten to do so or have stopped doing so due to inattention. The *muhtasib* may prevent a person who is eating in public during fasting times if that person has no legitimate excuse according to the *shari'a*. The *muhtasib* can make those who appear in the public sphere in clothing that is not befitting of Islamic dignity to observe the minimum religious standards. Similarly, if a merchant over prices goods or withholds from selling, the *muhtasib* can require them to be fair. Even if a person expresses an interpretation of religion that contradicts that which is accepted, then the *muhtasib* has the authority to prevent that person from speaking or writing.[30] The *muhtasib* does not allow the commission of anything forbidden or the departure from what is required in the public sphere. It is the *muhtasib*'s job to be curious in the public realm about the observation of religious criteria and values.

The *muhtasib* and other agents of the office of accountability have – with permission from a judge – the right of immediate prosecution of a number

---

29 Muhammad ibn Muhammad al-Qurashi Ibn Al-Ukhuwwa, *Ma'alim al-Qurba fi Ahkam al-Hisbah* (*Milestones of Proximity in the Rulings of the Enforcement of the Law*), ed. Reuben Levy (Cambridge: Cambridge University Press for the Trustees of the "E. J. W. Gibb Memorial"; London: Luzac, 1938), 22–25.
30 Ibid., 29.

of cases. These are called *ta'zir* and are a part of *ta'zirat* in accordance with *shari'a*. Put another way, the *muhtasib* may use the following levers for cleaning up the public sphere: force the carrying out of requirements, as well as some that are recommended and permitted if it is in the public interest to do so; stop that which is forbidden as well as some things that are deplorable and some that are permitted as long as it is in the public interest to do so; inflict *ta'zir* punishment on offenders and violators such that it is less than the limit of *hadd* (fixed *shar'i* punishment), for example by inflicting monetary penalties, detention and corporal punishment (such as whipping).[31] It is clear that the *muhtasib* does not have the right to transgress against people's private realm and their homes; the inspector is not permitted to inspect, as long as the issue is not linked to the public sphere.

In cases where there is doubt over whether an issue belongs to the private or public sphere, the *muhtasib*'s view becomes the determining standard. For example, suppose a person has invited friends to his or her home and within this private space those friends engage in diversion (*lahw*) and fun (*la'ib*) activities in a way that is not appropriate for the public sphere, does this belong to the private sphere (and therefore inspection into that sphere is forbidden and it is necessary to tolerate the probable sin), or does it belong to the public sphere (and therefore it is necessary to stop the sinners and the wrongdoing?). Another example is the question of whether the space within a person's private transportation vehicle counts as private or not?

The inspection authority is doubtless among the Islamic state's strong levers for purging society of that which is contrary to *shari'a*. Through his representative (the *muhtasib*), the Islamic ruler can organise the public sphere in accordance with the tastes of *shari'a*. Therefore, careless and immoral people will not have the opportunity to assert themselves in public. On the other hand, the *muhtasib*'s boundless authority is a serious threat to the private sphere and it may be used to deny people's freedom to act in the public sphere, including in what apparently pertains to their private and personal affairs. Put another way, the private sphere is almost reduced to the private home, and all of a person's manifest actions outside the home, even if they are completely private and personal, will be considered to be part of the

---

31 Ali ibn Muhammad Al-Mawardi, *Al-Ahkam al-Sultaniyya wa'l-Wilayat al-Diniyya* (*The Ordinances of Government*) (Cairo: Dar al-Hadith, 2006), the discussion of *al-hisbah*, 349–373.

public sphere. Exclusive control over determining this domain will be out of that person's hands, and the Islamic ruler and the *muhtasib* will make such determinations. They will force the person to commit or refrain from actions without the person's consent, and in case of violations, they will punish the person. The *muhtasib* may even limit or deny the freedom of speech.

If a ruler considers the control and expansion of the public sphere to be a duty in accordance with *shari'a*, then the ruler has complete leeway. It is clear that with an active inspection authority, the private sphere becomes very small and is sometimes completely reduced to the private realm of the home. In the conventional Islamic reading, whether in the Sunni or Shi'a traditions, the public sphere is vast and strong and the private realm (outside the private realm of the home) is very small and weak.

The Limits of the Islamic State's Authorities

The amount of the state's authority is in inverse relation to the extent of the private realm and legal freedoms of the people. In a society where the state has absolute authority and the laws have not limited its hand in transgressing against the private sphere of citizens, private life and individual freedoms are extremely small. This problem is not exclusive to religious societies, but is a general problem of all human societies. In totalitarian states and dictator- ships, the private sphere is more threatened than in other kinds of societies and essentially the private sphere has no meaning in these societies.[32] If the religious state also follows the line of a dictatorship or totalitarian state, the private sphere is even more damaged than in other societies, because dic- tators and totalitarian leaders are rulers of the earth rather than of divine Heaven, and create a human hell for their citizens.

In a healthy society, citizens cultivate "civil society" in order to limit the power of the state. One of the signs of a healthy society is the provision of minimum legal boundaries for the private sphere that states may not violate under any circumstances. Critics and those in opposition to states are more vulnerable to transgressions against their private spheres. In religious societ- ies ruled by religious states such as the caliphate (in Sunni societies) and the *Welayat al-faqih* (in Shi'ite societies), reference to public interest is a winning weapon that can be easily used to cut down the private sphere.

---

32 Hannah Arendt, *The Origin of Totalitarianism* (New York: Schocken, 1951).

If the *maslahat al-nizam* (interest of the state) is considered to be more important than the requirements of *shari'a*,[33] it means that the Islamic state even has the right to temporarily violate the orders of *shari'a* if it is in its interests to do so. Thus, if its interests require it, inspecting personal affairs and private lives becomes not only permissible but required. Interest is the catalyst that can turn all copper to gold.[34] Officially recognising the absolute and boundless interests of the state means giving it permission to violate and enter private lives. The authority of states in times of emergency must be determined precisely in the law and a limited time set for the state to use that authority. The state must also be held accountable at the earliest possible time for actions taken. Uninhibited claims of public interest – especially if undertaken by a religious state – are the biggest threat to private life and permitted freedoms.

To prevent the great corruption that can arise from absolute interests, the following must take place. First, stable legal boundaries must be set and officially recognised to determine those absolute rights of all individuals which no state can violate, no matter what the excuse. Second, the exact determination of stable legal boundaries is the prerequisite of these stable legal boundaries; these are boundaries that under no circumstances, in no place or time, by no one and with no interests can be reinterpreted or changed. Third, the institutions that determine public interest must be independent of the state. If it is not separate from the state, religion will be expended for the sake of political power. Determining and interpreting religion and religious interests cannot be the institutionalised responsibility of the state. Otherwise, religion will be in serious danger. Fourth, the institution for determining public interest must be chosen by the people, be accountable before other legal institutions, and be under the supervision of civil society. Lastly, the concentration of power and the granting of absolute authority to one person surely leads to corruption and the violation of religious criteria.[35]

---

33 Mohsen Kadivar, "*Qalamro-e Hokumat-e Dini az Didgah-e Emam Khomeini*" ("The Domain of the Religious State according to Imam Khomeini"), in *Daghdagheh-haye Hokumat-e Dini* (*The Concerns of the Religious State*) (Tehran: Nashr-e Ney, 2000), 111–134.
34 Mohsen Kadivar, "*Rohaniyat, Nabz-e Qodrat va Eksir-e Maslahat-e Nezam*" ("The Clergy, the Pulse of Power, and the Elixir of the State's Interest"), in *Daghdagheha-ye Hokomat-e Dini* (*The Concerns of the Religious State*) (Tehran: Nashr-e Ney, 2000), 560–571.
35 Mohsen Kadivar, "*Hokumat-e Dini va Maslahat*" ("The Religious State and Interest"), in *Daghdagheha-ye Hokomat-e Dini* (*The Concerns of the Religious State*) (Tehran: Nashr-e Ney, 2000), 254–256.

Raising Religious Conscience

It seems that the great reliance on the principle of *al-amr bi al-ma'ruf wa al-nahy 'an al-munkar* (without following its nuances), the predictions of the state's office of accountability (*da'ira al-hisbah*), the absolute authority of the religious state, considering the state's interest to be above all standards of the *shari'a*, have all been carried out with the good intentions of strengthening religion and deepening *shari'a*. Yet these four solutions have been unable to bring about this positive goal. These approaches lead to the domination of the "appearance (*zahir*) of *shari'a*" in society. But as much as believers or the state are able to use force in encouraging the proper and uprooting that which is forbidden, the essence of religiosity and religious faith will have been weakened. Duplicity, discord and pretensions of religiosity are the certain results of forced religion. What is the value of having a public sphere that is in accordance to the *shari'a*, when the private spheres – homes – are contrary to *shari'a*?

Believers do not have responsibilities beyond those of their prophets. The Prophet of Islam was responsible for bringing Islam to the people, not to impose or force it.[36] The principle of *al-amr bi al-ma'ruf wa al-nahy 'an al-munkar* is one of the Prophet's orders of *shari'a* and it must be understood in the context of Islam as a religion of mercy. Its meaning is rooted in creating the foundations and facilitating the execution of the proper and the prevention of the forbidden. The aim of this progressive principle is to persuade those who have left the proper and engage in the forbidden. What is important is that the religious conscience of the society be rebuilt. The abominable act arises from a weak and careless conscience. Forcing the appearance of the religious action without curing the patient's ailment of a religious conscience is not the correct way of solving the problem. God wants his servants to freely choose to have faith and do good.[37] If it were about force, then God would be the one with the right to force it.[38] God did not even permit his

---

36 "The Messenger's duty is only to deliver the message" (Q. 5:99); "There is no compulsion in religion" (Q. 2:256)

37 "Let those who wish to believe in it do so, and let those who wish to reject it do so" (Q. 18:29).

38 "Had your Lord willed, all the people on Earth would have believed. So can you [Prophet] compel people to believe?" (Q. 10:99)

Prophet permission to use force in religion.[39] The condition for the effectiveness of the principle of *al-amr bi al-ma'ruf wa al-nahy 'an al-munkar* is in this nuanced point.

Paying attention to the religiosity of others requires codification in law, a law that officially recognises the minimum stable and unchangeable boundaries of private life. The inspection authority need not be a state institution. The institution can emerge from the people as an institution of civil society. So, as long as it is based on the above-mentioned law, the civil society institution of accountability (*hisbah*) will be defensible and will prevent many social corruptions. An absolute state with interests that are not bound to the stable boundaries of religion is alien to Islamic thought. In *fiqh*, there is a very important principle of caution regarding people's lives (*dima'*), dignities (*a'rad*), honours (*nawamis*) and property as a stable religious minimum. In officially recognising these limits and basing laws upon them, private spheres in Islamic societies will be immune to transgressions by rulers and a particular religious class.

Adhering to such points will lead to the stable balance of private and public spheres in Islamic societies. The roots of this point of equilibrium are found throughout Islamic texts, although over time Muslims seem to have forgotten them. Reaching this point of equilibrium where the private sphere has its healthy function within a religious framework alongside that of the public sphere, is tied to the "new *ijtihad*" and a new look at our Islamic heritage. The author is very optimistic about this approach. May it be that a critical analysis of the challenges of the private sphere in prevailing Islamic thought will lead us to a favourable situation for the private and public spheres in Islamic society, a situation where both the rights of the private and public spheres are respected. God willing, the details of this will be taken up in another piece.

Epilogue

This chapter describes the public and private debate in Islamic culture in its historical context. It raises some questions and concerns about the

---

39 "So [Prophet] warn them: your only task is to give warning, you are not there to control them" (Q. 88:21–22); "If it had been God's will, they would not have done so, but We have not made you their guardian, nor are you their keeper" (Q. 6:107).

historical description and contemporary prescription of this debate. The mainstream understanding of *shari'a* has been that it represents rulings (*ahkam*). However, *shari'a* can also be understood as representing ethical values and moral standards. Rulings or laws are limited to the conditions of time and place and are consequently time-bound. Ethical values and moral standards can be universal and exist beyond the restrictions of time and place, and can therefore be timeless and permanent. Imposing the rulings and legal formulations of the modest socio-economic conditions of the Hijaz in the seventh century on complex modern societies in the twenty-first century is problematic. State law in Muslim-majority countries could be inspired by *shari'a* if understood as Islamic ethical values and moral standards, but *shari'a* understood as rulings and as a major part of state law is a significant misunderstanding.

Although Islamic teachings are not exclusive to individuals and while Muslims without doubt also have public responsibilities and duties, this does not mean that the ideal state in Islam is a theocracy or an Islamic state. Muslims could also run their Islamic public activities in civil society under a democratic secular state. Islamic states or theocracies have been shown to be problematic in both theory and practice.

The traditional understanding of *al-amr bi al-ma'ruf wa al-nahy 'an al-munkar* (enjoining the proper and forbidding the improper) is problematic and paradoxical in terms of major elements of Islamic teachings. Although this dynamic obligation has at least four conditions, the observation of which is not easy for anyone, it unfortunately represents the best weapon for the violation of individual freedom in the public domain. The main way in which this obligation is misunderstood is that it provides religious permission to address an individual in person in order to force them to do what is proper or avoid the improper through sayings or physical actions. The correct meaning of *al-amr bi al-ma'ruf wa al-nahy 'an al-munkar* (enjoining the proper and forbidding the improper) is expanding Islamic values and standards publicly through media and social networks and building a cultural atmosphere that encourages individuals to do what is proper and to avoid the improper without any force, compulsion, conflict or interference at all. Exact implementation of this duty means to do what is proper and to avoid the improper in order for people to follow you as a role-model. This is exactly what the Shi'ite master Shaykh al-Ta'ifah al-Tusi (995–1067) explicitly expressed in his book of *fatwas* titled *al-Nahaya*.⁴⁰

Al-amr bi al-ma'ruf wa al-nahy 'an al-munkar (enjoining the proper and forbidding the improper) is essentially the duty of people versus the state and not vice versa. The office of accountability (*da'irat al-hisbah*) was a medieval institution based on a restricted and incomplete understanding of this duty. *Hisbah* was part of an Islamic state or theocracy, on the one hand, and a legal understanding of *shari'a*, on the other – both of which are problematic. The time of *hisbah* is over.

---

40 Abu Ja'far Muhammad b. al-Hassan al-Tusi, *Al-Nahaya fi Mujarrad al-Fiqh wa al-Fatawa* (*The End in Mere Jurisprudence and Fatwas*) (Beirut: Dar al-Kutub al-'Arabi, 1980), 299–300.

Section Two
Islam and Human Rights

4
Imam Sajjad and the Rights of Mankind[1]

The teachings of the fourth Shi'a Imam, Sajjad 'Ali b. al-Husain Zayn al-'Abidin[2] (48–94 H/658–713 AD), can be considered from two angles. One is from the perspective of practical life (or biography; *sirah*) and one from his scholarship. His scholarly legacy, in turn, can itself be divided into three separate sections. The first is his prayers. To quote the late 'Ali Shariati, "he has the most beautiful soul of a worshipper".[3] The prayer of Abu Hamza Thumali is one of the prayers of this gallant Imam. Some of the prayers of Imam Sajjad have been collected in the *Al-Sahifa al-Sajjadiyya* (*Scripture of Imam Sajjad*). Second is his *Treatise on Rights* (*Resalat al-Huquq*) which is the subject of this chapter. Last are the other narratives of Imam Sajjad which are mostly ethical teachings. This chapter is devoted to the critical analysis of Imam Sajjad's *Treatise on Rights*, which is, in fact, a letter he wrote to one of his companions.

The discussion of the treatise will include the following: first, a brief consideration of the sources of the treatise, assessing the documents of the treatise, determining the most accurate text of the treatise among differing versions, and a general review of the introduction and categorisation of the fifty-one rights listed in the treatise. Following this, the chapter will address

---

1 Kadivar, *Emam-e Sajjad wa Hoquq-e Mardom.*
2 For more information about this Imam, see Zayn al-'Abidin, *The Psalms of Islam*, trans. and Introduction William Chittic (London: Muhammadi Trust, 1988).
3 Shari'ati's sermon in 1972. Ali Shari'ati, "*Zibatarin Rouh-e Parastandeh*" ("The Most Beautiful Soul of a Worshipper"), in *Niyayesh* (*Invocation Prayer*), *Majmou'e Athar* (*Complete Works of Dr. Ali Shari'ati*), vol. 8 (Tehran: Elham, 1991).

the meaning of "rights" in the *Treatise of Rights*. To do so, the chapter will distinguish various terminologies of right in the Qur'an, the hadith as well as in philosophy, theology, ethics and *fiqh*, and compare Imam Sajjad's notion of "right" with the concept as it appears in the philosophy of law, political philosophy and law. Finally, and as an example, the chapter will analyse the section on political rights (*al-huquq al-asasi*), that is, the rights of the sultan and the people (the ruler and the ruled) in relation to one another.

The Sources and Documents of the Treatise on Rights

The oldest sources that have cited the *Treatise on Rights* include: first, Hassan b. Ali b. Hussain b. Shu'ba al-Harrani (d. 991) in *Tuhaf al-'Uqul*[4] (*Masterpieces of the Mind*); second, in three books by Muhammad b. Ali b. Babawaih al-Qummi (823–991), known as al-Shaykh al-Saduq (the truthful scholar), *Man la Yahduruhu al-Faqih*[5] (literally, "for him who is not in the presence of a jurisprudent"), *al-Khisal*[6] (*The Book of Characters*), and *al-Majlis* (*The Book of Meetings*) or *al-Amali*[7] (*The Book of Dictations*); and, lastly, in the book *Makarim al-Akhlaq*[8] (*Nobilities of Character*) by Hasan b. Fadl b. Hasan al-Tabrisi (the son of the compiler of *Majma' al-Bayan*, thirteenth century).

In later compilations of narratives (in the seventeenth and eighteenth centuries), Muhammad Muhsin al-Fayd al-Kashani in *Kitab al-Wafi*[9] and

4 Hassan b. Ali b. Hussain Ibn Shu'ba al-Harrani, *Tuhaf al-'Uqul 'an Al al-Rasul* (*Masterpieces of the Mind in the Reports of the Household of the Prophet*), ed. Hussain al-A'lami (Beirut: al-A'lami, 2002), 182–193.

5 Al-Shaykh Muhammad b. Ali b. Babawaih al-Qummi al-Saduq, *Man la Yahduruhu al-Faqih* (*For Him Who is Not in the Presence of a Jurisprudent*), ed. 'Ali-Akbar al-Ghaffari (Tehran: Maktabat al-Saduq, 1972), chapter on the rights, No. 1, 2:618.

6 Al-Shaykh Muhammad b. Ali b. Babawaih al-Qummi al-Saduq, *al-Khisal* (*The Book of Characters*), ed. 'Ali-Akbar al-Ghaffari (Qom: Islamic Publication Institute, 2013), chapter of 50 and more, No. 1, 2:126.

7 Al-Shaykh Muhammad b. Ali b. Babawaih al-Qummi al-Saduq, *al-Amali* (*The Book of Dictations*) (Qom: Mu'assasat al-Bi'tha, 1996), No. 59, 222.

8 Hasan b. Fadl b. Hasan al-Tabrisi, *Makarim al-Akhlaq* (*Nobilities of Character*), ed. Hussain al-A'lami (Beirut: al-A'lami, 1972), 230.

9 Muhammad Muhsin al-Fayd al-Kashani, *Kitab al-Wafi* (*The Adequate*) (Esfahan: Maktaba al-Imam Amir al-Mu'minin 'Ali al'Aamma, 2009), chapter 108 of *al-iman wa al-kufr*, No. 1, 5:713–719.

al-Hurr al-'Amili in *Wasa'il al-Shi'a*[10] have considered the *Treatise on Rights* to be a part of the hadith collection *Min la Yahduruhu al-Faqih*. However, in *Bihar al-Anwar* Muhammad al-Majlisi has referenced it as part of the hadith collection *Tuhaf al-Uqul*.

Among the five main sources, the *Treatise on Rights* does not have any transmitters (*faqid al-isnad*) in *Tuhaf al-Uqul* and *Makarim al-Akhlaq*. The chain of transmitters in al-'Amili is the same as *Min la Yahduruhu al-Faqih*. Therefore, the treatise has two chains of transmitters in total, one through *al-Khisal* and one through *Man la Yahduruhu al-Faqih*. The direct narrator of the treatise is Thabit b. Dinar, known as Abu Hamzah al-Thumali (d. 767), one of the distinguished companions of the four Imams Sajjad, Baqir, Sadiq and Kazim. 'Ali b. Muhammad b. Mousa in the transmitters of the treatise in *al-Khisal* has not been authorised (*tathiq*). This problem also concerns Jafar b. Muhmmad b. Masrour (one of al-Saduq's masters (*mashayikh*)) in the transmitters of the treatise in *Man la Yahduruhu al-Faqih*. Although al-Saduq recalls him with prayers such as, "may Allah be pleased with him" and "may Allah be merciful to him", neither these prayers (*tarahhum*) nor the *rijali* principle of "the master of the trustworthy is trustworthy" (*mashayikh al-thiqa thiqa*) are accepted as authorisation.[11]

If the *Treatise on Rights* had *fiqhi* content, two chains of transmission would be considered weak.[12] It is important to note that in his book *al-Rijal*, al-Najashi (d. 1058) provided different transmitters for Imam Sajjad's *Treatise on Rights*. The transmitters of this new chain were authorised (*sahih*), except Muhammad b. Fudial who is considered doubtful, between weak and credible. The chain of transmission even in this new way is therefore not authentic.[13] However, al-Najashi has not noted the content of the treatise. In

---

10 Al-Hurr al-'Amili, *Tafsil Wasa'il al-Shi'a*, ch. 3 on *jihad* of the soul, No. 1, 15:72–180.

11 *Treatise on Rights* is a hadith. According to the consensus of scholars of *'ilm al-rijal* (the science of qualifying transmitters of the hadith) all transmitters of the hadith should be qualified as trustworthy (*thiqa*). Although a few *rijali* scholars authorised the masters of al-Saduq according to their prayers (*tarahhum*) and the principle "the master of the trustworthy is trustworthy", these two justifications were not accepted by contemporary scholars of *rijal*, such as Sayyid Abu al-Qasim al-Musawi al-Khu'i (ed.), in *Mu'jam Rijal al-Hadith wa Tafsil Tabaqat al-Ruwat* (*Encyclopaedia of the Hadith Transmitters and their Generations in Details*) (Beirut: Mu'assasa al-Imam al-Khu'i, 1989), 1:74.

12 See al-Khu'i, *Mu'jam Rijal al-Hadith*, 3:166.

13 Ibid., 3:392.

any case, the treatise has a weak chain of transmission in the framework of jurisprudence (*alsina'at al-fiqhiya*).

Determining the Correct Text and Providing an Overview Report of the Substance of the Text

In comparing the primary sources of the treatise, we find that its text is briefest in *Man la Yahduruhu al-Faqih* and that it starts with the phrase "God's Right is greater than you" and without introduction. The text of the treatise in *al-Khisal* is the same as the one that is noted in *Man la Yahduruhu al-Faqih* with the difference that in *al-Khisal* it starts with an introductory overview on rights. There are fifty-one rights under discussion in these two sources. However, in the introduction to *al-Khisal*, the right of *hajj* is not mentioned. The text of the treatise in *Tuhaf al-Uqul* is quite different from that which al-Saduq noted in his three books. While the text in *Tuhaf al-Uqul* has an overview introduction on rights like the one in *al-Khisal*, in general the terms used in *Tuhaf al-Uqul* are explained and expanded upon more and the text is not free from obscure, adulterated, unclear and disgraceful repetitive words, "the reason for which can be attributed to changes by copyists".[14]

Whether in the overall introduction or the discussions in the main text, the number of rights in *Tuhaf al-Uqul* are fifty without mention of the right of *hajj*. Relying on the transmitters of al-Saduq in all three of his works, the untransmitted (*mursal*) nature of the text in *Tuhaf al-Uqul*, the strength of the terms in al-Saduq's version as compared with what appears in *Tuhaf al-Uqul*, circulation of *Man la Yahduruhu al-Faqih*, and the excess material in *Tuhaf al-Uqul* as compared with al-Saduq's version, the narration of al-Saduq, especially his *al-Khisal*, is selected as the most correct one. *The Treatise on Rights* begins with these words: "Know that God Almighty has rights upon you, that surround you, in movement or in calm, in any place or position, in any body part that you move, and in any instrument, that you use. Thus, God's biggest rights upon you are his blessedness and greatness which he made necessary for himself and are the bases of rights. Thus, what

---

14 Seyyed Ja'far Shahidi, *Zendeghani-e Ali b. Hussein* (*The Life of Ali b. Hussein*) (Tehran: Office of Islamic Culture Publications, 1986), 170.

he has made necessary for you, applies to you from head to toe, with all the various organs that you have."

The fifty-one rights under discussion in the treatise are categorised in order as follows:

First, the right of God (right 1).

Second, the rights of self and the rights of the parts of the body: tongue, ear, eye, hand, feet, stomach, private areas (rights 2–9).

Third, the rights of the acts of worship: prayer, hajj, fasting, charity, sacrifice (rights 10–14).

Fourth, the rights of rulers and subjects: the sultan, teacher, landowner, peasant, student, spouse, slave (*mamluk*) (rights 15–21).

Fifth, the rights of the womb: mother, father, child, brother (and sister) (rights 22–25).

Sixth, the rights of others: master (*mawla*), freed slave, good samaritan, muezzin, prayer leader, participant in social gathering (*jalis*), neighbour, friend, partner, loan applicant, companion (*mu'ashir*), the opponent who demands something from you, the opponent from whom you demand something, consultant, adviser, recommender, counsellor, elder, minor, beggar, a person who is begged of, a person who makes you happy, a person who wrongs you, the people of your creed, and the People of the Book (rights 26–34 and 36–51).

Seventh, the rights of property (right 35).

The Five Meanings of "Haqq"

"Right" is one of those terms that are both simple and impossible. Everyone who uses the term in general understands its meaning but explaining it as an end is difficult. Furthermore, referring to its use, on the one hand, in the Qur'an and the Tradition, and in the philosophical, theological, ethical and *fiqhi* texts, on in the other hand, as well as it how it appears in law, philosophy of law and philosophy of politics, shows that "right" has various meanings and idioms. Distinguishing among these meanings and paying attention to the differences in these idioms is necessary in order to avoid mixing meanings and overlapping terms. *Haqq* (right) and its plural, *huquq* (rights), have been used in five different senses and with five different idioms in the above-noted texts. These five meanings are as follows below.

First, *haqq* or "true" fundamentally means conformity and correspondence, correspondence with the requirements of wisdom or belief, promise or action, reality and actual fact (*nafs al-amr*).[15] "Right" is in opposition to that which is futile, erroneous and misguided, and is used to mean that which is permanent in existence and true. For example, one of the beautiful names of God is *Haqq Ta'ala* ("Exalted True"). Here, "*Haqq*" is not used as a genitive construction (*'idafah*) and is the adjective for belief, promise and action.[16] This is how "right" has been used a lot in the language of the Qur'an and philosophical and theological texts: "Do not mix truth with falsehood" (Q. 2:42); "We have sent you [Prophet] with the truth" (Q. 2:119); "The truth is from your Lord" (Q. 1:147); "On that Day the weighing of deeds will be true" (Q. 7:8); "That is God, your Lord, the Truth" (Q. 10:32); "God created the heavens and earth for a true purpose" (Q. 45:22).

Second, *haqq* or "rule" in the second to the fifth meanings is used as a genitive construction (*'idafah*) and here "*haqq*" is a construct state (*mudaf*). In the second meaning of "*haqq*", it has always been attached to God: *haqq Allah*, "*huquq Allah* means something obligatory, necessary".[17] In this genitive construction (*'idafah*), God is the inventor of *haqq* (not the owner of *haqq*), *haqq Allah* means what must be of God, that which has been invented by God and acting upon it is necessary. In this meaning, *haqq Allah* is synonymous with *hukm Allah* (order or rule of God), it is a divine obligation and duty. One has *haqq* (*man lahu alhaqq ya dhawi al-haqq*) and it could be applied to God, humans, things, nature, animals and plants. For example, the right of the mother is the duties that God has determined for mothers, the right of property means the duties that God has determined for the possessions of humans. The use of the term "right" in this regard adds to the terms rule (*hukm*), obligation (*taklif*) or duty (*wazifih*) in that it has also considered the rightful when addressing right. Unlike the first meaning, "right" here is among the mentally posited (*i'tibari*) and the promulgated

---

15 Abu al-Qasim Hussain b. Muhammad al-Raghib al-Isfahani, *Al-Mufradat fi Gharib al-Qur'an* or *Mufradat alfaz al-Qur'an* (*A Dictionary of Qur'anic Terms*), ed. Safwan 'Adnan Dawudi (Damascus: Dar-al-Qalam, 2009), 165.

16 See Muhammad b. Ibrahim al-Qawami Sadr al-din al-Shirazi (Mulla Sadra), *al-Hikmat al-Muta'alyah fi al-Asfar al-'Aqliyya al-'Arba'a* (*The Transcendent Philosophy of the Four Journeys of the Intellect*) (Beirut: Dar Ihya' al-Turath al-'Arabi, 1990), 1:89

17 Fakhr al-Din al-Turayhi, *Majma' al-Bahrain* (*The Confluence of the Two Seas*), ed. Ahmad al-Hussaini (Beirut: Mu'assasa al-Tarikh al-'Arabi, 2007), 3:93.

(*maj'ul*) terms, and eliminating and replacing it with the divine *hukm* does not create any problems. Here "right" contains obligatory and non-obligatory orders, and includes legal and ethical affairs and is not limited to those things which if not practised, will be equivalent with committing a crime or subject to punishment in this world. *Haqq Allah* as such is used abundantly in ethical hadiths and texts.

Third, are *haqq Allah* and *haqq al-nas*. *Khums* (a 20 per cent tax), *zakat*, public endowments and *had* (fixed punishment) paid for adultery and sodomy are examples of *haqq Allah*. Other issues such as marriage, divorce, retaliation in kind (*qisas*), obligation to pay (*dain*), debt, usurpation (*ghasb*), representation (*wikalat*), family linage (*nasab*) and last will are considered *haqq al-nas*.[18] *Haqq* in this meaning is a specific *fiqhi* term in chapters of judgement (*qadha*), testimony (*shahadat*) and fixed punishments (*hudud*). Based on this, claims and conflicts are divided into two types. Those that have a private plaintiff are considered *haqq al-nas* and those cases where there is no private plaintiff and divine orders have been overstepped are considered *haqq Allah*. In some cases, both may be true as in the case of defamation (*qadhf*) and theft punishments.

Haqq al-nas means the ruling which God has promulgated for humans and which he has given to the people to act upon within the framework of *shari'a*. Thus, attaching "right" to the people is attaching right to the rightful and is a possessive grammatical construction. The term "*nas*" is not the plural noun, and does not mean the totality of people, but people individually, not from the public aspect. *Haqq Allah* here means what God has made necessary in society in order for religious criteria to be followed. Put another way, *haqq Allah* is an allusion to *haqq Din Allah* (the rule of God's religion) which can be interpreted as the "public aspect in a religious society". Attaching *haqq* to *Allah* is the genitive construction of right to the rightful and is different from *haqq Allah* in the second sense, which attaches right to the promulgater (*ja'il*) of the right. Between *haqq Allah* and *haqq al-nas* there are differences in the standard of proof in prosecution, number of witnesses, the gender of the witnesses, the manner of confessions, the process of the prosecution, reneging on confessions, the judge's intuition and the pardoning of the convict.

---

18 For example, see Sayyid Abu al-Qasim al-Musawi al-Khu'i, *Mabani Takmilah al-Minhaj* (*The Foundations of the Righteous Platform*) (Najaf: Mu'assasat al-Khu'i al-Islamiyya, 1976), 1:12, 35, 107, 177, 307; and Ayatollah Ruhollah Khomeini, *Tahrir al-Wasilah*, 2:478–480

Whether in *haqq Allah* or *haqq al-nas*, *haqq* is among the legal rules (*al-ahkam al-shar'iya*) whose violation is considered a crime in accordance with *shari'a* and has punishments in this world. While right in the second sense does not have such a contingency, right in the third sense (*haqq Allah* and *haqq al-nas*) has a legal aspect (in the conventional sense used in the legal field) and is not limited to ethical standards. These two are part of Islamic criminal law terminology and are considered to be among the *shar'i* mentally posited (*i'tibarai*) and promulgated (*maj'ul*) terms. Put another way, they are considered to be the *shari'a* rules (*ahkam*). The total of *haqq Allah* and *haqq al-nas* in this sense is more specific (*akhass*) than *haqq Allah* in the previous sense.

Fourth, right (*haqq*) in opposition to the rule (*hukm*). Right as such is a term of *fiqh* and is used in the framework of transactions. The right to property, the right of custody, the right of pre-emption (*shuf'ah*),[19] the right to withdraw a contract (*khiyar* [*al-faskh*]), and the right of priority (*awlawi-yah*)[20] belong to this sense of "right". *Shari'a* declaratory (*wadh'i*) affairs[21] are of two types, they are either right (*haqq*) or ruling (*hukm*). "Right" in the fourth sense has three characteristics: first, it is usable; second, it is transferable; and, third, it can be inherited. However, a declaratory ruling (*al-hukm al-wadh'i*), on the other hand, cannot be omitted (*isqat*), is not transferable, nor can it be inherited.[22] Right in this sense is a type of promulgated *shar'i* (*maj'ul*), and its genitive construction is always one of the explanatory genitive constructions (*al-idhafa al-bayaniya*), that is, a right whose type is of property or custody. Right in this sense is more specific than the previous two. Meaning every right opposite to ruling (*hukm*) (fourth meaning) is *haqq al-nas* (third meaning), but every *haqq al-nas* is not the opposite of a ruling. In the fourth sense, *haqq* is a participant of an external object and benefit. That which is transferable is either an object, benefit or a right. Right

---

19 The right of *shuffa* or pre-emption is a right whereby a party has the first opportunity to buy an asset (immovable shared property) before it is offered to a third party.
20 The right of priority (*haqq al-sabq*) in the use of public places (such as mosques, shrines and gardens), as well as in the restoration of lands, gives priority to a person which others are not allowed to violate.
21 *Shar'i* affairs are two types: injunctive (*taklifi*) and declaratory (*wadh'i*). The former includes five rules: obligatory (*wajib*), prohibited (*haram*), recommended (*mandub*), unfavourable (*makruh*) and permissible (*mubah*). All other *Shar'i* affairs are declaratory (*wadh'i*).
22 For example, see al-Ansari, *Al-Makasib*, 3:8–9, and its commentaries.

in this sense speaks of a kind of attaching and belonging to the rightful and one can consider it among the special *shar'i* rulings with the three noted characteristics.

Fifth, right as opposed to obligation (*taklif*). The right to live, the right to resist injustice, the right to be equal before the law, the right to determine one's own destiny, the right to choose one's religion and beliefs, the right to a fair hearing in court, the right to choose one's occupation and residence, the right to security, the right to freedom, and the right of social security are among the particulars of right in the fifth sense. Previously, these rights were introduced as innate or natural rights. However, over time, they took on a completely secular, declaratory and contractual meaning, and were considered to be necessities that arose from human dignity. These rights transcend particular belief, religion or ideology. The origin of these rights are human and human contracts. Individual and social responsibilities and duties are born of rights. No official or law can take these rights away from people. The meaning of right here is those things which enable the minimum healthy life of a human being. Violation of these is considered a "crime" and one can take the transgressor against this domain to court. It is not correct that the offender of the right is "only" guilty of a religious sin with punishment in the other world. The totality of these rights makes up "legal studies" (*'ilm al-huquq*), which is distinctly different from the study of ethics. The violation of ethical standards does not necessarily have punishments in this world, while the violation of law is a crime and has punishments in this world. In legal studies, philosophy of law and philosophy of politics, whenever "right" is spoken of, it is in this fifth sense. This is the meaning of "right" in "human rights" too.

This sense of "right" has not been used in religious texts. However, based on the fact that most of the particulars of rights in this sense are reasonable (*'uqala'i*), they can be considered to be in the category of those rulings which are endorsed (*imdha'iyyat*) by religion.[23] This is especially the case given that most of the above-mentioned rights not only do not contradict Islamic teachings but also contribute to reaching the lofty goals of religion.

---

23 *Shar'i* rulings are divided into new (*ta'sisiyyah*), which literally means established, and endorsed (*imdha'iyyah*) rulings. The former means that the ruling does not have any background in the other traditions, and is completely innovative. The latter means that the ruling is in approval of or in conformity with the ruling in the previous traditions, either completely or with a little reform.

Claiming divine roots for human rights does not take away from the value of these rights; on the contrary, it increases their practical enforcement. This is because by attaching otherworldly punishment to punishment in this world for the one who violates these rights, and attaching otherworldly rewards to rewards in this world for those who respect these rights, the credibility of these rights is doubled. Elsewhere, I have compared the rights-oriented secular system (neglecting religious obligation) and the religious system oriented on obligation (*taklif*) (neglecting human rights) with the system that is a composite of human rights and religious obligations.[24] Here the goal was only to outline the different meanings of "right" in the contemporary humanities and traditional Islamic literature.

The Meaning of "Right" in the Treatise on Rights

Now is the time to respond to the main question of this section: what is the meaning of "right" in the treatise of Imam Sajjad? Which of the five meanings of right did Imam Sajjad have in mind? It is clear that Imam 'Ali b. Hussein did not present the fifth meaning of right, i.e. right as opposed to obligation (or law as opposed to ethics), or the fourth meaning (rights as opposed to ruling with its three features), or the third meaning (*haqq Allah* or *haqq al-nas* or a combination of *haqq Allah* and *haqq al-nas*), or the first meaning (*haqq* meaning a true belief, word or deed and corresponding to facts, as opposed to being in vain); rather, Imam Sajjad presented the second meaning. Divine rights in this treatise mean divine rulings, duties and obligations, and that which God has made necessary for humans in relation to various things. The rights under discussion in the treatise are not rights in the sense of philosophy or theology (first meaning of right: true), or rights in their dual *fiqhi* meanings, namely, the criminal *fiqhi* term of *haqq Allah* and *haqq al-nas* (third meaning), and the transactional *fiqhi* term of *haqq* as opposed to ruling (*hukm*) (fourth meaning). It is clear that in containing human rights (fifth meaning) the *Treatise on Rights* is not synonymous with it. Rather, this treatise contains the duties according to *shari'a* that a believer has in relation to God, the parts of the body, actions, kin, social classes and his or her property. The term "*haqq*" in the treatise can be turned into ruling

---

24 Mohsen Kadivar, "*Haqq wa taklif dar din*" ("Rights and Obligation in Religion"), in *Daghdagheha-ye Hokumat-e Dini* (*The Concerns of a Religious State*) (Tehran: Nashr-e Ney, 2000), 305–319.

(*hukm*), or duty or obligation without any problem. These *huquq* are not limited to the obligatory duties of the believer but also include those that are non-obligatory (such as recommended).

The rights under discussion are not limited to those rulings whose violation brings punishment in the other world. It is not even limited to those affairs whose violation ends in punishment of *hadd* and *ta'zir* in this world. Rather, the *Treatise on Rights* contains the "ethical duties" of a believer. However, this does not mean that the treatise is free of *fiqhi* obligations. Rather, the point is that the dominant undergirding of the treatise is not one of law or *fiqh*, but is one that is ethical and pedagogical. The rights and ethical duties under consideration in the treatise have been addressed in fragments of the hadiths of other Imams. However, the collection and orderly expression of these rights in one independent treatise is unprecedented.

Here it is necessary to make two points. First, in the *Treatise on Rights* there is no discussion of rights pertaining to the environment, primates, plants, places, times and certain items. These rights have been discussed in fragments in certain hadiths. Therefore, the treatise does not contain all *shari'a* rights, but one can say that the most important of these rights have been addressed. Second, ultimately the treatise has considered each right in brief and does not necessarily address all aspects of each right. For example, the rights of brothers in faith in relation to one another that has been considered extensively in other hadiths are far beyond what has been addressed in this treatise. One can say that some, but not all, aspects of each right have been discussed in the treatise.

Given the determining role of ethical criteria in religious society, the *Treatise on Rights* can play a significant role in generating the ethical conscience of a society of believers. Ethical values and advice will elaborate and deepen the *fiqhi* rulings, and legal principles. We must be sure that without following the nuances presented in Imam Sajjad's treatise, we will never witness a society that would satisfy the Prophet. If we find our society is a stranger to following the fiftyfold rights outlined by Imam Sajjad, we can be sure that we are Muslim and Shi'a in name and appearance only, not in reality and practice. As Imam Sajjad has said: "Beware that the most hated people before God are those who follow the tradition of an Imam without following his actions (in practice)."[25]

---

25 Ibn Shu'ba al-Harrani, *Tuhaf al-'Uqul*, 280.

The Rights of the Ruler and the People in the *Treatise on Rights*

Among the rights mentioned in the *Treatise on Rights* is the "Right of the Ruler over the Ruled" and the "Right of the Ruled in relation to the Ruler":

> The right of the ruler is to know that God has made you a trial (*fitna*) for him, God is testing him through the authority he has given him over you. You should not expose yourself to his anger, for thereby you cast yourself by your own hands into destruction,[26] and become his partner in his sin when he brings evil down upon you.
>
> The right of subjects over whom you rule is to know that they have been your subjects because of their weakness and your strength. Thus, it is incumbent upon you to treat them justly, and to be like a compassionate father to them, to forgive their ignorance, and not rush to punish them, and be thankful for the power that God has bestowed on you.

The ruler under discussion in the treatise is not limited to the Imam and the just ruler. The rulers who must not be angered are the common rulers and leaders of societies. Put another way, Imam Sajjad has considered rulers realistically rather than in an idealistic manner. In the area of the rights of the ruler over the ruled (the ethical duties of the ruled in relation to the ruler), two points have been made. First, the people are the instruments for testing rulers. Rulers are tested with the powers that they have been given. It is the ultimate ignorance for someone to be deceived by the test instruments. Second, the people must do their best not to anger the ruler. This is because disagreeing with the ruler often leads to the people being denied their rights and social benefits. This, too, is a realistic recommendation to the majority of the people who cannot withstand hardships. Not angering the ruler is not the same as appeasement in the face of incorrect policies and passivity in the face of injustice. Negative resistance and *taqiyyah* (dissimulation) are compatible with the above-noted ethical recommendation. In addition, if the state tends to go astray, it is the duty of religious scholars and reformers to follow the same pronouncements and actions of Imam Sajjad's great father

---

26 Allusion to Q. 2:195.

(Imam Hussein).[27] In other words, this right is usual but is not general or permanent.

In the area of the right of the ruled in relation to the ruler (the duties of the ruler in relation to the people), the following is noted in the treatise. First, the fact that you are the ruler and the others the ruled derives from your force and might. It does not necessarily mean that you have merit and are deserving and they are incompetent. All power and strength is from God's formation, and God is to be thanked for granting it. It is clear that this does not that mean that the strength of every unjust ruler and tyrant is legislated by God and that it can be used to justify injustice and determinism. Second, the ruler is obligated to treat his people justly as "justice is the basis for the rule". Third, the ruler must be to his people like a kind father is to his children. He must forgive their mistakes and not rush to punish them. He must be tolerant towards them and refrain from harsh policies. Comparing this part of the *Treatise on Rights* with the corresponding rights of the ruler and the ruled in sermons 34 and 216 of *Nahj al-Balagha*[28] shows that the treatise discussed only some and not all of the rights of the ruler in relation to the ruled or the rights of the ruled in relation to the ruler. Furthermore, these were not even the most important of these rights, but those that were appropriate given the specific audience and circumstances of their time.

Evin Prison, Tehran
March 2000

Epilogue

This chapter is based on one of my first introductory articles towards a critical analysis of the legacy of the Shi'ite Imams. Seven years later, I published an article "The Forgotten Interpretation: Reconstruction of the Theory of Virtuous Scholars (*al-'ulama' al-abrar*); the First Approach of Shi'ite Islam to the 'Principle of Imamate'".[29] I began my examination of the legacy of the

---

27 Uprising against an unjust ruler.
28 Al-Sayyid Muhammad ibn al-Hassan al-Musawi al-Sharif al-Radi, *Nahj al-Balagha*, ed. Subhi Salih (Cairo and Beirut: Dar al-Kutub al-Misriyya and Dar al-Kitab al-Lubnani, 2004), 79, 332–335.
29 Mohsen Kadivar, "*Qara'at-e faramush-shodeh: bazkhvani-ye nazariyyeh-ye 'Ulama-ye Abrar', talaqqi-ye avvaliyye-ye Eslam-e Shi'ite az asl-e emamat*", *Madreseh*, quarterly, Tehran, 1(3) (2006): 92–102.

Imams with an elaboration of the concept of "'right". Can we find principles for human rights in the teachings of the Imams? The best source for this analysis was Imam Sajjad's *Treatise on Rights*.

Haqq has at least two meanings: true and right. The former is an existential and philosophical concept beyond the scope of this chapter. The chapter therefore focuses on the second meaning of "right". *Haqq* or right is a mentally posited concept (*al-mafhum al-i'tibari*). It can be divided into two types according to its origin and domain. Its origin can be religious or secular. In other words, this promulgated (*maj'ul*) concept could be religious (*shar'i*) or secular (*'urfi*).

The Islamic (*shar'i*) concept of "right" is divided into two types: an injunctive ruling (*al-hukm al-taklifi*) and a declaratory affair (*al-amr al-wadh'i*). *Haqq* in the former is always attached to something and has been used in two ways: first, *haqq Allah*, meaning His ruling (*hukm Allah*), both obligatory and non-obligatory. Second, *haqq* is attached to *Allah* and people (*al-nas*) and means "obligatory ruling" (*al-hukm al-ilzami*) in both cases. *Haqq* in reference to a declaratory affair (*al-amr al-wadh'i*) is the opposite of ruling (*hukm*). *Haqq* has three characteristics in this sense. In all three of these *shar'i* uses of *haqq*, it simultaneously means "right" in reference to an injunctive ruling (*al-hukm al-taklifi*), or right in reference to a declaratory affair (*al-amr al-wadh'i*). The secular version of "right" does not have this diversity.

The domains of rights in the secular (*'urfi*) and *shar'i* frameworks are different. In the former, right refers to a human as he or she is human, regardless of anything else. In the latter, the domain of rights is determined by the Lawmaker (*shari'*). Most of these rights are recognised only for believers or Muslims, free persons (not slaves) and usually limited to males.

Besides these two differences, there is common ground between the *shar'i* and secular approaches to "right". There are many specific meanings assigned to the concept of "right" in the *shari'a* that are not considered as such from the secular perspective. There are also a few specific meanings from the secular perspective that are not recognised in the *shari'a*. However, most of those from the secular perspective are acknowledged as "right" in the *shari'a* as well. As such, we should be careful about the meaning, origin and domain of "right" in Islamic texts, as well as their exact differences from modern concepts of right.

This conclusion is crucial for preventing any misunderstandings in discussions about Islam and modernity. It is therefore also the essential introduction to the next chapter.

5

Human Rights and Reformist Islam[1]

Preface

The relationship between human rights and the rulings (*ahkam*) of Islam is among the most important examples of the challenges between modernity and tradition. As one of the most prominent legacies of tradition, what relationship should religion have with human rights, which are among the products of modernity? General and sometimes opaque answers have been given to the question of the relationship between religious rulings and human rights, but none of these responses have indicated all of the conflicting issues, nor have they provided a credible or strong theory to investigate the roots of these conflicts. When an answer is unsuccessful at the stages of "description" and "explanations and delineations", then how can one expect it to provide a functional and theoretically sound solution?

The current interview, which will be printed completely and without summation in two issues due to its importance, was carried out with the aim of taking the first step towards providing a description of the points of conflict and inconsistency between religious rulings and human rights. After inducting these points of conflict, the interview will provide an explanation and analysis of the nature and roots of these conflicts. Providing a solution

---

1 Interview published in *Aftab* bimonthly, Tehran, June 2003, 27:54–59 and August 2003, 28:106–115. The topic of the written interview was "*Hoquq-e Bashar wa Roshanfikri Dini*" (literally: "Human Rights and Religious Intellectual"). I prefer "Human Rights and Reformist Islam".

and prescription for the relationship between human rights and Islamic rulings makes up the final segment of the interview. Due to the lack of necessary sources for researchers, there is an extensive discussion in the descriptive section on these conflicts. The interviewee has attempted to complete this description on two levels. He has first laid out the field of these conflicts and has outlined its examples. He has then pointed to the depth of these conflicts and has shown that they are not limited to those arising between *fatwas* and existing interpretations of religion, but that the appearance of Qur'anic verses and the hadiths mentioned in credible religious texts also reflect this incompatibility.

Based on our research, we could not find these points of conflict in any of the sources on human rights and the rulings of *shari'a* to the extent of the details found in this interview. The emphasis on these details is to gain comprehensive knowledge of the problem, and in order to precisely clarify the subject. It was necessary for these points of conflict to be comprehensively described in detail and categorised so that they could be openly examined in broad daylight without any ambiguity. The analysis of these conflicts, especially by those who have religious attachments, shows a great joint attempt to elevate religious thought and to revive religion in the modern world.

The interviewee is among the defenders of the message of religion in the contemporary world, but with admirable effort he has been able to outline the conflicts between [traditional] religion and human rights as a neutral observer. One must point out that this ability to remain neutral and refrain from judgemental assessment at the stage of explanation and delineation is a serious lesson to be learned from this interview. Thus, in the section on the description of the conflicts one cannot fight any sort of judgement (either about human rights or about the traditional interpretation of Islam). Of course, the interviewee is not without his views or positions, but has intentionally, and for the purpose of maintaining scholarly method, refrained from issuing judgements in this section. Readers must be patient until the end of the interview, when they will receive their reward by reading the interview in its entirety.

In the first section of the interview it will become clear that there is a fundamental conflict between the traditional and conventional interpretation of religion, religious rulings and human rights. Contrary to some superficial responses to the issue, this is a conflict that cannot easily be passed over or dealt with through trivial innovations. We hope that these sorts of interview continue so that innovative thinking about religion deepens and expands in general in our contemporary society. The interviewee is not an unknown figure. As a *mujtahid* (a qualified jurist) who has studied Islamic sciences in the seminary, he is now at the stage of invention (*istinbat*),[2] and as one who has studied philosophy in the modern academy, he is now at the stage of professorship and teaching. With gratitude for his patience and collaboration, we bring your attention to the text of the interview.

Aftab

* * *

Question: it seems that in recent years your attention to human rights has gradually increased: *The Political Rights of People in Islam: The Right to Determine One's Destiny* (1998),[3] *Freedom of Belief and Religion in Islam* (2001)[4] and *The Dilemma of Slavery in Contemporary Islam* (2002).[5] In these articles you have attempted to create a kind of compatibility between Islam and human rights or to present a picture of Islam that is compatible with human rights. There are a lot of questions about this topic, and particularly about your most recent article. Permit me to begin the discussion with this introductory question: did you take up the topic of human rights incidentally and without prior plans or did you do so as part of a "research plan", as was the case with your work on the topic of "political thought in Islam"?

Answer: in around 1989 I began to focus my study and research on the field of political thought in Islam. This research programme has not yet reached its halfway point. I have not even been able to publish what I have written on this subject. It seems that the obstacles to discussion, dialogue and publication in this field increase daily. However, I have not yet lost hope and continue my efforts.

---

2 *Istinbat* (literally, stream forth), or applying *ijtihad*, is the process of extracting theories and principles, on the one hand, and deriving rulings and *fatwas*, on the other, from detailed primary sources (the Qur'an, the Tradition of the Prophet and Imams, the consensus and reason).

3 Mohsen Kadivar, *Hoquq-e Siyasi-e Mardom dar Eslam: Haqq-e Ta'yeen-e Sarnevesht*, in *Daghdagheha-ye Hokumat-e Dini* (*The Concerns of the Religious State*) (Tehran: Nashr-e Ney, 2000), 320–337.

4 Chapter 8, this book.

5 Chapter 12, this book.

The first written nod towards human rights came from the perspective of political thought in Islam. For the fiftieth anniversary of the ratification of the Universal Declaration of Human Rights, there was a gathering in Tehran. I selected the topic of the right to determine one's destiny as an axis of the political rights of people in Islam, and gave an affirmative presentation that did not consider the critiques of past thinkers in this regard.

The heinous murder of dissidents by some security agents in the autumn of 1998 had me constantly thinking. "Religion, Tolerance, and Violence",[6] "The Consequences of Violence of the Right to Live in a Religious Society"[7] and "The Religious Prohibition of Terror",[8] were the titles of three speeches I had presented in objection to the violation of human rights, the last one of which caused my imprisonment.[9] Inevitably, the discussion on the right to live and the prohibition on terror arose, but not from a set plan.

During my last year in prison, I was eventually spurred towards human rights. I suddenly felt that all of my studies on the critique of violence, on the one hand, and human rights, on the other, had become focused on Islamic thought. The assassination attempt on Saeed Hajjarian[10] by the mercenaries of a pressure group[11] in the winter of 1999 increased my research in this area. I went through an entire series of *fiqh*[12] from the perspective of human rights and took notes. I elaborated a lot on the viewpoint of *fuqaha* (jurists) and believers (*mutasharri'in*) on human rights. I also revisited Islamic texts, especially the Qur'an and the hadiths of the Prophet and the Imams, from the perspective of human rights. I read more and wrote less. The article "Imam

6 Mohsen Kadivar, "*Din, Modara va Khoshounat*", in *Daghdagheha-ye Hokumat-e Dini (The Concerns of the Religious State)* (Tehran: Nashr-e Ney, 2000), 859–883.

7 Mohsen Kadivar, "*Payamadha-ye zir-e pa kozashtan-e Haqq-e Hayat dar Jame'e-ye Dini*", in *Daghdagheha-ye Hokumat-e Dini (The Concerns of the Religious State)* (Tehran: Nashr-e Ney, 2000), 823–836.

8 Mohsen Kadivar, "*Hormat-e Shar'i-e Teror*", in *Daghdagheha-ye Hokumat-e Dini (The Concerns of the Religious State)* (Tehran: Nashr-e Ney, 2000), 837–858.

9 For more information, see Mohsen Kadivar, *Baha-ye Azadi: Defa'iyat-e Mohsen Kadivar dar Dadgah-e Vizheh-ye Rohaniat (The Price of Freedom: Kadivar's Defence in the Special Clerical Court)*, ed. Zahra Roodi (Tehran: Nashr-e Ney, 2000).

10 A reformist political strategist, pro-democracy activist member of Tehran's city council, and adviser to President Mohammad Khatami (b. 1953).

11 The terrorist was Saeed 'Asghar (b. 1980 in Shahr-e-Rey) a member of *Basij*, the militia of *Sepah* (the Revolutionary Guard). He was twenty years old at the time of Hajjariyan's assasination.

12 *Fiqh* consists of about fifty parts (called *kitab*) from *tahara* (cleanliness) to *diyat* (blood money).

Sajjad and the Rights of People"[13] (March 2000) is a product of that time. One of the important conclusions of this article is the noteworthy point that the notion of "right" that is used in Imam Sajjad's *Treatise on Rights* and in various other Islamic sources is in the sense of "divine obligation" and the "ethical duty of a person", and is fundamentally different from the term "right" as it is used in the humanities and human rights.

The death sentence on charges of apostasy that my reformist friend Hasan Yousefi Eshkevari[14] received was the main reason I wrote the article "The Freedom of Belief and Religion in Islam and in Human Rights Documents".[15] In this article, in addition to critiquing the death penalty for charges of apostasy in traditional Islam, I presented a new reading of Islam to defend the absolute negation of worldly punishment for converting in religion or belief.

Finally, in mid-2001, the article "From Traditional Islam to Islam as an End in Itself"[16] was completed. I consider this article to be a turning point in my scholarly life. I presented a theory in this article, a model for a research project which I think will solve many of the problems in contemporary Islamic thought. All of my subsequent work is based on this research. As an example, it is worth noting the article "The Dilemma of Slavery in Contemporary Islam"[17] which generated a lot of discussion. This article considers the prohibition of slavery in contemporary times as a primary ruling (*al-hukm al-awwali*) (and not a secondary or state ruling) on the basis of it being unjust and unreasonable. Overall, I have only just begun the discussion on the master project "Islam and Human Rights" and hope to have the opportunity to complete it.

The Six Axes of the Conflict between Traditional Islam[18] and Human Rights

Question: you explicitly stated in your two articles on apostasy and slavery that the traditional reading of Islam is incompatible with human rights regarding these two issues. Is it true that the tension between traditional Islam and human

---

13 Chapter 4, this book.

14 He was born in 1950. For more information, see Ziba Mir-Hosseini and Richard Tapper, *Islam and Democracy in Iran: Eshkevari and the Quest for Reform* (London: I. B. Tauris, 2014).

15 Chapter 8, this book.

16 Chapter 1, this book.

17 Chapter 12, this book.

18 I think the term "traditional Islam" expresses my idea better than "historical Islam".

rights is limited to only these two issues? Is traditional Islam in general incompatible with human rights? Within that framework, can one uphold rights that humans have on the basis of their humanity and independent of their religion, culture, etc.?

Answer: the incompatibility of the traditional readings of Islam with human rights is not limited to slavery or the death penalty for apostasy. The points of conflict are many more than these. To make the discussion more objective and to avoid generalisations, when I speak of human rights, I mean the legal system outlined in the Universal Declaration of Human Rights (UDHR, 1948), and the International Covenant on Economic, Social and Cultural Rights and the International Covenant on Civil and Political Rights (ICCPR, 1966). What I mean by the traditional reading of Islam is the Islam whose main centres of teaching are the University of Al-Azhar for the Sunni and the seminaries of Najaf and Qom for the Shi'a. Their outputs are booklets of *fatwa* such as *al-'Urwah al-Wuthqa, Tahrir al-Wasilah, Minhaj al-Salihin*[19] or *Jawahir al-Kalam* by al-Najafi; *al-Makasib* by al-Ansari; *al-Mughni* by ibn al-Qudama; *Kitab al-Mabsut* by al-Sarakhsi; *Nayl al-Awtar* by al-Shawkani in argumentive jurisprudence.

From the perspective of traditional Islam, the *shar'i* rulings are incompatible with the documents on human rights on several axes. Put another way, in comparing traditional Islam with the criteria of human rights, we see several areas of conflict. There are many offshoots and issues arising from each of these areas, to the extent that even a list of them could make up an entire book. Before any kind of pre-judgement, analysis or search for the roots of the problem, the only option is to present a comparative description of these two legal systems.

Axis One: The Lack of Equality between Muslims and Non-Muslims

In the rulings of traditional Islam, we find an undeniable discrimination among the believers of different religions. From this perspective, humans are divided into three, or rather, four classes. The first class of Muslims are those

---

19 The authors of these three *fatwa* booklets are, respectively, Muhammad Kazim al-Tabataba'i al-Yazdi (1831–1919), Ruhollah Musavi Khomeini (1902–1989) and Abu al-Qasim al-Musawi al-Khu'i (1899–1992).

of the Saved sect (*al-firqa al-najiyah*).²⁰ The second class are the Muslims of other sects. People of the Book such as Christians, Jews and Zoroastrians are considered third class, as long as they have accepted the conditions of protection (*dhimmi*), as well as non-Muslims who have signed treaties with Islamic governments. All other humans, meaning warring non-believers (*al-kafir al-harbi*) who are made up of non-Muslims with no treaties or *dhimma* agreements, are considered fourth-class humans.

First-class humans, meaning those Muslims of the Saved sect, enjoy all of the religious rights accorded by *shari'a*, as well as all the religious privileges. Second-class Muslims, meaning those of other Islamic sects, enjoy most of the rights accorded by *shari'a*, but they are denied some of them as well as many of the religious privileges. Third-class humans, meaning protected (*dhimmi*) People of the Book, enjoy some *shar'i* rights, while unbelievers who have signed treaties with Islamic governments do not enjoy many *shar'i* rights, depending on their treaties. Fourth-class humans, meaning non-believers who do not have *dhimma* status, or who have not signed treaties, are denied almost any rights or sanctity.

These differences based on *shari'a* are among the axioms of *fiqh*. Sheikh Fazlollah Nouri,²¹ who was among the representatives of this way of thought, considered these types of discrimination to be among the necessities of *shari'a*; From this perspective, he ridiculed the notion of egalitarianism and considered it to be contrary to *shari'a*. In his opinion, seeing people as equal and considering differences in denomination and religion to be irrelevant to legal discrimination was equivalent to exiting from traditional Islam.²² These

---

20 There is a controversial hadith attributed to the Prophet that says: "Those who came before you of the People of the Book split into seventy-two sects, and this *ummah* will split into seventy-three: seventy-two in Hell and one in Paradise." Sunni Muslims claimed that the Saved sect was the *jamaa'ah* (main body of Muslims), meaning it was them. However, the Shi'ite Muslims claimed that the saved sect was them.

21 Sheikh Fazlollah Nouri (1843–1909) was a prominent *faqih* in Tehran in his time. Despite his initial sympathy with the Iranian Constitution Movement for its opposition to tyranny and rule of law, he soon turned his back on it when he realised that the movement established a Western-style government with secular law rather than a government with Islamic law. He was executed for treason by Constitutionalists. Nouri is the first example of political Islam in Iran and was admired by Ayatollah Khomeini.

22 Sheykh Fazlollah Nouri, "*Tazkirat al-Ghafil wa Irshad al-Jahil*", in *Rasi'il, I'lamiyeh-ha, Maktoubat wa Rouzname-haye Sheikh Shahid Fazlollah Nouri* (*Treatises, Declarations, Writings and Journals of Martyr Sheikh Fazlollah Nouri*), compiled and ed. Muhammad Turkaman (Tehran: Rasa, 1983), 1:59–60.

legal differences and discriminations can be found aplenty among the books and *fatwa*s of *shari'a*, although I do not recall that these discriminations have been extracted and compiled anywhere in a single place. I will use this opportunity to outline the most important of these four categories of legal difference.

In *shar'i* discussions and *fiqhi* rulings, the term *mu'men* (believer) is different from that of Muslim. A believer is a Muslim who is a believer in the True sect (*al-madhab al-haqq*). Muslims who believe in other sects (*madhahib*) of Islam are called the opposite (*mukhalif*). For example, from the perspective of Shi'ite religious leaders, a believer is a Shi'ite Muslim and a *mukhalif* is a Sunni.[23] To hold religious positions such as ruler (*wilayat al-amr*), source of emulation (*al-marji'ayyat al-diniyah*), judge, witness, Friday and congregational prayer leader (imam), having faith (as defined in each *madhab*) is an additional condition to being Muslim. That is to say, Muslims of other sects do not meet the necessary conditions to serve in the six positions named above. Their testimony is not heard, their judgement is not credible. They cannot be ruler (*wali*), or the leader of the Friday or group prayer. Of course, it is clear that in cases where the sects are the same, the problem does not exist, meaning, for example, that among Sunni Muslims their judgement or testimony would be accepted.

Faith (as defined in each *madhab*) is a condition for those who receive *khums* (20 per cent tax) and *zakat*. Therefore, based on *shari'a*, one cannot make payments from *shari'a* funds to the poor or orphaned of the *mukhalif* (people of other *madhab*s). *Khums* and *zakat* are exclusive to the *mu'min* (true *madhab*) Muslim.

In traditional Islam, the forbidden nature of some sins is not absolute, but relative instead. It is not the case that a particular action is considered a sin no matter who it is carried out against, but it is only a sin when committed against a *true madhab Muslim*, and is permissible when carried out against others. Speaking behind another's back (*ghibah*), uttering falsehoods (*buhtan*), gossip (*namimah*) and defamatory poems (*hija'*) are among these sins. It is forbidden to speak behind a true *madhab* Muslim's back, but it is not a sin to speak behind the back of a Muslim *mukhalif*. That is to say, one

---

23 From a traditional Sunni perspective, Muslim means Sunni (the people of the Sunna and *Jama'ah*), and other Muslims were considered "heterodox", especially the Shi'ite, who were sometimes called *Rafidhis*.

can speak behind the back of Muslims from other sects without fear of the Hereafter. It is a sin to utter falsehoods about a true *madhab* Muslim, but accusing and defaming others is not forbidden nor is it a sin and is permissible. Gossiping and ruining the relations of true *madhab* Muslims is a sin, but ruining the relations of other Muslims is not contrary to *shari'a*. It is forbidden to make fun of a true *madhab* Muslim, but making fun of or ridiculing and defaming other Muslims is not considered a sin. The meaning of the permissibility of speaking behind the back of non-true *madhab* Muslims, to ridicule them, and to utter falsehoods and gossip about them, is that the non-true *madhab* Muslim does not have respect, sanctity or dignity. In the language of *shari'a*, it means that they have no "inviolable dignity" (*al-'irdh al-mutaramah*). People who have "unprotected dignity" (*mahdur al-ihtrim*) lack cultural security. Having permission in accordance with *shari'a* to utter falsehoods is enough to ruin the character of a person. Out of caution, a *mu'mina* woman cannot marry a Muslim man from another sect (*madhab*), as such a marriage would be unfavourable (*makruh*). Paying attention to the above issues leaves no doubt that from a traditional viewpoint the true *madhab* Muslims are considered first-class humans and that Muslims of other sects are considered second class. At least ten legal discriminations can be observed in the *shari'a* between the two.

Legal differences between Muslims and non-Muslims are among the necessities of *shari'a* in traditional Islam. The body of a Muslim is considered to be clean (*tahir*) but the body of an unbeliever is considered as one of the unclean objects (*al-a'yan al-najisah*). This applies to all types of unbelievers, including idolaters, apostates, original unbelievers (*al-kafir al-asli*), protected unbelievers (*al-kafir al-dhimmi*) and People of the Book (non-*dhimmi*). This means that all non-Muslims are absolutely considered unclean (*najis*) and that according to the *shari'a*, this uncleanliness must be avoided.

Being an unbeliever is one of the reasons that marriage to a Muslim is forbidden. A Muslim is absolutely not allowed to marry a non-Muslim (excluding People of the Book). However, a Muslim female cannot marry People of the Book either. Such a marriage is null according to *shari'a*. One of the obstacles to inheritance is being an unbeliever. An unbeliever cannot inherit anything from a Muslim, although a Muslim can inherit from an unbeliever.

One of the conditions for carrying out *qisas* (retaliation in kind), whether it is of the soul (*qisas al-nafs*) or a body part, is belonging to the same religion. Therefore, a Muslim will not be killed for killing an unbeliever, but it is clear that an unbeliever may be killed for murdering a Muslim. Even if an unbeliever kills another unbeliever and the murderer converts to Islam, the avengers of blood will not have the right of *qisas* against the murderer. If a Muslim cuts off the hand of an unbeliever, the victim will not have the right to *qisas* and retaliation in kind.

From a monetary perspective, the value of a Muslim is completely different to that of a non-Muslim. The *diya* (blood money) of a Muslim man is 10,000 dirham. The *diya* of a non-Muslim man of the *dhimma* (a Christian, Jew or Zoroastrian who has accepted the conditions of *dhimmi*) is 800 dirham. People of the Book who have not accepted the conditions of *dhimma*, members of other religions, and unbelievers and idolaters generally do not have *diya*; which means that if someone kills them, the murderer is not subject to revenge (*qisas*) nor does blood money (*diya*) have to be paid. From the point of view of *shariʿa*, these people are not "the holders of sacred life" (*al-nafs al-mohtarama*). Their blood has neither sanctity nor value. It is the religion of truth that creates the value of life. Adhering to false religions and beliefs takes the value from life. The unbeliever is as dead. From a legal perspective they are as the dead, thus they are neither given the right of blood money (*diya*) nor the right of revenge (*qisas*). If someone wants to guarantee his or her life, property, honour or dignity, he or she must convert to the honour of Islam and become a Muslim.

Of course, the People of the Book, such as Christians, Jews and Zoroastrians, will enjoy some rights, such as the right to security of life, property and honour, in an Islamic society once they accept the *dhimma* agreement. The most important condition of the *dhimma* is the payment of *jizya*. *Jizya* is a type of tax that is paid annually by the men of these three religions to the Islamic government. Of course, if the ruler sees fit, he may take more from the people of the *dhimma*. The way in which the *jizya* is paid must be humbling and the people of *dhimma* must always feel lowly. The people of *dhimma* are not allowed to build new churches, synagogues or fire temples in the land of Islam (*dar al-Islam*). If the Islamic state feels endangered by the past temples of the people of the *dhimma*, it may destroy them. The people of the *dhimma* do not have the right to construct their buildings higher than those of Muslims. They have no right to appear contrary to the *shariʿa* in public gatherings. The people of the *dhimma* have no right to prevent their children from attending Islamic meetings. As soon as they violate the terms of the *dhimma*, they will be expelled from Muslim lands. The *dhimma* agreement does not guarantee their dignities (*'irdh*). This means that they are not protected from slander, falsehood, gossip, defamation, insult, deceit, etc. These sort of sins are forbidden only when carried out against Muslims and are not absolute. The *dhimma* agreement is exclusive to the followers of the three recognised religions (People of the Book). Other unbelievers are not allowed to enter into it.

Another difference between Muslims and non-Muslims is the impermissibility of eating the slaughtered animals of non-believers. Muslims can only eat meat that was butchered by a Muslim. This condition holds for hunting on land as well.

One of the punishments stipulated in the *shari'a* is the punishment for falsely accusing someone of adultery (*hadd al-qadhf*). The victim has to be a Muslim for this punishment to apply. In other words, falsely accusing a non-Muslim in this way carries no punishment.

The testimony of a non-Muslim against a Muslim is not heard, just as their verdicts as judges lack legal validity for Muslims. Non-Muslims are different from Muslims not only in life but in death. They cannot be buried in Muslim cemeteries. The prohibition against exhumation only holds for Muslims as well.

Attending to the above points leaves no doubt that Muslims and non-Muslims are totally different in terms of *shari'a* rights and that non-Muslims are denied many rights. Of course, Christians, Jews and Zoroastrians gain access to some important rights, such as that of life and property, once they accept the *dhimma* contract. Even given this, there is no doubt that people of *dhimma* are third-class humans as compared with Muslims and true *madhab* Muslims.

Followers of other religions and creeds, atheists, unbelievers and idolaters can obtain rights similar to those of *dhimma* via two ways. One is through "the assurance of protection contract" (*'aqd al-istiman*), and the other is through a treaty. The former is when a non-Muslim comes to the lands of Islam to learn about Islamic teachings. During that time, he or she is held in security by Muslims and after that, if the person has not accepted Islam, he or she will be returned to his or her lands. Non-believers who enter into a treaty with an Islamic government will have protections in accordance to the terms of that treaty.

However, a non-Muslim who does not have the status of *dhimma*, *istiman* or who has not signed a treaty, which makes up the majority of non-Muslims, is considered a warring unbeliever (*al-kafir al-harbi*) and has no rights.[24] His or her life, property and honour does not have sanctity and in the language of *shari'a* is *hadar* (waste). Waste of blood (*mahdur al-dam*), waste of property (*mahdur al-mal*) and waste of dignity (*mahdur al-'irdh*). If someone assaults them, steals from them, ruins their dignity, takes their life, that person cannot be pursued, there can be no revenge (*qisas*) or blood money (*diya*). These are losses that a person accepts if they do not convert to the religion of the truth, or enter into a treaty (*dhimma*) or assurance of protection (*istiman*) contract. If a person wants to enjoy a minimum of rights, he or she must accept the protection treaty (*dhimma*) or *istiman* conditions, and if that person wants to enjoy the maximum of rights, he or she must convert to the honour of Islam and become Muslim.

It is clear that in traditional Islam "the human in respect of being human", regardless of religion and sect, does not have rights. From this point of view, there is nothing that can be called "essential human rights", or this is certainly very rare. In traditional Islam, religion, sect and belief take precedence over a human being's humanity: tell me what religion and sect you are so I can tell you what rights you have. In the traditional reading of Islam, it is faith and Islam that are the sources of rights, not the humanity of humans. Humans have rights in respect of being Muslims, and do not have rights in an absolute sense. Thus, the human who is an idolater, atheist or an unbeliever is devoid of rights; or there are the humans who are People of the Book and have *dhimma* agreements and who therefore enjoy some rights, but who are still devoid of many. In *shari'a* one can speak of the rights of the Muslim, the true *madhab* Muslim, or at most, the rights of the people of *dhimma*, but what is called "human rights" has no meaning. In traditional Islam we have Muslim rights, not human rights. The rights of Muslims in the *shari'a* are akin to human rights in contemporary thought. Although it does seem that by turning a blind eye to some of the ethical rules, even these rights of the *mu'min* and Muslims are less than human rights.

Based on Article 1 of the UDHR, that "all human beings are born free and equal in dignity and rights", or Article 2 that "Everyone is entitled to

---

24 This is a challenging point. Although these unbelievers did not sign an agreement with Muslims, they have neither fought against Muslims, nor have they driven Muslims out of their homes, and they have not helped others to drive Muslims out. So according to the Qur'an (60:8–9): "the Muslims should deal kindly and justly with them".

all the rights and freedoms set forth in this Declaration without any discrimination particularly because of religion",[25] or Article 3, which says that "Everyone has the right to life, liberty and security of person", or Article 7, which says that "All are equal before the law and are entitled without any discrimination to equal protection of the law. All are entitled to equal protection against any discrimination in violation of this Declaration and against any incitement to such discrimination" – all of these are in open and explicit conflict with the rulings of the *shari'a* in traditional Islam.

In traditional Islam, all people potentially have equal dignity, but are not necessarily born with equal rights. Individual humans have different rights based on their religions. Although true *madhab* Muslims are equal before religious law just as Muslims of different sects are equal before religious law. *Dhimmi* People of the Book are similarly equal before the *dhimma* agreement that they have signed, if their agreements are alike. Others have no rights and are in this sense, of course, equal to one another.

It is noteworthy in the traditional reading of Islam, that non-true *madhab* Muslims or non-Muslims are seen as guilty (*muqassir*), or at most ignorant with shortcomings (*al-jahil al-qasir*), and are deprived of many rights on the basis of this guilt or shortcoming. They are people who have gone astray and who, in addition to the Hereafter, will be punished in this world via loss of some or all social rights.

Axis Two: Inequality between Women and Men

Question: in traditional Islam, are all true *madhab* Muslims, or all Muslims of the same sect, equal before the law? If we neglect religious- and sect-based differences and discriminations, can we speak of equal rights in *shari'a*?

Answer: the answer is negative. In traditional Islam the differences between the rights of humans is not limited to differences in religion and sect. In fact, the second axis of tension between traditional Islam and human rights is the inequality between men and women. Based on this, gender is the second source of legal discrimination in traditional Islam. Of course, this difference

---

25 Article 2: "Everyone is entitled to all the rights and freedoms set forth in this Declaration, without distinction of any kind, such as race, colour, sex, language, religion, political or other opinion, national or social origin, property, birth or other status."

does not apply to all rights. In many of the rulings pertaining to the rights of commerce or worship, men and women are equal. However, from another perspective, in civil and criminal rights, gender is the reason for legal difference. In a few of these cases, this discrimination is to the advantage of women. For example, as long as a woman is obedient to her husband, *nafqa* means the household expenses are the man's responsibility, and even if the woman has financial resources, she has no obligation towards these. In case of separation, too, the woman has no financial obligation to her children, and the father is financially responsible for them until maturity in the case of boys and until marriage in the case of girls. Women are exempt from serving in *jihad* and military war. It is not permitted to kill women on the battlefield. Women of the Book are exempt from having to pay *jizya* to Islamic governments. Women are not required to attend Friday prayers. Unlike a male apostate, a female apostate will not be executed, but will instead be sentenced to prison with hard labour.

However, in numerous cases women have less rights as compared with men. Women are absolutely excluded from five important religious positions. In traditional Islam, being a man is a prerequisite for becoming the source of emulation, a judge, a statesman or ruler, Friday prayer leader or congregational prayer leader (of course, in cases where the worshippers are men). Traditional Islam is of the view that women are not qualified to hold high political office, to be judges or to be religious leaders.

The *diya*, or blood money, of a woman is half that of a man. Based on this perspective, it would not be out of turn to say that a woman is a second-rate creature and is worth only half a man economically. If a Muslim woman is intentionally killed by a Muslim man and the avenger of the victim's blood wants *qisas*, they must first pay the equivalent of the *diya* of the woman to the murderer and then have the *qisas* carried out. In terms of the blood money for body parts too, if the blood money of the body part is more than a third of the blood money for a life, the blood money of the woman's body parts is calculated as half of that of a man's.

In a number of cases, traditional Islam absolutely does not accept the testimony of women in a court of law. This is the case regarding many religious punishments (*al-hudud al-shar'iya*), such as those for waging war against God (*muharaba*),[26] theft, drinking alcohol, falsely accusing someone of adultery

---

26 *Muharib* is an armed robber or gangster. There is no political or religious motive in *muharaba*. It is a crime primarily against the security of citizens and society.

(*qadhf*), sodomy (*liwat*), pandering (*qawwadi*) and lesbianism (*musahiqa*). Women's testimonies are also totally invalid in non-financial disputes, such as those pertaining to consanguinity (*nasab*), Muslim-ness, puberty, invalidating and validating narrators of hadith (*al-jarh wa al-ta'dil*), exemption from revenge (*al-'afw min al-qisas*), identifying the new moon, being a lawyer, last will and testimony, and also in divorce (*talaq*), mutual divorce (*khul'* and *mubarat*), and in the revocation of a divorce. The testimony of dozens of women would not be worth the testimony of two men in these cases. There are also many instances in which women's testimonies are invalid unless a man's testimony is appended to it. This means that the independent and separate testimonies of women are not heard in these cases, including that of marriage, blood money and usurpation, as well as in financial disputes such as those involving mortgages, rent, endowments and financial legacies and debts, and the crime of adultery (*hadd al-zina*) which leads to lashing. Even in instances where, conventionally, the relevant information is at the disposal of women and where women's testimonies are accepted on their own without the appended testimony of a man, testimonies by men are also accepted either separately or as an appendage. These include issues such as birth, fostering, virginity and defects deemed specific to women. Therefore, the testimony of a just man is absolutely heard. But the testimony of a just woman is either totally inadmissible, or it is accepted only if accompanied by that of a man. A woman's testimony is only accepted without a man's appended testimony in four instances. In any case, the testimony of two women is equal to that of one man. This means that in the realm of judicial testimony, a woman's testimony is either worth only half that of a men or their testimony counts for nothing, is worthless and without credibility.

In a marriage contract, although the equal consent of both sides is a prerequisite of the contract's validity – moreover, the woman is considered to be the cause (*moujib*) and the man, the recipient (*qabil*) – in traditional Islam, divorce is in religious terms a one-sided legal act by the man (*al-iqa' al-shar'i*) where a woman's consent, or even knowledge of it, is not relevant.

Whenever a man wills it, he may divorce his wife according to *shari'a*. Even in cases of mutual divorce (*khul'*) where a woman forgoes (*badhl*) the dowry, or even more than that and a woman requests a divorce from a man, carrying out the divorce will ultimately be in the hands of the man. In the case of another type of mutual divorce (*mubarat*), separation also occurs by forgoing all or part of the dowry along with the consent of the husband.

In sum, if a man does not desire it, a woman cannot divorce unless she goes through the *shari'a* judge and proves "distress and hardship" (*al-'usr wa al-haraj al-shar'i*). In traditional Islam, in addition to divorce, a man can even terminate a marriage forever and against his wife's consent by injurious assimilation of wife to mother or sister (*zihar*), abandonment of intercourse via swearing (*ila'*), or solemn imprecation (*li'an*). In terms of defects leading to the annulment (*faskh*) of a marriage (without divorce), again there are differences between men and women. If a woman has leprosy (*judham*), vitiligo (*baras*) or is paralytic (*iq'ad*), a man has the right to annul marriage, but the same defects in a man do not give a woman the same right.

A Muslim woman absolutely does not have the right to marry a non-Muslim man. But a marriage between a Muslim man and women of the Book (Christian, Jews and Zoroastrians) is permissible.[27] It goes without saying that the favourite system for women by nature is monogamy, but in traditional Islam men can simultaneously have four permanent wives and unlimited temporary wives. In addition, a man can have sexual relations with his female slaves without any limitations, but it is clear that any such relation for a woman and her male slave is prohibited without marriage.

In inheritance, the share of the daughter is half that of the son. The share of the wife from a husband, in case there are children, is one-eighth of the bequest (*taraka*). Without children, her share is one-fourth. This is while a husband's share in these same circumstances is one-fourth and one-half of the bequest, respectively. This means that, again, the woman's share is exactly half that of the man. In addition, a wife can only inherit movable property, buildings and trees but not land; this is while a husband inherits everything from his wife whether movable or not. If a husband is the deceased wife's sole heir, he inherits all of his wife's property. However, if the wife is the husband's sole heiress, she only inherits one-fourth of his movable inheritance and buildings and the rest counts as property without heir and goes to the *shari'a* judge. The share of inheritance for a mother as compared with a father is in most cases based on inequity. In cases where the parents are the sole heirs of their children, and where no one objects to this inheritance (*hajib*), the mother receives one-third and the father two-thirds. In cases where there is an obstacle to the inheritance (*hajib*), the mother receives one-sixth and the father five-sixths. These comparisons between the inheritance

---

27 Permanent marriage (Sunnis) and temporal marriage (most Shi'ites).

of the daughter and son, wife and husband, and mother and father, show that women either inherit half of what men inherit or less.

From the perspective of traditional Islam, the age when people are criminally culpable is different for men and women. From the point of view of *shari'a*, the age of puberty is the same as the age of criminal culpability, the age of marriage and the age where worship duties are determined. Based on this, a nine-year-old girl is subject to *hudud* punishments in the same way as an adult, but a fourteen-year-old boy is a minor who is exempt from such responsibility and is treated as a child.

Due to caution, if her father and paternal grandfather are alive, a girl absolutely cannot marry without the permission of at least one of them. This is while a boy does not need any such permission for marriage. Guardianship over minors until the age of puberty belongs to the father and the paternal grandfather. As such, according the *shari'a*, a mother has no right to interfere in affairs pertaining to her child whether they concern finances, criminal issues or marriage, no matter whether before or after the age of puberty. Even in cases where the children's father and paternal grandfather are deceased, the executor of their will (*wasii*) has precedence over the mother in accordance to *shari'a*. If the parents separate, the custodian of boys under two and girls under seven will be the mother if she does not remarry, otherwise the father will have custody.

According to *shari'a*, the man is the head of the household. A wife cannot leave the house without her husband's permission. A woman is obligated to absolutely obey (*tamkin*) her husband and, in the absence of an excuse that is acceptable in *shari'a*, she cannot prevent her husband from having sexual relations with her. However, a man is not obligated to respond to his wife's desires whenever she has them. According to *shari'a*, her right is limited to once every four months. Without her husband's permission, a wife has no right to swear any oaths, just those bound in *shari'a*, since it is not correct for a wife to take a vow (*nadhr*) that may be disagreeable to her husband's rights. A recommended (*istihababi*) fast by a woman is not valid without the permission of her husband or if he forbids it. A woman's seclusion (*i'tikaaf*) is only correct with the permission of her husband. In terms of prayer and fasting during travel, a wife is subordinate to her husband's intention. In cases where a wife does not obey and becomes belligerent (*nashizi*), a husband has the right to beat and discipline (*ta'dib*) her without going to court, with certain conditions. In cases where a man does not carry out his duties as required by *shari'a*, a woman can only go to court to complain about her husband. It is not forbidden by *shari'a* for a husband to curse and speak ill to his wife.

If a person is murdered by his or her father or grandfather, the murderer is exempt from revenge (*qisas*), although he (the murderer) will be sentenced to payment of blood money to the victim's heir. However, if a person is murdered by his or her mother, the murder will not be exempt from *qisas*. If a woman aborts her foetus for unnecessary reasons, she must pay the blood money of her foetus to her husband. In the case of a boy, the blood money of a foetus with a soul is the full amount, but for a girl it is half that amount.

In cases of speculative evidence (*lawth*), an intentional murder is proven on the basis of compurgation (*qasama*), that is, the oath of 50 just men. In case there are not enough men, an individual man may swear more than once. However, as long as there are men who meet the conditions to swear the oath, women are prohibited from doing so.

Consideration of the above points leaves no doubt that from the perspective of traditional Islam, the rights of women are less than those of men in numerous instances, and that traditional Islam has accepted gender discrimination in many cases and does not tolerate the legal equality of men and women. In family law, civil law and judicial law, women are second-rate human beings in accordance with *shari'a*.

Gender discrimination in the orders of *shari'a* are in conflict with Articles 1, 2 and 7 of the UDHR. According to these Articles, all human beings are born with equal rights and dignity, and every person, without discrimination, especially as it pertains to gender, has all the same rights and freedoms. All are equal before the law and have the right to be equally protected by it without any sort of discrimination. In traditional Islam, women are not born with rights and dignity equal to that of men. In many of the *shari'a* rulings, women face legal discrimination. In many instances of family, civil and judicial laws, women and men are unequal. In addition, traditional Islam is in explicit conflict with Article 16 of the UDHR. This Article states that: "men and women are entitled to equal rights as to marriage, during marriage and at its dissolution". In traditional Islam, while men and women are equal in the act of marriage, they are absolutely not equal in their rights during marriage and especially at its dissolution. A woman has less rights during the marriage and in separation she is almost lacking in any rights accorded by the *shari'a* (unless she gains some, but not all, of these rights through means such as conditions set during the marriage contract). In addition, traditional Islam does not accept that "Men and women of full age, without any limitation due to religion, have the right to marry and to found a family."

Article 3 of the ICCPR (1966), ratified by the Iranian parliament in 1975, states that: "The states party to the present covenant undertake to ensure the equal rights of men and women to the enjoyment of all civil and political rights set forth in the present covenant." Article 23 states that: "States party to the present covenant shall take appropriate steps to ensure equality of rights and responsibilities of spouses as to marriage, during marriage and at its dissolution." It is clear that traditional Islam is in obvious conflict with both of these.

In Article 1 of the International Declaration on the Elimination of Discrimination Against Women, ratified by the United Nations General Assembly (UNGA) in 1975, it states that: "Discrimination against women, denying or limiting as it does their equality of rights with men, is fundamentally unjust and constitutes an offence against human dignity." Article 6, in addition to noting the freedom of travel and movement of women, outlines the equal rights of women and men in the marriage contract as well as in its resolution, in addition to the equality of parents in relation to their children. It is clear that the above-noted issues in this international document are unambiguously in conflict with traditional Islam.

One of the latest and most important documents on the human rights of women is the Convention on the Elimination of all Forms of Discrimination Against Women, ratified by the UNGA in 1979. In this convention, the terms of discrimination against women refer to any sort of differentiation, prohibition or limitation based on gender whose goal and result is to damage or cancel the identification, benefit or carrying out of human rights and fundamental freedoms of women, in political, economic, social, cultural, civil or any other arenas regardless of their marital status and based on the equality between men and women. Article 16 of this convention outlines the equal rights and responsibilities of men and women during marriage and separation, in instances relating to children, and in terms of the guardianship and custody of children. Each of the rulings of traditional Islam that is based on the legal differences between women and men is in direct conflict with this convention. It is clear that traditional Islam cannot accept the elimination of all the points of discrimination against women.

In traditional Islam, gender precedes being human. In this system of thought, one cannot speak of the innate rights of humans. Tell me if this person is a woman or a man and then I will tell you that person's rights. In traditional Islam, we have the rights of men and women, but we do not have human rights. In the traditional reading of Islam, the biological and physiological differences between men and women are as self-evident as their legal differences. In traditional Islam, from a legal perspective, men are first-rate humans and women are second-rate humans. Women are humans whose lives cannot flourish without their attachment to a man and their reliance on him. From this perspective, it is therefore natural that women should not be considered in social arenas such as leadership, a judge, a source of emulation, a prayer leader, divorce, guardianship over children, a witness in various instances and in many other areas, such as inheritance, blood money and bearing witness in financial matters, where they count as half a man or as a half a human. In any case, gender discrimination is one of the axioms of *fiqh* in traditional Islam and not only does it not consider this discrimination to be ugly, but it also considers it to be among the natural correlates, innate disposition and perfection of the *shari'a*. However, there is no doubt that the *shari'a* rulings pertaining to gender-based discrimination are in clear conflict with numerous human rights documents.

Axis Three: The Inequality of Slaves versus Free Human Beings

Question: can one say that there is equality among true *madhab* Muslim men in the traditional reading of Islam? Is there in this view legal equality among true *madhab* Muslim women?

Answer: here too the answer is negative. All male Muslims of the same sect are not equal before the law. Similarly, all female Muslims of the same sect are not equal from a legal perspective. In fact, we have reached the third axis of the conflict between traditional Islam and the system of human rights, which is the difference between a free human being and an enslaved person who is property (*'abeed* and *ima'*). On the one hand, traditional Islam has committed to creating and keeping slaves. Second, it has determined different and many fewer rights for the enslaved than the free. Although today slaves in the traditional sense do not exist, traditional Islam is of the view that, given the right circumstances, this auspicious tradition should be revived and its benefits exploited within the framework of the *shari'a*.

Enslaving a human or the reasons for slavery can occur in seven ways, the most important of which is being taken captive in war. If captured men do not obtain their release without exchange or in exchange for captured Muslims, they are considered slaves. The women and children of conquered lands, with certain provisos, are viewed as the spoils of war and as slaves, and all slaves are distributed among the soldiers. The main condition for enslavement in this form is that the captured person must be an infidel. However, the conversion of a slave to Islam does not annul their enslavement. If people are kidnapped from enemy territory (*dar al-harb*) to the territory of Islam (*dar al-Islam*) via abduction, treachery, trickery, pillage or force by civilians or by soldiers but without military force and, on the whole without war, they are viewed as booty and treated as slaves. If infidels at war (*al-kuffar al-harbi*) are willing, for whatever reason, to sell their family members, such as their wives, daughters, sisters or female children, it is permissible to buy them. After they have been bought, they are considered as purchased female slaves. If a father and mother have become slaves via one of the accepted methods, then all of the children born to them when they were enslaved will also be slaves. If a sane, autonomous adult who is an affirmed (*iqrar*) slave, his or her slavery is accepted as long as he or she is not known to be free. A foundling (*laqit*) in war territory (*dar al-harb*) is considered to be a slave in certain circumstances. It is permissible to buy slaves from a non-Muslim market after which the purchased humans are considered legitimate slaves.

In numerous instances, male and female slaves are deprived of the rights accorded to free people, meaning they are generally either deprived of any rights or enjoy very few rights. The slave is the property of his or her owner, and the owner is free to do whatsoever he or she pleases with his or her property based on *shari'a*. The consent of the slave is not required in any of the owner's actions. A slave has to live in accordance with their master's wishes. Without their master's consent, a slave does not have the right of ownership. A slave has no right to choose an occupation that he or she pleases, but is required to do the work that their master has determined. Any money that a slave earns in the course of work goes to their master. Male and female slaves have no right to marry without their owner's consent. For married couples, their marriage becomes nullified without divorce as soon as they are taken as slaves. A man's ownership of a female slave is tantamount to marriage. Thus, any sort of sexual gratification from his female slaves is permitted, even if they are not Muslim. In this sexual relationship the consent of the woman is absolutely not necessary. In obtaining gratification from a slave woman, there is no restriction, unlike in permanent marriage. Similarly, in terms of the number of simultaneous wives permitted. The owner of a female slave can marry her off to someone without her consent. He can even place her at another man's disposal without marriage, even if the other man is his male slave. This action, which is known as "making lawful" (*tahlil*) in the *shari'a*, licenses all forms of sexual gratification. With the permission or an order from their master, it is permitted for a male or female slave to marry a free person. The master even has the right to nullify the marriage of his female and male slaves without divorce.

Once the children of a male and female slave reach the age of maturity, their master can separate them from their parents and sell them. Whether male or female, a *mujtahid* or a commoner, just or unjust, a master can prosecute and sentence his or her slave who has committed an offence without going to a judge or a court, and implement the appropriate religious punishments (*al-hudud al-shari'a*). These punishments are less severe and are half of those of free humans. The blood money for a slave is his or her price as long as it does not surpass the blood money of a free human. If a free human deliberately kills a slave, he or she will not be subject to *qisas*, the murderer only has to pay the price of the slave to the owner. However, if a slave kills a free human deliberately, the blood custodian of the victim is permitted to carry out *qisas* or to enslave him or her. Under certain conditions, a master may inherit from his or her freed slave, but a slave absolutely does not inherit from their master.

According to Articles 1 and 4 of the UDHR and Article 8 of the ICCPR, all people are born free and are equal in dignity and rights, and no one may be kept in slavery – the slave trade is forbidden in any form. Traditional Islam is in direct conflict with human rights documents on slavery. In this reading of Islam, a child whose parents were slaves is born a slave. Slaves have different and far fewer rights than other humans in numerous issues. Being a slave is more lowly than free humans and a bit higher than animals. A slave does not live according to his or her desires, but must absolutely adjust to the desires and requests of their master. A slave performs forced labour, with his or her earnings going to the owner, and his or her marriage and divorce is in the hands of another. In sexual enjoyment, his or her consent is never an issue. If a non-slave kills him or her, the murderer is not subject to *qisas*. Without the owner's permission, he or she cannot partake in rest, leisure, a private life, education or participate in the public sphere.

The incompatibility of traditional Islam with human rights in relation to the discrimination of slaves is so clear that no proof or explanation is necessary. The acceptance of slavery is itself against human rights. One can thus explicitly say that in traditional Islam humans do not have inherent rights. Humans do not have rights on the basis of being human. One cannot therefore speak of human rights in traditional Islam. First say if you are free or a slave and then I will tell you your rights. The free, true *madhab* Muslim man has the highest of rights, then the free, true *madhab* Muslim woman, then the free man of the Book, then the free woman of the Book. Male and female slaves are in the next category and at the very end are the non-believers and the idolaters. In reality, religious rights are firstly and essentially the rights belonging to religion, sect, gender and freedom, and do not belong to humanity and humanness. In this way of thinking we have the rights of the religious, male, female, free and enslaved, but we do not have human rights.

Based on these three aspects, the most important point of human rights, meaning the equality of humans, is scraped away in traditional Islam: once from the aspect of religion and sect; second, from the aspect of gender; and, third, from the aspect of freedom and servitude or freedom and slavery.

Axis Four: Inequality of Commoners and *Fuqaha* in Public Affairs

Question: in traditional Islam, are legal discriminations limited to the three that are based on religion, gender and slavery, or are there are other discrimi-nations based on *shari'a*? In other words, are free, true *madhab* Muslim men equal to one another? Is there legal equality among free, true *madhab* Muslim women? In general, is there a meaningful sense of legal equality in *shari'a*?

Answer: the answer in the private realm is affirmative. Meaning, free, true *madhab* Muslim men are equal to one another in the private sphere. However, in the realm of public affairs, especially in constitutional law, there are two different views among Islamic theologians and jurists. One viewpoint sees special political rights based on *shari'a* for jurists (*fuqaha*), but another view does not officially recognise such special rights for jurists in constitutional law.

Although in relation to specific issues where there is no specific guarantor, such as guardianship of minors without guardians or public endowments, and similar cases which are known as non-litigious (*hisbiya*) affairs, they do recognise jurists (*fuqaha*) as the specific individuals (*al-qadr al-mutayyaqan*) who have precedence in regulating (*awla bi al-tassaruf*) these affairs.[28] However, in the public sphere, specifically as it pertains to political affairs and affairs of constitutional law, it does not assign a privilege and special duty for jurists. According to the second viewpoint, discrimination based on *shari'a* is limited to the three discriminations of religion and sect, gender and slavery. Based on this, free, true *madhab* Muslim men really are equal to one another whether in private or public affairs. Similarly, free, true *madhab* Muslim women enjoy equal legal rights, whether in the private or public sphere. Thus, the second viewpoint is not in conflict with human rights in this respect.

However, the first viewpoint, meaning those who believe in special rights for jurists in the public sphere or, in other words, those who believe in *wilayat-i faqih* based on *shari'a* in the public sphere, suffer from a kind of legal discrimination in human rights. In fact, this is the fourth form of discrimination and conflict between the rulings of traditional Islam and human rights. While there is also precedent in the Sunni tradition for the special rights of jurists and theologians in the public sphere, and the system of the caliphate has, at least theoretically, been based on this, with credible sources such as Mawardi's *al-Ahkam al-Sultaniyya*,[29] which also set knowledge of *ijtihad* as a condition for being a caliph, in practice, this view has not been enacted since the Rashidun Caliphate and has lost credibility. Among the Shi'ite too, this viewpoint is in scholarly terms neither a dominant nor a popular (*mashhur*) standpoint. However, in the last century and a half, despite it being the minority view, it has transformed into a serious viewpoint in practical terms and has become the official driver in Iran. Thus, it appears that its technical analysis in relation to human rights will be useful. In any case, one must not forget that this approach is not the dominant orientation in traditional Islam.

Believing in the special rights of jurisprudents (*fuqaha*) in the public sphere brings politics under the umbrella of *shari'a* and *fiqh* and is based on the thought that *fiqh* and *shari'a* are prerequisites for politics, and that

---

28 In sum: the jurists are the only permissible people for handling these affairs (*hisbiya*) based on the *shari'a*.
29 Al-Mawardi, *al-Ahkam al-Sultaniyya*, ch. 1, s. 2, p. 19.

political leadership is the responsibility of the jurists and scholars of *shari'a*. On this basis, statesmanship, leadership and reigning must all be entrusted to jurists based on *shari'a*, and believers and followers of *shari'a* are obligated to obey them and assist them in this grave task. Based on this perspective, not only are public law, and especially constitutional law, sub-branches of the science of *fiqh*, but also of politics, including the philosophy of politics, the science of politics and realpolitik. However, due to the lack of adequate circumstances, historically these important branches of *fiqh* have not developed very much, although they are potentially very strong and sturdy. From this point of view, *fiqh* is the science for administering all aspects of society and one can expect it to solve political, economic, social, cultural, legal and military dilemmas. As a result, the science of *fiqh* does not remain limited to deriving general rulings from *shari'a*, and issuing variable rulings that are suited to particular times and places, which are among the necessities of politics, realpolitik and policy making, is also included in its agenda. In this view, jurists do not confine themselves to the identification and extraction of general rulings (*al-ahkam al-kulli*), but determining subject (*mawdhou'*) and particular (*misdaq*), which are among the necessities of realpolitik, is also acknowledged as part of the status (*sha'n*) of the jurist. A "*fiqhi* administration" that strives to extract rulings and the subjects that relate to the management of society from religious teachings is different from a "scientific administration" that aims to manage society based on humanities and human experiences. In *fiqhi* administration, all the key positions in society are either in the hands of the jurists or can only be completed with their permission or authorisation.

On the one hand, *fiqhi* administration sees the relationship between the ruler and the people as based on guardianship (*wilaya*), meaning the *wilayat al-faqih* over the people (he does not rule on behalf of the people or as a representative of them). Hence, a corollary of *fiqhi* administration is "a guardian-based state" (*hukuma wila'iyya*). Second, it considers the ruler to be the appointee of God and does not acknowledge his legitimacy via the election by the people. Thus, the other corollary of *fiqhi* administration is known as "appointed state". Third, either the ruling *faqih*'s prerogatives embrace the entire public sphere, but are circumscribed by the primary and secondary rulings of the *shari'a* – this is known as "general guardianship" (*wilaya 'amma*) – or the ruling *faqih*'s prerogatives rest on respect for the system's interests and are higher than the primary and secondary rulings of the *shari'a* and human-made laws – this is known as "absolute guardianship" (*wilaya mutlaqa*), a particular form of absolutist rule.

According to the first aspect ("*wilaya*-based state"), those individuals who have not reached the inspired disposition (*malaka qudsi*) of *ijtihad*, meaning the majority of the people who are considered "the commoners" (*'awam*),[30] are under the rule of the just jurists based on *shari'a*, and are called "wards" (*muwalla 'alayhim*). In the realm of guardianship (*wilayat*), public affairs and politics, inequality holds. In political and social administration, ordinary people (commoners) and just jurists are not equal in the eyes of *shari'a*. Just jurists, the guardians of the people (*awliya'*) based on *shari'a*, have religious prerogatives, abilities and capabilities for running political affairs and for governing society. In all public and political affairs and matters that concern society – especially in delineating guidelines for policies – the people known as "wards" (*muwalla 'alayhim*) lack the required capabilities and qualifications for administration and management, and need a guardian based on *shari'a*. In this view, while the people are capable (*rasheed*) in the arena of private affairs, they are "legally incompetent" (*mahjur*) to run public affairs based on *shari'a*. Any kind of intervention or action by the people in the arena of public affairs requires the permission of the ruling jurist prior to the act, or his authorisation thereafter. Given that people will go astray without the guidance, counsel and the rule of the jurists, and will ignore what is in their interest and make improper decisions under the influence of devils and enemies of Islam, mature wisdom and divine grace requires that in order to make up for the weakness and inability of the masses, they be under the *shari'a*-based supervision of jurists. From this point of view, "there is no difference between the nation's guardian and the guardian of minors in terms of position and responsibility".[31]

As "wards" (*muwalla 'alayhim*), the people have no role in the appointment or dismissal of the ruling jurist. Just jurists have been appointed by the Lawmaker and will be automatically discharged if they lose their qualities of justness or their expertise as a jurist. People either have no right to intervene in public affairs or, if they have rights, they are not able to exercise their rights in this sphere because of their "legal incompetency" (*mahjuriyyat*).

---

30 Opposition to elites (*khawass*) who are the jurist here.
31 Ruhollah Mousavi Khomeini, *Welayat-e Faqih: Hokoumat-e Eslami (The Guardianship of Jurist: Islamic State)*, in *Mawsu'a al-Imam al-Khomeini (Complete Works of Imam Khomeini*, No. 21) (Tehran: Institute for Compilation and Publication of Imam Khomeini's Works, 2013), 51.

As "wards" (*muwalla 'alayhim*), the people do not have the right to intervene in the exercise of guardianship in, or supervision over, jurist-ruler administration either in terms of being kept informed (*istitla'i*) or in terms of approbatory (*istiswabi*) supervision.

The criterion for decision-making in the public sphere is the opinion of the ruling jurist. He is the guardian over the people, and is not the people's representative. Thus, in contrast to the lawyer who should follow the views of his clients, the ruling jurist is not obligated to respect the views of the people in administration. It is the people who must harmonise and fit their actions with his views, not the other way around.

Any kind of intervention by the people in the public sphere is legitimate only if it is accompanied by either the prior permission or the subsequent endorsement of the ruling jurist. Of course, if the ruling jurist sees fit, he can entrust some minor political and social affairs (but not overall policies) to the people, while maintaining the right to approbatory (*istiswabi*) supervision for himself. But even in these instances, the ultimate authority and endorsement rests with the religious ruler. He can, at any stage, modify and alter the decisions of the people's elected representatives in any way he sees fit. The legitimacy of all public institutions rests on their link to the ruling jurist in two ways: either if the operators of public institutions are appointed by the ruling jurist, or if they are run under the approbatory supervision of the representatives of the ruling jurist. The people are duty-bound to convey to the ruling jurist – in a way that does not lend itself to exploitation by the enemies of Islam, that is, confidentially – any information at their disposal that relates in some way to the public sphere, and they must rest assured that the ruling jurist recognises the interests of the people better than they do themselves.

The religious guardianship (*wilayat* based in *shari'a*) over the people is compelling (*qahri*) and not by choice. This means that the jurists, whether they want to or not, are obligated by the sacred Lawmaker to take charge of public affairs. The people, for their part, are duty-bound to pledge allegiance to the ruling jurist, which is also obligatory. Pledging allegiance to the religious guardian is to declare that you accept their guardianship; otherwise, the people's acceptance or non-acceptance has no bearing on the fact of guardianship affirmation. The duty to pledge allegiance and declare obedience (*tawwali*) is different from the right to choose and elect. In the right to elect, the people can elect whomever they want. However, in pledging allegiance and its declaration of obedience, the people are duty-bound to accept the *wilayat-i faqih*, and in case they fail to do so, they are sinners. The jurist's guardianship over the people is permanent and lifelong, not temporary. As long as the religious conditions are met, the guardianship continues.

The *shari'a*-based guardian of jurists is just in a universal sense, which means that it applies to all the people of the world regardless of gender, colour, race, nationality, religion and sect. This guardianship is not limited by geographical borders, and all the people of the world, not only Muslims and Shi'ites, are obliged to obey him as a "man in charge (*wali amr*) of the world's Muslims". The jurists are independent in exercising their guardianship and do not need to receive the permission of anyone, including the people. The guardianship of jurists is not a contract and so it cannot be circumscribed through the stipulation of conditions in the contract, such as respect for the constitution. In its scope, this guardianship is subject to religious criteria, not to the consent, wishes and will of the people.

The *shari'a*-based guardianship of the jurist over the people is only compatible with having been appointed by the divine Lawgiver. Guardianship cannot be based on election. Women lack the authority to be religious guardians. In other words, women are not qualified to occupy the religious post of the people's guardian, even if they have attained a high degree of just expertise in Islamic jurisprudence (*ijtihad*). The ruling jurist is required by *shari'a* to act in the public sphere in accordance with the interests of the people. Of course, the authority that identifies the people's interests is the ruling jurist himself or his appointees. The guardianship of jurists over the people is a sacred position.[32] In any case, a guardian-based state means a state that is in charge of society's public affairs on behalf of the Lawgiver, not on behalf of the people, not as a representative of the people and not on the basis of a contract with the people. It is appointed, not elected. The idea that the people are "legally incompetent" (*mahjur*) in public affairs is integral to the guardian-based state.

Concerning the second point, that is, an appointive state, it has to be said that an appointment is a kind of kingly creation (*insha'*), a governmental

---

32 I have provided a detailed account of the discussions relating to guardianship and appointment in my books *Hokumat-e Wela'i* (*Governace by Guardianship*), vol. 2, and *Hokumat-e Entesabi* (*Appointive/Non-Elective State*), vol. 3, Political Thought in [Shi'ite] Islam series (Tehran: Nashr-e Ney, 2008).

decree that is issued from on high for running affairs down below. On this basis, the only legitimate religious state is a state that is appointed by God. The non-appointed state is tyrannical (*taghout*), illegitimate and idolatrous. Given that according to this viewpoint, people, first, do not recognise what is good or evil and are incapable of discerning their own true interests, second, are easily influenced by devils, tricked and led astray, and, third, that the sphere of public affairs is God's due (*haqq Allah*), and not the people's due (*haqq al-nas*), the people must entrust this sphere to those who are competent; that is, to jurists appointed by the Lawgiver. Appointment by the Lawgiver cannot be combined with election by the people. Election is appropriate when the people can freely elect or not elect someone; or accept or not accept a policy. If a particular person or class has been appointed in advance to exercise guardianship over the people, there is no room left for election.

Concerning the third point, that is, "absolute" government, the ruling jurist is above the law. In general, the legitimacy of the constitution and ordinary laws basically emanates from his endorsement, derives from his will and is validated through his authorisation. An underling can never circumscribe and restrict the superior. The ruling jurist is not accountable to any human institute. It is the people who must harmonise themselves with the ruling jurist, it is not the ruling jurist who is duty-bound to harmonise himself with public opinion or national will. The votes of the people, in case the Guardian Jurist does not accept them, are worthless and without religious validity.

In sum, the state that is favoured by this viewpoint is jurist aristocracy, jurist reign or religious kingship. By analogy with Plato's philosopher king, we can speak in this context of a "jurist king" or the kingship of the jurists. Of course, in states like these, the required condition of expertise (of being a jurist and *mujtahid*) is rapidly diluted and it turns into a kind of rule by clerics or a clerical state. This does not really affect our discussion, since the point of concern for us is "a special political right" for a particular profession, be it philosophers, jurists or clerics. This is the problematic point that conflicts with human rights.

According to Articles 1, 2 and 7 of the UDHR, "All people are equal in rights and dignity and all can enjoy all the rights and freedoms without discrimination, all people are equal before the law." According to Article 21 of this international declaration, "Everyone has the right of equal access to public service in his country. The will of the people shall be the basis of the authority of government; this will shall be expressed in periodic and genuine elections which shall be by universal and equal suffrage and shall be held by secret vote or by equivalent free voting procedures." In Article 25 of the ICCPR, it says that, "Every citizen shall have the right and opportunity without discrimination . . . to participate in public affairs directly or via freely chosen representatives, and to vote and to elect in genuine periodic elections which shall be by universal and equal suffrage . . . to have access on general terms of equality to public service in his country." According to Article 26 of this international covenant, "all persons are equal before the law . . . in this respect, the law shall prohibit any discrimination".

Accepting a special right for jurists and clerics in the public sphere or the theory of an absolute, appointed, guardian state run by jurists or the clergy is in conflict with human rights. This conflict can be summarised in the points below:

First, inequality between jurists and clerics and the people in the sphere of public affairs; second, guardianship and leadership are the special right of a particular strata, that is, jurists or clerics; third, the sphere of public affairs is not the people's due (*haqq al-nas*), or the right of the people, but is God's due (*haqq Allah*), or the right of God, and whose management has been vouchsafed by God to jurists; fourth, guardianship and leadership is not chosen by public election, but is determined (*ta'yeen*), discovered (*kashf*) or recognised (*tashkhis*) by a particular strata, that is, jurists or clerics; fifth, guardianship and leadership is a post for life and is not temporary or periodic; sixth, the approbatory supervision of the appointees of the ruling jurist over the representatives of the people is a correlation of such a state; seventh, the guardian or ruler is not accountable to any human institution; eighth, the guardian and ruler is above the law and all public institutions and laws obtain their legitimacy from him; ninth, the opinion of the ruling jurist or that of his appointees is above that of the people; tenth, the ruling jurist or his appointees have a right of veto in all public affairs.

The special rights of jurists or clerics in public affairs and the theory of an absolute, appointed, guardian state run by jurists or the clergy are in obvious conflict with the notion of human rights. People who believe in these special clerical rights and in this kind of state cannot accept the system of human rights. Their two beliefs allow them to reject human rights. Based on this, it is clear that human rights are cancelled in this view, and one must speak separately of the rights of clerics and jurists, on the one hand, and the rights of the masses and commoners, on the other. First tell me whether you are a jurist or a commoner and then I will tell you what rights you have. Yes, the masses and commoners, with attention to the previous three forms of discrimination, have equal rights.

Based on this important point, legal equality, which is the cornerstone of human rights, is violated on four counts by traditional Islam: first, the legal discrimination between a Muslim and a non-Muslim, as well as between believers in a particular sect of Islam and the believers of other sects of Islam; second, legal discrimination between men and women; third, legal discrimination between free people and slaves; fourth, discrimination in the realm of public affairs between jurists and non-jurists. Traditional Islam is based on legal discrimination in these four arenas and is in conflict with human rights. Of course, the former is based on a minority view in traditional Islam and is not accepted by all the adherents of this reading of Islam.

Axis Five: Freedom of Belief and Religion and the Punishment for Apostasy

Question: based on what you have said, traditional Islam cannot accept the equality of humans and, given its recognition of the four forms of legal discrimination, it is in conflict with the notion of human rights. Does this reading of Islam have any other conflicts with human rights other than its violation of the fundamental point of equality?

Answer: the answer is affirmative. In fact, the fifth axis of the conflict between traditional Islam and the notion of human rights is the freedom of belief, religion and speech. Articles 18 and 19 of the UDHR and Articles 18 and 19 of the ICCPR, state that:

Everyone has the right of freedom of thought, conscience, and religion. This right includes the right to change one's religion and belief and also includes the freedom to express one's beliefs and religion and also includes religious education and carrying out religious ceremonies. Everyone has this right as an individual or as a group either privately or publicly. Everyone has the freedom of belief and expression and the aforementioned right includes that one need not have fear for having one's beliefs and to be free without geographical constraint to gain information and to publish and have access to all necessary instruments for doing so.

Given the legal discrimination among Muslims, the People of the Book and others, it seems that the issue of freedom of religion in the above three cases can be considered. In the first area, meaning Muslims, although they have the most religious freedoms, in many instances their religious freedoms are limited and in this sense their human rights have been violated. I will point to the most important of these.

First, Muslims are not free to change their religion, whether it be to another religion like Christianity or Buddhism, or whether to unbelief or atheism. The apostate is severely punished. The *fitri* apostate[33] is executed, his wife becomes forbidden to him, his property is divided among his heirs. The *milli* apostate[34] is allowed three days to repent, on the fourth day he has the same sentence of death, his wife is made forbidden to him and his property is divided. For a Muslim woman who becomes an apostate, her husband becomes forbidden to her, and if she does not repent she will be sentenced to imprisonment with hard labour until she repents or dies in prison.

Second, Muslims are not free to theoretically deny matters that are considered by contemporary experts to be part of Islam. If a Muslim denies something that is considered to be an essential element of religion on the basis of contemporary convention – and is thereby equivalent to denying the Prophet's mission, rejecting the Prophet or diminishing the *shari'a* – he or she will be considered an apostate, even if he or she considers him- or herself to be a Muslim, and the sentences for apostasy will apply.

Third, an adolescent with parents one or both of whom is Muslim, is not free after maturity to choose a religion other than Islam. If for whatever reason he or she does not choose Islam, the sentence for a *milli* apostate will be carried out against him or her (execution for a boy and imprisonment and hard labour for a girl).

Fourth, Muslims are not free to ignore religious obligations or to carry out religious prohibitions. If they do so knowingly and deliberately, they will be sentenced to punishment at the judge's discretion (*ta'zir*), such as lashes.

---

33 Literally, renouncing the first nature (*fitra*). *Fitri* apostate is someone whose parents, one or both of whom were Muslim when he or she was born, and he or she was also a Muslim, until after having reached puberty, that person converted to being a non-Muslim.

34 Literally, an apostate from the community (*milla*). *Milli* apostate is an apostate who is not a *fitri*. In other words, a person who was born of a non-Muslim parent, converted to Islam, and later rejected the religion.

Fifth, Muslims believing in other Islamic denominations are not permitted to preach their beliefs among true *madhab* Muslims. For example, Sunni Muslims are not permitted to preach their denomination (*madhab*) among the Shi'ite and vice versa.[35] Hence, in a land where one of the denominations is dominant, Muslims of other denominations are not permitted to have their own mosques or buildings.[36]

The traditional reading of Islam on the people of *dhimma*, that is, Christians, Jews and Zoroastrians who have accepted the protection (*dhimmi*) contract, has a number of conflicts with the freedom of belief and religion, such as: first, the people of *dhimma* are not free to raise their children in a way that will encourage them to follow their fathers' religion, meaning they cannot forbid them from attending Islamic preaching centres and meetings. Rather, they are obligated to leave their children free to choose their own way, it being clear that they will choose Islam as it is the religion of *fitra* (first nature). Second, the people of *dhimma* are not free to build churches, synagogues, monasteries or fire temples. Third, the people of *dhimma* are not free to preach or spread their religion and to weaken the beliefs of Muslims. The dissemination of their views is considered to amount to leading people astray and is forbidden. Fourth, the people of *dhimma* are *a fortiori* not free to critique Islamic teachings. Fifth, the people of *dhimma* are not free to openly perform acts which are permitted in their religion but forbidden in Islam. Sixth, other than converting to Islam, the people of *dhimma* are not free to convert to any other religions or they will be killed.[37]

From the perspective of traditional Islam, non-Muslims who have failed to enter into either a *dhimma* contract (which is for People of the Book), or a treaty with a Muslim state, are counted as warring infidels (*kafir harbi*). Islam must be presented to them, and if they do not accept, *jihad* will be carried out and will continue until they either accept Islam, enter into

---

35 However, when one of these two main Islamic *madhab*s are in the majority and in power, it is in practice permissible to preach their *madhab* among the fellows of the other *madhab*.

36 There is no theoretical evidence for this case. Indeed, in practice see, for example, the policy of Saudi Arabia on Shi'ite mosques in the big Sunni-majority cities, and the Islamic Republic of Iran's policy on Sunni mosques in the big Shi'ite-majority cities.

37 The other opinions in this case, are that the people of *dhimma* are free to convert to any religions which are allowed in their traditions, or from one of these three recognised religions to another, as well as Islam in both opinions, but that they will be killed if they convert to any religion other than those which are allowed in their tradition or than these three.

dhimma contract or treaty, are killed or are taken captive. These types of people basically do not have the right to life, so they can hardly have the freedom of belief and religion.

In any case, in the face of the dominance and expansion of the traditionalist reading of Islam, the freedom of belief and religion is almost negated. The fact that traditional Islam does not tolerate the freedom of belief and religion seems to be beyond dispute. From this point of view, the publication of books and articles that promote ideas or opinions that are anti-Islamic or have been written to critique or deny the views and teachings of Islam, are considered as an effort to lead people astray (*kutub dhalal*), and their publication, distribution or possession for safekeeping is forbidden and a sin. Other cultural products such as films, paintings, cartoons, speeches, the internet, satellites and others are also included in this.

In its political dimension, the freedom of expression in a state based on special rights for jurists and clerics will be subject to multiple limitations. All in all, in these types of religious states, the freedom of speech, the freedom of expression, and the freedom of belief and religion are null and void. The violation of the freedom of belief and religion, speech and expression in the traditional reading of Islam is out of the question. The traditional reading of Islam sees such freedoms as being in direct contradiction with religiosity and the upholding of the *shari'a*, and in order to safeguard people's faith, it will easily issue *fatwa*s to violate or threaten these types of freedom.

Axis Six: Arbitrary Punishments, Harsh Punishments and Torture

Question: other than the four types of legal discrimination and the violation of the freedom of belief and religion, can one say that traditional Islam does not have any other issues with human rights? Or are there other areas of conflict?

Answer: so far, five axes of conflict between traditional Islam and human rights have been highlighted, but they are not exhaustive. The sixth axis is the violent and degrading punishments of the *shari'a*. In fact, the problem concerning this is criminal law in traditional Islam. Article 5 of the UDHR states that: "no one can be subject to torture, or to cruel, inhuman, or degrading treatment or punishment". Article 6 of the ICCPR considers that "every human being has the inherent right to life . . . No one shall be arbitrarily deprived of his life . . . Sentence of death may be imposed only for the most serious crimes in accordance with the law . . . This penalty can only be carried out pursuant to a final judgment rendered by a competent court . . . Sentence of death shall not be imposed for crimes committed by persons below eighteen years." Article 7 states: "No one shall be subjected to torture or to cruel, inhuman or degrading treatment or punishment." One of the most important international documents in this regard is the Convention against Torture and Other Cruel, Inhuman or Degrading Treatment or Punishment, ratified in 1984, which has meticulously defined torture.

In traditional *fiqh* (Islamic jurisprudence), some of the punishments stipulated in the *shari'a* can be carried out by any Muslim adult (*mukallaf*) based on their own judgement and without recourse to a judge or a court. It is even possible for a death sentence to be carried out as a religious duty. One of the conditions of death as blood-vengeance (*qisas al-nafs*), is that the victim's blood must have esteem; that is, blood-protected (*mahgoun al-dam*), not deserving death (*mahdur al-dam*) or someone whose life is of no worth.

Based on this, the *fitri* apostate, someone who insults the Prophet (*sabb al-nabi*) or who pretends to be a prophet, may be killed without the need for proof in a fair court, or the right to self-defence by the accused, or the right to have an attorney, or a jury's verdict or other similar formal procedures. In the case of a permissible killing, the *qisas* does not apply. The same rule applies to the killing of a person who deserves to be put to death in accordance with *qisas* (of course, with the permission of the avenger of the blood), or subject to the *hadd* punishment of execution. If someone kills such a person on the assumption that his life is of no worth, the killer does not risk being put to death as *qisas*. If a man sees his wife in bed with another he is permitted to kill them both.

One of the elements of the general obligation of *al-amr bi al-ma'ruf wa al-nahy 'an al-munkar* (enjoining good and forbidding wrong), is to inhibit evil-doers practically through physical attacks. Although, in the opinion of most jurists, killing an evil-doer is only allowed with the formal permission of a *mujtahid* and believers are not allowed to go this far on the basis of their own judgement. However, some jurists consider it permissible for the evil-doer to be injured in the process of being inhibited. Jurists are also collectively of the view that formal permission is not required for the beating of an evil-doer. In the same way, a husband beating a disobedient wife is permitted and does not need judicial permission. Some jurists have even expressed the verdict that it is permissible to administer discretionary punishments (*ta'zir*) (based on the rulings of judges) to wives and slaves. There is no doubt that based on the norms of human rights, any kind of beating or injury would require judicial authorisation and can only be carried out by judicial authorities. Giving ordinary individuals a free hand to do this is viewed as a violation of human rights. It is clear that the punishment of execution can never be carried out outside the courts and without going through the judicial system or without the threefold stages of the trial, appeals and endorsement by the supreme court. Allowing ordinary individuals to carry out executions is in direct conflict with the norms of human rights.

Today, punishments such as throwing offenders into a fire, throwing them from the top of a mountain or from a high place with their feet and hands tied, stabbing them with a sword and then throwing them into a fire, stoning them, subjecting them to prison with hard labour, or harsh treatment such as beating them at the time of ritual prayers or restricting their food and water, nailing them to a cross, cutting off their right arm and their left leg, or cutting off four of their fingers, or flogging, are considered to be cruel, inhuman and degrading punishments. Hence, all the sentences (*al-hudud al-shar'iya*) that demand the implementation of these afore-mentioned punishments are considered to be violations of human rights. The purpose of including these harsh punishments in the *shari'a* was to eradicate serious crime. But the notion of human rights is moving in the following directions: first, to completely eliminate physical and bodily punishments; second, the death sentence is likely to be severely restricted and gradually eliminated; and, third, violent forms of the death sentence and harsh punishments in general are likely to be eliminated. On this basis, all the punishments stipulated in the *shari'a*, that is, *hudud* and the discretionary punishment (*ta'zir*) of lashes, will be in violation of human rights norms.

The third point within this area of conflict consists of the discretionary punishments (*al-ta'zir al-shar'i*) for extracting information from a suspect, or for breaking his resistance or for making him cooperate with the judge. Human rights thinking views any kind of physical or psychological pressure on a suspect – even by authorised agents – aimed at extracting information and the like as "torture" and the Convention against Torture has been approved precisely to prevent these kinds of action.

It is clear that the penal law of traditional Islam conflicts with the notion of human rights on at least three counts: arbitrary punishments, harsh punishments and torture. The free hand that judges have with some *shari'a* punishments and variations in sentencing, ranging from one year in exile to crucifixion or killing, is another flaw of traditional Islam from the perspective of human rights.

It seems that the main axes of the conflict between human rights and traditional Islam are these six discussed above. Although *jihad*, children's rights and labour rights are other potentially problematic areas, elaborating on these would overly lengthen our discussion here. So far, I have attempted to compare two legal regimes, that is, that of traditional Islam and human rights. The treatment has been descriptive only, that is, a technical account without passing judgement, evaluation or taking sides. I have no doubt that a description of these six areas has been enough to show that traditional Islam conflicts with human rights. As to whether this conflict is good or bad, how it can be resolved, and whether it is even necessary to strive to resolve it – this is a separate matter.

The Depth of the Conflict between Traditional Islam and Human Rights

Question: are the *shari'a*-based rulings that you outlined the rare and odd opinions of some traditional jurists, or is it the conventional, unanimous and consensual view of traditional Islam?

Answer: the conflict between one or two rare or odd opinions and human rights is not a problem, but the conflict between the conventional or consensual or agreed-upon view of traditional Islam and human rights is seriously problematic.

The *shari'a*-based rulings that are in conflict with human rights along the six axes described above are not rare or odd opinions of unknown jurists. The overwhelming majority of these views are the mainstream (*mashhur*) (or at least mainstream in our time). Of course, among these mainstream views, agreed-upon, or even so-called consensual views are not few. Many of these views are the agreed-upon views of traditional jurists. Some of these are consensual. Of course, consensual does not mean the absence of dissenting views. Diversity in opinions is the conventional common ground of *fiqh*. In any case, *shari'a*-based rulings that are in conflict with human rights in traditional Islam are views that are mainstream, agreed-upon, and in many cases are either so-called consensual or are actually consensual; traditional Islam is these very rulings, nothing else.

Question: was this conflict because of the particular mentality of the theologians, jurists and *shari'a* followers, or did it arise from religious sources? For example, does one find documentation in the hadiths of the Prophet and the Imams for these conflicts with human rights?

Answer: if you mean that the scholars of traditional Islam knowingly and intentionally expressed a view that was contrary to human rights norms, that is not correct. Generally, in the course of deducing these rulings of *shari'a*, such matters were not taken into account, either for or against. Of course, it is undeniable that a jurist's specific understanding of humans and their rights will impact his *fatwas*. But to be fair, the sin of conflict with human rights norms, if it is a sin – sin in the sense of a conventional sin and not a religious one – cannot be merely blamed on jurists and theologians. One cannot think that religious sources did not have any role in this regard and that the jurists arbitrarily came up with these conclusions.

The references for most of these rulings are the hadith. From the point of view of the jurists who have referenced these hadith, these sources were acceptable and relevant. Of course, not all of the references of the above-noted rulings are authentic or validated hadiths. But among them authentic and credible hadiths are not rare. Based on the standards of traditional Islamic *fiqh*, it is a credible presumption (*zann m'utabar*) that these hadith are the words of the Prophet and the Imams. From the perspective of traditional Islam, it is really believed that these *shari'a*-based rulings that conflict with human rights are either derived from, or are the actual teachings of, the Prophet and the Imams. Of course, within the compilations of hadith as the heritage of the Prophet and Imams, compatibilities with human rights can also be found. But for whatever reasons, those hadith have not been the reference for the *fatwas* of traditional jurists. If we want to speak explicitly and without platitudes, we should say that the numerous hadiths that have been recognised as authentic and credible by traditional *fiqh*, are in serious conflict with the criteria of human rights. One can even be certain that some of the hadith were really issued by the primary authorities of the religion and are certainly not fake or fabricated. Thus, the issue of resolving the conflict with human rights becomes more difficult. Overall, looking at *Wasa'il al-Shi'a*, which is among the most credible sources of hadith in Shi'ite *fiqh*, shows the undeniable conflict between the hadith referenced by jurists and the criteria of human rights. The same can be seen in Sunni *fiqhi* hadiths.

Question: but the main religious source is the Qur'an, the Book of God, which takes precedent over the hadiths of the Prophet and the Imams. Does the domain of this conflict, that is, the conflict with human rights, reach to some verses of the Qur'an? In other words, can we find any verses that are the word of God and are in conflict with human rights?

Answer: in some of the above-noted *shari'a*-based rulings, the verses of the Holy Qur'an have been referenced by the jurists. From the traditional point of view, the Qur'an does not tolerate human rights norms. From this perspective, therefore, the system of human rights that believes in the equality of all human beings and is against discriminating between the rights of Muslims and non-Muslims, men and women, and the free and enslaved, is an anti-Islamic and anti-Qur'anic system. Of course the majority of the *shari'a*-based rulings under discussion in the six axes of conflict have no Qur'anic reference, but there are verses on the legal differences between Muslims, the People of the Book and idolaters, and the legal differences between men and women such as in divorce, inheritance and testimony, as well as the legal differences between free people and enslaved men and women, and regarding criminal law and *shari'a*-based *hudud*, such as the amputation of hands, lashings or crucifixion. Perhaps one can derive compatible opinions with human rights from the Qur'an by using particular absolute expressions (*iqlaqat*), general expressions (*'umumat*) and other verses. Nonetheless, one cannot get around the fact that according to the fundamentals of the conventional methodology (*usul*) of *fiqh*, the domain of conflict with human rights also leads to the Book of God. The conflict is deeper than one can imagine and is not limited to the opinions of theologians and jurists, but extends to the conflict between the religious text, that is, some of the Qur'anic verses and many hadiths, with human rights norms.

The Muslim who allows human rights notions into their mentality and consciousness must be aware that with the arrival of this new guest in their mind, they will have to cope with epistemic mayhem and must respond to deep conflicts. Human rights is a system of thought that is based on specific epistemic, philosophical, and anthropological prerequisites and assumptions. One cannot accept this system of thought without accepting these fundamentals and assumptions. It is clear that this thought is not comparable with every legal regime. In fact, each legal regime has its own specific fundamentals and assumptions. That legal regime that sees religion, sect and belief as preceding over the humanness of humans, that gives precedence to gender, or man- and womanhood, over the humanness of humans, or that gives official recognition to female and male slaves, has first drawn the world and humans in a particular way, and has then accepted propositions based on legal discrimination based on this anthropology and cosmology. There is no doubt that until a special epistemological relationship had been established between the theology and beliefs of this legal regime, these conclusions were not acceptable. One of the principles of epistemology in dealing with various different legal regimes or different propositions is "the principle of impossibility of gathering contradictories together". The human mind cannot at once accept two completely contradictory or conflicting propositions. Thus, it is clear that the system of human rights thought cannot be combined with legal regimes which are antagonistic and in conflict with it on the bases of assumptions and fundamentals (and arising from that, also in terms of corollaries and conclusions).

As a system with a faith-based epistemology, traditional Islam also has a special legal system with its own particular fundamentals and assumptions. This system includes the text of God's scripture and the traditions of the authorities of the religion, the technical opinions of the religion's scholars (such as the *fatwa*s of jurists, the ethical opinions and the theological propositions) and also the practical life styles of Muslims, the pious and the adherents of *shari'a* throughout history.

Traditional Islam believes, first, that in regard to all three, the conflict with the notion of human rights is certain, and, second, on this basis, believes that the notion of human rights is void, incorrect and to be rejected. With a minor correction, one can agree with the first proposition and accept it, that is, I believe that in the practical lifestyles of Muslims and adherents of *shari'a* throughout history and even today, abundant cases of conflict with human rights can be found. Second, in the opinions and *fatwa*s of the experts of religion, there are plenty of propositions that conflict with human rights. Third, in the verses of the Qur'an and hadiths attributed to the Prophet and the

Imams, one can find cases that conflict with human rights. There are fewer of these in the verses of the Qur'an and more so in the hadiths. In addition, the conflict of traditional Islam with human rights is not minor, superficial and rudimentary. It is a conflict that is serious, deep and rooted. Accepting and preferring either side of this conflict has important corollaries, conclusions and consequences that one must not neglect.

The Theoretical Underpinnings of the Conflict of Traditional Islam with Human Rights

Question: actually, what are the epistemological, theological, anthropological or cosmological underpinnings on which traditional Islam arrives at shari'a-based rulings that are in conflict with human rights? What are the assumptions and suppositions on which these rulings and propositions are based and which require revision with the arrival of human rights elements?

Answer: in traditional Islam, humans are not the focal point of discussions, so that their rights are of concern in the formulation of rulings. Rather, God is the focal point, and the axis of religion and divine duties makes up the body of the *shari'a*. The concern of traditional Islam is to identify and implement these obligations which are called *shari'a* rulings. If we carefully examine the works of traditional experts, we find that strenuous efforts have been made to infer and extract these duties and rulings, and that they have tried to keep their mind and conscience free from all other issues and points in order to bar any other non-divine sources or issues from their minds. In facing the consequences and phenomena of the modern era, such as human rights, democracy, civil society and so forth, traditional Islam has had a comprehensive and stable formula, that is: if these kind of issues have a role in the true happiness of humans, and are intrinsically correct and valid, then they have been noted in the texts of the *shari'a* in a complete and all-encompassing way, and if they are not factors in the true happiness of people, then they are condemned to nullification. If one insists on asking whether, at the end of the day, ideas such as human rights are credible or not, do they have a role in human happiness or not, the answer will at once come from an *a priori* position, that in the divine duties and *shari'a* rulings the "true rights of humans" have been absolutely regarded more so and more deeply than the modernists realise and that there is nothing to worry about in this regard. In the Divine mature wisdom everything has been accounted for, including the "true rights of humans". Given the growing acceptance of human rights in Islamic societies, the experts of traditional Islam have in practice taken two approaches. On the one hand, as much as possible, they have removed conflicting rulings from the religious rulings and have tried to somehow justify them. On the other hand, they try to showcase the supportive points from Islamic texts that confirm human rights and in sum to remove Islam from the accusations of its conflict with human rights.

If we want to judge fairly, the "true rights of humans" are different from "human rights". Given that the conflict between traditional Islam and human rights is based on *a posteriori* research, that is, the rulings of traditional Islam were compared with the UDHR and other international conventions, the conclusion is that there is conflict along at least six fundamental axes. It is unlikely that believers in traditional Islam would be able to deny this conflict. From an *a priori* position, they try to avoid this pitfall through the notion of the "true rights of humans". An explanation of the "theory of the true rights of humans" reveals the epistemological, theological and anthropological bases of traditional Islam. The true rights of humans are a set of intrinsic interests (*masalih nafs al-amr*) that have been completely taken into account by the wise God in setting the rulings of *shariʿa*. These rights are stable and unchanging throughout different times and conditions in the evolution of human lifestyles across various places. The maker of these rights is the creator of humans, that is, God. Implementation of the divine duties and rulings of the *shariʿa* is the most certain way in which to observe the "true rights of humans". So now the question arises of how we recognise the true rights of humans? The only credible way to recognise these rights is to refer to the Divine Revelation, meaning that which the Lawmaker has provided in the Book of God or the Traditions of the Prophet. The trustworthy way to acknowledge the true rights of humans is thus the narrative method of the text-oriented approach. From the Shiʿite perspective, consensus does not constitute an independent source and is a secondary method for proving the Traditions. As the discoverer of the rulings of *shariʿa*, reason (*ʿaql*) too can take us from one *shariʿa*-based ruling to another *shariʿa*-based ruling that is the corollary of the first ruling. Idiomatically, this is called non-dependent rational evidence (*dalil gair-mustaqillat ʿaqliya*) and there is no doubt that it can be accepted.

Question: the fundamental issue is the possibility for discovering the true rights of humans via human reason without help from the *shari'a*, the revelation or the narratives. Can humans recognise their own true rights?

Answer: the acceptance of rational good and evil (*husn wa qubh 'aqli*) by the Shi'ite and the Mu'tazila could have formed the basis for an affirmative response. Based on this principle, the only issue that "reason" has the ability to discover is the good of justice and the evil of injustice and whatever reason orders here, so does *shari'a* (principle of correlation). Thus, that which reason has found just must be obligatory in accordance to *shari'a*, and that which reason has found unjust must be forbidden in accordance to *shari'a*. This principle of *fiqhi* methodology has not been reflected much in *fiqh*. As Muhammad Baqir al-Sadr notes at the beginning of *Al-Fatawa al-Wadhihah*, "one can infer an entire course of demonstrative *fiqh* without having to clasp even once to the ruling of reason".[38] Why? Because it is effectively impossible for human reason to achieve an all-embracing grasp of the hidden interests and harms (*masalih wa mafasid khafiya*) of subtle and minor matters. The ruling of reason is either certain and definite (*qat'i*) or presumptive (*zanni*). The certain and definite comprehension of the intrinsic interests and harms of affairs such as the true rights of humans is practically impossible. The indefinite and presumptive comprehension is also not credible or trustworthy. Therefore, discovering the true rights of humans via human reason is not possible. The only way to lift the veil from these rights is to refer to the text of the *shari'a*, the revelatory narration, and nothing else.

In traditional Islam, the "true rights of humans" is delivered in terms of the rulings of the *shari'a* or the religious duties of humans. Whatever those true rights are, they are intrinsic (*nafs al-amr*) matter inscribed in an immutable scroll (*lawh thabit*) which is beyond human comprehension and reason. However, the divine duties and *shari'a*-based rulings are accessible via a narrative way. The "true rights of humans" do not lend themselves to discussion, but the rulings of *shari'a* are discussable, at least among experts of religion. With this, allow us to speak no further of the "true rights of

---

38 Muhammad Baqir al-Sayyid al-Sadr, *al-Fatawa al-Wadhihah wifqan li Madhab-i Ahl al-Bayt* (*Clear Fatwas According to the Shi'i Doctrine*) (Qom: Center of Professional Discussions and Studies on the Martyr al-Sadr, 2001), 1:111.

humans" and focus our discussion on the *shari'a*-based rulings for humans. It is clear that the *shari'a*-based duties and the religious rulings for humans differ on the basis of religion, sect, gender, status as free or enslaved, or even being or not being a jurist. Of course, from this traditional viewpoint, these differences never mean discrimination, but are instead true justice, meaning that each ruling is observed as an essential merit (*istihqaq dhati*) of the person to whom it applies. Because God is wise and just, every single *shari'a*-based ruling must thus definitely be just and wise.

The most important basis of the epistemology, theology and anthropology of traditional Islam in our discussion has to do with the limits of human reason. Reason is unable to comprehend the true rights of humans. The inherent incapacity and congenital faultiness of the human mind in comprehending what is abundantly important in a person's life, is the basis and mother of the other principles of this traditional thought. Included in these principles based on the faultiness of reason, are the serious incapacity and limitation of human reason in a comprehensive understanding of the particulars of justice. The logical conclusion of this sort of principle is the practical monopoly of the understanding of justice and injustice in the statements of the sacred Lawmaker. When the human mind is unable to recognise the justness of a ruling, then the only option is that justice is that which the Lawmaker says is just, and injustice is that which the Lawmaker says is unjust. This means that traditional Islam has in practice succumbed to the Ash'arite[39] methodology. The second principle based on the faultiness of reason, is the inability to legislate for this worldly life. Faulty and incapable human reason does not have the competence to make laws. Given the failure to comprehensively understand the true needs of human beings and their true happiness, and because human beings are swayed by appetites and carnal desires, human legislation will lead to social struggles and conflicts. To establish peace and calm, there is no option other than divine laws, meaning the *shari'a* and the divine Lawgiver, that is, God. The importance of this principle is such that an argument on the necessity of the prophecy has been

---

39 Ash'arite theological school, a dominant strand within Sunni Islam alongside the Maturidi school, founded by Abu al-Hasan al-Ash'ari (d. 936). The most famous figure of this school was al-Ghazali. According to this school: "God is all-powerful, therefore all Good and Evil is the result of His decree. What God does or commands is per definition just and what God prohibits is by definition unjust."

secured on its basis, an argument that the majority of Muslim theologians and even some Muslim philosophers refer to. Based on this, it is obvious that human laws – including the documents on human rights – would be condemned at the outset as being defective, void and a failure. Given that the *shariʿa* rulings have been made by the wise God and that human laws arise from the defective and limited reason of humans, it is obvious that divine duties and the rulings of *shariʿa* are superior to human laws. Thus, in comparing any order of *shariʿa* with its counterpart in human laws, it is evident at the outset that the rulings of *shariʿa* are superior. This superiority is such that it never needs to be tested or proven. Given its inherent limitations and defectiveness, human reason cannot be a judge in this arena. This superiority is the necessary conclusion of accepting the mature wisdom of the Divine and is the third principle that is based on the faultiness of human reason.

Among the other bases of the epistemology and theology of traditional Islam is the possibility of making stable and unchanging laws, laws that have not changed in all of the different circumstances of life, ranging from the simple circumstances of life in the past to the complicated circumstances of life today, because if laws are a manifestation of hidden intrinsic interests and harms, then they are time-less and space-less. All the rulings of *shariʿa* are as such. The Divine duties set out in the Qurʾan are stable rulings beyond time and space. The same is true for the majority of the rulings of *shariʿa* in the traditions of the Prophet and the Imams which are reflected in the honourable texts of *fiqh*. This belief results in two logical consequences: first, the primary importance of the science of *fiqh* among the Islamic sciences, such that the writings of Muslim scholars in this honourable science have been regarded with more importance and respect than their writings in other Islamic sciences, such as ethics, theology, exegesis of the Qurʾan, hadith, history, biographies, philosophy and mysticism, and jurists have been accorded more esteem and importance. Second, is the abundant importance of the narrative sciences and *shariʿa* as compared with the rational sciences, intuitive sciences and experimental sciences, and that the way to gain happiness is via narrative and *shariʿa* studies and one's efforts and attention must be spent on studying this sort of knowledge.

In traditional Islam, humans essentially lack honour and dignity, although they potentially form an honourable jewel. The closer humans get to the axis of dignity and honour, the more nobility they gain, and the further away they get from this divine axis, the more degraded they become. Thus, humans can inhabit a position as high as divine saints and as close to God's creations as possible, down to a level that is below that of four-legged animals and the most degraded of creatures. The status of human beings depends on their closeness or otherwise to divine virtues and perfection. In the same way, the true rights of humans are related to a person's status in faith and religion. Based on this, to speak of human rights and the inherent equal rights of all humans, whether man or woman, Muslim or non-Muslim, free or enslaved, is useless and unjust.

In this system, the world must be understood in the shadow of the Hereafter. Comparatively, therefore, this world is called *dunya*, which is the lower and more degraded world. The management of this world has to be in terms of the other, and a person's efforts must not be limited and expended only towards his or her worldly welfare. Thus, it is natural that the affairs of this world have secondary value.

What has been said so far is a brief analysis of the epistemological, theological, anthropological and cosmological bases of traditional Islam. It is appropriate to compare the synopsis of these bases with the bases of human rights notions. The pillar of human rights thought is the belief in the relative capacity of human reason to comprehend the needs, interests and harms of humans. Autonomous critical reason is the foundation of modernity and human rights is one of its fruits. From this perspective, reason, and especially human reason, has the ability to discover and establish human rights.

Under the shelter of the continuous experiences of human societies, the collective reason of humanity takes on this task of discovery and establishment and it does not consider its conclusion to be final and unchangeable. Instead, it is ready to complete and reform its rulings in accordance with new experiences. The documents of human rights are the result of the latest experiences of the collective reason of contemporary humans and it holds that in observing them, the lives of every single person will include more peace, calm and justice. This thought emphasises the ability of human reason to find the rules of justice and holds that collective human reason has the ability to recognise the particulars of justice and injustice in human laws and relations. In the same way, humans can establish just laws for managing their societies and environments. The documents of human rights, including international laws, are made by the collective reason of contemporary humanity. Given the diversity of religions and sects in human societies and the fact that each one determines its own rules for its followers, human rights, in addition to respecting all religions and sects, also officially recognises them in the private sphere of human lives, and takes a neutral position in relation to religion and sects in the public sphere. This means that these rights are established for humans as humans, before they come to believe in this or that religion or sect. Put another way, a person's religion or sect does not bring about any benefits or change to his or her legal status and the principles of human rights do not support any particular religion or creed.

The important point is that human rights have been organised in accordance with an *a posteriori* method, meaning that it is based on human experiences, and through comparison of different practical ways on the confidence in the priority of this method over others. This way of thought is not based on secrets, codes or points that are beyond human reason and understanding. Its superiority to competing ways is therefore easily proven and is shown through its success in practice. In following the criteria of human rights, each person has the opportunity to freely and with total authority build their life in the way they see fit; whether in the style of a believer or as an atheist, this is their business and no one else's. The system of human rights is neither atheist nor monotheist.

The comparison of traditional Islam with the foundations of the documents of human rights shows the deep and fundamental differences between these two systems. Accepting either one requires negating the other, unless one superficially believes in both with closed eyes, without paying attention to the corollaries and consequences, and with ignorance of their roots and foundations. Up to this point, the conflict between traditional Islam and human rights has been described and analysed.

The Preference of Human Rights Thought over the Position of Traditional Islam

Question: what must one do about the deep and fundamental conflict between traditional Islam and human rights? Which of these two systems should one accept? What should be done with the other?

Answer: the question pertains to judgement. It is not easy to answer. Before answering, I want to bring your attention to several points. First, one side of the conflict is traditional Islam, and not Islam per se. Traditional Islam is a particular reading of this Divine religion. Criticism of it, or indeed its negation, is not attached to a criticism or negation of Islam. One can be a Muslim and be a believer in the Oneness of God, the truth of Judgement Day, and the Prophecy of Muhammad b. 'Abdullah, but still have a different reading of Muhammad's creed, a reading that is different from the traditional one. One must therefore enter this judgement in a free, fair, neutral and scholarly way, rather than in a way that is set in belief, bias and mimicry. The second preliminary point is that, given the issues that were raised in response to the previous question, one can interpret this conflict as being between reason (autonomous human "reason") and narration ("sayings" of an authority such as God or His Prophet). The method of traditional Islam is through narration and that of human rights is based on rationality. The interpretation of narration and reason is much more realistic than other terminology, for example, those that see the conflict as being between "revelation and reason" or between "religion and reason".

As a third point, it appears that in making a judgement about the two sides of this conflict one cannot use an "*a priori* method" of investigation since the birth of this conflict was precisely due to using the "*a posteriori* method". In other words, numerous propositions from religious duties and rulings have been declared in conflict with the criteria of human rights, and using the "*a priori* method" is not convincing. Put another way, in judging, we cannot rely on credentials ("who said"), since it is the word of God or the Prophet, and consider that we are exempt from proving the credibility of the "what is said" separate from the "who said". This is exactly what the "*a posteriori* method" is, comparing two statements in terms of their own rightfulness, credibility and validity. In the contemporary world, one must defend the rulings of *shari'a* in terms of their being reasonable, just and superior as compared with similar solutions.

The fourth point is that the system of human rights belongs to the era of modernity and was never an issue in the premodern period. Traditional Islam is also under discussion during the era of modernity; in the premodern era the traditional reading of Islam did not face any problems in terms of conflict with human rights. In other words, this conflict is a new phenomenon (*mas'ala mustahdatha*) which belongs to a new era and it cannot be attached to eras of the past. In facing the problems of the past, traditional Islam was successful and proud.

Lastly, the final point is that this conflict is one of the branches of the discussion on tradition and modernity. In this conflict, traditional Islam is the representative of tradition and human rights notions represent modernity.

Turning now to judging the conflict between traditional Islam and human rights notions, this conflict has been described and analysed in terms of six axes. To be more precise in judgement, we will assess each of the above axes separately. In the first axis of conflict, that is, the legal inequality between Muslims and non-Muslims, one cannot defend the position of traditional Islam in the contemporary world. Religion and sect must not be the basis of legal discrimination among people. Faith in the true religion and good deeds (*'amal salih*) will lead to access to the sublime life in the afterlife in accordance with the judgement of the just and wise God. However, in this world, legal equality and the lack of discrimination based on religion and sect is closer to justice. In a world where followers of different sects and religions live, where each considers their own religion and sect to be the best or only means of salvation, that the believers of other creeds are misguided or ignorant, and that there should be special rights for the followers of their own religion, the most just way would be to negate all of these special rights and disregard religious belief in favour of human rights. If God has placed natural blessings at the disposal of all people without any difference or discrimination, why would we not act in such a way? According to what rational argument does belief, faith and religion cause discrimination or legal difference? In a legal egalitarian situation, facing and accepting a particular religion occurs in a more genuine and pure way than the fleeting sweet benefits of this world. If we do not want to accept the *shari'a*-based arguments of traditional Islam based on the legal differences between Muslims and non-Muslims, and members of one sect and those of another, in a devotional (*ta'abbudi*) way, or we do not want to assess the sayings based on who said them, and, instead, we want to officially recognise reason as the judge of the dispute, we will have no doubt that egalitarianism is closer to justice and truth than religious discrimination.

In terms of the second axis, that is, the inequality between men and women, the priority of gender over humanity lacks reason. On what basis is physiological or biological difference the reason for differing legal rights? If differences in race or skin colour cannot be the basis for legal differences, then why is gender difference the basis for legal difference? The absolute subordination of women and the absolute superiority of men lacks any kind of credible reason. The criterion of excellence in the Hereafter is based on virtue and "being mindful of God" (*taqwa*), not gender. In this world as well, one must prepare equal opportunities and chances for healthy competition. Women are no less than men in mental capacity or in gaining scientific and professional skills, or in the arenas of politics, economics, and culture. In sum, the egalitarian position regardless of gender is in accordance with common sense, while gender discrimination in terms of the rights of women as compared with those of men, is in conflict with fairness, justice and reasonability.

In regard to the third axis, that is, the inequality of the rights of slaves and free people, this legal discrimination is not only lacking in any rational argument (*dalil*), but rational argument is against it. While the multiplicity of religions and sects and genders among humans cannot be eliminated, slavery can be, and today it has been eliminated in its traditional form. Common sense, justice and fairness do not tolerate slavery. Furthermore, they do not approve of discrimination against the rights of slaves. One cannot have any doubts regarding the rightness of the human rights position on the abolition of slavery and its rejection of discrimination on account of it.

Unlike the previous three axes, the fourth axis, that is, the inequality between the masses and jurists in the public sphere, is not among the certainties of traditional Islam, but arises from differing views within traditional Islam. The special rights of jurists or clerics in the public sphere is first of all lacking in credible *shari'a*-based documentation (at least from the point of view of intra-religious critics). Second, it lacks rational argument. Third, and most importantly, rational argument is against it. According to which argument should the public sphere and the political domain be entrusted to jurists, and why should their opinions and views have priority over that of public opinion? Why should a jurist or cleric have special rights to determine crucial policies and key professions in society? What is the reason that juristic policies have priority over scientific or common sense (*'uqala'i*) policies? The preference of democracy over autocracy, monarchy or theocracy is clear. Nonetheless, I have published several books and articles to prove all of these issues.[40]

---

40 *Andishe-ye Siyasi dar Eslam [-e Shi'ite]*, Political Thought in [Shi'ite] Islam Series, vol. 1: *Nazariyeha-ye Dolat dar Fiqh-e Shi'a* (*The Theories of State in Shi'ite Law*), vol. 2; *Hokumat-e Wela'i* (*Governance by Guardianship*), vol. 3: *Hokumat-e Entesabi* (*Appointive/ Non-Elective State*); *Daghdagheha-ye Hokumat-e Dini* (*The Concerns of Religious Rule*, a collection of political papers and lectures); *Shari'at wa Siyasat: Din dar 'Arse-ye 'Umumi* (*Shari'a and Politics: Religion in the Public Sphere, A Case Study of Contemporary Iran*), Kadivar web-book, 2010; *Siasat-nameh-ye Khorasani* (the spiritual leader of the Iranian Constitutional Revolution of 1906); "*La naissance du 'souverain juriste': Généalogie de la théorie de l'État Shi'ite*" ("The Birth of Guardianship Jurist: The Genealogy of Shi'ite Theory of Governance"), transl. into French Anoush Ganjipour, *Les Temps Modernes*, Paris (Aril–June 2015), 110–128.

Now to the fifth axis, that is, the freedom of belief and religion and the punishment for apostasy: freedom of belief and religion is the requisite of egalitarianism and the rejection of religious discrimination. The freedom of belief and religion, the freedom of expression and religion, the freedom to carry out religious rituals and ceremonies, the freedom to stop religious practice, the freedom to change belief and religion, and the freedom to preach belief and religious teachings are all among the elements of this axis. Common sense defends the freedom of religion and does not tolerate worldly punishments for changing religion. Denying or limiting the freedom of religion and setting punishments, such as execution or imprisonment with hard labour for apostasy, displays a weak and unreasonable picture of traditional Islam. The way to guard the faith of believers is to strengthen their religious knowledge, not to strip them of the freedom of religion and belief. One cannot doubt the rational preference of the position of human rights in defending freedom of belief and religion. I have proven this in an independent article.[41]

Now to the sixth axis, that is, arbitrary punishments as well as violent punishments and torture: today, human conventions do not accept that a person can be punished or even executed without the sentence of a legal court and without the ability of the accused to defend themself. In punishing criminals, current thinking tends towards eliminating crime and public warnings not to commit offences, more than towards bodily punishments, execution and any form of punishment in general. In many instances, violent punishments have lost their effectiveness in this regard. In today's world, any kind of torture in order to obtain information, or for breaking a prisoner's resistance, is considered forbidden. If criminal rulings and penal codes in traditional Islam are not devotional (*ta'abbudi*) in comparison with the criteria of human rights, the preference is with human rights notions in regard to the three above-named axes.

Thus, regarding the six axes, that is, egalitarianism and the rejection of the four types of discrimination based on religion, gender, slavery and status as a jurist, as well as the freedom of belief and religion and the rejection of arbitrary and violent punishments and torture, the positions taken in the human rights documents as compared with those of traditional Islam are more defensible, reasonable, just and preferred. In contemporary times, the rulings of traditional Islam are not acceptable in relation to these positions.

---

41 See Chapter 8, this book.

The Solutions of Traditional Islam for the Elimination of Conflict

Question: on the one hand, you came to believe in the fundamental conflict between traditional Islam and the notions of human rights, and, on the other, in the position of judgement, you defended the preference of human rights in these six axes over traditional Islam. Can traditional Islam escape these problems? Can these conflicts be eliminated by the criteria of traditional *fiqh* and conventional *ijtihad* in the seminaries, that is, *ijtihad* in secondary branches (*furu' fiqhi*)? And if so, to what extent?

Answer: the answer is negative. Traditional Islam has obligatory criteria and standards that cannot be cast aside without departing from the whole framework. And adhering to these criteria and standards leaves the conflict unresolved.

First, the reference for some of the rulings that conflict with human rights are the verses of the Qur'an. Traditional Islam considered these verses to be the stewards of unchanging rulings, absolute expression (*mutlaq*: those that are not restricted to the circumstances of time and place), and non-abrogated (*ghair mansoukh*). If we want to judge fairly and remain faithful to the *prima facie* meanings (*zawahir*) of these sort of verses, we have no choice but to accept the legal inequality of Muslims and non-Muslims, men and women, slaves and free people, as well as the lack of freedom of religion and belief, and acceptance of violent bodily punishments. The traditional jurist has no choice but to embrace the rulings of *shari'a* that are in conflict with human rights.

Second, the references for the overwhelming majority of the rulings of *shari'a* that are in conflict with human rights, are hadiths narrated from the Prophet or the Imams. The chains of transmission for many of these hadiths are authentic (*sahih* or *muwaththaq*), and are as a whole considered to be credible and unproblematic in accordance with the criteria of *fiqh*. The implication of the content of these hadiths is explicit in terms of purpose and *prima facie* meaning (*zuhur*) in rulings which are understood today to be in conflict with human rights. Traditional *fiqh* considers these credible hadiths to be the vehicle for stable and permanent rulings and believes that "what was permitted (*halal*) according to Muhammad is permitted until the Day of Judgement and what was forbidden (*haram*) by him is forbidden until the Day of Judgement".[42] In some detailed issues, there is a non-mainstream approach, such as those pertaining to the age of maturity for girls, which also has hadith references, but the contrary approach in the case of many of the rulings under discussion lacks any kind of hadith reference. In other words, the approaches which are compatible with human rights in the majority of the particulars pertaining to the six axes are lacking references in the Qur'an or hadiths. Even if it is possible to apply generalities (*umumat*) and absolute expressions (*itlaqat*), the issue is afflicted by conflicting verses and authentic hadiths. Given these sources and the framework of these criteria, the traditional jurist cannot distance himself very much from the existing *fatwa*s.

Third, many of the rulings of *shari'a* that are in conflict with human rights are consensual (*ijma'i*). In many of these cases, opposition can rarely be found and the ruling is unanimous. The majority of these cases are the mainstream (*mashur*) opinion. Above all, some of these rulings that are in conflict with human rights are considered to be a necessity of *fihq*, or a necessity of the *madhab* or a necessity of religion. In traditional *fiqh*, these type of rulings are unchangeable. How can one consider it possible to eliminate conflict with human rights while remaining faithful to such criteria?

Fourth, if the rulings pertaining to transactions (*mu'amalat*), like rulings pertaining to worship (*'ibadat*), are based on hidden interests (*masalih khafiya*), independent reason[43] (*'aql mustaqil*) does not have the capacity to comprehend these interests. Thus, traditional jurists cannot use rational rulings in support of human rights, since from this point of view "independent reason" cannot issue any rulings in this regard. The way of reasonable people (or rational common sense) (*sira al-'uqala*)[44] has also been denied in the audibility and visibility of the Lawgiver.[45] What greater deterrence can there be

---

42 Al-Kulaini, *al-Kafi*, 1:58.

43 An argument that all its promises are purely rational, and that none of them derived from divine revelation or the Tradition of the Prophet, so its validity is independent of *shari'a*.

44 This is an important term in the methodology of *fiqh*. Comprehension of good and evil by reasonable people is the foundation of independent rational arguments. The comprehension of these people is reasonability (pure reason) and nothing else. It is more than common sense. This rational common sense is called *sira al-'uqala*.

45 If an existing custom (*'urf*) has not been denied in the audibility and visibility of the Lawgiver, it is the indication that its validity and permissibility has been confirmed and approved by the Lawgiver.

than the credible and sourced verses and hadiths of these rulings of *shari'a* that are in conflict with human rights? In the sphere of *shari'a* rulings, justice too cannot be comprehended with certainty, in the same way that reason has no way to reach the criteria of the rulings, unless the Lawmaker himself says so.

Yes, minor and super-structural reforms are not impossible. For example, some of the rulings close to human rights in relation to women can be accepted as a "condition required by the contract" (*shart dhimn 'aqd*) for marriage, as long as they are not contrary to the requirements (*muqtadha*) of the marriage contract. This includes the right of a wife to be an attorney on behalf of her husband in her own divorce. The second means of reform within traditional *fiqh* is through applying the principle of secondary rulings, that is, the principle of distress and constriction (*'usr wa haraj*) or urgency (*idhtirar*). In proving this principle, the wife can refer to the judge and obtain a divorce without the consent of her husband. Claiming the "weakening (*wahn*) of Islam" is the third way of reform. For example, implementation of stoning (*rajm*) can be halted if the weakening of Islam can be proven, or if for the same reason the open implementation of *hudud* punishments can be stopped, especially whipping or lashing. In the case of the fifth and sixth axes of conflict, the fourth solution is to stop *hudud* punishment during the time of the Mahdi's occultation. In stopping these *hudud* punishments during this period, the problem of the conflict with human rights notions is eliminated. It is clear that the capacity of these kinds of solution is very small. One cannot address the majority of *shari'a*-based rulings using conditions set during the marriage contract or by using the principle of distress and constriction. The use of "weakening of Islam" is also very difficult.

The claim to being able to recognise hidden interests and harms is outside the criteria of traditional Islam. If these sorts of secondary rulings and principles are relied upon and turn into a regular procedure and become used more often than the primary rulings, then this shows the difficulty of recognising the primary rulings. In other words, those rulings which jurists consider to be primary are not so, otherwise they would not require so many amendments and additional sections.

While traditional *fiqh* believes that rulings are divided into stable and changing, it also believes that what has been under discussion in *fiqh* all belongs to the stable orders. In addition, the problem that traditional jurists face today, that is, the conflict with notions of human rights, is entirely in the realm of rulings which are considered to be stable by traditional Islam. Put another way, the problem concerns the conflict between stable rulings and notions of human rights. Thus, dividing rulings into stable and unchanging does not eliminate the problem when the problem is exclusive to the stable rulings.

One of the figures who has correctly grasped the inability of traditional *fiqh* and conventional *ijtihad* to solve the problems of the contemporary world and who tried to reform them in accordance to the requirements of the time and place by relying on the element of the interest of the system (*maslahat-i nizam*) was Ayatollah Khomeini (1902–1989). In his view, the issues that have been discussed at the scholastic seminaries in the framework of theory cannot be solved.[46] In response to the objection to his new *fatwa* on chess, he said that with this sort of fanatical analysis of the hadiths, new civilisation would be completely eliminated and people would either live in caves or the desert forever.[47] Ayatollah Khomeini found the solution to this problem in the absolute rule (*wilayat mutlaqa*) of the state over *fiqh*. According to him, "the state can prevent any act, whether or not it is an issue related to worship, that is against the interests of Islam for as long as it remains so". He explicitly considered the elimination of some rulings, such as those pertaining to farming partnership (*muzara'a*) and limited partnership (*mudharaba*), to be under the authority of the government. According to Ayatollah Khomeini, *shari'a*-based rulings are accidental purposes, instrumental affairs, and tools for executing government and expanding justice. Based on this, the ruling jurist can suspend all *shari'a*-based rulings that do not fit the circumstances of time and place, or that do not suit the interests of the system, for as long as they are such, and he may also submit rulings required for the interests of the system or by the circumstances of time and place.[48]

Question: now, supposing the state that has been established in accordance with the theory of Ayatollah Khomeini considers the observation of human rights to be in the interests of the system, or in accordance with

---

46 Komeini, *Sahife-ye Imam*, 21:217–218; letter of 29 December 1988.
47 Ibid., 21:149–152; letter of 9 September 1988.
48 Ibid., 20:451–452; open letter to President Khamenei, 6 January 1988.

the requirements of time and place, does this state have the authority to prevent those rulings which are in conflict with human rights?

Answer: certainly, the answer is affirmative. The solution of interest-oriented jurisprudence (*fiqh al-maslaha*) or governmental ruling (*hukm hukumati*) is more efficient than all four of the previous solutions (setting conditions during the marriage contract, the principle of distress and constriction, the weakening of Islam, and the stopping of *hudud* punishment in the time of occultation). This is because all the *shari'a*-based rulings, whether they be related to worship or not, can be prevented for as long as they are contrary to the interests of the system. In addition, any ruling whose establishment may benefit the system, may be established by the jurist ruler. Thus, if the absolute jurist-ruler or his appointees consider the observance of human rights to be in the interest of the system, they may overturn all *shari'a*-based rulings which are considered "stable rulings" by traditional Islam and even those orders which are considered the necessities of the religion, *madhab* or *fiqh*, which are seen to be in conflict with human rights. There is no doubt that with this innovation, the conflict between traditional Islam and human rights would be eliminated.

However, this respectable solution has suffered several problems; the most important of which is that it departs from the framework of traditional Islam and conventional *ijtihad*. According to many traditional jurists, the theory of *wilayat al-faqih* (rule of the jurist) in the public sphere is lacking in credible *shari'a*-based references. The absolute rule of the jurists over *fiqh* is accepted only by its innovator and some of his students, but is not accepted by traditional jurists. Traditional *fiqh*, whether in regard to the attainability of interests or in the absolute priority of rulings based on interest over all *shari'a*-based rulings, especially rulings pertaining to worship, does not think in this way and acts very cautiously. This point in itself is not a problem. If the solution of acting in accordance with the interests or the rule of the jurist is the correct way, one must accept it, whether it be in the framework of traditional *fiqh* or outside it. But one cannot consider the solution of interest-oriented *fiqh* as an answer to traditional *fiqh*. Invoking the interest of the system is a departure from the criteria of traditional Islam for solving the problem of conflict with human rights.

However, fundamentally, interest-oriented *fiqh* does not solve the problem, since access to governmental rulings or interest-oriented rulings is a temporary and situational solution and not a permanent one. This is because the stable rulings of *shari'a* are protected by their own credibility and it is only when the invocation of necessary interest by the ruling jurist or his appointees is overturned, and only while this interest endures practically (and not theoretically in terms of *shari'a*-based credibility), that followers are religiously obligated to act in accordance with rulings that are interest-oriented or governmental. As soon as the government does not see the interest, and the governmental ruling is cancelled, believers are called to act in accordance with the previous stable ruling. The governmental ruling is not a permanent solution that would fundamentally eliminate the problem of the conflict with human rights; rather, like a pain-relieving pill, it temporarily soothes the pain of conflict, without curing the cause of the problem.

Second, interest-oriented *fiqh* places *shari'a* and *fiqh* in the domain of government and political power. The absolute authority and rule of the state over *fiqh* subordinates *shari'a*-based rulings to state interests, making them followers of political power and subordinate to daily politics. In addition, a state that sees the observation of human rights to be in the interests of the government, has in truth previously rejected the special role of jurists and clerics in the public sphere and in political affairs, which translates into the rejection of the absolute rule of the jurist in the public sphere. Put more precisely, invoking such interests leads to the negation of the legitimacy of such a state and what state do we know of that would honestly reveal its own legal incompetence to the people? The system of human rights is in fundamental conflict with the theory of interest-oriented *fiqh*, that is, the absolute and appointive rule of the jurist.

Third, given the above-noted problems, if, on the one hand, the number of governmental rulings became so abundant that it would benefit society to temporarily suspend the majority of stable *shari'a*-based rulings, and, on the other, that the time that these interests endured increased to more than several years and decades, such that it was in the interests of society that these orders be suspended for many years, would these two issues not indicate our error in how we have adduced the stable rulings of *shari'a*? Without mincing words, the repeated reliance on interest to suspend the stable rulings of *shari'a*, and the gradual extension of the time period when these rulings are suspended, means the practical admission that *mujtahids* have been erroneous in recognising *shari'a*-based rulings. In other words, those rulings which have been introduced as stable rulings of *shari'a* are not in fact permanent and stable rulings of God, otherwise they would not need to be cobbled together with so many amendments and additional sections.

Although the innovations of Ayatollah Khomeini can be seriously critiqued, his courage in criticising traditional *fiqh*, while also showing his appreciation of it, and admitting to the inefficiency of conventional *ijtihad* in dealing with the issues of the modern world is admirable.

Traditional Islam, and its *fiqh* in particular, does not have the capacity to exit this dead-end without a revision of its criteria and bases. It seems that *ijtihad* in secondary branches is reaching the end of its historical life. The inefficiency of conventional *ijtihad* (meaning *ijtihad* in secondary branches without *ijtihad* in the principles and foundations) and traditional *fiqh* in our time must not prevent us from being grateful to this legal system for its service in past eras. New methods are all indebted to this successful predecessor and draw from its rich scientific legacy. In addition, traditional *fiqh*'s method of induction in orders pertaining to worship such as prayer, fasting and *hajj* continue to be credible and reliable since rational argument does not enter into the realm of worship and it does not conflict with human rights.

An Investigation of National and International Efforts to Integrate Traditional Islam with Human Rights

Question: some efforts have been made on both the national and international level to integrate Islam and human rights. On the international level, there was the Islamic Declaration of Human Rights in Cairo in 1990. On the national level, the laws of the Islamic Republic of Iran are notable. Have the conflicts you mentioned not been eliminated in these documents? In general, what is your assessment of these efforts?

Answer: on the level of international efforts in the last quarter of a century, six declarations and draft declarations have been issued by the European Islamic Council (1980 and 1981), the Kuwait Conferences (the International Commission of Jurists, together with the University of Kuwait and the Union of Arab Lawyers, 1980), and the Organization of Islamic Conferences (Mecca 1979, Ta'if 1981). The latest and most official declaration of Islamic human rights was approved by the nineteenth conference of the foreign ministers of the member states of the Organization of Islamic

Conferences[49] in Cairo in 1990, which was based on a Tehran draft titled the "Cairo Declaration on Human Rights in Islam (CDHRI)". Other than these declarations, which represent the maximum of what is understood to be shared among Muslims in terms of human rights, it has not been possible to ratify a binding convention, treaty or agreement. Nonetheless, even these non-binding declarations should be seen as a good sign. One can see them as indications of the necessity for Islamic societies to consider the case of human rights. These declarations have attempted to foreground elements of international human rights documents that are compatible with traditional Islam and to extract these from the crevices of Islamic teachings and prove the precedence of Islam in observing human rights. As compared with the international documents on human rights, the Cairo Declaration includes new points, such as Article 11, which officially recognises the right to resist colonialism as "one of the most evil forms of enslavement", and the right to enjoy a pure, spiritual and ethical environment in Article 17: "Everyone shall have the right to live in a clean environment, away from vice and moral corruption, an environment that fosters self-development; and it is incumbent upon the state and society in general to afford that right." The Cairo Declaration also took a big step in relation to the discrimination between the legal rights of a free person and a slave and explicitly believes in the abolition of slavery. Article 11 stipulates that: "Human beings are born free and no one has the right to enslave, humiliate, oppress or exploit them, and there can be no subjugation but to Allah the Almighty."

These declarations, including the Cairo Declaration, were however unsuccessful in relation to the five other axes of conflict between traditional Islam and human rights. They dealt with these issues with generalities, ambiguities, brevity or silence, which in practice confirmed the conflict. For example, Article 10 of the Cairo Declaration states: "Islam is the religion of unspoiled nature. It is prohibited to exercise any form of compulsion on man or to exploit his poverty or ignorance in order to convert him to another religion or to atheism." It is worth asking whether it is permitted to use pressure for the purpose of the persistence of Islam? In any case, like traditional Islam, this declaration has not accepted the freedom of religion and in general has

---

49 The new name of this organisation since 2011 is the Organization of Islamic Cooperation (OIC).

officially recognised completely legal discrimination arising from religion. In other words, contrary to the international documents on human rights which are neutral on religion, this declaration is legally conditional on, and bound to, Islam. Regarding the axis of gender-based discrimination, the Cairo Declaration has not been able to move beyond the equality based on innate humanity and considers the *shariʿa*-based rights of women to be appropriate in relation to women's responsibilities. Article 24 considers all of the rights and freedoms noted in the declaration to be conditional on their concordance with the Islamic rulings of *shariʿa*. This means that the five axes of conflict between the *shariʿa* in traditional Islam and human rights have permeated the declaration. The Cairo Declaration represents the greatest effort of traditional Islam in the field of human rights, but it suffers from the five fundamental conflicts between traditional Islam and human rights notions. The conservative tradition that dominates the legal associations of Islamic countries was only successful in eliminating the conflict in one axis, that of slavery, and nothing more. The Cairo Declaration suffers, first, from the legal discrimination arising from religion and a lack of religious tolerance; second, from the legal discrimination arising from gender; third, from legal discrimination in the public sphere (it has, of course, been silent on the special rights of jurists which have been reduced in a vague sense to general positions based on the rulings of *shariʿa*); fourth, in not officially recognising the freedom of belief and religion, and, fifth, in the implicit official recognition of violent and arbitrary punishments.

The constitution of the Islamic Republic of Iran represents the height of the efforts by traditional Shiʿite Islam to address the field of human rights. It officially recognises the different legal status of Muslims and non-Muslims and Shiʿite and Sunni Muslims, in Articles 12, 13 and 14 of the document. The legal difference between men and women has been subtly placed in Articles 20 and 21. It is totally silent on the issue of slavery, although the principle in Article 4 creates the basis for returning with full force to all of the *shariʿa* rulings in traditional Islam. The Constitution explicitly and officially recognises the discrimination between jurists and the masses in the public sphere in Articles 5, 57, 109 and 110. Although Articles 23 and 24 officially recognise the freedom of opinion in general, freedom of religion, including the right to change religion, preaching the religion and so on, is out of the question in view of the fact that Article 4 states that the *shariʿa* absolutely governs all absolute expressions (*itlaqat*) and generalities (*ʿumumat*) of the Articles of the Constitution and all other laws and regulations. Article 38 of the Constitution explicitly bans all forms of torture, while Article 36 rejects arbitrary punishments and states that the conviction and execution of punishments can be carried out only via a fair court and in accordance to the law. Based on this, the status of the sixth axis of conflict, that is, the issue of punishments, is better than the situation of the other four axes. This is because it has outlawed torture and arbitrary punishment and is silent on harsh and degrading punishments. However, relying on Article 4 means that the possibility for the threefold rulings of the sixth axis to enter without much justification remains.

All in all, the Iranian Constitution of 1979, with revisions in 1989, is explicitly in conflict with human rights along three axes: first, the inequality between Muslims and non-Muslims and the Shiʿite and the Sunni; second, the inequality between men and women; and, third, the inequality between the rights of jurists and the masses in the public sphere. Although it is silent on three of the axes of conflict, given the general application of Article 4 and the conflict between traditional Islam and human rights on these issues, the Constitution is implicitly in conflict with human rights notions in the following: first, the freedom of religion; second, harsh punishments; and, third, slavery.

In terms of the sixth axis, the Constitution has moved in the same direction as human rights by explicitly forbidding torture and arbitrary punishments in two sections. However, Article 4 of the Constitution, in leaving the potential for turning to *shariʿa*-based *taʿzir* punishments and the supremacy of the *shariʿa* rulings regarding unprotected life (*mahdur al-dam*), means that even these two adventive points raise questions and ambiguities.

An investigation of the official opinions and interpretations of the Guardian Council of the Constitution shows that the current procedures of this council in the area of human rights are much more difficult and further from reality than the procedures of the Assembly of Experts of the Constitution (constitution-makers). Among the regular laws of the Islamic Republic, the Islamic Penal Code is the most problematic from the perspective of the criteria of human rights and is much further from human rights as compared with civil law. With traditional Islam, one cannot make much more progress in the domain of human rights than was made in the Cairo Declaration or the Constitution of the Islamic Republic of Iran. Attention to these two documents is confirmation of the theory that traditional Islam does not observe the criteria of human rights. Without *ijtihad* in the principles and foundations and a fundamental change in the thinking of jurists, the conflict between the laws of Islamic countries and human rights notions in the above-mentioned axes will not be eliminated.

Abuse of Human Rights and its Causes

Question: the opponents of human rights generally raise several complaints: one is that in the contemporary world, human rights are a political weapon and are used as leverage by the United States and the European Union against developing countries, and especially against Islamic societies, while the violation of human rights by allied countries, in particular by Israel, is overlooked. The other is that human rights fit with Western lifestyles and societies. Accepting them means to surrender to the West. As Muslims, we have no need of the consequences of the unbelievers of the world. Are there any flaws in our religion that we need to make up for by turning to the products of unbelievers and the enemies of Islam? As a Muslim defender of human rights, what is your response to these issues?

Answer: it is unfortunate that such superficial critiques are brought up in the name of religion and that religion and faith are placed in opposition to human rights notions. In response to the first problem, one can say that as compared with developed nations, the criteria of human rights are more often violated in developing countries. However, in relation to other societies, developed countries are not too concerned about the violation of human rights. Indeed, if their interests are in conflict with the observation of the rights of people in developing countries, they show no hesitation in placing their interests above anything else, including human rights! Human rights are the "necessary condition" for a perfect world, but it is not its "sufficient condition". The observation of human rights requires a guarantee of execution. The absence of this guarantee is not a flaw of human rights notions, it is a problem regarding the lack of ethics, spirituality and faith in the contemporary world. We are not saying that one flower will make a spring and that by believing in human rights all the problems of contemporary humanity will be solved. We have a more modest proposal which is as follows: in observing the criteria of human rights "some" of the problems of contemporary humanity will be solved.

In addition, the possibility of abuse applies to any desirable issue. There has been no small amount of abuse of religion throughout history. Have tyrannical states not used religion, which is the source of mercy, as an instrument for the cruelty, confirmation and justification of power? Human rights abuses are also not excluded. However, such abuses never count as a reason for the undesirability of religion or human rights.

In response to the second problem, one should say that human rights are either right or wrong. In the rightness or deviance of ideas geography is not a factor. An idea being Eastern does not make it more right in the same way that an idea being Western does not prevent it from being right. None of the principles of the UDHR, ICCPR or ICESCR is exclusive to or appropriate only for Western lives and societies. Defending human rights is not because of its Western origins, it is because of it being right, reasonable and concordant with justice and fairness. Throughout the history of Islam, logic and philosophy were similarly critiqued. The phrase *"man tamantaqa faqad tazandaqa"* ("anyone who applies logic becomes heretic") took centuries until it was clarified that formal logic had nothing to do with idolatry and monotheism. For centuries, philosophy was called the "infidels' saliva" (*su'r al-kuffar*) because of its Greek origins. However, today it is clear that no system of thought, even religious knowledge, can reply to its critics without rational explanation. Accepting human rights is not surrendering to the West, it is surrendering to the way of reasonable people (*sira al-'uqala*) and justice. Religion responds to specific human needs, not to all human requirements. At one time, people had medical expectations of religion. The evidence of this is in the following hadith collections: *Tibb al-Nabi, Tibb al-Sadiq* and *Tibb al-Ridha* (*The Medicine of the Messenger, The Medicine of the Sixth Imam* and *The Medicine of the Eighth Imam of the Shi'ite*). But today no one expects religion to write medical prescriptions. If it is not expected that religion provides the answers to questions in physics, chemistry and biology, why should one have economic, political or legal expectations of it? One must have religious expectations of religion. To change religion into a legal regime is the demotion of religion, not its elevation. From religion one must expect faith, rightful action and the cultivation of humans. A comprehensive discussion of this requires another opportunity, but in any case, opposing human rights in the name of defending religion is a great blow to religiosity and religious faith and provides the best excuse for those who hate religion.

Question: it seems that your *fiqh* viewpoint has changed. In works published before your imprisonment, you raised some new issues from a position within religion that drew from the capacities of traditional *fiqh*. The new *ijtihad* in *fiqhi* problems is among the features of your work during this period. In your book (*Hukumat-I Wila'i (Guardianship-based State)*), all of the new issues or critiques you brought up were raised within the framework of traditional *fiqh*. In the arena of human rights, too, such as the discussion of apostasy (*'Asr-i Ma*, 1998),[50] and especially in the article "Islam, Tolerance, and Violence" (*Kian*, 1998),[51] you tried to paint a picture of the compatibility of Islam with human rights while observing the criteria of traditional *fiqh*. However, in articles published after your imprisonment, such as "From Traditional Islam to End-Oriented Islam" (2001) and "The Dilemma of Slavery in Islam" (2003),[52] we see a sort of *ijtihad* in the fundamentals, and your new theory does not fit within the framework of traditional *fiqh* and conventional *ijtihad*. Are we seeing a paradigm shift in Kadivar here? What were the factors that led to this change in thinking?

Answer: your assessment is correct. I have reached a turning point and I thank God for this attention. In the critical analysis of the theory of the absolute appointed rule of the jurist (*wilayat intisabi mutlaqa faqih*) I completely followed all the criteria of traditional *fiqh*, whether in books published before I went to prison or in articles published thereafter. For example, in *Hukumar Intisabi (State by Appointment)*, like in *Guardianship-based State*, I proved that in accordance to the standards of conventional *fiqh* the appointment of the jurist by the Lawmaker to have guardianship over the people in the public sphere is unfounded. In my first steps in the field of human rights, I tried to use all of the capacities of traditional *fiqh*. For example, in the discussion of apostasy or violence, which can now be read in the book *The Concerns of a Religious State*, I reached the limit of what can be said via *ijtihad* in the secondary branches of *fiqh*. During that time, I believed that one could use this method to present a desirable picture of Islam from the Scripture, Tradition and reason (rational correlations). For about two decades I

---

50 Mohsen Kadivar, "Marzha-ye Azadi az Manzar-e Din" ("Borders of Freedom from a Religious Perspective"), in *Daghdagheha-ye Hokumat-e Dini (The Concerns of the Religious State)*, (Tehran: Nashr-e Ney, 2000), 495–543.

51 Ibid., 859–883.

52 Chapters 1 and 12, this book.

studied, researched and taught on the basis of this belief. In Evin prison, I spent long months carefully studying the *fatwas* of the most important Sunni and Shi'ite jurists from the fourth century to contemporary scholars on the specific issue of *shari'a*-based punishments (*hudud* and *ta'zirat*), physical confrontation in prohibiting the improper (*nahy 'an al-munkar*), and the subject of unprotected life (*mahdur al-dam*). I took notes and, more than anything else, I contemplated, and I reached some initial conclusions. I organised numerous questions which I raised with various Shi'ite authorities and senior experts after prison, and I again reflected on their answers. In 2001, I clearly wrote out in two pages the headlines of the conflicts between traditional *fiqh* and the UDHR, and I made inquiries about them with one of my most important mentors.[53] After waiting for several months and following up numerous times, it became clear that traditional *fiqh* could not solve these dilemmas and that the response was tied to the development of a new *fiqh*. The mentor kindly encouraged the disciple to provide the response, with the recommendation of being cautious, however. In any case, after three years of constant reflection and complete examination of the solutions, I felt that I had reached tranquillity. I had reached the legal proof (*hujjat shari'iya*) by way of the pious predecessor (*salaf salih*), which could at least be discussed as a possibility within academic gatherings and be critiqued and assessed by experts. It is clear that with debate, critique and discussion this study will be enriched. Put another way, the publication of "From Traditional Islam to End-oriented Islam" started the second phase and that article suggested a sort of *ijtihad* in foundations and principles. It was a suggestion that was made after the complete disappointment in the manner in which old methods were responding to new issues, a suggestion that arose from honesty and sincerity for the elevation of faith and the influence of Islam.

The Solution of Reformist Islam for the Dilemma of the Conflict between Traditional Islam and Human Rights

Question: after explanation, analysis and assessment, it is now time for providing a solution. What is your solution for eliminating the conflict between

---

53 *Dar Mahzar-e Faqih-e Azadeh Ustad Ayatollah Montazeri (In the Presence of a Noble Theologian Ayatollah Montazeri* (1922–2009), A Collection of Exchanges between the Mentor and the Disciple), 2015, letter of 8 August 2001, 35–37.

traditional Islam and human rights? In accepting human rights, what kind of "Islam" does reformist Islam offer instead of traditional Islam? What are the dimensions of this "Islam"? What characteristics does it have?

Answer: in facing modernity and its outcomes, such as human rights and democracy, and after the inadequacy of the responses of traditional Islam was proven, we have witnessed the birth, growth and blossoming of a new movement among Muslims that is unique neither to the Sunni or the Shi'ite, is not particular to Iran or the Arab countries nor limited to the Middle East or Far East. Among all Muslim elites, there have been various similar attempts to present a new picture of Islam and a re-reading of the creed of Muhammad, a new take on the Scripture and Tradition. This movement, which is known as reformist or re-visiting Islam, while adhering to the immortal message of God's revelation, believes that in traditional Islam this holy message is entwined with the customs of the age of Revelation. In addition, it believes that all the critiques that can be made of traditional Islam in the new age are in relation to the segment that pertains to the customs of traditional Islam, and that the holy message can still be defended with pride. The main duty of the insightful experts of Islam is to once again extract the message of Islam and to cast aside the sediments of custom. Hence, this solution is not confined to resolving the conflict between traditional Islam and human rights; it will also resolve conflicts such as those of reason, science and democracy with traditional Islam. This is the solution of the conflict between traditional Islam and modernity, and it can be explained as follows.

One can divide all Islamic teachings into four sections: first, affairs of faith and belief, meaning faith in the Great, Almighty, Wise, Just, Omniscient, Omnipotent, Compassionate and Merciful God, faith in the Hereafter and the Day of Judgement and Resurrection, and faith in the prophecy and mission of the last prophet, Muhammad b. 'Abdullah (Peace be upon him and his household); second, moral affairs such as the cultivation of the self, and the grooming of oneself with an honourable character and moral values as the most important goal of the mission of the Prophet; third, affairs pertaining to rituals and worship such as devotion and intimate supplication, prayer, fasting, *hajj*, *zakat* and charity as the most important demonstrations of servitude to God and surrendering to Him; fourth, the rulings of *shari'a* that do not relate to worship which are known as the *fiqh* of transactions, including the rulings of civil law, commercial law, criminal law and penal codes, public and private international law, constitutional law, and the rulings pertaining to food and drink.

More than 98 percent of the Qur'an is dedicated to explaining the first three, that is, the affairs pertaining to faith, morals and worship, and only about 2 per cent is dedicated to the *fiqh* of transactions. Although the volume of *fiqh* orders that are not about worship are greater in the hadiths than in the Qur'anic verses, in total they do not take up more than 10 per cent of our hadith tradition. In traditional Islam, the fourth section, meaning the *fiqh* of transactions, has gained an unaccountable importance that has cast itself on the sections of religion pertaining to faith, morals and worship. In worship, too, its *fiqh*-based form and face has cast a shadow on the other dimensions of these integral parts of the religion. The main feature of the new reading of Islam is the great and primary attention paid to affairs pertaining to faith, morals and worship as the main body of the divine religion. This means that these three are deepened and regain their Qur'anic position and blossom and spread as the main characteristics of religiosity. The major difference between the traditional and new reading is in the fourth section, that is, the *fiqh* of transactions. Reformist Islam does not deny the necessity of *shari'a* and *fiqh*, but it is critical of them, and has differing views from jurists in the past in relation to numerous rulings. It therefore presents a new *fiqh* that, although it shares some rulings with traditional *fiqh*, is fundamentally different in terms of certain rulings such as the *shari'a* rulings that conflict with human rights. In terms of volume, the new *fiqh* is smaller than traditional *fiqh*, and in terms of some of the bases of its *ijtihad*, it differs from the methodology of traditional *fiqh*.

Every single *shari'a* order from the time of the Revelation (non-ritual) had three features: first, they were considered reasonable (*'uqala'i*) according to the rationale of that time; second, they were considered just in accordance to the rationale of that time; and, third, as compared with the rulings of other religions and schools of thought, they were considered to be better solutions. In having the above-noted features during the time of the Revelation, all these rulings were considered to be progressive and in the service of bringing about a successful religious order. The collective intellect of people during that time did not have a better solution, and the style of reasonable people (*sirah 'uqala'i*) at the time undersigned the reasonableness of these rulings. None of them were judged to be unjust, violent, degrading or unreasonable and inferior to competing solutions.

Put another way, all of the rulings of *shari'a* were established by the Wise Lawgiver in accordance with what was best for his worshippers. "Species interests" (*maslaha naw'iya*) formed the basis of the formulation of *shari'a* "must dos", and "species harms" (*mafsada naw'iya*) formed the basis of *shari'a* "must not dos", such that one cannot find a ruling of *shari'a* that was established without observing this standard of what is in the species interests and what is harmful. One of the most important features of "species interests" is justice. As such, the forging of the rulings of *shari'a* was based on justice and fairness, and the rationale of the age of Revelation completely sensed this justice and fairness.

As long as it fits this criterion of interest, every ruling of *shari'a* will have credibility. Rulings from this perspective are of two categories: the first is orders which are permanently concomitant with that which is in the interest or harmful, meaning they will continually have the features that they had from the beginning and thus do not change their requirements in differing conditions of time and place. Rulings such those pertaining to the necessity of fairness, gratefulness to the benefactor, the prohibition on injustice and treachery, the necessity of keeping one's promise and trusteeship, the prohibition against lying, and so forth, will remain unchanged. The second category is one in which changing the subject of good to evil, or the reverse, is permitted. This means that in some conditions these rulings are good and have interests, and in other conditions they are evil and lack interests. The majority of transactional rulings belong to the second category, which means that in some circumstances of time and place they are beneficial, and in others they are credible in accordance with the *shari'a* when these interests hold. In dividing the rulings of *shari'a* into these two categories, there is no doubt that the second category exists among the rulings of *shari'a* and that this division is always prevalent in the philosophy and methodology of *fiqh*. The conflict under discussion, between the rulings of *shari'a* and human rights, is never considered among the first category of rulings, which means that none of the rulings of *shari'a* which are permanently concomitant with permanent or essential interests or harms are in conflict with human rights. The problem of conflict concerns the second category of rulings.

In the real world, the first category of *shari'a* orders is established to be absolute, permanent and eternal. But the Wise Lawgiver, who is more aware than anyone of the capacity of actions, conditions and the various aspects of every action, as well as the contingencies of time and place, places the orders in the second category to be conditional on the situation, temporary in accordance with particular circumstances, and dependent on them to remain credible.

In the substantive realm (*'alam thubut*), the first type of *shari'a* rulings are announced to be absolute, permanent and eternal. But the Wise Lawgiver – knowing better than anyone the potential of actions, circumstances, the different aspects of each action, and the different requirements of time and place – makes the second type of rulings conditional on the continuation of the circumstances and bound to the remaining aspects and considerations (*wujuh wa i'tibarat*), as well as temporary to a particular period. In other words, the rulings concerning actions that may be beneficial in some circumstances and harmful in others have not been formulated by God as permanent and unchanging rulings; from the outset, they were made temporary and conditional on the continuation of the relevant circumstances.

But in the affirmative realm (*'alam ithbat*), virtually all *shari'a* rulings (i.e., even the rulings of the second type) are presented in an absolute and permanent form and without any particular conditions or specific time attached. There was a particular advantage to not stipulating a timeframe for *shari'a* rulings that were, in fact, temporary and conditional on the circumstances: it was unnecessary to stipulate that a ruling was temporary long before the relevant circumstances had expired, since it is easier for people to act on a permanent ruling than on a temporary, conditional one.

Given that the conditions and duration of the first are different from the conditions and duration of the second in terms of interest, if the Lawgiver set the rulings of *shari'a* in accordance to the conditions and durations of the second, this ruling would lack interest in the conditions and durations of the first. It would be abominable if the Wise Lawgiver were to set a ruling that is lacking in interest, and if He were to give continuity to the first *shari'a* ruling in the framework of the conditions and durations of the second, given that this first ruling lacks interest in the conditions and duration of the second, it would be abominable if the Lawgiver did not abrogate them. Thus, in relation to these acts, which have various aspects and considerations and whose interests and harms change in various times and places, there is no choice but to set "temporary rulings". These acts do not deserve permanent rulings.

The lack of a permanent ruling of *shari'a* for these acts arises from the flaws, shortcomings and undeserving nature of the acts themselves, otherwise the agency of the Wise Actor is complete. In regard to acts which have traits in opposition to good and evil, and which gain interest or harms that vary with different aspects and considerations, there is no choice but to make (*ja'l*) temporary rulings that are determined in accordance with the durability of their interest in the substantive realm (*'alam thubut*). Since the dominant interest framed in the affirmative realm (*'alam ithbat*) is the assertion of the ruling in absolute and non-temporary form, the frame of the vast majority of *shari'a* rulings has been issued as absolute expression (*mutlaq*), whether in relation to time or conditions. However, as Sheikh Tusi (995–1068), the most distinguished jurist (*faqih* and *usuli*), put it precisely in his statement about *shari'a* rulings in *al-'Uddat fi Usul al-Fiqh* (*The Tools of Fiqh Methodology*), *shari'a* commands and prohibitions are always bound to the maxim "as long as interest exists" and should ensure the implementation of duties according to this condition.[54] This means that all of the *shari'a* rulings (of the second type) are in fact conditional, restricted and temporary. Conditional and restricted to the condition and restriction of "continuance of interest", and temporary according to the "time of existence of that interest".

The rulings of *shari'a* present in the Qur'an and the traditions of the Prophet and the Imams are not external to the two categories noted above. To put it more precisely, the majority of what is commanded and prohibited, as well as the situational rulings (*ahkam wadh'iya*) set in the Scripture and Traditions, are of the second category, that is, while the context of the indication (*shar'i* ruling) is absolute and unconditional, in the substantive realm it is conditional and restricted to "continuance of interest", and temporary according to the "time of existence of that interest". The Qur'anic nature of a *shari'a* ruling does not mean that it is one of the permanent rulings correlated with continuous interest, rather, many of the *shari'a* rulings whose interests change according to various aspects and considerations also have Qur'anic sources. In fact, the discussion of abrogating (*nasikh*) and abrogated (*mansukh*) *shari'a* rulings is among the most important discussions in Qur'anic studies, theology and the methodology of *fiqh*. Abrogation means the elimination of a stable *shari'a* ruling as a result of the expiration of its time and duration.

---

54 Abu Ja'far Muhammad b. al-Hasan al-Tusi, *al-'Uddat fi Usul al-Fiqh* (*The Tools of the Principles of Fiqh*), ed. Muhammad Rida al-Ansari al-Qomi (Qom: the editor, 1997), ch. 7: "Abrogating and abrogated", s. 3: "possibility of abrogation in *shar'i* affairs", 2:511–512.

The main condition of abrogation is that the abrogated ruling be from the second category of *shari'a* rulings, that is, from the rulings that are not correlated with permanent interests or harms, and that a change in their interest or harm in changing conditions of time and place and various aspects and considerations is possible. As such, there is no abrogation in regard to the first category of *shari'a* rulings, but in the second category, not only is abrogation possible, but it has also taken place in this category. It is clear that the meaning of abrogation in the Qur'an is the abrogation of the ruling without the abrogation of the recitation of the Qur'an (*naskh al-hukm la al-talawa*). This means that at the same time that it is accepted that the abrogated verse was revealed to the Prophet by God and will forever be part of the Qur'an, and one can continue to refer to it in terms of its recitation, miracle-ness, rhetoric and other Qur'anic discussions, its ruling has been abrogated by another verse in the Qur'an. This means that the abrogated verse was indicated by a temporary and conditional ruling, although it was presented in a non-temporary and unconditional context. With the revelation of the second verse, we find that the time or duration of the ruling has expired and its interest is cancelled, therefore the duty is to follow the second verse (meaning the abrogating verse). As Imam Ali has said, a person who cannot distinguish the abrogated from the abrogating will perish and cause others to perish. In any case, the knowledge of abrogating and abrogated is among the necessities of the knowledge of interpretation of the Qur'an. Among the most important instances of abrogation in the Qur'an is that of the *Najwa* (secret conversation) verse (Q. 58:12), along with the next verse of the same sura; the abrogation of the number of fighters (Q. 8:65) by the next verse of the same sura; the ruling of the waiting period (*'idda*) for widows (Q. 2:240) and verse 234 of the same sura; the ruling of the punishment of prostitution (Q. 4:15–16); the ruling of the role of faith in inheritance (Q. 8:72) by 33:6, and the change of the *qiblah* from Jerusalem to Mecca (Q. 2:142–150). Referring to the books of Qur'anic studies and an examination of abrogating and abrogated verses, leaves no doubt that a *shari'a* ruling that is based on the Qur'an could not only be abrogated by the widespread transmission (*mutawatir*) of the tradition, but abrogation has also occurred in identified particulars. The *shari'a* ruling that has been proven by a singular hadith (*khabar wahid*) is also subject to the possibility and occurrence of abrogation.

Question: while there is no doubt in the possibility and occurrence of abrogation in the verses, the widespread transmission (*mutawatir*) of hadiths, and singular hadith (*khabar wahid*), discussion is required with regard to the abrogating (*nasikh*) evidence. The abrogating indicator cannot be weaker than the abrogated indicator. The abrogating of a Qur'anic verse is a Qur'anic verse or a *mutawatir* hadith of the Prophet that "he does not speak from his own desire" (Q. 53:3); the abrogating of a *mutawatir* hadith is a verse of the Qur'an or another *mutawatir* hadith. A speculative singular hadith is not eligible for abrogating a verse of the Qur'an or a *mutawatir* hadith. Does rational indication (*dalil 'aqli*) have the eligibility to abrogate a *shari'a* ruling?

Answer: the gist of our discussion in response to this is a key question. One can change this question to another question, which is: what is one to do with conflicts between indications based on narration and reason? If the rational indication (*dalil 'aqli*) is certain (*yaqini*), then it would be the contextual evidence (*qarina*) of changing (*tassuruf*) the *prima facie* meaning (*zahir*) of the narrative indicator (*dalil naqli*). This means that the narrative indicator is hermeneutically interpreted (*ta'wil*) by the rational indicator; or, put more precisely, the rational indicator is preferred over the narrative indicator. This is the collective view of the "People of Justice" ('Adliya), including both the Mu'tazila and Shi'ite schools. The consequence of this firm basis is the possibility of the abrogation of narrative *shari'a* rulings by a certain rational ruling. For experts who acknowledge reason ('*aql*) to be one of the four *shari'a* indicators, the discussion in fact turns to the possibility of abrogation of a narrative *shari'a* ruling by a rational *shari'a* ruling. If all of the second type of *shari'a* rulings (meaning rulings pertaining to actions whose interests and harms change in accordance with different aspects and considerations and with different conditions of time and space) are in fact conditional to the continuance of the interests and are temporary, and if reason in any way definitely discovers that the interests of this *shari'a* ruling have been eliminated in this time, it becomes clear that this *shari'a* ruling has been abrogated by the rational ruling. After the rational ruling, the previous *shari'a* ruling is no longer considered a duty to be carried out (*taklif bi al-fi'l*). If reason is eligible for discovering the *shari'a* ruling, then there is no doubt that it is eligible for discovering the duration and time of the *shari'a* ruling as well. Saying that a rational ruling is abrogating means nothing other than that it has the ability to confine the time of the *shari'a* ruling.

It seems that in theology, the methodology of *fiqh*, and the interpretation of the Qur'an, traditional thinking does not have a problem with the various steps of this argument, except for one point. This is that if a definitive reason (*'aql qat'i*) comprehends it as such, it is evidence (*hujjat*). However, definitive reason has not come to such a comprehension on which one can refer. In fact, the challenge with such scholars will be on the minor premise and not the major premise; that is, there is no disagreement with them on the basis or principles, the disagreement is in the particulars. However we interpret this disagreement, it will have far-reaching consequences. In exploring the roots of this issue, until about one or two centuries ago no conflict was observed between rational and narrative indications. In addition, jurists would find the answers to the questions of their time via deductions based on Scripture and Tradition such that they had no need to refer to rational argument. This was the case even among the People of Justice ('Adliyah) and Usulis (scholars of the methodology of *fiqh*), who also acknowledged reason to be evident, and who were not much different in the procedure of deductions from the Akhbaris[55] or the Ash'ari, each of whom deny the validity of reason in the *shari'a*. Thus, in the discussions at hand

---

55 Shi'ite *fiqh* was divided into two schools, the Usulis and the Akhbaris. Although their ancestors can be found from the eleventh century onwards, the second revival of the Akhbaris occurred five centuries later in the time of the Safawids. The former were those jurists who believed in *usul al-fiqh* (the principles of jurisprudence) and their name came from this knowledge. The juridical procedure of deduction of *shari'a* rulings from the four major sources is called *ijtihad*, and jurists in this school are known as *mujtahids*. Muhammad Baqir Wahid Bihbahani (1706–1791) was the founder of this school. In this school, reason was the fourth source of *shari'a*, and *usul al-fiqh* was a type of reasoning. Usulis classified all hadiths, including the content of four major hadith collections, to be authentic or weak based on the qualification of the chain of transmission. Attributing anything to a text has principles that are gathered in linguistic discussions (*mabihith al-alfaz*), that is, the first large chapter of *usul al-fiqh*. In contrast, Akhbaris, or people of *akhbar* or hadiths, do not need to have knowledge of *usul al-fiqh*. For them, the exclusive source of *shari'a* is the hadiths. All the details and particulars that are needed in *shari'a* can be found in hadiths. The *prima facie* meaning of the Qur'an is not evident (*hujjat*), and its correct understanding requires hadith references. Human reason is not sufficient to be a source of *shari'a*. Any believer is able to find their *shar'i* duty in hadith without needing *usul al-fiqh* or the difficulty of *ijtihad*. The founder of the Akhbari school was Muhammad Amin Astar-Abadi (who died in *c*. 1626). Following a deep conflict between these two schools, the Usulis won and became the dominant figures in Shi'ite academies. The Usuli–Akhbari juridical challenge in Shi'ite Islam can be compared with the Mu'tazilite–Ash'arite theological challenge in Sunni Islam, but in contrast to the Shi'ite challenge, the winner in Sunni Islam was the Ash'arite school which was less rational. The rational Mu'tazilites were marginalised and eliminated completely by the thirteenth century.

about human rights, there is no noteworthy difference between the *shari'a* rulings of the jurists of the Ash'ari, Mu'tazila, Maturidi,[56] Akhbari and Usuli schools. For example, in the six axes under discussion, it is enough to refer to the opinions of al-Sarakhsi (who died in approximately 1096), a Hanafi jurist; al-Ghazali (1058–1111), an Ash'ari theologian and Shafi'i jurist; Ibn Rushd (1126–1198), a Maliki jurist; Ibn Taymiyya (1263–1328), a Hanbali theologian and jurist; Yusuf al-Bahrani (1695–1772), an Akhbari jurist; and al-Najafi, the author of *Jawahir al-Kalam* (1788–1850), an Usuli jurist, in order to be certain about the extent that the rational argument was relevant in the deduction of the *shari'a* ruling.

The main feature of the modern age is the blossoming of human reason. Critical reason does not officially recognise any red lines and has begun to questions all issues, even those that in previous times were unquestionable. The contemporary human being has understood many things that in the past were adrift in a halo of secrets and symbols. This does not mean that contemporary humans know everything and that nothing remains unknown to them. On the contrary, the realm of his or her knowledge has both increased and he or she has also come to understand the depth and extent of his or her ignorance.

He or she asks courageously and answers modestly. No theologian or jurist can consider him- or herself to be exempt from the need for new rational research, such as the content analysis of methodology, methodology of interpretation, especially of the scriptural texts (hermeneutics), philosophy of religion, critical theology, sociology of religion, psychology of religion, historical method, philosophy of law, philosophy of ethics and so forth. One cannot close the door to all critiques and objections by considering all transactional rulings to be devotional (*ta'abbudi*) or beyond the rational (*tawqifi*),[57] or by linking them to hidden interests or harms. Today in the realm of non-ritual

---

56 Maturidi is a Sunni theological school founded by Muhammad b. Mahmud al-Samarkandi al-Maturidi (853–944). Maturidi and Ash'arite schools are in the same theological camp. Maturidi – the largest Sunni theological school – is a little bit more rational than the Ash'ari school. Maturidis are mostly Hanafi (the largest Sunni legal school), and Ash'arites are mostly Shafi'i and Maliki in *fiqh*. Hanbilism is the smallest Sunni theological and legal school.

57 *Tawqifi* issues are subjects or rulings that cannot be comprehended except through the statements of the Lawmaker. Human reason is not able to comprehend them. So their definitions and rulings depend on *shari'a*. Although these issues are not irrational or non-rational, they are beyond rational or supernatural.

shari'a rulings, the contemporary human thinks that he or she has access to the interests or harms of various commands and prohibitions. Certainly, the contemporary human considers slavery to be unjust, unreasonable and evil. They do not consider legal discrimination on the basis of religion, creed or gender to be just and rational. They find it unfair and irrational that jurists and clerics should have special rights in the public sphere. They pronounce any limitations on the freedom of religion to be a restriction of the essential rights of humans, and do not tolerate harsh physical punishment. Wherever reason comprehends a ruling, it is evident, an essential evident (*hujjat bi al-dhat*). The contemporary human has no doubt in his or her comprehension of these affairs. If someone has not yet reached such comprehension, he or she is not permitted to condemn the comprehension of others and contemporary rational common sense.

For contemporary Muslims, reason is not compatible with the narrative indications of some of the *shari'a* rulings of traditional Islam, rather it is contrary to them. The strength of today's reason is such that it can change the narrative indications as the contextual evidence (*qarina*), and discover their temporariness. The discussion of reason is much more extensive and in depth than the simple discussion of yesterday, which was limited to independent reason and the issues of the good and evil of reason. Cleaving apart this fundamental discussion requires more research.

In any case, contemporary Muslims are witness to two ways of thinking alongside one another in the texts of religion, meaning the Scripture and Tradition. The first is the way of thinking that is compatible with human rights and which includes two propositions: one, is the proposition that does not have any conflict with human rights notions; and the other is the proposition that explicitly indicates that the essential rights of human beings are based on their humanness. These types of proposition are evident in the frame of the generalities (*'umumat*) and absolute expressions (*itlaqat*) referenced mostly in the Mecca verses, the Tradition of the Prophet in Mecca, and which are also included in the Tradition of Imam Ali during his leadership. The second is the way of thinking that is incompatible with human rights, and includes propositions that are explicitly in conflict with human rights and explicit textual indications (*nass*) regarding discrimination in the rights of humans based on religion, sect, gender, status as free or enslaved, and status as a jurist or one of the masses, which are explicit in denying the freedom of religion, and in support of violent and impaired punishments, representative of a weakening of Islam (*wahn al-Islam*) to one that is distant from mercy and compassion. These are explicitly found in parts of the Tradition of the Prophet in Medina and some of the hadiths of the Imams.

In dealing with the above two ways of thought, traditional Islam has found the indications of the second category to be stronger, since those of the first group are not outside of the three categories of general (*'amm*), absolute (*mutlaq*) and indeterminate (*mujmal*) indications. In addition, there is no doubt that the indications from the second category are specifically applicable (*khass*), restricted (*muqayyad*) or determined (*mubayyan*) in the collection of indications (*jam' dilali*) which have become prioritised based on their restriction (*taqyyeed*), determination (*tabyeen*) and being specific (*takhsees*). In this collection, all of the *shari'a* rulings from the first and second category are considered to be stable, unchanging and non-temporary. This way of collecting indications in our time is assessed to be in conflict with human rights.

In the solution that has been offered, the narrative indication of the first category is strengthened by the rational indication. The rational indication is the context that changes absolute expressions based on time (*itlaq zamani*) in the second category of rulings, discovers their restriction (*taqayyud*) in terms of the interests that no longer exist, and makes them temporary to the continuance of the interest. Put another way, the rational indication that is confirmed (*mu'ayyad*) by the narrative indications of the first category, abrogates the narrative indications of the second category that are in conflict with human rights, and provides information about the negation of their interests. In this de-activation of the conflicting indications and their abrogation, the conflict is eliminated from its foundations.

The three conditions of being reasonable, just and better than the solutions offered by other religions and schools of thought are not just the conditions of the age of Revelation. Rather, in any age, non-ritual *shari'a* rulings must meet the above three conditions in accordance with the rational conventions (*'urf 'uqala*) of that time. The certain opposition of a ruling with the conventions of reasonability (*sira 'uqala*) of our time, its conflict with the standards of justice of our time, or its inferiority to the solutions of a new era, reveal the temporariness, impermanence and abrogation of these types of rulings. This means that such rulings were appropriate for the requirements of the age of Revelation and are not among the permanent and stable *shari'a* rulings of the Lawgiver. When people start speaking about the requirements of time and place, it means that they have accepted the idea that a *shari'a* ruling can be temporary. The requirements of time and place are not necessarily stable, but they are changing and varied. The philosophy of the existence of such rulings in the texts of the Scripture and the authentic Tradition is necessary for the resolution of problems of the age of the Revelation and similar eras. If the Lawgiver did not set these types of *shari'a* rulings, which are in accordance with the time of the Prophet and the customs of the time of Revelation, and if he left people on their own, especially considering the great need of the people of that time for these types of rulings and the insufficiency of the experience of human collective reason in this regard, it would not have been in keeping with the mature wisdom of God. In all his completeness, the Prophet could not solve the numerous problems and issues, organise the religious regulation and administer society without the direct help of God. In many instances, he waited for the Divine Revelation to rain down. Thus, there was no solution other than to set the temporary *shari'a* rulings that were restricted to the continuance of the interest in the sub-stantive realm (*'alam thubut*) alongside the *shari'a* rulings that were stable and unchanging, and put them in the text of the Scripture and Tradition. The absolute expression based on time (*itlaq zamani*) of the indication's context (*lisan dalil*), and even the explicit statement of eternity (*ta'beed*) (the eternal nature of the ruling) with the *prima facie* meaning of the abrogating indicator, does not prevent the first *shari'a* ruling from being abrogated. The pious predecessor (*salaf salih*) has altogether accepted this point.

Ijtihad means distinguishing those rulings which have been set in accor-dance with the requirements of the time, place and conditions of the age of Revelation from the stable and permanent rulings of *shari'a*. To mix these two categories and to introduce all of the *shari'a* rulings from the Scripture and Tradition as permanent and stable Islamic rulings that apply to all times and places shows an inability to understand the true meaning of reli-gion, the goal of the Prophet's mission and the telos of *shari'a*. Those who consider the secondary rulings and practical forms of *shari'a* to be superior to the goals and ends of religion, and consider not just the customs of yesterday but the customs of the age of Revelation to be sacred, while they have suspended the sacred ends of religion and the high aims of *shari'a*, are far from the correct *ijtihad*. The persistent repetition of past *fatwas* and the conversion of the most precautionary (*ahwat*) to preferable (*awla*),[58] is nothing other than emulation of the pious predecessor. The *shari'a* rulings are the objective of religion by accident (*matlub fi al-'aradh*), and the transcendent final goals of religion are the objectives of religion itself (*matlub bi al-dhat*). To put it in another way, secondary *shari'a* rulings are the means for achieving the main and sacred ends of religion; every path is credible only until it takes us to that destination. There is no "objectivity" (*mawdhu'iyyat*) in this path, it has "instrumentality" (*tariqiyyat*). Each path is valid only if it is determined by certainty (and not by speculation, presumption or guessing) that a ruling no longer has instrumentality and its benefit has been cancelled and it is no longer conducive to the destination. In that case, it is clear that it was credible when it was instrumental and not in absolute terms. If insightful *mujtahids*, expert jurists, and informed theologians of Islam who are aware of the necessities of the time do not rise up in this regard, they can be sure that serious religious and cultural problems and crises will marginalise religion and *shari'a*. It is clear that distinguishing between rulings that are temporary and conditional on interests from those that are stable and permanent is a matter for experts. It requires deep professionalism concerning the Scripture and Tradition, on the one hand, and knowledge of the capacities and limits of reason in the age of modernity, on the other.

If it happens that someone fears permanent abrogation (with the completeness of the arguments and the observation of the necessary cautions), they can use temporary abrogation, meaning that the possibility of return to the ruling that has been abrogated in case of changing conditions of time and place in the future is not eliminated. This means that both indicators of abrogating and abrogated are considered to be temporary and conditional on interest and will be carried out in accordance with what is in the interest of lawmaking. The issue of a temporary abrogation is not unprecedented in scholarly Qur'anic discussions.[59]

---

58 These are two minor *fiqhi* terms which are repeatedly used in *fatwa* handbooks. The major differences between *fatwa*s are these two terms. The *fatwa*s of jurists, regardless of these two minor terms, are the same. They indicate lack of *ijtihad* and emulation in practice.

59 For instance, see Ma'rifat, *al-Tamhid fi 'Ulum al-Qur'an, al-Naskh al-Mashrut* (conditional abrogation), 2:285–286.

In addition, the true interests and harms of the rulings of *shari'a*, which are occasionally noted as hidden interests and harms, or as interests or harms in themselves (*nafs al-amr*), are completely different than the interest of the system in the *fiqh* of public interest (*fiqh al-maslaha*) or in governmental *fiqh* (*fiqh hukumati*). In the former, the interests of the human species are at issue and in the latter, it is the interests of a political regime, or that which the ruler considers to be in the interest of the people. Determining what is in the interest of the species is the duty of rational conventions (*'urf 'uqala*) and theologians, and determining the interest of the state is the responsibility of politicians and the ruling councils. The former is in the position of promulgation (*ja'l*) of *shari'a* rulings and the latter belongs to the promulgation of state rulings.

Question: there is no doubt that your theory will further aflame the fires of reformist Islam in Iran and that it will be a source of great criticism and confirmation. In advance, we ask that you publish more details on this new viewpoint, as well as more explanation, so that its various dimensions are further clarified. With every single one of the subject matters you bring up, new questions arise, but we must at some point end the interview. In addition to wishing you success, please let us know if there are any remaining points, or if you have any recommendations for the readers of this theory.

Answer: the conversation has become lengthy but issues remain. I hope to have the opportunity and luck to explain and expand on the issue. I ask that all readers who have critiques or recommendations, in particular those who are learned members of seminaries and believers in traditional Islam, to do me the great favour of cautioning me about the shortcomings and flaws of this work. I hope that *Aftab*, the monthly, will also provide the opportunity for such scholarly critiques to be published. It is without doubt that with the multiplication of opinions, critiques and assessments, the theory will become more developed.

At the end, to eliminate any providential objection, I think it is appropriate to bring the attention of the followers of the official reading of Islam to a *fatwa* of the late Ayatollah Khomeini. In his *Kitab al-Tahara* (*Book of Purity*), he stated: "If we know that someone has accepted the principles of religion (*usul deen*) and accepts as a whole that the Prophet has some rulings, but if he or she has doubts about the mandatory nature (*wujub*) of prayer or *hajj*, and assumes that these rulings were mandatory during early Islam but are no longer in recent years, followers of religion do not consider such a person to be a non-Muslim, as there are enough arguments for that person to be a Muslim."[60] Peace.

Epilogue

1. In this chapter, I have focused my discussion on human interactions (*mu'amalat*), or the non-ritual parts of *fiqh*. Although it can be accepted that there is no clash between worship and human rights, this does not mean that structural *ijtihad*, or *ijtihad* in foundations and principles, is exclusive to human interactions, or that it includes ritual and worship. Although the essence of worship is dictated and devotional (*ta'abbudi*), this does not prevent reform in other aspects of ritual such as non-obligatory *khums* (one-fifth tax) of business profit (*arbah makasib*), obligatory *zakat* on trade, as well as the nine traditional subjects which include saving, the permissibility of sacrifice outside of Mena (Mecca) during the *hajj*, Ramadan fasting over long days in the territory between 43° and 66° latitude, discovering the new moon, the minimum distance of *shar'i* travel, and particular issues around purity and impurity. I reached this conclusion after thorough inductive inquiry.

2. In this chapter, I mentioned three criteria for revisiting the validity of *shari'a* rulings: reasonability (*'uqala'i*), justice (*'adala*) and functionality. Because of the importance of ethical standards, I added a fourth criterion in 2006: that all *shari'a* rulings were ethical in the age of early Islam. This is not only a primary condition, but it is also necessary for this condition to remain continuous for a *shari'a* ruling to remain valid. There are some rulings in the *shari'a* that were ethical in the age of early Islam according to the conventions of reasonable people at that time, but which are not ethical according to the conventions of reasonable people today. The best example of changing ethical standards is slavery. If a *shar'i* ruling definitely fails to meet an ethical criterion, it demonstrates that this ruling *was* a specific *shari'a* ruling,

---

60 Ruhollah Mousawi Khomeini, *Kitab al-Tahara* (*Book of Purity*) (Tehran: Institute for Compilation and Publication of Imam Khomeini's Work, 2013), 3:445.

but that it is not anymore as soon as it *is* no longer ethical. This is a sign of rational abrogation.

The overlap between these criteria is undeniable, but the case for rational abrogation would be stronger if more than one criteria pointed towards it. In other words, when an issue is unreasonable, unjust, unethical and less functional than equivalent solutions, there will be more certainty around its abrogation as more than one of these criteria applies. Although the domain of ethics is larger than the domain of justice, the importance of justice makes it necessary for it to be a separate criterion.

3. The key point in this theory is "rational indication", which is reasonable, just, ethical and more functional than competing solutions. All four criteria are rational. The abrogating indication is rational too. This means that if there were no narrative indications, this theory would be valid. However, there are many narrative indications that support the rational indication. These narratives include the Qur'anic verses or prophetic hadiths which are "confirmed" (*mu'yyid*), not argued (*dalil*). These confirmed narratives can mostly be found (but not always) in the general statements (*'umumat*) and absolute expressions (*itlaqat*) of the Mecca period, including the Qur'anic verses and prophetic hadith (mostly in the hadith heritage of Imam 'Ali in the Shi'ite collection of hadith). These narratives are rulings for guidance (*ahkam irshadi*) on the rational indication. Most (but not all) of the abrogated rulings belong to the Medina period, including Qur'anic verses and prophetic hadiths (as well as the hadiths of other Shi'ite Imams).

4. There is an ambiguous point concerning infidels from the perspective of traditional Islam. By infidels, I mean non-Muslims who are not People of the Book who applied for the *dhimmi* contract with Muslim authorities, as well as non-Muslims who are not People of Treaty (*mu'ahad*). Are all of these non-Muslims, non-*dhimmi*, non-*mu'ahad* infidels at war with Muslims (*kafir harbi*) without any human rights at all? The answer is no according to the unequivocal textual meaning (*nass*) of the Qur'anic verses (Q. 60:8–9), which states that Muslims are not allowed to enter into war against those unbelievers who did not declare war against them, did not try to exclude them from their homes, and did not interfere in their religious affairs. As a result, people were divided into six classes: (1) Muslims of the true *madhab*; (2) other Muslims; (3) *dhimmi*s (People of the Book who have entered

into contract with Muslim authorities); (4) *mu'ahad*s (People of Treaty); (5) unbelievers who have neither signed a treaty with Muslims nor entered into war or displayed any hostility towards Muslims; and (6) unbelievers who have declared war against Muslims (*kafir harbi*). Even in traditional Islam, neglecting the fifth category and combining the fifth and sixth as *kafir harbi* is incorrect.

6

Questions and Answers about Human Rights and Reformist Islam

Preface

Mohsen Kadivar's views on "Human Rights and Reformist Islam",[1] which were published in issue 3 and 4 of *Aftab*,[2] raised many questions for readers and experts. We are grateful to him for being willing to respond to the questions received, and we bring the attention of readers to these replies.

The Comparison of Ratified Rulings (ahkam imdha'i) and Conventions of Reasonable People (sira al-'uqala)

Question one: based on historical research (for example, in the book *The Detailed Pre-Islamic History of Arabs*[3]) and according to many researchers of Islam (for example, Dr Mehdi Haeri Yazdi (1923–1999)), the main body of Islamic *shari'a* on human transactions addresses ratified rulings (literally, signed, *ahkam imdha'i*), as opposed to positive rulings (literally, established, *ahkam ta'sisi*). The late Haeri Yazdi believed that with the exception of those

---

1 Chapter 5, this book.
2 "Porsesh wa Pasokh-e Hoquq-e Bashar wa Roshanfekri-ye Dini", *Aftab* No. 6 (March 2006); No. 8 (August 2006); No. 9 (November 2006). This *Aftab* is a literary, social and cultural journal published by Iranian students at Waterloo University in Canada and is different from the Iranian bi-monthly journal *Aftab*.
3 Jawad 'Ali, *al-Mufassal fi Tarikh al-'Arab qabl al-Islam* (*The Detailed Pre-Islamic History of Arabs*) (Baghdad: University of Baghdad, 1993), 10 vols.

pertaining to worship, less than 5 per cent of the rulings fall into the category of positive rulings. In other words, this historical fact demonstrates that it cannot be other than that the Legislator (*shari'*) has followed the conventions of reasonability (*'urf al-'uqala*) in non-worship issues.

A. Given the above, could one not suppose that none of the ratified principles are mandatorily permanent and eternal?
B. Human rights is the symbol and sum of the conventional reason of contemporary humans. What is the difference between the pre-Islamic conventional reason of humans whose principles were approved by the Legislator and the conventional reason of contemporary humans?
C. Given that the non-worship rulings are usually ratified and also circulated in the pre-Islamic period, the rejection of contemporary human rational achievements (including human rights) because of conflict with *shari'a* rulings (the pre-Islamic conventions which were confirmed by the Legislator), in fact is nothing other than the rejection of rational achievements of contemporary humans due to conflicts with the rational achievements of those who came before. Will elaborate differentiation between ratified and positive rulings not be one of the keys for solving this issue?

Answer: among the prevalent ways of categorising *shari'a* rulings in traditional *fiqh* is to divide rulings into ratified and positive rulings. Positive rulings are the Legislator's innovative rulings that were unprecedented. The ratified rulings are those that existed prior to Islam and were accepted as a whole, or with some revisions by the Legislator. These rulings were ratified because they were in accordance to the conventions of reasonable people. It is clear that the credibility of ratified rulings is dependent on consideration of the criterion of its promulgation (its accordance with the conventions of reasonable people). The dominant reception of the conventions of reasonable people by traditional *fiqh* has been that they are stable, eternal and permanent. This means that the rational convention, or conventions of reasonable people, has arisen from the rational aspect of humans and is not subject to change with the varying circumstances of time and place and thus always remains stable.

One of the expansions over the last half a century in the area of ratified rulings is to rely on the "possibility" of the signing of the ruling by the Legislator rather than the "occurrence" of the signing. This means that the criterion for the ratification of the ruling by the Legislator among previous jurists has been the occurrence of the rational convention before the eyes and ears of the Legislator, without lack of rejection and prevention by the Legislator, as long as ratification and confirmation could be detected from this lack of rejection. Some jurists[4] did not find the occurrence of the rational convention before the eyes and ears of the Legislator (or occurrence during the time of the Revelation) to be necessary, but, rather, they put a new justification on the table: would the Legislator reject the rational convention, if He faced it? If the answer is negative because it unconsciously springs to mind among reasonable people (*irtikaz 'uqala'i*) and rejection is negated, in such cases of rational innovations (*musdahdath*) one can believe in the Legislator's ratification. Based on this solution, all rational conventions that are not based in precedent during the time of Revelation, and are considered to be new and innovative if they pass the above-noted test (which, in fact, is no more than an emphasis on being true rational conventions), will count as ratified rulings of *shari'a*. While this solution is noteworthy and solves problems in cases of rational rulings without precedence in early Islam, it requires a supplement in the case of other rational rulings.

One of the neglected issues in traditional Islam and *fiqh* is the possibility of changes in rational conventions. In this traditional epistemic system, rational conventions in themselves have been studied, *a priori*, and imperatively, and they have been ruled to be permanent, unchangeable and stable. While if rational conventions are studied from *a posteriori*, historical and phenomenological points of view, it is not unexpected to find changes in some rational conventions (but not all of them). It suffices to compare rational conventions in regard to the three issues below during two different time periods. One is the older era until about two centuries ago, and the other is during the past two centuries. The first issue is slavery, the second is the case of women, and the third is violent punishments. The conclusion is that ratified rulings can be divided into two categories, temporary or changing rulings and stable or permanent rulings, and that both of these are ratified rational conventions. One is the rational conventions that have changed,

---

4 For example, al-Sayyid Muhammad Baqir al-Sadr (1935–1980), *Durus fi 'Ilm al-Usul* (*Lessons in the Science of Principles of Fiqh*), *al-halqa al-thalitha* (*the third episode*) (Qom: Center of Professional Discussions and Studies on the Martyr al-Sadr, 2000, 143 (with some restricted conditions).

and the other is those that have not yet changed and somehow will never change either. Based on this, a ratified ruling neither correlates with it being a permanent and stable ruling (as is thought in traditional Islam), nor is it an indication of it being a temporary and changeable ruling (as was raised in the question).

Human rights are one of the symbols of the rational conventions in our time. It is clear that the rational convention is different from convention (*'urf*). Not every conventional issue necessarily arises from rational conventions. Conventions can have sources that are different from rational conventions. Based on this, conventional rationality is also different from rational conventions. The latter means actions arising from reasonable people based on their reasonableness. Compared with the rational conventions of our time, those during the period of early Islam were general and specific in some respects (*'umum wa khusus min wajh*). What are shared between these two disciplines are the stable rulings. The rational rulings of the age of Revelation that are no longer considered to be reasonable (a few examples of which have been noted above) certainly count among those rulings of *shari'a* whose validity has expired. Rational rulings without precedent during the age of Revelation are not valid in traditional Islam and only have validity in the expansion noted earlier in accordance with the rational convention (which I believe is defensible).

With ratified rulings, pre-Islamic conventions are not relevant. The criterion in traditional *fiqh* in this regard is the way of reasonable people (*sirah al-'uqala*) (and not convention (*'urf*)), which has been confirmed by the Legislator and is considered immortal and unchanging. In reformist Islam, in cases of conflict between ratified rulings and the conventions of reasonability (the contemporary conventions of today) – of course, with confidence in the rationality of these conventions – the conventions take precedence over the previous ratified rulings. These circulated rational conventions become the context for abrogation of the *shari'a* ruling, or, put another way, it indicates the temporary nature of that ruling and the expiration of the duration of validity of that ruling.

Therefore, one of the clearest points of difference between traditional and reformist Islam is in the conflict between the conventions of reasonable people (contemporary, and without precedence in early Islam) and the ratified rulings of early Islam. Traditional Islam has issued a *fatwa* on the invalidity of the conventions of reasonable people and generally does not consider a ruling that has not been ratified by the Legislator to be reasonable. On that basis, most of the propositions of human rights are rejected according to the *fatwa* of traditional Islam and *fiqh*. Reformist Islam considers the ratification of the Legislator to be conditional on the continuity of the validity of the conventions of reasonable people, and after changes in these conventions in this case, it announces ratified rulings based on previous conventions to be abrogated and turns to giving orders in accordance with contemporary conventions.

Given the above points, it becomes clear that turning to the distinction between ratified and positive rulings is not the key to solving the problem.

Question two: in presenting your recommended solution, you implicitly assume that the precedence of justice over religion is understandable and distinguishable and that religion must be just. This presumption itself, how-ever, is not very obvious or clear. Although I am aware that this conflict is an old one and I am not unaware that the opinion of Shi'ite theologians is in some ways closer to that of the Mu'tazila, nonetheless, the question remains difficult. In many Qur'anic stories (as well as in many historical events from early Islam), the actions of the prophets and saints seem both immoral and unjust in accordance with the standards of humanity. Among these, perhaps there is no clearer example than that of Abraham and the slaughter of Ismael (Q. 37:102–103). If we consider morality and justice to precede and to be inde-pendent of a divine order, Abraham's decision to kill his child is highly immoral and unjust, even in accordance with the standards of his time. The same is true of *Khidhr*'s activities when facing Moses (Q. 18:65–82). What is to prevent believers from supposing that Divine issues (which appear to be in conflict with human rights) have a wisdom and secret that is not revealed to us (just as the wisdom and secret of *Khidhr*'s activities were not clear)? Based on this evi-dence, how can believers be sure that that they are able to rely on their reason to determine good from evil and the just from the unjust?

Answer: if we believe that all of the non-worship rulings are based on wis-dom that is impossible to reveal to human reason, and that good and evil are beyond the grasp of human reason, and that justice gains meaning in the light of religion, then one must not dwell on the conflict of divine rulings with human rights which are born of the poor reason of humans. What arises from mature Wisdom, even if it is not comprehensible to us, is absolutely preceded. Based on this, there is no discussion and there is nothing to say to a believer on this basis.

However, if we go through the Akhbaris and People of the Hadith, and in the historical quarrel between the Mu'tazila and the Ash'arites, we chose the basis of People of Justice and considered justice to be precedent over religion, and wanted religion to be just, and did not consider justice to be religious. According to the sequence of *mujtahids* (Usuli jurists), we also considered reason to be one of the official sources of *shari'a*, and we did not imagine all of the non-ritual rulings to be devotional (*ta'abbudi*) and beyond rational (*tawqifi*). We also considered the rulings of the time of the Prophet to include time-bound and time-sensitive rulings (as well as timeless rulings) and we considered the rulings of *shari'a* to be the duty of all and not a specific responsibility of elites. This is when the big problem of the conflict of some of the rulings attributed to *shari'a* with the conventions of reasonable people of this period presents itself to the wise believer and requires an appropriate answer.

The source of duties as determined by the *shari'a* is the exoteric meanings (*zahir*) of religion and not their esoteric meanings (*batin*). The specific commands to Abraham and the "pious servant" (*Khidhr*) cannot be generalised to others, and if someone in delusion attempts to follow these men of good name by punishing someone before a crime, or attempting to kill their child, they will have unequivocally committed a sin (prohibited act) according to the *shari'a* and can be legally prosecuted. With the end of the Revelation and the last prophet, the era of specific Divine missions ended and all human beings are without exception bound by the *shari'a* of the Prophet Muhammad. The *shari'a* of the Prophet Muhammad denotes the *prima facie* meaning of the Book and the Tradition, and nothing else. In this regard as well, both traditional and reformist scholars of religion agree, and not a single person has referred to the command test of Abraham or the mystical teachings that Moses was taught by the pious servant (*Khidhr*) in order to extract the rulings of *shari'a*. It is clear that there are different stages (*maqamat*). The hidden wisdom of the station of nearness of the most senior saints is completely distant from the stage of legislation of the public juridico-moral obligations of servants. We as average humans are absolutely duty-bound by morality and justice, and have no choice other than comprehension of religious *prima facie* too.

Human Rights: An Achievement of Contemporary Humans

Question three: the historical evolution of an idea is the test of that idea. According to what you have noted, the interpretation of traditional Islam conflicts with human rights, and even if your interpretation of Islam today is a correct interpretation and that the rulings of Islam are not in conflict with human rights, this problem remains steadfast: why is Islam so prone to misunderstanding and conflicting understandings of human rights? Is it not far from the wisdom of God to determine His *shari'a* such that the majority understand it in an unjust way and interpret it in a way that conflicts with human rights?

Answer: the historic occurrence of an idea is one of the factors (but not the only factor) for qualification of that idea. One of the standards (*shakhis*) (but not the only standard) in judging religions and ideologies of our era (but not in all eras) is the compatibility of that religion or ideology with the conventions of reasonable people, and specifically one of its manifestations, that is, human rights. To impose standards belonging to the circumstances of a time and place of a past era on our current era is just as wrong as using standards from a contemporary time and place as criteria for judging past eras. One must refrain from making a standard absolute, and using it in different conditions and times. Human rights is one standard of "contemporary" rationality. In different eras, humans had different standards. One cannot use this standard to judge the ancient civilisations of Greece, Iran, Egypt, China or the medieval civilisations of Europe. Similarly, one cannot use it to judge Islamic culture and civilisation from Muhammad's Mission (*bi'that*) until the last one or two centuries. Human rights is an achievement of "contemporary" humans and one can use it to ask questions about the situation of Islam over the past one or two centuries.

Throughout its history, traditional Islam has had relative success and, as compared with its rivals, has left behind a defensible report card of itself. Muslims had a more humane and tolerant stance towards followers of other religions, and had a greater share in elevating the collective of human knowledge and culture. What is under discussion is traditional Islam outside the context of its own time: or, more precisely, Islam in the circumstances of time and place prior to the twenty-first[5] century in the circumstances of time and place from the twenty-first century onwards. I believe that the imposition of the circumstances of time and place of Arabia in the first century of Islam on all of the teachings of Islam is openly unfair to the Islam of the Prophet. Among the teachings of the Divine Scripture and the Tradition of the Prophet, one may also find rulings that transcend time and place, and Islam is universal and immortal on the basis of the validity of these stable rulings. However, this does mean that immortality and stability perpetuate all of the rulings attributed to God and the Prophet. In order to manage the Arabia of the first century AH, there was no choice but for God and the Prophet to make temporary *shari'a* rulings. It is debatable whether these temporary rulings can be used in other eras as stable and eternal rulings. Reformist Islam has taken up the role of eliminating this historic mistake.

In the texts of the Scripture and Tradition, there is much contextual evidence that may be given in support of the reformist interpretation of Islam. In Islamic societies, reformist Muslims have great general support, even though the roots of the masses supporting the traditional readings cannot be ignored. Nonetheless, the growth of the reformist reading is noteworthy. The future lies with this progressive reading. The wise God, whether via the internal messenger, meaning reason, or through the external messenger, meaning the Prophet Muhammad, has arranged Islam and its understanding in such a way that it is possible for the majority of people in all times to be able to have a just and realistic understanding of it.

Question four, part A: your opinions have been about traditional Islam. In contrast to this, your reader must imagine a "non-traditional Islam". Where is this non-traditional Islam? At what date and in which corner of the Earth has it been shaped? How do believers worship and undertake their religious activities? How can one carry out statistical and scholarly research (using today's standards) on this? The writer of these lines believes that "religion" and "language" are similar to one another in the sense that they both produce the goods of their consumers. The same way that the experience of creating the language of Esperanto (despite all of its rational principles and standards) was not successful, the scholastic logic (even if strong) that wants to build a religion, will not take shape either. The sum of these questions is as follows: how

---

5 "Twentieth century" in the original text.

can we be sure that in solving the conflict under discussion in the interests of the reading of supporters of human rights will leave us with something that is still a religion with people who have faith with sincerity and belief?

Answer: traditional Islam is the consequence of the understanding of the majority of Muslims about Islam (the Book of God and the Tradition of His Messenger) in the premodern era. This understanding of Islam continues to live on, with the difference that in the modern era another understanding of Islam, meaning the reformist understanding of the Qur'an and the Prophet's Tradition, has gradually taken shape among some Muslims. This new understanding, like the previous one, believes in God and the Day of Judgement, believes that implementation of the teachings of the Prophet is a necessity for achieving happiness, and considers the Qur'an and the Divine Revelation to be the unchanging foundation of being a Muslim. However, it does not believe in the authority (*hujjiyat*) of the conditions of time and place of the age of Revelation or the understanding of Muslims during the early years of Islam. Nor does it believe that it is the telos of Muslims to think with the rational conventions of that time or to perpetuate the conditions of that time to this era. The reformist Muslim accepts him- or herself as the child of his or her time, thinks with the rationality of today, and guards his or her faith in the modern world. They have neither accepted modernity altogether, nor have they rejected it, rather, they have faced it critically and selectively. Their approach to traditional Islam is the same: critical and selective. Their criterion in these two critical positions has been an honest adherence to religious faith and reason (or external and internal authority). The reformist Muslim recognises the right of human reason and the Divine Revelation fairly and believes that there is no conflict between these two God-given sources. If there is a conflict to be found, it is an indication of improper understanding, whether it be an improper understanding of rational ruling or an improper understanding of the ruling of Revelation. The reformist Muslim neither sees her- or himself to be needless of secular (*bashari*) knowledge, nor does he or she consider human knowledge to be fruitful if it ignores Divine values. Reformist Islam claims that it is possible to have Islamic faith in the age of modernity and to have a modern reading of the Islam of Prophet Muhammad.

Reformist Islam faces two types of criticism: one from traditional Muslims who think that Islam is the equivalent of their own understanding of the

Book and traditions; and the other is from followers of modernity who consider any type of faith and religiosity to belong to a premodern era.

Non-traditional (reformist) Islam is the reading of a great number of Muslims over the last two centuries in Iran, Arab countries, Turkey and Central Asia, the Indian subcontinent, Southeast Asia, Europe and America. It has taken shape gradually at the same time in various lands, and it has been articulated by various thinkers who were unknown to each other. It is therefore not indebted to a particular thinker. Rather, it is the outcome of the works of dozens of thinkers who are Iranian, Egyptian, Pakistani, Turkish, Sudanese, Indonesian, Indian, Algerian, Moroccan, Syrian, etc.

Religious worship and rituals are not much different in these two readings of Islam. This is because they are in the realm of the devotional (*ta'abbudi*) and reason has no role in determining their specifics.[6] Like traditional Muslims, reformist Muslims pray five times a day; fast during Ramadan; journey to Mecca for the *Hajj*; give charity for God, which can be in the various forms of *zakat*, one-fifth tax (*khums*), almsgiving (*sadaqah*), expiation (*kaffarah*), and interest-free loan (*qard al-hasana*); are committed to offering prayers, intimate supplication and invocation; are familiar with recitation of the Qur'an; follow what is permitted and forbidden in terms of drink and food; refrain from any kind of sexual relations outside legitimate marriage; protect the sanctum of the family; do not pollute his or her economic affairs with methods that are prohibited according to the *shari'a* such as usury; refrain from lying in testimony and any kind of lying in general; and consider trustworthiness and observance of treaties and agreements as *shari'a* obligations. It is clear that despite the shared fundamental issues pertaining to worship and human interactions – examples of which were given above – there are some differences in some of the details based on *ijtihad* (similar to the differences in this regard between the *fatwa*s of traditional *mujtahid*s). These include the conditions for the prayers of a traveller, the conditions when *khums* is necessary, the possibility for directly using *shari'a* taxes, some of the conditions for the slaughter of animals, as well as other issues whose discussion would require another opportunity. It is noted that like traditional Islam, reformist Islam is concerned with religion and *shari'a* and has a distinct border separating itself from carelessness.

---

6 See my comments in the Epilogue to the previous chapter.

Undertaking a statistical and scholarly study of the followers of reformist Islam is possible and useful. Some information and statistics can be extracted from the field research that has been carried out over the last half a century on the religious beliefs, activities and lifestyles of Muslims. Based on these sociological studies, although incomplete, one can grasp the undeniable conclusion that reformist Islam is a reality.

The familiarity with traditional Islam no doubt causes one to be pessimistic in dealing with any new takes on Islam. Some extremists even encourage this pessimism outside scholarly criteria. To make a judgement on traditional Islam and reformist Islam is to make a judgement on the rationales of yesterday and today and nothing more. The main axis of the disagreement rests on reading the conventions of the age of Revelation and the temporary rulings as religious standards and as permanent rulings. With reformist Islam, not only is there no harm to faith and sincerity, but they become deeper. Yes, accepting reformist Islam requires the bravery to bid farewell to the understanding of theologians and jurists of past centuries and to put aside the religious conventions of yesterday. This equates to a surgical procedure which separates the gem of Islam from the sedimentation of the human understanding of past theologians and jurists, the conventions of yesterday and temporary rulings. This is not an easy procedure, it is possible that errors may occur, it is after all a human task. However, it is a necessary step, because inhaling these sediments has made it difficult for the gem of religion to breathe. Reformist Islam is a form of religious reform. Those who are satisfied with traditional knowledge and whose faith faces no problems in dealing with the modern world will remain with the traditional reading. Reformist Islam provides an answer to those Muslims who are neither convinced by traditional knowledge, nor those who have exclusively accepted all of modernity, they are the Muslims who have "concerns" about the modern world. We leave those who have no concerns alone, but we modestly offer our human efforts to those who have reached the state of having concerns and who have felt pain. There is no doubt that taking precautions in protecting the gem of religion is the essential advice of reason and the recommendation of the Revelation. In this difficult position, we have entrusted our hearts to God since ". . . We shall be sure to guide to Our ways those who strive hard for Our cause: God is with those who do good" (Q. 29:69). It is hoped that this path is one of His.

Question four, part B: Islam has four parts: rulings, faith, morals and worship. You have also said that the last three form the overwhelming majority of the Book and the Tradition. What remains is a negligible segment which has created a very large area called *fiqh*. You have implicitly complained that abandoning that which was the principle and the major concern of the Book and the Tradition, and clinging to this segment of rulings is not legitimate. Furthermore, that the illegitimacy of the foundation of traditional Islam is due to this same *fiqh*-based Islam which, inadvertently or not, thinks that the basis of Islam is this small segment. With these introductory comments, I mean to ask why has it been like this? I have no doubt that one of the reasons has been the historical concern to make this segment somehow compatible with the rest of religion. In fact, that is why *fiqh* has expanded, so that it may try to explain this kind of incompatibility and unreasonableness. If Islam did not have rulings from the beginning, then naturally thinkers would more easily contemplate in other areas and would entrust lawmaking to secular institutions. Why did our mystics bury their books and say the science of love cannot be placed in a book,[7] was not the reason for this no other than them wanting to free themselves from the noise and these controversies and to reach what they thought was the main principle? If after all this effort you have accepted that the outcome of our *fiqh* is not compatible with reasonability (here in the form of human rights), is it necessary to accept that the project of Islam is a defeated project, meaning that some of its segments, even if small, are not combinable with its other segments, and it must now go back and eliminate these incompatible segments.

Answer: Islamic teachings have four parts: faith, morality, worship and rulings. *Fiqh* has been an agent of the latter two (the *fiqh* of worship and the *fiqh* of transactions). All four parts are necessary in their place and the lack of any one would cause problems. Practical rulings are a part of Islamic teachings. In considering the importance of this part, one should not be an extremist and imagine it to be more important than faith and morality and to summarise Islam by it; nor should one go to the other extreme of considering Islam to have no need for it. *Fiqh* is a necessary part of Islamic knowledge, even if it

---

7 Extracted from the poetry of *Divan-e Hafez: ghazal* No. 158, 1:332.

is not the most important. In traditional Islam, *fiqh* has grown more than necessary in comparison with other parts of Islam which have not had similar growth. Reformist Islam has tried to respect the place of all aspects of the religion. Thus, reformist Islam is not Islam without *fiqh*. This reading of Islam has its own specific *fiqh*, which is different than traditional *fiqh*. The main difference is in the *fiqh* of transactions (as noted above, the differences in the *fiqh* of worship are few). In accepting human rights, some of the non-ritual rulings (but not necessarily all of them) will evolve. From the point of view of reformist Islam, the rulings under discussion are the temporary and imper-manent *shari'a* rulings. These rulings were justified and useful during their time of validity. The fact that they perpetuated beyond the duration of their validity was a mistake of *ijtihad* and neglectful of their conditions of time and place. Not only has the project of Islam not been defeated, but given that it has had the highest growth of all of the religions across all continents in the last century, it is the religion that is most alive in our time.

Reasons for the Lack of Explicit Expression of the Temporary in Changeable Rulings

Question four, part C: You have mentioned that "people more easily implement a permanent, stable ruling than a restricted and temporary one", which you have held up as proof for why the Qur'an uses a permanent and stable tone in laying out some of the temporary verses, meaning you consider it far from the Divine Wisdom to let go of a more influential tone. My question is: which people more easily implement the stable and permanent rulings? The believer who is a qualified *mujtahid* after fourteen hundred years and who wants to provide a reading of Islam that fits with the issues of the day, but has no choice but to accept that the audiences of this religion cannot be restricted to the sphere of one particular time and place. What measures have been thought out in this regard? Is it not far from the Divine Wisdom for Him not to specify the temporary nature of a ruling and, for the price of bringing the Arab tribes of Najd around Arabia to have faith during the advent of Islam, risking that billions of Muslims of yesterday, today and tomorrow be at risk of ignorance?

Answer: temporary rulings may be presented in two ways: one is those that are specified in terms of the time of the validity of the ruling, and the other is those that are expressed in absolute terms without any indication of the duration of their validity. If the temporary ruling is given in the first way, then after the time reference has passed, the ruling is no longer valid. In cases where the temporary ruling is given in the second way (i.e., with no indication of the duration of its validity), then at the end of the period of its validity, the Legislator must "abrogate" the ruling. Only those rulings that were expressed in the second sense are abrogated. A ruling that has been specified to be temporary is not one that can be abrogated. With the process of abrogation, one discovers that the ruling was temporary from the time it was set, but it was not beneficial to specify its temporariness.

Both ways of expressing a temporary ruling can be seen in human and Divine legislation. Choosing one over another is subordinate to thinking about which way of expressing a ruling would be beneficial. What is beneficial at the time of primary legislation or at the establishment of the ruling, is not a negligible issue that can be easily ignored.

The *fiqh* rulings under discussion have legally organised the social life of Muslims for over thirteen centuries without having any conflict with the rationales of their time. This issue therefore goes beyond what was in the interests of Arabs living in the Hijaz during the time of the Revelation. What was in the interest of a human in the fifteenth century AH, cannot be supposed to be the standard interest in all centuries and eras. As a dominant norm, the notion of human rights is less than a century old. We have no right to judge past generations or cultures using the standards of today's rationale. The criteria of our judgement of those who came before should be based on the accepted rationale of that time. When the right to vote for women only goes back to the early decades of the twentieth century in most European countries, how can we expect the same of societies from six or seven centuries ago? Religious knowledge, like other aspects of a culture, is limited to the conditions of time and place, even if the text of a religion can contain teachings that transcend various times. The problems begin when we try to understand religion and make it understood through the rationales and conventions of the past. More so than in the text of religion, the problem lies in the understanding of believers and their epistemological and theological presuppositions. It is not impossible to have a reading of the text of the Book and the Tradition that is compatible with human rights. The claim of impossibility is borne of the presupposition that religion belongs to a premodern era.

Question five: how many of these issues are confirmed in pure Islam and how many are extras that some authoritarians and utilitarians have added to Islam in the name of Islam? And also, in general, are ratified human rights in accordance with primordial nature (*fitra*)? Or, does it too have problems that we will witness with the passing of time?

Answer: every religion, including Islam, is always (even during the time of the Revelation and when the Prophet was present) expressed in ways that are limited by the conditions of time and place and is understood with the limitations of human understanding. Thus, a "pure Islam" or pure religion is unattainable in this world. In understanding the text of religion, in addition to the text and its creator (God), there is a role for the believing reader. In the text itself, one can find propositions that are principles and those that are not (explicit and equivocal). Among the propositions that are principles of Islam (such as the principle of the dignity of humankind; the principle of the equality of all humankind in closeness to God and true happiness; the universal principle of justice and fairness that has no exceptions; the principle of the lack of compulsion in religion; the principle of human responsibility), one cannot find any instances that are incompatible with human rights. All of the examples of incompatibility belong to the propositions that are not principles of Islam, or to the temporary and time-bound rulings, which were, of course, just and reasonable during the time of their validity. These cannot be considered the constructions of authoritarians and utilitarians. In the museum of traditional anthropology these can be found aplenty.

The Articles of the Universal Declaration of Human Rights are reasonable. The bases of these Articles relate to primordial nature. From another perspective, one can consider them in the category of natural rights. Affairs pertaining to reasonability, primordial nature or natural rights are desirable and acceptable. There is, however, no collective or consensus agreement on which affairs are reasonable, or pertain to primordial nature or natural rights. One could say that the above-named declaration includes Articles that are reasonable, or are related to primordial nature or natural rights. However, it is debatable whether it includes all of these types of Articles. For example, today's humans need an "International Declaration of Human Responsibilities and Duties". In addition, in our time, the human rights approach is less problematic as compared with other approaches; although we have no guarantee that in the future it will remain a dominant approach as well.

Two Forms of Human Knowledge about Divine Religion and Human Rights

Question six: human rights are among the constructions and innovations of humans. It consists of the constructions and innovations of several thinkers which have been ratified and signed by various states. Why is it necessary for religion to harmonise itself with the innovations of thinkers? If in the future, other thinkers suggest and prescribe a set of different rights for humans, would religion again have to harmonise itself with those laws? Is there a red line?

Answer: the UDHR is the result of the reasonability of contemporary humans. Human knowledge, including Islamic knowledge in our time, consists of the understanding of the contemporary believer or Muslim of the text of religion or Islam. Religious knowledge is in exchange and dialogue with other knowledge of its time. Whether we want to or not, we face the questions of our time. Reformist Islam is an attempt in this direction. Thus, the discussion is not about harmonising Divine Religion with human achievements, but about the engagement of two kinds of "human knowledge": the knowledge of Divine religion and the rights of humans. In the realm of thought and exchange, there is no red line, but there are winners and losers. The idea that remains is the one that in the battlefield of thoughts convinced its followers and became dominant by demonstrating its advantages in comparison with its competition.

Question seven: as someone who is aware of international principles, when I have tried to refer to some of the traditions of the Imams to justify to my non-Iranian counterparts that there is compatibility between Islam (from the Shi'ite viewpoint) and human rights, whether by convention or treaty, like you I completely agree that there are also some fundamental conflicts. My question is, summoning some of the traditions of the Imams, can one not cross out and void at least some issues relating to the viewpoints of traditional Islam? It seems that the key is the insistence on the explicit unequivocal verses of the Qur'an and interpretations based on the text without using the method of the Imams, as credible proof in the interpretation of the fundamentals of the Qur'an. In your research, have you considered Islamic rules regarding the support of individuals during war? Generally, in international law, these principles are thought of as humanitarian law, although many believe that these two fields (human rights and humanitarian law) are in fact one branch of international law.

Answer: as in the Tradition of the Prophet, it is clear that some of the criteria of human rights are observed in the Tradition of the Imams, although in some of the hadiths one can see that in the Tradition of the Imams or the Prophetic Tradition, there are some conflicting, or at least unclear points, in this regard. In terms of the validity of the sources, these hadith are interpreted as changing and time-bound rulings, and the first category of religious narratives is counted as stable and permanent rulings. One example of this auspicious scholarly effort can be found in the small but rich work of Ayatollah Montazeri's *Treatise on Rights*. It is possible to reference the credible hadiths of the Imams as the third level among the sources of Shiʻite Islam (after the Qurʾan and the Tradition of the Prophet), but referring to this legacy does not change the main frame of the discussion (the conflict of traditional Islam with the UDHR and the possibility of its compatibility with reformist Islam). This is because the reference for the majority of the *fatwa*s related to the first proposition (conflict) are hadith of the Prophet's Household, although some of the references in relation to the second proposition (compatibility) are also their hadith. It is worth asking why, over many centuries, scholars of religion did not refer enough to the second category of hadith in deducing the religious rights of people alongside their mature extraction of *shariʻa* duties.

My research has focused on human rights, in particular the UDHR (1948) and the ICESCR and ICCPR (1966), and did not include humanitarian law (human rights during war). I hope that on another occasion I will have the opportunity to examine this area as well. I will say in general that the position of traditional Islam in the sphere of humanitarian law is better than its position in that of human rights.[8]

---

8 In this regard, it is worth noting the research of the Islamic law expert Muhammad Hamidullah (1908–2002), *Majmuʻa al-Wathʻiq al-Siyasiyya lil-ʻAhd al-Nabawi wa al-Khilafa al-Rashida* (*The Political Covenants in the Prophetic Age and the Age of the Righteous Caliphate*) (Beirut: Dar al-Nafaʾis, 1987), and his other works.

Question eight: can you please clarify your opinion on the rights of Baha'is according your understanding of Islamic law?

Question nine: I would be very thankful if you could clarify the rights of Baha'is according to your modern interpretation of Islamic law?

Question ten: According to the Qur'an, what status is assigned to Baha'is? Are they infidels? What are their rights?

Answer: human rights apply to all humankind regardless of religious beliefs. No person can be denied the minimum human rights (the rights outlined in the UDHR and the two Covenants) on the basis of his or her religious beliefs, even if those beliefs are wrong from our point of view. Enjoying these rights has no correlation with the correctness of religious beliefs and dogmas. Fundamentally, human rights are the rights of all humankind, not only the rights of monotheists, the pious and orthodox believers.

The Qur'an recognises the Abrahamic religions as Divine religions, and considers their followers to be People of the Book. The beliefs that form the bases of Islam – as presented in the Qur'an – are the belief in God, belief in the Hereafter, and belief in the Prophecy of Muhammad (PBUH). The Qur'an explicitly identifies Muhammad as the Seal of Prophets and Islam as the final divine religion, and any claims that conflict with these bases are considered void and outside the boundaries of faith. Muslims all share these bases without any difference.[9]

Homosexuality and Human Rights

Question eleven: one of the issues that has not been mentioned in the discussion is the conflict of traditional Islam with human rights in the sphere of sexual choice. Does traditional *fiqh* not deal with the choice of one's sexual partner (same-sex partner) in a discriminatory manner? Where does this discrimination fit within any of the previously mentioned axes?

---

9 For more explanation, see Epilogue to this chapter, below.

Answer: first, sexual relations with someone of the same sex (homosexuality) has not been recognised in the UDHR, ICESCR and ICCPR. The efforts of homosexuals to gain recognition as a minority (sexual minority) through the main consensual international documents have not yet been successful. As far as I know, the only place where this has been implicitly addressed is in a secondary document about the refugee status of those individuals who face the danger of death in their own country as a result of this issue.[10] In some European countries, efforts have begun to officially recognise homosexuals and families made up of same-sex couples. However, the most success they have had is that sexual relations pertain to one's personal rights and as long as they are carried out with the consent of both sides no one has the right to oppose or dismiss them.[11] Throughout the world, homosexuality faces serious critique, whether among the followers of the Abrahamic religions (Muslims, Christians and Jews) or among secular people who are not religious. At present, homosexuality has not received consensual international support as one of the particular human rights.

Second, the controversial point about homosexuality is its reasonability and whether it is a humane act or whether it strays from the correct path of humanity. Traditional Islam and reformist Islam are in the same camp in

---

10 The 1951 Convention Relating to the Status of Refugees: "Article 33 prohibition of expulsion or return ('refoulement') 1. No Contracting State shall expel or return ('refouler') a refugee in any manner whatsoever to the frontiers or territories where his life or freedom would be threatened on account of his race, religion, nationality, membership of a particular social group or political opinion" (*Conventions and Protocols Relating to the Status of Refugees*, Geneva, United Nations High Commissioner for Refugees (UNHCR), December 2010, 30). There is no explicit terminology regarding sexual orientation or gender identity in this document. However, since 1988, in the view of UNHCR, individuals who fear persecution on account of their sexual orientation or gender identity may be considered members of a "particular social group".

11 The Treaty on the Functioning of the European Union makes provision in Articles 10 and 19 for combatting discrimination on the grounds of sexual orientation. These provisions were enacted by the Treaty of Amsterdam in 1999 (signed: 2 October 1997, effective: 1 May 1999). Article 10: "In defining and implementing its policies and activities, the Union shall aim to combat discrimination based on sex, racial or ethnic origin, religion or belief, disability, age or sexual orientation." Article 19: "1. Without prejudice to the other provisions of the Treaties and within the limits of the powers conferred by them upon the Union, the Council, acting unanimously in accordance with a special legislative procedure and after obtaining the consent of the European Parliament, may take appropriate action to combat discrimination based on sex, racial or ethnic origin, religion or belief, disability, age or sexual orientation." Treaty of Amsterdam Amending the Treaty on European Union, the Treaties establishing the European Communities and Certain Related Acts, *Official Journal of the European Communities*, C 340/143, 10 November 1997.

terms of supporting family and the restriction of sexual relationships through a legal marriage contract between females and males. From this perspective, this is the only reasonable and humane style of marriage. The discussion between opponents and proponents of homosexuality based on reasonability is a big challenge. Neither side accepts the claim of the other side. In this way, in relation to reasonability, homosexuality is an antinomy. Having a reasonable and justified foundation is the necessary condition for accepting any issue as a particular human right. Based on reasonability, homosexuality has not been unanimously accepted as a human right. There are strong doubts about it as a human right. Considering these doubts, discussion of the discrimination of sexual minorities is problematic. Same-sex sexual relationships are denounced and prohibited in all Abrahamic traditions, including Islam. The Qur'an disapproves of it in the most severe tones in its discussion of Lot. Traditional jurists – both Shi'ite and Sunni – forbid it in accordance with the *shari'a* and accord it the harshest of punishments. The consent of both sides in a sexual relationship does not work in an act that is emphatically forbidden by *shari'a*. The *shari'a* prohibition against sodomy (*lawat*) and tribadism (*musahaqa*) are among the permanent and unchanging rulings of *shari'a*. In dealing with this issue which lacks reasonable support, reformist Islam has a similar position to that of traditional Islam in forbidding it in accordance with *shari'a*. Although public same-sex relationships are considered a crime, violent and harsh punishments are generally negated in reformist Islam, including in this case. Of course, spying on the private sphere of people is also forbidden.[12]

Question twelve: does the theory of the *wilayat al-faqih* (Guardianship of the Jurist) conform to the Qur'an? Is it compatible with human rights?

Answer: in my books,[13] I have provided detailed arguments to show that the Guardianship of the Jurist in all its forms – including absolute or restricted, appointed or elective, in non-litigious (*hisbiya*) affairs, or in the certain particulars (*al-qadr al-mutayyaqan*) of those affairs – is lacking any credible

---

12 A few sentences of this answer were rephrased or revised in the translation, in order to protect the original message of the text. For more explanation, see the Epilogue to this chapter, below.

13 *Hukumat-i Wela'i (Guardian-based State); Daghdagheha-ye Hokumat-e Dini (The Concerns of a Religious State); Hukumat-e Entisabi (Appointive/Non-Elective State).*

Qur'anic evidence, has no credible verification in the tradition of the Prophet or the Imams, and rational argument is in fact against it, as well as it being in open conflict with human rights. The inseparable correlative of the *wilayat al-faqih* is that the people, as wards (*muwalla 'alayhim*), are legally incompetent (*mahjur*) at running public affairs. To put it in plain terms, if people were qualified to control their own affairs they would never need a *shari'a*-based guardian. The Qur'an, the Tradition of the Prophet and the Imams, and sound reason provides the evidence for nullifying the special anthropology that forms the basis of the *wilayati al-faqih*, namely, that every person is incompetent to run public affairs.

Epilogue

1. Discussing the rights of Baha'is was taboo among Shi'ite Muslims. I was the first to recognise their human rights and to publish an article on this subject in November 2006 when I was in Iran. Less than two years later in May and June 2008, my mentor Ayatollah Montazeri issued two innovative *fatwa*s about citizenship rights for Baha'is. I did not discuss this issue with him. "Although the Baha'i cult was not acknowledged as a religious minority in the Constitution of the Islamic Republic of Iran, because in contrast to Jews, Christians and Zoroastrians they do not have divine scripture", he wrote in the first *fatwa*, "they are Iranian, and have citizenship rights. They too should be offered Islamic graciousness." He mentioned the Qur'an (Q. 60:8) and letter 53 of Imam Ali in *Nahj al-Balagha* addressing the ruler of Egypt that "your citizens are of two types, your brother in religion or the same as you in creation".[14] My book *Haqq al-Nas* was released in October 2008. It was the first book published in Iran to include the rights of Baha'is.

I would like to add a few more words from my recent e-papers.[15] The creed and belief of a person, Muslim or non-Muslim, regardless of which dogma he or she believes, is not a reason for the prevention of human rights. This principle is far removed from traditional Islamic thought. Baha'is in Iran, Ahmadiyya in Pakistan and Mormons in the United States are three

---

14 *Sug-Name-ye Faqih-e Pakbaz Ustad Hossein Ali Montazeri Najaf Abadi (A Tribute to the Virtuous Theologian, my Mentor Hossein Ali Montazeri Najaf Abadi)*, Kadivar web-book, 2015. The citizenship rights of Baha'is from the Mentor's perspective, 36–38.

15 *Ba Baha'iyan chegoune barkhord konim? (How Should We Treat Baha'is?)*, 15 May 2016.

contemporary examples of religious groups who face difficulties in their societies. Of course, the first two groups face many more problems than the latter. Baha'ism identified itself as a new religion, but Muslims have not recognised it as such. Theological discussions in seminars and universities should be followed seriously and fairly.

However, if Baha'ism is discounted as an invalid cult and a deviant doctrine, this does not mean that its believers should be deprived of their human rights because of their particular beliefs. It is not acceptable to say that the right to fair trail does not apply to them because they are infidels; or that their lives, property and dignity, even their corpses in the cemetery, are without sanctity, because they are non-Muslims and are not People of the Book; or that any Baha'i who does not hide his or her beliefs is necessarily a spy from Israel, and consequently deprived of the right to higher education. These rulings are illegitimate and irreligious. Traditional Shi'ite jurists mostly prohibited any communication and transactions with Baha'is as a secondary ruling. They issued *fatwa*s on impurity and invalidity of marriage with Baha'is as the followers of a deviant cult.

In reformist Islam, Baha'is are not infidels. Attributing this to those who identify themselves as monotheists is problematic. The primary principle is the "essential purity of humans". Baha'is believe in the prophecy of Muhammad, but do not accept him as the Seal of Prophets (the last one). According to Islam, this is an invalid creed and a non-divine religion. But an invalid religion and wrong beliefs are not necessarily the cause of impurity, and attributing impurity to people who believe in monotheism and the prophecy is problematic. The conclusion to this discussion is therefore that the Baha'is are pure.

Denying Islam and denial of the Prophet as the Seal of Prophets (*khatamiyyat*), denying the existence of the twelfth Imam and the existence of God, and frankly to be an infidel, unbeliever or atheist does not deprive anyone of basic civil rights, human rights and citizenship rights. These rights are not related to religion, sect, thought or belief. There is no valid religious argument for the prevention of Baha'is from human rights, citizenship rights and basic civil rights.

2. In traditional Islam two types of rulings apply to same-sex sexual relationships: first, an injunctive ruling, or *shari'a* obligation: it is prohibited and a cardinal sin. Second, is a declaratory (*wadh'i*) ruling: a penal code that is more severe than that for adultery. The subject of these rulings includes sex with and without the consent of two partners, whether one partner is

a minor or both are adults. There is no doubt that sex without consent (by force, rape) and sex with a minor, or someone who is under-age, even with his or her consent, is illegal and a crime. The particular challenge is therefore a sexual relationship between two same-sex adult partners with consent.

By the 1970s, homosexuality was classified as a mental disorder by many medical and mental health professionals, as well as in the behavioural and social sciences. In the last quarter of the twentieth century the doctrine that homosexuality was a variation of human sexual orientation gradually became dominant in the behavioural and social sciences, as well as in the health and mental health professions, although the doctrine of homosexuality as a disorder continued to exist. Although the proponents of homosexuality highlight the former doctrine as the general consensus, the marginal existence of the other doctrine is undeniable. According to the dominant doctrine in which homosexuality is a variation of human sexual orientation, not only can it not be considered a crime, but any discrimination against homosexuals is also considered improper.

Although advocates of the doctrine of homosexuality as a variation of human sexual orientation have tried several times to ratify a declaration, covenant or even a resolution by the end of the first decade of the twenty-first century, they were not able to convince the majority of the members of the United Nations. The first document on this issue in the history of the UN was issued on 17 November 2011. It was a report titled "Discriminatory Laws and Practices and Acts of Violence against Individuals based on their Sexual Orientation and Gender Identity", issued by the office of the UN High Commissioner for Human Rights (OHCHR). According to its official summary, this report is "a study documenting discriminatory laws and practices and acts of violence against individuals based on their sexual orientation and gender identity, and how international human rights law can be used to end violence and related human rights violations based on sexual orientation and gender identity". The most important and applicable international standards and obligations are still, however, in the first article of the UDHR (1948) and the ICCPR and ICESCR (1966) on universality, equality and non-discrimination. The conclusion of the report issued by the OHCHR is this warning: "the Council formally expressed its 'grave concern' regarding violence and discrimination based on sexual orientation and gender identity".

It is obvious that the members of the UN did not reach any agreement on the rights of LGBT people as a particular of human rights, neither in the form of a universal declaration, nor in the form of an international covenant or resolution until now. The achievement is only an annual report for the purposes of study. The main sources for this report are the generalities or absolute expressions of the UDHR (1948) and the ICCPR and ICESCR (1966). These generalities, or absolute expressions, were, however, ratified several decades before the doctrine of homosexuality as a variation of human sexual orientation became dominant. I am sure that at the time of ratification (i.e., 1940s and 1960s) of these three main sources for the 2011 Report, homosexuality was still classified as a mental disorder. This means that the arguments in this report are not able to support its conclusion. We can therefore at least strongly assert that there is no universal agreement, or valid UN-ratified document (declaration, covenant or resolution), on homosexual rights as a particular of human rights. In the absence of a UN document, it is possible to state that at present there is no evidence for accepting homosexual rights as the conventions of reasonable people. This means that the conventions of contemporary humans need more evidence in order to accept their reasonability as a standard notion of human rights.

Although the reasonability of homosexual rights was not accepted, this does not mean that these scientific achievements were completely invalid and in vain. What can be learned from the 2011 Report is the elimination of a penal code for LGBT people based on a new argument. The punishment for any homosexual action can neither be justified as a variation of human sexual orientation, nor as a mental disorder. There is no third doctrine. When there is no punishment or crime with regard to the sexual orientation of LGBT people, it is obvious that any discrimination in public life for non-sexual issues is not acceptable. Public regulations are managed according to the legal framework of each society.

At present, from my perspective, reformist Islam has first of all not come across sufficient documentation for accepting homosexuality as a particular human right. Second, it believes the only *shari'a* premised sexual relationship is defined between a female and male under legal marriage. As such, same-sex marriage or any sex outside of marriage is illegal. Third, there is no punishment for LGBT sexual orientation. Fourth, no discrimination of LGBT people is accepted in the public domain regarding non-sexual affairs.[16]

---

16 This is the second draft of a subsection of this article on homosexuality and UN documents: Mohsen Kadivar, *Noandishi-ye dini va kheradvarziha-ye shakhsi (Reformist Islam and Personal Rationality)*, BBC Persian, 5 September 2018. I have not focused on research on homosexuality and have not published any articles on this yet, but hope to do so in the future.

7
Human Rights, Secularism and Religion[1]

Human rights is one of the most important, inclusive and recommended discussions in human society of the last seventy years. So much so, that following its criteria has become the key axis for assessing the health, progress and development of a society, and their violation has become the most legitimate reason or excuse for condemning regimes which do so. Aside from the principles of international law, human rights have been able to find a place at the forefront of the demands and desires of developing societies in peripheral countries. The fruits of valid international agreements, such as the Universal Declaration of Human Rights (ratified by the UN General Assembly in 1948), the International Covenant on Economic, Social and Cultural Rights, and the International Covenant on Civil and Political Rights (both ratified by the UN General Assembly in 1966) have meant that human rights are more transparent, clear and organised as compared with other human demands such as justice, democracy and freedom.

One of the questions that has been posed of human rights relates to its relationship with religion and religious values. This question is more important and more difficult in societies where religion is among the strong

---

1 Mohsen Kadivar, "*Hoquq-e Bashar, Laïcité wa Din*", paper presented at the Interdisciplinary and International Conference on the Relationship between Laïcité, Secularism, and Human rights: Citizenship and Religion, the UNESCO Seat of Human Rights, Peace and Democracy, Shaheed Beheshti University, Tehran, 18 December 2004; *Laïcité wa Hoquq-e Bashar (Secularism and Human Rights)*, Proceedings of the Conference, Amir Nikpay (ed.) (Tehran: UNESCO Seat of Human Rights, Peace and Democracy, Shahid Beheshti University, forthcoming), 113–125; *A'een (Ritual)*, monthly journal, Tehran, No. 4 (October 2006): 64–67.

components of national identity and the powerful indicators of social life. In arenas where human rights articles and religious teachings confront one another, and the citizens, states and laws of these societies are incapable of choosing between the two, a battle of strength ensues between religious traditions and modern conventions. However, case studies of different societies show the prevalence of human rights as well as interpretations, hermeneutic commentary and re-readings of religious teachings in the light of human rights.

Axes of the Challenges of Religions and Human Rights

First, the most important axis of the challenge of human rights versus traditional readings of religions pertains to the equal rights of humans. While in many religions inequality before the law and racial discrimination have been completely negated, legal equality in matters of gender, religion, sect and sometimes the negation of slavery have not been officially recognised, such that in numerous cases women do not enjoy as many of the rights that men enjoy. Believing in a particular religion, or a particular sect, provides the believers of that religion or sect with more benefits and rights compared with the followers of other religions or sects, and in general as compared with those who do not believe in any religion or sect. Sometimes, it is even the case that theologians, jurists and clerics have special rights and unique benefits in the political sphere. Not abrogating the rulings on slavery and the serious differences between the rights of slaves and those of free people is another indicator of the lack of legal equality among humans.

The second axis of this challenge pertains to freedom of religion and thought. In the traditional reading of some religions, leaving that religion (apostasy) results in heavy punishments, including death. Proselytising among followers of the state religion is seriously limited. Open display (*tajahur*) of the fact that one is not implementing religious obligations and carrying out religious prohibitions is not permitted.

The third axis of the challenge pertains to the followers of religion who consider its rulings and teachings not to be subject to criticism or discussion. In other words, that religious criteria and rulings have no need of rational justification, and that by having faith in the principles of belief, one must accept those orders devotionally (*ta'abbudi*); and that in cases where those rulings are in conflict with human rights, which are a human affair and therefore fallible, religious rulings and teachings, which are divine and infallible, are considered to have the right to veto and essential precedence.

In the reformist reading of the Abrahamic religions, which in the past century has gradually become the dominant reading among the followers of the most important Abrahamic religions, all three axes of the challenge of human rights versus traditional readings of religion have been resolved in favour of human rights. Meaning, from the point of view of reformist thinkers, that none of these three axes were inherent to the religion but rather pertained to its changeable and time-bound rulings. Based on this, every single human being has equal rights without discrimination in accordance with religion, gender, race, belief, etc. In addition, no special rights or privileges are acceptable for any particular social group or strata. This right is a continuous right rather than a disposable one. In the same manner, people are free to leave their religion, sect and beliefs. No one can be forced or punished for carrying out or discontinuing a religious practice, as it is religious. Third, while all religious propositions are respected by believers, they are also subject to discussion, criticism and questioning. Placing a holy halo around religious beliefs does not result in strengthening them, rather, it leads to them remaining weak. Until the necessary justification for accepting religious propositions has been provided through wise discussion or public reasoning, and until religious values have become dominant, it is not right to make them obligatory by law.

In regard to all three axes in our time, or at least in the last half a century, these three issues have been accepted from a human rights perspective according to rational conventions. Gradually, from the perspective of the conventions of believers, legal equality, religious freedoms, and that all rulings pertaining to humans are subject to discussion, have also been accepted and religiosity has been harmonised with the three rights noted above. In fact, after accepting that the above are indeed human rights, in dealing with the conflict of religious rulings with the above rights, the precedence of human rights over traditional religious propositions is established by means such as abrogation, the changeable or situational (*maosimi*) ruling, the place-and-time-bound ruling, and so forth.

The Secular Approach to Human Rights

Following the universalisation of the articles of human rights and the passing of several decades after the ratification of its first declaration, the expansion of human rights and its domain and the additions to its Articles, as well as the non-restricted interpretation of its past Articles that in practice lead to the expansion of the realm of human rights, have been considered in legal circles. The expanded Articles are among the serious challenges between the two systems of *laïque* (secular) and religious thought. The subject under consideration here is a preliminary discussion of this issue. The discussion is preliminary, first, in the sense that this discussion does not have much or any precedence in Persian; and second, each and every particular under discussion requires its own separate investigation, and after all of the research is complete, one can take up the main general discussion. Naturally, the criticisms and recommendations of experts will enrich this discussion.

I begin the discussion from the point of view of *laïcité* (laicism). *Laïcité* is a French term meaning non-religious.[2] *Laïcité* (secularism) has two components:

> one is the separation of the state (which includes the three branches) and the public sectors of society from the institutions of religion and the church and specifically the independence of the state in relation to religions and religious references, and second the secular state guarantees and supplies the freedom of all beliefs, including religious and non-religious ones. Separation of state and religion means citizenship and having citizenship rights is not linked to the religion of the members of a society. State and social institutions do not determine their policies according to religion, in light of religion, or based on conformity with religious principles. Finally state and public institutions do not make the religious belief of citizens a criterion for determining citizenship rights and freedom.[3]

From the *laïque* (secular) standpoint, one of the pillars of the independence of the state from religion is the independence of human rights, citizens' rights, constitutional and non-constitutional laws, and public policy and policy-making from religion, in the sense that none of the above are determined on the basis of, in the light of, or in accordance with the principles of religion. Put another way, religion does not provide any source of

---

reference for determining laws or public policy, meaning that in the public sphere religion does not serve as a source of reference. Thus, although those who are religious are free to practise their religion in civil society, none of the public institutions (including the state, municipalities, public education institutions, etc.) are permitted to be managed according to religious criteria and values. Distinguishing and separating public institutions from religious ones guarantees the freedom and independence of both. Religious institutions have no right to interfere in the public sphere and the state, and other public institutions are also not permitted to intervene in religious affairs. In the public sphere, there are neither special rights nor privileges for believers, even if they make up the majority of society; nor is it expected that religion and religious values be a source for public laws and regulations. Thus, in this view, human rights are to be identified as independent of religion.

Among the corroborations of the *laïque* (secular) approach to human rights is that if we suppose that religion is a permitted source and reference for human rights, given the diversity and great number of religions, which religion would be chosen as the source of human rights? If we choose several longstanding religions the prior question still remains. In addition, every religion has several sects. If we were establishing human rights according to one particular religion, which of its sects would be granted the status of being the source? In the third stage, supposing we picked a particular religion and sect, what reading of it should be granted the status of a source? If we pick a particular religion, sect and reading, two other problems arise: first, the rights of the followers of other religions (sects and readings) are not respected, and, in general, the rights of absolute non-believers in religion (deists, agnostics and atheists) are ignored. Thus, no solution remains other than to make human rights independent of absolute religious and non-religious beliefs, that is, we consider rights to be for humans and special rights or privileges are not accorded to any particular religious dogma. Second, in general, we should not reference any religious teachings in the codification of human rights, so that human rights are not determined in the light of any religion and that no religious values are considered as the source of human rights. In a word, we should be *laïque* (or secular) in the arena of human rights.

Based on this, in issues pertaining to the expansion of human rights, like human rights itself, one cannot allow references to religious values and teachings to enter the realm of human rights. In every single one of these instances, if the only obstacle is religious teachings, values, and affairs, without doubt one must ignore the objections of believers and remark that while they are free to be religious in their personal affairs, human rights goes beyond these and religions are not permitted to assert themselves anywhere other than in personal life and civil society. The public sphere is close to religious teachings and values. Thus, without any concerns, one must welcome the expansion of human rights and in accepting them prove that religion has no place outside of personal life and civil society.

The Religious Approach to Human Rights

From the opposing point of view, meaning that of the religious approach, the *laïque* (secular) approach is not acceptable, and the problems that this approach raises for the possibility of religious values serving as a source for human rights can be answered and rejected. Believers hold that those of a *laïque* (secular) persuasion have relied on unproven and challengeable bases for pushing religion out of the public sphere, and on the basis of this they have assumed special rights and privileges for themselves that are not defensible in any way. Believers express their views about how religion should appear in the domain of human rights in several points.

Point one: humans are completely equal in human rights. Believers and non-believers are equal from a legal perspective. Believing in a particular religion does not produce special rights or privileges. Based on this, non-believers and secularists must also not receive special rights or privileges. That followers of religions do not have a right to use symbols of their faith in the public sphere (specifically government offices and public institutions of health and education), violates religious freedoms set out in Articles 18 and 19 of the UDHR and the ICCPR. It is a form of discrimination against religions and to the benefit of *laïcité* (secularism). The public sphere is the common property of all citizens and the impermissibility of personal religious symbols such as the head scarf of Muslim women in the public sphere (in countries such as France) is against human rights and lacks the necessary legal references.

Point two: existing religions, especially those with the most followers worldwide, including the Abrahamic religions (Judaism, Christianity and Islam) which make up half the people of the world,[4] have numerous shared

---

4 According to Pew Research Center, in 2015, at least 55.3 per cent of the world population were the believers of these three religions.

teachings and values. These shared features are to the extent that one can create a camp of the followers of these religions, specifically the Abrahamic ones, who have the same demands and expectations in the realm of human rights. These are demands and expectations that stand in contrast to *laïcité* (secularism). Belief in human dignity, God giving meaning to life, belief in another realm, the elevated place of morality in life, the prohibition on what is against public morality and security, and the respect for family are among the shared teachings and values of these religions. The source for human rights is not those issues that are different among various religions, sects and readings, and so it does not lead to a discussion about these and ultimately the setting aside of religious values in absolute terms. Thus, the problems indicated by secularists in this regard are not acceptable.[5]

Point three: each person is permitted to live how he or she pleases in terms of personal affairs, in the private realm and in civil society. People also have complete legal equality in the public sphere. There is no difference regarding these two statements between believers and non-believers. However, the main debate is about the rights, laws and regulations of the public sphere, including those pertaining to human rights and citizens' rights. What do religious values lack as a source of reference in this domain? On what philosophical and epistemological bases has being a source of reference been taken from religion?[6]

Categorisation of the Orders of the Public Sphere as Compared with Religious and Secular Values

To further clarify this fundamental question, orders in the public sphere, including those of human rights, can be divided into two categories as they compare with religious and *laïque* (secular) values:

First category: these are issues on which three positions can be taken: that of being conditional on religiosity; of being conditional on denying religiosity (or conditional on the *laïque* or secular or lay approach); and, being without any requirement in relation to religion. The meaning of the third position is to be indifferent and neutral towards religion. In such a position, the ruling issued is neither for nor against religion, and is neither for nor

---

5 For more explanation, see the Epilogue to this chapter.
6 Ibid.

against *laïcité* (secularism). In issues where it is possible to take the three positions, the fairest one is the one that is neutral. In taking such a position, the same rights and rulings will be issued to both those who are religious and *laïque* (secular) and will be executed similarly in relation to those who believe in religion and those who do not. The principle of the legal equality of humans and the freedom of belief and conscience is placed in this sphere. This means that instead of taking a position in support of those who are religious (the equality of the rights of religious people and the freedom to have religious beliefs), or taking a position that is against the religious (the legal equality of non-believers but the lack of human rights for believers, and the freedom of belief and opinions of non-believers), the indifferent and neutral position vis-à-vis religion is chosen, meaning that all humans have equal legal rights, and special rights or privileges are in general denied, and that there is freedom of religious and non-religious belief and conscience. But the important question is whether taking the third position (the one that is neutral in relation to religion) is possible in all cases.

Second category: these are issues where in relation to shared religious values, a position of rejection or proof must be taken, meaning either one must take a religious position and give a ruling based on religious values, or one must take a *laïque* (secular) position and give an order based on non-religious beliefs and secular values. In such cases it is not possible to take up an indifferent and neutral position in relation to religion. In these instances, cutting off the hand of religious values and taking away religion as a source of reference in the public sphere or for human and citizens' rights is based on the presupposition of detestation (*marjouhiyya*) or rejection of religion. This presupposition is acceptable to those who deny religions (atheists) and who are of *laïque* persuasion. But why should this special belief dominate the public sphere? This presupposition is in conflict with religious faith and the religious will not tolerate it.

In issues where accepting religious values revolves around the issue of proof or rejection, accepting *laïcité* means cutting off the hand of religion in the public sphere or keeping religion away from this sphere. The religious ask on what universal basis, or on which accepted international principle, are religious values being denied as a source of reference and are *laïque* and secular values dominating the public sphere?

When it comes to the challenging issues pertaining to religious and *laïque* (secular) approaches, one cannot at the outset and without reference to credible reasons make the *laïque* (secular) approach dominant over the religious one in the domain of human rights. Rather, one must raise the issue in an intellectual dialogue, and if one side can convince the other and provide a justified and reasonable explanation for their position, then this approach can become the basis for human rights. And if neither side is able to convince the other, or if the arguments of both sides were equivalent (*mutikafi'*), no solution remains other than the practical one, which is to submit to the vote of the majority, meaning submission to a democratic solution. Do we know of another solution for such challenges?

There is no doubt that the number of believers in the contemporary world and in the majority of countries is far more than those who do not believe in religious values,[7] and that in a democratic election, the religious approach would take precedence over the *laïque* and secular approach. Shared religious values should thus be the basis for explaining questionable issues in the sphere of human rights.

Particulars of the Challenges of Religion and Secularism

These questionable issues are among today's most important challenges in the sphere of human rights. They are not hypothetical discussions or probabilities far from reality. Pointing to some of these dubious particulars shows the importance of having this discussion.

First, not only in public elementary education but also in all compulsory education in general, should this education be organised such that it is based on the existence of God, or as though God is dead? It is clear that parents have the right to raise their children in private religious or *laïque* (secular) schools in accordance to their beliefs, but what should be done in state (non-private) schools? Especially in societies where believers are in the absolute majority, should public education ultimately be explained in reference to shared religious beliefs or should they be rejected and propagate the bases of *laïcité* (secularism) instead? It is clear that elementary education is among the most important aspects of the public sphere and that is has great influence in shaping the world's cultural future.

---

7 According to the Pew Research Center, in 2015, 83.76 per cent of the world's population were religious believers.

Second, in relation to public media, should radio and TV shows be organised in reference to shared religious beliefs or their rejection? One should not remain unaware of the tremendous role of public media in the production of culture. Religious believers and non-believers have the right to have their own media. But which policy should be used in managing public media (such as state media and corporate media)? The media policy on sexual content could be discussed as an example.

Third, are free sexual relations outside marriage (especially before marriage) part of human rights? The *laïque* (secular) answer to the question is positive, what is important is the consent of both partners. The religious answer to the question is negative. In addition to the consent of the girl/ woman and the boy/man, the consent of the Creator is also a necessary condition and God hates any sexual relations outside marriage. In the religious approach, the institution of the family has the greatest importance and is the only institution within which sexual relations are permitted. From the religious standpoint, any type of sexual relationship outside marriage is prohibited and does not count among human rights, while from a *laïque* (secular) perspective these types of relationship are included in human rights.

Fourth, is homosexuality a human right or not? The *laïque* (secular) answer is affirmative, what is important is the consent of both partners. Sexual inclination towards the opposite or same sex depends on both partners and the denial of religion cannot be an acceptable source for negating this right. From the dominant religious perspective, homosexuality is impermissible and against the Divine order. It is an intruder on the foundation of the family and counting it within the category of human rights is problematic.[8]

Fifth, mercy killing (euthanasia) or the killing of patients who are ill or elderly and for whom doctors see no hope for recovery or a cure. Is it permissible to make arrangements for their death, or to relieve them from their pain and suffering with the permission of their dependants, or with the patient's own prior consent? Is this included in human rights or not? Believers are much more strict than secular individuals in this case, and consider this permissibility as losing hope in God's mercy. They believe that life and death is in the hands of God and that as long as humans are alive and breathing, even with the help of equipment, it is not permissible either in accordance

---

8 For further explanation, see the Epilogue to Chapter 6, above.

to morality or *shari'a* for us to bring about a person's death. The human soul is venerable and suicide or killing someone else does not count as a human right under any circumstances. In contrast, those who do not believe in God or the Hereafter consider the easing of a patient's suffering or even making the patient's dependants comfortable as important. They believe that it is permissible to kill out of mercy (euthanasia) on the basis of the permission of either of these parties.[9]

Focusing on the five examples above of the challenges facing *laïcité* (secularism) and religiosity in the sphere of human rights, shows that this discussion is essential. In this important discussion, one cannot rely on unproven propositions which cannot be discussed or criticised in the modern era, such as the idea that "the public sphere or human rights are inherently *laïque* (secular)". Here, two completely fundamental issues are relevant: one is the belief in the acceptance of religion and religious values; and the other is the belief, at least in relation to the public sphere, that it should be arranged without even the slightest interference from religion or God. Choosing either of these two beliefs returns one to the question of accepting or not accepting religion, or at least to determining the domain of the influence of religious values. One cannot answer this fundamental question with unproven propositions and with the indefensible reply that "the public sphere is independent from religious values as a source of reference".

Conclusion

First, in regard to the three axes of the challenges concerning the teachings of traditional religion in relation to human rights, the problem has been solved by giving precedence to human rights over traditional readings of religion. These three axes include: the equality of the rights of humans; freedom of religion and thought; and the permissibility of critique and dialogue in religious propositions.

Second, the most important challenge between *laïcité* (secularism) and religiosity is whether or not shared religious values have a place in the public sphere as a source of reference. The *laïque* (secular) approach holds that there is no place for religion outside the private sphere and civil society and

---

9 For further explanation, see the Epilogue to this chapter.

defines the public sphere by excluding religion. Based on this, any reference
to religious values is denied in human rights, even in societies where almost
everyone is a believer.

Third, the religious approach, by leaning first on the principle of the
equality of humans, disagrees with the special rights and privileges granted
to non-believers in the public sphere, including the permission denied to
religious people to use religious symbols in the public sphere; second, shared
religious values can be one of the bases and sources of reference for organising the public sphere; and, third, the rulings of the public sphere in relation
to religion are not excluded in two instances.

In the first instance, it is possible to take a neutral position in relation
to religion. In these instances, the fairest stance is to take a neutral position
vis-à-vis religion, and both those with a *laïque* (secular) stance and religious
believers will have similar rights and opportunities. The principle of equality
of humans and the freedom of belief and conscience are of this kind.

In the second instance, it is not possible to take a neutral position and
the issue requires denial or proof. In these cases, removal of religious values
is based on the consideration that religion is detestable or to be rejected. This
presupposition lacks any sort of philosophical basis or firm epistemological
underpinning. In these cases, there is no solution but to submit to democratic action by submitting to the vote of the majority. Given that in the
contemporary world and in the majority of countries, the religious segment
of society forms the majority, removing religion from the public arena and
cutting off the hands of religious values in organising the public sphere is
not justifiable.

Among the most important examples of the challenges between *laïcité*
(secularism) and religiosity in the public sphere, one can cite elementary
education not only in public schools but also in compulsory public education, as well as media, free sexual relations outside marriage, homosexuality
and mercy killings (euthanasia). In the above-noted cases, it is not wise to
deny shared religious values as a source of reference.

Epilogue

1. The focus of this chapter is a comparative study between *laïcité* (secularism) and religious beliefs in the domain of human rights. *Laïcité* is a French
version of secularism that is much less neutral than other versions, such as the

American example, regarding religion in the public sphere. This chapter is the outline of a long project. The categorisation of rulings related to the public sphere discussed in this chapter adds a third dimension to the debate which previously focused only on religious and *laïque* issues. Focusing my discussion on the five particulars of rulings on religion in the public sphere as related to human rights is an innovative point that has capacity for expansion.

The discussion is not limited to the UDHR, the ICESCR and the ICCPR, but also highlights the main challenging issues between *laïcité* and religiosity, predominantly in Europe. Although these issues were not among the rights explicitly discussed in the aforementioned UN documents, it is clear that these are areas of future focus for human rights. The most challenging of these is the right to be homosexual. I discussed this in the Epilogue to Chapter 6.

2. Euthanasia should first be defined, after which its permission or prohibition can be discussed. This is because the rulings on its various types are not the same:

> Euthanasia may be classified into three types, according to whether a person gives informed consent: voluntary, non-voluntary and involuntary. Voluntary euthanasia is conducted with the consent of the patient. Non-voluntary euthanasia is conducted when the consent of the patient is unavailable. Involuntary euthanasia is conducted against the will of the patient. Voluntary, non-voluntary and involuntary types can be further divided into passive or active variants. Passive euthanasia entails the withholding of treatment necessary for the continuance of life. Active euthanasia entails the use of lethal substances or forces (such as administering a lethal injection).[10]

What is the position of Islamic reformists on these types? (1) Involuntary euthanasia is absolutely prohibited. (2) Non-voluntary euthanasia (regardless of whether it is passive or active), such as in the case of brain death, is

---

10 Hugh LaFollette, *Ethics in Practice: An Anthology* (Oxford: Blackwell, 2002), 25–26; R. W. Perrett, "Buddhism, Euthanasia and the Sanctity of Life", *Journal of Medical Ethics* 22(5) (1996): 309–313; Michael Wreen, "The Definition of Euthanasia", *Philosophy and Phenomenological Research* 48(4) (1988): 637–653.

permitted by decision of a committee including family members, a team of physicians, a jurist from the tradition that the patient practised and a representative of the state. If a will from the patient is available, the case is easier. Either way, permission in this case is reasonable because the patient is not a living human. This case is really excluded from mercy killing. (3) The challenge is voluntary euthanasia. The proponents of euthanasia refer to the right to die and violation of human dignity because of the incurable condition and extreme suffering of a patient. The opponents of euthanasia refer to the necessity of hope in God and resistance in difficult situations. From their perspective suicide or assisted suicide is prohibited and the right to die belongs exclusively to the Creator and no one else. They refer to the many cases where incurable diseases were healed. Although physicians were not able to explain these cases based on their medical knowledge, they confirm their occurrence. Religious believers reject voluntary euthanasia, especially its active variants.

Section Three

Freedoms of Belief, Religion and Politics

8
The Freedom of Belief and Religion in Islam and Human Rights Documents[1]

Preface

The freedom of belief and religion means the right of each person to choose and adhere to any religion or belief. These include the right of thinking, believing and having faith; expressing one's faith and belief; stating beliefs and implementation of religious rituals and activities; teaching religious issues to children and believers; inviting, preaching and promoting religious teachings in society; establishing temples; losing one's faith and leaving a religion (apostasy); ending religious acts and criticising religious teachings, as long as the person's religious practices do not take away from the rights and freedoms of others and do not cause a disruption in the general order and morals. Freedom of religion and belief is realised when a person's religion or belief – whatever it may be – is not considered a crime and does not lead to that person's individual and social rights being violated in this world.

In the conventional Islamic reading, people are divided into three groups: Muslims, People of the Book and unbelievers. Each of these three categories have limitations and prohibitions in all or some of the above aspects which result in the denial of freedom of religion and belief in Islam. This reading is based on certain verses of the Qur'an and hadiths.

1 Mohsen Kadivar, *Azadi-ye 'Aqideh wa Mazhab dar Eslam wa Asnad-e Hoquq-e Bashar*, paper presented at the First International Conference of Human Rights and the Dialogue of Civilizations, Mofid University, Tehran, with the collaboration of UNESCO and the International Center for the Dialogue of Civilizations, 2 May 2001 (*Conference Proceedings*, Mofid University, Qom, 2001, 263–265); *Aftab* bimonthly, Tehran, 23 (2003): 54–63.

From my viewpoint, the freedom of belief and religion is good and desirable from a rational perspective, and is also worthy of praise from the viewpoint of the conventions of reasonability. In seven groups of outstanding verses, the Qur'an has recognised the plurality of beliefs and religions in the world, in addition to introducing the religion of truth and correct belief. It has left people free to choose, and has strictly forbidden force and reluctance in turning to religion; it has not set any temporal punishment for choosing the wrong religion or belief, although it promises suffering in the afterlife for those who deny the Truth.

For three reasons, the arguments for the execution of the apostate do not meet the necessary criteria for credibility. The rulings pertaining to the people of *dhimma*, like those pertaining to slaves, are among the time-bound rulings of the Qur'an, and the meaning of *jihad* is to eliminate coercive obstacles in non-Muslim societies so that people can "freely" choose their desired religion or belief.

Thus, with renewed *ijtihad* based on the authentic criteria of the Book and the Tradition, the freedom of belief and religions in Islam may be supplied.

One of the hypotheses of the theory of the dialogue of civilisations is the acceptance of plurality and diversity of beliefs and religions. Civilisations are based on differing cultures, and differing cultures are based on various beliefs, schools and religions. The dialogue of civilisations and cultures is not possible without the freedom of belief and religion.

The dominant culture in Iran – the proponent of the theory of the dialogue of civilisations – is based on Islam as religion. However, the conventional reading (traditional and official) of Islam apparently does not tolerate the freedom of belief and religion. Thus, the noted theory arises from another reading of Islam. This chapter draws on a reading of Islam that determines the freedom of belief and religion in Islam.

To achieve this aim, it is necessary to answer the following questions: what is the meaning of the freedom of belief and religion? And what place do they have in the documents of international human rights? What is the conventional viewpoint in Islam about the issue of the freedom of belief and religion, and what religious evidence is it based on? Is the freedom of religion and belief something desirable and beneficial or is it something harmful and blameworthy? What are the features of and evidence for the viewpoint that considers Islam to be compatible with the freedom of belief and religion?

The assumption of this chapter is that the freedom of religion and belief is desirable and beneficial, and that its observation in Islam requires following the fundamental criteria of Islam and renewed *ijtihad* in some rulings of *fiqh*.

This chapter is made up of several sections.[2] The first section analyses the conventional Islamic reading of the issue of freedom of belief and religion, as well the evidence it is based on. The second section addresses the task of proving that the freedom of religion and belief is desirable and beneficial. In looking at original Islamic texts, extracting the fundamental criteria of the religion, and criticising the arguments of the conventional reading, the third section provides the evidence for the freedom of belief and religion in Islam. Given the great sensitivity of this topic, from the outset the author welcomes criticism of this introductory step.

Section One: Freedom of Belief and Religion in Traditional Islam

In terms of belief and religion, people can be divided into three groups: first, Muslims; second, Jews, Christians and Zoroastrians; and, third, others. Traditional Islam has different rulings for each of these groups regarding religion and belief. First, I will review these orders according to their most credible sources and I will then review the evidence for them.

First Group: Muslims

Muslims are free to manifest their religion, to express their religious beliefs, and to implement their rituals and religious practices individually or as a group. They are free to instruct children and believers in the teachings of their religion, and to preach and promote Islamic teachings in society. They are free to build mosques. They have the right to criticise other religions and beliefs, and to expose their shortcomings and show the superiority of Islam. No one has the right to force a Muslim to wash his or her hands of his or her religion and beliefs or prevent him or her from implementing religious practices. On these issues there is consensus and no difference in opinion.

---

2 The first section setting up the main concepts under discussion has been deleted. These definitions are clear and can be found in each section.

However, in the following matters, freedom of religion and belief has not been observed.

First, a Muslim is not free to change his or her religion. For example, he or she cannot become a Christian, or a Buddhist or an Atheist. A Muslim who leaves Islam for whatever reason, that is, a Muslim who has become an apostate, will be severely punished. A man who is born Muslim and who accepts Islam after maturity but then becomes an apostate, that is, a *fitri* apostate (literally, renouncing their innate disposition, *fitra*), has the following rulings against him: (1) his repentance and his Islam will apparently not be accepted; (2) he will be executed; (3) his spouse will be considered dead to him without obtaining a divorce; and (4) his properties will be divided among his heirs.

A man who was not born Muslim but who accepted Islam after maturity and then left Islam (i.e., a *milli* apostate: literally, apostate from the *milla* community) will be called to repent. If he repents by the third day and returns to Islam, he will be freed; otherwise he will be executed. In addition, the spouse of the apostate will be separated from him without divorce. For a Muslim woman who becomes an apostate, her spouse will be separated from her without divorce and she will be obligated to enter into a waiting period. Second, she will be called to repent. If she accepts, she will be freed, otherwise she will be sentenced to prison and hard labour until she repents or dies.

Therefore, for a Muslim who becomes an apostate and is not willing to return to Islam, in the case of a man he must be executed, and in the case of a woman she must face life in prison with hard labour.[3]

Second, a Muslim is not free to theoretically deny issues that are known as elements of Islam in the discipline of believers (*'urf mutasharri'a*). If a Muslim

---

3 The above rulings have been derived from the *fatwa* of Shi'a jurists. For example, see Ayatollah Ruhollah Khomeini, *Tahrir al-Wasilah*, chapter on inheritance, the obstacle of inheritance, *al-Kufr*, No. 10, 2:394 and chapter on punishment (*al-hudud*), apostasy, No. 1, 2:528–529; Ayatollah Mousawi Khu'i, *Mabani Takamila al-Minhaj*, apostasy, 1:324 and 327 and No. 271, 1:330. The hard labour includes hitting during times of prayer, imposing very difficult labour, prevention from eating and drinking beyond the necessary amount, and the wearing of harsh clothing (*Mabani Takmila al-Minhaj*, 1:331–332). Sunni jurists have consensus on the mandatory killing of the apostate in case there is no repentance. Only the Hanafi school considers the punishment for a woman apostate to be imprisonment with hard labour until she either dies or converts. Second, they consider giving the chance to repent to be recommended rather than required. See Wahba al-Zuhayli, *al-Fiqh al-Islami wa Adilatahu* (*Islamic Jurisprudence and its Proof*) (Damascus: Dar al-Fikr, 1985), 6:183–193.

denies an issue that is considered in Islamic convention to be a necessity of
the religion, which is therefore concomitant with denial of the prophecy or
a rejection of Muhammad the messenger of God, or attributes shortcomings
to the *shari'a*, he or she will be counted an apostate, and will be penalised
with the punishment for apostasy, even if he or she identifies him- or herself
as a Muslim.[4] The new approaches of religious rulings by some Muslim theologians can easily be included under the auspices of the above rulings, and
throughout history it has not been rare for many distinguished philosophers
or mystics to be sentenced as blasphemers and apostates.[5]

Third, an adolescent whose parents were either both, or one of them,
Muslim, is not free to choose any other religion than Islam after maturity. If
for whatever reason he or she does not become a Muslim, they will be punished as an apostate, meaning he or she will be asked to repent. If they fail

---

4 "When we discuss a *kafir* (non-believer), we mean one who rejects the existence of God, or His
Oneness, or prophecy, or one of the essential elements of Islam in a way that turns their rejection
into a rejection of prophecy. It is precautionary to avoid one who absolutely rejects essential [ele-
ments of Islam] without his/her attention to its essentiality" (Muhammad Kazim al-Tabataba'i
al-Yazdi, *al-'Urwah al-Wuthqa* (*The Firmest Hand-Hold*), with glosses by Shi'i authorities (Qom:
Islamic Publication Institute, 2001–2005), chapter on purity (*tahara*), section on impurities
(*nijasat*), subsection 8, 1:138–139). In defining impurity "A person who attributes himself to
a religion except Islam, or attributes himself to Islam but rejects an issue that is defined as a
necessity of Islam in a way that turns his rejection into a rejection of prophecy, or denial of the
Prophet Muhammad, or the attribution of shortcomings to *shari'a*, or that results in doing or
saying something that requires his disbelief (*kufr*) . . ." (Ayatollah Ruhollah Khomeini, *Tahrir
al-Wasilah*, chapter on purity (*tahara*), section on impurity (*nijasa*), subsection 10, 1:124). "One
who attributes himself to Islam, and rejects an issue that is known as a part of Islam in a way
that turns his rejection into rejection of prophecy [i.e., leaving Islam], however rejection of resurrection is the cause of becoming an absolute non-believer". (Sayyid Abu al-Qasim al-Musawi
al-Khu'i, *Minhaj al-Salihin*, (*The Righteous Platform*) (Qom: Madina al-'Ilm, 1990), chapter on
purity (*tahara*), section on impure objects, 1:109). To become familiar with the *fatwa*s of Sunni
jurists, see, for example, this *fatwa*: "The apostate is a person who converted from Islam to non-
Islam (*kufr*) . . . or who premises something that is prohibited consensually . . . or prohibits
something that is promised consensually . . . or denies the obligatory that is consensual, or
believes in the obligation of something that is not obligatory by consensus . . . or intends to
become an unbeliever tomorrow, or becomes doubtful [about Islam]" (al-Zuhayli, *al-Fiqh al-
Islami wa Adilatahu*, 6:183).
5 The examples of the ruling for anathema (*takfir*) are plenty among the biggest scholars of Islam,
including Avicenna (980–1037), Suhrawardi (1154–1191), Ibn Arabi (1196–1240), Mulla Sadra
(1571–1640) and even recently among the jurists of Sheikh Muhammad Hadi Tehrani (known as
Mukaffar) (1837–1903).

to do so, a boy will be executed and a girl will be sentenced to prison with hard labour, the end of which will be determined by death or repentance.[6]

Fourth, a Muslim is not free to abandon mandatory aspects of their religion or to undertake anything their religion prohibits. If he or she does so knowingly and on purpose, then he or she will receive *ta'zir* punishment under the supervision of a jurist of *shari'a*[7] (the most significant aspect of *ta'zir* is lashing).

Second Group: People of the Book

The People of the Book are Jews and Christians. Zoroastrians are also attached to the People of the Book (Q. 22:17). The Sabians[8] are among the People of the Book in the more acceptable view (*azhar*).[9] Other unbelievers are absolutely not considered to be People of the Book.[10] It is obligatory for Muslims to go to war with the People of the Book until they accept one of the following ways: either accept becoming Muslim or pay tax (*jizya*) to become humbled (*sagharoun*) and be accepted as people of the *dhimma*.

If the People of the Book accept the conditions of *dhimma*, then their life, property and dignity (*namous*) will be safeguarded. The amount of tax (*jizya*) is determined by the ruler and the conditions of *dhimma* will be in accordance to what he sees fit. In a manner that might be conducive towards them becoming Muslim, the people of *dhimma* have the right to manifest their religion and express their religious beliefs. And in cases where the ruler allows it, they are able to keep their temples and carry out their rituals and religious practices individually or as a group, and instruct their co-religionists in their teachings. They can leave their religion and turn to other religions

---

6 See Ayatollah Ruhollah Khomeini, *Tahrir al-Wasilah*, chapter on punishment (*al-hudud*), section on apostasy, No. 4, 2:529.

7 Al-Khu'i, *Mabani Takmila al-Minhaj*, No. 282, 1:337. According to Khomeini, abandoning obligations and implementing what is prohibited will be subject to *ta'zir* punishments if they are among the cardinal sins (Ayatollah Ruhollah Khomeini, *Tahrir al-Wasilah*, chapter on punishments (*al-hudud*), the punishment of false accusation of adultery (*hadd al-qadhf*), subsection on branches, No. 5, 2:510)

8 Sabians are mentioned three times in the Qur'an as being People of the Book (Q. 2:62, 5:69 and 22:17).

9 Al-Khu'i, *Minhaj al-Salihin*, 1:337 and 391, chapter on *jihad*, No. 62.

10 Ibid., 1:391 and Ayatollah Ruhollah Khomeini, *Tahrir al-Wasilah*, the supplement on punishments (*al-hudud*), *ahkam al-dhimma*, No. 2, 2:532.

(which are permitted according to their own religion). In any case, changing their religion to Islam is permitted. They may also leave their own religious practices, and criticise their own religious teachings.

The rulings pertaining to the people of *dhimma* deny the freedom of belief and religion in the following points. First, the people of *dhimma* are not free to raise their children in such a way that they may turn to the religion of their fathers, meaning that they cannot forbid their children from attending meetings and centres for preaching Islam. Rather, they must let their children be free to choose their own paths – it being clear that this path leads to the choosing of a religion based on innate disposition (*fitra*), meaning Islam.[11] Second, the people of *dhimma* are not free to establish synagogues, churches, monasteries or fire temples.[12] Third, the people of *dhimma* are not free to preach or to promote their religion and weaken the beliefs of Muslims. The publication of their views is prohibited.[13] Fourth, based on the preferable method,[14] the people of *dhimma* are not free to criticise Islamic teachings. Fifth, the people of *dhimma* are not free to openly carry out acts that are forbidden in Islam but permitted in their religion.[15] Sixth, the people of *dhimma* are not free to change their religions to anything other than Islam, Christianity, Judaism or Zoroastrianism. Otherwise, they will be killed.[16] Seventh, the people of *dhimma* are not free to remain in Islamic

---

11 Al-Khu'i, *Minhaj al-Salihin*, chapter on *jihad*, No. 81, 1:397.
12 Ayatollah Ruhollah Khomeini, *Tahrir al-Wasilah*, the conditions of *dhimma*, No. 6. 2:537; Al-Khu'i, *Minhaj al-Salihin*, chapter on *jihad*, No. 85, 1:399.
13 "Non-believers, regardless of whether they are *dhimmi* or not, do not have the right to preach their corrupted religion, to publish their heterodox books, or to invite Muslims and their children into their invalid religion in the land of Muslims; their punishment (*ta'zir*) is required [if they violate those three rights], and the senior governors of Islamic States must prevent them from doing so through any appropriate means. It is mandatory for Muslims to avoid their books and meetings, and to prevent their children from attending them [any activities of the non-believers]. If Muslims have received any of their heterodox books or declarations, they must eliminate them, because their scriptures are nothing but falsified and are therefore without any sanctity; May almighty God protect Muslims from the evils and scheming of the enemies, and transcend the Word of Islam" (Ayatollah Ruhollah Khomeini, *Tahrir al-Wasilah*, chapter on punishment (*al-hudud*), the details of *dhimma* rulings, No. 4, 2:542).
14 Preferable syllogism (*qiyas al-awlawiya*) is one of the well-known forms of reasoning in the methodology of *fiqh*.
15 Ayatollah Ruhollah Khomeini, *Tahrir al-Wasilah*, chapter on punishment (*al-hudud*), the details of *dhimma* rulings, No. 2, 2:541; Al-Khu'i, *Minhaj al-Salihin* chapter on *jihad*, No. 80, 1:393.
16 Ayatollah Ruhollah Khomeini, *Tahrir al-Wasilah*, ibid., No. 1, 2:541.

society if they violate the conditions of *dhimma*. There are two opinions on whether they are free to go to a safe place or if the ruler has the right to kill, enslave or to demand ransom from them.[17]

Third Group: Unbelievers

Non-Muslims, including People of the Book who are not willing to accept the conditions of *dhimmi*, and other idolatrous non-believers (who have not entered into a protection treaty with Muslims, or who have attacked Muslims, or have expelled them from their lands and forced them to leave Islam),[18] are considered infidels of war (*kafir harbi*), and it is mandatory to impart Islam to them. If they accept Islam, then there is nothing more, but otherwise they must be approached through *jihad*. War with them shall continue until they accept Islam or are killed.[19] Their women and children will be enslaved and all of their properties and lands will be given to Muslims as bounty.[20] However, the popular view among Shi'ite scholars is that this initiation (*ibtida'i*) of *jihad* is not permitted during Imam Mahdi's occultation.[21] Nevertheless, the other contemporary view is that initiating *jihad* is permissable, which means that the ruling on this type of *jihad* is not conditional on the presence of the infallible (Prophet or Imam).[22]

Based on this, in general, a non-Muslim who is non-*dhimma* and who does not accept Islam does not have the right to live. Furthermore, it is clear

---

17 Al-Khu'i, *Minhaj al-Salihin*, chapter on *jihad*, No. 82, 1:398: Ayatollah Ruhollah Khomeini, *Tahrir al-Wasilah*, the conditions of *dhimma*, No. 8, 2:538.

18 As such, the non-Muslims who have entered into a *dhimmi* treaty with Muslim rulers (exclusive to the People of the Book), or who have entered into a protection treaty with Muslim rulers (this includes all forms of non-believers such as pagans, idolaters, polytheists and atheists) and are called the People of Treaty (*mu'ahad*), as well as non-Muslims who did not enter into a protection treaty with Muslims, but who did not attack Muslim lands, did not expel Muslims from their lands, did not force Muslims to leave Islam and did not commit anything against Islam, are not considered warring unbelievers. For further explanation, see the Epilogue at the end of this chapter.

19 Al-Khu'i, *Minhaj al-Salihin*, chapter on *jihad*, 1:360

20 Ibid., chapter on *jihad*, bounties, 1:379–381.

21 Ayatollah Ruhollah Khomeini, *Tahrir al-Wasilah*, chapter on enjoining right and forbidding wrong, conclusion, No. 2, 1:513.

22 For example, see Mohammad Mo'men Qomi, *Kalimat Sadidah fi Masa'il Jadida* (*The Correct Words in New Issues*) (Qom: Islamic Publication Institute, 1995), chapter on initiating *jihad*, 315–358; al-Khu'i, *Minhaj al-Salihin*, chapter on *jihad*, bounties, 1:379–381.

that based on the preferable method he or she will not enjoy other rights either. Thus, the rulings pertaining to non-believers are completely at odds with the freedom of belief and religion.

Given the rulings applicable to the above three categories, one can conclude that in its extended form, the conventional reading of Islam almost completely denies the freedom of religion and belief. Given the issues discussed above, it would seem that there is no argument about the fact that the conventional reading of Islam does not tolerate the freedom of religion and belief. I will now turn to a discussion of the most important reasons given for the rulings above. For each category of these rulings, I will select one ruling and examine the strongest argument given for its validity. The three chosen rulings include the execution of a Muslim apostate, the *jizya* tax levied on the People of the Book, and the absence of the right to life for non-*dhimma* unbelievers.

The source for the heavy punishment of Muslim apostates can be found in particular hadiths. The Sunni refer to the authentic hadith of the Prophet, which refers to killing anyone who changes his or her religion.[23] The references to the punishment of a *fitri* apostate include the validated hadith of 'Ammar Sabbati: "I heard from Imam Sadiq who said that any Muslim who leaves Islam and denies the Prophecy of Muhammad and contradicts him, it is permitted for the person who hears this to spill his blood, and his wife will be separated from him from the day of the apostasy, his property will be divided among his heirs, his wife will take the waiting period of death, and it is required that the Imam kill him and not ask him to repent either."[24]

The authentic hadith of 'Ali b. Ja'far is among the references for the punishment of a *milli* apostate. He asked Imam Moussa b. Ja'far about a Muslim who becomes Christian, and he said: "he will be killed and not asked to

---

23 'Abdallah b. 'Abbas narrated that the Prophet said: "Whosoever changes his religion, kill him" (al-Bukhari, 6922, Ahmad b. Hanbal: 1871, al-Tirmidhi: 1458, Abu Dawud: 4351, Ibn Majah: 2536, al-Nisa'i: 4059). For more information about this hadith, see my introduction to *Blasphemy and Apostasy in Islam: Debates in Shi'a Jurisprudence*.

24 Al-Kulaini, *Al-Kafi*, 7:257, hadith No. 11; al-Saduq, *Man la Yahdhuruh al-Faqih*, 3:98, hadith No. 333; Abu Ja'far Muhammad b. al-Hassan al-Tusi, *Tahdhib al-Ahkam (Refinement of Rulings)*, ed. Hassan al-Musawi al-Khirsan (Tehran: Dar al-Kutub al-Islamiyya, 1970), 10:136, hadith No. 541; Abu Ja'far Muhammad b. al-Hassan al-Tusi *al-Istibsar fi ma Ukhtulifa min al-Akhbar (Reflections on the Disputed Reports of the Perspicacious)*, ed. Hassan al-Musawi al-Khirsan (Tehran: Dar al-Kutub al-Islamiyya, 1970), 4:353, hadith No. 957; al-Hurr al-'Amili, *Tafsil Wasa'il al-Shi'a*, chapters on the punishment of apostasy, ch. 1, hadith No. 3, 28:324.

repent". He asked, "what if a Christian becomes Muslim and then becomes an apostate?" He said, "he will be asked to repent. If he repents, then nothing will happen. Otherwise, he will be killed."[25]

The authentic hadith of Hammad is among the references for the punishment of a woman apostate. He asked Imam Sadiq about the punishment of a woman apostate and he said: "she will not be killed, she will have to do hard labour, and will be prohibited from food and drink other than that which sustains her life. She shall wear rough clothes and be beaten during times of prayer."[26]

The most important of the references for rulings pertaining to the People of the *dhimma* is the following verse of the Qur'an:

Fight those who believe not in God and the Last Day and do not forbid what God and His Messenger have forbidden – such men as practice not the religion of truth, being of those who have been given the Book – until they pay the tribute out of hand and have been humbled. (Q. 2:29)

The most important references for the rulings pertaining to the non-believer who is not of the People of *dhimma* are some verses of the Qur'an:

Fight the unbelievers totally even as they fight you totally. (Q. 9:36)
Then, when the sacred months are drawn away, slay the idolaters wherever you find them, and take them, and confine them, and lie in wait for them at every place of ambush. But if they repent, and perform the prayer, and pay the alms, then let them go their way; God is All-forgiving, All-compassionate. (Q. 9:5)
Fight them [unbelievers], till there is no persecution and the religion is God's entirely; then if they give over, surely God sees the things they do. (Q. 8:39)

---

25 Al-Kulaini, *Al-Kafi*, 7:257, No. 10; al-Tusi *Tahdhib al-Ahkam*, 10:138, hadith No. 548; al-Tusi, *al-Istibsar*, 4:354, hadith No. 963; al-Hurr al-'Amili, *Tafsil Wasa'il al-Shi'a*, chapters on the punishment of apostasy, ch. 1, hadith No. 5, 28:325.
26 Al-Kulaini, *Tahdhib al-Ahkam*, 10:143, hadith No. 565; al-Saduq, *Man la Yahdhuruh al-Faqih*, 3:89, hadith No. 335; al-Hurr al-'Amili, *Tafsil Wasa'il al-Shi'a*, chapters on the punishment of apostasy, ch. 4, hadith No. 1, 28:330.

Reflecting on these examples of references shows that the conventional read-ing of Islam about the freedom of belief and religion has notable sources in the Book and the Tradition. The critical analysis of these arguments will be covered in Section Four.

Section Two: *The Desirability and Goodness of the Freedom of Belief and Religion*

In this section, I will consider the issue of freedom of belief and religion from a rational perspective that is free from a narrative view. First, I will attempt to sketch the rational framework of those who deny the freedom of belief and religion and then by critiquing it, I will rationally show the desirability and goodness of the freedom of belief and religion.

The freedom of belief and religion is not among the dictated and devo-tional (*ta'abbudi*) issues and is beyond rational (*tawqifi*) issues, so its interests and harms may be hidden from human reason. Thus, its discussion is per-missable. Without doubt, whoever has voiced an opinion on this issue has done so after weighing up its pros and cons. Religious scholars, theologians and jurists are not excluded from this principle. The person who issues a *fatwa* against the freedom of belief and religion undoubtedly considers the costs, harms and corruptions of this freedom to be greater than its benefits, while the person who confirms the importance of the freedom of belief and religion certainly considers its interests, benefits and uses to be greater than its harms. If the issue of freedom of belief and religion is a rational one, then before a consideration of the narrative ruling – which will no doubt be in the form of guidance (*irshad*) to the rational ruling – the status of the issue must be clarified in terms of reason and reasonability.

Aside from the rational and non-dictated essence of the freedom of belief and religion, it is an *a priori* religious issue. It is an antecedent to the choos-ing of religion and belief. With its acceptance, religion and belief are chosen. How can a religion that requests its followers to research and accept religious beliefs with evidence and arguments and which invalidates immitation in the arena of beliefs, deny the freedom of religion and belief?

One cannot impose the results of research at the outset. It is inadequate to say that people are free to research among various religions and beliefs but must choose Islam for certain. If they are free, then the result cannot be determined at the outset, and if the result is determined at the outset and there is no choice but to give into it, then they are not free. What is the difference between a person who is born in a Muslim family, and who has matured in an Islamic society and as a result is a Muslim, and a person who is born into a Christian family, and who has matured in a Christian society and is therefore a Christian? Rewards and punishments are the course of an individual's choices based on consciousness. How can a religion that denies the freedom of belief and religion expect that others be free to choose it, but if they do choose it, their freedom will be denied?

Unfortunately, the issue of freedom of belief and religion has not been discussed independently by scholars of religion. Thus, its principles and foundations have not been described in a clear and convincing manner. It is natural that in deducing some of the rulings of *fiqh*, such as those pertaining to the punishments of an apostate, the conditions of *dhimma*, and the absence of the right to life for non-*dhimma* non-believers, the theological bases and the general criteria of religion have not been adequately observed.

Critique of the Assumptions behind the Denial of the Freedom of Belief and Religion

In addition to these assumptions, the general framework in which these rulings were issued was based on the following points:

First, the possibility of realising a closed society. This means that the cultural atmosphere of a society can be controlled such that no unwanted opinions can pollute the general atmosphere, and that people cannot be informed about false beliefs and religions and would therefore not be influenced by them and become deviant.

Second, the positive influence of heavy penalties on society. Human nature is such that people must be forced away from falsehoods with pressure and violence. Otherwise, meaning if they are left free, they will become deviant and the devils will have control over their life. If leaving Islam carries the death penalty, then no one will be tempted to become an apostate. If the People of the Book feel the abjection of *dhimma*, they will become Muslim, and if non-believers are stuck with a choice between Islam and death, they will doubtlessly choose Islam. In general, there is no other way than this for the religion of truth to reign globally.

Third, the great passivity of people in the face of promotion. People are such that if they are placed behind the blindfold of preaching and promotion for various beliefs and religions, they will be easily deceived, come under the influence of devils, and will lose their religion and beliefs. The only way for people to live a life of religion and beliefs is to prohibit the preaching and promotion of other religions. Otherwise, there will be no guarantee for the survival of one's own religion.

Fourth, the heavy penalties and violent confrontations in dealing with religions and beliefs are not restricted to a particular one. In the last millennium, various religions and beliefs had hostile relationships with one another. These sorts of rulings were therefore not limited to Islam, and were generally prevalent in the Old World, and were thus not considered to be deficient or a fault.

Fifth, the issue of the spread of Islam for the sake of appearances (*Islam zahiri*).[27] It is clear that converting to Islam because of the fear of death, or to escape the payments of tax (*jizya*), and that remaining Muslim to avoid the death penalty for apostasy is on the face of it compatible with Islam for the sake of appearances. However, we have no evidence for this not to apply to real and internal Islam in any circumstances, although it is difficult to accept that these rulings would lead to the deepening of religious knowledge and faith, and the dissemination of religion. In addition, do scholars of religion not have a duty when it comes to the religious conscience (*batin diyanat*) of society?

There is no doubt about the compatibility of the rulings noted above with the five bases that were mentioned earlier. However, there is doubt about the accuracy and completeness of every one of these axes. I will point to these briefly, and move on.

First, the amazing progress of mass communications in our time makes a closed society impossible. Whether we like it or not, it is possible to gain general knowledge about various beliefs and religions from those who hold them.

Second, while violence, heavy punishments and intimidation may work in the apparent acceptance of religions and beliefs, the impact in terms of the penetration of faith in the hearts of people is certainly reversed. Clearly, we have to reconsider our anthropology. We must trust

---

27 Islam for the sake of appearances (*Islam zahiri*) occurs by confessing the Oneness of God and the Prophecy of Muhammad (*Shahadatain*). Real and internal Islam (*Islam batini*) is faith or confession of the heart.

the human individual, as he or she will choose right over wrong in free circumstances; what is important is that he or she be convinced and choose freely.

Third, in today's world the hostile confrontation between religion and beliefs leaves no place for acceptance. These types of rulings bring about repulsion and hatred towards religion and beliefs and are therefore not instruments for attracting people to religion.

Fourth, if there is an issue that causes the reduction in true faith and the belief in the human species, and given that the goal of religions is to bring about internal changes in people, how can one vote for such an issue?

The Rational Rulings on Freedom of Belief and Religion

Following a brief account and criticism of the theological bases of the denial of freedom of belief and religion, I will move on to discussing the rational reason for the freedom of belief and religion:

1. Belief and religion are issues of choice that humans choose or let go of freely. Choosing a particular belief or religion is based on reasons and preliminaries, the realisation of which leads to the acceptance of a religion and the denial of which leads to that belief being left underfoot. If the reasons and preliminaries exist, pressure and coercion can never cause the elimination of or change in that belief, and if the reasons and preliminaries do not exist, then pressure and coercion can never bring them about. That which pressure and coercion produces is no more than belief and religion in appearance and in words, not internally and of the heart.

2. It is clear that all beliefs and religions that exist among people are not on equal footing in terms of their correctness or credibility. In addition, there is no doubt that some of these beliefs and religions are false. Nonetheless, many people believe and are pious in the same beliefs that we may consider to be false. The best way of changing and reforming false beliefs and religions is to convince those who follow them, and convincing does not occur anywhere other than in a free space. If people do not accept, then we have no other duty. This means that we are not free to force them to have the same belief and religion as us. Denying the freedom of belief and religion results in forcing others to accept a particular belief or religion. Force and fear in the realm of beliefs and religions leads to them going underground and becoming hidden, but it will not lead to them being uprooted.

As long as people see benefit in their particular faith or religion, such as the achievement of happiness, or the negation of temporal suffering or reaching a transcendent destination, they will not let go of it. Throughout history, the survival of every religion and belief indicates its beneficial function for its believers. People are strict when it comes to changes in belief, especially regarding religion, and change their beliefs and religion with difficulty. This change will occur only when they become *convinced* and not if they are *forced* to do so.

3. On the other hand, the world is full of plurality, diversity, trials and tests. Among the various opinions, beliefs and religions of the world, people are free to choose their own way, a choice that may be right or false, correct or incorrect, and in the other world – according to our beliefs – they will see the results of their choices with their own eyes. If it was supposed to be the case that people should be forced to choose right over wrong in this world, or if there were circumstances where people had no choice but to take the path of the right (or be killed), God would have prioritised such coercion and lack of freedom to guarantee the determination of truth; He would have created humans like angels and made their world like the world of incorporeal beings, a world that does not contain the contradictions of what is true and false. If this were the case, what meaning would eternal penalties have and what would be the consequences for wrongdoers and the rewards for those who do right?

4. The plurality of beliefs and religions among people is ineradicable. At least, so far, the history of human ideas has shown this to be the case. The denial of freedom of belief and religion among this plurality leads to hypocrisy, duplicity and two-faceness. If those who hold forbidden beliefs and religions would be penalised with the death penalty, or be denied many rights and social benefits for having a different belief or religion, or for expressing their thoughts, they would have no choice but to pretend to follow the dominant religion of the time. Duplicity is like a degenerative disease for faith. And with an increase in hypocrites, one cannot establish a society of faith and religion. The prevalence of duplicity and hypocrisy is the logical and inescapable result of the denial of the freedom of belief and religion.

5. Many religions and beliefs consider themselves to be the most complete, the best, the most comprehensive and the final religion. Their respective followers believe these claims as well. There is no doubt that these claims will be tested in the other world and that right will be distinguished from

wrong. But in this world, for centuries, every religion has presented its arguments on the basis of this momentous claim, and these reasons have apparently been unable to convince others. If it is to be the case that believers of every religion and belief prohibit all other beliefs and religions on the basis of having a monopoly over being complete and comprehensive, and only give their own followers the freedom of belief and religion (without the right to change one's religion), then religious societies will become closed and secular societies will be open. The biggest danger for a religion is to be restricted in a closed society or atmosphere, as it will lead to stagnation and a lack in its flourishing. To merely be able to breathe in a free atmosphere, the followers of such religions and beliefs will lose their religion and belief, and will become weak in their religion.

6. The denial of the freedom of belief and religion, even within that religion and belief itself, will lead to the solidification of an official reading. As a result, any kind of *ijtihad* and new thinking within the religion will face serious problems. Rulings pertaining to apostasy, blasphemy and accusations of atheism are the definite products of such a society, and the result will be that members of that society will be denied the opinions of its strongest thinkers.

7. If the followers of a religion and belief do not give freedom to the followers of other religions and beliefs (and do not even give followers of their own religion the freedom to change religion), and come to a confrontation outside the lands of their own particular religion and belief, and the others reciprocate and limit or prohibit this particular religion, who will be harmed other than this particular religion or belief?

8. The corruption and harm caused by the denial of the freedom of belief and religion is such that if they were recognised, no wise person would give into it. The scholars who have issued rulings based on the denial of belief and religion have thought that in this way, that which is beneficial to the religion will be better observed. There is no doubt that if they too were placed in this atmosphere, they would reconsider their previous opinions. Perhaps they would refer to the harm caused by the freedom of belief and religion, and the possibility that it would lead to deviance among children and adolescents. It is clear that there are standards for instruction and promotion among children and adolescents and that parents play the greatest role in the religious teachings of their children. In addition, all of the activities of those with various beliefs and religions in society are according to laws, and no religious

person or believer has the right to step on the legal rights and freedoms of others, or the security, order and public morals of society using the excuse of acting in accordance with his or her religious beliefs.

9. Religions and beliefs which have strong and steady foundations should have no fear of being in the arena of the freedom of belief and religion. It is clear that religions and beliefs with weak foundations fear competition from different opinions, as well as the conflict between different beliefs and faiths, and make up for these weaknesses by eliminating the freedom of belief and religion.

10. This view, which has established a difference between the freedom of thought and the freedom of belief by accepting the former on the basis of it being reasonable and by denying the latter because some views may not be rationally correct, is not an acceptable position.[28] This is because thinking does not require permission from an authority and in general it is not preventable, so one cannot act as though a favour is being done for thinkers by allowing freedom of thought. Where there is room for critique and dispute is the freedom to *express* one's views and the freedom to act in accordance with one's views. Thus, making a distinction between thinking and belief does not solve the problem. What belief considers itself to be false and incorrect? Those who are faced with such a division will take their place on the side of those who deny the freedom of belief and religion.

Thus, from a rational point of view, one can conclude that freedom of belief and religion is good and admirable among reasonable people, and that it is therefore a desirable and beneficial issue.

Section Three: Freedom of Belief and Religion in Reformist Islam[29]

In this section I will first present the religious arguments for the freedom of belief and religion in Islam. Second, I will provide a critique of the arguments of those who deny the freedom of belief and religion. Before addressing these, I will answer the preliminary question of whether the key principle in religion and belief is freedom and whether the denial of this freedom requires

---

28 Morteza Motahhari, *Piramoun-e Jomhuri-e Eslami* (*About the Islamic Republic*) (Tehran: Sadra, 1989), 87–136; Morteza Motahhari, *Piramoun-e Enqelab-e Eslami* (*About the Islamic Revolution*) (Tehran: Sadra, 1989), 6–22.
29 "Another Reading of Islam" is translated to "reformist Islam".

discussion, or the opposite? It is clear that the meaning of freedom of belief and religion is the freedom in this world; in the face of the righteousness of belief in a particular religion – Islam – and the eternal happiness for its true followers, is the belief in different religions and sects considered a temporal crime and do punishments apply? Therefore, the importance of establishing this principle is to determine whether it is based on the temporal criminalisation and punishment of non-Muslims (including apostates, the People of the Book and non-*dhimma* non-believers), as proving their innocence from temporal punishment requires arguments; or is it the opposite, with the principle based on the innocence of everyone from criminalisation and temporal punishment, except something that is considered to be a crime by the religion and which requires punishment? It seems that the principle is innocence from criminalisation and temporal punishment, and that proving the punishment for apostasy, restrictions for the People of the Book as *dhimma*, and the lack of the right to life for the non-*dhimmi* non-believer requires reasoning. It is necessary to point out that the discussion is absolutely not about the status of apostates, *dhimmi* and non-*dhimmi* non-believers as sinners in the other world. There is no doubt that if, despite the knowledge of the rightfulness of Islam, the above three groups are selected as sinners, the discussion is about their status as a temporal crime and their punishment in this world. Every sin is not a crime in this world, thus many sins have neither a *hadd* nor *ta'zir* punishment. Therefore, if there is a credible reason to be found for the criminality and punishment of these three categories, then one must stick with the principle of innocence.

First Stage: The Qur'anic Arguments for the Freedom of Belief and Religion in Islam

I will use this opportunity to analyse the most important verses of the Qur'an which in some way or another prove the freedom of belief and religion. These will be analysed in the following seven categories.[30]

---

30 In his treatise *Hurria al-fikr wa al-'itiqad fi al-Islam* (*The Freedom of Thought and Belief in Islam*) (Cairo: Dar al-Fikr al-Islami, 1998), Jamal al-Banna has provided a classification of Qur'anic verses that is close to this classification.

First Category: The Denial of Coercion and Compulsion in Religion and Faith

The most important verses in this category are the three verses below:

> There is no compulsion in religion: true guidance has become distinct from error, so whoever rejects false gods and believes in God has grasped the firmest hand-hold, one that will never break. God is all hearing and all knowing. (Q. 2:256)

The above verse is probable for negation (*nafie*) and prohibition (*nahie*). It negates the idea that God has called for faith by pressure and coercion, and it prohibits forcing another to have faith, since forcing faith or lack of faith has no credibility. The denial of coercion in this verse equates to accepting freedom in religion. Its consequences are therefore freedom in two areas: freedom to enter a religion and the freedom to leave it. To give people the option of choosing either a particular religion or death, is to deny freedom and to accept coercion in religion. If people are left free to accept religion, but upon accepting the religion are no longer free to leave that religion, their remaining in the religion is forced through fear of punishment. At the same time, the Qur'an has shown that faith in God is right and that it represents true guidance. It considers the distinction between true and false very clearly and openly, but does so without wanting to force people into accepting the religion of truth: "The Qur'an has not limited the freedom of belief and lack of coercion to Islam, based on the absolute expression that is achieved from the verses [of the Qur'an: 2:256], but has declared the prohibition of any kind of pressure or coercion from all religions, and furthermore, based on abolition of the specialty (*ilgha' khususiyyat*) of the case, has declared the prohibition of any kind of coercion from all beliefs and thoughts. This type of freedom which has a natural and essential relationship with human essence, can neither be designated nor taken away."[31]

In terms of the occasion of the Revelation of this verse, the following narration has been cited from *Mujahid*: a man from the *Ansar* (supporters of the Prophet) forced Sabih, his black servant, to accept Islam; this verse was

---

31 Mahdi Haeri-Yazdi, *Islam wa I'lamiye Hoquq-i Bashar* (*Islam and Human Rights*), *Maktab-e Tashayo'* (Shi'a School), Annual 1341 Qom, 4 (1962): 67–76.

revealed and prevented Muslims from carrying out this act. Others have narrated the occasion of the Revelation of this verse as follows: a man from the *Ansar* who was called Abu al-Hussain had two sons who sometimes cooperated with foreign merchants in trade. Some oil merchants who were Christians entered Medina and invited Abu al-Hussain's sons to become Christian. The sons converted to Christianity and headed towards Sham with their new co-religionists. Their father, who was among the Prophet's companions, told the Prophet about what had happened to his two sons. The verse was revealed: there is no compulsion in religion.[32]

There is no doubt that punishments for apostasy, such as execution and life sentences, or forcing non-believers to choose between Islam and death, are examples of coercion in religion and that they contradict the honourable verse above.

> Had your Lord willed, all the people on earth would have believed.
> So, can you [Prophet] compel people to believe? (Q. 10:99)

While believing in God and the Hereafter is true, God has not willed existentially (*takwini*) that people have faith, for in such a case the choice of humans would be denied, and reward and punishment as consequences for belief and non-belief would be useless. Religion and faith only have value when humans freely choose them. When the Prophet worried about the lack of faith of some people and insisted on them becoming Muslim, God would remind him: when your God does not approve of coercion in faith and religion, how could you approve of it? He asked in "denying question" style.[33] Do you make people believe? And the answer is clearly in the negative. If force and coercion is not permitted for making others into believers and Muslims, then how can it be permissible for force and coercion to make others stay Muslim and to keep their faith? Becoming a believer and a Muslim is right, nonetheless God has not permitted us to force this right, so how can one force others to choose between Islam and execution? In the same way, remaining a believer and not changing one's belief to unbelief is right. Are

---

32 Fadl b. al-Hassan al-Tabrisi, *Majama' al-Bayan fi Tafsir al-Qur'an (Complex Statements in the Exegesis of the Qur'an)* (Beirut: Dar al-Murtada/Dar al-'Ulum, 2005/6), 3:363–364.

33 "Denying question" is a style of asking where the reply is denial and rejection.

we permitted to consider punishments such as life sentence in prison and the execution of people in order to force them to keep their faith and Islam?

> He said, "My people, think: if I did have a clear sign from my Lord, and He had given me grace of His own, though it was hidden from you, could we force you to accept it against your will?" (Q. 11:28)

When Noah shared his divine message with the people, he was faced with their rejection and they called him a liar. In discussion with his people, he called on them to think about whether he had proof from his God and that this proof remained hidden from them. Is the prophet permitted to force people to accept the right when they express hatred? This style of question is a "denying question", that is, it is clear that the prophet has no such permission. If the prophet has no such permission, are the followers of prophets permitted to force others to follow Islam or to use threats of punishment to force them to remain in their faith and in Islam?

From these three verses one can derive the strong Qur'anic principle that one cannot and should not force anyone else to have religion and faith. The freedom of religion is nothing other than the denial of force and coercion in this sphere.

Second Category: Freedom to Choose the Temporal Option of Guidance or Deviation

> Say, "Now the truth has come from your Lord: let those who wish to believe in it do so, and let those who wish to reject it do so." We have prepared a Fire for the wrongdoers . . . (Q. 18:29)

While there is no doubt as to the rightfulness of Islam, nonetheless the Qur'an explicitly declares that anyone who chooses so may accept and believe, and anyone who chooses can decline to accept and be a non-believer. God has only provided a reminder of the punishment for non-belief in the other world. But should it be that someone is punished for their beliefs in this world? If this were the case, then saying that whoever wants to can believe or not would have no meaning. In this verse, God sets out the basis of the freedom of religion in this world and the punishment in the other world for the wrong choice. Believers have no right to turn away from the steadfastness of this Divine logic and turn to the logic of violence, force and threats in making others become religious.

> Say, "People, the Truth has come to you from your Lord. Whoever follows the right path follows it for his own good, and whoever strays does so to his own loss: I am not your guardian". (Q. 10:108)

There is no doubt that the Qur'an does not consider the right path and the wrong one, and Islam and non-belief, to be on the same level. That humans truly choose the right way is an art and deserving of reward, otherwise if in this world only one path was set before people – the right path – and if everyone was forced to take that path otherwise they will lose their life, then what need would there be for being tested in this world and for reward and punishment in the other world? The master principle of resurrection in the other world is possible only with the freedom of religion in this world.

> We have sent the Scripture down to you [Prophet] with the Truth for people. Whoever follows the guidance does so for his own benefit, whoever strays away from it does so at his own peril: you are not in charge of them. (Q. 39:41)

The Qur'an has represented the truth to the people, but people in this world are free to accept the truth or to ignore it and the Hereafter is the place of assessment and reward. We are not free to carry out what God did not permit his Prophet to do to people. God and his Prophet left people free in their acceptance of religion and, of course, have advised them about the truth. The Hereafter is the place of comfort and happiness for those who have accepted the truth freely and willfully.

> [Say Prophet], "What I am commanded to do is to serve the Sustainer of this town, which He has made inviolable. Everything belongs to Him; I am commanded to be one of those devoted to Him; I am commanded to recite the Qur'an." Whoever chooses to follow the right path does so for his own good. Say to whoever deviates from it, "I am only here to warn." Say, "Praise belongs to God: He will show you His signs so that you will recognise them." Your Lord is never unmindful of what you all do. (Q. 27:91–93)

The Prophet warns people of the consequences of false religions and beliefs. He recites the Qur'an for them and shows them the right faith and religion. Those who accept, then good for them, and those who do not accept have harmed themselves and will see the results of their unpleasant choice in the Hereafter. God is a clear-eyed observer and monitors all choices.

This category of verses – some of which have been discussed and which emphasise the freedom in this world to choose guidance or deviation – is among the foundations of freedom of belief and religion.

Third Category: The Duties of the Prophet, the Delivery of Truth not the Forcing of Truth

In the Qur'an, the lofty status and place of the Prophet Muhammad as he relates to people's religion has been determined with great care. The duties of the Prophet were to bring the message and to deliver guidance and edification. He does not have the right to pressure or coerce people into accepting the religion of truth.

> So [Prophet] warn them: your only task is to give warning, you are not there to control them. (Q. 88:21–22)

The duty of the Prophet is to deliver the message of religion, he warns the people of the truth. Whoever wants to, will accept and enjoy the tremendous benefits that come with it, and whoever does not wish to, does not accept and will, of course, suffer the tremendous detriments of going astray. The manifestation of truth and false phenomena will be fully shown in the Hereafter, the world is the place for being tested. The Prophet does not have the forceful control over people with which to make them have or keep their faith. If the Prophet has no such permission, can the Prophet's followers have the right to deny people the freedom of religion?

> We know best what the disbelievers say. You [Prophet] are not there to force them, so remind them, with this Qur'an, those who fear My warning. (Q. 50:45)
> We sent you only to give good news and warning. Say, "I am not asking for any reward for it, but anyone who wishes should take a path to his Lord." Put your trust in the Living [God] who never

dies, and celebrate His praise. He knows the sins of His servants well enough. (Q. 25:56–58)

Whether We let you [Prophet] see part of what We threaten them with, or cause you to die [before that], your duty is only to deliver the message: The Reckoning is Ours. (Q. 13:40)

The Messenger's duty is only to deliver the message: God knows what you reveal and what you conceal. (Q. 5:99)

If the Prophet, who is the first person in the world of Islam, has no other status other than to preach and encourage in relation to the religion of others, are others free to take on a role other than encouragement and preaching in relation to the religion of others and to deny people the freedom of religion and belief? If assessing the religion of humans is the work of God, and delivering the way is the work of the Prophet, then denying people the freedom of belief and religion and dragging the reward and punishment of the other world to the stage of this world is like playing God, something that God has not approved for humans and his Prophet has not done.

Fourth Category: Disapproval of Punishment for Change in Religion

The use of force for the purpose of making people religious and heavy punishments for apostasy have long been a subject of discussion. The Qur'an has laid out and disapproved of punishment in three scenarios regarding change in religion.

His people's arrogant leaders said, "Shu'ayb, we will expel you and your fellow believers from our town unless you return to our religion." He said, "What! Even if we detest it?" (Q. 7:88)

The arrogant aristocrats gave two choices to the Prophet Shu'ayb and the believers of his time: they must either accept exile or change their religion. They must become apostates and turn from faith to unbelief. The Prophet Shu'ayb responded: should we change our religion even if we are not willing? Is it possible to change religion and faith while unwilling and with coercion? We cannot leave our religion with force. Shu'ayb's logic is accepted by the Qur'an.

One cannot say that it is not mandatory to change the true religion to false, but changing the false religion to the truth may be mandatory, and in the analysis of the Qur'anic verse against coercion in religion (Q. 2:256), we found that the Qur'an has given the news of denying pressure and coercion in the absolute terms of belief and religion.

> They said, "We believe in the Lord of the Worlds, the Lord of Moses and Aaron!" but Pharaoh said, "How dare you believe in Him before I have given you permission? This is a plot you have hatched to drive the people out of this city! Soon you will see: I will cut off your alternate hands and feet and then crucify you all!" (Q. 7:121–124).

After seeing the miracle of Moses, the magicians came to have faith in God. They let go of unbelief and changed their religion. To put it another way, they became apostates. The Pharaoh became upset that they changed their religion without first gaining permission from him. He called the magicians' change of religion a conspiracy for leading the people astray and he immediately declared the punishment for the apostates to be hanging and the cutting off of their hands and feet. The punishment for apostasy and the changing of religion is death according to the religion of the Pharaoh: in the land of the Pharaoh, whoever changes his religion will be killed. The Qur'an does not accept this logic and disapproves of it. The logic of the Qur'an is to deny pressure and coercion in religion; in other words, its logic is that of freedom of belief and religion.

> . . . and Pharaoh said, "Leave me to kill Moses – let him call upon his Lord! – for I fear he may cause you to change your religion, or spread disorder in the land." (Q. 40:26)

In the Pharaoh's religion, people changing their religion (from unbelief to belief) carried the punishment of death. He threatened Moses with execution because Moses wanted to change the people's religion and, according to the Pharaoh, he wanted to create corruption on Earth. The Qur'an rejects the Pharaoh's logic. The people are free to change their religion. No one has the right to pressure or coerce them into accepting this or that religion. The path of guidance is clearly distinguishable from that of misguidance.

From these and similar verses we find that they reject the way of the arrogant and the Pharaohs in relation to the phenomena of apostasy and changing religion. At the same time, they consider the truth of faith in God, consider faith and unbelief in this world to be elementary and on a continuum, or in other words, consider the choice of religion and belief to be a free one.

Fifth Category: The Critique of how People of Different Religions Relate to One Another and the Will of God Concerning Differences in Human Beliefs

> If your Lord had pleased, He would have made all people a single community, but they continue to have their differences – except those on whom your Lord has mercy – for He created them to be this way, and the word of your Lord is final: "I shall definitely fill Hell with both jinn and men." (Q. 11:118–119)

It has not been Divine Will that everyone thinks the same. In other words, God has recognised that it is beneficial to have different beliefs and religions in this world and has promised that the misguided will suffer in hell. Forcing the beliefs and religions of the world to fit an official ideology is exactly the opposite of the Islamic and Qur'anic view.

> The Jews say, "The Christians have no ground whatsoever to stand on," and the Christians say, "The Jews have no ground whatsoever to stand on," though they both read the Scripture, and those who have no knowledge say the same; God will judge between them on the Day of Resurrection concerning their differences. (Q. 2: 113)

The Qur'an disapproves of every religion, considering all others to be worthless. The place of judgement is in the Hereafter and not in this world. In this world, people are free to choose whatever religion and belief they want. Of course, the Divine prophets will tell people of the true religions, but the choice is with the people themselves and the test is nothing other than this.

> Say [Prophet], "Disbelievers: I do not worship what you worship, you do not worship what I worship, I will never worship what you worship, you will never worship what I worship, you have your religion and I have mine." (Q. 109:1–6)

Sura 109 (*kafirun*: disbelievers) is one of the strongest pieces of evidence for the freedom of religion and belief in Islam. Can Muslims face other religions and beliefs in any other way than this?

Sixth Category: The Lack of Temporal Punishment for Apostasy

While the Qur'an disapproves of changing one's faith to unbelief, based on its own steadfast logic, it notifies one of the bad ending in the other world and does not call for any temporal punishments such as execution or life imprisonment. Here, I will consider two of the most important verses on the issue of apostasy.

> . . . If any of you revoke your faith and die as disbelievers, your deeds will come to nothing in this world and the Hereafter, and you will be inhabitants of the Fire, there to remain. (Q. 2:217)

The verse speaks of the death of the apostate and the word used for death (*fa-yamut*) means natural death rather than death by execution or murder. If it were the case that the apostate was killed (executed), He would have used this expression (*fa-yuqtal* or *fa-yuslab*): "If any of you revoke your faith and are slaughtered, or crucified." We learn from the expression "die as a disbeliever" (*fa-yamut wa huwa kafir*) that it is also possible to "die as a believer". This means that, first, after apostasy, it is necessary for the person to "live in unbelief" so that the punishments of the subsequent verse apply. Second, the repentance of an apostate is accepted in ordinary situations if he finds the opportunity to repent. The punishments predicted in the verse include the cancellation of the apostate's deeds (*habt*), meaning that his rewards will decay in this world and the Hereafter, and that he will be in perpetual hellish punishment. All of these pertain to the Hereafter and in no way is there a discussion of the temporal execution or imprisonment of the apostate.

> If anyone seeks a religion other than "Islam"[34] complete devotion to God, it will not be accepted from him: he will be one of the losers in

---

34 The other meaning of Islam is submission to God, the general meaning of Islam is the shared name of divine religion, such as Islam and Muslim in these verses: Q. 2:132, 133 and 136; 3:52, 64 and 67; 5:111; 6:163, 7:126, 10:72, 84 and 90; 12:101; 22:78; 27:31, 38 and 42.

the Hereafter. Why would God guide people who deny the truth, after they have believed and acknowledged that the Messenger is true, and after they have been shown clear proof? God does not guide evildoers: such people will be rewarded with rejection by God, by the angels, by all people, and so they will remain, with no relief or respite for their suffering. Not so those who afterwards repent and mend their ways – God is most forgiving and merciful – [although] the repentance of those who, having believed, then increase in their disbelief, will not be accepted. They are the ones who have gone [far] astray. (Q. 3:85–90)

While the Qur'an explicitly announces that after the mission of the final messenger of God (Prophet Muhammad), no religion other than Islam will be accepted from anyone, and that whoever has another religion will be among the losers, it does not determine any temporal punishment for followers of other religions. In addition, the punishments in the Hereafter that are predicted in the verse apply only to "those who know the Truth but put it underfoot because of obstinacy and malice", meaning those who are apostates in practice and politics instead of those who are apostates in theory and in philosophical terms; those who choose a false religion due to ignorance, will not even be punished in the Hereafter. The punishments in the Hereafter for the apostate in practice and politics are curses from God, the angels and the people, as well as eternal suffering and a lack of reprieve from that suffering. These punishments are carried out in case the apostate does not repent in practice. If he or she repents, God is forgiving and the probability of forgiveness is not impossible. Although the apostate who is excessive in their unbelief will not find the opportunity to repent. The lack of acceptance of repentance in the Hereafter is not a reason for the lack of temporal acceptance of his repentance.

Reflecting on all of the verses related to apostasy, a sample of which has been discussed above, leads to the following conclusions:

1. Changing from faith to unbelief is absolutely undesirable, rejected and disapproved of. The change from faith to unbelief can be of two kinds: first, it can come through theoretical and scientific discussions and research that in a mistaken way leads a person to deny God, the Hereafter and Islam, or to doubt the truthfulness of Islam (theoretical and scientific apostasy); or it can come about that a person knows the Truth but ignores it and changes religion because of lust, political deviation, or satanic insinuations and the

mundane, meaning the apostasy occurs for the person's material benefit and not due to theoretical suspicions (political and practical apostasy).

2. For theoretical and scientific apostasy, the Qur'an predicts no punishments, neither temporal nor in the Hereafter. It is clear that such a person would be existentially bereft of the blessings and benefits of not being connected to the Truth.

3. For practical and political apostasy (meaning apostasy after the truth has been clearly revealed to the person), the punishments in the Hereafter and perpetual suffering in hell have been predicted. Every time apostasy is discussed in the Qur'an, the meaning of apostasy has been as such.

4. The Qur'an sets absolutely no temporal punishments for the apostate such as execution or life imprisonment.

Seventh Category: Ways of Being Invited to Religion

[Prophet], call [people] to the way of your Lord with wisdom and good teaching. Argue with them in the most courteous way, for your Lord knows best who has strayed from His way and who is rightly guided. (Q. 16:125)

The logic of the Qur'an regarding the invitation of people to religion, calls for a peaceful and reasonable way, a way that uses people's rationality and mind, and reminds and advises them, and finally augments them in a good way. Fear, intimidation, coercion or murder have no place in this logic. Islam is the religion of mercy and being invited to it is also merciful.

Conclusion of the Qur'anic Arguments

In reflecting on the verses of the Qur'an on the issue of the freedom of belief and religion, the most important of which were considered in the seven categories above, the following conclusions can be reached:

First, Islam has introduced people to the true religion and correct beliefs with the clearest of criteria and has outlined the corruptions and harms of the inclination to falsehoods.

Second, Islam considers that the true happiness of humans is to belong to the religion of truth and correct beliefs and greatly disapproves of deviation from it.

Third, from the point of view of Islam, people are free to choose their religion and belief, and nobody can pressure or force another into accepting the religion of truth and correct beliefs.

Fourth, after the Divine invitation to the religion of truth, Islam recognises the plurality of religions and beliefs, meaning that some will follow the Divine invitation and others will remain in error. There are numerous categories and groups of those who remain astray.

Fifth, from the point of view of Islam, those who have not followed the Divine invitation and who have chosen false beliefs will be punished in the Hereafter.

Sixth, in Islam, no temporal punishments have been set for having a false religion or belief.

Seventh, the logic of Islam in inviting others to the religion of truth is reasonable, peaceful, merciful, and removed from violence and force.

Eighth, one cannot force another into changing his or her religion. Apostasy has no temporal punishment, but if it comes with odium (*jahd*) and obstinacy (*'inad*), then it will come with great suffering in the hereafter.

Given the above points, it becomes clear that freedom of belief and religion has been approved in Islam. But this conclusion is complete only when the arguments of those who deny the freedom of religion and belief have been critiqued in such a way that they cannot dispute the above reasons. This important step will be taken up in the second stage of this discussion.

Second Stage: Critique of the Evidence Used in the Traditional Reading

Detailed critique of the arguments of those who deny the freedom of religion and belief requires a widespread discussion that is beyond the scope of one chapter. However, in this case, I have chosen to discuss three known rulings from the numerous rulings related to the lack of the freedom of religion and belief mentioned earlier. I believe that these three are the most important rulings about the issue in the conventional and traditional reading of Islam. They include the ruling for execution of a male apostate and life imprisonment for a female apostate, the ruling of tax (*jizya*) for the People of *dhimma*, and the lack of the right to life for the non-*dhimma* non-believer. The most significant sources for these three important rulings were covered at the end of the first section of this chapter. Here, I will assess and critique

these sources against the backdrop of the previously discussed arguments for
the freedom of belief and religion.

First: The Ruling for the Temporal Punishment of the Muslim Apostate

The sources for rulings about the execution of the apostate are some of the
hadiths that have been attributed to the Prophet (in Sunni jurisprudence)
and some of the hadiths attributed to the Imams (in Shi'a jurisprudence).
According to conventional and traditional jurisprudence, some of these
hadiths are considered credible in their transmissions. If their indications
(contents) are also complete, then despite all of the absolute expressions and
generalities of the rational and Qur'anic arguments, we would have no choice
but to accept them. But in this regard a number of points should be noted:

First, the debate is not about carrying out the rulings pertaining to the
apostate, whatever they are, during the lifetime of, or by, the Prophet and the
Imams. Since they themselves were aware of all aspects of *shari'a* better than
anyone else, as well as all the benefits and deficiencies of the Divine rulings,
there is absolutely no doubt about what they carry out as a ruling of *shari'a*.
What is under discussion is the rulings pertaining to the apostate at the time
when the Prophet and the Imams are not present. Assuming the correctness
of all aspects of these arguments, does carrying out the *shari'a* punishments
(*hudud*) as they were during their time apply to all periods regardless of their
presence, therefore counting among the timeless religious rulings? In this
regard, there are two different approaches between the Shi'a jurists. The most
famous approach[35] is the impermissibility of the implementation of *hudud*
when the Prophet and Imams are not present;[36] some have even claimed consensus on this issue.[37] Given that the punishments for apostasy are from the
conventional point of view among the type of *hudud* from the *shari'a*,[38] this

35 Khwansari, *Jami'al-Madarik fi Sharh-i al-Mukhtasar al-Nafi'*, 5:411.
36 Al-Muhaqiq al-Hilli, *Sharayi'al-Islam fi Masa'il Al-Halal wa Al-Haram* (*Paths of Islam on the Issues of Permitted and Forbidden*), ed. 'Abdul-Hussain Muhammad Ali (Najaf: al-Adab, 1969), 1:344, see al-Najafi, *Jawahir al-Kalam*, 21:386, for interpretation of al-Hilli's approach.
37 Ibn Idris al-Hilli, *al-Sara'ir al-Hawi li Tahrir al-Fatawi* (*The Mind, Container for Editing of the Rulings*) (Qom: Islamic Publication Institute, 1989), 2:25.
38 The other approach considers apostasy to be subject to *ta'zir* and not *hudud*, see al-Hilli, *Sharayi'al-Islam*, 4:147.

hadd (singular of *hudud*), like the other *hudud* of the *shari'a*, is not carried out when the Prophet and Imams are not present. The importance of this approach becomes clearer in the light of the many problems that apply to this ruling in our time, especially given that in the conventional view initiating (*ibtida'i*) *jihad* is among the special rulings of the time of the Prophet. These two subjects have a shared axis which is Islam: one is entry into Islam (initiating *jihad*), and the other is remaining in Islam (the punishments for apostasy).

Second, the sources for the above-noted rulings on the punishment for the execution of the apostate are *khabar wahid*.[39] The reason for its credibility and validity as a trustworthy hadith is the conventions of reasonability.[40]

In contrast to other issues, reasonable people do not confine themselves to *khabar wahid* in relation to serious and very important affairs. Protecting the lives of people is among the most important and momentous affairs (the right to life). One can only deny the right to life when having definitive (*qat'i*) evidence in hand, meaning the univocal clear text (*nass*) of a verse or a *khabar mutawatir*.[41] One cannot issue the ruling of execution based on *khabar wahid*, that is, carrying out a ruling of execution requires a definitive credible reason. Caution in blood (due to the extreme importance of life and the serious concern of the Lawgiver about this) requires that a ruling of execution should not be applied to anyone without definitive proof (not even credible speculative proof). As the distinguished *faqih* al-Ardabili (1500–1585) has said: "Murder is an immense issue because the Legislator

---

39 *Al-khabar al-wahid* does *not* mean a hadith that was narrated by a single person, as the phrase may imply, or a hadith of which the number of transmitters in each generation is singular. Its meaning is a narration of a hadith that is not regarded as *mutawatir*. In *mutawatir* the number of narrators in all generations of transmitters is enough to accept the authenticity of the hadith with certainty, which means that a common and intentional agreement to lie is absolutely impossible. The number of narrators in all generations of transmitters, or at least one generation, is not enough to accept the authenticity of a hadith with certainty. When all narrators of a non-*mutawatir* hadith in all generations are trusted individuals (*al-thiqahat*), it is an *al-khabar al-wahid al-thiqah* or *al-hadith al-sahih*. This type of hadith is counted as valid (*al-hujjah*) in *usul al-fiqh*. I am discussing the domain of this validity: is it absolute or does it include only matters of non-critical importance? According to the latter *al-khabar al-wahid al-thiqah* or *al-hadith al-sahih* are invalid in matters of critical importance.

40 Sayyid Abu al-Qasim al-Musawi al-Khu'i, *Misbah al-Usul* (*The Light of the Principles [of Fiqh]*) (Qom: al-Khu'i Islamic Institute, 2009), 2:196: "The main reason for credibility of the *hadith* is the convention of reasonability (*sira al-'uqala*) that is confirmed by the Lawmaker."

41 See fn. 43 for more explanation.

is greatly concerned with the preservation of life. This is because life is the centre of duties and happiness and that is why He made its preservation a duty. It is not even allowed to stop the preservation of life, for example, to get another killed to preserve one's own life. Reason also aids in this regard, as it merits that concerning this all precautions be taken."[42]

The great contemporary *faqih* Ahmad Khansari (1887–1985) has clarified as follows:

> the credibility of trustworthy or just hadith,[43] based on authorisa- tion or qualification by some of the scholars of *rijal*[44] according to the conventions of reasonability in dealing with some *khabar* [*wahid*] relating to matters of blood is not free of problems, especially given the great emphasis on blood, are you not aware that it does not suffice for reasonable people to rely only on trustworthy *khabar* in significant affairs, even though in other instances it is sufficient for them to rely on trustworthy *khabar*?[45]

Based on this caution about blood, al-Fadil al-Hindi (1651–1725) also believes that carrying out the *hudud* of shari'a, such as execution, is only limited to the Prophet and Imams.[46] Given that the evidence for the execu- tion of the apostate is made up of several *khabar wahid*, and that *khabar wahid* is lacking in credibility for proving the ruling of execution, the prin- ciple of caution in blood requires that the ruling of execution is not proven and is invalid.

Third, if someone is threatened with "if you do not become Muslim we will kill you", then there is not doubt that it constitutes coercion in religion. Hence, if someone is threatened with "if you leave Islam and become an

---

42 Ahmad b. Muhammad al-Ardabili, *Majma' al-Fayida wa al-Burhan fi Sharh-i Irshad al-Adhhan* (*The Complex of Interests and Proofs in the Commentary of Irshad al-Adhhan*), eds Mujtaba al- 'Iraqi, 'Ali Panah al-Ishtihardi and Husayn al-Yazdi (Qom: Islamic Publication Institute, 1983), chapter on punishments (*hudud*), 13:90.

43 A non-*mutawatir* hadith where all its transmitters in all generations are qualified.

44 Science of qualification of the transmitters of the hadiths.

45 Khwansari, *Jami'al-Madarik fi Sharh-i al-Mukhtasar al-Nafi'*, chapter on punishments (*hudud*), 7:35.

46 Muhammad b. Hasan al-Isfahani, known as al-Fadil al-Hindi, *Kashf al-Litham 'an Qawa'id al- Ahkam* (*Revealing the Veil of Qawa'id al-Ahkam*) (Qom: Islamic Publication Institute, 1995), 10:477.

apostate, we will kill you", then in the same way there has been coercion in religion. According to the univocal and clear text (*nass*) of the Qur'an, coercion in religion is negated and rejected. Thus, the ruling of execution for the apostate contradicts the verse in the Qur'an that states "there is no compulsion in religion" (Q. 2:256), in addition to numerous other verses that were mentioned at the beginning of this discussion. The narratives noted in relation to this ruling are against the Qur'anic provisions cited earlier. It is impossible to specify (*takhsis*) or limit (*taqyid*) these verses because they point to a rational ruling (as was covered in the section on the rational desirability and the goodness of the freedom of belief and religion). Thus, the credibility of such hadiths becomes void and we will leave their understanding to those who merit them. That is to say, the exact meaning of these provisions are not clear to us and we must turn to the Prophet and the Imams to remove doubt. Until that time, we cannot implement anything in accordance to the provisions of these hadiths.

Second: Rulings of *Dhimmi*s

The issue of *jizya* (protection tax) is the most important of the rulings pertaining to the People of *dhimma*. It is among the Qur'anic rulings which were absolutely carried out at the time of the Prophet and thereafter. The discussion is whether that ruling pertaining to the People of *dhimma* is among the stable, permanent and timeless rulings or whether it is among the special rulings of early Islam, and is considered among those changing and time-bound rulings of religion that are cancelled with the changing conditions of time and place. In its time, this ruling was of perfect interest, otherwise it would not have been legislated by God. In addition, this ruling does not count among the devotional (*ta'abbudi*) and beyond rational (*tawqifi*) rulings, and today, at least in relation to the seven axes discussed earlier, this order is not of benefit. The ruling of a *jizya*, like the rulings pertaining to slaves, was the provision of a specific time. The Qur'an, in addition to the timeless rulings, had no choice but to point to some rulings that were necessary during the early years of Islam. The ruling pertaining to the People of *dhimma* is among these.

It is interesting that in the topical laws of the Islamic Republic of Iran, which claims to be in accordance with the *shari'a*, there is neither mention of rulings pertaining to apostasy nor of rulings pertaining to the People of *dhimma*.

Third: The Absence of the Right to Life for the Non-*dhimma* Unbeliever

Jihad is one of the incontrovertible rulings of Islam. But contrary to the conventional understanding, it does not mean gathering armies to convert unbelievers to Islam or to make non-Muslims choose between becoming Muslim or dying. Rather, the meaning of *jihad* is that if lands under the rule of non-believers are such that people are denied the freedom of religion and that they are not free to turn as they like to *hanif* (pure faith) religion, and adequate religious information is not provided to the people, while at the same time Muslims have the opportunity to eliminate these problems from that oppressed and closed society, then they are obligated to remove the "burdens, and the iron collars"[47] from the feet of the people by fighting with the unbelievers and the idolaters, so that the people may freely choose their religion. Naturally, in free conditions, many people will choose the religion of truth. Thus, initiating *jihad* is in fact a kind of defensive *jihad*: defending the freedom of people in religion rather than forcing people towards any particular religion, even the religion of truth.

If a non-Muslim lives within or outside an Islamic society and does not enter into a war against Muslims, he or she will never be forced to choose between Islam and execution just because he or she believes in a religion or a belief other than Islam. Rather, if he or she wishes to keep his or her religion and belief – whatever it might be – then no Muslim has the right to attack them using the excuse of difference in religion or belief.

It seems that the timeless verses of the Qur'an express the above reading and not the conventional one.

Conclusion

Although the conventional reading of Islam does not tolerate the freedom of religion and belief in many instances, another reading of Islam that is based on the authentic criteria of the Qur'an and the Traditions, shows that freedom of belief and religion are compatible with the standards of human rights.

---

47 *Isr wa aghlal* (7:157)

Epilogue

One of the major points regarding freedom of religion and belief is the choice of non-Muslims between acceptance of Islam or execution (or enslavement). This choice is in deep conflict with the explicit verses of the Qur'an and the authentic Tradition of the Prophet Muhammad, which state that God does not allow this, and that the messenger of God never, ever did this. In addition to what I explain in this chapter, I will try to provide a brief but clear classification of non-Muslims and refer to the rulings that pertain to them in the Qur'an in the framework of traditional *fiqh* and *ijtihad*.

There are three types of non-Muslims. Type one is those non-Muslims who sign a treaty with Muslim authorities. They are known as *dhimmi*s and *mu'ahad*. The former include People of the Book (i.e., Jews, Christians and Zoroastrians) who sign a protection contract with Muslim authorities. The latter includes other non-Muslims (such as believers of non-Abrahamic religions, agnostics, deists, atheists, polytheists, idolaters, pagans, unbelievers and infidels) who sign a protection treaty with Muslim authorities. Both *dhimmi*s and *mu'ahad* (People of Treaty) are under the protection of Islam, the Qur'an and the Tradition of the Messenger of God.

The Qur'an obligates the fulfilment of contracts, treaties, pledges, bonds, covenants and agreements as a required duty of Muslims, regardless of whether the other party is Muslim or non-Muslim. Two examples: "You who believe, fulfil your bonds" (Q. 5:1) and "Honour your pledges: you will be questioned about your pledges" (Q. 17:36). The Prophet Muhammad made several treaties with various Jewish tribes and pagans in Medina, and honoured his treaties as long as they were not violated by the other party.

The second type is non-Muslims who do not sign a contract or treaty with Muslim authorities (non-*dhimmi* and non-*mu'ahad*), but who do not participate in any wars against Muslims, try to exclude them from their homes, or act with hostility against Muslims in their religious affairs. This type is potentially a very large portion of the world's population. Muslims are not only not allowed to attack them and start a war against them or pressure them into conversion to Islam or to sign a treaty with Muslims, but Muslims should also have peaceful, kind and just relationships with them.

The Qur'an is very explicit regarding this second type: "and He does not forbid you to deal kindly and justly with anyone who has not fought you for your faith or driven you out of your homes: God loves the just. But God forbids you to take as allies those who have fought against you for your faith, driven you out of your homes, and helped others to drive you out: any of you who take them as allies will truly be wrongdoers" (Q. 60:8–9). These two verses are the foundation of the timeless Islamic principle of peaceful coexistence and a mutual respectful relationship with non-Muslims.

The third type is those non-Muslims who not only do not sign a treaty with Muslim authorities, but who also declare war against Muslims, instigate hostilities towards them, drive them from their homes, or help others to drive them out. They are called non-believers at war with Muslims (*kafir harbi*) and Muslims are allowed to defends themselves against them. For example:

> Those who have been attacked are permitted to take up arms because they have been wronged – God has the power to help them – those who have been driven unjustly from their homes only for saying, "Our Lord is God". If God did not repel some people by means of others, many monasteries, churches, synagogues, and mosques, where God's name is much invoked, would have been destroyed. God is sure to help those who help His cause – God is strong and mighty. (Q. 22:39–40)

Sura 9 (repentance) of the Qur'an entirely concerns this third type of non-Muslims. Generalising this so that it applies to all non-Muslims and ignoring the first two types of non-Muslims is the major mistake made by certain ignorant Muslim fundamentalists, as well as by particular orientalists and political players in the contemporary Islamophobic scene.

9

The Rights of the Political Opposition in an Islamic Society[1]

Husain b. Ali as the Political Opponent of the Umayyads

What I have chosen for tonight's fine gathering is one of the aspects of Husain's movement that is not spoken of as much: the legal dimension of the Karbala movement. The question is: what had Husain done to cause the Umayyad rulers to dispense such a harsh punishment? Let us suppose that Husain did not have the character that we rightly attribute to him. That is to say, suppose he was not the son of Fatima, nor the grandson of the Prophet, nor one of the Imams, nor one of the companions. In that case, would it have been permissible to deal with him as such? Or not? Put in simpler language, the answer to this question is an "investigation of the legal dimension of the Karbala movement". Husain's actions at that time represented a form of opposition to the political regime of that era.

Husain b. Ali was the political opposition in the year 681 AD and the Umayyad caliph and his men did what they did to him. Certainly, according to the Shi'ite perspective, which considers Husain to be the rightly-designated Imam, the Umayyad caliph and his men undertook a very ugly act. The ugliest act possible. But let us suppose that someone does not consider Husain to be

---

1 Mohsen Kadivar, *Hoquq-e Mokhalef-e Siyasi dar Jame'e-ye Dini* (*The Rights of the Political Opposition in an Islamic Society*), presentation on the night of 'Ashura (4 April 2001) at the Office of the Islamic Association of Students of Iranian Universities (*Daftar-i Tahkim-i Wahdat*), Tehran, *Aftab* bimonthly, Tehran, 4 (April/May 2001): 4–13. The preface and a few paragraphs of the first section which did not focus on the topic of human rights have been omitted from the English translation.

the infallible Imam, they merely consider him to be someone who objected against the ruler of the time, what should be done with him? Does the political opponent in general have rights, whether he is Husain b. Ali or someone else? What are these minimum rights? No sanctities were respected with Husain. They killed him in the most cowardly and heinous way possible. They took his wife and children as prisoners, they stole his belongings. They rode their horses over the corpses. History knows of no other instance when people with this much dignity were treated in such a bold and vicious manner. What had Husain done? Do Islamic teachings in any *madhab* tolerate such things or not? Whether based in Shi'a or Sunni texts, or from an Islamic perspective in general, is it permissible to deal with someone in this manner, Husain or no Husain?

Husain was someone who was in political opposition. We will now examine Husain's actions in more detail to determine if they constitute a crime from a legal or *fiqh* perspective. If according to certain readings or *madhab*s what he did was a crime, what would the punishment be? And if someone who is not Husain carried out the same action, what would lie in store for them from a legal, *fiqh*, Qur'anic, hadith or religious perspective? What would he or she be called? That is to say, what would they call someone who had carried out what Husain did following the same methodology?

There is no doubt that the regime that confronted Husain was completely illegitimate. In any regime that considers itself to be religious and just, whether or not we would consider them religious or just, what is the administration for dealing with and confronting political opponents? If we merely say that the regime and system against which Husain fought was unjust, we have spoken correctly, but we will ask, do you know of any system throughout history that has pronounced itself to be unjust? Have a look, explore all of history pre-Islam or post-Islam, in this or any other country, in a religious or non-religious society, I do not recall any government that has declared itself to be illegitimate or considered itself to be unjust or oppressive. Throughout history, governments have considered themselves to be just, and no government has accepted that it is oppressive or illegitimate, neither the government of Mu'awiyah, Yazid and the Umayyads, nor the Abbasids, the Ottomans and others. There have been very few governments that were truly religious, just and based on the right like that of Imam Ali's rule. Thus, the claims of governments that they are based on rightfulness does not suffice, we need criteria to determine if they are legitimate or illegitimate.

It is also not the case that a state will always be 100 per cent right, like the rule of Imam Ali, or that it will be 100 per cent illegitimate like that of Yazid bin Mu'awiyah. Throughout history, governments have generally been a mix of right and wrong. A prevalent mistake is to over-simplify. We either see ourselves in the absolute right, and consider our opponent to be in the complete wrong. In the same way that I consider myself to be a devotee of Husain, someone who thinks differently to me may also consider him- or herself the same and call those standing in opposition to be a devotee of Yazid. This correspondence between interpretations and congruence between readings is a double-edged sword. Typically, other than the early years of Islam, notions of right and wrong have been mixed, as noted in *Nahj al-Balagha*,[2] and therein lies the difficulty in recognising the difference between what is right and what is illegitimate. They are never at issue in pure or absolute forms. Right and wrong are intermixed.

Have religion and ethics set minimum rights for the political opponent so that each state – whether legitimate or not – is bound to observing those minimums? What are the minimum rights of a political opponent in an Islamic society? This question has great importance. Because despite the fact that we always claim to be legitimate, unfortunately, states throughout history have been illegitimate.

Given that in the overwhelming majority of years after 'Ashura, illegitimate and oppressive governments have been in power, the issue of the minimum rights of the political opponent has been a question for everyday and not just a question for a particular day, place or time. One of the questions that is still current regarding 'Ashura and Karbala is therefore the question of the minimum rights of a political opponent. If this minimum is determined, then we can say why these rights were not observed in the case of Imam Husain, whether in other times they were observed or not, and whether on the mere fact of states considering themselves legitimate, any opposition to them is completely illegitimate.

In accordance with *fiqh*, the Qur'an, or the law, exactly what label can be accorded to what Imam Husain did? And as a result, what pretexts did the state of the time use to carry out these crimes? We want to compare the two approaches side by side. The two approaches consist of the Umayyad approach to dealing with a political opponent and the way of Ali, Husain

2 Sermon 50, 88.

and the household of the Prophet. How did Imam Ali deal with those who were active in his time in the role of overthrower. In the time of the Umayyads, Imam Husain would be considered by the conventional political discourse to be an influential dissident, a political opponent and someone who did not pledge allegiance to the caliph of the time. How did the Umayyads deal with this political opponent? That is when we will be able to judge – when we compare the logic of each against the other and see what the Qur'an has said in this regard.

The first response that comes to mind is to say that Imam Husain was carrying out *nahy 'an al-munkar* (forbidding what is wrong). Imam Husain was the agent of enjoining the good and forbidding what is wrong and wanted to reform the deviances of the corrupt society of the time. This is the response of the devotees of Husain. But the rulers at that time who carried out those heinous activities neither considered him to be a reformer nor someone who was enjoining the good and forbidding the wrong. In addition, if the action of a person is considered by one group to be reform and by another as misguidance and corruption, what should be done? What solution has religion provided?

The second answer to the question of the legal dimensions of Husain's action is the institution of *muharaba*. The literal meaning of the word *muharib* is someone who has risen up in war. Did the Umayyad state consider Husain a *muharib*, and, if they did, what could they do about him? The third answer to the afore-mentioned question is in the institution of *baghi*. Did the Umayyad government consider Husain to be *baghi*? *Baghi* means a rebel. It is a religious term that is used in the Qur'an as well. If he was designated as a *baghi*, what punishment did *shari'a* set for him?

So at minimum, we will examine three concepts together. *Muharib, baghi* and *nahy 'an al-munkar*, and what the differences are among these three.

The Right to Not Have Allegiance to a State

More than anyone, Imam Husain introduced his movement in the most fervent way possible. He explained and advertised what he said and what he wanted. The most beautiful way that Husain introduced himself came when the preliminaries of shaping a movement were taking place. It was during the year 680 (Rajab 60 AH) when Mu'awiyah died and Yazid came to power. In the peace treaty that had been signed between Imam Hassan b. 'Ali and

Mu'awiyah b. Abi Sufyan, there was a condition that Mu'awiyah had no right to designate his successor but that the people would determine who that would be.[3] Mu'awiyah violated this condition. For the first time in the history of Islam, a caliph had designated his son as the subsequent caliph in the way of a hereditory monarchy. First, according to the convention of the time, in cases where a designation (*nass*) had not come from God and the Prophet, caliphates would turn to the vote of the people or at least to the vote of the *Muhajirun* (the first Muslims in Mecca who emigrated to Medina with the Prophet), the *Ansar* (the early Muslims from Medina who supported the Prophet), and the vote of the *Ahl al-Hall wa al-'Aqd* (the people who are authorised to loosen and bind). Mu'awiyah ignored this notion. Second, he did not choose someone who was qualified in piety, Islamic knowledge or administration, or indeed any type of qualification. Instead, he imposed his unqualified son on society and tried to obtain allegiance for him. He sent a message to all that Yazid was not in power and that everyone must pledge allegiance to his son. This was when Imam Husain was in Medina.

This is the first question: in an Islamic state, is it mandatory to pledge allegiance to the caliph or the ruler? If someone refuses allegiance, what should be done with him or her? Is refusing allegiance a sin? Is refusing allegiance a crime? There is a difference between a sin and a crime, the two are not the same. Something may be a sin, but not a crime. A sin is something that has consequences in the Hereafter. A crime is something that may be punished in this world. If the ruler is legitimate, then the person who has not pleaded allegiance has certainly sinned. He or she will meet the consequences of that in the Hereafter. But what we seek to answer is whether not pledging allegiance to the ruler or the caliph is a crime or not? It is clear that not every sin is a crime, thus the *shari'a* punishments (*hadd* and *ta'zir*) cover some sins but not all of them. The first step that Husain took was not to pledge allegiance to Yazid. This is during the ten years that he lived at the time of Mu'awiyah. Imam Husain observed the treaty that his brother Imam Hassan had made with Mu'awiyah. But he had made no treaty with Yazid and had pledged no allegiance to follow him.

---

3 For details of the event, see Abu Ja'far Muhammad ibn Jarir al-Tabari (224–310 AH; 839–923 AD), *History of the Prophets and Kings* (*Tarikh al-Rusul wa al-Muluk, Tarikh al-Tabari*), vol. 18: *Between Civil Wars, the Caliphate of Mu'awiyah*, trans. Michael G. Morony (Albany, NY: SUNY Press, 1987); *vol. 19: The Caliphate of Yazid b. Mu'awiyah*, trans. and annotated I. K. A. Howard (Albany, NY: SUNY Press, 1990).

If a ruler is legitimate and qualified, like Imam Ali, then it is a sin not to pledge allegiance to him. But we have to assess whether Imam Ali would have considered this to be a crime and whether he would have punished the person? During the time of Mu'awiyah, was it a crime not to pledge allegiance to the Umayyad ruler or not? Two sets of logic confront one another. The Alawi logic says that people are free to pledge allegiance or not. If they pledge allegiance, they will be linked to the virtues of that government and the consequences of its blessings, and in the Hereafter they will receive the rewards. If they do not pledge allegiance, then they will be denied these virtues. But history has shown that there is not a single instance where Ali and his children forced a person to pledge allegiance. History has shown that there is not a single instance where those who did not pledge allegiance to Ali had one cent (*dirham*) deducted from what was due to them from public funds. Do you know of a case where someone who did not pledge allegiance to Imam Ali was imprisoned? Name a name. In their detailed histories, our senior historians have recorded the realities of that era.

The most prominent Shi'ite historian and jurist, Ibn al-Mu'allim, al-Sheikh al-Mufid (d. 1022), wrote several books about Imam Ali. One is the book *al-Jamal* (*Camel*), which was about the first civil war in his time, and the other is *al-Nusrat li-Sayyid al-'Itara fi Harb al-Basra* (*In Support of the Senior of the Household in the Basra War*). The senior of the household of the Prophet is 'Ali b. abi-Talib. He cites the names of those who pledged allegiance, which are many, and include all of the *Muhajirun* and the *Ansar*, led by Talha and Zubair and others.[4] He also cited those who did not pledge allegiance: Abdullah b. 'Umar, Usama b. Zaid, Hassan b. Thabit, Sa'd b. abi-Waqqas, Zaid b. Thabit, Mughayra b. Shu'ba Muhammad b. Maslamah – all of whom died of natural causes.[5] None of those who did not pledge allegiance to Ali faced any sort of difficulty during the time of Imam Ali. Their salaries from the public funds were not cut, exactly like everyone else. This is Alawi logic. On the other hand, what did Mu'awiyah do to Hujr b. 'Adi al-Kindi and 'Amr b. Hamiq al-Khiza'i? He hung them both.[6]

---

4 Muhammad b. Muhammad b. Nu'man al-Mufid, *al-Nusra li Sayyid al-'Itra fi Harb al al-Basra, Mawsou'a al-Sheikh al-Mufid* (*Complete Works of al-Mufid*) (Qom: Dar al-Mufid, 2010), 1:101–110.

5 Ibid., 1:94–100.

6 Al-Tabari, *History of the Prophets and Kings*, 18:137 and 144–152.

During the time of Yazid b. Mu'awiyah, Husain b. 'Ali was forced towards allegiance. Why did he flee Medina? Because he saw that if he stayed in Medina they would force him to pledge allegiance. Umayyad logic does not tolerate dissent in allegiance. From the Umayyad point of view, whoever lives in society is forced to obey the government. This means that the Umayyad did not tolerate political opponents and forced people to choose between servitude and rebellion, between abjection and insurrection. This is while Alawi logic explicitly states: you may live in my society without even accepting me. This is why we can take pride in Ali's leadership and believe that the political freedom that existed in Alawi society was unprecedented and rare. Imam Ali recognised the right of the political opponent at a time when this level of munificence could not be seen anywhere else.

When Marwan b. Hakam told Walid b. Utbah to cut the throats of those who did not pledge allegiance, Imam Husain says "We are of God and to Him we shall return, and Islam will be lost, if the community will be ruled by a ruler such as Yazid."[7] Speaking of "returning" (*inna lillah wa inna ilayhi raji'un* (Q. 2:156)) is for a time when a tremendous disaster has occurred. A ruler like Yazid is a great disaster for Islam. One must recite the *al-Fatihah* for Islam,[8] since the community has been transferred to a shepherd and ruler such as Yazid b. Mu'awiyah. He explicitly states: "I will not pledge allegiance. I am not willing to shake hands with a ruling system such as Yazid's." Mohammad b. Hanafiyya[9] is one of Husain's brothers. He was an honest and true-hearted man. He advised Husain that this path does not have a happy ending and asked him to stay. The Imam makes a point that has the greatest significance for our discussion. He says: "Oh brother, I swear by God that even if I find in this world no refuge or shelter, I will not pledge allegiance to Yazid."[10] This means that it is clear from the outset that whether he is in Medina or not, or wherever he may be, the Imam has reached his conclusion. He has to show that the real Islam cannot tolerate this way.

After emigrating from Medina to Mecca, Imam Husain wrote a will to Mohammad b. Hanafiyya whose text reflects Husain's goals. The text of the

---

7 Abu Muhammad Ahmad Ibn A'tham al-Kufi (d. 926), *Kitab al-Futuh* (*Book of Conquest*), ed. Ali Shiri (Beirut: Dar al-Adwa', 1991), 5:17.

8 To read the *al-Fatihah* in this context means to declare the death of Islam.

9 Muhammad b. Ali b. Abi Talib (633–700).

10 Ibn A'tham al-Kufi, *Kitab al-Futuh*, 5:21.

will reads as follows: "I have not risen up in revolt out of evil intent or greed, neither to perpetuate corruption nor wrongdoing."[11] I did not leave to selfishly have a good time. The issue is not a personal one. I do not have personal animosity towards Yazid. I have not left due to corruption or oppression either. "Rather I did so in quest of reform (*islah*) of the community of my grandfather. I want to reform the *ummah* in service of the Prophet." Husain was a reformer, even though the methods of reform we employ today are in opposition to his revolutionary and violent way. That is to say, reform here is in the commonly understood sense of taking up peaceful and legal means of ridding society of despotism and autocracy as opposed to violent means of forcing reform in the way that Imam Husain notes. I feel that Islamic society has become deviant, that society has become corrupted. Society has gone astray from the path that the Prophet determined, I have come to put society back in its place – in this sense, all prophets have been reformers.

"I want to enjoin the good and forbid the wrong." What is the wrong that happened? Oppression, transgression against the rights of the people, religious rulers engaging in debauchery and immoral lewdness, drinking wine, engaging in libidinous pleasures and foolish acts, but above all, Yazid does not observe the rights of the people. He transgresses against the life, property, dignity and reputation of the people. Thus, I want to eliminate this great wrong from society, "and [I want to] follow the example of my grandfather and my father Ali b. Abi Talib". I want to enjoin the good and forbid the wrong and in this way, take the path of my grandfather and my father Ali. That is to say, during these fifty years these ways have been cancelled, they have effectively become void; the way of Ali is no longer followed, the way of the Prophet has been forgotten and I want to re-establish those ways.

But gradually the Caliphate of the Prophet turned into the monarchy of the Umayyads. Someone like Husain needed to rise up to announce that this caliphate was not the simple and honest Caliphate of the Prophet. When the Prophet was sitting among a group and someone who did not know him entered, that person would ask, "Which one of you is Muhammad b. 'Abdullah?" It was not the case that the Prophet had a specific or differing face from others. Now the caliph sits in a castle. He has an officer at the gate. Bodyguards

---

11 Ibid.; Muhammad b. Ali Ibn Shahr Ashub, *Manaqib Al-i Abi-Talib* (*The Virtues of the Family of Abi-Talib*), ed. S. H. al-Rasouli al-Mahallati (Qom: 'Alammi, n.d.), 4:89.

surround him. How different is this from the ways of the Prophet? Husain has come to rid society of this way. In a letter to the people of Basra, Imam Husain wrote: "I summon you to the Book of God, the Sunna of His Prophet. Indeed, the Sunna has been killed while innovation (*bid'ah*) has been given life."[12] This means that in the society in which Husain lived, he was being enjoined to do wrong and forbidden from doing right. Enacting innovation, killing the Tradition and the style of the Prophet, the Prophet's administration had died and one must recite the *al-Fatiha* for it.[13] In place of it, innovations and the ways that are opposed to the Tradition of the Prophet have been vitalised. Thus, the first issue was that Husain did not pledge allegiance. In the Umayyad approach, not pledging allegiance was a crime. Outside the question of it being a sin, he does not care about the Hereafter. He does not even believe in the Hereafter. Husain has not pledged allegiance and he must be dealt with.

Accepting the Invitation of the Dissidents to Change the Oppressive Ruler

But why did Imam Husain leave Mecca? This is a secondary issue. Here, the people of Kufah wrote Husain b. Ali a letter. The number of letters is great, and they invite Husain to their city. They write that they too do not accept the caliphate of Yazid. They say they want a leader, be our leader. We will fight under your banner with Yazid. Abdullah b. Abbas warns the Imam that these people betrayed his father and brother, and they will not be loyal to him either. Thus, Imam Husain sends Muslim b. 'Aqil to Kufah to test whether the contents of these letters are true or not. In the first stage, Muslim finds the opportunity to write to Imam Husain and says, yes, I am here and those standing behind me in prayer number in the several thousands.[14] From here on, the Imam acts in the place of someone who has been invited to take on a leadership role to replace the caliphate. In fact, letters reached him that count as an invitation to rebel and overthrow the state in the political conventions of the time. Thus, in the first phase, the issue was not pledging allegiance. However, in the second phase, it is in fact about changing the caliph of the time and replacing a corrupt person with a righteous one.

---

12 Al-Tabari, *History of the Prophets and Kings*, 19:32.
13 Muslims recite the first sura of the Qur'an (*al-Fatiha*) when someone passes away.
14 Al-Tabari, *History of the Prophets and Kings*, 19:16–20.

Governments do not tolerate their own overthrow and act against those who reject their rule, but how do they act? If they do not tolerate it and consider it a crime, how do they address it? Thus, in the second phase, what Imam Husain was doing is exactly a rebellion. It was an uprising. It was an uprising against the government of the time. In the second phase, in addition to Husain not pledging allegiance to the corrupt ruler, there were those who pledged allegiance to him (Husain) so that he would be the ruler of the world of Islam. Yet Yazid is there sitting in his place. At the time these letters reached Husain, Yazid had spies, and he found out that these messages were coming and going and that some of the people who had written these letters to Husain had also written similar letters to Yazid. That is to say, two-faced people from Kufah also wrote some of these letters. They had signed both the letter to Husain and to Yazid. That way, if Husain was victorious, they would be with him, and if Yazid was victorious, then they would also gain something. But in response to the people of Kufah, when he sent his cousin Muslim b. Aqil to introduce his movement, Husain, in another sentence that is relevant to our discussion, also stated: "What is the imam except one who acts according to the Book, one who upholds justice, one who professes the truth, and one who dedicates himself to the essence of God?"[15] He introduced the Islamic ruler as one who must have these qualities: he must act in accordance to the Book of God, he must act in accordance to the Qur'an; second, he must act among the people in a measured way and with justice, he must make sure that the rights of every person are maintained, and that no one is transgressed against; third, he must maintain what is right and true in his piety and actions; and, fourth, he must be pure and refined, his breath is for the sake of the way of God. Having piety means putting on the brakes and avoiding sin. Someone who has piety and faces sin puts on the brakes and does not sin. He or she does not associate with sin. That is the answer he gives to those people.

Thus, in the second phase Imam Husain was a rebel. The question is: if someone rises up against the government of the time in the way that Husain did, considering that he had not yet taken up arms, although the people had invited him to do so, and he has accepted their invitation, what should

---

15 Ibid., 19:25–26.

be done with him or her? What does the Qur'an say? What does *fiqh* say? Does it count as a crime if someone has been invited and they accept the invitation, and no anxiety has been caused in society, no security has been undermined and no one has been killed? Until the time that Imam Husain was in Mecca and began to head towards Iraq, he had not undertaken any military actions.

We could say that he was armed, yes, but everyone in those days was armed. Being armed at that time was something ordinary. What is important is whether he used those arms or not. Until he reached Iraq, Husain had never taken up arms. If we examine this with Alawi logic, does this action constitute a crime or not? Let us return to the time of Imam Ali to see what the Qur'anic standards called those who acted against Imam Ali – not just those who refused to pledge allegiance to him, but those who started war against the just ruler, and headed to Basrah, like Talha, Zubair, *Umm ul-Mu'minin* (the Mother of Believers) 'Ayisha, and in the next phase, those like Mu'awiyah, and in the third phase the Khawarij of Nahrawan. These three groups, the Violators (*nakithin*), Deviators (*qasitin*) and Renegades (*mariqin*), fought three civil wars against him during the four and a half years that he was the ruler (the Leader of the Believers, or the fourth Righteous Caliph). What does the standard of Islam call those who took part in the battles of Camel, Nahrawan and Siffin? These are people who confronted and rebelled against the just and legal state of the time with military force. The Qur'an and *fiqh* calls them *baghi*.

Baghi *and Overthrow*

Baghi means a transgression. It denotes someone who disobeys, who transgresses. In the standard of *fiqh* it means someone who rebels against the government of the time. It is someone who does not accept pledging allegiance. Someone who does not pay taxes and rebels against the state with arms. What Talheh and Zubair did at the battle of Camel was *baghi*. Mu'awiyah's actions against the rulership of Imam Ali was *baghi*. What the Secedes (*Khawarij*) of Nahrawan did was *baghi*. All three groups are therefore considered *baghi*. Jurists in *fiqh* have set conditions for the punishment of *baghi*. This is a very important discussion: first, one must debate with the *baghi*, argue with them, have dialogue with them and make an effort to convince them. This is the case whether in the battle of Camel or the battle of Siffin. There are numerous letters from Imam Ali to Mu'awiyah[16] and others[17] that are published in the *Nahj al-Balagha* where he clearly and firmly exposes Mu'awiyah's insubstantial excuses. At that time, Mu'awiyah had used the blood of Othman as an excuse. Imam Ali points out that he had defended Othman. He never approved of Othman's murder. You could have done something at the time, why didn't you?

The first step for dealing with rebellions (*bughat*) is theory and dialogue. Because a *baghi* is someone who is apparently or actually opposed to the state based on a particular interpretation, a misgiving or, in today's language, on the basis of a particular theory. The difference between a *baghi* and a *muharib* is that a *muharib* undermines the security of the people, and their actions are not based on any theory, misgiving or viewpoint. They are interested in personal gain, theft and banditry. The thief and armed bandit are considered *muharib* in Qur'anic language. A *muharib* therefore acts against the security of the people based on personal interest and not against the political regime based on a political theory. However, if someone confronted the government based on a political theory, even a false one, this person is considered *baghi*. *Baghi* is therefore completely different from *muharib*. Talha and Zubair were Muslims, Mu'awiyah and the army of Levant were Muslims, they had recited the *Shahadas* (testifying Oneness of God and the prophethood of Muhammad). The Nahrawanis, or the Khawarij, were also practising, devoted and close-minded Muslims. Thus, all three groups were considered Muslim. Despite all of this, they did not accept the rule of Imam Ali. The first thing Ali did was to argue with them. He debated with them and attempted to convince them. War started when these phases reached their end. That is to say, when he saw that the issue would not be resolved by debate, persuasion or dialogue.

In the case of *bughat*, the ruler never has the right to start the war. Thus, in none of these cases did Ali start the war, neither in the case of the battle of Camel, nor Siffin, nor Nahrawan. The meaning of this ruling is that as long as a movement has not taken armed action against the government, the religious government has no right to take up arms against them and undertake military action. Compare this with the story of Karbala. If Husain b. Ali was a *baghi* from the point of view of the deviant government of the time, the

16 *Nahj al-Balagha*, letters Nos 6, 7, 9, 10, 14, 17, 32, 44, 48, 49, 55, 64, 65, 73 and 75.
17 Ibid., letters Nos 1, 2, 29, 54 and 58 on the battle of Camel.

government had no right to start a war against him. This was a ruling that Imam Ali held in high regard and left as a lesson for all Muslim governments: until a *baghi* takes up arms, you have no right to take military action against them. This is not only based on Islamic ethics, but is also a required principle of Islamic *fiqh*. You have no right to attack them. As a Muslim state, you can only defend. You are not allowed to attack your opposition. Thus, in none of the three wars noted above did Ali b. Abi Talib start the attack. Even when his companions wanted to start the war, he said that we will defend, let them start it, whether in the battle of Camel,[18] Siffin[19] or Nahrawan.[20]

The next point is that the *baghi* is not just any rebel. A *baghi* is a rebel who has a base. This base is outside the reach of the government, in a cave, or in the mountains or the jungle. It is a garrison where the government cannot easily bring them under its rule. These rebels must be numerous as one person cannot bring about *baghi*. It requires a group, an organisation. Thus, *baghi* is an organisation that wants armed revolt against the state. Therefore, if someone merely gives a speech or writes a critique of the government, they would not be considered *baghi*.

Baghi is someone who takes up arms against the ruling government based on a political theory. In *fiqh* it says *ahl al-rayba* (the people of suspicion) and *ahl al- ta'wawil* (the people of interpretation), that there is a theory behind this issue, and thus that the *baghi* intend to be on the political or governmental stage, and act to change it with an organisation, theory and arms. However, the eyes of a *muharib* are on the life, property and dignity of the people and are therefore individuals or groups that take up arms for personal gain. A *baghi* is a kind of political convict but a *muharib* is not. A *baghi* is someone who wants to change the ruling government by military attack and has a political theory. His or her hand might not be tainted with anyone's blood, but it might be. The Khawarij of Nahrawan did so, greatly upsetting the security of society and killing many innocent people.

From the point of view of the government, do the criteria of *baghi* apply to Husain b. Ali? Did Husain's caravan have a base? No. It was

---

18 Ahmad b. Yaya al-Baladhuri (d. 892), *Kitab Jumal-un min Ansab al-Ashraf (The Book of Sentences from the Lineage of the Nobles)*, eds S. Zakkar and R. Zarkaly (Beirut: Dar al-Fikr, 1996), 3:36.

19 Ibn A'tham al-Kufi, *Kitab al-Futuh*, 3:44–45.

20 Hanifa Ahmad b. Dawud al-Dinawari (d. 896), *al-Akhbar al-Tiwal (The Longest News [General History])*, ed. Abdul Mon'im 'Amir (Cairo: Wizarah al-Thaqafa, 1960), 210.

merely leaving the city. It was outside the city, but it did not have a specific base. The number of those around him were not enough to be considered a serious threat. Seventy-odd people are not much of a danger to
several thousand. But Husain was beloved and had serious backing from
the people. Thus, the ruling government greatly feared him. Governments
that do not have the people's backing fear every figure who is beloved
by the people and look for any opportunity to eliminate that person. A
beloved figure is a probable alternative ruler, therefore he must not exist.
While we know Husain as someone who forbade the wrong, let us suppose he fits the criteria of a *baghi* from the point of view of the government of the time. What are the punishments for a *baghi* according to the
Qur'an? This is a very important point. What should be done to a person
who has an organisation and is taking up arms against the government
of the time? After an ultimatum, one must turn to what is referred to as
"defensive war". War continues until the time that the organisation falls
apart. Thus, the aim is not the murder of rebels, it is merely the breaking
up of the organisation that has taken up arms against the current state.
If they happen to be accidentally killed during the war, then that is one
thing, but if it comes to an end without death, that is what should be
done. Thus, we have no penal code (*hadd* in *shari'a*) that calls for the
execution of the *baghi* outside the battlefield. If the organisation of the
rebels is broken up, those taken prisoner must not be killed and those who
have escaped must not be pursued; the injured must not be killed and in
any case women, children and elders must not be assaulted. The taking of
slaves is irrelevant in this context.[21] Permission was never given for setting
fire to tents, homes or gardens, or to the poisoning of water. The property
of *bughat* was not plundered. Their property is respected because they
are Muslim. In the battle of Camel, the companions supposed that the
women of their rivals could be taken as slaves. An angry Imam Ali said:
"which one of you will take 'Ayisha as a slave?" They all put their heads
down and stepped aside. In *baghi* both sides are Muslims, thus they neither lose their property, nor are their women and children subject to being
taken as slaves, nor will their people be assaulted. Their organisation is
merely disbanded. There is no penal code (*shar'i hadd*) for their execution

---

21 At the time slavery was an accepted part of war.

outside the battlefield. If they are killed on the battlefield then nothing remains, but outside the battlefield, the Qur'an, *fiqh* and the *shar'i* rulings have not determined that people who have acted against governments should be executed merely because they have rebelled.

In the Qur'an, the discussion of *baghi* appears in the following way: "If two groups of believers fight, you [believers] should try to reconcile them; if one of them is [clearly] oppressing the other, fight the oppressors until they submit to God's command, then make a just and even-handed reconciliation between the two of them: God loves those who are even-handed" (Q. 49:9). If two factions of Muslims (*baghi* is the actions of one group against another within the Muslim community) act to kill and confront one another, if they war with one another, Muslims are required to try to find compromise between them. They must listen to the arguments of both sides and reform corruption in an appropriate manner. The first duty in an Islamic community in the case of a dispute between believers is reconciliation. If one of the groups transgresses against the other, Muslims must enter into war against the oppressor and in defence of the oppressed. For how long, until when must we wage war against them? "Until they submit to God's command." They fought with the transgressors until they returned to God's command, and if they returned, then that is the time when you should cast judgement on them based on justice. What was the reason for the *baghi* and the transgression? Was someone killed unjustly, or was property stolen? Blood that has been unjustly shed is subject to retaliation (*qisas*), there is compensation for what was plundered, but for rebelling, there is no ruling of execution. No such penal code of *hadd* was predicted in the *shari'a*. All of these issues will be judged justly. Be fair and just, as God loves those who are just and fair.

If we do not consider Husain b. Ali to be a forbidder of wrong and we consider him to be a *baghi* from the point of view of the ruling government, were the Qur'anic duties carried out in relation to him? What were the duties of Muslims on that day? "Try to reconcile them." They ought to have come and tried to reconcile the situation. They ought to have inquired about what the rebels were saying. The logic of Husain is Muhammad and Ali's logic. It was the logic of reviving Islam. However, the logic of Yazid was that of force, compulsion and oppression. Should Muslims not have paid attention to these two logics? Should they not have acted for Truth and against falseness? The first step was reconciliation. When hearing the claims of both sides, it would have become clear who had transgressed. Did Husain b. Ali assault anyone? Husain said: "I will not pledge allegiance. A group of Muslims have invited me. I am heading towards those who have invited me." When al-Hurr b. Yazid al-Riyahi stopped Husain's convoy, Husain said: "four thousand letters have been written to me and I have them with me". Al-Hurr states that he knows nothing of the letters. He stopped the Imam's convoy, but the other commanders of the Umayyad army ignored all of the Qur'anic criteria. It was the Umayyad army who transgressed and not the army of Imam Husain. Husain had been invited, and once he heard that those who had invited him had retracted their invitation, he said he would return. They did to Husain what they should not have done. Who can defend the actions that were taken against the Imam, his family and his companions?

The minimum rights of the political opponent were not observed in the case of Husain b. Ali. Husain is someone who did not succumb to pledging allegiance to the unjust government of the time. He aimed to join his supporters. If the government had merely prevented him from joining his supporters, that would have sufficed, since Husain had no base outside the rule of the government of the time. He had also not carried out any armed actions, and had not attacked the army of the caliph. Thus, the title of *baghi* absolutely does not apply to him. Husain was not a transgressor, it was the government that started the war against him. The Umayyad army were considered as the "aggressor denomination" (*fi'ah baghiya*). Based on univocal Islamic criteria, Yazid was certainly *baghi*. In fact, the Umayyad government did not tolerate opposition. Thus, the Umayyad government immediately interpreted this lack of allegiance as rebellion and considered the disobedience to be *baghi* and attacked their opponents.

Elaborating on the verse quoted above (Q. 49:9) shows that there is no explicit discussion about the acts of an Islamic government against its opponents in the Qur'an. The discussion is about conflict between two groups of Muslims, which without doubt includes the conflict of a government with its opponents. It is as though the blessed and exalted God in his mature Wisdom had predicted that it would be usual for unjust governments to be ruling human societies. In the verse, there is no discussion of the right ruler or the wrong ruler only a discussion of fairness, justice and the absence of transgression. You fight with someone whom you consider to be against the ruling of God until that person observes the ruling of God, and He has not given permission beyond this. But, more importantly, another title may be noted, does this title apply to Husain b. Ali? Is Husain a *muharib*?

The Crime of Muharabah *and Armed Insecurity*

Muharib is also a Qur'anic word. Can a person who acts against the government be considered a *muharib*? Who is a *muharib*? A *muharib* is someone who takes armed action against the security of the people (not the government). This used to refer to bandits, but in today's language, *muharibs* are terrorists and gangsters.

"Those who wage war against God and His Messenger and strive to spread corruption in the land should be punished by death, crucifixion, the amputation of an alternate hand and foot, or banishment from the land: a disgrace for them in this world, and then a terrible punishment in the Hereafter, unless they repent before you overpower them – in that case bear in mind that God is forgiving and merciful" (Q. 5:33–34). Who is a *muharib*? *Hadd* is a punishment based in the *shari'a* that applies to those who carry out adultery, theft or the drinking of alcohol. One of these *hudud* of the *shari'a* is *muharabah*. Who is a *muharib*? The Qur'an says: "A person who wages war against God and His Messenger." What do God and His Messenger mean here? The jurists and theologians are in consensus that "security" is the highest achievement of an Islamic society. A society that is not secure, is not Islamic. In an Islamic society, whether a person is righteous or corrupt, he or she carries out his or her activities. The person who believes acts in accordance to his or her faith, and the person who is corrupt goes after worldly lusts and pleasures. Society is secure under the rule of God and the Messenger. Anyone who upsets this security is waging war against God and His Messenger. *Muharabah* with God and His Messenger means those who undermine the security of society. If you refer to any exegeses of the Qur'an (such as *Majma' al-Bayan*[22] and *al-Mizan*[23]), both Sunni and Shi'ite *tafsir* agree in their interpretation of the verse on *muharabah*, that taking away the security of society is tantamount to waging war against God and His Messenger.

---

22 Al-Tabrisi, *Majama' al-bayan fi Tafsir al-Qur'an*, 3:268.
23 Al-Tabataba'i, *al-Mizan fi Tafsir al-Qur'an*, 5:326–328.

But who is the *mufsid fi al-ard* (she or he who strives to spread corruption in the land)? Is a person who the government does not like, and whose presence the government does not tolerate, and who the government considers a troublemaker *mufsid fi al-ard*? The Qur'an points to people who try to corrupt the land as *mufsid fi al-ard*. What does it mean to strive to spread corruption in the land? Again, we see that interpreters have explained the term. It is clear that corruption does not occur in Heaven, and that all that we do, whether good or bad, we do on Earth or in the land. Therefore, corruption in the land means making it a place that is no longer appropriate for living or giving shelter. Thus, the Qur'anic interpreters have explained that those who undermine the security of society are *mufsid fi al-ard*. This means a person who takes security from society. Thus, the verse does not state "Those 'who' wage war against God and His Messenger and those 'who' strive to spread corruption in the land" (with two conjunctions), but states "Those 'who' wage war against God and His Messenger and strive to spread corruption in the land" (with one conjunction). Only one conjunction, *alladhina* (those who), appears before the expressions *muharabah* and *ifsad fi al-ard*, meaning those who go to war against God and His Messenger and strive to spread corruption in the land. These are both determining factors (*qaid*) for one act and both pertain to the issue of undermining security. Whoever upsets the security of society is a *muharib* and *mufsid fi al-ard*. This means that there are two topics for one crime: forcefully undermining the security of society. Jurists from both Sunni and Shi'ite schools are in consensus on this matter. Following this verse, there are also hadiths from the Imams in which they have defined *muharib*, we must try not to depart from our Islamic criteria. Who is a *muharib*?

It is appropriate here to quote from Ayatollah Khomeini's *Tahri al-Wasilah*. He has defined *muharib*, and the definition that he has provided is one that accords with that of the majority of jurists: "*muharib* is someone who takes up arms to scare people or to spread corruption in the land". Thus, the primary characteristic of a *muharib* is that they are armed. This condition is a consensus condition in Shi'ite *fiqh*. If someone does something in society without arms, force and intimidation, that person is not *muharib*. A *muharib* is someone who takes up arms to undermine the security of society. Someone who wants to scare people with force and arms, to steal something from them or to plunder. This is a *muharib*. As opposed to the *baghi*, where the *baghi* has an organisation, the *muharib* can be a single person or a group of people. A *baghi* acts against the state. A *muharib* acts against the people. The *baghi* says, I do not want you to lead, I want to lead. The *muharib* does not care about political issues. He or she wants property, wants to gain money with force and intimidation, and towards this end may even kill. There are thus four severe punishments that are laid out in the Qur'an (Q. 5:33–34): being killed, crucifixion, the amputation of an alternate hand and foot, and exile (each for the various parts of *muharaba*, and to be determined by a judge in accordance to the severity or weakness of the acts carried out).

Now the question is whether we can say that Imam Husain was a *muharib* from the point of view of the government. In response, we say absolutely not. In general, one cannot consider a political opponent as a Qur'anic *muharib*. In terms of the criteria of *fiqh* and the Qur'an, one cannot call someone who wants to overthrow a government a *muharib*. This is because a *muharib* is a bandit, a terrorist and an armed robber. But someone who is a political opponent will not necessarily be a *muharib*. Thus, if someone is in opposition to a government, regardless of whether it is legal or illegal, and they have not taken up arms, then they are neither a *baghi* nor a *muharib*. If the person is part of an organisation, has a military base outside the government's power, and is acting based upon a political theory, then that person is a *baghi*. In Shi'ite *fiqh*, *baghi* comes up in relation to the infallible Imam, thus in *Tahrir al-Wasilah* and other books of *fiqh*, you will not find the rulings of *baghi* during the time of the occultation. That is to say, in addition to the three conditions noted earlier, becoming *baghi* requires a fourth condition, the rising up against the Infallible Imam. However, an uprising against the governments during the time of occultation (since 847) has not been recognised as *baghi* in Shi'ite *fiqh*.

The Rights of the Political Opponent

A political opponent who peacefully critiques the state, the person of the ruler, or the policies and administrations of the state, and who has not taken up arms, has not committed a crime, so there is no discussion as to whether there should be punishment in accordance to *muharaba* or *baghi*. According to *shari'a*, it is forbidden to mete out punishment (*qisas*) before a crime has been committed.

Although Ali knew that the Khawarij wanted to act against him, why did he not act against them to extinguish the conspiracy? We must trust that Ali knew as much as us about politics, but that he was in the process of building a healthy political style. As long as the person had not taken up arms, Imam Ali gave the political opponent complete freedom. Imam Ali's red line was armed opposition, not verbal and written political opposition. How far removed are we from the way of Ali? A government that calls a political opponent, who has peacefully expressed critique both orally and in writing, a *muharib* has no familiarity with the way of Ali. The Violators (*nakithin*), Deviators (*qasitin*) and Renegades (*mariqin*) planned the overthrow of rule, and drew up plans so that Ali would not be in power. Knowing their bad intentions, Ali critiqued their false logic with strength and serenity, and as long as they did not take action and did not rebel with arms, he left them alone. Although he kept an eye on them, he neither arrested them nor subjected them to *ta'zir* punishments. Why? Because they had not yet committed a crime.

The intent to overthrow is neither a crime, nor is it *baghi* or *muharaba*. Yes, when the Khawarij of Nahrawan began their armed uprising against the Alawi state, that is when Ali rose up and confronted them in an assertive manner and made them pay for their shameful actions according to absolute Islamic criteria.

It is interesting that before taking office, the head of the judiciary had explicitly proven in an article titled "Who is a *muharib* and what is *muharaba?*"[24] that if someone uses words to corrupt society, whether orally or in writing, that person does not count as a *muharib*. A *muharib* is exclusively someone who undermines the security of society with arms. That is to say, in accordance with the criteria of *fiqh*, in which the head of the judiciary also believes, people who oppose the government either verbally or in writing do not qualify as *muharib* in the terms of *fiqh* and the Qur'an. The first point of an Islamic government is adhering to Islamic criteria. Based on absolute Islamic criteria, Husain is neither *muharib* nor *baghi*. Rather, he is a political opponent who, with the aim of preventing wrongdoing, did not pledge allegiance to the corrupt government of the time. Despite the fact that he intended to overthrow the oppressive government and had accepted the invitation of the people of Kufah, he had not initiated armed action against the

---

24 Mahmoud Hashemi Shahroudi, *"Mohareb Kist wa Moharebe chist?"* ("Who is the *Muharib* and What is *Muharaba?*"), *Fiqh Ahl-e Bayt Quarterly*, Persian, Qom, 11/12 (autumn/winter 1996): 143–200, 13 (spring 1997): 3–82.

Umayyad government and, after learning that the people of Kufah had gone back on their promise, he intended to go to a land that was not under the control of the oppressive government. Thus, none of the punishments that have been set for the *muharib* applied to his case.

I now want to address a more serious question. If there are two groups of believers, and one considers their actions as *nahy 'an al-munkar* (forbidding the wrong) and the other considers preventing those actions to be *nahy 'an al-munkar*, then what should be done? Husain considered his actions to be *nahy 'an al-munkar*. Yazid b. Mu'awiyah considered oppressing Husain to be *nahy 'an al-munkar*, since he considered the existence of a beloved figure like Husain to be a thorn in the side of his own government which had a weak foundation. The response to this question could be "the truth belongs to one who overcomes" (*al-haqq li man ghalab*), the right belongs to whoever is stronger. At that time, the apparent power was with Yazid, 'Ubaidullah and 'Umar b. Sa'd. Is it so? Absolutely not. As a matter of fact, from a political perspective, there is an issue known as public opinion. If we want to speak from an Islamic perspective, we could talk about fairness and justice. If we turn to history, we would say the judgement of history. Expanding on and explaining this matter requires another occasion. In any case, the fact that a state considers itself to be in the right is not proof of it being so. Which state does not consider itself to be in the right and confesses to its invalidity? Islam had taken note of the possibility that governments might abuse the notion of *baghi*, therefore it absolutely did not set punishments akin to those of the *muharib*. In *fiqh*, the highest punishments have been set for undermining the security of society with arms. The meaning of arms and force is swords, guns and the like. Opposition via speaking, writing and other peaceful means does not count as armed force. In general, given that governments always consider themselves to be in the right, if there are no minimum rights for the political opponent, then we will witness confrontations such as that which happened to Husain b. Ali. Thus, we must raise this question: do governments observe the minimum rights of the political opponent?

Imam Husain and the Duty of Forbidding the Wrong

Husain b. Ali was neither a *muharib*, nor a *baghi*. He was a dissident and political opponent who acted in accordance with the duty of *nahy 'an al-munkar* (forbidding the wrong). In a residence near Karbala, Husain quoted a hadith of the Prophet to the people, which counts among his most brilliant words in the Karbala movement: "People, the Apostle of God said: 'When anyone sees the unjust authorities making permissible what God has forbidden, violating God's covenant, and opposing the Sunna of the Apostle of God by acting against the servants of God sinfully and with hostility, when anyone sees all these incidents and does not upbraid them by deed or by word, it is God's decree to make that person subject to fortune.'"[25] Permitting what God has forbidden is no small issue. It means that society has become so deviant that wrongdoings are counted as good and that good is counted as wrongdoing.

In an Islamic society, four things, which are the most revered, are at issue. If these four are not observed, that society is not an Islamic society, even if it is filled with the call to prayer, recitation of the Qur'an and rituals. Jurists have required obligatory caution of these four: (1) the blood of Muslims; (2) the dignity of Muslims; (3) the reputation of Muslims; and (4) the property of Muslims. One can say, the blood of humans, the dignity of humans, the reputation of humans and the property of humans. A society in which the lives of people are cheap and where the government ruins the reputations of its political opponents, is not an Islamic society, even if it pretends to follow religion and practise *shari'a*. Many of the most bloodthirsty and oppressive governments of religious societies pretended to be religious, and despite claiming to be the representative of God on Earth, were worse than the devil. Permitting what God has forbidden and violating God's covenant means killing innocent people, ruining the reputation of believers because they have opposed the government, ravishment, and usurping the property of the people on the basis of capricious excuses.

The tradition of the Prophet was mercy. Our God began the Qur'an with "in the Name of God, the Lord of Mercy, the Giver of Mercy". The title of our Prophet is "the Merciful to all people". The Islamic way is accompanied by mercy, it is not accompanied by hardship. In a society where the rights of its citizens are violated, the people are oppressed, and sin and transgressions take place, there is no Islam. The biggest and most distinct sign of an Islamic society is the establishment of justice within it. A government that is inclined towards sin and oppression has no right to introduce itself as Islamic. It is a pity, a hundred-fold a pity, that rulers present their transgressive and anti-*shari'a* actions in the shell of religion.

---

25 Al-Tabari, *History of the Prophets and Kings*, 19:95.

After quoting the Prophet, Husain continues: "Indeed, these authorities have cleaved to obedience to Satan and have abandoned obedience to the Merciful, they have made corruption visible; they have neglected the punishments (*hudud*) laid down by God; they have appropriated the *fay*[26] exclusively for themselves; they have permitted what God has forbidden, and they have forbidden what He has permitted."[27] As we have noted, the most important things that God has forbidden pertain to the life, dignity, reputation and property of people.

In Karbala, Husain gives this sermon as a warning to Islamic societies throughout time: "Can you not see that truth is no longer something that men practice and that falsehood is no longer desisted from, so that the believer rightly desires to meet God [death]. I can only regard death as martyrdom (*shahddah*) and life with these oppressors as a tribulation."[28] I see nothing in death other than happiness and count living with oppressors as nothing but misery and shame. This sentence is bitter and biting: "People are the servants of this world and religion is the lick on their tongues. They spin it so that their livelihoods move along. When they are tested, the religious people are few."[29] In other words, people are slaves to the world, and as long as they live favourable and comfortable lives, they are loyal to religious principles. However, in times of hardship, the time of trials, true religious people are scarce. Husain strongly disapproved of the instrumental use of religion: those who have used religion as a ladder for obtaining worldly power, who hold prayer beads, who have a religious appearance in order to have what is sweet and rich in this world, but when are tested, few are found to be religious. When it is time for purification, meaning separating the pure from the impure, few will be counted as being successfully religious by the Divine test.

Epilogue

The massacre at Karbala was one of the biggest turning points in the history of Islam. In this chapter, I discussed this tragedy from the perspective of human rights, focusing on the rights of political opposition in the *shari'a*.

---

26 *Fay'* means what Muslims take from their enemies without war (Q. 59:7).
27 Al-Tabari, *History of the Prophets and Kings*, 19:95–96.
28 Ibid., 19:96.
29 Ibn Shu'bah al-Harrani, *Tuhaf al-'Uqul*, 245.

Husain b. Ali is the best example of political opposition against unjust rulers in the history of Islam. Muslims across the board, elites and ordinary people alike, fundamentally understand the importance of this example. Critical analysis of this tragedy, theological and sectarian orientations aside, is the starting point for any discussion of the right to protest in Muslim societies. Although this discussion focuses on the case study of Husain's opposition fifty years after the death of his grandfather, the Messenger of God, I have tried to highlight the general principles of the Qur'an and *shari'a* in this case.

There are three concepts that should not be confused: political opposition, *baghi* and *muharib*. Unfortunately, the former has been neglected in Islamic jurisprudence, almost to the point that the right to political opposition has not been recognised. It is important to clarify that the concepts of *baghi* and *muharib* do not include peaceful political opposition. *Muharib* refers to opposition in the form of terrorists and criminals, while *baghi* refers to regime changers or freedom fighters. These three categories are thus completely different from each other.

In theory, there is consensus and agreement in Sunni and Shi'ite *fiqh* that *haraba* or *muharaba* are among the most serious crimes punishable by the Islamic punishment code (*shar'i hudud*) since they represent armed violation of the security and order of society. They are not political crimes since they are not based on any political theories. Hence, the punishment for *haraba* or *muharaba* has been classified under *shar'i hudud* punishment.

However, *baghi* represents armed uprising or regime change and is based on an alternative political theory. It has a centre and military organisation. The concept of *baghi* is applied when these armed organised groups start physically fighting against the state. The fight between *bughat* and the state is regarded as civil war. However, it is incorrect to completely condemn *bughat*. It depends on the legitimacy of the state, on the one hand, and the support of public opinion, on the other. The first Islamic duty in the case of *bughat* is reconciliation between the two sides, identifying the oppressor and then fighting them, which could either be the state or the rebels, until submitting to God's standards. It is clear that punishment for *baghi* is not included under *shar'i hudud*. It is not absolutely categorised as a crime since it is possible that the state will be recognised as guilty instead of the rebels (*bughat*).

In practice, however, it is recognised that *bughat* are at fault and that they should be killed without trial. This means that the right to oppose, protest and object against the state or the government is not recognised. Any rebellion against the ruler, even an unjust ruler, is forbidden (*haram*). This is famously the approach of the Hanbalites[30] and is in practice the dominant Sunni approach. As a result, *baqhi* or any rebellion and uprising against the ruler, regardless of whether the state is just and legitimate or not, is without question regarded as a crime, even the most serious of crimes, to the extent that it has been regarded with zero tolerance throughout the history of Islam, except during the time of Imam Ali.

Although Shi'ite *fiqh* recognises the right to protest against an unjust ruler following the example of Imam Ali and Imam Husain, it restricts the definition of *baghi* to rebellion against the infallible Imam (i.e., more than a just or legitimate ruler). However, in practice Shi'ite rulers have not tolerated any uprisings against the state, just as Sunni rulers have not. This means that theocracy and tyranny do not tolerate alternatives or opposition regardless of religion, sect, history and geography.

The Islamic Republic of Iran is an example of the implementation of Shi'ite *fiqh*. Since its inception in 2013, the Iranian penal code (*Qanoun Mojazat Islami*) has defined any kind of armed opposition (and any connection – even non-military – to such organisations) against the Islamic state as *muharaba* punishable by capital punishment. In the latest revision of this penal code (2013), three concepts were distinguished: *muharib*, *baghi* and *mufsid fi al-ard*. *Baghi* is any armed uprising against the regime. It is the first time in the Shi'ite context that the punishment for *baqhi* is not restricted to the Infallible Imam (Article 287). In the same way as its Sunni counterparts, the Islamic Republic of Iran does not tolerate any alternatives or opposition. The ruling of *mufsid fi al-ard* (to spread corruption in the land) applies to any actions that undermine security and order, or to the publication of lies, and is punishable by death (Article 298). As a result, any lawmaking according to the *shari'a* (Sunni and Shi'ite) regarding political opposition is deeply problematic.

---

30 For more information about the Sunni perspective on *harabah* and *baghi*, see Wahba al-Zuhayli, *al-Fiqh al-Islami wa Adilatahu*, 6:128–147.

Section Four
Women's Rights

10

Reformist Islam and Women's Rights[1]

The discussion on women's rights is one about which much has been said and much remains to be said. It appears that to solve the problems in the sphere of women's rights, we must remove several obstacles from our way. In our society, there is both a problem of customs as well as of religion in this regard. In the sphere of women's rights, if we want to speak without mincing our words, there is a specific viewpoint that does not believe in women's rights. Given that the title of this chapter is "Reformist Islam and Women's Rights", it is important to discuss opposing viewpoints as well. Along the lines of the proverb that "things are understood in relation to their opposites", we will ask: which way of thinking should be critiqued and which should be affirmed?

Opposite to reformist thinking, there is "traditional thought" as well as fundamentalist thought, although the latter does not have much foundation in our society. We should therefore predominantly consider and reflect on "traditional thought" rather than fundamentalist thought. In prevailing issues, these two ways of thinking get mixed together. In considering traditional thought, we must look both at women's rights before the advent of Islam in Iran as well as women's rights after Islam. Namely, what rights did women have in the Hijaz, the land where the Prophet became God's Messenger, before and after Islam? What we have today is a cultural legacy that

---

1 *Roshanfekri-ye Dini wa Hoquq-e Zanan.* My presentation at *Jebhe-ye Mosharekati Iran-e Islami* (the Islamic Iran Participation Front), Tehran, 23 August and 6 September 2003, *A'yeen Monthly Journal* pre-issue 1 (December 2003): 9–17.

has taken root from three cultures: our religion (Islam); Iranian customs; and some elements of the modern world. This means that notions of women's rights in contemporary society are a compilation of three components: a religious component; a local and national component; and a contemporary and modern component.

There is no doubt that if we examine Iranian civil law, Islamic penal codes or the Iranian Constitution, we will conclude that in terms of women's rights, the section on religious rights, rulings and duties is much larger and more emphasised than the other two. If there are problems with women's rights in Iran today, it seems that the overwhelming majority of them pertain to the religious section. Before they were written by our ancestors, the Iranian laws that are the subject of our discussion were based on traditional Islamic laws and rulings of *shari'a*. If there are problems, one must critique these. Much has been said about the place of women in Islam. Thank God no one can say that in our society the place of women is not elevated. Even those who consider the international Convention on the Elimination of all Forms of Discrimination Against Women (CEDAW) to be forbidden and against *shari'a*, have often, at least in words, claimed respect for the rights of women.

It seems that the respect that is paid to women has two sources. Some think that the discrimination that women face is for their own benefit. From this perspective, the legal differences that are seen in the laws under discussion here are essential, inherent and Divine, and any change in them is a change in the honour of nature, the character of creation and religion of God. They consider the ultimate respect to women is to enact these same laws and duties of *shari'a*. They believe that if we follow these criteria, women's rights have been realised. From the traditional point of view, the forms and models that our women have inherited in *fiqh* are based on a kind of sacredness. They are all from the textual (*mansus*) and unchanging rulings of *shari'a* and thus following them is to follow the religion of God and the *shari'a* of the Prophet.

Requirement of Justice in Women's Rights

It is worth asking, since we are from the group of 'Adliyah (People of Justice) and since among the Islamic theological schools we give importance to God's attributes of Being Just more than his other attributes, what is the requirement of justice in the rulings of *shari'a*? The difference between the 'Adliyah and the Ash'arites is that the Ash'arites believed that whatever was sent down from God is justice itself. According to this view, outside Divine legislation and determination and outside *shari'a*, justice cannot be understood by human reason. Justice is religious, and the definition of justice must be requested from God, and God and the Prophet must define justice; otherwise, we do not have the capacity to understand justice with our intellects. According to the Ash'arites, our intellect is too poor to be able to understand the criteria of God's rulings in all their dimensions. Thus, all rulings of God must be just and all God's rulings during the age of Revelation were just. That is to say, conventional reason at that time considered the rulings to be just as compared with all other rulings. In contrast, the 'Adliyah are those who believe that we accept God's religion because He is Just. That is to say, we are able to understand justice prior to religion, and since we see God and His religion full of justice and fairness, we accept this religion, meaning Islam. This is at the forefront of the 'Adliyah programme: that not only is God Just, not only has Islam as a whole been woven on the axis of justice, but also every single one of the rulings of Islam must be just since no unjust act or ruling comes from God. If a ruling is to be eternal, it must always be just. Today, too, the rulings in the arena of women must be just. That is to say, in any time they must be just as compared with other similar rulings. If it is as such, then every ruling from the rulings of *shari'a* and in the case under discussion, every ruling from the rulings pertaining to women, must also be considered just today. If justice is supposed to be accessible to human reason, if reasonability (*sirah al-'uqala*) is to rule over the arena of justice, then regardless of who has set these rulings, regardless of them being *shari'a*, regardless of whether they were issued by God, the Prophet or some regular person, then in and of themselves, these rulings must be defendable.

Traditional thought has nothing to do with inherent assessment of the rulings of *shari'a*. They consider the rulings to be just since the maker and speaker of these rulings are clearly just. Since the infallible God and the Prophet have spoken and made them, there is no error or mistake in their rulings. But from the point of view of reformist Islam, many of the traditional rulings regarding women are not assessed to be just regardless of their connection to the Legislator. That is to say, if they are considered by a neutral mind, they will not be found just. Believers must provide an answer to this ambiguity. In the discussion on "Human Rights and

Reformist Islam",[2] I have shown that, in general, traditional thinking is not able to see the equality of the rights of women and men. The differences in the rights of men and women are among the necessities of traditional thinking, and if someone rejects that then they have left the paradigm of traditional thought. These differences are not merely those of the minds of the theologians and jurists, but evidence for it can be found in the remaining hadiths of the religion's first leaders and in the verses of the Scripture. Today, if someone wants to adhere to the legal equality of men and women, and if that person is religious, he or she must be aware of the great mental revolution that he or she will have to have in order to be able to hold the simple proposition that men and women are equal. One cannot achieve the rights of women and obtain legal equality of women and men using conventional *ijtihad*. I will express this explicitly, decisively and with transparency. That is to say, if someone does not want to leave the paradigm of traditional *ijtihad*, meaning if the person wishes to accept the scholarship on the methodology of *fiqh* (*usul al-fiqh*) as it is, then the conclusion will be unchanged. One may obtain very small and marginal reforms on the level of secondary rulings (*ahkam thanawi*) and conditions based on contract law (*shart dimn-i 'aqd*) that gain some benefits for women, such as can be seen in official marriage contracts in Iran. However, this is really the ultimate of what can be achieved within the confined framework of traditional *fiqh-e ahkam-e thanawi*, and if we want to remain faithful to that method, then in many instances our hands are tied. So what should be done? Of course, I am not the only one to ask this. The strongest jurist of our time, the late Ayatollah Khomeini, noted the failures and inabilities of the form of *ijtihad* that dominates in the seminaries. He put his finger on the foundational weaknesses of traditional *fiqh* at the same time as he defended it.[3] Now the question is, how do we solve this problem? Here we are with traditional thought. We want to maintain our beliefs, and to

---

2 Chapter 5, this book.

3 "The conventional *ijtihad* in the religious seminaries is not enough. In fact, if one person is the most learned in the specified sciences in the religious seminaries but could not identify the interest of the society or could not distinguish the righteous and important persons from the unrighteous ones and, in general, lacks the correct insight and power of decision-making on social and political aspects, that person is not a *mujtahid* on social and governmental issues and cannot administer the affairs of society" (*Sahife-ye Imam*, Khomeini's response to Mohammad Ali Ansari, 30 October 1988, 21:176–180).

be faithful to our beloved Islam. At the same time, in many instances we find traditional thought to be in conflict with the conventions of today. Today, if we look at traditional thinking using contemporary conventional reasonability, we will find many of the orders to be unjust, unreasonable and not preferable as compared with similar solutions. That is to say, we will not find them to be preferable. At least, these are the accusations that have been made against traditional Islam.

The three permanent criteria for rulings of *shari'a*. I believe that during the time that Islamic rulings were sent down, meaning during the time of Revelation and Prophecy, every ruling of *shari'a* that was given had three main characteristics. First, they were considered reasonable by the conventions of the day. They were not accepted on the credibility of the Prophet having spoken them, but because they were understood to be right in themselves. This is an important point: the Revelation was not accepted because a holy person said it but, when one thinks about it, one thinks that it is quite right, and that nothing better can be said. One could compare it with other religions and would see that it is superior. Thus, the second feature of the rulings of *shari'a* is their superior functionality as compared with similar solutions. Comparative functional superiority in relation to other religions, schools and other solutions. When you compared women's rights in Islam with the pre-Islamic period (the "Age of Ignorance"), you could see that Islam was superior. With every single ruling, if you compared it with the rights of women in ancient Iran, Rome and Greece, you could see that these rights were superior. And, finally, the most important feature of *shari'a* rulings is that they are just. According to the conventions (*'urf*) of the age of Revelation, these rulings were assessed to be the ultimate in terms of justice and fairness. I will return to this point in more detail at the end of this chapter.

The Evolution of the Approach of Human Reason in the Arena of Women's Rights

Today there have been developments in all three areas. That is to say, until about a hundred years ago, there had not been much change in the thought and consciousness of the world's Muslim societies and their requirements. In the last one hundred years, at least in Iran, we have been dealing with a way of thought in Islamic and Shi'ite societies where we cannot simply say that this ruling is accepted by today's approach of human reason, that it is just or superior. If each of us asks ourselves, when we hear about a ruling such as stoning, for example, our mind will anxiously question whether this way of punishment is the best way of punishment. Is this way the reasonable way, is it a just way? I believe that for each and every one of you, these questions have caused anxiety. In this regard, we also have the case of women not having equal rights to divorce as men. In marriage we see that women are the cause (*mujib*) and men are the ones who accept (*qabil*). That is to say, in entering this contract, the woman has the greater right, but for leaving the marriage – other than in cases of *'usr wa haraj* (distress and constriction), and even then via a judge and the courts and the giving up of the dowry or paying several times that amount in the case of *khul'* or *mubarat* (two forms of divorce) – the woman's hands are tied. And, separately, how can one defend that a woman's blood price is half that of a man at a time when female students make up more than 60 per cent of all college students in Iran?

The rulings in the arena of women's rights require deduction anew, an *ijtihad* in the foundation and principles being appropriate for the criteria of reasonability and justice. The Scripture and Tradition must be re-read through these lenses. The reason for bringing up the issue of women's rights in a society is that women in that society have legal problems. Every social group has their rights examined when there is discrimination or shortcomings in relation to their rights. For example, recently there have been discussions about labour rights and the rights of children. It is clear that there are problems in these areas. As a result, there have been discussions about these rights. Thus, if someone enters this arena and wants to speak about women's rights, that person has accepted at the outset that women in this society have faced some problems in regard to some of their rights.

If we want to speak with more precision, this problem can be found both in the area of the rights of Iranian women and the rights of Muslim women. Iranian women face problems with their rights specifically because many of these rights in our society are based on religious rights and the rulings of *shari'a*. Thus, if there are problems in the area of the rulings of Islam and the duties of *shari'a*, then these problems have carried over to national law as well and today we face laws that some claim are unjust in many areas. However, not everyone believes that there are problems in the area of women's rights. More than anything, our girls and women have to try to prove that there are problems with their rights because many do not believe that these rulings are oppressive. This group believes that the problem lies with the views and positions of the women themselves. Based on this, they believe that women are making a mistake or that people who claim that there are problems in the arena of women's rights must wash their eyes and see things in a different way. Thus, we have a long road ahead of us.

We must try to convince a part of our own society that there are problems in this area. The parts of our society that need convincing are the traditional segments of society. One must never underestimate the traditional segment in any society, especially in Iran. This segment has great strength and has managed to organise the laws from its own viewpoint and position. In the conflict of tradition and modernity, not just women overall, but also Muslim women feel the legal problem. This problem relates to the fact that they compare the Islamic rulings pertaining to them with rulings and laws about women in other societies, and in this comparison they likely reach conclusions that are not very desirable. They reach the conclusion that some of these laws are not preferable, that as compared to similar laws in other societies, these rulings are not better or preferable. They see problems with these rulings.

Reformist thinking believes that mistakes have been made or there are shortcomings in the deduction or understanding of these rulings, but at the same time women of this society are Muslims who want to remain faithful to their religion and beliefs. They worship God, believe in the Hereafter, and believe in the Prophets as the Messengers of God, and they want to live in this age with these fundamental threefold beliefs, and they do live in this age. The conflict that is seen now is between that of religious propositions and the results of the new age. No one can have a peaceful life in conflicted surroundings. It creates mental friction and internal struggle. With every act, there is a worry that it may be against Islam or *shari'a* and, on the other hand, there is a feeling that some of the things that have been introduced in the name of Islam and *shari'a* are not right. I believe that the picture I have sketched has been seen in most households. Every mother who has spoken with her young daughter or a father who has had a sincere conversation with his child can see this picture. It is a two-sided picture: on the one hand, there is a desire to preserve one's belief and faith, and, on the other hand, there is a desire to live in this age and the correlations of these two have no harmony with one another.

This disharmony is very profound and deep. If someone understands both sides correctly, then it will be clear how great a problem we have before us. The difficulty is that our traditionalists have little to no familiarity with the necessities of the modern world, and modernists rarely have a deep understanding of the traditions, culture and religion of their own society. Suppose there is a jurist who says, "I haven't read a newspaper in thirty years." Naturally, if there is someone who has not read the newspapers, has not listened to the radio or watched television (because he probably considered something in them to be contrary to *shari'a*) and who has not on principle ever consulted the Internet, has not watched satellite television, and now such a person wants to give opinions about the world in which he lives, how credible can his opinions be? If we present to the world what he considers to be reasonable, we will see that there are few of sound mind who will accept his views as reasonable.

Amidst these are people who are both familiar with the conditions of the modern world and who understand the traditions of their society. It seems that this group bears a heavier mission than the other two sectors. This is the group made up of those who both understand this culture and its most important religious components, and alongside it understand the world in which they currently live. They know that after the Renaissance in Europe the world's rationality changed. This is not a small issue. If you could express and prove this to al-Azhar University or in the theological seminaries of Najaf or Qom, then a great segment of the problem is resolved. There are things that are considered to be correct today that were considered incorrect 400 years ago. And, on the contrary, there are things that today are considered to be against values and convention that were once considered to be of value and that everyone defended. Today's rationality and yesterday's rationality are in many ways as different as night and day. We are not saying that everything has changed, but that many things have changed. If someone does not believe this, it means that the person has not understood the requirements of the time and place. Today, there are many issues that the pious push away from their religious frame. These are issues that yesterday were within the frame of believers and none protested them. However, today there are propositions that people try to hide, and when they are discovered, we are blamed for talking about them. Public taste has changed in relation to many issues. This taste was not the same in the past.

The very simple example is that of slavery. Until about 150 years ago, slavery was accepted throughout the world. That is to say, philosophers wrote treatises in support of it and almost no one considered it vile. But today, in the twenty-first century, one of the important Articles of the UDHR is the abolition of slavery. Today, it is considered among the vilest of acts. This while the philosophy of Plato and Aristotle is filled with discussions in support of it. Well, if someone does not recognise these cultural changes, then that person will not make correct decisions. Understanding the requirements of time and place precisely means to understand this part of the approach of human reason. It means it will be clear which features were characteristic of yesterday's reasonability versus today's reasonability.

Factors in the Development of Women's Rights

I want to move from this general introduction on the conflict between tradition and modernity to a more specialised introduction focusing on the difference between the views on women's issues in the past and present, and the difference in discussions and dimensions of women's rights in the past and today (this past is not limited to that of Islamic societies). Whether we look at scripture, hadiths or the customs and literature of nations, we find shared aspects in all of them. Thus, the issue is not limited to Iran and Islam. Prior to the Renaissance, women were considered second-class creatures who were vulnerable inferiors who had to remain under the protective umbrella of men, and if the protection of men were removed, then they would wilt like a flower or become like jewels stolen by bandits. Thus, they must always be protected by men: by father, brother, husband and son. This is the way it was practised in the majority of societies. If women were in command in some societies, we should not take those societies as exceptions. Even in those societies, the position of women was in passing and had not become a principle. We have to consider the lives of everyday women in society. The premodern period was a time when physical strength was held in high regard and the might of muscle prevailed. In the story of Talut and Goliath, which is also mentioned in the Qur'an, physical ability was one of the conditions for being a ruler (Q. 2:247–251). In the past, punishments were also corporal, and mental punishments were not even recognised as punishments at that time. It is clear that in a society where physical strength had the first word, women did not have much of a place.

The other factors were economic and livelihood issues. In the past, for a variety of reasons men typically provided for the livelihood of the family. It is natural that the person who provides the family's livelihood should be able to take their place as head of the family. Thus, if payment of the household expenses is in the hands of the man, then the rule of the family will be in his hands as well.

Alongside the economic and physical factors, there were other factors as well. In summary, it was the idea that women's minds were incomplete (you may immediately think of one particular religious text or idea that has been attributed to religion, but which texts of the past do you know of that did not think as such?). The cultures of the past considered women to be inferior. It is possible that some may try to use cases with very low credibility to try and turn some exceptions into a rule, but I think that any fair researcher would be able to see that the perception of women's inferiority was a rule in past cultures. But the views of the current world are different. In the new world, gender is not a factor in discrimination. In the past, in addition to gender, race, the colour of one's skin and religion were also factors in discrimination. "This person is black and so has less rights" was common and did not require argumentation. In some Persian proverbs, we also see traces of tribal and racial discrimination. But Islam came and said: "There is no favour of an Arab over a non-Arab, nor a non-Arab over an Arab, and neither white skin over black skin, nor black skin over white skin, except by righteousness."[4] That means that it cancelled privileges of race and skin colour, and this is what resulted in masses of people of different nations accepting the religion of Muhammad, "when you see people embracing God's faith in crowds" (Q.110:2). How do a Bilal Habshi, Salman Farsi, Suhaib Rumi, all of a sudden arrive at the same destination? They feel equality and justice. They feel that in this religion, race and colour do not take priority over humanity, and what God pays attention to is our faith and righteous actions. Even on the Day of Judgement, women and men are not different before God. If we look at the Qur'an from beginning to end, we do not find one instance when God

---

4 Farewell Sermon of Prophet Muhammad, Musnad Ahmad 22978, Ahmad b. Muhammad Ibn 'Abd Rabbih, *al-'Iqd al-Farid* (*The Unique Necklace*), ed. M. M. Qumayha (Beirut: Dar al-Kutub al-'Ilmiyya, 1983), 4:147–149; Ahmad b. abi Yaqub al-Ya'qubi, *Tarikh al-Ya'qubi* (*The History of al-Ya'qubi*), ed. Abdul Amir Muhanna (Beirut: al-A'lami, 2010), 2:110; Ibn Shu'ba al-Harrani, *Tuhaf al-'Uqul*, 29–30.

discriminates on the Day of Judgement: "I will not allow the deeds of any one of you to be lost, whether you are male or female, each is like the other [in rewards]" (Q. 3:195). It is a Qur'anic master principle. The criterion on Judgement Day is piety and nothing else. The conditions of the new world are such that the humanity of humans is the criterion for value and all those that cause incidental differences among humans cannot be the source of legal discrimination among them.

Slavery may be abolished, but being a man or a woman is a necessity of having a healthy society. A male society is not desirable, a society of men and women is dynamic and flourishes. So this difference must remain. However, the question is whether physical, biological and bodily differences can be the source of legal differences? What epistemological or philosophical argument can prove that because men and women have physiological differences their rights should be different as well? We have these physiological differences among different races and colours of people, too. Books have been written saying that white people are smarter than black people. In the nineteenth century, the superiority of the German race over other races was greatly advertised in pseudo-scientific books.[5] But today, we laugh at such talk. In my view, the issue is just as obvious in the case of gender differences as well. If differences arising from race and colour cannot lead to legal differences, then what is the reason for gender differences causing differences in legal rights? If someone thinks they have any arguments for this, they should submit them. The arguments that have been given here are based on the *shari'a* and not on rationality. We have no rational argument in this regard. Thus, a person of today believes that if men and women have equal opportunities, they can proceed like one another and each will reach their path naturally. During the last few decades where women in our own society (in Iran) have been given the opportunity, they have surpassed their male counterparts in many university majors. Who says that a woman's mind is less than that of a man? How can one prove this? Things have become so intense that governments have had to say they will not accept more than 50 per cent of women for some majors at university. If more than 50 per cent of men appear in a major, is that a rule but if more than 50 per cent women appear it is counter to the rule?

---

5 For example, see Arthur de Gobineau (1816–1882), *The Inequality of Human Races*, trans. Adrian Collins (n.p.: Ostara Publications, 2015).

The second part of the chapter argues as follows: when some of these propositions of *shari'a* are placed before a Muslim girl or woman, she feels that some of them are not compatible with the views of the world today. As a result, she feels that she is stuck within a duality where she both wants to keep her faith and religion, but also considers these legal principles with (human) reason, and therefore doubt arises. If there is doubt about these rulings, it must be discussed. One can be a believer but at the same time look at some of these rulings with doubt. In the story of resurrection, did Abraham not ask God to show him the resurrection? "And when Abraham said, 'My Lord, show me how You give life to the dead,' He said, 'Do you not believe, then?' 'Yes,' said Abraham, 'but just to put my heart at rest'" (Q. 2:260). Thus, if our women want to ask about certain rulings of *shari'a* so their hearts are put at rest, it is never the case that they have acted against *shari'a*. In fact, I invite more questions. Ask, request, so that the doors of scholarly discussion are opened, so that we can solve our problems with the help of one another.

Two Different Perspectives on Women in Islamic Texts

If we want to speak outside of generalities (since in the last two or three decades much has been said about Islam as highly considerate of the value of women, so I will not repeat that), there are two perspectives on women in our religious texts. One view is more Qur'anic: woman is a different kind of human but she stands alongside man. No inferior characteristics are seen in this first view. There are numerous verses with which each Muslim is familiar and in these there is no sense that "woman is lesser than man and is created for him, that she is made from his left rib and her mind and faith is lesser than that of a man". Rather, she is a human alongside man with her own specific duties. For example, this can be seen in famous verse Q. 33:35:

> For men and women who are devoted to God – believing men and women, obedient men and women, truthful men and women, stead- fast men and women, humble men and women, charitable men and women, fasting men and women, chaste men and women, men and women who remember God often – God has prepared forgiveness and a rich reward.

This verse notes a number of different characteristics in men and women without any discrimination or difference. Or in "The believers, both men and women, support each other; they order what is right and forbid what is wrong" (Q. 9:71), men and women have been considered the same in regard to the highest social responsibility of ordering what is right and forbidding what is wrong. Or in the case of economic rights for humans (regardless of whether the human is man or woman), these are the same in both what is for them and against: "Each gain whatever good it has done, and suffers its bad" (Q. 2:286). This view is a humanist perspective that we have no problems with today and all of my efforts are to strengthen this authentic and desirable view: meaning, the view of women from the viewpoint of the Prophet Muhammad and the Qur'an.

But the second view is more a view from the standpoint of *fiqh* and *shari'a*. This viewpoint paints an inferior, vulnerable and needy picture of women who need the protection of men. An inferior person means a second-class person (we see the not infrequent use of the term *da'ifa* (literally, weak female) in Persian culture). A vulnerable person is like a jewel that must be retained within a shell, and if that shell is cast aside, the jewel will become corrupted. This is a very common view. The face of Mary that we have seen in the Qur'an or even the women who are in our own religious traditions such as Khadija, Fatimah and Zainab remind us of the first view, and do not in any way recall the second view. In my opinion, this second view is the sediment of the view of the conventions of the past in Islam. This is exactly compatible with the culture that I just outlined. This culture is not just Arabic or Iranian and Eastern, but it was a world culture. Do you know of a civilised place in the past that did not look at women in this way? In medieval Europe things were not much better.

If we examine (Iranian) civil law, penal codes and political law, we see that the view reflected is the one in *fiqh* and *shari'a*. It is not very pleasant to outline it, but understanding symptoms are necessary for finding the cure. From the outset, I will note that I do not think everything that is in *fiqh* and *shari'a* is altogether dark or that what we see in women's rights in the West is altogether white. The chastity and decency that we find in our national and religious culture is worth more than the world. But alongside this positive view, I want to also point to the legal shortcomings in *fiqh* and *shari'a*, so that we can find a solution to them. A sampling of the rulings of the second view can be divided into two categories. One category makes up a majority of the rulings in quantity, and is based on the humanistic view of women as equal. According to this view, they are like men with differences that have nothing to do with discrimination and inferiority. These are found in rulings pertaining to worship, the rights of commerce and some issues pertaining to civil rights.

However, another category of rulings is based on the legal differences, discrimination and views of women as second-class citizens. These types of rulings can be found among discussions related to criminal law, political law and many aspects of civil rights. It seems that this latter category can and should be seen through a different lens and that there must be an effort to provide rulings that are in accordance to the first view, which is the humanistic view. Put another way, I believe a deep fundamental *ijtihad* is necessary in this type of ruling. These are not among the eternal and permanent rulings of Islam, but rather are those that were temporary and appropriate for the requirements of time and place of the era of Revelation. I will address some of these rulings that consider women in terms of the second view, meaning woman as an inferior creature, in the following three brief sections.

Section One: Women's Civil Rights

Women's civil rights from the perspective under consideration, namely, the view of women as inferior, can be discussed in terms of seven issues: marriage, married life, the rights of the mother, permissibility of the husband punishing the wife, separation and inheritance.

In terms of marriage, several points can be discussed, including the following: for marriage, the boy does not need his father's permission, but many of our jurists caution that in her first marriage, a girl must obtain her father's permission. If permission is needed, why not have it as necessary for boys as well? How much lower is a girl as compared with a boy? Both are in an emotional state. If being emotional is a criterion, then for the two in the intensity of youth, their feelings reign over their reason. But if legal consent is not required, and it is not, then girls are free like boys to marry independently.

The second point is about the permissibility of child marriage with the consent of the father or paternal grandfather. In the culture of the past, girls would marry before the age of maturity, and the permission for this marriage would come from the father or paternal grandfather. Today, it is very hard for us to imagine a circumstance where a child is made to marry another and has no right to object even after maturity. Here two points can be raised: why is the mother's approval not a condition here (both in the previous case and the case at hand)? In matters of marriage, mothers are even more insightful than fathers. During the time of marriage, which one of us considered our mother's recommendations to be lesser than our father's? I do not think if we changed this that the religion of God would be changed. The reason behind it is not very strong either. In addition, today the marriages of minors are legally considered null, or at a minimum many have misgivings about it. One of the conditions for marriage is maturity and the ability to marry from various aspects, such as sexual maturity, the ability to run a family, etc. whether for a girl or a boy.

The third point is the possibility for a Muslim man to temporarily[6] marry a woman from the People of the Book, while the marriage of a Muslim woman with a non-Muslim is absolutely forbidden (whether temporarily or permanently). Along the same lines, men can marry up to four women (in permanent marriage), and an unlimited number of women (in temporary marriage). We should add that in the past, men could have sexual use of female slaves without limits or accountability. It seems that any violation of the monogamy system for men must be restricted clearly to the case of emergency (*idtirar*) conditions, and to recognise the system of monogamy as the moderate and healthy system in normal and natural circumstances.

In terms of the second issue, that is, the rights of women in married life, the following points can be raised: first is the discussion of the man's leadership over the household. According to some, this leadership is an absolute rule and, like a dictatorship, the man gets the first and last word and if the woman objects even a little, her place is in hell. She has become disobedient (*nashizah*) and the rulings of being disobedient apply to her. Family life begins with the consent of man and woman, what is wrong with continuing this life with the consent of both parties? In the marriage contract in accordance to *shari'a*, the woman is the cause (*mujib*) and the man is accepter (*qabil*). That is to say, the woman is considered the first side and the man the second. But once they enter married life, then the woman's consent has no role in the family's destiny. Why? Should not a man who wants to lead the

---

6 This is based on Shi'ite *fiqh*. Sunni *fiqh* only allows the permanent marriage of a Muslim man with a woman of the People of the Book.

family do so with his wife's consent? What is wrong with saying that family affairs should be carried out in consultation with one another? Then if someone were to say: "consult with your wives and do their opposite!"[7] we will tell that person that this way belongs to the culture of the past and the time of acting this way in relation to women is gone. Today, one can consult with women, trust in their consultation and act accordingly.

The second issue is that they say a woman is not allowed to leave the house without her husband's permission, even if she observes the rights of the husband. Of course, this is to observe the rights of the man. When the husband is not at home, what is wrong with his wife leaving the house to study, or go to work or shopping as long as she observes chastity and decency? If both sides trust one another then all issues are resolved. If a person is unfit, she can bring corruption inside the house, and if someone is pure, she can be among society without suffering any damage. The idea of women's vulnerability has played a role here as well.

The third issue is the wife obeying the husband in relation to the place of residence. What is wrong with determining the residence based on the consent of both sides?

The fourth point is the woman's absolute obedience to the man in fulfilling his sexual needs. Absolute obedience is required at all times and in all places unless the woman has an excuse that is accepted by *shari'a*. Without doubt, sexual needs are not limited to men and exist in women as well. What is wrong with fulfilling sexual consent (*tamkin*) in a way that moves from one side to a way that includes both? Marital relations should be reformed from the manner of being a dry legal duty to the consent of both sides. And for women, too, one can go beyond the minimum of sexual relations once every four months so that their rights will be equal to that of men and the absolute one-sided fulfilment can be changed to the conditional consent of both sides.

The fourth issue is that of the rights of mothers in relation to their children. There are at least two rights in the family. One is the rights of guardianship and the other custody. Guardianship refers to who is responsible for children when they are not minors. In this regard, the rights have been given absolutely to the father and paternal grandparent. Even if the father

---

7 A series of weak hadiths attributed to the Prophet.

and paternal grandparent have died, they would have chosen an executor for the will of the father or paternal grandparent and the executor's opinions have precedence over that of the decisions of the mother. Unless a court has ruled that one of the parents is unfit, what would be wrong with having the mother and father have equal guardianship over their children? How is it that when someone goes to the see the Prophet and asks, "who should we respect more?", and he says, "the mother". The person asks a second time, and he says, "the mother". He asks a third time, and he says, "the mother". The fourth time he is asked, he says, "father".[8] Given that the goodness of the mother is so great in the mind and conscience of the Prophet, is a mother not fit to have guardianship over her own children?

Custody refers to keeping a minor (especially if an infant) until they are grown up. They say that in case the mother has not remarried, she has custody of her daughter until the age of seven and custody of her son until age two. After these ages, custody goes to the father. How fair is it to separate a two-year-old boy from his mother? At a minimum, we can say that unless a court rules based on reasons it has accepted that the mother is unfit, both daughter and son should be in the custody of a righteous mother until they reach puberty.

The fifth issue is the punishment of the wife by the husband. It is said that if the wife violates one of the rights that the man has been accorded as the head of the house such as absolute obedience (*tamkin*), then she may be punished. Punishment incudes verbal and bodily punishments. The former is uttering harsh words or insulting the wife. The latter is beating her if admonishing her and leaving her alone in the bedroom did not work in stopping her contumacy. In my opinion both of these rulings were time-bound and restricted to certain conditions that no longer exist today, and after negation of the ruling and the condition of the duty, the permission for verbal and bodily punishments of the wife by the husband is indefensible.

Woman is a human like a man, and if there is a disagreement, then a mediator must be chosen by both sides to act and resolve the conflict and if that does not work, then one cannot continue marital life by force and beating.

The sixth issue is that of separation, the most important of which is divorce. We know that married life begins with the consent of both sides.

---

8 Al-Kulaini, *al-Kafi*, 2:159.

It seems that the necessity for the Qur'anic view of woman is in continuity with the consent of both sides and in cases where there is not, then separation should happen with the consent of both sides as well. The idea that divorce is a unilateral masculine legal act (*iqa'*) that does not require the permission, consent or even informing the wife requires revision. While the process of *khula* (annulment) and *mubarat* could be started by the request of the wife, it takes effect only after payment of the dowry or more to the husband and finally by his acceptance. Thus, even return (*ruju'*) is a masculine act and not a bilateral one. What would be the matter with having the permissible but ill-regarded (*mabghudh*) act of divorce taking place with the consent of both parties, as is the case with entering marriage?

And, lastly, the seventh issue is that of inheritance. A daughter's inheritance is half that of the son. Similarly, in some cases, the inheritance of the wife is half that of the husband, with the difference being that the wife inherits property that is movable and constructed, rather than non-movable property such as land. The ratio of a mother's inheritance as compared with the father is 1:2 and in some cases 1:5. One cannot solve the issue of discrimination in inheritance in all instances with dowry and alimony (*nafaqah*). One instance is the case of women who never marry, and the other is that if this exchange were real, the woman could gain equal access to inheritance by refusing to accept a dowry or alimony. In any case, equality in inheritance is conceivable when both wife and husband participate in providing economically for family expenses. It should be said that the documents on the issue of inheritance are stronger than those pertaining to the issues raised previously, and that change in this area is more difficult.

In any case, it appears that all of these rulings are time-bound, conditional and not permanent. It was due to the problem of our lack of insight that we dealt with these rulings as though they were permanent. Issues that were in accordance with the conventions of the time of the Prophet are distinct from those rulings that are part of the everlasting message of the religion.

Section Two: Women's Criminal Law

The first issue is the blood price of women and men. Is it not the case that men and women both share in the economy of the household? Can one not hold that the blood price of the man and the woman is the same and still be pious? Solutions have been given for issues pertaining to the blood price of Muslims and non-Muslims which is 2/25 (meaning 800 Dirham for the blood price of a man from the People of the Book and 10,000 Dirham for a Muslim man). In these cases, they have reached a conclusion that the state will cover the difference between the blood price of a Muslim and a non-Muslim so that Islamic rules need not be reinterpreted. Can parliament not find a similar arrangement for the blood price of women? A woman is not less than a non-Muslim. The time for glossing over these issues has come to an end and fundamental solutions must be found.

The second point is the difference in the age for criminal responsibility in girls and boys. A fourteen-year-old boy is considered a child but a nine-year-old girl is considered an adult! Is there a direct relationship between physical maturity (and even that is around thirteen years for girls in this society) and criminal responsibility? Can the age for criminal responsibility for both girls and boys not be set at eighteen years old, for example?

The third point is the difference between the testimony of men and women. In many instances the testimony of women is absolutely not accepted, such as in the case of the majority of the *hudud* penal codes, non-financial disputes, divorce and the witnessing of the new crescent moon. In many other instances, too, the independent testimony of women is not accepted and the testimony of several women is required in addition to that of at least one man, for example, in the case of financial disputes, marriage and blood price. In any case, the testimony of two women is equal to one man. It is worth asking whether this discrimination was not specific to the particular conditions of the past? Can we today consider women's testimony to be null in many instances? Can the limits on the testimony of women not be considered among the temporary and conditional rulings of *shari'a*?

The fourth point is about women's judgement. In the second perspective, that is, of women being inferior, women's judgement is absolutely unacceptable. By contrast, in the first perspective, that is, in the humanist view of women, women's right to judge is the same as that of men.

Section Three: Women's Political Rights

In the case of women's political rights, women are exempt (to put it politely) from accepting key positions in society. For example, being a man is a condition for becoming the Supreme Leader in Iran, as well as the president and other positions. (Iran has had women vice-presidents but not ministers.[9] When this was about to occur, the extreme reactions of several religious forums forced the president to stop at the level of deputy minister.) These are all based on views from the past that women do not have the mental and scientific capacity for such roles. Apparently, the story of Queen Sheba has not appeared in the Qur'an (Sura 34). Or perhaps, that story has not reached the ears of some men. This point is referenced in Muhammad Hussain Fadlallah's (1935–2010) interpretation of the story of Queen Sheba in Sura 27.[10] If the Qur'an cites an issue and does not report it in negative terms, that means it has accepted it. Whatever reason we bring up alongside it is rejected. The late Mohammad Mehdi Shamseddin (1936–2001) wrote a book to prove that women are capable of holding political positions. The book *Woman's Capacity for Leadership* (*Ahliyyat al-Mar'a li-Tawalli al-Sultah*) has proven this using religious reasons and has rejected the conventional reasons that have entered religion.[11]

The five religious positions that women are allegedly excluded from holding include political leader and governor, judge, source of emulation (*marja'-i taqlid*), Friday prayer leader and prayer leader in general. A woman can be a *mujtahid* but she cannot be a source of emulation, why? If a woman has the capacity to carry out *ijtihad* why can she not be a source of reference for *shari'a* affairs? Why can female believers not emulate her at least? Which reason that can be defended by rationality and *sha ri'a* can support these issues? It is said that women cannot be general prayer or Friday prayer leaders either (in the case of a general prayer leader if the praying people are men). In the case where the general prayer leader is male and women are praying, we put up a curtain for segregation and no problems arise. What is the problem if the prayer leader is a woman with putting up a curtain in the same manner, or with the leader standing in a deep prayer niche (*mihrab*)?

---

9 Several years after this chapter was first written, Marzieh Vahid-Dastjerdi became the Minister of Health and Medical Education (August 2009–March 2013) during the presidency of Mahmoud Ahmadinejad. She has been the only woman minister in the Islamic Republic of Iran so far.

10 Muhammad Hussain Fadlallah, *Qara'a Jadida li Fiqh al-Mar'ah al-Huquqi* (*New Reading of the Legal Jurisprudence of the Woman*) (Beirut: Dar al-Thaqalain, 1997), 29–31. Fadlallah did not mention these points in his Tafsir. Muhammad Hussain Fadlallah, *Min Wahy-i al-Qur'an* (*From the Revelation of the Qur'an*) (Beirut: Dar al-Milak, 1998) 17:202–212.

11 Mohammad Mehdi Shamseddin. *Ahliyyat al-Mar'a li-Tawalli al-Sultah* (*Woman's Capacity for Leadership*), *Masa'il Harija fi Fiqh al-Mar'a* (Critical Issues in the Jurisprudence of Women series), No. 2 (Beirut: al-Manar, 1995).

Three Conditions for Permanent Shariʿa *Rulings*

If we look at the *shariʿa* rulings themselves rather than in terms of the credibility of those who uttered them, meaning not saying that they are right because God or the Prophet have issued them; if we are able to defend the rulings without reference to the source then that ruling is permanent. (There is only one place where we can accept the fact that something is right because God or the Prophet have issued it and that is in devotional (*taʿabbudi*) rulings pertaining to worship. We do not know why we must fast for one month or pray the way we do other than because God has said so.) But are all rulings devotional rulings? The solution to this problem is to say that in Islamic law, there are two types of rulings: one where they reflect the humanistic view of women as equal to men, such as in economic rulings, meaning if today a woman takes part in commerce, a man has no right to interfere in what is hers; and the rulings that belong to the second view of women, women as inferior to men, such as in criminal law and much of civil law.

But at the time of the Revelation, rulings and laws had to fulfil the three conditions of being reasonable, just and preferable, as compared with other rulings and laws in other schools and cultures in order to be accepted. It was not the case that the rulings were accepted because the Prophet was a good person. Rather, the rulings were accepted in accordance with the conventions of the time. These three characteristics do not hold only for the time of the Revelation. These are the permanent and continuous conditions of the rulings of *shariʿa*. This means that every *shariʿa* ruling that is to remain a part of *sha riʿa* must have these three characteristics. Every ruling from the rulings of *shariʿa* that is such will continue, and each ruling that loses one or some of these characteristics will be the context (*qarina*) for it to have been a temporary and time-bound ruling the credibility of which has expired. But who can claim that a ruling is temporary? Without doubt the scholars of Islam (theologians and jurists) can do so. It is not the case that I can say an order is null until I have accepted it. There must be a scholarly discussion around it. Each of these rulings requires a scholarly discussion so that we can prove if this ruling is unjust, unreasonable and that a superior solution exists as compared with it. All rulings will be permanent unless a reason is given for why they are conditional and temporary.[12]

---

12 I have expanded this discussion in Chapter 5 on "Human Rights and Reformist Islam".

My point in brief was that one can look at the rights of women in contemporary Islam from another point of view as well. We have no reason to
hold that the traditional view is the more religious one. With this view (the
reformist perspective), Islamic faith is strengthened and one can live in the
contemporary world while maintaining permanent aspects of Islam.

Questions and Answers

Question: what is the difference between the approach of human reason in
early Islam and the approach of human reason in the modern age as it relates
to women? What are the bases for being just? Superiority in relation to our past
conventions and historical traditions is being discussed, so what will happen
to us in the future and will we need a new messenger?

Answer: all rulings of *sha ri'a* given during the age of Revelation had to meet
the three conditions of being just, reasonable and superior when compared
with similar rulings in other religions and cultures. These conditions pertain not only to the time of Revelation. Every ruling that meets these three
conditions will remain a ruling of *shari'a*, but if any of these conditions or
all of them are eliminated, then the context will become clear that it was a
temporary and time-bound ruling and not a permanent one.

The Islamic reformist perspective requires that all rulings fulfil the condition of being reasonable, just and more functional than other rulings. It
is clear that a ruling that was made, was reasonable in accordance with the
criteria of the time of Revelation. If there is a problem, it is that the ruling is
not acceptable and reasonable in accordance with the criteria of reasonability
of our time. Traditionalists say that whatever was reasonable in the age of the
Revelation would also be reasonable in this time, indeed forever. One can
find numerous problems with this viewpoint. For example, in the past, slavery was considered both reasonable and just and Islam's approach to it was
preferable compared with other approaches. Indeed, none of the philosophers or thinkers of that time had given an absolute ruling on the abolition
of slavery. But in the current age, this is not the case. In fact, the real work
of the scholars of Islam is that they separate the true message of Islam from
the conventions of the past. If we do not do so, then we will be condemned
to elimination. Plenty of valuable jewels can be found in the original Islamic
texts, and those valuable jewels which are the authentic message of God

and the Prophet are eternal beyond space and time. Those issues that are critiqued about Islam today are not among these and the problems raised pertain to those rulings which were appropriate for the conventions of the time of the Revelation. There is nothing sacred about the conventions of the age of Revelation. Sacredness is unique to the main message of Islam. When some of the contemporary *mujtahids* such as Ayatollah Khomeini said that a *mujtahid* must pay attention to the conventions of his or her time and place in carrying out *ijtihad*, well I am applying this to past *ijtihad*s. Let us suppose that the Prophet wanted to carry out *ijtihad* in his own time, did he have to take into consideration the conditions of his time or not? Was it possible to issue a ruling of *shari'a* without taking into consideration the conditions of that time and place? Was it possible to speak with Arabic speakers in a language and culture other than the language and culture of Arabs? It was not possible. The Prophet spoke in the language and culture of the reasonability of his time. Today, it is we who must separate the stable and permanent rulings of the Prophet from the margins that were the conventions of that time.

Muslim women expect that our theologians and jurists separate the conventions of that time from the eternal message of Islam. *Mujtahids* today deal with the collection of all of these rulings as permanent rulings. Muslim reformists say that all of the rulings that have appeared in the books of *fiqh* are not permanent rulings of Islam and some of them were established in accordance to the conventions of the time of Revelation; and that if the Prophet were to undertake his mission today he would certainly speak in a different way. In our hadith tradition, it is stated that one of the characteristics of a society during the End of Days is that Imam Mahdi will fill the world with justice though it is filled with oppression. Is it not one of the criteria for justice according to contemporary rationality that women and men should be equal? This is something that the humans of yesterday did not understand. The other point is that certainly Imam Mahdi will not bring a new religion. He will interpret the Qur'an and make it understood in a way that people may think that a new book has been sent down. Is it not possible that one of the issues to which Imam Mahdi will pay attention is the importance of justice which is the basis for human rights?

We must understand how traditional thinking works. The main point of its proponents is that humans absolutely cannot understand rulings of *shari'a*. Today, when we bring up such critiques, women say we have understood and find this segment of rulings to be unjust. If many of us found

Islam to be what the official megaphones advertise it to be, we would not accept this religion. We did not accept Islam on account of stoning, lashing and such discriminations. We accepted Islam on the basis of the mercy of the Prophet, the justice of Imam Ali, the insight of Fatimah and the munificence of Zeinab. Today what keeps us in Islam is this eternal message and not the accidentals and the margins that were the conventions of the past.

Question: throughout the history of Islam, many different issues probably entered the religion such as *idhribuhunna* (hit them). According to what you have said, during that time they killed (buried live) infant females,[13] and Islam came and said at least hit them and do not kill them. However, when Moses is spoken about in the Qur'an *idhrib* is used in the sense of leaving rather than killing, why?

Answer: the literal meaning of *dharb* is hitting one thing with another, such as hitting with a hand, cane or sword. In the story of Moses in the Qur'an, it says "We revealed to Moses, 'Go out at night with My servants and strike a dry path for them across the sea. Have no fear of being overtaken and do not be dismayed.'" (Q. 20:77) In general, "*al-dharb fi al-ardh*" means travelling.[14] The conventional understanding of Q. 4:34 (If you fear high-handedness from your wives, remind them [of the teachings of God] then ignore them when you go to bed, then hit them) is compatible with the literal meaning (hitting). Women who become disobedient or discordant require three rulings that in the first degree involves admonishment, second is distance in bed and third is hitting. *Idhribuhunna* here means to hit and not to travel or leave. There is no contextual indication for putting aside the literal meaning and providing a figurative one. The problem that arises in understanding this

---

13 Q. 81:8; 6:151 and 17:31.

14 Seyyed Reza Sadr (1921–1994), the older brother of Seyyed Mousa Sadr (1928 – disappeared in Libya on 31 August 1978), in his Persian treatise *Dar Zindan-e Welayat-e Faqih* (*In the Prison of the Guardian Jurist*) narrated that Mohammad Muhaqiqi Rashti (d. 1968) the representative of Ayatollah S. Hussain Burujerdi (1875–1961) and the Imam of the Shi'ite Mosque in Hamburg, Germany, in his lecture on Islam in a German university interpreted Q. 4:34 in the following way: the exclusive meaning of *dharb* is not to hit. It has other meanings such as travelling, and it was used in the Qur'an in this meaning, and recited the travel verse (Q. 3:156). The Qur'an says: "If you cannot reconcile with your wives, travel and leave them." Sadr did not reject this meaning. I published this treatise with an introduction and annotation in November 2016 on my website.

verse is that in the past jurists deduced based on traditional thinking that one of the cases where punishment does not require going to court is this one. Of course, some thought it was possible that it was necessary to go to court and after receiving an order from the judge, the person to carry it out would be the husband.[15] But this is not prevalent. However, if marks stay on the woman's body as a result of the husband hitting her, then a blood price must be paid to the wife.

However, the other view (the reformist perspective) is that the mere presence of an issue in the Qur'an does not make that ruling eternal. There are many historical verses in the Holy Qur'an, such as the issues about the life of the Prophet, that have appeared in the Qur'an. There is no doubt that these verses are the Word of God and that it has reached us in the exact way in which it was Revealed. The only question is to know which are permanent rulings and which are changing and temporal. Separately it needs to be said that, considering a ruling to be permanent or changing does not damage the authenticity of it being a Qur'anic ruling. If this point is accepted, then we can say that these types of rulings were made in accordance with the time of the Revelation, and as long as those conditions remain so will these types of rulings. The eternal nature of the Qur'an is due to its containing eternal rulings. This does not cancel belief in rulings which are abrogated, temporary, time-bound and historical.

Question: if one ruling changes, then this will prepare the ground for all rulings of *shari'a* to be changed and this will become a trend, therefore should we stand against any kind of change? Also, is it not better to put aside *fiqh* and pursue a rational methodology?

Answer: the principle is the stability of the order unless it is proved with certainty that the ruling is contrary to the principles of justice, reason and superiority as compared with similar solutions. Our discussion is limited to rulings that do not pertain to worship and those rulings which can be

---

15 Zayn al-Din al-Juba'i al-'Amili al-Shahid al-Thani (1506–1558) in *Masalik al-Afham ila Tanqih Sharayi' al-Islam* (*The Routes of Comprehension in the Revision of Sharayi' al-Islam [Paths of Islam by al-Muhaqiq al-Hilli]*) (Qom: Mu'ssasa al-Ma'arif al-Islamiyya, 2005), 8:358, in his long discussion on this ruling mentioned: "Hitting is a punishment and *ta'zir*, and the principle in punishment is to be issued by the judge." He did not himself go in this way in his conclusion.

comprehended with reason. We have not claimed that all rulings can be comprehended, but whenever this comprehension is possible and applying reason leads one to conclude that these rulings are not just, then in that case this ruling will be declared time-bound, temporary and conditional, and as a result the ruling should be cancelled. As long as the jurists express their opinion in these matters before there is a crisis, there will not be a problem. In any case, rulings pertaining to belief are permanent such as the belief in God, the Day of Judgement, the Prophecy, and in rulings pertaining to worship such as prayer, fasting, *hajj* and charity. There are also plenty of permanent rulings among rulings pertaining to morality. In the arena of transactions, too, some rulings, such as those pertaining to marriage and family being made up of a man and woman, are among the permanent aspects of Islam. Not all that we have in religion is old-fashioned, we have plenty of progressive rulings even in relation to women, and even if there are discriminations in terms of inheritance, some of these discriminations can be compensated with dowry and alimony. But in traditional Islam the discriminations in benefit of men are more than the discriminations in benefit of women. What is permanent in religion is its lofty goals, such as human dignity, virtue, piety, justice, etc. As long as rulings move towards fulfilling these lofty aspects, they are credible, and when it is proven with certainty that they are in conflict with justice, they are abrogated. According to Ayatollah Khomeini, all rulings of *shari'a* are a path for establishing justice in society.[16] Thus, the rulings of *shari'a* are a means, not an end in themselves. That is, they show a path in order to reach a goal. If we reach this conclusion, then we must choose other rulings to find a path to reach the lofty goals of religion.

If the issues I have raised are not heeded, then there is fear that Islam will be accused of an inability to deal with contemporary problems. In this important matter, the responsibility of insightful theologians and the *mujtahid*s who understand the current time is serious and without their hurried action, becoming caught up in a crisis will be a certainty. What I have outlined here I discussed at length two years ago in the article "From Traditional Islam to End-oriented Islam".[17]

The *fiqh* pertaining to worship cannot be comprehended with the approach of reason. In matters not pertaining to worship, too, *fiqh* was a

---

16 Khomeini, *Kitab al-Bay'* (*The Book of Selling*), 2:633.
17 Chapter 1, this book.

guide to human action for a number of centuries before the time when the approach of reason was applied to some issues. Today also in a number of cases such as the affairs of the family, *fiqh* and *shari'a* are the guardians of morality and humanity. The approach of reason cannot replace *fiqh*, but it can provide a standard for the refinement and review of rulings not pertaining to worship.

Question: where can one deduce the Qur'anic view when in the verses of the Qur'an there are plenty of narratives and hadith about the second view (women as inferior humans)?

Answer: this discussion contains the generalities of extensive research. In terms of the Qur'an, we have two categories of verses: the Meccan verses and the Medinan verses. The dominant verses reflecting the first view of women are the Meccan verses, meaning the time when the Prophet was in the role of introducing and preaching his religion. The Medinan verses are from a time when rulings appropriate to managing a society were necessary. The Prophet alone was not able to manage society. If God had not come to his aid, he would not have been able to manage the society of that time. Many of the Medina verses are about the management of Medina. Thus, given that they were related to the management of Medina, the conditions of time and place had to be taken into consideration more. This is in contrast to the Meccan verses which are mostly of the first category. The Meccan verses pertain more to the messages of belief, morality and the permanent jewels of religion, while the Medina verses mostly have a legal tincture and for that reason are appropriate to the conditions of time and place of the age of Revelation. Much research has taken place about the differences between the Meccan and Medinan verses.

I have called the first view the Qur'anic view because I believe most of it is the message of Islam. Of course, alongside that, the second view has a small footprint in the Qur'an which is in no way as large as the first view in its permanent message. All of the rulings in the verses of the Qur'an number about five hundred verses, eighty of which are about issues that do not pertain to matters of worship. A small segment of these eighty verses relates to women. Now compare this volume with the number that have been used to introduce the first view. Of course, the message is not that there is no evidence for the second view. In the hadiths, both views are apparent, but in the *fiqhi* hadiths and the ruling verses (*ayat al-ahkam*) that do not pertain to worship, the second view (women as inferior humans) dominates. But the ruling verses do not make the entire Qur'an. When it is asked: "does the Qur'an not belong to all ages?", the answer is affirmative, the Qur'an is the eternal message of our Prophet. But if God wanted to help His Messenger, what path was he to take up other than Revelation? What is wrong with God having used Revelation to counsel him about the administration of Medina? Are the verses about the Badr and Uhud battles not particular to a specific time? Do we not have abrogating and abrogated verses in the Qur'an? A verse that has been abrogated by another is still a verse of the Qur'an. Thus, all of the issues that I have noted here can have a complete scholarly justification. But the Divine message of the Qur'an as a whole is an eternal message, and at the same time there is no contradiction with the inclusion of abrogated and temporal verses.

Question: is your view a novel one, one that none of the scholars of Islam has had over the last thousand years? Has there ever been a consensus view on the violation of the three conditions that a ruling must meet?

Answer: there is precedence for my views in the theological and *fiqh* books that one can refer to. But these problems are new and as a result the solution will be new also. In the last century, these were not issues for Islamic theologians and jurists. These issues pertain to the period after the Constitutional Revolution in Iran. This is besides those issues that traditionally have always been questioned, such the issues of blood price and inheritance.

However, about the three conditions that a ruling must meet: so that chaos does not ensue, the mainstream of scholarly and religious conventions must fulfil these three conditions, and it is the Muslim theologians and *mujtahid*s who must take up this responsibility. But ultimately everything will proceed gradually. Four hundred years ago, the views of Mulla Sadra were so new that even some of his students and his son-in-law did not follow him. It was only 150 years later that philosophers understood what Mulla Sadra was saying. Today, the scholars of the Qom theological seminaries take pride in the fact that their Qur'anic interpretation is based on his transcendental philosophy (*Hikmat Muta'aliyah*). In any case, a scholarly discussion is like water in a desert that will open its own path. Consider what they said about music in Iran thirty to forty years ago and what they say now?[18] So we have to be patient and not take the discussions outside a scholarly path.

Question: in terms of the relation between reason and Revelation, and if reason has precedence over the Book and Traditions, can you please explain why we then do not make reason the rule from the outset?

Answer: wherever reason comprehends, its comprehension is proof (*hujjat*). But it does not comprehend everywhere. That is the difficulty. Reason is an essential proof. We comprehend God with our reason, too. We also comprehend the proof of the Divine proofs, meaning the prophets and the Imams, with our reason. God has sent us two proofs (according to the hadith of Imam Kazim). The innate proof is reason.[19] We also comprehend apparent proofs such as the prophets with our reason. But this reason does not comprehend everything. How is the Hereafter? Whose reason can comprehend this? If God did not give us information via His Prophet, we would not know anything about the Hereafter. The only thing that reason can prove in this case is the necessity of resurrection and nothing else, the rest of the discussion is all via narrative arguments. In addition, all issues cannot be comprehended immediately and at once with human reason. Throughout the centuries and ages, issues have been understood gradually. People have different reasons for comprehension. God cannot only have the elite in mind. God must speak to the average person. If no Prophet had come along, would we still reach the same conclusions as we did with the coming of the Prophet? The saints may reach comprehension. But in every society, there are only a few of these people and the majority of the people require the guidance of prophets in salvation and true safety.

In addition, many of the issues that come up in Islamic texts are guidance on the rulings. These types of ruling are guidance rulings (*ahkam-i irshadi*) and not rulings of the master (*ahkam-i mawlawi*). The latter are rulings made by the Lawmaker (*mawla, shari'*), but the former are to guide us on issues that are possible to address through our reason and with these guidance rulings the ruling of reason is confirmed. If there was no Revelation, then we

---

18 It was forbidden almost absolutely at first, and gradually it has become almost accepted.
19 Al-Kulaini, *al-Kafi*, 1:16, chapter on the virtue of reason, hadith No. 12.

would not know many of the secrets of knowing God. Also, this Revelation is the highest backer of morality. If there was no Revelation, what reason would we have for the guarantee of moral values for ordinary people? If we take away the Hereafter and the Holy Observer, then, as is said: "If there is no God, then everything is permitted."[20] Some think that the only art of religion is in its *fiqh* and, thus, if there is fluctuation up or down in *fiqh*, religion will be lost. But the religion is religion on account of faith in God, the Day of Judgement, morality, worship and righteous actions. These are what have held religion up and, of course, this would not result without Revelation. The radical rationality of the contemporary time says that human reason has the ability to comprehend anything. The Akhbaris and the Ash'arites and some Zahiris say that human reason does not have the ability to understand any of the issues and all orders are rulings beyond rationality (*tawqifi*), and I believe in neither extreme nor shortcoming. Human reason has the ability to comprehend many issues and at the same time in relation to some issues in which their importance is not deniable, Divine Revelation is necessary.

Question: it seems that the two first conditions, that is, being reasonable and just, determine the situation of the third condition (superiority to alternative solutions). All are external to religion and pivot around reason. So why should religious reasonability be the pivot for accepting these conditions? The other question is that many issues are currently self-evident and proven, and reason has no objection to them. For example, the equality of men and women. That you say we have to hide certain things from the frame of religion itself shows that what exists in our *fiqh* does not have answers for the new age. So why should the jurists of *fiqh* be the ones who determine them?

Answer: I will start with the second question. If it is self-evident, is it also self-evident to the traditionalists? Your Lawmaker does not accept this self-evidence and it must be proven to him. Today, citing self-evidence does not suffice in epistemology. You have to make the knowledge public so that others are able to understand the obviousness of the issue.

But as for the first question, this is a very good and appropriate question. All three conditions (and not just two of them) are external to reli-

---

20 This is the message of Fyodor Dostoevsky's *The Brothers Karamazov*.

gion. Thus, being informed about the knowledge of the time and grasping the reason of the time and an expertise in at least one of the human fields of knowledge is a necessary but not sufficient condition. The other necessary condition for those who assess the three noted conditions is mastery in *ijtihad* on *shari'a* rulings, a deep understanding of the rulings of *shari'a* and of Islamic teachings. Assessing whether Islamic rulings meet the three conditions also requires the need to be an expert of reasonable standards as well as an expert in Islamic teachings and *ijtihad*. A lack in either of these two forms of knowledge will prevent the achievement of the desired outcome. There are nuances in Islamic knowledge that remain hidden from those who are not familiar with this knowledge. In addition, knowledge of *ijtihad* in Islam, including *shari'a*, among those who are assessing will result in their findings being accepted among believers and followers of *shari'a*, and they will trust that the principles and criteria of religion and *shari'a* have not been violated in the slightest. In total, one cannot issue a final opinion about an Islamic proposition without Islamic knowledge. Since the non-worship propositions have two dimensions pertaining to reasonability and Revelation, expertise and mastery in the two arenas is necessary and one-dimensional expertise does not relieve us of needing the other.

Epilogue

This chapter is based on one of my first attempts to address the rights of women in Islam, written in 2003, and forms Chapter five of this book. I outlined my new opinions on reformist Islam and women's rights a few months after this, resulting in this chapter. Ten years later, in 2013, I published my second general overview on this subject titled "Revisiting Women's Rights in Islam: 'Egalitarian Justice' in Lieu of 'Meritocratic Justice'".[21] What was initially described as a probability or a possibility in the first step was subsequently clearly actualised and realised in the second step. I walked a straight line.

The criteria for permanent rulings in the first step were three: reasonability, justice and functionality. A few years later I added a fourth criterion:

---

21 Kadivar, "Revisiting Women's Rights in Islam", 213–234. This chapter was originally written in Persian. In addition to English, it has been translated into Arabic (twice), Turkish and Bahasa-Indonesia.

morality. A *shar'i* ruling was moral and ethical according to the conventions of early Islam. It should be considered a permanent *shari'a* ruling as long as all of these four criteria are fulfilled, that is, the ruling is still reasonable, just, moral and more functional than other solutions according to the conventions of contemporary times. Immoral, unjust, unreasonable and less functional solutions as compared with others are the signs of an abrogated ruling. Although it was once considered a *shari'a* ruling, it is no longer. The judge represents the conduct of reasonable people in each era. This means that immoral, unjust, unreasonable or less functional rulings related to women in Islam cannot be accepted as a *shari'a* ruling or an Islamic teaching. This is the requirement of "reason" as the fourth source of *shari'a* in Shi'ite Islam.

11
Women's Rights in the Hereafter: A Qur'anic Theological Study[1]

Will women and men have equal rights in the Hereafter or will gender-based difference or discrimination continue in the mould of desert-based justice (*al-'idala-a-istihqaqiyya*)? Is gender a factor in the rewards and punishments of the eternal life in the Hereafter or do faith and righteous deeds set the eternal path without regard to gender? Does Divine grace apply equally to men and women or do men enjoy more of it because of what they intrinsically deserve? Are heavenly blessings and the material and spiritual pleasures of those who have prospered given equally to men and women, or does heaven have a masculine visage and have its blessings and pleasures been based on the tastes and leanings of men, and women are to follow men in second place in relation to what they receive of God's Grace?

This chapter seeks answers to such questions, and to determine and describe the place and situation of women in the Hereafter from an Islamic point of view and to explain the role of gender in resurrection. But before getting to the main discussion, it is necessary to note several introductory issues.

Introduction

First, why women's rights in the Hereafter? And why not in this world? Have women received their full rights in this world for us to now move

---

1 Mohsen Kadivar, *"Hoquq-e Zanan dar Ākherat: Motale'eye Qor'ani Kalami"* ("Women's Rights in the Hereafter: a Qur'anic Theological Study"), *Modaress-e 'Ulum-e Ensani*, Scholarly Research Journal of the Humanities College of Tarbiat Modares University, Tehran, 41 (spring 2005): 89–110.

to the Hereafter? In general, given that we have all of these problems and dilemmas concerning women's rights in this world, how did we get to a discussion of women in the Hereafter? Given the priorities of addressing critiques of women's rights in this world, is not a focus on such abstract discussions a kind of escape from existing difficulties? Put another way, the necessity to have this discussion itself needs to be outlined. In this regard, the following should be said.

First, women's place and women's rights in the Hereafter are in themselves a subject that can be discussed, and they are an issue for discussion in terms of scholarship and epistemology regardless of its conclusions or practical impact. In looking at the verses and narratives on the Hereafter related to the issue of women, serious problems and ambiguities arise that require solutions or at least require explanation. It was expected that the scholarship of Islamic theology or Qur'anic exegesis would take up this discussion, which for whatever reasons it has not. Providing new questions and issues in the field of women's rights imposes these discussions on the scholarship of Islamic theology or Qur'anic exegesis and makes discussion about them inevitable.

Second, the image of the Hereafter that is presented in every religion and sect has a direct relationship to the desired values of that religion or sect in this world. One can easily assess the this-worldly criteria and standards via an investigation and analysis of the desired situation in the Hereafter. If "this world is the field of Hereafter",[2] then by studying its results and productions one can learn about the ways of this field. If there is a religion that holds a second degree, subordinate and dispensable position for women in the Hereafter, then it is natural that that religion would recommend a subordinate position in the shadows for women in this world too. In fact, the situation of women in the Hereafter is a good guide for assessing women's place in this world.

Third, a critical analysis of women's rights in Islam, or put another way, women's rights in this world in Islam, and the reform of Islamic thinking

---

2 Prophetic hadith, Abu Hamid Muhammad ibn Muhammad al-Ghazali, *Ihya' 'Ulum al-Din* (*The Revival of the Religious Sciences*), ed. 'Abdul Rahim b. Hussain al-Hafiz al-'Iraqi (Dar al-Kutub al-'Arabi, n/a), 11:173; Muhammad Ali b. Ibrahim Ibn Abi Jumhuar al-Ahsa'i, *'Awali al-la'ali al-'Aziziyya fi al-Ahadith al-Diniyya* (*The Elevated Noble Pearls of Religious Reports*), ed. Mujtaba al-'Araqi (Qom: the editor, 1983), 1:267, No. 66.

about the time-bound and changing orders that are related to past conventions requires a safe and healthy environment. In addition, such debates require introductory arrangements and the acceptance of its principles and bases without acceptance of which the discussion will lead nowhere. The discussion of "women in the Hereafter" has been written to this end.

Second, the domain of the discussion is women in the Hereafter from an Islamic perspective focused on the point of view of the Qur'an, although the teachings of Tradition (Sunna) have not been ignored. The way of the discussion is *a posteriori* not *a priori*. Meaning instead of saying that women in the Hereafter ought to be such and such and have such and such a place, we have said that studying the verses shows that women will have such a place. In other words, we have reflected on the provisions of the verses and the hows and whys, and have tried to find the Qur'anic answers. As it was, these kinds of questions were not really an issue for exegetes of the Qur'an so they have not discussed them and have been silent. A look at the literature on women's studies shows that the topic of "women in the Hereafter" is a new one and until now has rarely been the subject of attention or research. This also adds to the difficulty of the issue.

Third, gender may have a role in the Hereafter in two ways. First, gender in this world can play a role in the rewards and punishments of the Hereafter, without gender being at issue in the Hereafter. At this stage, the impact of gender on spiritual resurrection can be debated. The question in this section is whether gender in this world or being a woman in this world has an impact on spiritual resurrection and reward and punishments in the Hereafter.

Second is the role of gender in life in the Hereafter in the sense of gender differences in bodily resurrection. Meaning, regardless of the legal differences between men and women in this world, will women and men in the other world have different rights and prerogatives, or will gender not play a role in enjoying material rights and prerogatives? It is clear that first, without a belief in bodily resurrection and the realisation of the human body during Judgement Day, this discussion is not possible; and, second, this discussion is separate from the first one. This is because in the first discussion the issue is the role of gender in this world in the rewards and punishments of the Hereafter without there being a material body for women and men during Judgement Day, and in the second the issue is the role of gender in the Hereafter, meaning the differences between the rights and prerogatives of women and men on Judgement Day without consideration of gender in this world.

On this basis, we will carry out the discussion in two sections. The first section will investigate the role of gender in this world on life in the Hereafter, and the second section will investigate the role of gender in the Hereafter in terms of rewards and consequences. While the first has been taken up by some exegetes of the Qur'an, the second discussion is novel and new. Given the difficulties of the discussion, I welcome critique and feedback on its shortcomings.

Section One: Investigation of the Role of Gender in this World on Life in the Hereafter

A precise examination of the verses of the Qur'an shows that the certain and unchangeable criteria for reward and punishments is "faith and righteous deeds", and that gender does not play the slightest role in this regard. Neither is being a man a condition for entering Heaven, nor does being a woman prevent one from becoming heavenly. Being male or not being female does not even have the smallest priority in reaching happiness in the Hereafter. To put it in more precise language, in terms of reaching eternal happiness, justice in the sense of absolute equality rules over Islamic thought. There is not the slightest difference between women and men in terms of the possibilities for happiness and spiritual resurrection. The current criterion and general standard is "goodness of deed and goodness of the agent". The meaning of goodness of deed is righteous deed (*al-'ama al-salih*), and the meaning of goodness of the agent is faith and belief in God and the Hereafter.

In this regard, I have chosen seven verses that explicitly and transparently prove the equality of men and women in life in the Hereafter and the absence of a role for gender in Judgement. First, let us review these seven verses:

Anyone, male or female, who does good deeds and is a believer, will enter Paradise and will not be wronged by as much as the dip in a date stone. (Q. 4:124)

Whoever does evil will be repaid with its like; whoever does good and believes, be it a man or a woman, will enter Paradise and be provided for without measure. (Q. 40:40)

God has promised the believers, both men and women, Gardens graced with flowing streams where they will remain; good, peaceful homes in Gardens of lasting bliss; and – greatest of all – God's good pleasure. That is the supreme triumph. (Q. 9:72)

To whoever, male or female, does good deeds and has faith, We shall give a good life and reward them according to the best of their actions. (Q. 16:97)

So as to admit believing men and women into Gardens graced with flowing streams, there to remain, absolving their bad deeds – a great triumph in God's eyes – and to torment the hypocritical and idolatrous men and women who harbour evil thoughts about God – it is they who will be encircled by evil! – who carry the burden of God's anger, whom God has rejected and for whom He has prepared Hell, an evil destination! (Q. 48:5–6)

On the Day when you [Prophet] see the believers, both men and women, with their light streaming out ahead of them and to their right, [they will be told], "The good news for you today is that there are Gardens graced with flowing streams where you will stay: that is truly the supreme triumph!" On the same Day, the hypocrites, both men and women, will say to the believers, "Wait for us! Let us have some of your light!" They will be told, "Go back and look for a light." A wall with a door will be erected between them: inside it lies mercy, outside lies torment. (Q. 57:12–13)

For men and women who are devoted to God – believing men and women, obedient men and women, truthful men and women, steadfast men and women, humble men and women, charitable men and women, fasting men and women, chaste men and women, men and women who remember God often – God has prepared forgiveness and a rich reward. (Q. 33:35)

The conclusions derived from the seven verses are as follows:

1. The punishment for an abominable deed is not more than it, but the reward for a good deed is more than it.
2. The condition for attaining the Hereafter in addition to good deeds is faith, faith in God and in the Judgement Day.
3. The accounting of people's deeds will take place justly and no one will suffer even the slightest wrong.
4. God forgives the bad deeds (*sayyi'at*) and minor sins of believers.

5. There is no difference between men and women in entering Heaven, the countless provisions, the obtaining of God's good pleasure (*ridwan min Allah*) which is greater than His Heaven, a good life (*hayat tayibah*), forgiveness of bad deeds (*sayyi'at*) and minor sins, benefiting from the Divine Light in the darkness of the Judgement Day, and Divine forgiveness and rich reward (*maghfira wa ajr*).

6. There is no difference between hypocritical men and women and polytheistic men and women in what they will face in suffering, Divine anger, and Hell.

7. In the rewards and punishments of the Hereafter, there is egalitarian justice in the sense of absolute equality between men and women, and gender in this world does not have the least impact on resurrection. Women and men are considered alike from the exact perspective of faith and righteous deeds. They are subject to mercy and pardon and forgiveness in the same way. They are subject to suffering in the same way, and benefit from attainment and happiness, light and Heaven, good pleasure and the good life in the same way. In general, it seems that in this arena there is no gender at work. It is humans who are assessed regardless of gender in terms of the rewards and punishment they will face in the Hereafter. There is not the slightest indication of gender discrimination on Judgement Day and there is justice in the sense of absolute gender equality.

Section Two: Investigating the Role of Gender in the Hereafter in Relation to Rewards and Consequences

If resurrection was limited to spiritual resurrection, and bodily resurrection was not in the picture, then gender in the Hereafter would not be an issue. This discussion is based on the acceptance and belief of bodily resurrection. Maleness and femaleness are characteristics of the physical human body, while the human soul is neither male nor female, especially after death when a physical body is lacking. Examining the verses of the Qur'an shows there is no discussion of gender or gender difference in the sphere of rewards, punishments and Hell, while in the area of rewards and Heaven there are many verses. Thus, an investigation of gender in the Hereafter is exclusive to the arena of benefiting from rewards. Gender in the hereafter can be examined in relation to two issues: one is the continuation in the Hereafter of gender as it is in this world, meaning that humans will manifest in the moulds of men and women in the Hereafter; and the other is the existence of Heavenly creatures that will be available in Heaven as rewards to the residents of Heaven whose gender plays a main factor in the role they play. Given the differences in the discussion of these two cases, we too will discuss them separately below.

First Topic: The Continuation of Gender in the Hereafter as It Is in this World

Regarding this subject, there are three categories of verses worth noting.

First Category: The Elimination of Family Relations and Kinship in Resurrection

This category of verses depicts the resurrection of people on Judgement Day, the horrors of that Day, and the stages before accounting is taken. At these times, family relations and kinship come undone. The difficulty and hardship of the events of that Day are such that one flees from one's brother, mother, father, spouse and children (Q. 80:33–37), mothers will abandon their infants and pregnant women will give birth and flee from their newborns (Q. 22:1–2). On that day the criminal is ready to sacrifice his or her children, spouse, brothers, family and all people so that he or she escapes from suffering (Q. 70:7–18). Finally, this verse provides a general principle about this: "On that Day when the Trumpet is blown, the ties between them will be as nothing and they will not ask about each other" (Q. 23:101). While this category of verses discusses gender and its continuity in the Hereafter, there is no sign of gender-based discrimination and difference. In the horrors of resurrection, women and men alike run after their destiny and no one, neither man nor woman, is safe from the panic of that Day and no one has special privilege.

Second Category: The Continuity of the Marriage of the Righteous in Heaven

The family relations of the righteous can continue in Heaven. If the members of a family have all been successful in faith and righteous deeds and have come out of the accounting for the Hereafter with their heads held high, they will enter Heaven together. A husband and wife who have been pious and who have followed the conditions of God's servants will also in Heaven have the success of continuing as a couple if they wish to do so and can enjoy the blessings of Heaven alongside each other for eternity.

In this regard, several verses are worth noting:

> They will enter perpetual Gardens, along with their righteous ances-tors, spouses, and descendants; the angels will go in to them from every gate. (Q. 13:23)
>
> Enter Paradise, you and your spouses: you will be filled with joy. Dishes and goblets of gold will be passed around them with all that their souls desire and their eyes delight in. There you will remain eternally.[3] (Q. 43:70–71)

Another verse (Q. 84:9) also depicts the return of the Companions of the Right (*ashab al-yamin*) to their families while smiling and happy after their easy assessment.

Reflecting on these verses, especially the second one, shows that: first, the meaning of spouses in both cases is the righteous earthly wives of the righ-teous husbands and not heavenly beautiful women (*hur'in*). This is because *hur'in* do not enter Heaven but are its correlations. Second, in addition to their simulations of entering Heaven, they speak of the companionship of the righteous couple in Heaven as continuing their worldly union. Third, given the context "with all that their souls desire and their eyes delight in" (Q. 43:71), the inclination of the woman and man towards continuing their companionship and union will be a criterion of action and not forced continuity of coupledom.

> The people of Paradise today are happily occupied – they and their spouses – seated on couches in the shade. There they have fruit and whatever they ask for. (Q. 36:55–57)

There are two possibilities concerning the meaning of the spouses of the people of Heaven in this verse: one is the righteous spouses of believers in

---

3 "Eternally" has been added to the translation taken from Abdel Haleem, *The Qur'an, A New Translation.*

this world whose companionship has continued in Heaven. Based on this possibility, they will be placed in this (first) position. The other possibility is heavenly beautiful women (*hur'in*), especially as it pertains to believers who had either not married in this world or whose spouses had not succeeded in entering Heaven. Based on this reading, the verse will be placed in the second position.

The fourth verse: in the three verses of the Qur'an (2:25, 4:57 and 3:15), the phrase "They will have pure spouses there" has been noted as the blessings of the righteous believers. There is the possibility in these types of verse that the pure spouses are the same spouses that the believers had in this world who have now in the Hereafter gained multiple material and spiritual purifications. However, the appearance (*zuhur*) of this phrase is in relation to the *hur'in* who have not entered Heaven from this world and are considered among Heaven's residents. Thus, it is likely that these types of verse pertain to the second position.

In any case, this category of verses also does not show any difference or discrimination between men and women, and the continuation of companionship in the Hereafter as it is in this world is based on the inclination of men and women, and with complete legal equality.

Third Category: The Availability of Whatever the Heart Desires in Heaven

Men and women believers who showed piety in this world and restrained themselves in the face of their own abominable desires and gave precedence to the Divine criteria over these worldly pleasures will enjoy a special privilege in Heaven. Whatever they want, desire, will or wish will be provided for them. There they will enjoy every pleasure in its highest form and without limitation. This applies to both spiritual pleasures such as approaching closeness to the Lord and God's good pleasure and material pleasures such as food, drink and sex (*ma'kulat, mashrubat wa mankuhat*). Whatever is willed and the soul wants is absolute (*itlaq*) in two aspects, one is who desires, meaning the requester and heavenly self, whether man or woman, and the other is what is desired, meaning the heavenly requested. Of course, it is clear that those who have reached this high level will not desire anything other than what God approves and in general with the availability of various permissible pleasures there is no need to desire anything forbidden. In any case, it is clear that this Heavenly privilege is not restricted to men and certainly applies to women as well.

The verses in this category can be divided into three groups.

The first group is about the availability of whatever they ask for: "Whatever they ask for [is ready]" (Q. 36:57 and 41:31).

The second group is about the availability of what they wish for: "They will enter perpetual Gardens graced with flowing streams. There they will have everything they wish. This is the way God rewards the righteous" (Q. 16:31). The phrase "for them whatever they wish" is also repeated in Q. 40:16. In Q. 39:34 and 42:22, this point is made with the phrase "They will have everything they wish for with their Lord." And, finally, in Sura 50:35, "They will have all that they wish for there, and We have more for them." This means, not only will We give them whatever they want but also We will provide them even with what they have not asked for.

The third category: whatever they desire: "And endlessly they will enjoy everything their souls desire" (Q. 21:102), "Where you will have everything you desire and ask for" (Q. 41:31), and "with all that their souls desire and their eyes delight in" (Q. 43:71).

Three phrases "whatever they ask for, whatever they wish, and what their souls desire and their eyes delight in" are absolute (*itlaq*) and certainly include material pleasures, especially the last phrase which appears as material pleasures, with one of the obvious particulars of material pleasures being sexual pleasures. In addition to this use, the three phrases from the other aspect are also absolute and men and women who have achieved attainment are included in both. The masculine pronoun or relative pronoun cannot be used to claim that these are peculiar to men. For it to be particular to men, it would have to be explicit. This is prevalent in all Qur'anic discussions. These verses express this reality that those who act according to the will of God in this world, God will act according to their will in the Hereafter, and in this regard there is no difference between men and women. This is an overall principle that tolerates no gendered difference or discrimination.

In any case, three categories of verses about the first position of the continuation of gender in the Hereafter as it is in this world, including the elimination of family relations and kinship in the resurrection, the continuation of the union of righteous people in Heaven, and finally the availability in Heaven of all that their souls desire, show complete gender equality with not the slightest difference or discrimination between men and women.

Second Topic: Heavenly Creatures as Companions to Those who Have Entered Heaven

In addition to righteous men and women who have entered Heaven, the Qur'an bears the news of two types of Heavenly creatures that will be companions in the service of those who enter Heaven: one is the Heavenly women who are perfect in beauty and completeness, and the other is Heavenly adolescent boys who are servants and servers in Heaven. We will therefore continue the discussion accordingly in relation to these two creatures.

First Type: Heavenly Women

The Qur'an has spoken about them at length and has counted their qualities of beauty and completeness. Sometimes they have been cited in relation to the phrase "pure spouses" (Q. 2:25, 3:15 and 4:57). Pure couples are spoken about, pure from any defect whether on the outside or inside.

Sometimes the phrase "We shall wed them to maidens with large, dark eyes" is used (Q. 44:54 and 52:20). The word *hur* is the plural of *haura'*, meaning a woman with intensely white and deep black eyes, with round eye sockets and thin eyelids.[4] The word *'in* is the plural of *'ayna'*, meaning a woman with large eyes. *Hur'in* in total alludes to a beautiful Heavenly woman. In the Qur'an, the verb for wedding is always transitive without a preposition, except in the case of marriage to the *hur'in* where it is used with a preposition (*ba'*). That is to say, contrary to the case of other marriages, "*zowwajnahum hura*" is not used. This indicates their difference from conventional marriage as it is known in this world.[5]

In Sura 55, a few other characteristics of Heavenly women have been provided in two groups of verses. First, "There will be maidens restraining their glances, untouched beforehand by man or jinn. Which, then, of your Lord's blessing do you both deny? Like rubies and brilliant pearls" (Q. 55:56–58).

Second, "There are good-natured, beautiful maidens. Which, then, of your Lord's blessings do you both deny? Dark-eyed, sheltered in pavilions. Which,

---

4 Ibn al-Manzur, Muhammad b. Mukarram, *Lisan al'Arab* (*The Tongue of Arabs*) (Beirut: Dar Sader, 1955), 2:219.

5 Al-Raghib al-Isfahani, *Mufradat alfaz al-Qur'an*, 385.

then, of your Lord's blessings do you both deny? Untouched beforehand by man or jinn" (Q. 55:70–74). Phrases such as "maidens restraining their glances" and "sheltered in pavilions" indicate that they confined themselves to their husbands, and their ultimate chastity and decency. The phrase "untouched beforehand by man or jinn" indicates their virginity. "Good-natured" indicates their spiritual completeness and "beautiful maidens" indicates their physical beauty. The comparison with rubies and brilliant pearls indicates their brilliance, attractiveness and high value.

Sura 56 also describes other qualities of these Heavenly women. First, "and beautiful companions, like hidden pearls: a reward for what they used to do" (Q. 56:22–24). Second, "with incomparable companions. We have specially created – virginal, loving, of matching age – for those on the Right" (Q. 56:34–38). Like the *hur'in*, being protected like pearls is an indication of their value and chastity. The high place is an indication of their spiritual completeness and physical beauty. God relates the creation of *hur'in* to Himself and removes the curtain from the difference in the creation of Heavenly women and earthly women. Earthly humans are the creations of God but from the loins of the father and the womb of the mother, but *hur'in* are the direct or primary (*ibda'i*) creation of God. Virginity is their continual characteristic not their primitive one, after every instance of intercourse they are virgins again. They love their spouses and all are of the same age, in the beginning of youth.

The characteristic of "nubile, well-matched companions" (Q. 78:33) indicates their youth. The phrase about being the same age is repeated in Q. 38:52. And, finally, it recalls them as such, "With them will be spouses – modest of gaze and beautiful of eye – like protected eggs" (Q. 37:48–49).

Of the collection of sixteen characteristics that the Qur'an has outlined for Heavenly women, and has sometimes repeated, one can gather that: (1) Heavenly women are distinguished from earthly women in how they are created; (2) they are the ultimate in completeness, high status and chastity; (3) they are the limit of beauty; (4) they are in their early youth; (5) virginity is their continuous characteristic; and (6) they are considered God's reward to righteous believing men.

Second Type: Heavenly Adolescent Boys

In explaining the moods of the Heavenly in the Qur'an, the terms *ghilman* and *wildan* come up three times. They are adolescent boys who serve those who have been admitted to Heaven, like cupbearers at a glorious party. First, "devoted youths like hidden pearls circulate around them" (Q. 52:24). Second, "everlasting youths will go round among them with glasses, flagons, and cups of a pure drink" (Q. 56:17–18). Third, "everlasting youths will circulate around them – if you could see them, you would think they were scattered pearls" (Q. 76:19).

Ghilman is the plural of *ghulam* and *wildan* is the plural of *walad* in the sense of adolescent boys who have the duty of being servants, and in particular to be cupbearers for those men who have been admitted to Heaven. They are beautiful and eternally stay the same age and are continually servants. They have no duties except serving the men who are the companions of the Heavenly women, and have no duty as independent servants of the women who are admitted to Heaven. There is no documentation that these youths have a distinct creation like that of the *hur'in*. Rather, certain narratives introduce them as the children of some people of the Earth.[6]

Based on this, *hur'in*, *ghilman* and *wildan* are the rewards of men who have been admitted to Heaven.

Examination and Reflection

Now we can reflect on the Heavenly companions of those who have been admitted to Heaven. It is clear that the weight of the discussion is focused on the first topic (Heavenly women).

While the three verses stating "and they will have with them their pure spouses" held the possibility that these pure spouses were the same righteous spouses of righteous men on Earth, the other verses on Heavenly women were explicit in their differences with earthly women.

In any case, on this issue the Qur'an describes how men who have been admitted to Heaven enjoy the blessing of the *hur'in*. Now the equivalent of such a situation for women who have been admitted to Heaven has not been depicted. That is to say, there is not the smallest indication of the existence of Heavenly men as a reward for righteous women. Put another way, the tone of the Qur'an in this regard is masculine. It addresses masculine desires and inclinations, and to encourage them makes promises of sexual pleasures by

---

6 Al-Tabrisi, *Majma' al-Bayan*, 9:277, two narrations from the Prophet and Imam 'Ali.

pointing to several of its dimensions in Heaven. In the initial view regarding this issue – in contrast to the previous topics where there was absolute gender equality between women and men – we find a kind of sexual discrimination: addressing men's desires and ignoring women's desires.

This is so much so that some have claimed that "the intended audience and goal of Heaven is for men and that for women nothing is a goal other than her body and her presence is linked to male lust. Heaven is condemned as dominated by the language of men and their lusty inclinations and women have a marginal presence, whether in this world or the Hereafter."[7]

In researching the views of past and contemporary scholars, at least four answers can be given in response to the problem of gender discrimination in the Hereafter, although some of these points were not directly provided in response to the above question or problem.

First Response

The problem arises from the term *hur'in*. *Hur'in* does not refer to beautiful Heavenly women, and in general the Qur'an does not promise something like this to righteous men: "The correct meaning of *hur'in* is 'white grapes' and not women with large, dark eyes. Based on this, the phrase '*rawwah-nā-hum bi hur'in*' ['We will let them rest with white grapes'] has mistakenly been recited as '*zawwag-nā-hum bi hur'in*' ['We shall wed them to maidens with large, dark eyes'] with the addition of two dots [on *rā'* and *hā'*]" (44:54 and 52:20).[8] The corroboration that *hur'in* means white grapes is the book *Hymns on Paradise* by St Ephrem the Syrian (306–373), which was written three centuries before Islam in Syriac and describes Heaven and its blessings. Many of these characteristics and blessings of Heaven have an unbelievable similarity to the Qur'anic Heaven, the only difference being that instead of women with large, dark eyes the blessing of white grapes is noted.[9] Two

---

7 Ibrahim Mahmoud, *al-Jins fi al-Qur'an* (Gender in the Qur'an) (Beirut: Riad el-Rayyes Books, 1998), 154.

8 Christoph Luxenberg, *The Syro-Aramaic Reading of the Koran: A Contribution to the Decoding of the Language of the Koran* (Amherst, NY: Prometheus, 2007), 247–283.

9 St Ephrem, *Hymns on Paradise*, Introduction and trans. Sebastian Brock (New York: St Vladimir Seminary Press, 1998). I first learned about Luxenberg's opinion in the review of his book in this article: Morteza Kariminia, "The Impact of Aramaic and Syriac Languages on the Language of the Qur'an", *Nashr-e Danesh Quarterly*, 20(4) (winter 2004): 45–56.

possibilities have been put forward for the change in meaning of *hur'in* from grapes to Heavenly women: one is that the phrases used in Ephrem's work to describe Heavenly grapes were the source of the meaning of *hur'in* in the Qur'an).[10] The other is that the phrase *hur'in* entered the Qur'an from the Syriac language and texts, and until the time that the Qur'an was Revealed the meaning was white grapes, but later in the history of exegesis and hadith a new meaning was imposed on it.[11] With this approach, the problem of gender discrimination in the Hereafter is completely solved.

Critique of the First Response

This response has serious problems.

First, the problem is not limited to the term's exegesis and so the issue of gender discrimination cannot be fundamentally resolved with proving the changes in the term's meaning. The description of the exegesis includes many characteristics of women (such as nubile, well-matched companions, being the same age, virginal, good-natured, beautiful maidens, sheltered in pavilions, untouched beforehand by man or jinn) which occur in numerous verses and can in no way be related to "grapes".

Second, the mere similarity of other Qur'anic characteristics to what is cited in St Ephrem's book does not prove that in cases where the two are not similar, the latter book has borrowed material from the first. These parallels show the great similarity, indeed, the unity, of the Christian Heaven and the Islamic Heaven.

Third, changes in the meaning of words do not happen instantly. How can one accept that before the Revelation of the Qur'an everyone understood *hur'in* to mean white grapes and that suddenly all the scholars of Islam and all Muslims mistakenly or with ill-will started to understand *hur'in* to mean Heavenly women? This extravagant claim lacks the necessary documentation and is nothing other than a baseless and unscholarly claim.[12]

---

10 E. Beck, "Eine Christliche Parallel zu den Paradiesjungfrauen des Korans", *Orientalia christiana periodica* 14 (1948): 398–405; Maher Jarrar, *"Houris"*, in J. D. McAuliffe (ed.), *Encyclopaedia of the Qur'an* (Leiden: Brill, 2002), 2:456.

11 Luxenberg, *Syro-Aramaic Reading of the Koran*, 247–283.

12 François de Blois, Review of *Die syro-aramäische Lesart des Koran: Ein Beitrag zur Entschlüsselung der Koransprache* ('Christoph Luxenberg', 2000, Berlin: Das Arabische Buch), *Journal of Qur'anic Studies* 5(1) (2003): 92–97. (Persian translation: Morteza, *Naqdi bar qara'at-e Arami Seryani-e Qur'an neweshte-ye François de Blois, Tarjuman-e Wahi*, bi-annual, 7(2) (February 2003): 120–128.

Second Response

Heavenly blessings are for all righteous believers, whether women or men, and the *hur'in* are among these blessings. The *hur'in* are partners of the believers, meaning every man and woman believer in Heaven will have a Heavenly spouse of the opposite sex with whom they will be intimate and enjoy themselves. The fact that *hur'in* has been misunderstood to be Heavenly women is due to the fact that Revelation occurred in a patriarchal society and had to be uttered in the language and culture of the people. It is clear that language, culture and historical adventures necessarily affect Revelation, and no prophet has spoken other than in the language of his community (Q. 14:4), otherwise, it is of the definite teachings of the Qur'an that humans have been created with the Divine spirit (Q. 15:29 and 38:72), and this Divine spirit is not limited to men. The gender difference between men and women is a material and this-worldly difference, and there is no trace of it left after death. The human body becomes dust after death and with the departure of the spirit from the body, it is neither masculine nor feminine, after which the spirit with a special form – whose details we do not know – will enter Heaven. There, God will create for it another form called the *hur'in*. For the men these are Heavenly women and for women, Heavenly men. The species name (*ism jins*) of this Heavenly creature created for the righteous person is *hur'in*.[13]

Critique of the Second Response

This response, which is an explicit and direct answer to the problem of gender discrimination in the Hereafter, is based on two theological and literary premises, both of which are incomplete.

The theological premise: it is clear that a righteous person is rewarded regardless of gender. However, one cannot provide rational proof for the claim that the righteous believer gains a new feminine or masculine body and its documentation is in the form of narrative proof. There is no narrative evidence, and especially no Qur'anic evidence, for there being Heavenly spouses for righteous believing women (like there are *hur'in* for righteous believing men).

---

13 Ahmed al-Gubbanchi, *al-Mar'a, al-Mafahim, wa al-Huquq: Qara't Jadida li Qadaya al-Mar'a fi al-Khitab al-Dini (Woman, Concepts, and Rights: A New Reading of Women's Issues in Religious Discourse)* (Beirut: Mu'assisa al-Intishar al-'Arabi, 2009), 54–55.

This premise, more than being *a posteriori* and arising from Qur'anic verses, is *a priori* and based on a particular philosophical hypothesis, which, while being desirable and defensible, is not provable from a Qur'anic perspective, or at least is not so in the existing Islamic literature, and thus remains on the level of a claim without proof.

The literary premise: the use of *hur'in* as Heavenly creatures by both men and women as the reward in the Hereafter for believing men and women is first lacking any evidence, because from the lexical perspective it is neither masculine nor does it apply to a shared characteristic of women and men, but exactly outlines the characteristics of women. Second, evidence contradicts it since all of the numerous characteristics that have been outlined (such as nubile, well-matched companions, being the same age, virginal, good-natured, beautiful maidens, sheltered in pavilions, untouched beforehand by man or jinn, like rubies and brilliant pearls, maidens restraining their glances, incomparable [female] companions, etc.) are all characteristics of women and in no way can be applied to men.

The above-noted justification is similar to an interpretation (*ta'wil*). While this interpretation about the spouse (pure marriage) of the righteous human including both men and women is acceptable, it certainly is not acceptable in regard to the *hur'in* and does not solve the problem.

Third Response

The term *hur'in* is evidence of the attractiveness of women as it suited the taste of Arabs during the time before Islam as well as at the time of the Revelation. It is highly unlikely that the Qur'an would express the dimensions of beauty (standards) on a worldwide scale for all women in all ages and lands. The expression of the Qur'an in this regard was according to the taste of an audience of a specific time. The term *hur'in* only comes up in the Meccan verses and is not even used once in the Medinan ones. The Meccan verses belong to the era when the audience for the Qur'an was limited to the Arabs in the Hijaz, while the Medinan verses belong to a time when the audience for the message of the Qur'an had greatly increased and was not limited to Arabs but included diverse audiences. In the Medinan verses, "*azwaj mutahhara*" (pure spouses) has been used instead of *hur'in*. The term *azwaj* means spouses, whether male or female. This means there is a pure man for the righteous woman believer and a pure woman for the righteous male believer in the Hereafter. In addition, and contrary to the understanding of most elegists, the plurality of *azwaj* in the phrase "*azwaj mutahhara*" (pure spouses) is not about polygamy in the Hereafter, but plurality as it applies to that of the believers. That is to say, for righteous believing humans, pure spouses will be available (for each righteous human, whether man or woman, there is one pure spouse, not more). It is clear that "*azwaj mutahhara*" is not the equivalent of *hur'in*, especially given that the *azwaj mutahhara* can be the same spouses from this world who have been admitted to Heaven, and not necessarily Heavenly-created women.[14]

Critique of the Third Response

Like the previous responses, this one is an explicit and direct response to the problem of sexual discrimination in the Hereafter. It is the first response from a woman to this problem and includes some defensible aspects. But at the same time, it also contains controversial aspects.

First, while it is true that the compound word *hur'in* has not been used in the Medinan verses and all three of its uses are in the Meccan verses (Q. 44:54; 52:20, 56:22), the fourth use appears without '*in* "dark-eyed, sheltered in pavilions" (Q. 55:72). While there are narratives on Sura 55 being among the Meccan verses, the more accurate narrative notes it as being a Medinan sura. This is because weak narratives and argumentations cannot resist those narratives on the agreed order of Revelation.[15] The al-Rahman sura is the 97th sura in terms of the order of Revelation. In addition, although the phrase *azwaj mutahhara* was used in the Medinan verses (Q. 2:25, 3:15, 4:57), the two following verses are in the Meccan suras,[16] and include both *azwajukum* and *azwajuhum*: "Enter Paradise, you and your spouses: you will be filled with joy" (Q. 43:70). "They and their spouses – seated on couches in the shade" (Q. 36:56). Without doubt, these spouses are also pure, though the adjective of being "pure" does not appear in the two verses. Thus, neither are the *hur* exclusive to the Meccan verses nor has the term *azwaj* only been used restrictively in the Medinan verses.

---

14 Amina Wadud, *Quran and Women: Reading the Sacred Text from a Woman's Perspective* (Oxford: Oxford University Press, 1999), 54–57.

15 Ma'rifat, al-*Tamhid fi 'Ulum al-Qur'an*, 1:151, 181–182.

16 Ibid., 1:173, 177.

Second, supposing that the *hur* or *hur'in* were only used in the Meccan verses and *azwaj* or *azwaj mutahhara* were only used in the Medinan verses, the problem would still not be solved, because if the Meccan verses on *hur'in* were not abrogated by the Medinan verses on *azwaj mutahhara*, and have indicative credibility in terms of the status of the credibility of the verses of the second category, then *hur'in* would be the specifier (*khass*) and *azwaj mutahhara* (based on the unity of the meaning) would be general (*'amm*), and the general would be specified (*takhsis*) by the specifier. Neither is a Meccan verse evidence of the temporality of the meaning (*madlul*) of that verse, nor is a Medinan one evidence for the permanence of the meaning (*madlul*) of the ruling. The view of some contemporaries is even completely opposite to that of Amina Wadud:[17] that is to say, some hold that the Meccan verses have the status of expressing the universal and timeless message of Islam and that the Medinan verses were time-bound verses revealed to aid in the establishment of government in Medina.[18] In any case, accepting that *hur'in* is the manifestation of women as they would have been attractive to Arabs during the time of the Revelation instead of being attractive in general is to accept verses in the Qur'an with a temporary meaning which were ultimately abrogated in the Qur'an (but an abrogation that is different from conventional abrogation in the Qur'an and the Sunna).

Fourth Response

This response is taken from mystical and philosophical principles.
From the viewpoint of the philosophers:

in terms of the *hur'in*, once the insightful view of the firm believer is opened by the kohl of success (*tawfiq*) and one becomes able to examine the mighty dominion (*malakut*) of two realms (*kawn*) as Abraham [did], "In this way, We showed Abraham [God's] mighty dominion over the heavens and the earth, so that he might be a firm believer" (Q. 6:75); he will observe the entrants of the presence of Glory (*'izzat*) who appear behind the curtain of the hidden (*ghaib*)

---

17 Wadud, *Quran and Women*, 54–57
18 Mahmud Muhammad Taha, *al-Risala al-Thaniya min al-Islam* (Sudan: n.p., 1969), 129–161, trans. An-Na'im *The Second Message of Islam*.

and manifest themselves in one speck of the specks of the creatures via the light of manifestation (*tajalli*); and inevitably each of them will represent themselves symbolically (*tamaththul*) in the best form of the creatures' forms, such as that which occurred in the story of Mary, "We sent Our Spirit to appear before her in the form of a perfected man" (Q. 19:17).

Since the enjoyment of that observation has not been formed other than through emanation of the effect of the world of unity – which requires the marriage of the essence and form together, in a way that leads to unification – so this marriage occurs with each of those forms that would be in place of one of the Heavenly *Huri*, "We shall wed them to maidens with large, dark eyes" (Q. 44:54, 52:20).

Since the faces of those who are behind the curtains are safe from the view of strangers and the people of contradiction: "Dark-eyed, sheltered in pavilions" (Q. 55:72); and according to its order the interpolation (*wasl*) of the strangers (non-*mahram* or *ghair al-mahram*) of the realm of multiplicity is impossible, including those people who have remained in the appearance of the terrestrial (*mulk*) world, and those people who are prevented from the interior of the mighty dominion (*malakut*), "untouched beforehand by man or *jinn*" (Q. 55:56 and 74); and since return to that situation each time affects the pleasure more than the first time, such as a lost love who is found again after suffering their loss – the virginity and celibacy of those pleasures will renew each time.[19]

From the viewpoint of the mystics:

Physical Heaven is the perceptual forms which rely on the imaginary soul. These perceptual forms are a reflection of what the soul is inclined towards and enjoys, and have no origin or manifestation other than the soul, and there is no agent or close originator [of those perceptual forms] except the soul . . . All that is in Heaven including trees, rivers, buildings, booths, all are alive in an inherent life, a life that is identical to the life of the soul that perceives and originates

19 Nasir al-din al-Tusi, *Aghaz wa Anjam* (*Start and Finish*), ed. and annotated Hasan Hasanzadeh Amoli (Tehran: Wizarat Farhang wa Irshad Islami, [1987] 2008), 69–70.

them. Perception of these forms is exactly their origination, since perception and origination are identical.[20]

In Heaven, the deed of the believer is exactly the divine action and his or her will (*mashiyyat*) is exactly the divine will . . . This is because whomever reaches the station of consent (*rida*) and servanthood ('*ubudiyya*), does not want anything other than what God wants.[21]

These are the teachings of Ibn 'Arabi.[22]

More clarification from transcendent philosophy:

hur'in means the illuminative spiritual entities (*dhawat nafsaniya nuriyya*) under intellectual supervision . . . because the relation of the soul to the intellect which perfects it via emanation (*ifadah*) and aspiration (*tashwiq*), is the relation of Eve to Adam . . . Rewards such as: couches (*surur*), [male] youths (*wildan*), a cup of a pure drink (*ka's min ma'in*), fruit, the meat of a bird, and *hur'in* are the rewards of deeds not of science and knowledge, because science and knowledge have no ends other than themselves, meaning union with the Sublime Realm (*mala' a'la*)[23] and to be adjacent to the Truth, observation of the mighty dominion (*malakut*), and the constant attention to His Mighty Face.

We have two heavens: the sensible heaven and the rational one . . . The sensible heaven is for the Companions of the Right (*ashab al-yamin*) and the rational one is for those who will be brought nearer to God (*muqarrabin*), meaning those of highest rankings ('*illiyun*).[24]

What those in Heaven desire will be provided for them . . . These are on several degrees: some are blessed with the glorifying (*tasbih*) God, sanctification (*taqdis*), and magnify (*takbir*) Him, and some are

20 Mulla Sadra, *al-Hikmat al-Muta'aliya fi al-Asfar al-'Aqliyya al-Arba'a*, 9:342.
21 Ibid., 9:343.
22 Muhyi al-Din Muhammad ibn 'Ali Ibn-'Arabi, *al-Futuhat al-Makkiyya* (*The Meccan Illuminations*), ed. Ahmad Shams al-Din (Beirut: Dar al-Kutub al-'Ilmiyya, 1999), chs 65 and 381, 1:478–486 and 6:305–313.
23 Muhammad b. Ibrahim al-Qawami Sadr al-din al-Shirazi (Mulla Sadra), *Tafsir al-Qur'an al-Karim* (*The Exegsis of the Noble Qur'an*), ed. Muhammad Khajawi (Qom: Bidar Publications, 1991), 7:39 and 44.
24 Mulla Sadra, *al-Hikmat al-Muta'aliya fi al-Asfar al-'Aqliyya al-'Arba'a*, 9:321–322.

about the sensible beneficences such as a variety of foods, drinks, soft chairs (*ara'ik*), marriage to the *hur'in*, the employment of everlasting youths (*wildan mukhalladun*) . . . There everyone enjoys to the extent of his or her ambition.[25]

The emergence (*nash'a*) of the Hereafter is an emergence between incorporeal intellectual beings and material corporeal beings. The tangible forms of that world considered to be an imaginary form in this world.[26]

The heaven of deeds and their blessings is tangible without any doubt, but although it is tangible, it is not of material nature. Its forms are forms in perception, whose objective existence (*al-wujud al-'ayni*) is just as their tangibleness . . . The emergence of Heaven (*nash'a al-jinan*) is the emergence of the souls.[27]

This spiritual–philosophical view can be summarised in simplified language below:

1. The righteous human will obtain the power in the Heavenly Hereafter to create what he or she desires.
2. This creation occurs via the imaginary faculty of the human soul.
3. Righteous humans are of two ranks: those righteous humans who will be brought closer to God (*muqarrabin*) have no request other than that of the spiritual and the sanctified. The Companions of the Right (*ashab al-yamin*) request tangible things such as food, drink, and sex.
4. The *hur'in* are the desire of the Companions of the Right, not those righteous who will be brought nearer to God (*muqarrabin*).
5. While corporeal requests are tangible, they are not material, they are a form of symbolic representation (*tamaththul*), and the constructions of the imaginary faculty. Based on the fact that carnal desire originates in the imaginary faculty, there is without a doubt no difference between men and women, both are able to have carnal desires. While those who will be brought nearer to God (*muqarrabin*) do not request anything other than the spiritual state of Nearness to Truth (*maqa qurb al-haqq*),

---

25 Ibid., 9:319–320.
26 Ibid., 9:335.
27 Ibid., 9:382.

the companions of the Right who have not joined that high state are pleased with corporeal requests and each request the opposite sex. The men request *hur'in* and the women request Heavenly spouses, and both take complete enjoyment from their imagination. While this imaginary creature is tangible, it is not material. It has an imaginary (*mithali*) form just as the symbolic representation (*tamaththul*) of Mary in the form of Gabriel.

Critique of the Fourth Response

In regard to the fourth response, the following points are worth noting:

First, on the bases of the noted philosophical and mystical foundations, any kind of gender discrimination in the Hereafter is eliminated and justice in the sense of absolute equality rules. In this regard, this response is a successful one. While the expressions of the philosophers and mystics are masculine, this formal problem is easily solvable.

Second, the references to *hur'in* as they appear in the Qur'an are such that, on the one hand, the majority of its audience in all eras ultimately have no end other than to be the companions of the Right, and those who will be brought nearer to God (*muqarrabin*) are in the absolute minority. On the other hand, at the time of the Revelation, in the majority of audiences male concerns were dominant and the requests of women were never explicitly considered and were addressed in accordance to male requests. In addition, the Book too has been Revealed in the language of the community of that time, but this does not mean that women do not enjoy a similar blessing, it is just that this blessing has not been explicitly explained in detail. Of course, it is clear that this esoteric response does not eliminate the exoteric problem of the Qur'an, and theologians and jurists consider it to be a kind of justification (*ta'wil*) and exoteric meaning (*zahir*), and reliance on the imaginary faculty as violation of the bodily resurrection criteria. A critical review of this controversy requires a separate article.

Further Reflection

Apart from the four responses above as to why the Divine Book has not addressed feminine blessings in Heaven, the following could be noted:

First, the shyness and chastity of women stand in the way of expressing these issues. Women do not like these issues to be spoken about.

Second, at the time of Revelation and the centuries thereafter, in various societies and cultures, patriarchy dominated and women's requests were never expressed independently and separately, and were always expressed in accordance to the requests and in the shadow of men. In these circumstances, it was natural that they speak of men's inclinations and desires in the Hereafter and ignore the desires and inclinations of women. The discussion of women's rights and their situation and demands is new and one cannot expect for them to have discussed this at the time of the Revelation. Having such expectations is to ignore the geography of what was spoken.

Critiques

However, the first argument is not satisfactory. As the Qur'an says: "God does not shrink from the truth" (Q. 33:53); looking at the details of the discussions in the Qur'an shows that God has spoken about many issues at length, even if they were not conventional issues to speak about. If sexual pleasure is a right for the Heavenly righteous people, one can point out that it is for men and women implicitly, and when it has been noted for men, it would have been possible to note it – in the same etiquette (*adab*) of the Qur'an – for women as well. Thus, this argumentation is not convincing.

The second argument is acceptable at first sight, but it requires accepting that at least some of the Qur'anic verses are time-bound and that they do not provide solutions in other circumstances and times. Not describing women's demands in the Hereafter like those of men was unproblematic during the time of the Revelation, but today this causes problems. The Qur'an's descriptions of Heaven are much more attractive to men than to women. If God's good pleasure (*ridwan*), state of Nearness to Truth and spiritual blessings are much more important than the banal material, corporeal and sexual pleasures, then in this regard there is no difference between men and women. Those who move forward devotionally (*muta'bbid*) in the arena of knowledge and beliefs, which is the arena of reasoning, do not have a problem. But for those who follow the Qur'an's invitation of reasoning and use the blessing of their God-given intellect to permit themselves to ask questions and speculate, the following question easily arises: why did the Book of God only speak in the taste of the humans of yesterday and only speak of the details of men's desires in the Hereafter, and not consider the demands of today regarding the equality of men and women in describing the details of the Hereafter? To say that the Wisdom of the Divine Will is hidden to us, will not convince the questioning person. To say this means that the theological claim on eternal inimitability was not at work at least in these segment verses. The critical analysis of this pretension requires a separate opportunity and article.

What will eliminate the problem in reality is a universal and general Qur'anic principle that has been noted before at length "*ma tashtahi al-anfus, ma yasha'un, ma yadda'un*" (everything their souls desire, whatever they wish, and whatever they ask for) is absolute (*mutlaq*) and is not particular to men and certainly includes women, and women who are admitted to Heaven enjoy all of the Divine blessings, including the blessing of the best spouse, and in this regard men and women enjoy the same rights. However, in fairness one must accept that in terms of the detailing, only men's demands are noted and women's demands in Heaven are not noted in the least. Put another way, there is equality as a general principle, but there are differences in the expression of the details and the explanations in the Qur'anic verses, with men's blessings noted, and silence in the realm of women's blessings.

Conclusion

Women in the Hereafter have equal and similar rights to men in all areas. This includes the conditions of attainment, the accounting of deeds, facing suffering, wrath and Hell, reaching Heaven, countless provisions, reaching God's good pleasure (*ridwan*) which is greater than his Paradise, the good life (*hayat tayibah*), forgiveness for one's minor sins, meeting the Divine Light in the darkness of resurrection, Divine Forgiveness and Reward, the elimination of family relations and kin on the Day of Judgement, continuing coupledom of the righteous couples in Heaven, and finally the availability of everything their souls desire in Heaven. In these cases, there is complete gender equality and there is not the least difference or discrimination between men and women.

Despite the complete equality of men and women in the general principle of the "availability of everything their souls desire in Heaven", this is one issue of which the details and explanations have been addressed only in terms of men's blessings and with no discussion of blessings specific to women in the Hereafter.

Section Five
Other Debates in Human Rights

12

The Issue of Slavery in Contemporary Islam[1]

The Necessity of the Discussion

The movement to abolish slavery began in the mid-nineteenth century and slavery – in the traditional sense – was uprooted to such an extent that today in public opinion and according to conventions of reasonable people (*bana' al-'uqala'*), slavery is something detestable, blameworthy (*qabih*), oppressive and unreasonable. Rejection of slavery (in all its senses, including its traditional and new forms) is among the essential principles of human rights. In one sense, no slaves exist for there to be a debate about its rulings other than from a historical perspective. However, for three reasons, it is necessary to examine and discuss the issue of slavery in contemporary Islam.

First, numerous verses in the Qur'an point to male and female slaves. In the tradition of the Prophet and the lives of the Imams, there are many discussions related to slaves. The question is how can a religion that claims to be the final one (*khatam*), that provides permanent exemplars (*uswah*), and a Book with an eternal calling, support something that is so blameworthy and unjust (at least in accordance with contemporary conventions)? What should we do with these verses and narrations?

Second, some contemporary Muslim scholars, including philosophers, jurists, exegetes and scholars of hadith explicitly defend the slavery noted in

---

1 Kadivar, "Mas'ale-ye Bardedari dar Eslam-e Mo'aser", *Aftab* 25 (May 2003): 80–89.

Islamic texts and consider it a matter of consensus consistent with the ruling of reason (*hukm al-'aql*). For example:

> In Islam, administrations and managements have considered the elimination of the system of slavery, but this does not mean that slavery is absolutely condemned in Islam. If in a legal (*mashru'*) war, Muslims defeat disbelievers and take them as captives (*asir*), the captured disbeliever under control of the victorious Muslims is recognised as a slave, and the rules of slavery apply to him or her. Today, too, if such a war occurs, the ruling is the same. It is not the case that slavery is completely eliminated and that the Chapter of Emancipation (*kitab al-'itq*) should be done away with. Of course, slavery in those days was based on racial discrimination. Black people and other vulnerable people would be trapped and sold. But if the matter is between killing the defeated enemy or capturing him, which is more humane? If the captured enemy is freed, he will start the same sedition again. If they kill him, the continuation of life and the path to return is closed. But if he is taken as a slave, then eventually he will be disciplined in *Dar al-Islam* (territory of Islam) and will become a worthy human. In any case, the issue of slavery has in itself been generally accepted in Islam and we defend it.[2]

This view is in complete contradiction with the principles of human rights. A critical analysis of these opinions is not a discussion for yesterday, but for today.

Third, the majority of Muslim countries, including Iran, have accepted all international conventions and protocols for abolishing slavery and have undertaken a pledge to uproot all instances of slavery. Reflecting on the religious teachings about slavery and responding to the scholars who defend it is one of the requirements of strengthening the foundations of human rights in Islamic societies.

---

2 Mohammad Taqi Mesbah Yazdi, *"Asl-e Azadi dar Eslam"* ("The Principle of Freedom in Islam"), *Ettelaat Daily*, Tehran, 2 October 1993, 20020:11. For more information about his viewpoints, see *Negai Gozhara be Hoquq-e Bashar az Didgah-e Eslam* (*Human Rights in Islam: A Brief Perspective*), ed. 'Abdulhakim Salimi (Qom: Mu'assisah 'Amuzeshi Pejuheshi Imam Khomeini, 2013), ch. 7 on slavery, 161–176.

The time for speaking in generalities and exorbitant claims about the compatibility of religion with human rights has come to an end. Today, we have no choice but to submit to scrupulous retroactive study of religious rulings in relation to the articles of human rights and to determine transparently and clearly the position of believers in relation to these types of modern challenges. Rest assured that circumventing issues, silence, stalling and buying time will not solve the problem.

Other than the inherent and essential benefits of having a discussion about slavery in contemporary Islam, it also has an accompanying benefit. This case study will provide a good benchmark for evaluating the capacity of contemporary Islamic thought, especially Islamic jurisprudence. The responses to this issue are not limited to this subject and can be applied to other challenging issues in contemporary Islam. The value of this accompanying benefit is no less than the main benefit. Failure even in this single problem is problematic and endangers all Islamic thought.

At this time, we are not at all concerned with discussing "slavery in Islam". It is not that difficult to explain slavery in the context of a time when some types of slavery were prevalent and accepted by the conventions of reasonable people. Our discussion is about the dilemma of slavery in contemporary Islam, that is, specifically in the last century (from the early twentieth century onwards), in an era when the conventions of reasonability consider slavery to be absolutely unjust and inhumane.

On the other hand, the meaning of slave and a subjugated person is broader than before. In workers' rights, children's rights and women's rights many issues come from those pertaining to slavery. Many of the categories belonging to neo-slavery were not considered as such a century ago. The subject of this chapter is that which Islamic thought considers a male slave (*'abd*) or female slave (*amah*) or people as property (*mamluk*), rather than all that would be considered slavery in the legal conventions of today. Until we agree on the definition of traditional slavery (which is very close to the notion of slavery that is noted in Islamic texts), we will not be able to have a fruitful discussion on neo-slavery (at least not in the framework of Islamic thought).

While the views of various Islamic schools (*madhahib*) are close to one another on the major points of the discussion on slavery, I have focused on the Shi'ite viewpoint for a number of reasons: one is to get into more depth on the issue, and the other, is that monographs on this issue have mainly been written from the Sunni point of view,[3] although there have been a few independent studies from the Shi'ite perspective. Third, a critical analysis of the defence of slavery in our time and society is considered pressing.

This chapter is made up of three sections. The first section is an outline of the rulings of slavery in contemporary Islam, meaning a description of the views of those who defend slavery. The second section is devoted to comparing these rulings with human rights documents. Finally, the last section provides a critical analysis of two completely conflicting viewpoints about slavery in contemporary Islam.

Given the grave paucity of case studies on this subject, I hope that this small step towards solving the problem will be helpful and will not be deprived of criticism and feedback from experts.

Section One: Rulings of Slavery

The Arabic terms *riqq, raqbah, mamluk, mamlukah, mawla, 'abd* and *qmah* are synonyms for the terms slaves, historical serf, vassal, thrall, archaic bondsman and bondswoman, as well as being antonyms for the Arabic terms *hurr* and *hurrah* (freeman or freewoman, and master). The meaning of slave is a human who is considered the property of another human and over whom the owner has full or partial rights of ownership.

The fundamental principle in this issue is the principle of freedom (*asl al-hurriyya*) or the negation of being owned (*'adam al-mamlukiyya*). As such, freedom is in accordance with the fundamental principle and does not require evidence. What requires evidence and proof is slavery.[4] All people are free, unless the contrary is proven.

Humans are divided in various ways. Gender, religion, sect (*madhab*), age of maturity (*rushd*), ignorance and knowledge are some of the criteria for these divisions. The sixth division of people is that between freedom and

---

3 For example, Ahmad Shafiq, *al-Riqq fi al-Islam* (*Slavery in Islam*), trans. from French to Arabic Ahmad Zaki (Maktabah al-Nafidha, 2010); Wahbah al-Zuhayli, *Athar al-Harb fi Fiqh al-Islami* (Damascus: Dar al-Fikr, 1998).

4 al-Sayyid Muhammad Jawad al-Husaini al-'Amili, *Miftah al-Karamah fi Sharh-i Qawaid al-'Allamah [ah-Hilli]* (*The Key of Dignity in the Commentary of Qawaid al-Ahkam [The Principles of Rulings] of al-'Allamah al-Hilli*), ed. Muhammad Baqir al-Khalisi (Qom: Mu'assah al-Nashr al-Islami, 2000), 17:601; al-Najafi, *Jawahir al-Kalam*, 24:136; Habib Allah al-Sharif al-Kashani, *Tashil al-Masalik ila al-Madarik fi Ru'us al-Qawa'id al-Fiqhiyyah* (Qom: al-'Imiyyah, 1983) 7.

slavery. Humans are either *hurr* and *hurrah* (freeman and freewoman) or *'abd* and *amah* (male and female slave). Like other divisions, this division reflects differences in rights and duties in accordance with *shari'a*.

Many contemporary scholars have been silent on the rulings of slavery in their work. However, within their works there are a number of points related to slavery that can be extracted. Some have also spoken explicitly about this matter. I have extracted the collection of rulings on slavery from the explicit opinions of scholars and will outline them in three sections: the causes of enslavement, the rights and rulings of slaves and, finally, the causes of emancipation.

Subsection One: Causes of Enslavement

Based on the principle of freedom (*asalah al-hurriyyah*), enslavement requires a credible *shari'a* cause. In total, there are seven *shari'a* causes given for enslavement. If any one of these occurs, then a person becomes the property of another, and he or she will be denied the rights of a free person and assume the duties of a slave.

Cause One: Capture in War

All those who are captured by Muslims in a war between Muslims and non-Muslims are considered slaves and property (*mamluk*) according to *shari'a*. Men who are captured by Muslims after the end of a war are subject to three rulings: (1) freedom without compensation; (2) freedom in exchange for ransom (*fidyah*) or in exchange for a captured Muslim; and (3) enslavement. The Muslim ruler decides in this matter, and in the case of choosing enslavement or receiving monetary compensation, they are considered as the spoils of war (*ghanimah*).

Women and children of the conquered lands are considered as the spoils of war, and are enslaved as soon as they are dominated by conquering Muslims. From all of the moveable spoils (including people and physical things), first, the ruler separates the king's fiefs (*qatayi' al-muluuk*), the best and most valuable property (*safaya al-amwal*) and what he – as per his absolute authority – considers to be appropriate, and considers them as war booty (*fay'*) for the Imam. After removing one-fifth (*khums*) from this as tax, what remains is distributed amongst the *mujahidin* or the soldiers who were present on the battlefield. This is such that each soldier will become the owner of some portion of the spoils, including male and female slaves. The main condition for enslavement in this case is the disbelieving status of the captured, including obstinate disbelievers (*kafir harbi*) or People of the Book, as long as they are not People of Treaty (*mu'ahad*), those who entered Islamic territory under a safe-conduct (*mus'taman*) and those who are loyal to the protection treaty (*dhimma*). Thus, Muslims cannot become slaves in this way. But if those who are captured convert to Islam after being captured, this conversion does not lead to the elimination of their slavery and he or she remains a slave.[5]

The ruling of slavery is not limited to those present in the battlefield or to the military, but to all residents of the territory of war (*dar al-harb*), including the military and civilians, women and men, and children and the elderly who have come under Muslim domination. All are subject to the aforementioned ruling.

Capture leading to slavery is the absolute result of wars between Muslims and non-Muslims and is not limited to offensive *jihad* (*al-jihad al-ibtida'i*) or defensive *jihad*. It is not even conditional on the presence of the Prophet, the Imam, or on their permission. It is only the case that during the time of the presence of Imams, if *jihad* was carried out without their permission (when it was possible to obtain permission), the spoils would belong to the Imam. In any case, during the time of the occultation, due to caution, taking the spoils of all of the wars between Muslims and non-Muslims, even if it is with the aim of conquering countries and taking spoils, is permitted after the deduction of *khums* (one-fifth tax).[6]

War has been the biggest cause of enslavement, and most slaves were obtained in this way. In this regard, the following points are noteworthy: first, slavery via war is not limited to the military and those present on the battlefield, and all residents of the territory of war (*dar al-harb*) who are under Muslim domination are subject to it.

---

5 Al-Najafi, *Jawahir al-Kalam*, 21:120–128; al-Khu'i, *Minhaj al-Salihin*, 1:373 and 379–380.

6 Al-Yazdi, *al-'Urwah al-Wuthqa*, 4:231–232; Ayatollah Ruhollah Khomeini, *Tahrir al-Wasilah*, 1:370; al-Sayyid Abu al-Qasim al-Musawi al-Khu'i, *Mustanad al-'Urwah al-Wuthqa (Documents of the al-'Urwah al-Wuthqa [The Firmest Hand-Hold by al-Sayyid Muhammad Kazim al-Tabataba'i al-Yazdi]), Kitab al-Khums*, written by Murtada al-Burujirdi (Qom: Mu'assah al-Khu'i al-Islamiyya, 2009), 16. It is clear that the required *khums* on a property is the evidence of permission (*ibahah*) for using that property and the legitimacy of the ownership of the property whose *khums* has been paid.

Second, about four-fifths of slaves acquired through war become the personal property of soldiers and more than one-fifth are at the disposal of the ruler and the appointee of the Imam. Put another way, the majority of slaves become the property of individuals and not the property of the government and state.

Third, men captured in war become slaves on the authority of the ruler, and after the end of the war not a single member of the enemy remains captive.

Fourth, slavery is not limited to *jihad* and legitimate war. The spoils of wars that have taken place outside the criteria of *shari'a*, including men, women and children who have been captured, are no different than spoils of *jihad* or the spoils of war in accordance to *shari'a*, as long as their *khums* has been deducted. This is especially the case during the time of the Imam's occultation.

Contrary to the opinions of some great contemporary scholars,[7] war is not the only legitimate way in Islam to acquire slaves. In *shar'i* texts we find a number of other ways through which slaves can be acquired.

Cause Two: Slavery through Overpowering (*tagallub*)

If anyone from the territory of war (*dar al-harb*), whether they reside there or not, are kidnapped (by theft, treachery, deceit, plunder, captivity and force) by civilians, or (without using force, and generally without war) by the military, and brought to the territory of Islam (*dar al-Islam*), then they are considered to be the spoils of war, and after deduction of one-fifth tax (*khums*), they become the property of the kidnappers. It is permitted for the kidnappers to use their property how they like, and selling and buying them is permissible. Even if these people are kidnapped by non-Muslims, it is permitted for Muslims to buy them from disbelieving kidnappers, even if they know that these people have been kidnapped by force or theft and have become the property of the disbelievers outside war.[8]

---

7 Tabataba'i, *al-Mizan fi Tafsir al-Qur'an*, 6:345.
8 Al-Muhaqqiq al-Hilli, *Sharayi' al-Islam, kitab al-tijarat*, ch. 9: the purchase of the animal, section 3, No. 7), 2:59; al-Najafi, *Jawahir al-Kalam*, 24:229; al-Yazdi, *al-'Urwah al-Wuthqa* (*Kitab al-Khums*, ch. 1, No. 1), 4:233; al-Khu'i, *Minhaj al-Salihin* (*kitab al-tijara*, ch. 13: the purchase of animals), 2:66.

The permissibility of taking slaves outside war is indicated by numerous hadiths.[9] The condition for taking slaves in this cause is just like the first cause, that is, that the kidnapped person should be non-Muslim at the beginning of their slavery. What is noteworthy about this cause is that although using means such as stealing and deception are against *shari'a*, forbidden and *haram*, the domain of these rulings (*haram*) is restricted to the respected property (*al-amwal al-muhtaramah*), and are not absolute. Since the obstinate disbeliever (*kafir harbi*) is devoid of any *shari'a* respect, thus rescuing them in any way is correct and permitted, and from the perspective of *shari'a*, the prohibitions on theft, deception, etc. do not apply. Indeed, transferring them to the territory of Islam (*dar al-Islam*) could be a source of insight and guidance for them. It is clear that slavery via overpowering and force would more often befall women and children.

Cause Three: Slavery through Purchase from Guardians

If obstinate disbelievers (*kuffar harbi*) are for whatever reason ready to sell female members of their family, such as their wives, sisters or daughters, it is permitted to purchase them and after the sale they become the female slaves of the purchaser. This is because obstinate disbelievers (*kuffar harbi*) are the *fay*[10] of Muslims and rescuing them in any way is permitted. In other words, ownership comes from the domination of a Muslim over the disbeliever and not from a purchase transaction, because it is clear that such a purchase is void. In this way, based on consensus and hadith, the sale of those misguided people taken as captives from the obstinate disbelievers (*kuffar harbi*) is permitted and the implications of a valid purchase apply. Although the property obtained from the second and third causes either belong to the Imam, or are at least subject to *khums*, during the period of occultation the Shi'ite were given the exception of having the opportunity to have female slaves.[11]

---

9 Al-Khu'i, *Minhaj al-Salihin*, 1:374.
10 *Fay'* literally means return, and taking as booty, and in *fiqh* means the property that the Muslims take from the obstinate disbelievers (*kuffar harbi*) without war.
11 Al-Najafi, *Jawahir al-Kalam*, 287.

Cause Four: Transmission of Slavery from Parents to Children

If a father and mother become slaves through legitimate means, all of their children who are born to them during their times as slaves, will also be slaves. Therefore, slavery transmits from parents to their children. The parents' conversion to Islam while enslaved does not prevent transmission of slavery from the parent to their children. The children of slaves represent growth (*nama'*) of the property and belong to the slave owner.[12] However, if one of the parents is free, the child is also free. Thus, it is not the case that all humans are born free, but that some are born from their mothers as a slave (congenital slave).

Cause Five: Slavery through Confession

If a mature person of sound mind freely confesses to be a slave, it will be accepted. This is on condition that the person is not commonly known to be free and that his or her lineage is not legally clear (*shari'a*).[13] In this regard there is no difference between Muslim and non-Muslim and man and woman. It is not even important whether the person's motivation for confessing to be a slave is poverty or something else.

Cause Six: Slavery of Foundlings (*laqit*) in the Territory of Disbelief (*dar al-kufr*)

If a child without guardians is found in the territory of disbelief (*dar al-kufr*) and they were not potentially born to Muslim or *dhimmi* parents, then it is permitted to enslave that child.[14] However, if protecting such a child is dependent on taking him or her under guardianship, then such an effort will count as collective obligation (*al-wajib al-kifa'i*).

Cause Seven: Purchase from the Market of Non-Muslims

If a person has become enslaved through whatever means other than the six previously mentioned ones and is put up for sale in the market of non-Muslims, it is legal and permissible for a Muslim to buy him or her and they are not required to ask how the person was enslaved. Even if the purchaser knows that

---

12 Ibid., 24:136; al-Khu'i, *Minhaj al-Salihin*, 2:66 and 313.
13 Al-Najafi, *Jawahir al-Kalam*, 24:150; al-Khu'i, *Minhaj al-Salihin*, 3:67 and 313.
14 Al-Khu'i, *Minhaj al-Salihin*, 2:136.

the person was enslaved by means other than war, force, theft or sale by husband, father or brother, the purchase is permissible and use of the slave is legal (*mashru'*). In general, when purchasing slaves from the marketplace of non-Muslims, it is not necessary to enquire about the permissibility of the cause by which they were enslaved. Even if the purchaser is certain that the cause was not among the accepted causes according to *shari'a*, they are permitted to purchase and make use of the slaves. Similarly, if the slave is a Muslim but is not able to provide clear evidence or witnesses (*bayyinah*) for his or her freedom, he or she will be subject to the aforementioned cause of slavery. According to this cause, Muslims are permitted to make use of and legitimately own slaves throughout the world, no matter the cause through which they became enslaved. Unlike the six previous causes, this cause does not create slaves, it provides the permission for transferring slaves to the marketplace of Muslims (*suq al-Muslimin*) and the territory of Islam (*dar al-Islam*), where there is a ruling for creating slaves in accordance with *shari'a*.

Reflections

The following points are worth mentioning about these seven causes for slavery: first, all of the causes had precedents in other societies, cultures and religions, and Islam was not the creator or innovator of any of the above-noted causes.[15] Thus, the rulings of slavery do not count among the ratified rulings (*al-ahkam al-imda'i*) of Islam, but are all among the positive rulings (*al-ahkam al-ta'sisi*) of *shari'a*.

Second, none of the above causes are exclusive to one particular denomination (*madhab*) of Islam, but some Islamic denominations that were in political power over numerous centuries have more widespread experience of and discussions about slavery as compared with the Shi'a.[16]

---

15 On slavery in other societies, see Ahmad Shafiq's *al-Riqq fi al-Islam*, 9–27. On slavery among Arabs before Islam, see Jawad 'Ali, *al-Mufassal fi Tarikh al-'Arab qabl al-Islam*, 5:486–487. On slavery in Jewish scripture, see *Tanakh: A New Translation of The Holy Scriptures According to the Traditional Hebrew Text* (Philadelphia, PA: Jewish Publication Society of America, 1985), Exodus 21:2–11 and 22:2, Leviticus 25:39–46, Numbers 31:26–27, Deuteronomy 20:10–11. On slavery in Christian scripture, see M. Jack Suggs et al. (eds), *The Oxford Study Bible: Revised English Bible with the Apocrypha* (Oxford: Oxford University Press, 1992), Ephesians 6:5–8, Colossians 3:22–25, Timothy 6:1, Titus 2:9–10, Peter 2:18 and Philemon 1:1–25.

16 For example, al-Mawardi, *al-Ahkam al-Sultaniyya*, 207–211; 'Abduallah b. Ahmad Ibn al-Qudamah al-Maqdisi, *al-Mughni* (*The Persuader*), ed. 'Abdullah b. 'Abdul Muhsin al-Turki and 'Abdul Fattah Muhammad al-Hulw (Riyadh: Dar 'Alam al-Kutub, 1997), 13:47–52.

Third, the evidence for the seven causes are the Tradition and cited narrations of the Prophet, Imams and the consensus of jurists. None of the causes for slavery are based on Qur'anic evidence. That is to say, the Qur'an has not negated or affirmed any of these causes of slavery, although it has addressed captivity (*isarat*) of war, on the one hand, and the rights and rulings of slaves, on the other hand, and has particularly addressed at length the causes of their emancipation. It is clear that there is a difference between being a prisoner of war and slavery.

Fourth, the causes of slavery would not have been actualised if Muslims never attained a dominant position. That is to say, when Muslims are not considered to be the superpower or regional power in international political transactions, their ability to have access to these causes is accordingly weakened or completely diminished. In such situations, what happens practically is the principle of reciprocity (*muqabala bi al-mithl*). Enslavement of non-Muslims can be followed by enslavement of Muslims.

Subsection Two: Rights and Rulings of Slaves

The rights of slaves refer to the slavemaster's or owner's responsibilities to the slave, and the rulings (*ahkam*) of slaves refer to those responsibilities that slaves are compelled to carry out for their owners.

First: The Rights of Slaves

First, the owner must provide provisions (*nafaqah*) for the slave. The costs of food, clothing and the slave's shelter are paid by the slave owner. In case the work of the slave does not sufficiently cover the cost of his or her expenses, *shari'a* requires that the slave owner makes up the difference.[17]

Second, the master has no right to force the slave to act against *shari'a*. In other words, the male and female slave are not free to obey the master outside the limits of *shari'a*. The famous hadith of the Prophet, "There is no obedience to creation in the disobedience of the Creator",[18] is the evidence for this right. What is permitted (*mubah*) in *shari'a* delimits the territory

---

17 Al-Khu'i, *Minhaj al-Salihin*, No. 1477, 2–228.
18 Al-Radi, *Nahj al-Balagha*, *hikmah* No. 165, 500.

of the slave's obedience to his or her master. Thus, observing the criteria of *shari'a* in all things is the right of the slave.

Third, in cases where there is no specific *shari'a* ruling pertaining to the slave, they have equal and similar rights to other people, that is, the same as free people. Thus, having a specific and different ruling for slaves requires evidence in *shari'a* and not the opposite.

Fourth, the master has no right to separate a child from the mother (female slave) during the period when the child is dependent on her.[19] Sale of the minor slave is therefore not permitted during the time of breastfeeding or before the age of discernment (*tamyiz*).

Fifth, a disbeliever does not become the slave of a Muslim from the outset. If a non-Muslim slave converts to Islam, a disbeliever is bound to sell him or her to a Muslim and receive his or her price.[20]

Sixth, it is good if the master considers his or her slaves as something entrusted by God, and treats them in a friendly, tolerant, kind and equal way. He should be fair and just in relation to them and refrain from oppression and injustice, and should not refrain from showing love and forgiveness.[21]

Second: The Most Important Rulings Pertaining to Slaves

First, both male and female slaves are the property of the owner and the owner is permitted by *shari'a* to use his or her property in any way appropriate. The slave's consent is not a condition for any of the owner's uses. The slave is required to satisfy the owner in the realm of permitted acts (*mubahat*). The slave is obligated to eat and drink what the owner provides, wear what the owner determines, and to live where the owner has provided as his or her residence. The slave must speak, act and make her- or himself up as the owner desires. The absolute expression (*itlaq*) of the verse "a slave controlled by his master, with no power over anything" (Q. 16:75) is predicated on nothing other than this.

Second, the slave cannot own anything without the permission of his or her owner. If through whatever means the slave receives some property,

---

19 Al-Khu'i, *Minhaj al-Salihin*, No. 306, 2:70.
20 Ibid., No. 288, 2:67.
21 Nasir al-Din al-Tusi, *Akhlaq-e Naseri*, ed. Mojtaba Minuwi and Alireza Heidari (Tehran: Kharazmi, 1985), 240–244.

for example, if the slave had some property at the time of enslavement, or inherits it or is gifted property, all such property will go to his or her owner, unless the owner gives him or her ownership of it.[22]

Third, a slave does not have the right to carry out work that is of interest to him or her, but is forced to undertake the work or occupation that the master determines for him or her. Whatever the slave earns from this work belongs to the master.

Fourth, male and female slaves cannot marry without their owner's permission.[23] If the owner allows his male slave to marry, the owner will have to provide the dowry and provisions (*nafaqah*). However, in the case where the wife of the male slave is a female belonging to another owner, the dowry will go to that owner and not the female slave herself.

Fifth, as soon as married men and women are taken as slaves, their marriage is annulled without the need for divorce even if they become the slaves of the same master.

Sixth, a man's ownership of a female slave is included under the same ruling as marriage. Based on this, all sexual enjoyments are permitted to the male owner in relation to his female slaves.[24] In these sexual relations, first, the woman's consent is absolutely not required, and, second, it is not necessary for the female slave to be a Muslim or of the People of the Book. Even if the female slave is a disbeliever and a polytheist, this relationship is permitted.[25] Third, unlike the case of permanent marriage, in gaining sexual enjoyment from a female slave it is not necessary to observe the limit of four. In the case of a female owner of a male slave, however, any kind of sexual relationship is not permitted outside marriage, and the male slave is considered a stranger (non-*mahram*) in relation to the female owner.[26]

Seventh, the master has the right to marry his female slave – even without her consent –to his male slave, the male slave of another (with the permission of the other owner) or to a free man.[27] In addition, he is permitted to place his female slave at the disposal of another man without marriage or without

---

22 Al-Najafi, *Jawahir al-Kalam*, 24:170–186; Al-Khu'i, *Minhaj al-Salihin*, 2:69.
23 Al-Khu'i, *Minhaj al-Salihin*, 2:275.
24 Ibid., 2:275; al-Yazdi, *al-'Urwah al-Wuthqa*, 5:495.
25 Al-Khu'i, *Minhaj al-Salihin*, 2:275.
26 Al-Yazdi, *al-'Urwah al-Wuthqa*, 5:497.
27 Ibid., 5:587–588.

her consent, even if the other man is his slave. In this act, called *tahlil*, it is not necessary to set a time or dowry, it is only permission for benefit (it is not a marriage). With *tahlil*, all sexual enjoyments are permitted unless the owner makes something an exception.[28]

Eighth, with the permission or command of the owner, it is permitted for a male slave to marry a free woman and for a female slave to marry a free man. During the time when a female slave is married to another slave with the owner's permission, the owner is forbidden from enjoying her sexually in any way.[29]

Ninth, the owner is required to verify the non-pregnancy (*istibra'*) of a female slave during the time of sale, marriage or *tahlil*.[30] The waiting period to verify non-pregnancy is the period of purity (*tuhr*) of one menstruation cycle up to a maximum of forty-five days.[31]

Tenth, the owner has the right to nullify (*faskh*) the marriage of his own male and female slaves without obtaining their divorce if both slave parties belong to him. However, if the marriage of a slave occurs with the owner's permission to a free person or slave (male or female) belonging to another master, the divorce is in the hands of the husband (not the master). The first case, that is, where both slaves belong to the master, means it is sufficient for him to order them to separate.[32] In all these cases of separation, the waiting period for divorce (*'idda al-talaq*) for the married female slave is the period of purity of two menstruation cycles, and the waiting period after the death of her husband (*'idda al-wafat*) is two months and five days (half the waiting period of a free woman).[33]

Eleventh, the female slave does not need to cover her hair, head and neck during prayer or otherwise.[34] Thus, the *hijab* for free women and girls is different than for female slaves.

---

28 Al-Najafi, *Jawahir al-Kalam*, 30: 307; al-Khu'i, *Minhaj al-Salihin*, 2:277.
29 Al-Khu'i, *Minhaj al-Salihin*, 2:277.
30 Sexual interaction is abstained from, during the period of *istibra'*.
31 Al-Khu'i, *Minhaj al-Salihin*, 2:67.
32 But if the marriage has been by the permission of the master with a free woman or a female slave of the other owner, the divorce is in the hands of the husband not the master (Al-Yazdi, *al-'Urwah al-Wuthqa*, 6:157; al-Khu'i, *Minhaj al-Salihin*, 2:276).
33 Al-Khu'i, *Minhaj al-Salihin*, 2:298.
34 Ibid., 1:136; al-Yazdi, *al-'Urwah al-Wuthqa*, 2:320; Ruhollah Khomeini, *Tahrir al-Wasilah*, 1:150.

Twelfth, after the children of slaves reach the age of maturity and discernment (*tamyiz*), the owner has the right to separate them from their parents and even to sell them.

Thirteenth, the owner – including female and male owners, *mujtahid* scholars and laymen, just and unjust people – has the right to carry out any punishments (*al-hudud al-shar'iya*) and punish their slave's wrongdoings without referring to a judge.[35] It is clear that the owner can carry out discretionary punishment (*ta'zir*).[36]

Fourteenth, the punishment (*shari'i hadd*) for a slave is lighter than that of a free person (half of it). For example, the *hadd* for a slave committing adultery, whether a chaste married man or a chaste married woman (*muhsin wa muhsinah*), is fifty lashes.[37]

Fifteenth, the blood money (*diyah*) of a slave is his or her price, as long as it does not exceed the blood money of a free person. If the price is higher, then it is not obligatory to pay more than the amount of blood money of a free man.

Sixteenth, one of the conditions of retribution (*qisas*) for a person or a limb is equivalence in freedom and slavery. If a free man or woman purposely kills a slave, they will not be subject to retribution (*qisas*). If the owner does not forgive the murderer, the murderer must pay the price of the slave to the owner, as long as that price does not exceed the blood money of a free person. However, if, on the contrary, a slave kills a free man or woman on purpose, the guardians of the victim can choose between execution of the murderer as retribution (*qisas*) or taking him or her as their own slave.[38]

Seventeenth, the master inherits from his freed slave under certain conditions (*wila' 'itq*), but a freed slave does not under any circumstances inherit anything from his or her owner.[39]

What has been noted above does not cover all of the rulings and duties of slaves, but these are the most important which have been gathered from the works of contemporary scholars and have been placed alongside one another. These selected rulings draw a complete picture of how those who have addressed the issue see slavery.

35 Al-Najafi, *Jawahir al-Kalam*, 21:387.
36 Al-Khu'i, *Minhaj al-Salihin*, 55.
37 Ibid., 36.
38 Ibid., 68.
39 Al-Khu'i, *Minhaj al-Salihin*, 2:374.

Subsection Three: Causes for the Freedom of Slaves

Slavery is not inherent and can be eliminated by certain causes. The causes for slavery can be divided into automatic, obligatory and voluntary. Automatic (*qahri*) causes are those where the occurrence of matters, according to *shari'a*, on their own leads to the freeing of the slaves, without requiring the consent of the slave or the permission of the owner. Obligatory (*ilzami*) causes are those matters where their occurrence comes with a *shari'a* requirement to free one or several slaves in the way of God. While specific slaves are freed by automatic causes, only the number and general conditions of emancipation are noted in the case of obligatory causes. Whether the believer doing this follows this *shari'a* necessity, or whether he or she frees this or that slave, is all up to the person carrying it out. Voluntary (*ikhtiyari*) causes are undertakings by the owner which lead to the freedom of his or her slaves. These voluntary causes are all in themselves recommended (*mandub*), but when they are achieved, slaves are emancipated and it is not possible for them to be re-enslaved. The voluntary causes include *shari'a* contracts (*'uqud*) and unilateral acts (*iqa'*). In the voluntary causes based on contract, the consent of the slave and his or her pledge is also a condition. I will briefly address the three causes for the elimination of slavery below.

First: The Automatic Causes for the Elimination of Slavery

First cause: the ownership of kin. No person may own his or her father, mother, grandparents, children or grandchildren. In addition, no man can own his close female relatives (*maharim*),[40] such as his sister, maternal and paternal aunt, and nieces. Those who have become kin through breastfeeding (*rida'*) are subject to the same ruling as those who are kin through genealogy (*nasab*). If such a case of ownership were to occur, the kin who are ownded will immediately be freed automatically.[41] A female slave who gives birth to a child with her owner (*umm walad*) will receive her child's inheritance on the death of her owner and is immediately freed on the basis of the above principle.[42]

---

40 Women whom *shari'a* does not allow one to marry.
41 Al-Khu'i, *Minhaj al-Salihin*, 2:67 and 313.
42 Ibid., 2:276.

Second cause: serious deficiency in a limb, blindness, leprosy and becoming paralysed will result in the freedom of a slave. If due to his or her master a slave is maltreated (*tankil*) or dismembered (*muthlah*), then the slave will automatically become free.[43]

Third cause: if a slave converts to Islam in the territory of war (*dar al-harb*) and enters the territory of Islam (*dar al-Islam*) before his or her owner, he or she will be considered free.[44]

Fourth cause: contagion (*siraya*). If a master partially frees his or her slave, then under certain conditions this partial freedom will extend to the remaining conditions of slavery and the slave will become completely free.[45]

Second: Obligatory Causes for the Elimination of Slavery

The first cause is atonement (*kaffarah*). To lessen or eliminate consequences in the Hereafter, the sinner is required by *shari'a* to atone for some of his or her sins. The canonical particulars for making atonement (*khisal al-kaffarah*) are freeing one slave in the way of God, fasting for two months in a row, and feeding sixty poor people. Depending on the strength or weakness of the sins, atonement is divided into three types. First, is voluntary (*mukhayyarah*) atonement. The person carries out one of the three options for atonement. The atonement for intentionally breaking each day of Ramadan fasting is of this type. Second, is atonement by degree (*murattabah*). The believer is required to carry out the first option of atonement, that is, to free a slave, and in case they are unable to do so will fast instead. In case they are unable to fast they will feed the poor. The atonement for unintentional murder is of this sort. Third, is additional (*jam'*) atonement. This means the requirement of carrying out all three canonical particulars (*khisal*) of atonement collectively. The atonement for intentionally killing a believer is of this sort.[46]

The second cause is the share of *zakat* to liberate those in bondage (*fi al-riqab*).[47] One of the types of people who deserve *zakat* are slaves. With

---

43 Al-Najafi, *Jawahir al-Kalam*, 34:189 and 191.
44 Ibid., 34:190.
45 Ibid., 34:152.
46 Al-Khu'i, *Minhaj al-Salihin*, 2:321; Ayatollah Ruhollah Khomeini, *Tahrir al-Wasilah*, 2:134–135.
47 Q. 2:177 and 9:60.

the *zakat* not only are these slaves set free in the way of God: but also *Mukatab* slaves[48] who are unable to pay their dues, slaves under pressure, in fact, all slaves can be purchased from their owners through this method and set free. Slaves who are freed with *zakat* must be Muslims.[49] *Zakat*, the tax required by *shari'a*, played a substantial role in freeing slaves in Islamic societies. The fact that a share of *zakat* is specifically set to liberate those in bondage (*fi al-riqab*) indicates the Lawmaker's (*shari'*) strong inclination towards freeing slaves, to the extent that freeing slaves is considered as worship, and the public treasury (*bait al-mal*) is put in the service of carrying it out.

The third cause is vow (*nadhr*), covenant (*'ahd*) and oath (*qasam*) and applies if someone makes a vow or a covenant with God, or swears to free a slave in the way of God in return for a permissible need or act he or she requires. It is absolutely obligatory for him or her to free the slave as soon as the condition of the vow, covenant or oath occurs.

Third: Voluntary Causes for the Elimination of Slavery

The first cause is manumission (*'itq*). Freeing slaves in the way of God is among the acts which are certainly recommended (*mandub*). It is greatly rewarded in the Hereafter and is very much encouraged by the Lawgiver.[50] Manumission is one of the unilateral acts (*iqa'at*) in *shari'a* and is enacted by the utterance (*insha'*) of a short formula: *"you are free"*. Manumission is the easiest way for a slave to become free and can come to fruition merely by the will and implementation of the owner.[51]

The second cause is suspension until the master's death (*tadbir*). If an owner suspends the slave's freedom until the time of his or her death, the slave becomes free upon the owner's death.[52] *Tadbir* is also one of the unilateral acts (*iqa'at*) in *shari'a*.

---

48 Q. 24:33. *Mukatabah* is an agreement between master and slave that the slave pays his or her price to the master through working and becomes free.

49 Ayatollah Ruhollah Khomeini, *Tahrir al-Wasilah*, 1:354 and 357; Hossein-Ali Najaf-Abadi Montazeri, *Kitab al-Zakat* (*The Book of Zakat*) (Qom: Tafakkur, 1992), 3:33–44.

50 Al-Najafi, *Jawahir al-Kalam*, 34:87.

51 Al-Khu'i, *Minhaj al-Salihin*, 2:313.

52 Ibid., 2:314.

The third cause is a *mukatabah* agreement. *Kitab* or *mukatabah* is a contract that is made between the master and slave based on the agreement that the slave will work with the consent of the owner and at determined times will make instalments towards his or her price, and at the end will be freed. In *mukatabah mutlaqah* (non-conditional agreement), the slave will be freed partially according to the ratio of the paid instalments versus the slave's price. But in *mukatabah mashrutah* (conditional agreement) the slave will be freed only if he or she pays their whole price to the owner.[53] In case the slave is unable to pay the rest of his or her price, the rest of the price will be paid from the share of *zakat* "to liberate those in bondage" (*fi al-riqab*), and then he or she will be freed, if he or she is a believer.[54]

In concluding the first section, it is necessary to mention several important points: first, none of the causes for slavery are particular to the past and in cases where Muslims gain power, the supporter of slavery can carry them out today; second, despite the abundant and great encouragement for freeing slaves, the obligatory causes for eliminating slavery are not so many as to be able to uproot slavery. Thus, given the rulings noted above, the continuation of slavery is not that unexpected; and, third, given the abundant attractions of slavery, such as having a virtually free or very cheap labour force and the widespread possibilities for sexual enjoyment, those societies which benefited from these possibilities were inclined to continue slavery.

In this section, I have tried to outline the conventional view of slavery in contemporary Islamic thought without casting any kind of judgement.

Section Two: A Comparison of the Rulings of Slavery in Islam with the Documents of Human Rights

Before assessing contemporary Islam on the rulings of slavery, it is necessary to look at what human rights have to say in relation to this discussion. After doing this, we will be able to judge whether the two are compatible with each other or not.

---

53 Ibid., 2:315.
54 Ayatollah Ruhollah Khomeini, *Tahrir al-Wasilah*, 1:357.

Subsection One: The Most Important Human Rights Documents on Slavery

The movement to abolish slavery began in the mid-nineteenth century. Prior to the Universal Declaration of Human Rights, the following are noteworthy as being among the most important documents that were ratified in support of abolishing slavery: International Agreement for the Suppression of White Slave Traffic (Paris, 1904); International Convention for the Suppression of the Traffic in Women and Children (1921); and the Convention to Suppress the Slave Trade and Slavery (Geneva, 1926).

The Universal Declaration of Human Rights, ratified in 1948, outlines the following: Article 1: "All human beings are born free and equal in dignity and rights"; and Article 4: "No one shall be held in slavery or servitude; slavery and the slave trade shall be prohibited in all their forms."

The Supplementary Convention on the Abolition of Slavery, the Slave Trade, and Institutions and Practices (Geneva, 1956), considers freedom to be the inherent right of every individual. In addition to welcoming new progress that had been made in eliminating slavery and the trade in slaves, it claimed that slavery and the sale of slaves, and practices and institutions resembling slavery had not yet been eliminated throughout the world. Thus, with the aim of amplifying national and international actions towards the elimination of slavery and the slave trade, it addressed practices and institutions that are like slavery. Article 7 of this convention states that "'Slavery' means, as defined in the Slavery Convention of 1926, the status or condition of a person over whom any or all of the powers attaching to the right of ownership are exercised." What they mean by the subjected person is someone who is in a situation such as: "A woman, without the right to refuse, is promised or given in marriage on payment of a consideration in money or in kind to her parents, guardian, family or any other person or group."

The International Covenant on Civil and Political Rights (1966), which is one of the most influential human rights documents, states in Article 8 that: "No one shall be held in slavery; slavery and the slave-trade in all their forms shall be prohibited. No one shall be held in servitude. No one shall be required to perform forced or compulsory labour."

The Cairo Declaration on Human Rights in Islam (1990), states in Article 11: "(a) Human beings are born free, and no one has the right to enslave, humiliate, oppress or exploit them, and there can be no subjugation but to

Allah the Almighty.[55] (b) Colonialism of all types being one of the most evil forms of enslavement is totally prohibited. Peoples suffering from colonialism have the full right to freedom and self-determination. It is the duty of all States and peoples to support the struggle of colonized peoples for the liquidation of all forms of occupation, and all States and peoples have the right to preserve their independent identity and control over their wealth and natural resources."

Subsection Two: Comparing the Rulings of Slavery with the Documents of Human Rights

Comparing the rulings of slavery in a specific reading of contemporary Islam with international human rights documents will leave no doubt that these two are in direct contradiction with one another and that accepting one equates to rejecting the other.

The most important principle of human rights in the abolition of slavery is that "All human beings are born free and equal in dignity and rights" (Article 1 of the UDHR). In comparison, this is what is cited in the aforementioned reading of contemporary Islam: first, children whose parents are slaves will be born slaves; and, second, people are not equal to one another in terms of rights and status (*haithiyyat*). A free person is different from a slave in a number of ways. The slave in these cases has far fewer rights. The slave is a being that is inferior to a free person and only slightly superior to an animal. The slave does not live according to his or her wishes, but their lives must absolutely coincide with the will and inclinations of the master. He or she is forced to labour, but cannot keep the pay for this work without the permission of the owner. The

---

55 The French and Arabic translation of this Article is as its English version. Unfortunately, in the Persian translation of the above, section A of Article 11 has been mis-translated as follows: "A person is born free, no one has the right to enslave, degrade, subdue, or use him or her other than God." This mis-translation means that God has the right to enslave, degrade, subdue or use humans. Put another way, it means that slavery without *shari'a* permission is forbidden and slavery with *shari'a* permission is allowed! The Persian translation of the 1990 Cairo Declaration can be found in Iran in: Hossain Mehrpour, *Hoquq-e Bashar dar Asnad-e Bainollmelali wa Moze'-e Jomhouri-e Eslami-e Iran (Human Rights in International Documents and the Position of the Islamic Republic of Iran)* (Tehran: Ettela'at Publications, 2007), 395–403 and in Afghanistan in: Independent Commission of Human Rights of Afghanistan, *Majmou'e-ye E'lamiyehaa-ye Hoquq-e Bashari (Collection of Declarations of Human Rights)*, (n.p.: n.p, June 2002), 18–33.

owner can punish the slave without going to court. A male owner is allowed to sexually enjoy the female slave without her consent or to put her at another man's disposal for his sexual pleasure. The marriage and divorce of a slave is in the hands of the owner. If the slave is killed by a non-slave, retribution (*qisas*) does not apply. Given these rulings, the slave is absolutely denied human rights.

The different perspectives of the documents of human rights as compared with the above-noted dominant readings of contemporary Islam can be illustrated in the table below. Examining this comparative table shows that the incompatibilities between the conventional view in contemporary Islam and human rights documents are so clear that they do not require explanation, argumentation or justification. If some God-fearing and pious slave owners do not practice some of the rights they have in relation to their slaves, this does not mean that we can turn a blind eye to the wide-ranging authority that owners have over their slaves in *shari'a*. In lawmaking, all aspects must be taken into consideration and the possibility of any kind of abuse must be prevented from the outset. On every issue, the causes for slavery and the duties and responsibilities of slaves are in direct conflict with the documents of human rights.

Row	Rulings of Contemporary Islam (Conventional Reading)	International Human Rights Documents
1	If the parents are slaves, the child is also born a slave.	All humans are born equal.
2	Slaves are different from free people in many instances related to dignity, rights and rulings.	All humans are equal in rights and dignity.
3	There are seven ways in which a free person may be enslaved.	A human cannot be enslaved in any way.
4	A person's status as a slave continues unless one of the causes for the elimination of slavery are realised.	No one can be kept in slavery.
5	Trading in slaves is permitted under the principles of *shari'a*.	Trading in slaves in any form is absolutely prohibited.
6	All residents of the territory of war who have come under the domination of the army of Islam, including soldiers and civilians, men, women and children are considered slaves and will be divided between soldiers, the ruler and the government.	Prisoners of war have specific rights and are absolutely not considered as slaves.

7	The slave only has the right to ownership with the permission of the master and the pay he or she receives belongs to the master.	All humans have the right to ownership and the pay they receive for work belongs to themselves.
8	It is not necessary for the slave to consent to his or her style of life, place of residence or work. He or she is compelled in all issues to obey the master and is compelled to realise the master's views within the limits of *shari'a*.	Every person has the right to freely determine his or her style of life, place of residence and work, and others have no right to impose on him or her.
9	The slave owner has the right to take a child from his or her mother and to sell the child after seven years of age. The slave owner has the right to nullify marriage between male and female slaves without their consent and without divorce. After enslavement, the marriage of the individuals who are enslaved is nullified.	No one has the right to break apart another person's family unit, separate parents from their children, or separate a husband and wife without their consent.
10	The marriage of a slave is completely in the hands of the owner. The owner may force a slave to marry whomever or prevent marriage to a specific person or in general not allow the slave to marry.	No one can be forcefully prevented from marrying or be forced into marriage with a specific person. Marriage without the permission of both sides is not allowed.
11	Taking a female slave is identical to marrying her. The owner of a female slave has the right to sexually enjoy her in any way they please even without her consent. The owner may place his female slave at the disposal of another man for sexual pleasure without marriage.	It is prohibited to sexually enjoy women or girls without their consent. No one has the right to place a woman or a girl at the disposal of another for the purpose of sexual pleasure.
12	The slave owner (even if they are a non-*mujtahid* and unjust individual) has the right to apply (*ta'zir* and *hadd*) punishments to the slave.	None has the right to punish another in the place of a judge or court.
13	The punishment for a slave is almost half of that of a free person. Free persons are not subject to retribution for the deliberate murder of a slave, but slaves are subject to retribution for the deliberate murder of a free person.	People are equal before the law and if they commit the same crimes will be subject to the same punishments.
14	The slave has no right to rest, leisure, private life, education and training without the permission of the owner.	All persons have the right to rest, leisure, private life, education and training.
15	Any interference in the public sphere by the slave is prohibited without the permission of the owner.	All persons have the right to participate in the management of the public sphere of his or her society.

Section Three: Contemporary Islam and the Issue of Slavery

The contemporary Muslim faces three definite propositions:

A. Rulings pertaining to slavery are widespread in Islamic texts, the Qur'an, the Tradition and in opinions in *fiqh* and ethics.
B. These rulings are in complete conflict with human rights documents.
C. The human rights movement in the last century has, first, forbidden slavery in all its forms, and, second, uprooted slavery in its traditional forms.

The question now is how contemporary Muslims should deal with the issue of slavery?[56] The simplest response is that in today's world there are no slaves so it is unnecessary to take a position on it. In other words, issues of male and female slaves and the rulings that pertain to them have gone outside the scope of applicable or commonly occurring rulings and there is no reason to spend time on them. The majority of Muslim scholars, by remaining quiet or not discussing the rulings on slavery, have tried to pass over the subject and to safely leave it behind without mention, without confirming or rejecting the issue, thereby avoiding the problem of having to answer a lot of questions.

This approach does not solve the problem and only delays the response. Some of the rulings on slavery are mentioned in the Qur'an. According to the belief of Muslims, discussions in the Qur'an pertain to all times and places. In addition, many religious discussions are tied to discussions of slavery such as discussion of atonement, *zakat*, *khums*, retribution, blood money, trade, marriage, divorce and *jihad*. No jurist of *fiqh* can extrapolate (*ijtihad*) in the above-noted areas without taking a definite stance on slavery. The fact that slavery is not currently applicable to people or a problem that they currently encounter does not eliminate the necessity for a scholarly debate.

---

56 It is appropriate to provide a sample of some contemporary Muslim scholars who have tried to respond to the dilemma of slavery in contemporary Islam. Mirza Abul Hassan Sha'rani (d. 1973): "slavery is permitted in Islamic *shari'a*, but is restricted to the case when during *jihad* based in *shari'a*, disbelievers are taken captive. At this time while the Imam is in occultation, the subject of slavery is negated, since *jihad* must take place with the presence of the Imam. The Declaration of Human Rights is at such a situation that all people should compromise with one another and there be no war to need defence." *Nathr-e Tuba* (*The Encyclopaedia of the Qur'an*) (Tehran: Islamiyya, 2000), 185.

Among the scholars of contemporary Islam, two positions can be discerned on the issue of slavery. The first position is to accept slavery as originally a religious issue, even in our era. The second position is to absolutely reject slavery as a religious issue in our era.

In this section, I will first identify and critique the first position. Then, I will examine the Qur'anic and narrative evidence (Sunna) for slavery. And, finally, I will present and discuss the second position.

Subsection One: Critical Analysis of the Conventional View

First, unfortunately the conventional view in Islamic thought has defended slavery in continuity with the past in the framework of *shari'a*, and has rarely attempted to clarify and justify its position. Among the strongest justifications in this regard is the short treatise on slaves and slavery (*Kalam fi al-Riqq wa al-Isti'bad*) by the great contemporary exegete and philosopher, Seyyed Mohammad Hossein Tabataba'i.[57]

Analysis of the Conventional View

According to Tabataba'i, servitude through capture in war is in accord with nature and is based on rational argumentation. This opinion is summarised and outlined below.

1. In respect to analytical meaning, man's servitude and bondage to God is taken from the rationale (*ra'y al-'uqala'*) of human bondage to other humans in human societies.

2. Man is by nature a subjugator and wishes to make everyone but him- or herself a servitor for him- or herself. This subjugation (*istikhdaam*) occurs through domination, ownership and taking control of the lives, honour (*a'rad*) and property of others. As such, the tradition of enslavement (*isti'bad*) and bondage (*istirqaq*) is based on the right to absolute and exclusive control and ownership which humans consider for themselves.

3. There are three main groups of people naturally subject to enslavement through domination, ownership, and enslavement of others: first, the transgressing enemy: the victor deems it permissible to murder, capture

---

57 Al-Tabataba'i, *al-Mizan fi Tafsir al-Qur'an*, 6:340–360.

and enslave the defeated enemy; second, the guardianship of the father over minors and that of male relatives over women; and, third, the defeated debtor to the defeating creditor.

4. From the three main causes for slavery, Islam has uprooted slavery through guardianship and debt, but has accepted the first cause, namely, slavery through war, albeit with some restrictions. This war is that of disbelievers who have set out to wage war with God, the Prophet and the believers, while slavery is not accepted in wars between Muslims against each other.

5. The reason for enslaving an unbeliever at war with Islam (*kafir harbi*) is that such a person is not considered a member of human society who enjoys social rights and benefits. A person who is outside religion, religious government, truce contracts with Muslims ('*ahd*) and religious protection (*dhimmah*), is outside human society. The army of Islam has the right to capture and enslave a person who has deprived him- or herself of respect. The enslavement of the person who goes to war against religion (*muharib*) and who will never submit to the Right is in accordance with the definite judgement of innate nature.

6. War with disbelievers starts when the wisdom, admonishment and better forms of disputation do not lead to a conclusion and the disbelievers have not been guided after clear evidence has been provided (*itmam hujjat*). In this case, if they are not in the category of people under contract (*mu'ahad*) or people of protection (*dhimmi*), those who enter the battlefield will be killed. However, the men who have surrendered and women, children and the elderly will not be killed. After the end of the war and domination by the army of Islam, all property and people who have come under the control of Muslims will belong to the Muslims.

7. Islam has provided many recommendations for slave owners to treat their slaves well, like a member of the family. There is truly no difference in Islam between a slave and a free person, other than the necessity for a slave to obtain the permission of the owner. It is among the necessities of Islamic teachings that the pious slave is above the corrupt free slaveowner. Islam has put great emphasis on manumission and the freeing of slaves, which causes the constant reduction of slave numbers in Islamic society. Manumission ('*itq*) as canonical particulars for making atonement (*khisal al-kaffarah*), the permission of *mukatabah mashrutah* (conditional agreement), *mukatabah mutlaqah* (non-conditional agreement) and suspension to a master's death

(*tadbir*) are all ways for freeing slaves and for removing the context of vileness and slavery.

8. The long-term efforts of non-Muslims in the nineteenth century to abolish slavery in the world pertains to abolishing slavery via guardianship and domination (through debt). However, enslavement through capture during war, which is accepted by Islam, was never the subject of their discussions.

9. Based on these, first, considering human freedoms to be unlimited is explicitly contrary to the legitimate innate nature of human beings. Second, the right of enslavement and taking into bondage the enemy of truthful religion who wages war with Islamic society is in accordance with the innate nature of *shari'a*. Freedom is taken from such people and they are absorbed into the religious society and become duty-bound by accepting slavery and the fact that they will be trained and disciplined according to religious manners so that they will eventually be freed and able return to free society.

10. Agreements on abolishing slavery, such as the 1890 Brussels Agreement, given the actions of the victorious nations who had signed such agreements at the conclusion of the Second World War in relation to the defeated nations, is playing with words and the practical acceptance of the Islamic approach to the issue. In any case, it is not accepted that the source of the abolition of slavery is the equality of every single person.

11. The philosophy behind a slave being unable to own anything without their master's permission is to avoid any conspiracies of the enemies who are at war with the Muslims. Its function is to destroy the economic foundations of the enemy causing the destruction of Islamic society. This is done by legislating such rules at the beginning of the period of their subjugation. Those who have no right to ownership will not have the ability and power for confrontation and waging war.

12. A slave's conversion to Islam does not cause the demise of slavery, because if this were the case, many slaves would pretend to accept Islam, leave slavery and begin strengthening themselves to fight against Islam.

13. While children of warring disbelievers (*kuffar harbi*) and their descendants who are born later and had no role in warring against Islam are victims of their parents, they wear the collar of slavery around their neck on account of their fathers' sins.

14. If an Islamic government considers the freeing of slaves to be to the benefit of an Islamic society, it may seek solutions such as the buying of slaves and freeing them as long as the solution of the ruler does not lead to the abrogation of the divine rulings.[58]

Critique of the Conventional View

Second, according to this philosopher and exegete of the Qur'an, first, the capture of warring disbelievers (*kuffar harbi*) is the only credible way of taking slaves; second, this way is based on the innate nature of humans and is defensible; third, Islam's position leans towards the Islamic nurturing of slaves and their eventual manumission; and, fourth, in cases where it is considered to be to its benefit, the Islamic government may in practice free all slaves, but it cannot abrogate divine rulings (including the rulings of slavery).

This master scholar has made a studious effort to provide a rational justification for the Qur'anic rulings on enslavement, and his texts in this regard are among the strongest defences for the enslavement of enemies at war with Islam. Despite all of this, there are numerous points that are flawed or controversial in his opinion on this matter.

First, human servitude to God does not have the same roots as human slavery to humans, so negating one does not negate the other. In the first instance, the master is a creature that is transcendental, worshiped, beloved, and the peak and epitome of human perfection, and in the other instance, the master is on the same level as those who are owned, is lacking in any inherent superiority, and has only come into such ownership via the route of force and domination.

Second, the causes of slavery in Islam are not only restricted to captivity in war, but rather, there are six other legitimate causes that can be derived from the *ahadith* and statements of the jurists (as discussed in detail in the first section of this chapter). Not one of these six causes are agreeable to innate human nature, and they cannot be defended with the justification for the first cause.

Third, the enslavement of those captured in war is not in accordance with a definite innate nature. There is no rational correlation between capture in war and slavery.

---

58 Al-Tabataba'i, *Al-Mizan fi Tafsir al-Qur'an*, 6:354–359.

Fourth, non-Muslims who for whatever reason are not willing to accept Islam but who have also not entered into war against Muslims are members of human society and have the right to life and freedom.

Fifth, capturing and enslaving civilians outside the battlefield, especially women, children and the elderly, is absolutely against sound reason (*'aql salim*) and innate nature.

Sixth, there is no doubt that Islam has many recommendations that slaves be treated well. However, these recommended (*mandub*) rulings do not have much impact as compared with the extensive rights that a master has over a slave, and the numerous rulings that pertain to what slaves must do (which were outlined in Section One, Subsection Two of this chapter). These non-obligatory rulings are only influential in the case of pious masters. The credibility of a legal regime is assessed in terms of its obligatory rulings.

Seventh, if the enslavement of disbelievers in war with Islam is in accordance with the definite judgement of innate nature, why does Islam seek numerous ways to continually reduce the number of slaves through freeing them? With all of this, there is no evidence for the superiority of the causes for eliminating slavery over the causes for slavery and therefore the continual reduction of slaves.

Eighth, human rights documents, especially those that were ratified by international bodies in the twentieth century, abolished all types of slavery and were not limited to particular kinds of slavery. In addition, they have absolutely prohibited slavery through war.

Ninth, doubting or denying the equality of human rights, especially those that pertain to freedom and servitude, require credible evidence.

Tenth, the fact that slavery did not disappear with conversion to Islam, especially after the first generation of slaves, is not justifiable or defensible.

Eleventh, the enslavement of the lineage of the obstinate disbeliever (*kuffar harbi*) for the sins of their forefathers is not in harmony with innate nature and reason.

Twelfth, if it is permitted to free all slaves with a governmental order on account that their freedom is in the temporary public interest, why can there not be an order to abolish slavery altogether. Particularly if we reach the conclusion that enslaving humans is contrary to justice and the ways of reasonable people, and that it is of permanent interest to eliminate it. Also, if we discover that the ruling to enslave was from its inception a temporary ruling, not a permanent one, and belonged to the changing rulings and not the stable and permanent rulings of *shariʿa*.

In any case, neither reason nor innate nature confirms the causes for slavery, including war. In the same way, none of the rulings and duties of slaves are in accordance to innate nature or reason. In fact, reason and innate nature welcome all the causes for eliminating slavery.

Subsection Two: Examining the Religious References to Slavery

I will examine the religious references to slavery in two discussions about the Qurʾan and the Tradition.

First: The Qurʾan and the Issue of Slavery

Which of the seven causes for slavery has the Qurʾan given its approval to? Is enslaving those captured in war based on Qurʾanic evidence? Which of the rulings and duties of slaves have been outlined in the Qurʾan? What is the position of the Qurʾan with regard to the causes for eliminating slavery? Does the Qurʾan approve of dividing humans into free people and slaves? Does the elimination of slavery and the absolute rejection of enslavement contradict Qurʾanic teachings?

Any discussion about the issue of slavery that does not study the position of the Qurʾan will be incomplete. The questions above are a sample of the questions about slavery that confront contemporary Muslims and which require a response. The position of the Qurʾan on slavery can be outlined as below:

1. The Qurʾan has not approved or confirmed any of the causes for slavery. Principally, the Qurʾan has not mentioned the origin of slavery and has not provided a negative or positive discussion of how a slave is taken. Based on this, none of the seven reasons for slavery have Qurʾanic evidence. The Qurʾan has not even mentioned the enslavement of those captured in war, let alone confirmed or approved this.

The most important verse on those captured in war is as follows:

When you meet the disbelievers in battle, strike them in the neck, and once they are defeated, bind any captives firmly – later you can release them by grace or by ransom – until the toils of war have ended. That [is the way] God could have defeated them Himself if He had willed, but His purpose is to test some of you by means of others. He will not let the deeds of those who are killed for His cause come to nothing. (Q. 47:4)

This verse gives two solutions for dealing with those captured in war. One is freedom without exchange, and the other is freedom with exchange, such as in exchange for Muslim captives or receipt of ransom or similar. However, a third solution, namely, enslavement, is neither noted explicitly in the verse nor can it be deduced from it. Rather, the enslavement of those captured in war is not definitely evidenced in the Qur'an. This ruling is derived from the Tradition (Sunna) and the narrations which will be addressed below.[59]

2. The issue of the freedom of slaves or the causes for the elimination of slavery has been the subject of attention and discussion in the Qur'an. Four axes for the elimination of slavery have been recognised, two of which are voluntary and two of which are obligatory as follows:

A. The encouragement for manumission: "Yet he has not attempted the steep path. What will explain to you what the steep path is? It is to free a slave" (Q. 90:11–13).
B. The encouragement to make contracts: "If any of your slaves wish to pay for their freedom, make a contract with them accordingly, if you know they have good in them, give them some of the wealth God has given you" (Q. 24:33).
C. The freedom of slaves via *zakat*: "Alms are meant only for the poor, the needy, those who administer them, those whose hearts need winning over, to free slaves and to help those in debt, for God's cause, and for travellers in need. This is ordained by God; God is all knowing and wise" (Q. 9:60). From the Qur'anic point of view, one of the characteristics of the virtuous is to pay for the freeing of slaves (Q. 2:177).

---

59 The other verses in the Qur'an that speak of capture in war are Q. 8:67 and 70, 33:26, 2:85, 76:8, and none of these provide the slightest reason for enslavement during war.

D. The freedom of slaves as the canonical particulars for making atonement. The Qur'an has set the freeing of slaves as atonement for three sins: first, murder by accident: "If anyone kills a believer by mistake he must free one Muslim slave" (Q. 4:92); second, is the atonement for breaking oaths (Q. 5:89); and, third, the atonement for injurious assimilation of wife to mother or sister (*zihar*) (Q. 58:3).

3. Rulings of slaves in the Qur'an. In total, the Qur'an has pointed to ten of the rulings pertaining to slaves.

First, the necessity of good conduct with slaves: "Worship God; join nothing with Him. Be good to your parents, to relatives, to orphans, to the needy, to neighbors near and far, to travellers in need, and to your slaves" (Q. 4:36).

Second, believers are encouraged to free their slaves and to allow righteous and believing slaves to marry with the consent of their owner: "Do not marry idolatresses until they believe: a believing slave woman is certainly better than an idolatress, even though she may please you. And do not give your women in marriage to idolaters until they believe: a believing slave is certainly better than an idolater, even though he may please you" (Q. 2:221). "If any of you does not have the means to marry a believing free woman, then marry a believing slave – God knows best [the depth of] your faith: you are [all] part of the same family – so marry them with their people's consent and their proper bride-gifts. [Make them] married women, not adulteresses or lovers" (Q. 4:25). In general, the Qur'an has greatly encouraged marriage for young and single individuals, including both free and enslaved people: "Marry off the single among you and those of your male and female slaves who are fit [for marriage]. If they are poor, God will provide for them from His bounty: God's bounty is infinite and He is all knowing" (Q. 24:32).

Third, the prohibition on coercing female slaves into prostitution: "Do not force your slave-girls into prostitution, when they themselves wish to remain honourable, in your quest for the short-term gains of this world, although, if they are forced, God will be forgiving and merciful to them" (Q. 24:33).

Fourth, the punishment for adultery for a slave is half of that of a free woman: "If they [female slaves] commit adultery when they are married, their punishment will be half that of free women" (Q. 4:25).

Fifth, in retribution (*qisas*), it is necessary to observe equality of status as free or enslaved: "You who believe, fair retribution is prescribed for you in cases of murder: the free man for the free man, the slave for the slave" (Q. 2:178). Thus, a free person who kills a slave is not subject to retribution.

Sixth, the female slaves of Muslim women are considered *mahram* and Muslim women need not observe the *shar'i* hijab before their female slaves (Q. 24:31). In addition, it seems that the addressees of the *shar'i* hijab are free believing women (Q. 33:59).

Seventh, in order to enter the bedroom of their married owners, female slaves must have permission for three specific times (Q. 24:58).

Eighth, it is permitted for the owner to sexually enjoy slaves as he enjoys his spouses: "If you fear that you cannot be equitable [to your wives], then marry only one [wife], or your female slave(s)" (Q. 4:3), and "who guard their chastity except with their spouses or their slaves – with these they are not to blame, but anyone who seeks more than this is exceeding the limits" (Q. 23:5–7 and 70:29–31).[60]

Ninth, it is permitted for an owner to sexually enjoy his married female slave after the period of verification of non-pregnancy (*istibra'*): "[It is forbidden for you to sexually enjoy] women already married, other than your female slaves" (Q. 4:24). This and the previous verse definitely forbid sexual relations (whether through marriage or as slaves) with fourteen categories of women. The fourteenth category are married women: "Based on this, the statement 'other than your female slaves' negates the prohibition of (sexually) approaching married slave-women. According to what has been mentioned in the Sunna, the master of a married female slave intercepts between the slave and her husband, he copulates with her after the period of verification of non-pregnancy (*istibra'*), and then returns her to her husband."[61] It seems that the epitome of ownership and the nadir of being owned is observable in this verse.

Tenth, inability of ownership for the slave. The Qur'an has pointed to an example of the inability of slaves to have ownership: "God presents this illustration: a slave controlled by his master, with no power over anything, and another man We have supplied with good provision, from which he gives alms privately and openly. Can they be considered equal? All praise belongs to God, but most of them do not recognise this" (Q. 16:75).[62]

---

60 In Q. 33:50 and 52 the rulings of the Prophet have been specifically cited in this regard.
61 Al-Tabataba'i, *al-Mizan fi Tafsir al-Qur'an*, 4:274.
62 Other issues in this regard are raised in Q. 16:76 and 71 and 30:28.

A precise look at the ten rulings of slavery in the Qur'an guides us to two points: first, the use of the owner is not absolute in relation to different dimensions of the slave and is bound by the criteria of *shari'a*. Second, the *shari'a* boundary set for the owner's use of the slave is very broad.

4. Given the complete investigation of the verses of the Qur'an about slavery in relation to the three general axes of the causes for slavery, the causes for the elimination of slavery and the rulings of slavery, the following conclusions are noteworthy.

First, the Qur'an, generally speaking, has approved of the issue of slavery, and has accepted that people are divided into free people and slaves, and that slaves have less rights in many areas.

Second, the causes of slavery have absolutely not been addressed in the Qur'an. That is to say, the Qur'an has remained silent on how people are enslaved. Furthermore, it has not put any emphasis on retaining the system of slavery, nor has it encouraged the taking of slaves. On the other hand, the Qur'an greatly encourages the freeing of slaves, which is considered in the category of worship.

Third, the collection of verses related to slavery shows how the Qur'an deals with the propositions of actuality (*qadiya kharijiya*) of slavery. Actuality propositions are time-bound and temporary. One cannot extrapolate rulings of permanent and substantial propositions (*qadiya haqiqiya*) from actuality propositions. I will return to this important issue later. What is of utmost importance in relation to slavery and the Qur'an, and which has been neglected, is the overall spirit of Islamic teachings and the anthropology of the Qur'an, which will be addressed in the last section of this chapter.

Second: The Issue of Slavery in the Narrations

All the issues regarding the causes for slavery, the causes for the freeing of slaves, and the rulings and duties of slaves that have been outlined in the three sections of the first part of this chapter, are evidenced in the narrations (hadiths). The number of these narrations, although not as great as those about worship, are based on the conventional technical standards (of *rijal* and *fiqh*). Indeed, there are quite a few narrations that can be found among these which are credible (*mu'tabar*)[63] based on two criteria: the criterion of

---

63 Credible (*mu'tabar*) hadith include authentic (*sahih*) hadith and trustworthy (*muwaththaq*) hadith.

the chain of transmitters (*isnad*) that ensures they were issued by the Prophet or the Imams; and the criterion of indication (*dilalat*), both of which have the capacity to provide arguments for the above-noted issues.

There is not enough space to address all of the hadiths discussing slavery. However, I will point to the narrative evidence for the most important of these, especially as they pertain to the causes for slavery.

1. Enslaving those captured in war: according to the credible narration of Talhah b. Zaid, Imam Sadiq said: "When war ends and the enemy is brought to their knees (defeated), the Imam will have authority over any captive who falls into the hands of the Muslims in this way. If he wants, he may do them a favour and free them (without exchange and ransom), and if he wants, he can free them in exchange for ransom (*fidya*: exchange of captives or receiving monetary compensation), and if he wants, he may take them as slaves."[64] Freedom without exchange and in exchange for captives has Qur'anic evidence (Q. 47:4), but the latter possibility, that is, the enslavement of the captive, is based on this narration and similar ones.

2. Permission to enslave civilians outside war: the reliable narration of Rafa'ah al-Nakkas (the slave-seller) asked Imam Kazim: "A group has raided the Romans (the Zanzibars) and the Slavs and has abducted their children, both girls and boys, has castrated the boys and then sent them (as slaves) to the merchants in Baghdad. What is your opinion about buying them, given that we know these male and female slaves have been stolen from their people and taken without there being a war?" The Imam responded: "There is no problem in buying them (and in buying them, they become your slaves). It is the case and nothing more than that they have been taken from the territory of the polytheists (*dar al-shirk*) and have been brought to the territory of Islam (*dar al-Islam*)."[65]

3. Enslavement by purchase from the guardians (*awliya'*): Abdullah Lahham asked Imam Sadiq about a man who purchased the daughter or wife of a polytheist: "Is it alright to get her [take her as a female slave]? He said: It is alright."[66]

---

64 Al-Kulaini, *al-Kafi*, 5:32, hadith No. 1; al-Tusi, *Tahdhib al-Ahkam*, 6:143, hadith No. 245; al-Hurr al-'Amili, *Tafsil Wasa'il al-Shi'a*, 15:71–72, hadith No. 20007.
65 Al-Kulaini, *al-Kafi*, 5:210, hadith No. 9; al-Tusi, *Tahdhib al-Ahkam*, 6:162, hadith No. 297; al-Hurr al-'Amili, *Tafsil Wasa'il al-Shi'a*, 15:131, hadith No. 20145 and 18:244, hadith No. 23596.
66 Al-Tusi, *Tahdhib al-Ahkam*, 8:200, hadith Nos 705 and 702; al-Tusi, *al-Istibsar*, 3:83, hadith Nos 282 and 280; al-Hurr al-'Amili, *Tafsil Wasa'il al-Shi'a*, 18:246 and 247.

4. Slavery through confession of exception from the principality of free-dom (*asala al-hurriya*): Adbullah b. Sanan narrated credibly from Imam Sadiq that Imam 'Ali said: "People are all free, apart from those who confess at the time of maturity against themselves that they are slaves, whether a female slave or a male slave, except if someone testifies to his or her slavery, and whether he/she is a minor or an adult."[67]

5. Marriage and control over the property of a slave without the permis-sion of the master is not correct: the narration of Adbullah b. Sanan from Imam Sadiq: "It is not permissible for a slave to be freed, marry or to use his own property except with the permission of his master."[68]

6. The contagion (*siraya*) of slavery from parents to children: "the child of a free father and an enslaved mother is free. If one of the parents is free, their children will be free."[69] The implicit meaning (*mafhum*) of this is that if neither of the parents are free, then their child will be born a slave.

7. The permissibility of giving a female slave to someone else for sexual purposes (*tahlil*): the narration of Fudail b. Sayyar from Imam Sadiq: "If the owner grants his female slave to his brother (in faith) [including for sexual purposes], she is permitted for him [non-owner]."[70]

8. The owner and the married slave woman: Muhammad b. Muslim asked Imam Baqir about verse (Q. 4:24), the Imam responded: "The owner orders the married slave to stay away from his wife and to not have sexual relations with her, then he locks up the female slave until she menstruates (and after being purified), the master can engage in sexual intercourse with her and after the next menstruation he will return her to her husband with-out having to marry again."[71]

9. The divorce of slaves is up to the owner and not up to themselves: Abu Salih Kinani's narration from Imam Sadiq: "when a male slave and a

---

67 Al-Kulaini, *al-Kafi*, 6:195, hadith No. 5; al-Saduq, *Man la Yahduruhu al-Faqih*, 3:141, hadith No. 3515; al-Tusi, *Tahdhib al-Ahkam*, 8:235, hadith No. 845; al-Hurr al-'Amili, *Tafsil Wasa'il al-Shi'a*, 23:54.

68 Al-Kulaini, *al-Kafi*, 5:477, hadith No. 1; al-Hurr al-'Amili, *Tafsil Wasa'il al-Shi'a*, 21:113, hadith No. 26663.

69 Al-Saduq, *Man la Yahduruhu al-Faqih*, 3:291, hadith No. 1381; al-Hurr al-'Amili, *Tafsil Wasa'il al-Shi'a*, 21:121.

70 Al-Kulaini, *al-Kafi*, 5:468, hadith No. 1; al-Hurr al-'Amili, *Tafsil Wasa'il al-Shi'a*, 21:125.

71 Al-Kulaini, *al-Kafi*, 5:481, hadith No. 2; al-Tusi, *Tahdhib al-Ahkam*, 7:346, hadith No. 1417; Muhammad b. Mas'ud al-Ayyashi, *Tafsir al-Ayyashi* (Qom: Mu'ssisa al-Bi'tha, 2000), 1:384, hadith No. 80; al-Hurr al-'Amili, *Tafsil Wasa'il al-Shi'a*, 21:149.

female slave belong to one owner, if the owner wants to he will preserve their marriage and if not, he will break it."[72]

10. The permission for slave women to keep their head uncovered: Mohammad b. Muslim asked Imam Baqir if a slave woman should cover her head during prayer. He said: "It is not required for a slave woman to have a head covering."[73] Hammad Lahham asked Imam Sadiq if a slave woman should cover her head during prayer, he said: "No, when my father (Imam Baqir) would see slave women covering their head during prayer, he would beat them so that the free women could be distinguished from the slave women."[74]

11. Encouragement for the freeing of slaves: Zurarah narrated credibly from Imam Sadiq that the Prophet said: "for whoever frees a Muslim slave, Allah the Most Powerful, the Compeller, will free one of their body parts from the fire (of hell) for every body part of the freed slaves."[75]

12. The requirement to treat slaves humanely: Abu Dharr al-Ghifari's narration of the Prophet about slaves: "slaves are your brothers and God has placed them under your authority. He whose brother is under his authority must give him to eat from what he eats and give him to wear from what he wears and not force him to do what he cannot bear, and if he does [what the slave cannot bear], he should help the slave."[76]

13. The disgrace (*kiraha*) of selling slaves: Ishaq b. Umar's narration of Imam Sadiq: "The Prophet said the worst people are those who sell people."[77] Selling slaves is among the occupations that narrations related to slavery, the following conclusions are noteworthy.

---

72 Al-Kulaini, *al-Kafi*, 6:168, hadith No. 1; al-Hurr al-'Amili, *Tafsil Wasa'il al-Shi'a*, 22:98.

73 Al-Kulaini, *al-Kafi*, 3:394, hadith No. 2; al-Hurr al-'Amili, *Tafsil Wasa'il al-Shi'a*, 4:409.

74 Al-Shaykh Muhammad b. Ali b. Babawaih al-Qummi al-Saduq, *'Ilal al-Sharayi'* (*The Shari'a Reasons*) (Najaf: al-Haidariya, 1966), 345–346; Ahmad b. Muhammad al-Barqi, *al-Mahasin* (*Advantages*), ed. Jalal al-Din al-Hussaini al-Muhaddith (Tehran: Dar al-Kutub al-Islamiyya, 1951), 318, hadith No. 45; al-Hurr al-'Amili, *Tafsil Wasa'il al-Shi'a*, 4:411, hadith No. 5562.

75 Al-Kulaini, *al-Kafi*, 6:180, hadith No. 2; al-Tusi, *Tahdhib al-Ahkam*, 8:216, hadith No. 769; al-Hurr al-'Amili, *Tafsil Wasa'il al-Shi'a*, 23:9.

76 Al-Majlisi, *Bihar al-Anwar*, 74:141, hadith No. 11.

77 Al-Kulaini, *al-Kafi*, 5:115, hadith No. 5; al-Tusi, *Tahdhib al-Ahkam*, 6:361, hadith No. 1037; al-Tusi, *al-Istibsar*, 3:62, hadith No. 208; al-Saduq, *'Ilal al-Sharayi'*, 530, hadith No. 1; al-Hurr al-'Amili, *Tafsil Wasa'il al-Shi'a*, 17:136.

First, the causes of enslavement, the causes for manumission, and the rulings on slavery are approved of in the narrations, and were confirmed and acted upon by the Prophet and the Imams in their own time.

Second, what the masters (*awliya'*) of the religion (Prophet and Imams) have approved was modified in comparison with the conventions of their time, and was accepted with some restrictions.

Third, the encouragement to free slaves and expand the causes for eliminating slavery are noteworthy in the narrations.

Fourth, as compared with other issues in jurisprudence (*fiqh*), the number of narrations about the causes for slavery are very few. Narrative evidence for rulings of slavery are also not many.

Fifth, there is no presumption in any of the narrations that the words of the masters of the religion were intended to be stable and permanent rulings.

Subsection Three: The Illegitimacy of Slavery in Contemporary Islam

In relation to the primary ruling (*hukm awwali*), the second approach to bondage and slavery considers it to be forbidden and illegitimate in contemporary times. Humans are absolutely not subject to being owned or enslaved and may not be sold, bought and used as per anyone's will. Holding any belief or religion does not permit ownership of a person who holds that belief or religion, in the same way that there is no action that can cause one to be held as a slave or servant as punishment. Humans are created free and no one has the right to turn them into slaves or property. The absence of servitude and the illegitimacy of slavery are among the inherent rights of humans as humans and cannot be taken away under any circumstances, even by the person themself. Enslavement is a crime and anyone who acts in any way to bring it about is a criminal.

Twelve Points

The above opinion is based on accepting the following points:

First, until a few centuries ago, servitude and slavery were prevalent and common in many parts of the world. Dividing people into free individuals and slaves was accepted. Reasonable people did not consider human servitude and slavery to be something ugly and disreputable, and they did not consider it to be contrary to justice and fairness. During that time, slavery was associated with people who were weak and inferior. Enslavement of war captives was a form of punishment and took place as a kind of reciprocity (*muqabala bi al-mithl*). The traditions of servitude and slavery during that time were among social traditions that were very strong and rooted.

Second, Islam arose at a time when slavery and servitude was dominant and strong, to the extent that eliminating and uprooting it was either impossible or very difficult. In those conditions, Islam approved servitude by modifying the rulings and setting some limits. On the one hand, it limited the causes for slavery and servitude, and, on the other hand, it counted manumission and the freeing of slaves as a form of worship and greatly encouraged it, as well as significantly expanding the causes for eliminating slavery. In a third way, it also provided a minimum of rights which owners could not violate and greatly emphasised that slaves should be treated in a humane, tolerant and kind way. The collection of Islamic rulings on servitude and slavery are ratified rulings (*al-ahkam al-imda'i*), and not positive rulings (*al-ahkam al-ta'sisi*). Servitude is not among the essentials (*daruriyyat*) of religion (*din*) or school (*madhab*) of Islam. It is neither considered to be a fundamental of the creed (*usul i'tiqadi*) nor a particular of it (*masa'il i'tiqadi*). Rather, it is a particular of jurisprudence (*furu' fiqhi*). Slavery is also neither among those rulings which are beyond rational (*tawqifi*) comprehension, nor is it among the devotional (*ta'abbudi*) rulings. Slavery is a declaratory ruling (*hukm wad'i*) that includes some action-orientated rulings (*ahkam taklifi*). The rulings pertaining to slavery are part of the rulings pertaining to human interactions (*mu'amalat*), and these rulings are dependent (*hashiya*) on conventions (*'urf*). During the time of the Revelation and for more than a millennium thereafter, these rulings were compatible with the conventions of the time and were considered just and reasonable.

Third, as the religion of innate nature (*fitrah*) and during the time of the Revelation, all Islamic teachings – whether in terms of the principles of faith, ethical criteria or in practical rulings and duties – were just and compatible with the conventions of reasonability (*sira 'uqala*) and were therefore welcomed by various classes of people. The two conditions of being just and reasonable are not limited to the time of the beginning of the Prophet's mission (*risalah*), but are the conditions for the continuity and duration of the religion. This means that religious rulings must be just and reasonable in other periods of time and places as well. Given that these two characteristics are necessary conditions of

Islamic rulings, their absence means that the ruling lacks legitimacy. Any ruling that in a particular context is unjust and unreasonable to the degree of certainty (*yaqin* and not speculative, estimation, guesswork or conjecture) is not legitimate in that context.[78]

Fourth, being just and reasonable is neither religious nor subordinate to religion. However, they are issues that precede religion and are placed in the chain of reason for religious rulings. It is religion that has to be just and reasonable, not justice and reasonability that have to be religious. The important dispute of the People of Justice (*'Adliyyah*) (the Sunni Mu'tazilah and the Shi'ite) points to such conclusions. People rely on their pure innate natures to choose a religion that is just and reasonable.[79]

Fifth, people's understanding of justice and reasonability, especially the conventions of scholars, has not been stable throughout time and has evolved and progressed. The criteria for justice and reasonability have become more precise and have deepened. There are many particulars that with today's common sense, and specifically from the perspective of conventional reasonableness (*mu'amilat*), are not considered just, but which in the past were considered just and fair. Today, the conventions of reasonability (*sira 'uqala*) do not tolerate what in the past was considered correct and good. Human understanding is inclined towards growth, and while it may have neglected issues in the past, today it uses its experience to critique the past. However, this does not mean absolute changes in human knowledge and science. What I have discussed is an *a posteriori* proposition and not an *a priori* one. It is a particular affirmative (*mujibah juz'iyyah*) proposition and not a universal affirmative (*mujibah kulliyyah*) proposition.

Sixth, as the final (*khatam*) religion, Islam – in addition to seeking solutions and providing alternatives and making rulings that apply to all times and places – cannot turn a blind eye and remain silent on solving issues that pertain to the time and place of the Revelation. As such, it is natural that among the corpus of Islamic rulings, there may be rulings that are seasonal, temporary, and particular to time and place. It is clear that this does not mean that all rulings of *shari'a* are of this type. Distinguishing the stable and

---

78 This issue has been outlined in detail in Chapter 1, above.
79 Morteza Motahhari (1919–1979) described this point on justice in his notes that were published after his death: *Barras-yei Ejmali-ye Maban-ei Eqtesad-e Eslami* (*Brief Review of the Fundamentals of Islamic Economy*) (Tehran: Hekmat, 1982), 14–15. I expanded it to reasonability.

permanent rulings from those that are temporary and seasonal is the main duty of expert *mujtahids* and researchers of jurisprudence. Any time that the insightful jurist finds with certainty that one of the rulings of *shari'a* is no longer just or reasonable, he or she will discover that such a ruling was one of the temporary and seasonal ones, and that its credibility (*i'tibar*) has expired, and is no longer legitimate. This does not mean the conventional abrogation (*naskh*), since legislation and abrogation of rulings are in the hands of God and His Prophet only, and it is not up to others, even jurists (*mujtahids*), to forbid what God has permanently allowed or to permit what God has permanently forbidden. But discovering the limit and duration of the credibility of a temporary ruling of *shari'a* is among the duties of the jurists and *mujtahids*. In addition, the temporary and seasonal orders of *shari'a* are not limited to governmental rulings (*ahkam hukumati*) and the commands of the Prophet and the Imams as rulers (*awamir sultani*).

Seventh, to observe utmost precaution in maintaining the permanent divine rulings, the primary assumption in the rulings of *shari'a* is permanence and continuity, and one must offer evidence for excluding a ruling on the basis of being temporary, seasonal and particular to a specific time and place. If no credible evidence is provided for a ruling being temporary and seasonal, then the ruling will remain stable and durable. Among the most important forms of evidence for a ruling being temporary and seasonal and belonging to a particular place and time, is to demonstrate with certitude that the ruling is not just and reasonable in another time.

Eighth, it is not the case that human reason is absolutely incapable of understanding the benefits and harms (*masalih wa mafasid*) of the rulings of *shari'a* pertaining to human interactions (*mu'amalat*), especially in the ratified rulings (*al-ahkam al-imda'i*) section. This does not mean that human reason understands all the benefits and harms of all the rulings of *shari'a*, but, rather that this is a point regarding partial or limited understanding (*dark fi al-jumlah*) of the aforementioned rulings (interactions), the same way in which the Usulis practically confronted the Akhbaris and the people of Hadith.

Ninth, servitude, humans as property and slavery are among the clearest issues in regard to which what people consider to be reasonable has completely shifted over the last century. If at one time the most famous philosophers such as Plato and Aristotle defended it, today slavery and servitude in all its forms is condemned by reasonable people and is found to be unjust and unfair. In contemporary times, the conventions of reasonability would never tolerate slavery and consider it to be contrary to human rights. The conventions of reasonability today consider servitude and slavery to be something ugly and disreputable which arises from the excessive desires of humans and transgresses against the absolute rights of others. The reasonable conventions of today consider humans to be superior to their beliefs and believe in a minimum of rights for all people regardless of their belief, religion, race, gender, colour and social situation. It holds that humans have a freedom that cannot be taken away and that it is absolutely unacceptable that people be owned as property. No human becomes property, even if he or she wants it. Any belief or religion or committing of a crime cannot lead to the permissibility of owning humans. Temporarily or permanently taking away someone's freedom as a result of committing certain crimes is never seen as permission to turn the criminal into property or a slave.

Tenth, with the elimination of the conventions of reasonability, which was the main basis for the ratified ruling (*huk imda'i*) on slavery and ownership of humans in Islam, it is natural that this ruling too be recognised as a temporary and seasonal ruling of *shari'a*, a ruling whose limit and duration of credibility has come to an end and which in these times is lacking credibility and legitimacy. That is to say, slavery, servitude and the owning of humans in such a context is illegitimate and forbidden (*haram*). This prohibition and lack of legitimacy does not question the legitimacy and permissibility of slavery in the past, since a subject such as slavery and humans as property can have two different rulings in two different contexts. In a context where slavery was confirmed by the conventions of reasonability of the time and was ratified (*imda'*) by the Legislator, it was permitted, and in a context where slavery is considered by the conventions of reasonability to be ugly, disreputable and unjust, it is forbidden and illegitimate. There is no evidence for permanent and continuous ratification (*imda'*) of the slavery ruling. All ratified rulings (*al-ahkam al-imda'i*) are conditional on continuity of justice and reasonability. Indeed, if the inclination of the Illuminated Law (*shar' anwar*) was towards the reduction and eventual elimination of slavery, and given that the global context of today's world is prepared for fundamentally uprooting servitude and slavery, why should we have any doubt about abolishing servitude and slavery and realising the ultimate goal of the Prophet of mercy.

Eleventh, it seems that the prohibition of servitude and the uprooting of slavery is also compatible with the spirit of the teachings of Islam and the lofty goals of *shari'a*. Slavery was among the incidental (*'aradi*) rulings whose elimination caused no damage to the pillar of *shari'a* and the essences of religion, and was such a refinement that it illuminated the beauty of religiosity even more. In Islamic anthropology, humans are the vicegerent of God on Earth (Q. 2:30 and 6:165) and have the biggest capacity for knowledge (Q. 2:31–33), humans are the trustees of God (Q. 33:72). "We have honoured the children of Adam and carried them by land and sea; We have provided good sustenance for them and favoured them specially above many of those We have created" (Q. 17:70). Humans have been created from a single soul (Q. 4:1). In Islam, superiority is based on piety (*taqwa*), not on temporal mundane authority such as wealth, ownership and mastership. "People, We created you all from a single man and a single woman, and made you into races and tribes so that you should recognise one another. In God's eyes, the most honoured of you are the ones most mindful of Him: God is all knowing, all aware" (Q. 48:13). Happiness in the Hereafter relates to faith and righteous deeds, and freedom and slavery plays no role in it: "As for those who believe and do good deeds – We do not let the reward of anyone who does a good deed go to waste" (Q. 18:30). The Prophet negated the superiority of Arabs over non-Arabs and the superiority based on colour except in piety.[80] In the view of the Prophet "people are equal like the teeth of a comb".[81] Imam Ali has said, "Oh human, do not be a slave to another person, God has created you free."[82] The complete abolition of slavery is aligned with the goals of the Prophet (Q. 7:157). In reality, what burden (*isr*) and iron collar (*aghlal*) is greater than slavery?

Twelfth, what if there is a delusion that the appearance of an issue in the Qur'an means that it is among the stable and permanent rulings of religion. First, the Qur'an has matters that are abrogating (*nasikh*) and abrogated (*mansukh*), and it is not considered wrong to cite abrogated matters, it is permitted to do so. Second, citing historical issues about past peoples and prophets and the Prophet of Islam, which is prevalent in the Qur'an, and claiming that it was specific to the past, does not undermine its goodness as

80 Ahmad b. Hanbal, *Musnad al-Imam Ahmad b. Hanbal (Collection of Hadith Compiled by Ahmad b. Hanbal)*, ed. Shu'aib al-Arnut et al. (Beirut: Resalah, 2001), 38:474, hadith No. 23489; and without mentioning the superiority based on colour: al-Ya'qubi, *Tarikh al-Ya'qubi*, 2:440.
81 Al-Saduq, *Man la Yahduruhu al-Faqih*, 4:379, hadith No. 5798.
82 Al-Radi, *Nahj al-Balagha*, 400, letter 31.

a verse of the Qur'an. Taking admonition from these stories is not limited to time. Third, none of the causes for slavery have been cited in the Qur'an. Fourth, slavery being unjust and unreasonable in this time is a definite indicator of its illegitimacy and its impermissibility in current circumstances but not in the past. The rulings of slavery were legitimate in the context where this temporary ruling was credible, but not outside that time. Abandoning the important foundation of the principle of freedom (*asalah al-hurriyyah*) is possible only with reliable evidence, and temporary rulings do not have the capacity to be excluded from this principle outside their context of validity.

13
The Rights of Non-Muslims in Contemporary Islam[1]

One of the issues facing contemporary Islam is the rights of non-Muslims in Muslim-majority societies. The issue originates in the fact that traditional *shari'a* determines a direct relationship between people's rights, on the one hand, and their religion and political situation, on the other. This means that from the first perspective, that is, religion, we are dealing with at least three different kinds of rights: the rights of Muslims; the rights of People of the Book (the followers of scriptures such as the Torah and the Gospel); and the rights of non-believers. And from the second perspective, that is, the political situation of a non-Muslim as compared with that of a Muslim, at least two scenarios are imaginable: one is peaceful with the mutual respect that usually occurs by agreement and treaty; and the other is one of hostility and enmity that can lead to war and armed conflict.

Based on this, the world is divided into three realms: the territory of Islam (*dar al-Islam*); the territory of war (*dar al-harb*); and the territory of treaties (*dar al-'ahd* or *dar al-mu'ahada*). The first realm is territories where Muslims are in the majority, or where they dominate the territory; the second are territories that have declared war on Muslims; and the third are territories that have signed treaties with Muslims and with which they have economic, cultural and political exchanges.

---

1 Mohsen Kadivar, *Hoquq-e Ghair-e Mosalmanan dar Eslam-e Mo'aser*, presented at the International Conference "Reframing Islam: Politics into Law", Irish Centre for Human Rights, National University of Ireland, Galway, 11 September 2005. The Persian version of this chapter was published in *A'een*, monthly, Tehran, 6 (March 2007): 69–72.

It is clear that not all residents of the territory of Islam are Muslims, but that since the early days of Islam, Jews, Christians and Zoroastrians have lived alongside Muslims. Non-Muslims who live in the territory of Islam are not limited to these three religions; any non-Muslim who can enter into a treaty with Muslims regardless of his or her religion will have the possibility of living peacefully in the territory of Islam. Similarly, on the other hand, the territory of the treaty is not limited to non-Muslims either, much less the Muslims who live in these lands. Although it is somewhat difficult to imagine Muslims living in the territory of war, it is not impossible.

In any case, in this threefold division of the world, we are faced with two minorities that cannot be ignored: the non-Muslim minorities in the territory of Islam and the Muslim minority in the territory of treaty. In Islamic literature, these non-Muslim minorities have been given *shari'a* titles such as the people of *dhimma*, *mu'ahad* and *musta'man*. The people of *dhimma* are those People of the Book who have signed a *dhimma* treaty (protection treaty) with a Muslim ruler and in exchange for the payment of a *jizya* tax, are thereby able to live in security among Muslims. *Mu'ahad* is a non-believer who has signed an agreement with a ruler of Muslims and who is treated in accordance to the terms of the agreement. *Musta'man* is a non-Muslim who has travelled to the territory of Islam to become familiar with Islamic teachings in accordance with a temporary agreement, which is usually less than a year.

Despite having a number of rights such as the right to life, security, property, trade, religious treatment, religious training of children, maintenance of temples and complete freedom in the private sphere, the people of *dhimma* are also denied some rights such as prohibition on religious proselytising among Muslims, visible actions that contradict *shari'a* in the public sphere, and the establishment of new temples. Non-Muslims who have not signed a *dhimma* agreement, but who are considered *mu'ahad* on the basis of having accepted another agreement, generally enjoy fewer rights. However, compared with warring non-believers, they have a great number of rights.

Independent books and treatises have been written about the rights of non-Muslims living in Muslim-majority lands, especially about the people of *dhimma*. In addition, in books of *fiqh* a detailed chapter has been written about the rulings that pertain to them, a list which would itself constitute a lengthy treatise. Experts in law have also carried out specialist debates about the rights of non-Muslims under the umbrella of discussions about international Islamic law. Historians have studied how Muslims have treated religious minorities. Overall, reports on how Muslims have treated non-Muslims residing in Islamic lands show that it was successful and defensible as compared with how non-Muslims have treated religious minorities (such as Jews and Muslims) in other lands. In this chapter, the task is not to review the actions of the past. I believe that the solutions of Islamic *shari'a* regarding the rights of non-Muslims was justified in its particular time.

Categorisation of the Shari'a *Rulings Pertaining to Non-Muslims*

The question I seek to answer is whether the rulings of *shari'a* pertaining to non-Muslims, such as those pertaining to the people of *dhimma*, belong to the stable and permanent rulings of *shari'a* that are necessary to carry out anyway? Or are they among the limited and conditional rulings of *shari'a*, the necessity of which to act upon depends on the realisation of their conditions, the most important being that Muslims are in power. Therefore, at a time when Muslims are not the regional or world power, are these rulings cancelled based on this condition not being met? Or are these rulings in general considered among the changing and time-bound rulings of *shari'a* whose duration of credibility has come to an end and are considered in the category of the abrogated rulings of *shari'a*, that is, that overall their legislation was appropriate for the conditions of a particular place and time, and with the shift in these particular conditions these rulings too are changeable?

If we hold any of these positions theoretically, there is no doubt that in current conditions none of these orders could be carried out practically. Even those who hold the first theory (that the rulings are permanent and stable), have no choice but to submit to the cessation of some of these rulings from a practical perspective, no matter how credible they find them theoretically. This chapter sets out to determine and prove a fourth view that is made up of the three views noted above, that is, the rulings on non-Muslims in the Qur'an, the traditions of the Prophet, and the manner of the people of *shari'a* (*sirah al-mutashirri'ah*), and that what we understand as Islamic *shari'a* is not all of one kind, but can be divided into the following: first, the stable and permanent rulings that can be called "principles and foundations of the rights of non-Muslims"; second, rulings that are limited to and conditional on the power of Muslims; and third, changing and time-bound rulings whose duration of credibility has come to an end and are considered abrogated.

The difference between the second and third rulings is that the second are credible and executable if the conditions are realised, while the time of the credibility of the third has come to an end.

To put it more precisely, the *shari'a* rulings on contemporary non-Muslims are of two types: first, the principles and foundations of the rights of non-Muslims which are stable and permanent; and, second, the conditional and changing rulings on the basis of which stable and permanent principles and foundations are designed. These are considered in the category of the policies of Islamic society that are limited to the observance of the public interest and national benefit of Muslims and which do not have a permanent and stable form. What is important, is finding and extracting those stable principles and foundations.

Some Muslims think that all of the rulings of the time of the Revelation are in the category of *shari'a* rulings which are stable and timeless. They have neglected the obvious point, that the Prophet, in addition to having the responsibility of clarifiying and issuing rulings of Islam that were permanent and timeless and placeless, had the duty of organising and administering the issues of his time, and that those rulings which he issued in relation to the second category are changing and temporary and not stable and permanent. In some instances, the Prophet was not able to deal with a problem on his own, and the issue could be solved only by Revelation. Based on this, some of the verses of the Qur'an may comprise some changing and temporary rulings. In any case, the majority of the rulings on non-Muslims in the narratives (*ahadith*) are conditional and changing rulings, and the principles and foundations of the rights of non-Muslims are mostly laid out in the Qur'an and sometimes in the Traditions of the Prophet.

Principles and Foundations of the Rights of Non-Muslims

The first principle is the essential dignity of human beings. In Islam, all humans regardless of their race, colour, gender, rank, religion and belief have essential human dignity. The evidence for this principle is in the verse "And We have honoured the children of Adam" (Q. 17:70). Without doubt, this honour is the basis of the rights whose observation is mandatory, the minimum rights which must be observed for every single person. Based on this, non-Muslims are included in this principle in the same way as Muslims.

The second principle is the plurality of religions and the differences of people in religion, which is a reality related to God's will. From the Islamic point of view, humans are free to choose a religion and no one can force them to become Muslim. If it was supposed to be the case that all people are Muslims, then God would have made it so. However, he has not done so and has seen the benefit and good in the plurality of religions and the differences of people in religion. The evidence for this important principle is found in numerous verses, including: "Say, 'Now the truth has come from your Lord: let those who wish to believe in it do so, and let those who wish to reject it do so'" (Q. 18:29); also "If your Lord had pleased, He would have made all people a single community, but they continue to have their differences" (Q. 11:118); and, finally, "Had your Lord willed, all the people on Earth would have believed. So, can your [Prophet] compel people to believe?" (Q. 10:99). This principle necessitates the acceptance of followers of other religions.

The third principle is that a Muslim is not obligated to question others about their religion. On the one hand, accounting and questioning and punishments are going to take place on Judgement Day, and, on the other hand, the judge is God and not fallible humans. To think that we are permitted to target and reproach non-Muslims on account of their religion is to step in the shoes of God and to bring Judgement Day to this world. A Muslim believes that in relation to the issue of religion, just judgement will be carried out by God on Judgement Day. This undoubtable Qur'anic principle has been affirmed by numerous verses, including: "and if they argue with you, say, 'God is well aware of what you are doing.' On the Day of Resurrection, God will judge between you regarding your differences" (Q. 22:68–69). In another place in the Qur'an, God reminds His Prophet to endure in his faith and to say: "to us our deeds and to you yours, so let there be no argument between us and you – God will gather us together, and to Him we shall return" (Q. 42:15).

The fourth principle is coexistence in peace and with respect. Muslims are obligated to be at peace with others and are not permitted to enter into hostile campaigns against those who have not acted against Muslims. Rather, they are obligated to be friends with these people and nations and to spread good and act in fairness. This principle, which is the source of foreign policies in Islamic lands, is the first principle of how to behave towards non-Muslims and has been explicitly affirmed by the Qur'an: "And He does not forbid you to deal kindly and justly with anyone who has not fought you for your faith or driven you out of your homes: God loves the just. But God forbids you to take as allies those who have fought against you for your faith, driven you out of your homes, and helped others to drive you out: any of you who take them as allies will truly be wrongdoers" (Q. 60:8–9). Based on this criterion, Muslims should deal with peaceful non-Muslims with goodness, justice and friendship, and must cut relations with oppressive and transgressing non-Muslims. This order of the Qur'an is exactly in accordance with the rational criteria of peaceful coexistence and mutual respect of international law.

The fifth principle is that all relations between Muslims and non-Muslims are based on agreements and contracts. The relationship between Muslim-majority countries and religious minorities must be based on agreements that are to the satisfaction of both sides. Thus, in the religious literature *dhimma* is an agreement that is established between the People of the Book and the ruler of Muslims. Similarly, agreements are made with non-Muslims who are not People of the Book and are called *mu'ahada*. The non-Muslim side of these agreements is called *mu'ahad* (non-believer). In *istiman* (requesting protection) as well, a temporary agreement is made between Muslims and non-Muslims that all Muslims should respect.

All three agreements are binding (*lazim*) for the Muslim side and non-binding (*ja'iz*) for the non-Muslim side. This means that the non-Muslim side can cancel the agreement at any point. Both sides are required to carry out the contract as long as both sides act on what they have agreed. Thus, if an Islamic government is not successful in providing security for the people of *dhimma*, then the non-Muslim side has the right to not pay the *jizya* tax. It is clear that the non-Muslim side is completely free as to whether or not to enter into the agreement or its provisions.

Being faithful to one's promise is among the necessities of *shari'a*. In the Qur'an, numerous verses emphasise the importance of being faithful to promises and agreements, and there is specific affirmation of being faithful to promises and agreements with non-Muslims as long as they have not violated the agreements. The following are examples: "You who believe, fulfil your contracts"[2] (Q. 5:1); "As for those who have honoured the treaty you made with them and who have not supported anyone against you: fulfil your agreement with them to the end of their term. God loves those who

---

2 In Abdel Haleem, *The Qur'an, A New Translation*, al-'uqud was translated as "obligations".

are mindful of Him" (Q. 9:4); "as long as they remain true to you, be true to them; God loves those who are mindful of Him" (Q. 9:7).

Relationships between Muslims and non-Muslims based on agreements that are to the satisfaction of both sides, whether it is with religious minorities within Islamic lands or with non-Muslims outside the borders of Islamic lands, is a reasonable principle that is harmonious with the criteria of contemporary international law. It is clear that both sides determine their own interests and benefits in the agreement, and it is obvious that the provisions of such agreements will not be the same in varying conditions of time and place.

The sixth principle is that of reciprocity (*muqabala bi al-mithl*) while observing justice. One of the ruling principles of the relationship between Muslims and non-Muslims is the principle of dealing with others the same way that one has been dealt with. This means that a Muslim or Islamic government has the right to act towards non-Muslims or non-Islamic states in the same way that the other side has acted towards them. The principle of reciprocity is reasonable and a deterrent. The Qur'an has noted the correctness of this reasonable principle in certain circumstances, such as: "So if anyone commits aggression against you, attack him as he attacked you, but be mindful of God, and know that He is with those who are mindful of Him" (Q. 2:194); "If you [believers] have to respond to an attack, make your response proportionate, but it is best to stand fast" (Q. 16:126).

However, the principle of reciprocity has been limited and restricted to the principle of justice. Muslims are obligated to precisely follow the principles of justice, fairness and being measured, and to not go beyond the framework of justice in carrying out the principle of reciprocity: "Do not let hatred of others lead you away from justice, but adhere to justice, for that is closer to awareness of God" (Q. 5:8). Both the principles of reciprocity and justice are reasonable and external to religion and apply to both Muslims and non-Muslims equally.

The Rights of Non-Muslims in Varying Circumstances

Given the above principles, it seems that there is no previously determined mould that applies to all times and places. It is natural that what is in the interest of Muslims is not the same in all times and places. In the same way, that which benefits non-Muslims also changes. At times Muslims are in power and at times they are in a position of weakness. How can one provide a single prescription for these relationships? Based on this, provisions such as the *jizya* tax and how much it should be, as well as other details of the *dhimma* agreement that are in the books of *fiqh*, are all rulings that were specific to a particular time and place, and there is no reason for their application to circumstances of a different time and place. All of the dimensions of the agreements, including *dhimma* and *mu'ahada*, are in the hands of the government elected by Muslims and the elected ruler sets the terms of these agreements in accordance with what is in the interest of, and of benefit to, his society. Whether there should be *jizya* or not, whether or not new temples should be built, whether religious minorities should serve conscription or not, and so forth, are all among the changing rulings which are never considered permanent or eternal.

In addition, there is another factor at work. This is the way in which to deal with Muslim minorities in other countries. The Muslim ruler considers the extent of the rights and freedoms Muslim minorities have in other countries as one of the factors in determining how to deal with religious minorities in his own country. Of course, this is only one of the factors, since even if others treat Muslims inhumanely and with violence, Islam does not allow Muslims to go outside the framework of justice.

Reflecting on the above clearly shows that the social rulings of Islam are linked to the political conditions of a specic time and one cannot blindly carry them out without observing the conditions of time and place. Put another way, in observing the principles and foundations of Islam, the majority of transactional rulings (*mu'amalat*) in Islamic *shari'a* have been made in observance of the conditions of time and place and have associated flexibility in various circumstances. This flexibility gives contemporary Islamic *ijtihad* the dynamism required to deal with different circumstances.

14
Social Security in Islamic Teachings[1]

Introduction

Social security constitutes the support that society provides in the face of social and economic upheavals that occur as a result of the severe decrease or lack of income resulting from illness, pregnancy, accidents or illnesses that are due to work, unemployment, inability to work, age, death, and also those that occur as a result of the increases in the costs of medical care and family care.[2]

Based on this, one can accept that "social justice cannot be realised without social security".[3] The Universal Declaration of Human Rights officially recognises social security among basic human rights: "Everyone, as a member of society, has the right to social security and is entitled to realisation, through national effort and international cooperation and in accordance with the organisation and resources of each State, of the economic, social

---

1 *Ta'min-e Ejtema'i dar Ta'alim-e Eslami. Gozaresh-e Nezam-e Jame'-e Refah wa Ta'min-e Ejtema'i* (*The System of Comprehensive Welfare and Social Security*) (Tehran: Research Council of the Institute of Advanced Research on Social Security, 1998). A concise version of this report was published publicly: *Nezam-e Jame'-e Refah wa Ta'min-e Ejtema'i, Khulase-ye Gozaresh* (*The System of Comprehensive Welfare and Social Security, Concise Report*) (Tehran: Research Council of the Institute of Advanced Research on Social Security, 1999), with a summary of my article on pp. 15–18.
2 C102 – Social Security (Minimum Standards) Convention, 1952 (No. 102) (paraphrase).
3 The main slogan of the International Labour Organization and the International Social Security Association in their 1994 Philadelphia declaration.

and cultural rights indispensable for his dignity and the free development of his personality."[4]

Based on experiences in this regard, the methods and strategies for providing social security in the last century can be divided into two main groups. The first group is the insurance system based on the financial participation of workers, employers and the government which covers the workforce of society. In this group, three strategies for providing social security are apparent. First, the strategy which consists of the obligatory participation of individuals in society who are supported in the form of insurance payments, including retirement insurance, disability, unemployment, and death and medical care insurance. Second, the strategy of reserve funds, which, like the previous strategy, is based on the participation of the individuals covered, with the difference that they enjoy the services of the fund in accordance to how much they contributed in payments to the fund. Third, the strategy of employer responsibility where the employer has direct responsibility for making social insurance payments for employees. This has been a less important and less prevalent strategy than the previous two.

The second group is the support system which covers all of the vulnerable segments of society, including those unable to work and those without guardians, and which is based on government support. In this group, there are two strategies for providing social security. The first strategy is where every person, whether working or not, has the right to receive social services assistance from general governmental resources when certain circumstances arise. These circumstances include ageing, illness, disability, unemployment and being without guardians. The second is where social services are particular to people who need various forms of support due to physical and mental conditions. This includes care for people who have no guardians, those with physical and mental disabilities, retirement, and the creation of job opportunities and skills for those in need (welfare services). Alongside insurance and support systems, there is another system called relief services which provides help to those hit by earthquakes, famine and other natural disasters, and which conventionally lies outside the system of social services.[5]

---

4 Article 22 of the UDHR, ratified by the UN General Assembly in 1948.

5 Obtained from Bahram Panahi, *Osoul wa Mabani-ye Nezam-e Ta'min-e Ejtema'i* (*Principles and Bases of Social Service Systems*) (Tehran: Research Council of the Institute of Advanced Research on Social Security, 1997).

Given the reforms, methods and strategies noted above, the following questions can be raised: as the last Divine religion, how has Islam looked at the issue of social security? From the point of view of Islam, what are the bases and principles for realising social security? In *shari'a* rulings and Islamic jurisprudence (*fiqh*), what ways, approaches and solutions have been predicted for realising social security? What are the similarities and differences between these approaches and solutions and those that are prevalent and known in other countries? Who is included in social security from the viewpoint of Islam? Who are the sources of social security; is it the government, the wealthy, the participation of those receiving it or are there underground sources? Is social security among the necessities (*ilzami*) of Islam, or is it among those things that are not necessary or which are perhaps considered recommended (*mustahabb*)? What role do Islamic teachings have in realising social security? This chapter has been written to provide answers to questions such as those above.

By Islamic teachings, I mean the verses of the Qur'an as well as the credible narratives of the Prophet and the Shi'ite Imams. In cases where there are differences in the rulings and opinions, I have relied on the Shi'a point of view, and in cases where there are differences among Shi'a jurists, I have used the dominant (*mashhur*) view.

The first section covers the foundations of social security in Islam. The second section addresses and assesses various systems of social security that have been predicted in Islamic jurisprudence (*fiqh*) and that have some similarity to prevalent categories of social security. The third section addresses prevalent ways of providing social security that were not considered in traditional systems of *fiqh* and assesses them from an Islamic perspective.

Section One: The Foundations of Social Security in Islam

The meaning of foundations here is the general and overall bases, goals, principles and rules that are considered to be the foundations of the Islamic orders and rules of social security, on the basis of which religious positions and policies are set in the arena of social security. In cases where Islam has not issued the necessary rulings, meaning issues that are innovative (*mustahdatha*), these foundations provide guidance for establishing the necessary laws for social security. These foundations, which have been taken from theological, *fiqhi*, interpretations of the Qur'an and commentaries on the narratives, are as follows.

The First Principle: The Principle of Liking One's Kind

In Islamic teachings humans have inherent dignity (Q. 17:70). Regardless of colour, race, gender, nationality, religion or sect, all come from one mother and father (Q. 4:1), and enjoy the same minimum of human rights. The people have been introduced as the family (*'yal*) of God.[6] The most beloved before God are those who are most beneficial to people – the family of God.[7] From the Islamic perspective, people only fall into two categories: they are either brothers (and sisters) in religion or they are of the same kind (human).[8] We are obligated by *shari'a* to deal with both groups with mercy, love and kindness, and to refrain from transgressing against their rights. Service to the people, eliminating their needs and solving their problems is a form of worship. Among the ways of becoming close to God and gaining His satisfaction is to provide service to people, and especially to provide help to those in need. Neglecting or not knowing about the needs of others, especially among one's family and neighbours, are among the factors that prevent prayers being answered and that bring about the anger of God. In total, one can say that humans are respected in Islam and meeting the rights and needs of humans is affirmed and recommended by religion.

The Second Principle: Fairness and Justice

God is Just, and commands justice. Instituting fairness (*qist*) was announced as the aim of sending prophets (Q. 57:25), and God has asked people to try to establish fairness and justice in society (Q. 4:135). Justice is a criterion of *shari'a* rulings, and the life and freshness of the rulings derive from justice.[9]

---

6 The Prophet says: "*al-khaq 'yal Allah*" (people are the family of God), al-Kulaini, *al-Kafi, Kitab al-Iman wa al-Kufr, bab* 70, hadith No. 6, 2:164.

7 Ibid.

8 Imam Ali, al-Radi, *Nahj al-Balagha*, letter 53 (to Malik al-Ashtar), 427.

9 Imam Ali: "*al-'adl hayat al-ahkam*", Abdul Wahid b. Muhammad al-Tamimi al-Amudi, *Gurar al-Hikam wa Durar al-Kalim* (*Exalted Aphorisms and Pearls of Speech*), ed. S. Mahdi Raja'i (Qom: Dar al-Kutub al-Islami, 1990), 31, No. 440; and "*al-'adl nizam al-imrah*", ibid., 46, No. 854.

The most important duty of governments is to establish justice. If societies had observed the criteria of justice and people's rights, poverty would have been eliminated from those societies.[10] Whatever counts as an example of the realisation of fairness and justice is obligatory according to *shari'a*. Social justice is not possible without social security, thus it is clear that in order to reach the high aim of social justice, carrying out social security in its conventional meaning is obligatory. The principle of justice is one of the most important goals and foundations of social security.

The Third Principle: The Abomination of Poverty

In Islamic teachings, poverty is considered abominable and a great distress,[11] and one must turn to God for shelter in the face of poverty, which stands in opposition to the rich, vast and expanding Divine blessings.[12] In the teachings of the Prophet a relationship between poverty and unbelief has been indicated.[13] For this reason, eliminating poverty and making fundamental efforts to help those in need are at the forefront of the social teachings of Islam. In the first place, Islam encourages its followers to work and put in effort, and has warned against laziness, disorder and uselessness; in addition, it has not approved of panhandling, claiming poverty and begging for anyone.[14] Rather, it has attempted to provide for the shortcomings of those in need in a manner and a way that preserves their honour and dignity.[15] Thus, it considers providing for their legitimate needs to be a human right and a *shar'i* obligation, which will be considered in the upcoming principles.

---

10 See Mohammad Reza Hakimi, Mohammad Hakimi and Ali Hakimi, *al-Hayat* (*The Life*) (Tehran: Dafter-e Nashr-e Farhang-e Eslami, 1989), 6:324–368.

11 Imam Ali: *"Ala wa inna min albala' al-faqa"* (al-Amudi, *Gurar al-Hikam wa Durar al-Kalim*, 178, No. 28). Imam Ali: "al-faqr al-mawt al-akbar" (al-Radi, *Nahj al-Balagh*, 500, *al-hikmah* No. 163,)

12 See Hakimi, *al-Hayat*, section 11, ch. 41, 5:27–58.

13 *"Kada al-faqr an yakuna kufra"*, al-Saduq, *al-Khisal*, 1:12.

14 The Prophet says: *"Al-mu'min iza lam yakun lahu hirfah ya'ishu bidinihi"* (Mirza Hussain al-Nuri al-Tabrisi, *Mustadrak al-Wasa'il wa Mustanbat al-Masa'il* (*The Emendation of Wasa'il [al-Shi'a by al-Hurr al-'Amili] and Discovered Issues*) (Qom: Mu'assasa Al al-Bayt li Ihya' al-Turath, 1991), 13:11); *"Mal'unun man alqa kallahu 'la al-nas"* (al-Hurr al-'Amili, *Tafsil Wasa'il al-Shi'a*, 21:543); Hakimi, *al-Hayat*, 5:332–333.

15 See Hakimi, *al-Hayat*, vol. 6, section 12.

The Fourth Principle: The Principle of Goodness (*ihsan*) and Charity (*infaq*)

A believer is someone who with satisfaction and enthusiasm gives in the way of God the same property that God has given to him or her as sustenance and provision. Charity in its conventional meaning is understood as a pillar of religiosity and among the fruits of faith to the unseen world (*iman bil-ghaib*) (Q. 2:3). Goodness and charity have a dual impact: on the one hand, in carrying out *jihad* with property and in cutting off the material hinge, a person gains access to a phase of perfection, edification of the self and the elevation of the spirit; and, on the other hand, the problems of the needy in society are eliminated and society will move towards fairness and justice.[16] To share property with the other, which is referred to in Islamic literature as *muwasat* (beneficence), proceeds in stages, some of which are recommended and optional, but some of which are obligatory and are a condition of faith.[17]

The Qur'an teaches believers that there is a specific amount of their property that belongs to the disenfranchised (Q. 70:24). Someone who follows the tenets of religion looks at goodness, charity and beneficence as observing the rights of the needy and as the carrying out of *shari'a* duties, and does not consider it as doing a favour for someone else. Tying faith to charity, the correlation of prayer and charity, and ascribing *jihad* to charity in Islamic texts is not accidental, but rather tells of the high place of this religious duty in social teachings.

The Fifth Principle: The Principle of Brotherhood in Faith

The Qur'an thrice calls believers brothers (in Q. 49:10, 3:103 and 33:5). The blessing of brotherhood in religion and faith creates certain rights and duties. Without doubt, brotherhood in faith and Islam are not just compliments and empty slogans, thus it is natural that the Legislator would speak of brotherly duties and rights and insist that His followers observe these rights and duties. The following are included in these rights: meeting their needs; eliminating their worries; providing their nutrition (the full believer does not eat if his brother or sister is hungry, the believer does not finish

---

16 See Hakimi, *al-Hayat*, 5:444.
17 Ibid., section 11, ch. 46, 5:111–122.

his drink when his brother or sister is thirsty); providing their clothing (the believer does not dress well while his brother or sister lacks clothing); and eliminating their financial problems.[18] Included in the Qur'anic teaching "mercy between them" (Q. 48:29) is that each Muslim should act to meet the needs of his or her Muslim brother or sister. The prevalent particulars of social security are all details of the rights of brotherhood in faith. It is necessary to note that the rights and duties of brotherhood in faith are divided into two sections of obligatory and recommended duties, and that only some of the obligatory ones are discussed, while there are numerous examples of recommended ones which make up the characteristics of an ideal society.[19]

Section Two: Systems Related to Providing Social Security in Shari'a

Research into *shari'a* rulings and the various sections of *fiqh* shows that some rulings and systems of *fiqh* have a direct congruence with the goals of providing social security. In addition to compiling and reporting these, I will provide a general comparison and highlight their similarities and differences with prevalent ways of providing social security.

First: *Zakat*

Zakat is one of the practical pillars of Islam and is among the *shari'a*-based taxes that are specifically allocated. The payment of *zakat* cleanses property and brings the owner closer to God.[20] Those who pay and provide *zakat* are the comfortable class of society whose property has reached a certain level,[21] and a specific segment of their property (about one-fortieth)[22] is annually accounted and spent on what religion has determined. There are

18 Al-Tabrisi, *Makarim al-Akhlaq*, 157; al-Hurr al-'Amili, *Tafsil Wasa'il al-Shi'a*, 16:341–370; Hakimi, *al-Hayat*, 5:114.
19 See Hakimi, *al-Hayat*, 5:114.
20 Q. 9:103: "Take from their wealth a charity to purify them and increase them by it."
21 After the Revelation of 9:102, the Prophet announced to the people that "The same way that God has made prayer obligatory for you, *zakat* is obligatory too. It is necessary that you pay *zakat* on gold and silver, camel and cow and sheep, wheat and oat and date and raisin and the rest has been given to you." al-Hurr al-'Amili, *Tafsil Wasa'il al-Shi'a*, 9:53 zakat, s. 8, hadith No. 1.
22 For example, the *nisab* (minimum amount of property liable to *muwasat* payment of the *zakat*) for gold is 20 Dinar and its *zakat* is half a Dinar. The *nisab* of silver is 200 Dirham and its *zakat* 5 Dirham. See Ruhollah Khomeini, *Tahrir al-Wasilah*, 1:339–340.

eight expenditures and these are allotted to the following: the poor, the needy, those who administer them, those whose hearts need winning over, to free slaves and help those in debt, for God's cause, and for travellers in need (Q. 9:60). I clarify each case briefly.

A poor person is someone whose source of income is not enough to support a life in accordance to his or her social class. Put another way, he or she cannot pay the yearly costs of him- or herself and those he or she supports.

A poor person is not necessarily unemployed or unable to work, that person may be working, or may have the minimum of life (without regard for his or her social class); what counts as poverty and wealth depends on the time, place and standards/class (*sha'n*) that accord to the person; this means the necessities of having a place of residence, a means of transport, a servant, proper clothes for the season, and home decor that is up to current conventions. If they do not have these things they are counted as poor. Those who have the ability to work (that accords with their class) and who have become poor because of laziness or inaction, do not deserve to receive *zakat* that is supposed to go to the poor. This ruling was established to encourage people to engage in legitimate work and to use *zakat* only in emergency conditions. The ceiling for the amount the poor receive is their annual costs and that amount cannot be exceeded. People who are poor in spite of working, receive *zakat* to cover the shortage of what they cannot pay. In claiming poverty, conventional confirmation suffices and there is no need to provide witnesses or sworn statements. In case conventional confirmation is not possible, however, a search for evidence of poverty becomes necessary.

The needy (*miskin*) are in a worse situation as compared to the poor (*faqir*). A person in need is someone who is not only unable to make an appropriate life for him- or herself, but the person's desperation and helplessness is such that he or she is not even able to have the minimum of a conventional life (outside the standards of his or her class) and the person's income does not reach the minimum required to meet the bare necessities of life. The needy are not necessarily out of work or unable to work, they may be employed but cannot pay for the costs of the minimum of a standard life.

Those who administer *zakat* get a share of it, carrying out their duty in collecting *zakat* and giving it to those who deserve to receive it. Put another way, the organisation of *zakat* is self-sufficient. The share of those who administer *zakat* is in exchange for the work, and there is no condition of there being poverty or the like.

Those who receive *zakat* for their inclination to the Truth, help Muslims in *jihad* and defence and the like, are from the category of those whose hearts need winning over. For these people, being Muslim, having faith or being poor is not a condition.

Freeing slaves and paying the costs of their freedom are covered by *zakat*.

Helping those in debt, debtors who cannot pay their debt are those who may receive *zakat* even if they are not considered poor, as long as their debt was not because of deficiency, intention, negligence and the result of activities that are contrary to *shari'a*.

Travellers in need or someone who is left behind, are those who are on a trip and away from home, lack access to property and family and friends, and need help to pay the costs of a trip back to their homeland. These people deserve to receive *zakat* as long as they are not able to get a loan and their trip was not contrary to *shari'a*.

The eighth use of *zakat* is *fi sabil Allah* (for God's cause). This category gives *zakat* great flexibility and dynamism since any good act can be covered as being for God's cause and be included as a recipient of *zakat*. Given the abovementioned foundations, all that is for the public interest and the benefit of people is for God's cause. Traditional examples of for God's cause include the building and repair of *madrasa*s (schools), mosques, hospitals, roads, bridges, making peace between people, eliminating evil and sedition, and preaching or spreading knowledge and perfection in society. What will be covered in the next section is an expansion of these particulars of God's cause which may include all of these cases of social security.

Other than those whose hearts need winning over, the condition for receiving other categories of *zakat* is that those receiving it be Muslim and have faith. The Islamic government is responsible for collecting, keeping and distributing *zakat* among those who deserve it. *Zakat* is not necessarily divided into eight equal or unequal shares. Rather, its use in each of these areas is in accordance to what the government assesses to be beneficial (and in cases where there is no legitimate government, it is assessed by the payers). In receiving and spending *zakat*, local priorities must be observed and transferral of *zakat* is not permitted before local needs have been met.[23]

---

23 Based on Montazeri's *fatwa*s, *Kitab al-Zakat*, vols 2 and 3, and *Dirasat fi Wilyat al-Faqih wa Fiq al-Dula al-Islamiya*, 3:32–36.

Second: *Khums*

Khums is one of the other *shari'a* taxes that in Sunni *fiqh* is more limited than *zakat* and which specifically applies to the spoils of war. However, in Shi'ite *fiqh* it is broader and more important than *zakat* because it covers profits from businesses, which is much broader than the nine specific matters of *zakat* (Q. 8:41). In addition, in terms of percentage, the amount of *khums* (about 20 per cent) is quite a lot more than *zakat* (around 2.5 per cent). *Khums* is divided into six shares. Three shares are for God and the Prophet and his family (*Ahl al-Bayt*), which are collectively called the Imam's share, and the three other shares go to orphans, the needy and travellers in need, which are collectively called the *sadat* (the title of the Prophet's descendants) share. In the latter three, being Muslim, having faith, *siadat* (being a descendant of the Prophet's line), and being poor or orphans are conditions of receiving *khums*. The authority to use *khums* during the time of the Imam's occultation is in the hands of the *mujtahid*s of the time (and in one telling the Islamic government), who after meeting the needs of descendants of the Prophet who are orphans, needy or travellers in need, will spend it as *zakat* as *fi sabil Allah* (for God's cause) in accordance to what would benefit Islamic society.[24]

Third: Penances (*kaffarat*)

In cases where Muslims have refrained from carrying out an obligatory action or have carried out a prohibited act, the fine for their deviation from *shari'a* goes to penances. Particulars vary based on the case, but penances include providing sustenance for sixty people in need, or sustenance and clothing for ten people in need. What counts as being in need in relation to penances is the same as what counts as poor in relation to *zakat*. Sustenance or clothing can be provided directly or via the payment of the fine.[25]

---

24 Ayatollah Ruhollah Khomeini, *Tahrir al-Wasilah*, 1:384–385; Hossein-Ali Najaf-Abadi Montazeri, *Kitab al-Khums* (*The Book of One Fifth*) (Qom: Arghawan-e Danesh, 2007), 324–354, and *Dirasat fi Wilyat al-Faqih wa Fiq al-Dula al-Islamiya*, 3:43–128.
25 Ayatollah Ruhollah Khomeini, *Tahrir al-Wasilah*, 2:134–143.

Fourth: *Zakat al-fitra*

Zakat al-fitra is *zakat* on the body. As opposed to *zakat* on property, which applies to what people own, this is the *zakat* that becomes necessary for Muslims each year on *Eid al-Fitr* (celebration that marks the end of Ramadan and a month of obligatory fasting). For each person, *zakat al-fitra* is about 3 kilogrammes of conventional food or its cost that is given to the poor and those in need. The conditions of the poor in relation to *zakat al-fitra* are the same as the conditions that apply to the poor in relation to the *zakat* on property.[26]

Fifth: Charity (*sadaqa*), Expenditure (*infaq*), Doing Good (*ihsan*) and Donation (*hiba*)

Charity (*sadaqa*) in the way of God is among the particular recommended acts of Islam, in the sense that a person willingly gives some of his or her property to people in need for the purpose of gaining God's satisfaction (Q. 2:267). Expenditure (*infaq*) and doing good (*ihsan*) bring great rewards in the Hereafter (Q. 2:261). People who receive charity do not have to meet the conditions of being poor, Muslim and having faith which the recipients of *zakat* have to meet.[27] Thus, what can be covered by charity and expenditure is quite broad. Put another way, all particulars of support for social security can be covered by people's charity and donations.

Sixth: *Hisbiya* Affairs

The meaning of *hisbiya* affairs is those issues that according to the Legislator should not be abandoned under any circumstances. These include taking care of orphans, the intellectually disabled (*sufaha'*) and people with a mental health disabilities (*majanin*), marrying girls without guardians, and in general all issues pertaining to the care of those in need.[28] Involvement in *hisbiya* affairs is the responsibility of the Islamic government. In cases where the government neglects these affairs, *mujtahid*s (Muslim jurists) are responsible for

---

26 Ibid., 1:363–368.
27 Ibid., 2:97–99.
28 al-Ansari, *Al-Makasib*, 3:535–580.

taking care of them, otherwise it is the responsibility of everyone. *Hisbiya* affairs are similar to social services and the cases related to welfare institutions in conventional systems of social security.

Seventh: Endowments (*awqaf*)[29]

In three cases, endowments are the source of social security: in cases where the endower of a property makes it an endowment for affairs of people in need, the poor and other groups that are included under social security; in cases where the endower of the property makes an endowment for the public good, in this instance social security will absolutely be a particular of the public good; if for whatever reason the direction of the endowment is not clear (for example, the endowment document has been lost), the returns on the endowment will be spent on the public good, including on social security, based on the view of the Islamic government (or *mujtahids*). The ruling of permission for free residence (*sukna*), permission for free residence for a specific time (*ruqba*), and permission for free residence for life (*'umra*) are the same as the ruling on endowments in the above cases.

Eighth: Vow (*nadhr*), Promise (*'ahd*) and Oath (*qasam*)

Vows, promises and oaths are among the *shar'i iqa'at* (unilateral obligatory legal actions) where a person is obligated to undertake action for God's consent in a particular manner.[30] The subject (*muta'allaq*) of vows, promises and oaths can be particulars of social security aimed at eliminating the needs of the poor.

Ninth: To Will One-third of One's Legacy

A person can will one-third of his or her wealth to be used as he or she sees fit.[31] In two cases, the willing of one-third of one's legacy goes towards the costs of social security: in cases where the text of the will specifies that it be spent on eliminating the needs of the poor and the like; and in cases

---

29 Ruhollah Khomeini, *Tahrir al-Wasilah*, 2:67–96.

30 Ibid., 2:119–133.

31 Ibid., 2:100–118.

where the text of the will states that it should be spent on charity, then certainly social security is among the absolute particulars of good deeds or charity.

Tenth: Interest-free Loan (*qard al-hasana*)[32]

Qard al-hasana, or interest-free loan, is one of the areas of *takaful* (mutual inter-community help and a type of cooperative insurance) and social resources, because to each Muslim who gives an interest-free loan to someone who needs it, eighteen times that amount of reward is promised in the Hereafter. While if this same property were given in the way of God as charity, its reward would only be tenfold.[33] Helping others via interest-free loans is among the fine traditions of Islamic societies.

Eleventh: Property without Owners

Luqata, or property that has been found,[34] property whose owner is unknown, the inheritance of deceased without heirs, and in general all property that has no particular owner is considered public property and treasury (*bait al-mal*), and is spent under the supervision of the Islamic government on what is in the public interest, including the provision of social security.

Twelfth: *Anfal* and *fay'*

Anfal refers to public property such as uncultivated lands, mountains, valleys, forests, meadows, seas and seashores, big rivers and mines. *Fay'* refers to lands that have come under the control of Islamic governments without war. *Anfal* and *fay'* are managed by the Islamic government as public property and are used for the public interest.[35] Social security is among the most important of public interests.

---

32 Ibid., 1:693–698.
33 Prophetic hadith, al-Saduq, *Man la yaduruhu al-Faqih*, 1:22.
34 Ruhollah Khomeini, *Tahrir al-Wasilah*, 2:238–251.
35 Montazeri, *Kitab al-Khums, anfal* section, 419–502, and *Dirasat fi Wilyat al-Faqih wa Fiq al-Dula al-Islamiya*, 4:1–228 and 3:317–362.

Thirteenth: *Kharaj* and *Jizya*

Kharaj is the tax on certain types of land that is taken from Muslims. *Jizya* is the tax that is taken from the People of the Book in accordance with the contract of *dhimma* (contract of protection between Islamic governments and the People of the Book) based on farm land or each individual. What is obtained from *kharaj* and *jizya* is spent on the public interest under the supervision of the Islamic government.[36] Social security is among the most important public interests.

Fourteenth: Taxes

In case the methods set by *shari'a* for covering the management of society are not enough, the Islamic government is free to tax people for the purpose of covering the expenses of running society.[37] Social security is among the necessities for managing a healthy society and one can use taxes to pay for it. It is clear that using taxes, *kharaj* and *jizya*, *anfal* and *fay'* in social security occurs when previous means do not suffice for social security.

Concluding Remarks

The points covered in Section Two can be outlined as follows.

First, there are fourteen institutions related to the provision of social security in Islamic *shari'a*, which can be categorised as follows. The first category is institutions that explicitly include certain particulars of social security, including *zakat*, *zakat al-fitra*, *khums*, penance, charity, interest-free loans and *hisbiya* affairs. The second category is systems where expenses are predictable or explicitly mentioned, or in which social security is provided under the umbrella of charity and public interests: endowments, vows and the willing of one-third of one's legacy. The third category is institutions that in general may spend on social security for the public interest: property without owners, *anfal* and *fay'*, *kharaj* and *jizya*, and taxes.

Second, in terms of payments being obligatory or voluntary, these institutions can be divided into two. The first includes voluntary ones such as charity, interest-free loans, endowments, vows and wills. The second includes the rest which are obligatory.

---

36 Montazeri, *Dirasat fi Wilyat al-Faqih wa Fiq al-Dula al-Islamiya*, 3:363–507.
37 Ibid., 4:286–295.

Third, in institutions of *shari'a* related to social security, thirteen issues pertaining to specific expenditures are noteworthy: one and two, eliminating the needs of the poor and people in need (*zakat, zakat al-fitra, khums*); three, food and clothing for the poor (penances); four, eliminating the needs of orphans (*khums*); five, freeing of slaves (*zakat*, penances); six, paying for travellers in need (*zakat, khums*); seven, paying the debts of those in debt (*zakat*); eight, the guardianship of those with mental disabilities (*hisbiya* affairs); nine, the guardianship of those without guardians (*hisbiya* affairs); ten, those whose hearts need winning over (*zakat*); eleven, helping others and providing loans (interest-free loan); twelve, those who administer *zakat* (*zakat*); and thirteen, for God's cause (*zakat*). In addition, charity, endowments, vows and wills are used for expenditures and *anfal, kharaj* and property without owners. Taxes are also considered public property that may be spent on social security where necessary.

Fourth, institutions of *shari'a* related to social security are all supportive (non-insurance). *Hisbiya* affairs are close to social services. Institutions of *shari'a* that are close to the approach of social assistance include *zakat, zakat al-fitra, khums*, penances, charity, endowments, vows, wills and interest-free loans.

Fifth, in institutions of *shari'a* related to social security, the diversity of those who receive *zakat* and the like is more than that found in prevalent institutions of social security (for example, the expenditures for travellers in need, paying the debts of those in debt, those whose hearts need winning over, etc.). However, the existence of specific conditions, such as Islam, faith and, in some cases, direct *siyadat* (descent from the Prophet) distinguishes these recipients from those who receive social assistance. Of course, these specific conditions apply to the obligatory systems such as *zakat, khums* and penances, but the recipients of charity and expenditure are not bound by these specific conditions.

Sixth, the general term *fi sabil Allah* (for God's cause) has provided a particular flexibility to institutions of *shari'a*, such that any expenses that are for the good and the public benefit may be paid through this method. In addition, the Islamic government is completely free to cover the costs of social security and other public benefits through *anfal* and *fay', kharaj* and *jizya*, properties without owners, and taxes. It faces no obstacles in this regard.

Section Three: New Ways of Social Security from an Islamic Perspective

1. While in *fiqhi* institutions, cases such as *daman al-jarira, daman al-ʿaqila* and *diman al-darak*[38] are accepted as limited insurances, insurance in the prevalent sense is a modern (*musdahdatha*) institution and is placed under the generalities (*ʿumumat*), such as the mandatory fulfilment of contracts, that are considered correct and executable.[39]

Thus, health insurance, unemployment insurance, and retirement and disability insurance which are established with the participation of citizens, the government and employers are correct from an Islamic perspective and their fulfilment is obligatory.

The institution of "reserve fund" is acceptable and executable regarding the conditions of *mudarabah* (profit- and loss-sharing); as well as the approach of employer responsibility via the rent (*ijara*) contract and given that conditions during the making of the contract (*sharait dimn al'aqd*) are met. In general, issues that have not been explicitly outlined in the above-mentioned institutions of *shariʿa* can be accomplished in several ways: first, through *fi sabil Allah* (for God's cause) in *zakat* and charity; second, the institutions need to be mentioned explicitly or to be included in "public affairs" such as endowments, vows and wills; and, third, the institutions of the public budget such as *anfal* and *fayʾ, kharaj* and *jizya*, properties without owners, and taxes.

2. In general, new methods of social security are executable on the basis of the following two principles in Islamic societies: first, all of the reasonable issues that have no contradictions with the criteria of *shariʿa* are considered to be confirmed affairs (*al-umur al-imdai*) of *shariʿa*; and, second, the expenses

---

38 These are guarantee contracts or actions. *Daman al-jarira*: a guarantee contract between a person without heirs and another individual who will defend the former through payment of *diya* in exchange for their inheritance, even though they are not relatives. *Daman al-ʿaqila*: the male relatives of someone who commits murder by mistake are responsible for paying the victim's *diya* to his or her family on behalf of the murderer. *Diman al-darak*: the third party in a purchase contract guarantees that should there be any problems with the purchase or sale, he or she will pay for any damages or harm incurred.

39 See Morteza Motahhari, *Reba, Bank, Bimeh* (*Usury, Bank, Insurance*) (Tehran: Sadra, 1985); Muhammad Khamenei, *Bimeh dar Hoquq-e Eslam* (*Insurance in Islamic Law*) (Tehran: Tolid-e Ketab, 2002).

related to the public interest will be paid from the public funds of the Islamic government when it cannot be obtained from the customary sources set by *shariʿa*.

3. Social security is a right of all citizens of an Islamic society regardless of religion, sect, gender, colour, race, etc., which is accorded to the citizen by the society at particular times. Islamic society is bound to providing this right for its citizens to have social security from its specific resources. When a ruling government in an Islamic society submits to Islamic teachings, the management of social security counts as a right and providing it is the responsibility of the government.

4. Taking a position on social security from the point of view of Islam must be such that it encourages people to work and that it only provides social security in particular circumstances. Thus, the direction of social security is also towards encouraging voluntary and spontaneous actions by people themselves. Traditional Islamic institutions such as religious authorities, the clergy and mosques can make up part of the services of social security. These sectors, in cooperation with other sectors of social security, will carry out their duties under the supervision of the Islamic government.

Epilogue

1. Although this chapter is the last chapter of the book based on subject order, chronologically speaking, it was the first chapter to be written. I wrote it before my three paradigm shifts took place, the first shift being from traditional *ijtihad* in secondary *fiqhi* rulings to *ijtihad* in principles and foundations (*al-usul wa al-mabani*);[40] the second shift from *shariʿa* as a system of law to *shariʿa* as moral virtues and ethical values; and the third shift from the possibility of an Islamic democratic state to a secular democratic state. Local, elected *zakat* committees, such as charities and the like, that are independent of the state and monitored by Muslim communities in civil society in cooperation with Islamic religious scholars (*ʿulama*), could decide on the distribution and expenditure of Islamic financial resources.

---

40 "Ijtihad in Usul al-Fiqh: Reforming Islamic Thought through Structural Ijtihad". More information can be found in the introduction to Chapter 5 in this book.

2. One of the fruits of *ijtihad* in principles and foundations can be found in the rulings of *zakat* and *khums*. *Zakat* is not restricted to nine properties, but includes all properties and businesses. The *khums* of annual business profits (*khums arbah al-makasib*) has been a temporal ruling since the time of the seventh Shi'ite Imam and is not counted as a permanent ruling in Islam today. As such, the annual obligatory Islamic tax (*zakat*) for each Muslim is around 2.5 per cent of all business revenues, as well as all savings.

Bibliography

Persian Books

Haeri-Yazdi, Mehdi, *Hekmat va Hokumat* (*Wisdom and Government*) (London: Shadi, 1994).

Hafez Shirazi, Shams al-Din Mohammad, *Divan* (*Poetry Court*), ed. Parviz Natel Khanlari (Tehran: Khwarazmi, 1996).

Javadi Amoli, Abdollah, *Falasafe-ye Huquq-e Bashar* (*The Philosophy of Human Rights*) (Qom: Esra', 1996).

Kadivar, Mohsen, *Baha-ye Azadi: Defa'iyat-e Mohsen Kadivar dar Dadgah-e Vizheh-ye Rohaniat* (*The Price of Freedom: Kadivar's Defence in the Special Clerical Court*), ed. Zahra Roodi (Tehran: Nashr-e Ney, 2000).

Kadivar, Mohsen, *Hokumat-e Wela'i* (*Governance by Guardianship*), Political Thought in [Shi'ite] Islam series, vol. 2 (Tehran: Nashr-e Ney, 2008).

Kadivar, Mohsen, *Nazariyeha-ye Dolat dar Fiqh-e Shi'a* (*The Theories of State in Shi'ite Law*), Political Thought in [Shi'ite] Islam Series, vol. 1 (Tehran: Nashr-e Ney, 2008).

Kadivar, Mohsen, (compiler and ed.), *Siasat-nameh-ye Khorasani* (*Political Works of Akhond Molla Mohammad Kazem Khorasani*) (Tehran: Kavir, 2008).

Kadivar, Mohsen, *Haqq al-Nas: Islam va Hoquq-e Bashar* (*The Rights of People: Islam and Human Rights*) (1st print, Tehran: Kavir, Mehr 1387/September 2008; 4th print, Sharivar 1388/August 2009).

Kadivar, Mohsen, *Shari'at wa Siyasat: Din dar 'Arse-ye 'Omumi* (*Shari'a and Politics: Religion in the Public Sphere: A Case Study of Contemporary Iran*), Kadivar web-book, 2010, available at: https://kadivar.com/wp-content/uploads/2009/04/Shari%CA%BFat-wa-Siyasat.pdf, last accessed 8 June 2020.

Kadivar, Mohsen, *Hokumat-e Entesabi* (*The Appointive/Non-Elective State*), *Andishe-ye Siyasi dar Eslam [-e Shi'ite]*, Political Thought in [Shi'ite] Islam series, vol. 3, Kadivar web-book, 2014, available at: https://kadivar.com/

wp-content/uploads/2014/05/Hokumat-e-Entesabi.pdf, last accessed 8 June 2020.

Kadivar, Mohsen, *"Dar Mahzar-e Faqih-e Azadeh Ostad Montazeri"* ("In the Presence of a Noble Theologian Ayatollah Montazeri"), *A Collection of Exchanges between the Mentor and the Disciple*, Kadivar web-book, 2015, available at: https://kadivar.com/wp-content/uploads/2015/08/Dar-Mahzar-e-Faqih-e-Azadeh.pdf, last accessed 8 June 2020.

Kadivar, Mohsen, *Ebtezal-e Marja'iyyat-e Shi'a: Estidhah-e Marja'iyyat-e Maqam-e Rahbari S. Ali Khamenei* (*The Trivialization of Shi'ite Marja'iyyat: Impeaching Iran's Supreme Leader on his Marja'iyyat*) (Kadivar web-book, 2015), available at: https://kadivar.com/wp-content/uploads/2015/05/Ebtezal-e-Marja%E2%80%99iyyat-e-Shi%E2%80%98a.pdf, last accessed 8 June 2020.

Kadivar, Mohsen, *Sug-Name-ye Faqih-e Pakbaz Ustad Hossein Ali Montazeri* (*A Tribute to the Virtuous Theologian, my Mentor Ayatollah Montazeri*), Kadivar web-book, 2015, available at: https://kadivar.com/wp-content/uploads/2015/08/Sug-Name-ye-Faqih-e-Pakbaz.pdf, last accessed 8 June 2020.

Khamenei, Seyyed Mohammad, *Bimeh dar Huquq-e Islam* (*Insurance in Islamic Law*) (Tehran: Tolid-e Ketab, 2002).

Khomeini, Ruhollah Mousavi, *Sahife-ye Imam* (*The Speeches and Declarations of Imam Khomeini*) (Tehran: Institute for Compilation and Publication of Imam Khomeini's Works, 2010), vols 20 and 21.

Khomeini, Ruhollah Mousavi, *Welayat-e Faqih: Hokoumat-e Eslami* (*The Guardianship of the Jurist: Islamic State*), in *Mawsu'a al-Imam al-Khomeini* (*Complete Works of Imam Khomeini*), No. 21 (Tehran: Institute for Compilation and Publication of Imam Khomeini's Works, 2013).

Mehrpour, Hossain, *Hoquq-e Bashar dar Asnad-e Bainollmelali wa Moze'-e Jomhouri-e Eslami-e Iran* (*Human Rights in International Documents and position of Islamic Republic of Iran*) (Tehran: Ettela'at Publications, 2007).

Mesbah Yazdi, Mohammad Taqi, *Negahi Gozara be Hoquq Bashar az Didgah Eslam* (*Human Rights from an Islamic Perspective: A Brief Review*), ed. 'Abdul-Hakim Salimi (Qom: Imam Khomeini's Educational and Research Institute, 2013).

Motahhari, Morteza, *Barras-yei Ejmali-ye Maban-ei Eqtesad-e Eslami* (*Brief Review of the Fundamentals of Islamic Economy*) (Tehran: Hekmat, 1982).

Motahhari, Morteza, *Reba, Bank, Bimeh* (*Usury, Banks, Insurance*) (Tehran: Sadra, 1985).

Motahhari, Morteza, *Piramoun-e Enqelab-e Eslami* (*About the Islamic Revolution*) (Tehran: Sadra, 1989).

Motahhari, Morteza, *Piramoun-e Jomhori-ye Eslami* (*About the Islamic Republic*) (Tehran: Sadra, 1989).

Motahhari, Morteza, *Eslam wa Muqtazayat-e Zaman* (*Islam and the Time Specific Requirements*) (Tehran: Sadra, 2001).

Na'ini, Mirza Mohammad Hossein Gharavi, *Tanbih al-Ummah wa Tanzih al-Milla: Hokoumat az nazar-e Eslam* (*The Awakening of the Community and Refinement of the Religion: Governance in Islam*), with an introduction and commentary by Seyyed Mahmoud Taleqani (Tehran: Ferdowsi, 1954).

Panahi, Bahram, *Osoul wa Mabani-ye Nezam-e Ta'min-e Ejtemai* (*The Principles and Basics of a Social Security System*) (Tehran: Research Council of the Institute of Advanced Research on Social Security, 1997).

Qorbani, Zayn al-'Abedin, Mohammad [Mojtahed] Shabestari, Ali Hojjati Kermani, 'Abbas-Ali 'Amid [Zanjani] and Hossain Haqqani, *Zan va Entekhabat* (*Woman and Election*), with Introduction by Nasser Makarem Shirazi, *Az Eslam cheh midanim?* What We Know about Islam? series (Qom: n.p., n.d.)

Sadr, Seyyed Reza, *Dar Zindan-e Welayat-e Faqih* (*In the Prison of the Guardian Jurist*), ed., with Introduction and annotation by Mohsen Kadivar, Kadivar web-treatise, November 2016, available at: https://kadivar.com/15651, last accessed 8 June 2020.

Shabestari, Mohammad Mojtahed, *Jame'e-ye Ensani-e Eslam, Ketab-e Avval: Osoul-e Fekri* (*Humanistic Society of Islam, Book One: The Theoretical Principles*) (Tehran: Sherkat-e Sahami-ye Enteshar, 1968).

Shabestari, Mohammad Mojtahed, *Hermeneutic, Ketab wa Sonnat* (*Hermeneutics, the Scripture and the Tradition: The Process of Interpretation of the Revelation*) (Tehran: Tarh-e No, 1996).

Shabestari, Mohammad Mojtahed, *Iman wa Azadi* (*Faith and Freedom*) (Tehran: Tarh-e No, 1997).

Shabestari, Mohammad Mojtahed, *Naqdi bar Qara'at-e Rasmi az Din: Bohranha, Chaleshha va vah-e Halha* (*A Critique of the Official Reading of Religion: Crisis, Challenges and Solutions*) (Tehran: Tarh-e No, 2000).

Shabestari, Mohammad Mojtahed, *Ta'ammolati dar Qara'at-e Ensani az Din* (*Reflections on Humane Reading of Religion*) (Tehran: Tarh-e No, 2004).

Shabestari, Mohammad Mojtahed. *Qara'at-e Nabavi as Jahan* (*The Prophetic Reading of the World*), a collection of Shabestari's presentations and notes posted on his website in thirty-one parts, January 2008–November 2015. Available at: http://mohammadmojtahedshabestari.com/, last accessed 8 June 2020.

Shabestari, Mohammad Mojtahed, *Naqd-e Bonyadha-ye Feqh va Kalam: Sokhanraniha, Maqalat va Gofteguha* (*Critique of the foundations of fiqh and Theology, Speeches, Articles and Dialogues*) (Shabestari web-book, 2017), available at: http://mohammadmojtahedshabestari.com/upload/book/Naqd%20Bonyan.pdf, last accessed 8 June 2020.

Shahidi, Seyyed Ja'far, *Zendeghani-e Ali b. Hussein* (*The Life of Ali b. Hussein*) (Tehran: Office of Islamic Culture Publications, 1986).

Sha'rani, Mirza Abul Hassan, *Nathr-e Tuba* (*The Encyclopaedia of the Qur'an*) (Tehran: Islamiyya, 2000).

Shariati, Ali, "*Zibatarin Rouh-e Parastandeh*" ("The Most Beautiful Soul of a Worshipper"), in *Niyayesh* (*Invocation Prayer*), *Majmou'e Athar* (*Complete Works of Dr. Ali Shari'ati*), vol. 8 (Tehran: Elham, 1991).

Soroush, Abdolkarim, Mohammad Mojtahed Shabestari, Mostafa Malekian and Mohsen Kadivar, *Sonnat wa Secularism* (*Tradition and Secularism*) (Tehran: Serat, 2002).

Tabandeh, Nour-Ali, *Hoquq-e Tatbiqi* (*Comparative Law*) (Qom: Tehran University, College of Judicial and Administrative Sciences, 1978).

Tabandeh, Nour-Ali, *Majmou'e Maqalat-e Feqhi wa Ejtema'i* (*The Collection of Fiqhi and Social Articles*) (Tehran: Haqiqat, 1999).

Tabandeh, Nour-Ali, *Majmou'e Maqalat-e Hoquqi wa Ejtema'i* (*The Collection of Legal and Social Articles*) (Tehran: Haqiqat, 2002).

Tabandeh, Sultan Hussein, *Nazar-e Madhabi be E'lamiye-i Hoquq-e Bashar* (*Muslim Commentary on the Universal Declaration of Human Rights*) (n.p., 1966; reprinted in 1975), 98 pp.

Taleqani, Seyyed Mahmoud, *Islam wa Malekiyat* (*Islam and Ownership*) (Tehran: Enteshar Publications, 1981).

Tabataba'i, Seyyed Mohammad Hossein, *Barresiha-ye Eslami* (*Islamic Investigations*) (Qom: Dar Al-Tabligh-e Islami, 1976).

Tabataba'i, Seyyed Mohammad Hossein, *Eslam wa Ensan-e Moaser, Barresihay-e Eslami* (*Islam and the Contemporary Human*), in *Barrasiha-ye Eslami* (*Islamic Investigations*), vol. II, ed. Seyyed Hadi Khosrowshahi (Qom: Resalat, 1977).

Bibliography

al-Tusi, Nasir al-din. *Aghaz wa Anjam* (*Start and Finish*), ed. Hasan Hasanzadeh Amoli (Tehran: Ministry of Culture and Islamic Guidance, 1987).

al-Tusi, Nasir al-din, *Akhlaq-e Naseri* (*Naseri's Ethics*), ed. Mojtaba Minuwi and Alireza Heidari (Tehran: Kharazmi, 1985).

Vasmaghi, Sedigheh, *Zan, Fiqh, Islam* (Tehran: Nashr-e Samadiyah, 2008).

Vassigh, Chidan, *Laicite Chist?* (*What is Laicism?*) (Tehran: Akhtaran, 2005).

Arabic Books

Ibn 'Abd Rabbih, Ahmad b. Muhammad, *al-'Iqd al-Farid* (*The Unique Necklace*), ed. M. M. Qumayha (Beirut: Dar al-Kutub al-'Ilmiyya, 1983).

Ahmad b. Hanbal, *Musnad al-Imam Ahmad b. Hanbal* (*Collection of Hadith Compiled by Ahmad b. Hanbal*), ed. Shu'aib al-Arnut et al. (Beirut: Resalah, 2001).

'Ali, Jawad, *al-Mufassal fi Tarikh al-'Arab qabl al-Islam* (*The Detailed Pre-Islamic History of Arabs*) (Baghdad: University of Baghdad, 1993).

al-'Amili, al-Sayyid Muhammad Jawad al-Husaini, *Miftah al-Karamah fi sharh-i Qawaid al-'Allamah [al-Hilli]* (*The Key of Dignity in the Commentary of Qawaid al-Ahkam [The Principles of Rulings] of al-'Allamah al-Hilli*), ed. Muhammad Baqir al-Khalisí (Qom: Islamic Publication Institute, 2000).

al-Amudi al-Tamimi, Abdul Wahid b. Muhammad, *Gurar al-Hikam wa Durar al-Kalim* (*Exalted Aphorisms and Pearls of Speech*), ed. S. Mahdi Raja'i (Qom: Dar al-Kutub al-Islami, 1990).

al-Ansari, al-Shaykh Mortada, *al-Makasib* (*The Book of Buying*) (Qom: Majma' al-Fikr al-Islami, 1999).

Ibn-'Arabi, Muhyi al-Din Muhammad ibn 'Ali, *al-Futuhat al-Makkiyya* (*The Meccan Illuminations*), ed. Ahmad Shams al-Din (Beirut: Dar al-Kutub al-'Ilmiyya, 1999).

al-Ardabili, Ahmad b. Muhammad, *Majma' al-Fayida wa al-Burhan fi Sharh-i Irshad al-Adhhan* (*The Complex of Interests and Proofs in the Commentary of Irshad al-Adhhan [The Guidance of Minds of al-'Allamah al-Hilli]*), eds Mujtaba al-'Iraqi, 'Ali Panah al-Ishtihardi and Husayn al-Yazdi (Qom: Islamic Publication Institute, 1983).

Ibn A'tham al-Kufi, Abu Muhammad Ahmad, *Kitab al-Futuh* (*Book of Conquest*), ed. Ali Shiri (Beirut: Dar al-Adwa', 1991).

al-Ayyashi al-Samarqandi, Muhammad b. Mas'ud, *Tafsir al-Ayyashi* (*The Exegesis of Ayyashi*) (Qom: Mu'ssisa al-Bi'tha, 2000).

al-Baladhuri, Ahmad b. Yaya, *Kitab Jumal-un min Ansab al-Ashraf* (*The Book of Sentences from the Lineage of the Nobles*), eds S. Zakkar and R. Zarkaly (Beirut: Dar al-Fikr, 1996).

al-Banna, Jamal, *Hurria al-Fikr wa al-'Itiqad fi al-Islam* (*The Freedom of Thought and Belief in Islam*) (Cairo: Dar al-Fikr al-Islami, 1998).

al-Barqi, Ahmad b. Muhammad, *al-Mahasin* (*Advantages*), ed. Jalal al-Din al-Hussaini al-Muhaddith (Tehran: Dar al-Kutub al-Islamiyya, 1951).

al-Bashir, 'Abdullah al-Fakki, *Sahib al Fahm al-Jadid lil-Islam, Mahmud Muhammad Taha wa al-Muthaqqafun: Qarat-un fi al-Mawaqif wa Tazwir al-Tarikh* (*The Holder of a New Understanding of Islam: Mahmoud Mohamed Taha and Intellectuals, A Reading of Situations, and the Deception of History*) (Cairo: Roueya, 2013).

Al-Beyhaghi, Abu Bakr Ahmad ibn al-Hussain, *al-Sunan al-Kubra* (*Major Traditions*) (Haydarabad Dakan: Da'ira al-Ma'arif al-'Uthmaniyya: 1936).

al-Bukhari, Muhammad b. Isma'il, *al-Sahih* (*The Authentics*) (Beirut: Dar al-Fikr, 1980).

Abu Dawud, Sulayman ibn al-Ash'ath, *Sunan* (*Traditions*) (Damascus: Dar al-Risala al-'Alamiyya, 2009).

al-Dinawari, bu Hanifa Ahmad b. Dawud, *al-Akhbar al-Tiwal* (*The Longest News [General History]*), ed. Abdul Mon'im 'Amir (Cairo: Wizarah al-Thaqafa, 1960).

Fadlallah, Muhammad Hussain, *Qara'a Jadida li Fiqh al-Mar'ah al-Huquqi* (*New Reading of the Legal Jurisprudence of the Woman*) (Beirut: Dar al-Thaqalain, 1997).

Fadlallah, Muhammad Hussain, *Min Wahy-i al-Qur'an* (*From the Revelation of the Qur'an*) (Beirut: Dar al-Milak, 1998).

al-Ghazali, Abu Hamid Muhammad ibn Muhammad, *Ihya' 'Ulum al-Din* (*The Revival of the Religious Sciences*), ed. 'Abdul Rahim b. Hussain al-Hafiz al-'Iraqi (Dar al-Kutub al-'Arabi, n.d.).

al-Ghazali, Mohammad, *Huquq al-Insan bain Ta'alim al-Islam wa I'lan al-Umam al-Muttahidah* (*Human Rights between the Teachings of Islam and the Declarations of the United Nations*) (Cairo: Nahdat-i Misr, 1965).

Hakimi, Mohammad Reza, Mohammad Hakimi and Ali Hakimi, *al-Hayat* (*The Life*) (Tehran: Dafter-e Nashr-e Farhang-e Eslami, 1989).

Hamidullah, Muhammad, *Majmu'a al-Wath'iq al-Siyasiyya lil-'Ahd al-Nabawi wa al-Khilafa al-Rashida* (*The Political Covenants in the Prophetic Age and the Age of the Righteous Caliphate*) (Beirut: Dar al-Nafa'is, 1987).

Bibliography

al-Hilli, Ibn Idris, *al-Sara'ir al-Hawi li Tahrir al-Fatawi* (*The Mind, Container for Editing of the Rulings*) (Qom: Islamic Publication Institute, 1989).

al-Hilli, Ja'far b. Hassan (al-Muhaqiq), *Sharayi' al-Islam fi Masa'il Al-Halal wa Al-Haram* (*Paths of Islam on the Issues of Permitted and Forbidden*), ed. 'Abdul-Hussain Muhammad Ali (Najaf: al-Adab, 1969).

al-Hilli, Hassan b. Yusuf, *Kashef al-Morad fi Sharh Tajrid al-E'tiqad* (*The Discovery of the Intention in the Commentary of Tajrid al-I'tiqad*), ed. Hassan Hassanzadeh Amoli (Qom: Islamic Publication Institute, 2012).

al-Hindi, Muhammad b. Hasan al-Isfahani al-Fadil, *Kashf al-Litham 'an Qawa'id al-Ahkam* (*Revealing the Veil of Qawa'id al-Ahkam [the Principles of the Rulings of al-'Allama al-Hilli]*) (Qom: Islamic Publication Institute, 1995).

al-Hindi, Ali al-Muttaqi ibn Hisam al-Din, *Kanz al-'Ummal fi Sunan al-Aqwal wa l-Af'al* (*Treasures of the Doers of Good Deeds*) (Beirut: Resalah, 1985).

Al-Hurr al-'Amili, Muhammad ibn al-Hassan, *Tafsil Wasa'il al-Shi'a ila Tahsil Masa'il al-Shari'a* (*Details of the Means of the Shi'a regarding the Collection of Shari'a Issues*) (Qom: Mu'assasa Al al-Bayt li Ihya' al-Turath, 1994).

Ibn Abi Jumhur al-Ahsa'i, Muhammad Ali b. Ibrahim, *'Awali al-La'ali al-'Aziziyya fi al-Ahadith al-Diniyya* (*The Elevated Noble Pearls of Religious Reports*), ed. Mujtaba al-'Araqi (Qom: the editor, 1983).

al-Fayd al-Kashani, Muhammad Muhsin, *Kitab al-Wafi* (*The Adequate*) (Esfahan: Maktaba al-Imam Amir al-Mu'minin 'Ali al'Aamma, 2009).

al-Gubbanchi, Ahmed Hasan Ali, *al-Mar'a, al-Mafahim, wa al-Huquq: Qara't Jadida li Qadaya al-Mar'a fi al-Khitab al-Dini* (*Woman, Concepts, and Rights: A New Reading of Women's Issues in Religious Discourse*) (Beirut: Mu'assisa al-Intishar al-'Arabi, 2009).

Ibn Khaldun, Abd ar-Rahman ibn Muhammad, *Muqaddimah* (*The Introduction*), ed. Abdullah Muhammad al-Darwish (Damascus: Dar Ya'rib, 2004).

Kashif al-Ghita', Shaykh Jaffar, *Kash al-Ghita'a an Mubhamat al-Shariat al-Gharra'* (*The Revealing of the Covering from the Ambiguities of the Brilliant Shari'a*) (Qom: Maktab al-I'lam al-Islami, 2001).

Khwansari, Sayyid Ahmad, *Jami' al-Madarik fi sharh-i al-Mukhtasar al-Nafi'* (*The Comprehensive Evidence of the Commentary of al-Mukhtasar al-Nafi' [fi Fiqh al-Imamiyya] [Useful Manual on the Shi'i Fiqh of al-Muhaqiq al-Hilli]*), ed. 'Ali Akbar al-Ghaffari (Tehran: Maktabat al-Saduq, 1976–1981).

Khomeini, Ruhollah Mousawi, *Kitab al-Bay'* (*The Book of Selling*), *Mawsu'a al-Imam al-Khomeini* (*Complete Works of Imam Khomeini*), No. 16 (Tehran: Institute for Compilation and Publication of Imam Khomeini's Work, 2013), vol. 2.

Khomeini, Ruhollah Mousawi, *Kitab al-Tahara* (*Book of Purity*) (Tehran: Institute for Compilation and Publication of Imam Khomeini's Work, 2013).

Khomeini, Ruhollah Mousawi, *Tahrir al-Wasilah* (*The Editing of* Wasilah al-Nijat *[The Means of Salvation by al-Sayyid Abul-Hassan al-Isfahani]*) (Tehran: Institute for Compilation and Publication of Imam Khomeini's Work, 2013).

al-Khu'i, Sayyid Abu al-Qasim al-Musawi, *Mabani Takmilah al-Minhaj* (*The Foundations of the Righteous Platform*) (Najaf: Mu'assasat al-Khu'i al-Islamiyya, 1976).

al-Khu'i, Sayyid Abu al-Qasim al-Musawi, *Al-Bayan fi Tafsir al-Qur'an* (*Explanation of Qur'anic Exegesis*) (Qom: Anwar al-Huda, 1981).

al-Khu'i, Sayyid Abu al-Qasim al-Musawi (ed.), *Mu'jam Rijal al-Hadith wa Tafsil Tabaqat al-Ruwat* (*Encyclopaedia of the Hadith Transmitters and their Generations in Details*) (Beirut: Mu'assasa al-Imam al-Khu'i, 1989).

al-Khu'i, Sayyid Abu al-Qasim al-Musawi, *Minhaj al-Salihin* (*The Righteous Platform*) (Qom: Madina al-'Ilm, 1990).

al-Khu'i, Sayyid Abu al-Qasim al-Musawi, *Misbah al-Usul* (*The Light of the Principles [of Fiqh]*), written by S. M. S. W. H. al-Bihsudi (Qom: al-Khu'i Islamic Institute, 2009).

al-Khu'i, Sayyid Abu al-Qasim al-Musawi, *Mustanad al-'Urwah al-Wuthqa* (*Documents of the al-'Urwah al-Wuthqa [The Firmest Hand-Hold by al-Sayyid Muhammad Kazim al-Tabataba'i al-Yazdi]*), Kitab al-Khums, written by Murtada al-Burujirdi (Qom: Mu'assah al-Khu'i al-Islamiyya, 2009).

al-Kulaini, Muhammad b. Ya'qub, *al-Kafi* (*The Sufficient*), ed. Ali-Akbar Ghaffari (Tehran: Dar al-Kutub al-Islmiyya, 1984–1988).

Ibn Majah, Muhammad ibn Yazid, *Sunan* (*Traditions*) (Cairo: Dar Ihya' al-Kutub al-'Arabiyya, 1955).

al-Majlisi, Muhammad Baqir, *Bihar al-Anwar al-Jami'a li Durar-i Akhbar al-A'ima al-Athar* (*Seas of Lights, the Collection of the Pearls of the Reports of the [Shi'i] Pure Imam*) (Qom: Ihya' al-Kutub al-Islamiyya, 2009).

Ibn al-Manzur, Muhammad b. Mukarram, *Lisan al-Arab* (*The Tongue of Arabs*) (Beirut: Dar Sader, 1955).

Ma'rifat, Muhammad Hadi, *al-Tamhid fi 'Ulum al-Qur'an* (*An Introduction to the Sciences of the Qur'an*) (Qom: Dar al-Ta'aruf, 2011).

Al-Mawardi, Ali ibn Muhammad, *al-Ahkam al-Sultaniyya w'al-Wilayat al-Diniyya* (*The Ordinances of Government*), ed. Ahmad Jad (Cairo: Dar al-Hadith, 2006).

Mahmoud, Ibrahim, *al-Jins fi al-Qur'an* (*Gender in the Qur'an*) (Beirut: Riad el-Rayyes Books, 1998).

Mo'men Qomi, Mohammad, *Kalimat Sadidah fi Masa'il Jadida* (*The Correct Words in New Issues*) (Qom: Islamic Publication Institute, 1995).

Montazeri, Hossein-Ali Najaf-Abadi, *Dirasat fi Wilayat al-Faqih wa Fiqh al-Dawlat al- Islamiya* (*Studies on the Guardianship of the Jurist and Islamic State Law*) (Qom: Maktab al-I'lam al-Islami, 1988).

Montazeri, Hossein-Ali Najaf-Abadi, *Kitab al-Zakat* (*The Book of Zakat*) (Qom: Tafakkur, 1992).

Montazeri, Hossein-Ali Najaf-Abadi, *Kitab al-Khums* (*The Book of One Fifth*) (Qom: Arghawan-e Danesh, 2007).

al-Mufid, Muhammad b. Muhammad b. Nu'man, *al-Nusra li Sayyid al-'Itra fi Harb al al-Basra, Mawsou'a al-Sheikh al-Mufid* (*The Complete Works of al-Mufid*), vol. 1 (Qom: Dar al-Mufid, 2010).

al-Najafi, Muhammad Hassan, *Jawahir al-Kalam fi Sharh Sharay'i' al-Islam* (*Jewels of Speech in the Commentary of Sharay'i' al-Islam [The Paths of Islam by al-Muhaqiq al-Hilli]*), ed. 'Abbas Quchani (Tehran: Dar al- Kutub al-Islamiyya, 1988).

al-Nasa'i, Ahmad b. Shu'ayb, *al-Sunan al-Kubra* (*The Major Traditions*) (Beitut: Resalah, 2001).

Nöldeke, Theodor, *Tarikh al-Qur'an* (*The History of the Qur'an*), trans. George Tamer (Zürich: Dar Nashr Goerge Elmes, 2000).

Nouri, Sheykh Fazlollah, "*Tazkirat al-Ghafil wa Irshad al-Jahil*", in *Rasi'il, I'lamiyeh-ha, Maktoubat wa Rouzname-haye Sheikh Shahid Fazlollah Nouri* (*Treatises, Declarations, Writings and Journals of Martyr Sheikh Fazlollah Nouri*), compiled and ed. Muhammad Turkaman (Tehran: Rasa, 1983).

al-Nuri al-Tabrisi, Mirza Hussain, *Mustadrak al-Wasa'il wa Mustanbat al-Masa'il* (*The Emendation of Wasa'il [al-Shi'a by al-Hurr al-'Amili] and Discovered Issues*) (Qom: Mu'assasa Al al-Bayt li Ihya' al-Turath, 1991).

Ibn al-Qudamah al-Maqdisi, 'Abduallah b. Ahmad, *al-Mughni* (*The Persuader*), ed. 'Abdullah b. 'Abdul Muhsin al-Turki and 'Abdul Fattah Muhammad al-Hulw (Riyadh: Dar 'Alam al-Kutub, 1997).

al-Qurtubi, Abu 'Abdullah Muhammad ibn Ahmad, *Tafsir al-Qurtubi: Al-Jami' li Ahkam al-Qur'an* (*Comprehensive [Interpretation] in Rulings of the Qur'an*) (Beirut, Resalah, 2006).

al-Radi, al-Sayyid Muhammad ibn al-Hassan al-Musawi al-Sharif, *Nahj al-Balagha*, ed. Subhi Salih (Cairo and Beirut: Dar al-Kutub al-Misriyya and Dar al-Kitab al-Lubnani, 2004).

al-Raghib al-Isfahani, Abu al-Qasim Hussain b. Muhammad, *Al-Mufradat fi Gharib al-Qur'an* or *Mufradat alfaz al-Qur'an* (*A Dictionary of Qur'anic Terms*), ed. Safwan 'Adnan Dawudi (Damascus: Dar-al-Qalam, 2009).

al-Sadr, al-Sayyid Muhammad Baqir, *Lamha Fiqhiya Tamhidiya 'an Mashru' Dustur al-Jumhuriya al-Islamiyat-i Iran* (*Introductory Juristic Glance at the Constitution of the Islamic Republic of Iran*), Majmu'a al-Islam Yaqudu al-Hayat, Islam Guides Life Series, No. 1 (Qom: al-Khayyam, 1979).

al-Sadr, al-Sayyid Muhammad Baqir, *Durus fi 'Ilm al-Usul* (*Lessons in the Science of Principles of Fiqh*), *al-Halqa al-Thalitha* (*The Third Episode*) (Qom: Center of Professional Discussions and Studies on the Martyr al-Sadr, 2000).

al-Sadr, al-Sayyid Muhammad Baqir, *al-Fatawa al-Wadhihah wifqan li Madhab-i Ahl al-Bayt* (*Clear Fatwas According to the Shi'i Doctrine*) (Qom: Center of Professional Discussions and Studies on the Martyr al-Sadr, 2001).

Sadr al-din al-Shirazi, Muhammad b. Ibrahim al-Qawami (Mulla Sadra), *al-Hikmat al-Muta'alyah fi al-Asfar al-'Aqliyya al-'Arba'a* (*The Transcendent Philosophy of the Four Journeys of the Intellect*) (Beirut: Dar Ihya' al-Turath al-'Arabi, 1990).

Sadr al-din al-Shirazi, Muhammad b. Ibrahim al-Qawami (Mulla Sadra), *Tafsir al-Qur'an al-Karim* (*The Exegsis of the Noble Qur'an*), ed. Muhammad Khajawi (Qom: Bidar Publications, 1991).

al-Saduq, al-Shaykh Muhammad b. Ali b. Babawaih al-Qummi, *'Ilal al-Sharayi'* (*The Shari'a Reasons*) (Najaf: al-Haidariya, 1966).

al-Saduq, al-Shaykh Muhammad b. Ali b. Babawaih al-Qummi, *Man la Yahduruhu al-Faqih* (*For Him Who is Not in the Presence of a Jurisprudent*), ed. 'Ali-Akbar al-Ghaffari (Tehran: Maktabat al-Saduq, 1972).

al-Saduq, al-Shaykh Muhammad b. Ali b. Babawaih al-Qummi, *al-Amali* (*The Book of Dictations*) (Qom: Mu'assasat al-Bi'tha, 1996).

al-Saduq, al-Shaykh Muhammad b. Ali b. Babawaih al-Qummi, *al-Khisal* (*The Book of Characters*), ed. 'Ali-Akbar al-Ghaffari (Qom: Islamic Publication Institute, 2013).

Bibliography

al-Sarakhsi, Shams al-Din Muhammad b. Ahmad, *Kitab al-Mabsut* (*The Extensive*) (Beirut: Dar el-Ma'refah, 1989).

Shafiq, Ahmad, *al-Riqq fi al-Islam* (*Slavery in Islam*), trans. from French to Arabic Ahmad Zaki (n.p.: Maktabah al-Nafidha, 2010).

al-Shahid al-Thani, Zayn al-Din al-Juba'i al'Amili, *Masalik al-Afham ila Tanqih Sharayi' al-Islam* (*The Routes of Comprehension in the Revision of Sharayi' al-Islam [Paths of Islam by al-Muhaqiq al-Hilli]*) (Qom: Mu'ssasa al-Ma'arif al-Islamiyya, 2005).

Ibn Shahr Ashub, Muhammad b. Ali, *Manaqib Al-i Abi-Talib* (*The Virtues of the Family of Abi-Talib*), ed. S. H. al-Rasouli al-Mahallati (Qom: 'Alammi, n.d.).

Shamseddin, Mohammad Mehdi, *Ahliyyat al-Mar'a li-Tawalli al-Sultah* (*Woman's Capacity for Leadership*), *Masa'il Harija fi Fiqh al-Mar'a*, Critical Issues in the Jurisprudence of Women series, No. 2 (Beirut: al-Manar, 1995).

al-Sharif al-Kashani, Habib Allah, *Tashil al-Masalik ila al-Madarik fi Ru'us al-Qawa'id al-Fiqhiyyah* (*The Facilitation of Routes to the Documents of the Heads of Fiqhi Principles*) (Qom, al-'Imiyyah, 1983).

al-Sharafi, 'Abdul Majid (or Abdelmadjid Charfi), *al-Islam wa al-Hidathah* (*Islam and Modernity*) (Tunisia: Al-Dar al-Tunisiyya, 1991).

al-Shatibi, Abu Ishaq, *Al-Muwafaqat fi Usul al-Shari'a* (*The Reconciliation of the Fundamentals of Islamic Law*) (Saudi Arabia: Dar Ibn 'Affan, 1997).

al-Shawkani, Muhammad b. Ali, *Nayl al-Awtar (Sharh-i Muntaqa al-Akhbar min Ahadith Sayyid al-Akhyar)* (*Achieving the Purposes: The Commentary of Muntaqa al-Akhbar min Ahadith Sayyid al-Akhyar [Selected Reports from the Reports of the Master of Good Men, by Abul Barakat Ibn Taymiyya]*), ed.'A. al-Sababiti (Cairo: Dar al-Hadith, 1993).

Ibn Shu'ba al-Harrani, Hassan b. Ali b. Hussain, *Tuhaf al-'Uqul 'an Al al-Rasul* (*Masterpieces of the Mind in the Reports of the Household of the Prophet*), ed. Hussain al-A'lami (Beirut: al-A'lami, 2002).

Suhrawardi, Shahabuddin Yahya, *Majmu'a Mussanafat-i Shaikh Ishraq* (*Complete Works of the Master of Illuminative Philosophy*), vol. II, ed. Henry Corbin (Tehran: Institute of Humanities and Cultural Researches, 1993).

Tabataba'i, Seyyed Mohammad Hossein, *al-Mizan fi Tafsir al-Qur'an* (*Balance in the Exegesis of the Qur'an*), 20 vols (Qom: Jama'a al-Mudarissin, [1954–1972] 2009).

al-Tabrisi, Fadl b. al-Hassan, *Majama' al-Bayan fi Tafsir al-Qur'an* (*Complex Statements in the Exegesis of the Qur'an*) (Beirut: Dar al-Murtada/Dar al-'Ulum, 2005/6).

al-Tabrisi, Hasan b. Fadl b. Hasan, *Makarim al-Akhlaq* (*Nobilities of Character*), ed. Hussain al-A'lami (Beirut: al-A'lami, 1972).

Taha, Mahmoud Mohamed, *Nahwa Mashru' Mustaqbali lil-Islam* (*Towards a Future Project of Islam*), with Introduction by Taha's daughter Asma and his student an-Nur Muhammad Hamad (Morocco and Lebanon: Al-Markaz al-Thaqafi al-'Arabi, 2002). It contains: *al-Risalat al-Thaniya min al-Islam*, *Risalat al-Salat* and *Tatwir Shari'a al-Ahwal al-Shakhsiyya* (*Developing the Shari'a of Civil Status*).

Taha, Mahmoud Mohamed, *al-Risalat al-Thaniya min al-Islam* (*The Second Message of Islam*) (Sudan: n.p., 1967).

al-Tirmidhi, Muhammad b. 'Isa, *Al-Jami' al-Kabir* (*Great Comprehensive [Traditions]*) (Beirut: Dar al-Gharb al-Islami, 1996).

al-Turayhi, Fakhr al-Din, *Majma' al-Bahrain* (*The Confluence of the Two Seas*), ed. Ahmad al-Hussaini (Beirut: Mu'assasa al-Tarikh al-'Arabi, 2007).

al-Tusi, Abu Ja'far Muhammad b. al-Hassan (Shaykh al-Ta'ifa), *al-Istibsar fi ma Ukhtulifa min al-Akhbar* (*Reflections on the Disputed Reports of the Perspicacious*), ed. Hassan al-Musawi al-Khirsan (Tehran: Dar al-Kutub al-Islamiyya, 1970).

al-Tusi, Abu Ja'far Muhammad b. al-Hassan, *Tahdhib al-Ahkam* (*Refinement of Rulings*), ed. Hassan al-Musawi al-Khirsan (Tehran: Dar al-Kutub al-Islamiyya, 1970).

al-Tusi, Abu Ja'far Muhammad b. al-Hassan, *Al-Nahaya fi Mujarrad al-Fiqh wa al-Fatawa* (*The End in Mere Jurisprudence and Fatwas*) (Beirut: Dar al-Kutub al-'Arabi, 1980).

al-Tusi, Abu Ja'far Muhammad b. al-Hassan, *Al-'Uddat fi Usul al-Fiqh* (*The Tools of the Principles of Fiqh*), ed. Muhammad Rida al-Ansari al-Qomi (Qom: the editor, 1997).

al-Tusi, Nassir al-Din, *Tajrid al-E'tiqad* (*Abstraction of the Belief*), ed. Muhammad Jawad al-Hussaini al-Jalali (Qom: Maktab al-I'lam al-Islami, 1987).

Ibn Al-Ukhuwwa, Muhammad ibn Muhammad al-Qurashi, *Ma'alim al-Qurba fi Ahkam al-Hisbah* (*Milestones of Proximity in the Rulings of the Enforcement of the Law*), ed. Reuben Levy (Cambridge: Cambridge University Press for the Trustees of the E. J. W. Gibb Memorial; London: Luzac, 1938).

Bibliography

al-Ya'qubi, Ahmad b. abi Yaqub, *Tarikh al-Ya'qubi* (*The History of al-Ya'qubi*), ed. Abdul Amir Muhanna (Beirut: al-A'lami, 2010).

al-Yazdi, al-Sayyid Muhammad Kazim al-Tabataba'i, *al-'Urwah al-Wuthqa* (*The Firmest Hand-Hold*), with glosses by Shi'i authorities (Qom: Islamic Publication Institute, 2001–2005).

al-Zarkashi, Muhammad Ibn 'Abdullah, *Al-Burhan fi 'Ulum al-Qur'an* (*The Perfect Guide to the Sciences of the Qur'an*) (Cairo: Maktaba Dar al-Turath, 1984).

Zayd, Mustafa, *Al-Naskh fi al-Qur'an al-Karim, Dirasah Tashri'iyah, Tarikhiyah, Naqdiya* (*Abrogation in the Qur'an, a Legal, Historical and Critical Study*) (Cairo: Dar al-Wafa, 1987).

al-Zuhayli, Wahba, *al-Fiqh al-Islami wa Adilatahu* (*Islamic Jurisprudence and its Proof*) (Damascus: Dar al-Fikr, 1985).

al-Zuhayli, Wahba, *Athar al-Harb fi Fiqh al-Islami* (*The Effect of War in Islamic Jurisprudence*) (Damascus: Dar al-Fikr, 1998).

English Books

Abdel Haleem, M.A.S., *The Qur'an, A New Translation* (Oxford: Oxford University Press, 2005).

Abou El Fadl, Khaled, *Reasoning with God: Reclaiming Shari'a in the Modern Age* (Lanham, MD: Rowman & Littlefield, 2017).

Arendt, Hannah, *The Origins of Totalitarianism* (New York: Schocken, 1951).

Bielefeldt, Heiner, Nazila Ghanea and Michael Wiener, *Freedom of Religion or Belief* (Oxford: Oxford University Press, 2016).

Böckenförde, Ernst-Wolfgang, "The Fundamental Right of Freedom of Conscience", in Mirjam Künkler and Tine Stein (eds), *Religion, Law, and Democracy: Selected Writings* (Oxford: Oxford University Press, 2020).

Burton, John, *The Sources of Islamic Law: Islamic Theories of Abrogation* (Edinburgh: Edinburgh University Press, 1990).

Dostoevsky, Fyodor, *The Brothers Karamazov*, trans. Richard Pevear and Larissa Volokhonsky (London: Vintage Digital, 2017).

Saint Ephrem, *Hymns on Paradise*, Introduction and trans. Sebastian Brock (New York: St Vladimir Seminary Press, 1998).

Fatoohi, Louay, *Abrogation in the Qur'an and Islamic Law: A Critical Study of the Concept of "Naskh" and its Impact* (London: Routledge, 2014).

Gobineau, Arthur Comte de, *The Inequality of Human Races*, trans. Adrian Collins (n.p.: Ostara Publications, 2015).

Habermas, J., *The Structural Transformation of the Public Sphere*, trans. Thomas Burger with the assistance of Frederic Lawrence (Cambridge, MA: MIT Press, 1989).

Haleem, M. A. S. Abdel, *The Qur'an: A New Translation*, Oxford World's Classics series (Oxford: Oxford University Press, 2005).

Ignatieff, Michael, *Human Rights as Politics and Idolatry* (Princeton, NJ: Princeton University Press, 2001).

Kadivar, Mohsen, *Blasphemy and Apostasy in Islam: Debates in Shi'a Jurisprudence*, trans. Hamid Mavani (Edinburgh: Edinburgh University Press in association with the Aga Khan University Institute for the Study of Muslim Civilisations, 2021).

al-Khu'i, Sayyid Abu al-Qasim, *The Prolegomena to the Qur'an*, introduction and trans. Abdulaziz A. Sachedina (Oxford: Oxford University Press, 1998).

LaFollette, Hugh, *Ethics in Practice: An Anthology* (Oxford: Blackwell, 2002).

Little, David, John Kelsay and Abdulaziz Sachedina, *Human Rights and the Conflict of Cultures: Western and Islamic Perspectives on Religious Liberty* (Columbia, SC: University of South Carolina Press, 1988).

Luxenberg, Christoph, *The Syro-Aramaic Reading of the Koran: A Contribution to the Decoding of the Language of the Koran* (Amherst, NY: Prometheus, 2007).

Mawdudi, Abu'l A'la, *Human Rights in Islam* (Lahore: Zahid Bashir Printers, 1976).

Mayer, Ann Elizabeth, *Islam and Human Rights: Tradition and Politics*, 5th edn (London: Routledge, 2019).

McCarthy, Mary, *Memories of a Catholic Girlhood* (New York: Open Road Media, 2013).

Mir-Hosseini, Ziba, Lena Larsen, Christian Moe and Kari Vogt (eds), *Gender and Equality in Muslim Family Law: Justice and Ethics in the Islamic Legal Tradition* (London: I. B. Tauris, 2013).

Mir-Hosseini, Ziba and Richard Tapper, *Islam and Democracy in Iran: Eshkevari and the Quest for Reform* (London: I. B. Tauris, 2014).

Moore, B., *Privacy: Studies in Social and Cultural History* (London: Routledge, 1984).

Morsink, Johannes, *The Universal Declaration of Human Rights: Origins, Drafting, and Intent* (Philadelphia, PA: University of Pennsylvania Press, 1999).

An-Na'im, Abdullahi Ahmed, *Toward an Islamic Reformation: Civil Liberties, Human Rights and International Law* (Syracuse, NY: Syracuse University Press, 1990).

An-Na'im, Abdullahi Ahmed (ed.), *Human Rights in Cross-Cultural Perspectives: A Quest for Consensus* (Philadelphia, PA: University of Pennsylvania Press, 1992).

An-Na'im, Abdullahi Ahmed, *Islam and the Secular State: Negotiating the Future of Shari'a* (Cambridge, MA: Harvard University Press, 2008).

An-Na'im, Abdullahi Ahmed, *Islam and Human Rights: Selected Essays of Abdullahi An-Na'im*, ed. Mashood A. Baderin (Farnham: Ashgate, 2010).

An-Na'im, Abdullahi Ahmed, *Muslims and Global Justice* (Philadelphia, PA: University of Pennsylvania Press, 2011).

Nöldeke, Theodor, Friedrich Schwally, Gotthelf Bergsträßer and Otto Pretzl, *The History of the Qur'an*, ed. and trans. Wolfgang H. Behn (Leiden: Brill, 2013).

Rahman, Fazlur, *Islamic Methodology in History* (Karachi: Central Institute of Islamic Research, 1965).

Rahman, Fazlur, *Islam* (Chicago: University of Chicago Press, 1979).

Rahman, Fazlur, *Islam and Modernity: Transformation of an Intellectual Tradition* (Chicago: University of Chicago Press, 1982).

Rahman, Fazlur, *Revival and Reform in Islam* (Oxford: Oneworld, 2010).

Rahman, Fazlur, *Major Themes of the Qur'an* (Chicago: University of Chicago Press, 2013).

Sachedina, Abdulaziz, *Islamic Messianism: The Idea of Mahdi in Twelver Shi'ism* (Albany, NY: State University of New York Press, 1981).

Sachedina, Abdulaziz, *The Just Ruler in Shi'ite Islam: The Comprehensive Authority of the Jurist in Imamite Jurisprudence* (Oxford: Oxford University Press, 1988).

Sachedina, Abdulaziz, *The Islamic Roots of Democratic Pluralism* (Oxford: Oxford University Press, 2000).

Sachedina, Abdulaziz, *Islam and the Challenge of Human Rights* (Oxford: Oxford University Press, 2009).

Sachedina, Abdulaziz, *Islamic Biomedical Ethics: Principles and Application* (Oxford: Oxford University Press, 2010).

al-Shatibi, Abu Ishaq, *The Reconciliation of the Fundamentals of Islamic Law*, trans. Imran Ahsan Khan Nyazee, review Raji M. Rammuny (Reading: Centre for Muslim Contribution to Civilization in association with Garnet Publishing, 2011).

Suggs, M. Jack et al. (eds), *The Oxford Study Bible: Revised English Bible with the Apocrypha* (Oxford: Oxford University Press, 1992).

[Suhrawardi], *The Mystical Visionary Treatises of Shahabuddin Yahya Suhrawardi*, trans. W. M. Thackston Jr. (London: Octagon Press, 1982).

Tabandeh, Sultan Hussein, *Muslim Commentary on the Universal Declaration of Human Rights*, trans. F. J. Goulding (London: F. T. Goulding, 1970), with Foreword by Abulfazl Hazeqhi and letter of permission from the author to the translator.

al-Tabari, Abu Ja'far Muhammad ibn Jarir, *History of the Prophets and Kings* (*Tarikh al-Rusul wa al-Muluk, Tarikh al-Tabari*), *vol. 18: Between Civil Wars, the Caliphate of Mu'awiyah*, trans. Michael G. Morony (Albany, NY: SUNY Press, 1987).

al-Tabari, Abu Ja'far Muhammad ibn Jarir, *History of the Prophets and Kings* (*Tarikh al-Rusul wa al-Muluk, Tarikh al-Tabari*), *vol. 19: The Caliphate of Yazid b. Mu'awiyahh*, trans. and annotated I. K. A. Howard (Albany, NY: SUNY Press, 1990).

Taha, Mahmoud Mohamed, *The Second Message of Islam*, trans. Abdullahi Ahmed An-Na'im (Syracuse, NY: Syracuse University Press, 1987).

Tanakh: A New Translation of the Holy Scriptures According to the Traditional Hebrew Text (Philadelphia, PA: Jewish Publication Society of America, 1985).

Turkel, G., *Law and Society: Critical Approaches* (Boston, MA: Allyn & Bacon, 1995).

Wadud, Amina, *Quran and Women: Reading the Sacred Text from a Woman's Perspective* (Oxford: Oxford University Press, 1999).

Weiss, B. G., *The Spirit of Islamic Law* (Athens, GA: University of Georgia Press, 1998).

Zayn al-'Abidin, *The Psalms of Islam*, transl. and Introduction William Chittic (London: Muhammadi Trust, 1988).

Books in Other Languages

Kadivar, Mohsen, *Gottes Recht und Menschenrechte. Eine Kritik am historischen Islam* (*God's Rights and Human Rights: A Critique of Historical*

Islam), trans. and introduced Armin Eschraghi, Buchreihe der Georges-Anawati-Stiftung, Modernes Denken in der Islamischen Welt, Band 7 (Freiburg: Herder, 2017).

Larousse French–English, English–French Dictionary, eds Janice McNeillie and Marie-Hélène Corréard (Paris: Larousse, 2007).

Persian Articles and Book Chapters

De Blois, François, "*Naghdi bar Qerat-e Arami Siryani Quran*" ("A Critique of the Syro-Aramaic Reading of the Quran"), trans. Morteza Kariminia, *Tarjoman Wahy Journal* 7(2) (February 2003): 120–128.

Ghaffari, Farhad, "Human Rights from the Perspectives of Ayatollah 'Abdollah Javadi Amoli and Dr Mohsen Kadivar", Master's thesis, Mofid University, Faculty of Law, Department of Public Law and Human Rights, Qom, 2 February 2013.

Haeri-Yazdi, Mehdi, "*Islam wa I'lamiye Hoquq-i Bashar*" ("Islam and Human Rights"), *Maktab-e Tashayo*, Annual, Qom, 4 (1962): 67–76.

Hashemi Shahroudi, Seyyed Mahmoud, "*Mohareb Kist wa Moharebe chist?*" ("Who is the *Muharib* and What is *Muharaba?*"), *Fiqh Ahl-e Beiyt Quarterly*, Qom 11/12 (autumn/winter 1996): 143–200, 13 (spring 1997): 3–82.

Independent Commission of Human Rights of Afghanistan, *Majmou'e-ye E'lamiyehaa-ye Hoquq-e Bashari* (*Collection of Declarations of Human Rights*) (n.p.: n.p., 2002), 18–33.

Kadivar, Mohsen, "*Ta'min-e Ejtema'i dar Ta'alim-e Eslami*" ("Social Security in Islamic Teachings"), in *Nezam-e Jame'-e Refah wa Ta'min-e Ejtema'i, Khulase-ye Gozaresh* (*The System of Comprehensive Welfare and Social Security, Concise Report*) (Tehran: Research Council of the Institute of Advanced Research on Social Security, 1999), 15–18.

Kadivar, Mohsen, "*Din, Modara va Khoshounat*" ("Religion, Tolerance, and Violence"), in *Daghdagheha-ye Hokumat-e Dini* (*The Concerns of the Religious State*) (Tehran: Nashr-e Ney, 2000), 859–883.

Kadivar, Mohsen, *Emam-e Sajjad wa Hoquq-e Mardom* (*Imam Sajjad and the Rights of Mankind*), Tehran, *Sobh-e Emrouz* (*This Morning*), daily magazine, 17 April 2000, 8.

Kadivar, Mohsen, "*Haqq wa taklif dar din*" ("Rights and Obligation in Religion") in *Daghdagheha-ye Hokumat-e Dini* (*The Concerns of the Religious State*) (Tehran: Nashr-e Ney, 2000), 305–319.

Kadivar, Mohsen, "*Hokumat-e Dini va Maslahat*" ("The Religious State and Interest"), in *Daghdagheha-ye Hokomat-e Dini* (Tehran: Nashr-e Ney, 2000), 254–256.

Kadivar, Mohsen, *Hoquq-e Siyasi-e Mardom dar Eslam: Haqq-e Ta'yeen-e Sarnevesht* (*The Political Rights of People in Islam: The Right to Determine One's Destiny*), in *Daghdagheha-ye Hokumat-e Dini* (*The Concerns of the Religious State*) (Tehran: Nashr-e Ney, 2000), 320–337.

Kadivar, Mohsen, "*Hormat-e Shar'i-e Teror*" ("The Religious Prohibition of Terror"), in *Daghdagheha-ye Hokumat-e Dini* (*The Concerns of the Religious State*) (Tehran: Nashr-e Ney, 2000), 837–858.

Kadivar, Mohsen, "*Marzha-ye Azadi az Manzar-e Din*" ("Borders of Freedom from Religious Perspective"), in *Daghdagheha-ye Hokumat-e Dini* (Tehran: Nashr-e Ney, 2000), 495–543.

Kadivar, Mohsen, "*Payamadha-ye zir-e pa kozashtan-e Haqq-e Hayat dar Jame'e-ye Dini*" ("The Consequences of Violence of Right to Live in a Religious Society"), in *Daghdagheha-ye Hokomat-e Dini* (Tehran: Nashr-e Ney, 2000), 823–836.

Kadivar, Mohsen, "*Qalamro-e Hokumat-e Dini az Didgah-e Emam Khomeini*" ("The Domain of the Religious State according to Imam Khomeini"), in *Daghdagheha-ye Hokomat-e Dini* (*The Concerns of the Religious State*) (Tehran: Nashr-e Ney, 2000), 111–134.

Kadivar, Mohsen, "*Rohaniyat, Nabz-e Qodrat va Eksir-e Maslahat-e Nezam*" ("The Clergy, the Pulse of Power, and the Elixir of the State's Interest"), in *Daghdagheha-ye Hokomat-e Dini* (*The Concerns of the Religious State*) (Tehran: Nashr-e Ney, 2000), 560–570.

Kadivar, Mohsen, "*Azadi-ye 'Aqideh wa Mazhab dar Eslam wa Asnad-e Hoquq-e Bashar*" ("The Freedom of Belief and Religion in Islam and Human Rights Documents"), in *Proceedings of the First International Conference of Human Rights and the Dialogue of Civilizations* (Qom: Mofid University, 2001), 263–265.

Kadivar, Mohsen, *Hoquq-e Mokhalef-e Siyasi dar Jame'e-ye Dini* (*The Rights of the Political Opposition in an Islamic Society*), *Aftab* bimonthly, Tehran, 4 (April/May 2001): 4–13.

Kadivar, Mohsen, "Azadi-ye 'Aqideh wa Mazhab dar Eslam wa Asnad-e Hoquq-e Bashar" ("The Freedom of Belief and Religion in Islam and Human Rights Documents"), *Aftab* (*Sunshine*), bimonthly, Tehran, 23 (March 2003): 54–63.

Kadivar, Mohsen, "*Hoquq-e Bashar wa Roshanfekri-ye Dini*" ("Human Rights and Reformist Islam"), *Aftab* bimonthly, 27 (June 2003): 54–59, 28 (August 2003): 106–115.

Kadivar, Mohsen, "*Mas'ale-ye Bardedari dar Eslam-e Mo'aser*" ("The Issue of Slavery in Contemporary Islam"), *Aftab*, bimonthly, 25 (May 2003): 80–89.

Kadivar, Mohsen, "*Roshanfekri-ye Dini wa Hoquq-e Zanan*" ("Reformist Islam and Women's Rights"), *A'yeen Monthly Journal* pre-issue 1 (December 2003): 9–17.

Kadivar, Mohsen, "*Hoquq-e Zanan dar Akherat: Motale'eye Qor'ani Kalami*" ("Women's Rights in the Hereafter: a Qur'anic Theological Study"), *Modaress-e 'Ulum-e Ensani*, Scholarly Research Journal of the Humanities College of Tarbiat Modares University, Tehran, 41 (spring 2005): 89–110.

Kadivar, Mohsen, "*Mas'ale-ye Bardedari dar Eslam-e Mo'aser*" ("The Issue of Slavery in Contemporary Islam"), *Proceedings of the Second International Human Rights Conference (the Theoretical Bases of Human Rights)* (Qom: Mofid University, 2005), 263–265.

Kadivar, Mohsen, "*Hoquq-e Bashar, Laïcité wa Din*" ("Human Rights, Secularism and Religion"), *A'een* (*Ritual*), monthly journal, Tehran, 4 (October 2006): 64–67.

Kadivar, Mohsen, *Porsesh wa Pasokh-e Hoquq-e Bashar wa Roshanfekri-ye Dini. Aftab*, 6 (March 2006), 8 (August 2006), 9 (November 2006), available at: http://www.aftab-magazine.com/archive, last accessed 18 June 2020.

Kadivar, Mohsen, "*Hoquq-e ghair-e Mosalmanan dar Eslam-e Mo'aser*" ("The Rights of Non-Muslims in Contemporary Islam"), *A'een*, monthly, Tehran, 6 (March 2007): 69–72.

Kadivar, Mohsen, *Ta'ammoli dar Mas'aleye Hejab* ("A Reflection on the Issues of *Hijab*" [*Women's Head Scarf*]), series of articles, Kadivar website, 2012, available at: https://kadivar.com/10843, last accessed 18 June 2020.

Kadivar, Mohsen, "*Ba Baha'iyan chegoune barkhord konim?*" ("How Should we Treat the Baha'is?"), Kadivar website, 15 May 2016, available at: https://kadivar.com/15243, last accessed 18 June 2020.

Kadivar, Mohsen, "*Layeheye Qesas wa hokm-e ertedad-e Jebhe-ye Melli*" ("Retaliation Bill and the Apostasy Sentence of the National Front"), series of articles, Kadivar's website, 2017, available at: https://kadivar.com/16159, last accessed 18 June 2020.

Kadivar, Mohsen, "*Noandishi-ye dini va kheradvarziha-ye shakhsi*" ("Reformist Islam and Personal Rationality"), BBC Persian, London, 5 September 2018, available at: https://www.bbc.com/persian/blog-viewpoints-45420271, last accessed 18 June 2020.

Kadivar, Mohsen, "*Hoquq-e Bashar, Laïcité wa Din*", in Amir Nikpay (ed.), *Laïcité wa Hoquq-e Bashar* (*Secularism and Human Rights*), Proceedings of the Interdisciplinary and International Conference on the Relationship between *Laïcité* and Human Rights: Citizenship and Religion (Tehran: UNESCO Seat of Human Rights, Peace and Democracy, Shahid Beheshti University, forthcoming).

Kadivar, Mohsen, "*Qara'at-e faramush-shodeh: bazkhvani-ye nazariyyeh-ye 'Ulama-ye Abrar', talaqqi-ye avvaliyye-ye Eslam-e Shi'ite az asl-e emamat*", *Madreseh*, quarterly, Tehran, 1(3) (2006): 92–102.

Kariminia, Morteza, *Mas'ale-ye Ta'thir-e Zabanha-ye Arami va Siryani dar Zaban-e Qur'an: naqd wa mo'arefi-ye Ketab-e Christoph Luxenberg* (*The Influence of Aramaic and Syriac Languages on the Language of the Quran: Critique and Introduction of Christoph Luxenberg's Book the* Syro-Aramaic Reading of the Koran: A Contribution to the Decoding of the Language of the Koran, Berlin 2000), *Nashr-e Danesh Quarterly*, Tehran, 20(4) (winter 2004): 45–56.

Mesbah Yazdi, Mohdammad Taqi, "*Asl-e Azadi dar Eslam*" ("The Principle of Freedom in Islam"), *Ettelaat Daily*, Tehran, 2 (October 1993): 20020:11.

Shabestari, Mohammad Mojtahed, "*Din va 'aql*" ("Religion and Reason"), *Kayhan-e Farhangi*, monthly, Tehran, 42 (August 1987): 12–14; 44 (October 1987): 20–23; 48 (February 1988): 10–11; 51 (May 1988): 10–13; 57 (November 1988): 28–29; 62 (April 1989): 14–17; 65 (July 1989): 14–15.

Arabic Articles and Book Chapters

Kadivar, Mohsen, "*Huriyyat ud-Din wa al-'Aqida fi il-Islam, Mutala'a Fiqhiyya*" ("The Freedom of Religion and Belief Islam, a *Fiqhi* Issue"), trans. Ali al-Wardi, *Al-Ijtihad wa al-Tajdid*, quarterly, 3 (2008): 9–10:11–57.

Bibliography

Kadivar, Mohsen, "*Huriyyat ul-'Aqida wa ad-Din fi il-Islam*" ("The Freedom of Belief and Religion in Islam"), trans. Haidar Najaf, *Qadaya Islamiyya Mu'asira*, quarterly, Baghdad, 13 (2009): 39–40:146–178.

Kadivar, Mohsen, "*Usul Insijam il-Islam wa al-Hidatha*" ("The Principles of Compatibility between Islam and Modernity"), trans. Mushtaq 'Abdi Manaf, *Qadaya Islamiyya Mu'asira*, quarterly, Baghdad, 51/52 (2012): 302–314.

al-Makki, Basim, "Mahmoud Mohamed Taha", in *A'lam tajdid al-fikr al-dini (Outstanding Men of the Renewal of Religious Thought), vol. I: Tajdid al-fikr al-Islami: muqaraba naqdiyya (Renewing Islamic Thought: A Critical Approach)*, ed. Bassam al-Jamal (Rabat, Morocco: Mominoun without Borders, 2016), 31–32.

Kadivar, Mohsen, "*Fahm al-Islam bain al-Qara'at al-Taqlidiyya wa al-Qara'at al-Maqasidiyya*" ("From Traditional Islam to End-Oriented Islam"), trans. Tawfiq Alsaif, *Al-Kalema (The Word)*, quarterly, Beirut, 25 (2018): 100:141–172.

English Articles and Book Chapters

Bauer, Karen, "Debates on Women's Status as Judges and Witnesses in Post-Formative Islamic Law", *Journal of the American Oriental Society* 130(1) (2010): 1–21.

Bhargava, Rajeev, "Reimagining Secularism: Respect, Domination and Principled Distance", *Economic and Political Weekly* 48(50) (2013): 79–92.

Burton, John, "*Naskh*", in *The Encyclopaedia of Islam*, 2nd edn (Leiden: Brill, 1993), 7:1009–1012.

Burton, John, "Abrogation", in Jane Dammen McAuliffe (ed.), *An Encyclopaedia of the Qur'an* (Leiden: Brill, 2001), 1:11–19.

Calhoun, Craig J. (ed.), "Public Sphere and Private Sphere", in *Dictionary of the Social Sciences* (Oxford: Oxford University Press, 2003), 392.

Gavison, Ruth, "Privacy: Legal Aspects", in Neil J. Smelser and Paul B. Baltes (eds), *International Encyclopaedia of Social and Behavioural Science* (Amsterdam: Elsevier, 2001), 12067.

Jarrar, Maher, "*Houris*", in J. D. McAuliffe (ed.), *Encyclopedia of the Qur'an* (Leiden: Brill, 2002), 2:456.

Kadivar, Mohsen, "An Introduction to the Public and Private Debate in Islam", *Social Research* 70(3) (2003): 659–680.

Kadivar, Mohsen, "Freedom of Religion and Belief in Islam", in Mehran Kamrava (ed.), *The New Voices of Islam: Reforming Politics and Modernity – A Reader* (London: I. B. Tauris, 2006), 119–142.

Kadivar, Mohsen, "From Traditional Islam to Islam as an End in Itself", *Die Welt des Islams (International Journal for the Study of Modern Islam)* 51 (2011): 459–484.

Kadivar, Mohsen, "Genealogies of Pluralism in Islamic Thought: Shi'a Perspective", in Mohammed Hashas (ed.), *Pluralism in Islamic Contexts: Ethics, Politics and Modern Challenges*, Philosophy and Politics – Critical Explorations series (Basel: Springer, forthcoming).

Kadivar, Mohsen, "Human Rights and Intellectual Islam", trans. Nilou Mobasser, in Kari Vogt, Lena Larsen and Christian Moe (eds), *New Directions in Islamic Thought: Exploring Reform and Muslim Tradition* (London: I. B. Tauris, 2009), 47–74.

Kadivar, Mohsen, "Ijtihad in Usul al-Fiqh: Reforming Islamic Thought through Structural Ijtihad", *Iran Nameh* 30(3) (2015): 20–27.

Kadivar, Mohsen, "The Issue of Slavery in Contemporary Islam", trans. Sadiq Meghjee, Syed Ali Imran and Syed Hadi Rizvi; adviser, Jonathan Brown (Georgetown University), *Iqra Online: Shi'ite Islamic Sciences Repository*, September 2018, available at: https://www.iqraonline.net/the-issue-of-slavery-in-contemporary-islam, last accessed 24 February 2019.

Kadivar, Mohsen, "Revisiting Women's Rights in Islam: 'Egalitarian Justice' in Lieu of 'Desert-based Justice'", in Ziba Mir-Hosseini, Lena Larsen, Christian Moe and Kari Vogt (eds), *Gender and Equality in Muslim Family Law: Justice and Ethics in the Islamic Legal Tradition* (London: I. B. Tauris, 2013), 213–234.

Matsunaga, Yasuyuki, "Human Rights and New Jurisprudence in Mohsen Kadivar's Advocacy of 'New-Thinker' Islam", *Die Welt des Islams* 51(3/4) (2011): 358–381.

Oevermann, Annette, "Taha, Mahmud Muhammad", in *The Encyclopaedia of Islam*, 2nd edn (Leiden: Brill, 2000), 10:96–97.

Perrett, R. W. "Buddhism, Euthanasia and the Sanctity of Life", *Journal of Medical Ethics* 22(5) (1996): 309–313.

Stepan, Alfred C., "The World's Religious Systems and Democracy: Crafting the Twin Tolerations", in Alfred Stepan, *Arguing Comparative Politics* (Oxford: Oxford University Press, 2001), 213–253.

Wreen, Michael, "The Definition of Euthanasia", *Philosophy and Phenomeno-logical Research* 48(4) (1988): 637–653.

Articles and Book Chapters in Other Languages

Beck, E., "Eine Christliche Parallel zu den Paradiesjungfrauen des Korans", *Orientalia christiana periodica* 14 (1948): 398–405.

Kadivar, Mohsen, "Vom historischen Islam zum spirituellen Islam" ("From Traditional Islam to Islam as an End in Itself"), in *Unterwegs zu einem anderen Islam, Texte Iranischer Denker*, ed., trans. and annotated Katajun Amirpur (Freiburg: Herder, 2009), 80–105.

Kadivar, Mohsen, "*La naissance du 'souverain juriste': Généalogie de la théorie de l'État Shi'ite*" ("The Birth of Guardianship Jurist: The Genealogy of Shi'ite Theory of Governance"), trans. into French Anoush Ganjipour, *Les Temps Modernes*, Paris (April–June 2015), 110–128.

Internet Sources

Constitution of the Islamic Republic of Iran, available at: https://en.parliran. ir/eng/en/Constitution, last accessed 15 June 2020.

Human Rights in Arab countries (Arab Gateway), available at: https:// al-bab.com, last accessed 15 June 2020.

Naqd wa Barrasi-ye Ketab-e Haqq al-Nas (The full text and bibliography of all of the reviews of *Haqq al-Nas* (*The Rights of People: Islam and Human Rights*)), available at: https://kadivar.com/13826, last accessed 15 June 2020.

United Nations Human Rights Documents, available at: https://www.un.org/ en/sections/general/documents, last accessed 15 June 2020.

Glossary

adab	etiquette
'adam al-mamlukiyya	negation of being owned
ahkam hukumati	governmental rulings
ahkam-i irshadi	guidance rulings
ahkam imdha'i	ratified rulings
ahkam thanawi	secondary rulings
Ahl al-Hall wa al-'Aqd	authorised people to loosen and bind
ahl al-rayba	people of suspicion
ahl al- ta'wawil	the people of interpretation
ahkam-i mawlawi	rulings of the master
al-ahkam al-kulli	general rulings
al-ahkam al-ta'sisi	positive rulings
al-amwal al-muhtaramah	respected property
al-firqa al-najiyah	the Saved sect, referring to Muslims
al-haqq li man ghalab	"the truth belongs to one who overcomes"
al-hukm al-awwali	primary ruling
al-hukm al-wadh'i	declaratory ruling
al-jahil al-qasir	ignorant with shortcomings
al-jarh wa al-ta'dil	invalidating and validating narrators of hadith
al-kafir al-harbi	warring non-Muslims, refers to non-Muslims who have no treaty or protection agreements with Muslims
al-kuffar al-harbi	infidels at war
al-madhab al-haqq	True sect
al-nafs al-mohtarama	holders of sacred life
al-ta'zir al-shar'i	discretionary punishments
al-waifs al-kifa'i	that which is required of everyone
al-wajib al-kifa'i	collective obligation
al-wujud al-'ayni	objective existence

al-amr bi al-ma'ruf wa al-nahy 'an al-munkar	enjoining the proper and forbidding the improper
al-'idala-a-istihqaqiyya	desert-based justice
al-'irdh al-mutaramah	inviolable dignity
al-'uqala'i	reasonable, common sense
al-'usr wa al-haraj al-shar'i	distress and hardship
al-'afw min al-qisas	exemption from revenge
amah	female slave
anfal	public property such as uncultivated land, mountains, valleys, forests, meadows, seas and seashores, big rivers and mines
Ansar	the early Muslims from Medina who supported the Prophet
'aql salim	sound reason
aradi	incidental
ara'ik	soft chairs
ashab al-yamin	Companions of the Right
asl al-hurriyya	principle of freedom
asl 'adam al-wilaya	principle of excluded guardianship
'awam	commoners
awamir sultani	position of rulers
awlawiyah	right of priority
awliya'	guardians of the people
awqaf	endowments
ayat al-ahkam	ruling verses
baghi/bughat	rebel/rebellions
bait al-mal	public treasury
bana' al-'uqala'	public opinion and the conventions of reasonable people
baras	vitiligo
bashari	secular
batin diyanat	religious conscience
batin	Esoteric meaning
bayyinah	clear evidence or witness
bi'that	Mohammad's Mission
buhtan	speaking falsehoods
dain	obligation to pay

dalil gair-mustaqillat 'aqliya	non-dependent rational evidence
dar al-harb	enemy territory
dar al-Islam	the land of Islam
dar al-kufr	territory of disbelief
dar al-shirk	territory of the polytheists
dar al-'ahd or	
dar al-mu'ahada	territory of treaties
dark fi al-jumlah	general understanding
daruriyyat	essentials
da'irat al-hisbah	office of the Islamic state whose duty is to to ensure accountability
dhawat nafsaniya nuriyya	illuminative spiritual entities
dhimmi	People of the Book, such as Christians, Jews and Zoroastrians who have accepted the Islamic conditions of protection
dilalat	criterion of indication
din	religion
diya	bloody money
faqir	Poor
faskh	annulment
fa-yamut	death by natural causes
fay'	what Muslims take from their enemies without war
fidyah	ransom
fiqh al-maslaha	interest-oriented jurisprudence
fiqh hukumati	governmental *fiqh*
fitra	primordial nature
fi sabil Allah	for God's cause
fitri	apostate: literally renouncing the first/ primordial nature (*fitra*). *Fitri* apostate is one whose parents or one of them were Muslims when he/she was born, and he/she him-/herself was also a Muslim, utill after having reached the puberty, and thereafter he/she converted to become a non-Muslim.
fi'ah baghiya	aggressor denomination
fuqaha	jurists

ghaib	hidden
ghair mansoukh	non-abrogated
ghanimah	spoils of war
ghibah	speaking behind another's back
habt	deeds
hadd/hudud	fixed punishment(s)
hadar	waste
hadd al-qadhf	false accusation of adultery
hadd al-zina	crime of adultery
hajib	Muslim court official
hanif'	pure faith (religion)
haqq Allah	God's Right; the duty of humans before God
haram	prohibited
hayat tayibah	good life
hiba	donation
hija'	defamatory poems
Hikmat Muta'aliyah	transcendental philosophy
hujjat bi al-dhat	essential evident
hujjat shari'iya	legal proof
hujjiyat	authorativeness
hukm hukumati	governmental ruling
hukm	rule
hukuma wila'iyya	A guardian-based state
hurr/hurrah	freeman/freewoman
hur'in	heavenly beautiful women
husn wa qubh 'aqli	rational good and evil
ibtida'i	initiating in relation to carrying out *jihad*
'idafah	genitive construction
'idda	waiting period for widows
'idda al-talaq	waiting period for divorce
'idda al-wafat	waiting period after death of husband
idhtirar	urgency
idtirar	emergency conditions
ifadah	emanation
ihsan	doing good
ijara	rent

ijma'i	consensual
ikhtiyari	voluntary
ilgha' khususiyyat	abolition of specialty
'illiyun	those of the highest ranking
'ilm al-huquq	legal studies
ilzami	obligatory
iman bil-ghaib	fruits of faith to the unseen world
'inad	obstinacy
infaq	charity
insha'	kingly creation
insha'	requisition
iqa'	unilateral act
'iqab	Judgement Day
iqlaqat	absolute expressions
iqrar	affirm
'irdh	dignity
irshad	guidance
irtikaz 'uqala'i	uncontentious mind of reasonable people
isnad	chain of transmission
istibra'	verification of non-pregnancy
istihqaq dhati	essential merit
istikhdaam	subjugation
istiman	requesting protection
istinbat	invention or the the application of *ijtihad* in the process of extracting theories and principles, on the one hand, and deriving rulings and *fatwa*s, on the other hand, from detailed primary sources
istirqaq	bondage
istiswabi	approbatory
itlaq(at)	absolute expression(s)
itlaq zamani	absolute expression based on time
i'tibari	mentally posited
i'tikaaf	seclusion
'itq	manumission
'izzat	presence of Glory
jahd	odium

jam' dilali	collection of indicators
ja'il	promulagater
ja'iz	non-binding
judham	leprosy
kaffarah/kaffarat	expiation(s), atonement, penance(s)
kashf	discovered
kawn	two realms
ka's min ma'in	cup of pure drink
khabar wahid	singular hadith
khass	specifier/specific
khawass	elites
khisal al-kaffarah	canonical particulars for making atonement
khiyar	withdraw (right to)
khul'	mutual divorce
khula	annulment
khums	one-fifth tax
kiraha	disgrace
kitab al-'itq	Chapter of Emancipation
kutub dhalal	publications that are anti-Islamic and considered to be efforts to lead people astray
laqit	foundling
lawat/liwat	sodomy
lawh thabit	immutable scroll
lawth	speculative evidence
lazim	binding
luqata	property that has been found
mabghudh	permissible but ill-regarded
madhab/madhahib	school(s) of Islamic thought
mafsada naw'iya	species harms
maghfira wa ajr	rich reward
mahdur al-dam	waste of blood
mahdur al-ihtrim	unprotected dignity
mahdur al-mal	waste of property
mahdur al-'irdh	waste of dignity
mahjur	legally incompetent
majanin	people with mental health disabilities
maj'ul	promulgated

makruh/makruhat	deplorable or unfavourable act(s)
malaka qudsi	inspired disposition
malakut	mighty dominion
mala' a'la	Sublime Realm
mandub	recommended acts
maosimi	situational
maqamat	stages
maqa qurb al-Haqq	spiritual state of Nearness to Truth
mariqin	(the) Renegades
marja'-i taqlid/ *al-marji'ayyat al-diniyah*	source(s) of emulation
marjouhiyya	detestability
masalih nafs al-amr	intrinsic interests
masalih wa mafasid	benefits and harms
masalih wa mafasid khafiya	hidden interests and harms
mashhur	dominant view/mainstream
maslaha naw'iya	species interests
maslahat al-nizam	interest of the state
mas'ala mustahdatha	new phenomenon
mawdhou'	determining subject
mawdhu'iyyat	objectivity
ma'kulat, mashrubat wa mankuhat	food, drink and sex
imdha'iyyah/imdha'iyyat	endorsed
milli	apostate: literally, apostate from the community (*milla*). *Milli* apostate is an apostate who is not *fitri* one. In other words, a person who was born of a non-Muslim parent, converted to Islam and later rejected the religion.
misdaq	particular
miskin	the needy
mithali	imaginary
mokhalef	followers of other Islamic schools
moujib	the cause (of)
mu'ahad	non-Muslims who have made a treaty with Muslims (People of Treaty) and are not People of the Book

mubah/mubahat	permitted act(s)
mubarat	mutual divorce
mubayyan	determined
mudaf	construct state
mufsid fi al-ard	someone who strives to spread corruption in the land
Muhajirun	first Muslims in Mecca who immigrated to Medina with the Prophet
muharaba	waging war against God
muhtasib	director of *da'irat al-hisbah*
mujibah juz'iyyah	particular affirmative
mujibah kulliyyah	universal affirmative
mujib	cause
mujtahid	a qualified jurist
mukallaf	adult Muslim
mukatabah mashrutah	conditional agreement
mukatabah mutlaqah	non-conditional agreement
mulk	terresterial
muqabala bi al-mithl	principle of reciprocity
muqarrabin	those who will be brought nearer to God
muqassir	guilty
muqayyad	restricted
mursal	untransmitted
musahaqa	tribadism
musahiqa	lesbianism
musdahdath	rational innovations
mustahabbat	recommended acts
mustahdatha	innovative
mutasharri'in	believers
muthlah	dismembered
mutikafi'	equivalent
mutlaq	absolute
muwalla 'alayhim	wards
muwasat	beneficence
muzara'a	farming partnership
mu'amilat	transactional rulings
mu'men	believer in Islam

nadhr	vow
nafaqah	provisions
nafie	negation
nahie	prohibition
najis	unclean
nakithin	(the) Violators
nama'	growth
namimah	gossip
namous	dignity
nashizah	disobedient
nashizi	belligerent
nash'a al-jinan	emergence of Heaven
nash'a	emergence
nasikh	abrogating
naskh al-hukm la al-talawa	abrogation of the ruling without abrogation of the recitation of the Qur'an
qabih	blameworthy
qabil	recipient
qadhf	defamation
qadiya kharijiya	proposition of actuality
qahri	compelling
qard al-hasana	interest-free loan
qarina	contextual evidence
qasama	compurgation
qasitin	(the) Deviators
qatayi' al-muluuk	king's fiefs
qawwadi	pandering
qa'idat al-saltanat	sovereignty principle
qisas	retaliation in kind
qist	fairness
qiyas al-awlawiya	preferable syllogism
rajm	stoning
rasheed	capable
rida'	kin through breastfeeding
ridwan min Allah	God's good pleasure
rijali	attributed to the science of *rijal*, which is the qualification or evaluation of the transmitters of hadith.

sadaqah	almsgiving
sadat	title of the Prophet's descendants
safaya al-amwal	the best and most valuable property
sagharoun	to become humbled
sahih	authorised
salaf salih	pious predecessor
sayyi'at	bad deeds
shakhis	standards
shari'	Lawmaker
shart dhimn 'aqd	condition required by the contract (for marriage)
shar' anwar	Illuminated Law
shar'i iqd'at	unilateral obligatory legal action
sha'n	status
shuf'ah	pre-emption (right of)
siadat	a descendant of the Prophet's line
sira al-'uqala	conventions of reasonability, rational common sense
siraya	contagion
sufaha'	intellectually disabled
suq al-Muslimin	marketplace of Muslims
surur	couches
tagallub	overpowering
taghout	tyranny
takhsis	specified
tahlil	making lawful
tajalli	light of manifestation
takaful	mutual inter-community help and a type of cooperative insurance
takbir	magnify
takfir	anathema
taklif	obligation
takwini	existential
tamaththul	symbolic representation
tamkin	obey
tamyiz	discernment
tankil	maltreated
taqiyyah	dissimulation

taqyid	limit
taraka	bequest
tariqiyyat	instrumentality
tasbih	glorifying (God)
tashkhis	recognised
tashwiq	aspiration
tawqifi	beyond rational
tawwali	declare obedience
ta'abbudi	devotional
ta'beed	explicit statement of eternalness
ta'dib	discipline
ta'sis al-asl	fundamental principle
ta'sisiyyah	new, literally established
ta'yeen	determined
'ubudiyya	servanthood
umm walad	a female slave who gave birth to a child with her owner
'umum wa khusus min wajh	general and specific in some respect
'umumat	general expressions/generalities
'uqala'i	reasonable
'urf	convention/custom
'urf mutasharri'a	elements of Islam in the discipline of believers
'usr wa haraj	distress and constriction
uswah	permanent exemplars
wahn	weakening (of Islam)
wajib	obligatory acts
wasii	executor of a will
wasl	interpolation
wilaya mutlaqa	absolute guardianship
wilayat al-amr	ruler
wildan	youths (male)
'yal	family
zahir/zawahir	exoteric and *prima facie* meaning(s)
zann m'utabar	credible presumption

Index

Index

Index

EU representative:
Easy Access System Europe
Mustamäe tee 50, 10621 Tallinn, Estonia
Gpsr.requests@easproject.com

www.ingramcontent.com/pod-product-compliance
Lightning Source LLC
Chambersburg PA
CBHW050622280326
41932CB00015B/2493